'If I had only one book to help me under: would go for. Skilfully edited by Dr Phili scholars not only give a comprehensive su but also provide four chapters introd Testaments (Story, Background, Theol an important chapter "Between the Tes............ . accessible, requires no specialist knowledge, and combines sound scholarship with an evident love for the Bible. Students and church members alike will find it invaluable. I commend it wholeheartedly.'

Dr Michael Green, former Principal of St John's College, Nottingham, Professor of Evangelism at Regent College, Vancouver, and Archbishops' Advisor on Evangelism

'This splendid book provides a clear, structured and accessible overview of the whole Bible. Its genius is in blending qualities that might easily cancel each other out. For instance, it provides the essential tools and information to make Bible study illuminating and productive, but does so without readers realizing they are being taught a wide range of literary, historical and theological issues.

Some recent Bible overviews have provided a major motif running like a motorway from Genesis to Revelation, but haven't shown the reader how to navigate the minor roads with profit. This work, by contrast, gives enough detail to explore, and sufficient direction not to get lost. Finally and perhaps most importantly, it blends an academic rigour with a godly humility – essential to hearing God's Word. Brian Rosner conveys this well (p. 183):

The biggest obstacle to right reading is not a dull mind, nor the absence of specialized knowledge, but a hard heart. As God's word to the world the message of the NT is accessible to all who come to it in faith.

I warmly commend this timely book.'

Richard Cunningham, Director, UCCF

'Both the Bible itself and the field of biblical studies are large and complex. But they are also immensely rich and rewarding. Here is a clear introduction by evangelical scholars who know what they're talking about. It is substantial enough to deliver what it promises without being ponderous and technical. A good introduction for the interested non-specialist. I warmly recommended it.'

Dr Barry Webb, Research Fellow in Old Testament, Moore College, Sydney, Australia

'Anyone who makes a serious effort at reading the Bible soon finds that it is not easy. This book is designed to help by providing both specific information and general perspective for today's readers. It does not assume much prior knowledge, but nor does it "talk down". Be prepared for some demanding reading, as acknowledged experts distil their specialist knowledge into an accessible text. And be prepared too to be led, gently but firmly, out of your "comfort zone": the Bible is not a comfortable book, and this volume does not disguise the fact. But if you are ready to be stretched, welcome to an exciting voyage of discovery that will last a lifetime.'

Dr Dick France, former Principal, Wycliffe Hall, Oxford

The IVP
Introduction
to the Bible

EDITED BY
Philip S. Johnston

IVP Academic
An imprint of InterVarsity Press
Downers Grove, Illinois

InterVarsity Press
P.O. Box 1400, Downers Grove, IL 60515-1426
Internet: www.ivpress.com
E-mail: email@ivpress.com

InterVarsity Press® is the book-publishing division of InterVarsity Christian Fellowship / USA®, a student movement active on campus at hundreds of universities, colleges and schools of nursing in the United States of America, and a member movement of the International Fellowship of Evangelical Students. For information about local and regional activities, write Public Relations Dept., InterVarsity Christian Fellowship / USA, 6400 Schroeder Rd., P.O. Box 7895, Madison, WI 53707-7895, or visit the IVCF website at <www.intervarsity.org>.

Unless otherwise indicated, Scripture quotations are taken from the Holy Bible, Today's New International Version. *Copyright ©2001, 2005 by International Bible Society. All rights reserved.*

The Epilogue: "Reading the Bible" is adapted from the article "Reading Plans: How to Approach the Job" by John F. Balchin in The Bible User's Manual *(Inter-Varsity Press, 1991).*

Cover design: Cindy Kiple

Cover image: King David: Giraudon / Art Resource, NY
The Tribute Money: Detail of two apostles, Jesus and Peter: Erich Lessing / Art Resource, NY
The Tribute Money: Detail of four apostles and St. Peter: Erich Lessing / Art Resource, NY

ISBN 978-0-8308-3940-7

Printed in the United States of America ∞

Library of Congress Cataloging-in-Publication Data

IVP introduction to the Bible / edited by Philip S. Johnston.
   p. cm.
Includes bibliographical references and index.
ISBN 978-0-8308-2828-9 (cloth / casebound: alk. paper)
1. Bible—Introductions. I. Johnston, Philip, 1954- II. Title:
Introduction to the Bible.
BS475.3.I97 2007
220.6'1—dc22

2006101782

P	18	17	16	15	14	13	12	11	10	9	8	7	6	5	4	3	2	1
Y	26	25	24	23	22	21	20	19	18	17	16	15	14	13	12	11		

Contents

Dedicated to all our children –
of flesh and blood or of faith and spirit

List of contributors

Desmond Alexander, Director of Christian Training, Union Theological College, Belfast, Northern Ireland

Jamie Grant, Tutor in Biblical Studies, Highland Theological College, Dingwall, Scotland

Philip Johnston, Director of Studies and Tutor in Old Testament, Wycliffe Hall, Oxford, England

Tremper Longman III, Robert H. Gundry Professor of Biblical Studies, Westmont College, Santa Barbara, USA

Ernest Lucas, Vice-Principal and Tutor in Biblical Studies, Bristol Baptist College, England

Howard Marshall, Honorary Research Professor of New Testament, University of Aberdeen, Scotland

Carl Mosser, Assistant Professor of Biblical Studies, Eastern University, St Davids, USA

Ian Paul, Dean of Studies and Lecturer in New Testament, St John's College, Nottingham, England

Brian Rosner, Senior Lecturer in New Testament and Ethics, Moore Theological College, Sydney, Australia

Mark Strauss, Professor of New Testament, Bethel Seminary, San Diego, USA

Introduction

Philip Johnston (editor)

The Bible and the IVP Introduction to the Bible

The Bible is a truly wonderful book. It leads us to faith in Jesus Christ, nourishes us as we grow in faith, and guides, moulds and corrects that faith throughout our lives. Millions of Christians through the ages and across the world have treasured it as their most valued possession.

Much of the Bible is immediately clear to any reader, like the general storyline in the Old Testament, the ministry of Jesus in the Gospels, and the rapid spread of the early church in Acts. This is why Christians often insist that anyone can read and understand the Bible for themselves.

But many details remain fuzzy until we find out more about their historical or literary setting, like the minor prophets, or specific instructions in the letters. This *IVP Introduction to the Bible* is intended to reduce the fuzziness, in two complementary ways. First, there are four general chapters (1, 2, 7, 8) dealing with overall background issues to the whole Bible and to each testament, as well as filling in the gap between the testaments. Secondly, there are eight chapters (3 – 6, 9 – 12) dealing with all the main sections and each biblical book in turn. So the great biblical panorama is brought to life, first with broad brush strokes and then with fine art work.

This *IVP Introduction* is written by an international and inter-denominational team of evangelical scholars, all involved in teaching Biblical Studies at a theological college, seminary or university, and each writing in their area of specialization. They are all experienced writers and able communicators, and can guide you expertly through the detail so that your understanding of the Bible and its message is enhanced.

Readers of the IVP Introduction to the Bible

Many different readers can benefit from this *IVP Introduction*:
- young Christians, who have a real desire to grow in their faith and to know more about its foundation document;
- older Christians, who have a mature faith but whose knowledge of Scripture is patchy;
- non-Christians, who have a genuine desire to find out more about this book that means so much to their Christian friends.

You can read it in several ways:
- rapidly, right through, to get a thorough overview of the Bible in all its diversity and richness;
- slowly, section by section, reading the text of each biblical book alongside it, to absorb the detail.

Whichever way you choose, you should have a Bible open to check the main references and to follow up as much detail as you can.

You can use any version of the Bible as you read. All quotations are taken from the TNIV, or Today's New International Version, though the authors are aware of different modern versions as well as the original languages. (See ch. 1, E.3, pp. 15–17, for a guide to Bible versions.) Abbreviations are used throughout for Old Testament (OT) and New Testament (NT), and for all the biblical books (see p. xii). Everything else is fully explained.

Further reading

Each chapter concludes with a few suggestions for further reading (cited where possible in British editions). These are helpful resources, with more detailed information and interpretation, and they give further bibliographies for advanced study. Note also:

Reference volumes:

A one-volume commentary and a one-volume dictionary are both extremely useful for further study. We recommend:

New Bible Dictionary, edited by Howard Marshall and others (IVP, 3rd edn 1996).

New Bible Commentary, 21st Century Edition, edited by Don Carson and others (IVP, 1994).

Commentary series:

There are two excellent and inexpensive series of commentaries accessible to everyone, though neither yet covers the whole Bible:
Bible Speaks Today, individually titled *The Message of...* (IVP).
New International Biblical Commentary (Paternoster).

There are many other excellent series accessible to everyone, at varying prices, including:
Tyndale Commentary (IVP) – also good value, with more background detail than the two series above.
NIV Application Commentary (Zondervan) – recent and detailed, with emphasis on application.
IVP New Testament Commentary (IVP) – very helpful for the New Testament.

Abbreviations

LXX – Septuagint (Greek version of OT)
MT – Masoretic Text (Hebrew text of OT)
NT – New Testament
OT – Old Testament
p. (pp.) – page(s)
v. (vv.) – verse(s)

Old Testament
Gen. – Genesis
Exod. – Exodus
Lev. – Leviticus
Num. – Numbers
Deut. – Deuteronomy
Josh. – Joshua
Judg. – Judges
1 & 2 Sam. – 1 & 2 Samuel
1 & 2 Kgs – 1 & 2 Kings
1 & 2 Chr. – 1 & 2 Chronicles
Neh. – Nehemiah
Esth. – Esther
Ps. (Pss.) – Psalm (Psalms)
Prov. – Proverbs
Eccl. – Ecclesiastes
Song – Song of Solomon

Isa. – Isaiah
Jer. – Jeremiah
Lam. – Lamentations
Ezek. – Ezekiel
Dan. – Daniel
Hos. – Hosea
Obad. – Obadiah
Jon. – Jonah
Mic. – Micah
Nah. – Nahum
Hab. – Habakkuk
Zeph. – Zephaniah
Hag. – Haggai
Zech. – Zechariah
Mal. – Malachi

New Testament
Matt. – Matthew
Rom. – Romans
1 & 2 Cor. – 1 & 2 Corinthians
Gal. – Galatians
Eph. – Ephesians
Phil. – Philippians
Col. – Colossians
1 & 2 Thess. – 1 & 2 Thessalonians
1 & 2 Tim. – 1 & 2 Timothy
Philm. – Philemon
Heb. – Hebrews
Jas – James
1 & 2 Pet. – 1 & 2 Peter
Rev. – Revelation

1. Introducing the Bible

Mark Strauss

A. Diversity and unity

Though 'Bible' (from Greek *biblos*, 'scroll' or 'book') is a singular term, the Bible is not one book but a library, a collection of diverse writings concerning God and his relationship to the world. Perhaps the best way to begin an orientation to the Bible is with the terms *unity* and *diversity*. Diversity means that the Bible is a diverse collection of books written over a period of some 1,500 years by many authors from a wide range of experiences and walks of life. The Bible arose in a variety of historical and cultural contexts and contains an array of literary forms: prose, poetry, genealogies, laws, psalms, proverbs, history, philosophy, prophecy, letters, etc. This diversity may be described as the human side of the Bible, since it encompasses a vast range of human experiences and perspectives.

Side by side with the Bible's diversity is its unity, the claim that despite its many differences the Bible represents one grand story or meta-narrative. This story may be summed up as the actions of God in redeeming the world. This unity was achieved because the Bible is more than a human book. It is the inspired and authoritative Word of God.

B. Inspiration and authority

Inspiration means that the Bible is not just a record of religious reflections or human experiences of God, but is God's self-revelation, his meaningful communication to human beings. Scripture claims this inspiration for itself, both implicitly and explicitly. The prophetic literature of the OT carries the sense of 'Thus says the LORD ...' and NT writers frequently cite the OT by stating, 'God said ...' or 'the Holy Spirit said ...' A good example appears in Acts 4:25, where an OT citation from Ps. 2:1–2 is introduced, 'You [the Lord] spoke by the Holy Spirit through the mouth of your servant, our father David'. Here we see the convergence of the human and divine in the inspiration of Scripture. The Lord spoke by means of the Holy Spirit through David his human instrument.

Inspiration is claimed explicitly in 2 Tim. 3:16, traditionally translated: 'All scripture is given by inspiration of God (Greek: *theopneustos*), and is profitable for doctrine, for reproof, for correction, for instruction in righteousness' (AV). The term *theopneustos* was apparently coined by Paul and means 'God-breathed' (as in TNIV). Inspiration means that the Holy Spirit influenced the human writers in such a way that they recorded not just their own words, but God's Word – his divine message. 2 Pet. 1:21 similarly says that 'prophecy never had its origin in the human will, but prophets, though human, spoke from God as they were carried along by the Holy Spirit'.

How this inspiration took place in the minds and hearts of human authors remains a mystery, but certain qualifications can be made:

(1) Inspiration does not mean dictation. While in some cases God may have spoken directly to authors, as in prophetic utterances ('the LORD says ...'), in most cases inspiration means that God worked *through the author's own circumstances, thoughts and intentions* to communicate his divine message. This is evident from the unique human styles and personalities which emerge in these writings. Mark, for example, writes in a rather rough Semitic style, while Luke and the author of Hebrews have more polished literary styles.

(2) Nor does inspiration deny the use of written or oral sources. The author of Chronicles drew from passages in Samuel and Kings, as well as non-canonical sources. Luke explicitly refers to written and oral accounts from which he probably borrowed (Luke 1:1–4). Paul at times quotes from pagan poets and philosophers (1 Cor. 15:33; Titus 1:12; cf. Acts 17:28) and the letter of Jude cites the apocryphal work known as 1 Enoch (Jude 14–15).

(3) It follows that inspiration lies not with the sources or traditions behind the text, but with the author and the text produced. The inspired author's selection, editing and composition were guided and 'carried along by the Holy Spirit' (1 Pet. 1:21), so that the result was authoritative Scripture – God's Word.

The terms *plenary* and *verbal* are often used to qualify inspiration. Plenary means 'full' and refers to the fact that all Scripture is equally inspired. Verbal means that the words themselves, not just the ideas, are inspired by God. Here we must be cautious, however, since words are arbitrary signs which indicate conceptual content. It is the *meaning* of these words – the message which they convey – which is ultimately inspired by God. In this way a translation of Scripture which accurately represents the meaning of the text remains God's Word. Another necessary qualification for verbal inspiration is that all language carries a measure of ambiguity and imprecision. Though the Holy Spirit who inspired Scripture may be perfect and precise, the vehicle of transmission (human language) is subject to ambiguity and imprecision. Our comprehension of divine revelation is therefore always partial and incomplete (1 Cor. 13:12).

If the Bible is the inspired Word of God, then it naturally follows that it is *authoritative* for all who worship and serve God. Its theological tenets are to be believed and its commands are to be obeyed. For more specifics on how theology may be gleaned from the text of Scripture and how its truths are to be applied, see the sections 'OT Interpretation' and 'NT Interpretation'.

C. Biblical criticism

The term 'criticism' is not meant to be negative, but refers to a variety of methodologies developed to analyse and interpret the biblical text. In one sense, Jews and Christians have always engaged in biblical criticism, since there has always been a need to identify and interpret the sacred text. Modern biblical criticism arose during the period of the Enlightenment in the eighteenth and nineteenth centuries, when the Bible was placed under the same historical and scientific scrutiny as other works of literature. Though biblical criticism is sometimes viewed as a negative discipline which undermines the authority of Scripture, this is not a necessary conclusion. The human side of this divine–human book makes careful analytic study a necessity. The Bible did not fall from the sky, but arose in the crucible of the challenges and trials of the people of God. The more we understand the settings and situations in which its various books arose, the better we will understand God's revelation to us today.

Biblical criticism can be divided into two broad areas. Historical criticism refers to a variety of methods developed to analyse the history of the text – how it came to be through various compositional phases. Literary criticism refers to the analysis of literary features of the text, apart from its composition history.

1. Historical criticism

Form criticism is the identification and analysis of oral (spoken) traditions which lie behind written documents. Form critics recognize that religious tradition is generally passed down by word of mouth before being codified in written form, and that these 'forms' (or mini-genres) of oral tradition have various functions in religious communities. Forms such as miracle stories, pronouncement stories and parables were analysed to determine their formative context (or *Sitz im Leben*, literally 'setting in life') in the early church. The term *tradition criticism* is sometimes used for the analysis of how these oral traditions changed and developed as they were passed down.

Source criticism seeks to identify the written sources which lay behind biblical texts. NT source criticism has primarily focused on the 'synoptic problem', the literary relationship between the first three Gospels. The most widely held solution is the two-source theory: Mark wrote first; Matthew and Luke (independently) used Mark and another common source ('Q'). The primary competitor to Markan priority is the two-Gospel hypothesis. This is the view that Matthew wrote first, Luke used Matthew as a source, and Mark combined and abridged their two accounts.

Redaction criticism arose in the mid-twentieth century as a reaction against the tendency of form criticism to treat the gospel writers and others as mere compilers, stringing together bits of oral tradition. Building on the results of form and source criticism, redaction critics seek to analyse how the gospel writers edited, arranged and altered their sources to achieve a particular theological purpose (a 'redactor' is an editor).

2. Literary criticism

The term 'literary criticism' has sometimes been used of all methods employed to analyse the biblical text, including those discussed above. More recently, the term is used specifically of methods which examine the biblical documents in their final form, without reference to sources or composition history.

Narrative criticism arose as a correction to the tendency of form and redaction critics to focus on the component parts of the gospels at the expense of their narrative unity. While redaction criticism studies the history of composition of a text, narrative criticism analyses its literary nature, seeking to determine how plot, characters and settings function to produce the desired effect on the reader. Narrative criticism has been particularly helpful in analysing OT narratives, the gospels and the book of Acts.

Rhetorical criticism analyses how authors use literary devices to persuade or influence readers. *Rhetoric* is an ancient art which became the foundation of the educational system of the Greco-Roman world, and treatises on rhetoric were composed by Aristotle, Cicero and others. Modern rhetorical critics utilize these ancient (and some modern) categories to determine the literary strategies of the biblical writers. Rhetorical criticism has proved especially useful in the study of epistolary literature like the letters of Paul, and discourses found in narrative, like the sermons of Jesus and the speeches in Acts.

Canonical criticism, like narrative and rhetorical criticism, focuses on the biblical writings in their final form. Yet it goes beyond these by examining the role these books have played as an authoritative canon in the life of the church (see discussion of the canon below). Some canon critics focus on the history of interpretation, while others on the hermeneutics of canon, that is, how various faith communities read and interpret the Bible as authoritative Scripture.

Structuralism combines insights from linguistics and anthropology, claiming that literature, like language, functions at the level of conventional patterns and rules. Just as there are rules of grammar which govern the way we speak, so there is a 'grammar' of literature which determines how stories operate. While on the surface, stories may have different plots, settings and characters, below this is a 'deep structure' – subconscious for both author or reader – which follows certain universal patterns. By identifying and categorizing these structures (plot movements, character types, kinds of action, etc.), stories can be objectively analysed according to their essential meaning. According to structuralists, meaning does not reside in the author's intention or in a reader's response, but in this deep structure intrinsically encoded in the text.

Reader-response criticism claims that meaning is determined by the reader, not structure of the text or the intention of the author. Reader-centred approaches are diverse, with some claiming there is no 'correct' meaning in the text since each reader creates meaning. Others speak of right or wrong meanings as determined by particular reading communities; still others treat a text's meaning as a dynamic interplay between text and reader. Some reader-response approaches are historically focused, examining how the original readers would have responded to the text. This approach is sometimes called audience criticism.

Liberationist and *feminist* approaches to biblical criticism are closely related to reader-response criticism since they seek to read the text from a particular viewpoint, whether that of women, ethnic minorities, the poor or the oppressed. In general, feminist readings of Scripture assert that the patriarchal character of the Bible is culturally determined rather than divinely sanctioned, and argue for an egalitarian reading which affirms the value, dignity and historical contribution of women.

D. Text and canon

How did we get the Bible we have today? This is the question of text and canon. Textual criticism concerns the preservation of the biblical text. The study of the canon refers to how these particular books came to be viewed as inspired Scripture.

1. Textual criticism

The necessity and goal of textual criticism. How did the books of the Bible come down to us? Before the invention of the printing press, all literature was copied by hand by scribes or copyists. The books of the Bible were copied again and again to disseminate them among God's people and to pass them down to future generations. Of course, when a document is hand-copied, errors inevitably result. Of the thousands of biblical manuscripts, no two are exactly alike. How can we be sure that we have an accurate Bible? The science and art of textual criticism has been developed to reconstruct as accurately as possible the original text of Scripture.

An *autograph* refers to the original document penned by the author. Not surprisingly, considering the ravages of time, no autograph of a biblical book has survived. The goal of textual criticism is to work backwards from the many surviving manuscripts, reconstructing the autograph as closely as possible. This is accomplished by judging where scribes made unintentional errors or intentional changes. Textual criticism is a science, in that there are rules and principles which govern the procedure. It is also an art, in that nuanced decisions must be made from the best available evidence. While one hundred per cent reliability is never possible, there is widespread agreement among scholars today that the text of the Bible has been preserved and restored with a very high degree of reliability.

Old Testament textual evidence. The standard Hebrew text of the OT is called the *Masoretic text* (MT) because it is based on the textual tradition of the Jewish scholars known as the Masoretes, who meticulously standardized and copied the text from the sixth to tenth centuries AD. The Masoretes treated the sacred Scriptures with the highest regard, revering and protecting them. This had a positive and a negative consequence. On the positive side, they did their work with precision and accuracy, thus maintaining a high level of consistency. On the negative side, they tended to destroy old scrolls to protect them from defilement. For this reason our oldest copies of the MT come from the tenth and eleventh centuries, over a thousand years after the last books were written.

Supplementing the MT are both recent finds and ancient translations. The Dead Sea Scrolls (DSS) were discovered from 1947 onwards in caves near the ancient settlement of Qumran on the shores of the Dead Sea. They are important because of the insight they give us into the Jewish community which produced them in the first century BC, and because they contain a wealth of information on the text of the OT. Fragments from almost every book in the OT were discovered. The DSS have pushed back the textual history of the OT almost a thousand years. The greatest find was a magnificent scroll containing almost the entire text of Isaiah.

Another witness to the text of the OT is the Samaritan Pentateuch. When the Samaritans separated from the Jews in the post-exilic period, they came to accept only the Pentateuch, the first five books of the OT, as authoritative Scripture. The value of the Samaritan Pentateuch is disputed among scholars. Some view it as a late revision of the Masoretic text. Others consider it an independent and valuable pre-Masoretic tradition.

Other important witnesses for the OT text are the early translations or 'versions' made from the Hebrew text. The most important of these is the Septuagint, produced by Jews in Egypt beginning in the mid-third century BC. The name comes from the Latin word for 'seventy' (*septuaginta*), a rounded-off reference to the seventy-two scholars who – according to an ancient legend – completed the work in seventy-two days. The Roman numeral LXX is used as an abbreviation. The Septuagint is a valuable witness to the OT, since it represents pre-Masoretic traditions. Other ancient versions utilized by textual critics include the Aramaic Targums (translations with some additions), the Syriac 'Peshitta', Old Latin, the Vulgate and Arabic.

New Testament textual evidence. The manuscript evidence for the NT is much greater than for the OT, including over five thousand manuscripts in Greek. Most of these are fragmentary, containing portions of the NT (e.g. Gospels or epistles). The oldest manuscripts (second to seventh centuries AD) are made of papyri, a paper-like material made from a reed grown in Egypt. There are approximately 100 extant papyri. The majority of manuscripts are made of parchment, or animal skins. These come in two writing styles. The older uncials, similar to capital letters, date from the fourth to the ninth centuries. The later miniscules, similar to lower case, date from the ninth century onward. pproximately 300 uncial and 3,000 miniscule manuscripts. to these, there are over 2,000 lectionaries, church reading itaining selected liturgical readings for the church calendar. Thes. ate from the ninth to the fourteenth centuries.

As with the OT, translations of the NT into other languages provide another important textual source, including versions in Latin, Syriac, Coptic, Ethiopic, Armenian, Georgian and Slavonic. Prepared by missionaries to aid in evangelism, these originated in the second and third centuries. Finally, citations of Scripture found in church fathers provide a fourth important source for NT textual critics. These citations, which are many and varied, give insight into the ancient texts available to church leaders at various places and times.

The method of textual criticism. Textual criticism of the OT and NT have tended to be quite different enterprises. For the OT, the standard Masoretic text is widely accepted. Most English versions have tended to follow the MT closely, occasionally introducing variant readings from the LXX or the DSS. NT textual criticism is a more developed discipline because of the wealth of early manuscript evidence and the greater variation among manuscripts.

Contemporary NT textual criticism focuses on two kinds of evidence, external and internal. External evidence relates to the date and value of manuscripts. Based on a comparison of their readings, manuscripts have been grouped into four 'families': Alexandrian, Caesarean, Western and Byzantine. These families are named for the geographical regions in which scholars believe each family arose. The great majority of manuscripts are Byzantine. These are also the latest manuscripts, most from the ninth century onward. The external evidence tends to favour the Alexandrian family, since these are the earliest manuscripts. The two most important Alexandrian manuscripts are Codex Vaticanus and Codex Sinaiticus.

Internal textual evidence refers to the tendencies of copyists and authors. Textual critics have derived certain principles or 'rules' from the kinds of mistakes copyists tended to make. The most basic rule is to choose the reading that best explains how the other readings might have been made. Another common rule is that the shorter reading is usually original, since a copyist was more likely to add a clarifying phrase than to drop one. A third is that the 'harder reading' is usually the original, since a scribe was more likely to smooth over a difficulty than to create one.

Applying these rules of internal evidence to the manuscript evidence results in a text closest to the Alexandrian family. This is not to say that Alexandrian readings are always the best, but in general this family seems to represent the earliest text. Since both the external evidence and the internal evidence favours the Alexandrian family, almost all textual critics consider this to be the earliest and most reliable family.

Textual criticism and modern English versions. The Greek text derived by following the principles of textual criticism is known as the 'critical text'. There are two standard editions, Nestle-Aland (NA, 27th edn) and the United Bible Societies (UBS, 4th edn). Almost all modern English versions utilize the critical text. The exception is the *Revised Authorized Version*, which uses the so-called *Textus Receptus*, the Greek text which lies behind the *Authorized Version* of 1611. The *Textus Receptus* was based on a very limited number of late Byzantine manuscripts available in the sixteenth century.

There are thousands of variant readings throughout the OT and NT, but most are very minor (many in the OT involve spelling), and no doctrine of the Christian faith rests on any of these divergences. Furthermore, the wealth of manuscript evidence and the strong consensus among scholars concerning the practice of textual criticism, together confirm the accuracy and reliability of the text of Scripture.

2. The canon of Scripture

The word canon comes from a Greek word meaning 'measuring rod', and hence a 'rule' or 'standard'. The canon of Scripture are those books recognized by the church as the authoritative Word of God. When did a book become part of the canon? The ultimate answer is when that book was completed by a Spirit-inspired author or authors (2 Tim. 3:16–17; 2 Pet. 1:21). No council or committee made a book part of the canon. Rather, through the centuries the people of God – filled and guided by the Holy Spirit – have recognized those writings which exhibit the power and presence of the Spirit (1 John 2:20, 27).

Nor did formal recognition of the canon occur through a single council or decree. The canon was rather the result of a gradual process of collection, recognition and confirmation. Local canons and collections gradually grew into the widespread affirmation by the church.

The Old Testament canon. The Jewish Scriptures, sometimes called the Tanak, contain the same books as the Christian OT, but ordered differently. TaNaK is an acronym of the Hebrew words Torah (Law), Nevi'im (Prophets), and Kethuvim (Writings). Torah means the five books of Moses (Genesis to Deuteronomy); Nevi'im are the four 'former prophets' (Joshua, Judges, Samuel and Kings) and the four 'latter prophets' (Isaiah, Jeremiah, Ezekiel and the Book of the Twelve, meaning the minor prophets); Kethuvim are the three main books of

The Old Testament

Order in the **Hebrew Bible**

Law (Torah)

Genesis	Exodus	Leviticus	Numbers	Deuteronomy

Prophets (Nevi'im)

Joshua	Judges	Samuel	Kings

Isaiah	Jeremiah	Ezekiel	The Twelve (Hosea–Malachi)

Writings (Kethuvim)

Psalms	Proverbs	Job

Ruth	Song of Songs	Ecclesiastes	Lamentations	Esther

Daniel	Ezra–Nehemiah	Chronicles

Order in the **English Bible**

Pentateuch or Law

Genesis	Exodus	Leviticus	Numbers	Deuteronomy

Historical Books

Joshua	Judges	Ruth	1 & 2 Samuel	1 & 2 Kings	1 & 2 Chronicles	Ezra	Nehemiah	Esther

Poetic Books

Job	Psalms	Proverbs	Ecclesiastes	Song of Songs

Prophetic Books

Isaiah	Jeremiah	Lamentations	Ezekiel	Daniel	Hosea	Joel	Amos	Obadiah	Jonah	Micah	Nahum	Habakkuk	Zephaniah	Haggai	Zechariah	Malachi

poetry (Psalms, Proverbs, Job), the five 'scrolls' (Ruth, Song of Songs, Ecclesiastes, Lamentations and Esther), and three other writings (Daniel, Ezra–Nehemiah and Chronicles). Hence there are twenty-four books in the Jewish canon, which are identical to the thirty-nine books in the Christian OT (see chart).

While one cannot speak definitively of a time or event when the OT canon was 'closed', it seems clear that by the NT period this tripartite division had achieved authoritative status. For instance, Jesus refers once to the 'Law of Moses, the Prophets and the Psalms' (Luke 24:44). Psalms is the first and main book of the Writings, so indicates the whole section. There was also a widespread tradition in Judaism that the prophetic voice of God had ceased after the post-exilic prophets: 'With the death of Haggai, Zechariah and Malachi, the latter prophets, the Holy Spirit ceased out of Israel' (*Tosefta Sotah* 13:2, from the mid-third century AD; cf. Talmud *b. Sanh.* 11a). The so-called 'council' of Jamnia in the decades after the destruction of Jerusalem in AD 70 debated the authority of various books among the Writings, but ultimately affirmed them all. Melito of Sardis writing around AD 170 produced the first known list of all OT books (except Esther).

The New Testament																			
Gospels				Acts	Paul's Letters										Other letters				Reve-lation
Matthew	Mark	Luke	John	Acts	Romans	1 & 2 Corinthians	Galatians	Ephesians	Philippians	Colossians	1 & 2 Thessalonians	1 & 2 Timothy	Titus	Philemon	Hebrews	James	1 & 2 Peter	1, 2 & 3 John	Jude	Revelation

The New Testament canon. As with the OT, there is no definitive point at which the NT books received canonical recognition. 2 Pet. 3:15–16 suggests that even in the first century AD Paul's writings were being preserved and read as authoritative Scripture. The early church fathers frequently quote from the NT writings and attribute authoritative status to them. Impetus for formal recognition of the canon arose especially from external challenges, such as when the second-century Gnostic heretic Marcion established his own truncated canon made up of portions of Luke's Gospel and ten letters of Paul (c. AD 140). The church responded with discussions and lists of its own. The Muratorian fragment, dated about AD 170, contains a list which contains our NT with some minor variations. In the fourth century Eusebius categorized books under four headings: accepted, disputed, rejected and heretical. Those 'accepted' contain all our NT books except James, Jude, 2 Peter and 2 and 3 John, which are identified as disputed. Eusebius also identifies Revelation as accepted by some but rejected by others. The first list which is identical to the twenty-seven NT books was produced by Athanasius of Alexandria in his Easter letter of AD 367.

Apocryphal Books		
Roman Catholic Deuterocanonical Books		Other Books
Tobit, Judith, 1 & 2 Maccabees, Wisdom of Solomon, Ecclesiasticus, Baruch	Additions to Esther, Additions to Daniel	1 & 2 Esdras, 3 & 4 Maccabees, Prayer of Manasseh, Psalm 151

The Apocrypha. The most significant canonical debate among Christians concerns the books of the Apocrypha, a group of Jewish works mostly written between the times of the OT and the NT. These are included in our earliest complete copies of the LXX (fourth century AD), produced by Christians, but we do not know when they were first included with the OT. The canonicity of the Apocrypha was rejected by Martin Luther and the Protestant Reformers, following the tradition of Jerome (translator of the Vulgate). Roman Catholics accept the Apocrypha as 'deuterocanonical'. This does not mean it is less inspired than the proto-canonical books, but rather a 'second canon' beside the first. Catholics claim that the Apocrypha has been read and cherished by Jews and Christians from antiquity, and was included in the Septuagint. Protestants counter that these books were not part of the Hebrew Scriptures as recognized by Jesus, that they contain historical and doctrinal errors, and that they lack the prophetic power of inspired Scripture.

Historical tests of canonicity. For the OT, its acceptance as Scripture by Jesus and his apostles has been sufficient authority for Christians.

For the NT, we can discern certain tests which the people of God applied to writings to test their authority and canonicity.

(1) *Apostolic origin.* Does the book show evidence of divine authority? Jesus commissioned his apostles to pass down the authoritative message. When judging books for canonicity, the early church placed great emphasis on apostolic authority. Even those books that were not written directly by an apostle (e.g. Mark, Luke) bore the stamp of apostolic authority because their authors were closely associated with the apostles.

(2) *Theological consistency with the rest of Scripture: the rule of faith.* Since God is a god of truth, new revelation will not contradict earlier revelation, but will conform to the body of tradition passed down by the authentic community of faith.

(3) *Recognition by the Spirit-filled community.* Although this test does not reject differences of opinion or debates about canonicity, in time the church has recognized the presence of the Spirit in truly inspired writings.

(4) *Transforming power.* Has the work demonstrated the power of God to change lives? God's Word is recognizable by its living and dynamic capacity to renew and restore people's lives (Heb. 4:12).

Is the canon of Scripture closed? There is no explicit evidence for this in the Bible, but that is not surprising, since no NT author wrote with the intention of establishing the NT canon. Yet two thousand years of church history have confirmed that God's people have all they need in these sixty-six books to know God's nature, purpose and plan for the world.

E. Translating the Bible

Most people in the world do not read the Bible in its original languages, but in translation. The history of Bible translation begins in the third century BC and continues today, as scholars and linguists around the world labour to make God's Word understandable to people everywhere.

1. The languages of the Bible

The Bible was originally written in three languages: Hebrew, Aramaic and Greek. Most of the OT was written in Hebrew, the ancient language of the Jews. A few passages were written in Aramaic, a related Semitic language which served as the trade language for the ancient Near East. By the first century, most Jews in Israel spoke Aramaic as their native tongue. Hebrew was restricted to religious contexts (rather like Latin in the Middle Ages). Since the conquests of Alexander the Great in the third century BC, Greek had replaced Aramaic as the common trade language of the eastern Mediterranean. Jews engaged in commerce and administration with non-Jews (Gentiles) needed to speak Greek. Jesus was probably trilingual, speaking and teaching primarily in Aramaic, reading Hebrew in the synagogue and conversing with non-Jews in Greek. As Christians began proclaiming the gospel outside Palestine, they spoke and wrote mainly in Greek. The whole NT was written in Greek, except for a few of Jesus' words recorded in Aramaic (e.g. Mark 5:41; 7:34; 14:36).

2. The history of Bible translation

Ancient versions. By the third century BC, the Jews of Egypt were speaking Greek instead of Hebrew and the need arose for a Greek version of the Hebrew Scriptures. The result was the Septuagint (LXX; discussed above). By the first century the Septuagint was the primary Bible for Jews of the *diaspora* (or 'dispersion'), i.e. those living outside of Israel. A similar need arose in Israel since most Jews now spoke Aramaic rather than Hebrew. After the Hebrew text was read in a synagogue service, an Aramaic paraphrase or explanation, called Targum, would be given so the people could understand. These Targums were eventually put down in written form.

The need for translation also arose in the early church, as Christian missionaries began spreading the gospel beyond Greek-speaking regions. Versions in Latin and Syriac were produced in the second century, and many more followed: Coptic (the language of Egypt), Armenian, Georgian, Slavic, Ethiopic and others. The most enduring of ancient versions was the Latin Vulgate, produced by the early church father Jerome in the late fourth century. Commissioned by Pope Damasus I, the Vulgate was intended to replace the Old Latin version. Jerome's magnificent translation became the standard Bible of the Catholic church for over a thousand years. 'Vulgate' comes from the Latin word for 'common' and refers to the vernacular, the everyday language of the people.

Early English versions. Although the Vulgate was intended to be a common language translation, by the Middle Ages its Latin was understood only by the elite. Fearing the potential for heresy if everyone interpreted the Bible for themselves, the church placed strict limits on the production of vernacular versions. Yet people like Oxford theologian John Wycliffe believed that God's Word was meant for everyone. In 1382 Wycliffe and his associates produced the first English translation of the entire Bible.

With the invention of the printing press by Johannes Gutenberg in 1450, and the Protestant Reformation in the early sixteenth century, Bible publication flourished. In 1526 William Tyndale produced the first printed version of the NT in English. Tyndale's excellent translation, the first English version rendered directly from the Greek, set the standard for accuracy and style and became the model for all subsequent English versions. Yet vernacular translations were still illegal in England, and Tyndale was forced to flee to continental Europe to finish his work. He was eventually kidnapped, imprisoned and executed. Tyndale's legacy lives on today as international Bible translators suffer hardship and even martyrdom to take God's Word to the remotest parts of the world.

The Authorized or King James Version. The changing political climate of Britain as well as the popularity of Tyndale's work resulted in an easing of restrictions and the proliferation of English versions. The *Authorized Version*, known in North America as the *King James Version* (KJV), was commissioned by James I of England in 1604 as a compromise between two competing versions, the *Bishop's Bible* (1568), the official Bible of the Church of England, and the *Geneva Bible* (1560) favoured by the Puritans. The translation work was completed in seven years by forty-seven of the leading biblical scholars in Britain and published in 1611. Though – like all new versions – the AV was initially rejected by some, it quickly became the most widely used English version of its day and, eventually, the most popular English Bible of all time.

Revisions of the Authorized Version. Though the AV remained the pre-eminent English Bible for over 300 years, changes in the English language, advances in biblical scholarship, and the discovery of older and more reliable manuscripts resulted in the need for revision. In 1870 the Church of England commissioned the *Revised Version* (RV, 1881–85). A separate revision, the *American Standard Version* (ASV) was published in 1901 to reflect the preferences of North American scholars. Though neither of these versions challenged the popular dominance of the AV, they launched an era of translation and revision which continued throughout the twentieth and into the twenty-first centuries.

3. Contemporary versions and modern translation principles

English Bible versions today can be categorized in a variety of ways. One distinction is between those versions which are in a direct line of revision from the AV and its predecessors, and those which are 'new' versions translated directly from the Hebrew and Greek. Some of those in the AV tradition include the *Revised Standard Version* (RSV, 1952), the *New American Standard Bible* (NASB, 1971), the *Revised Authorized Version*

(RAV, 1982), the *New Revised Standard Version* (NRSV, 1990), and the *English Standard Version* (ESV, 2001). New versions without direct link to the AV include the *New English Bible* (NEB, 1970), *Good News Bible* (GNB, 1976), *New International Version* (NIV, 1978), *New Century Version* (NCV, 1986), *Revised English Bible* (REB, 1989), *Contemporary English Version* (CEV, 1995), *New Living Translation* (NLT, 1996), and *Today's New International Version* (TNIV, 2005). Most of these would be categorized as 'Protestant' versions, since their translation teams were primarily Protestant. Recent versions which are predominantly Roman Catholic include the *Jerusalem Bible* (JB, 1966), the *New American Bible* (NAB, 1970), and the *New Jerusalem Bible* (NJB, 1985). In 1985 the Jewish Publication Society released the *Tanakh*, a modern Jewish translation of the Hebrew Scriptures.

Another more significant distinction between modern Bible versions is their translation philosophy. *Formal equivalent* versions, also called 'literal' or 'word-for-word' versions, seek as much as possible to follow the lexical and grammatical form of the original Hebrew or Greek. *Functional equivalent* versions, also known as dynamic equivalent or idiomatic versions, seek first to translate according to the *meaning* of the text, regardless of the form. For example, the RSV renders Acts 11:22 quite literally: 'News of this reached the ears of the church at Jerusalem...' Recognizing that 'the ears of the church' is a Greek idiom rather than an English one, the GNB translates 'The news about this reached the church in Jerusalem'. While the RSV reproduces more closely the form of the Greek, the GNB captures the meaning in natural, idiomatic English.

There are no pure versions of either translation philosophy. Since no two languages are the same, all versions must frequently introduce idiomatic renderings in order to make sense. The difference is how much freedom translators take to alter the form in order to produce natural-sounding English. All Bible versions lie on a spectrum between form and meaning. Some recent versions which are generally formal equivalent include RSV, NASB, RAV, NRSV and ESV. Functional equivalent versions include GNB, CEV, NCV and NLT. Versions somewhere in between are the NIV, REB, NAB, NJB and TNIV, and many Christians use one of these as their 'all-purpose' Bible. (Most quotations in this *IVP Introduction* are taken from the TNIV.)

There are strengths and weaknesses of both formal and functional translations, and students of the Word should be encouraged to use a variety of versions from across the translation spectrum. Both kinds of translations have an important place in Bible study. Formal equivalent versions are helpful for examining the formal structure of the original text, identifying Hebrew or Greek idioms, locating ambiguities in the text, and tracing formal verbal allusions and recurrent words. Functional equivalent versions are more helpful for communicating accurately the meaning of the text, and for providing clarity, readability, and natural-sounding language. The weakness of functional equivalence is the danger of misinterpreting the original and so misleading the reader. The weakness of formal equivalence is producing obscure and awkward English when the text was clear and natural to its original readers.

Bible translation continues to be a critical concern of the church. God's Word was meant to be for all people everywhere, yet there are ethnic groups around the world which do not yet have Scripture in their native tongue. There is also the continual need for updating existing versions. Language changes over time, requiring periodic revision to keep up with contemporary idiom and to eliminate archaic language (e.g. the AV's archaic use of 'pitiful' in the sense of 'compassionate' in Jas 5:11). Advances in biblical scholarship and archaeological discoveries also create the need for ongoing assessment and improvement of existing versions. While no Bile version is perfect, the steadfast goal remains to communicate the meaning of the sacred text with accuracy and clarity.

Further reading

On inspiration and authority:

Howard Marshall, *Biblical Inspiration* (Paternoster, 1995) – well-written standard summary.

Howard Marshall, *Beyond the Bible: Moving from Scripture to Theology* (Baker, 2004) – helpful reflections in accessible lectures.

Richard Bauckham, S*cripture and Authority Today* (Grove, 1999) – thoughtful, booklet response to postmodernism.

Tom [N. T.] Wright, *Scripture and the Authority of God* (SPCK, 2005) – very readable, with helpful application to church life. Published in the USA as *The Last Word* (HarperCollins, 2006).

On text, canon and translations:

F. F. Bruce, *The Books and the Parchments* (Zondervan, 1991) – very readable survey of all the issues.

David Dewey, *Which Bible? A Guide to English Translations* (IVP, 2004) – now the best straightforward introduction available.

Dick [R. T.] France, *Translating the Bible: Choosing and Using an English Version* (Grove, 1997) – excellent booklet introduction, though it pre-dates the TNIV.

Bruce Metzger, *The Bible in Translation: Ancient and English Versions* (Baker, 2001) – another good survey, with more detail on the ancient versions.

2. Introducing the Old Testament

Desmond Alexander, Jamie Grant, Philip Johnston

OLD TESTAMENT STORY

One of the most remarkable features of the Bible is the way in which this library of sixty-six books forms an overarching story or meta-narrative that begins in Genesis with an account of the divine creation of the earth and ends in Revelation by describing the coming of a new earth. Between these two events the Bible paints a picture of human history that quickly moves from a 'good' creation (Gen. 1 – 2) to a state of imperfection due to the rebellion of Adam and Eve against the Creator (Gen. 3). Thereafter, the Bible provides a detailed, but selectively focused, account of how the Creator sets about redeeming and restoring the whole of creation. Central to this is the coming of Jesus Christ who, as the perfect God-man, atones for human sin, setting in place the means by which individuals may be both justified and sanctified.

As the first three-quarters of the biblical meta-narrative, the OT plays an indispensable role in illuminating how Jesus Christ stands at the heart of God's redemptive activity in the world. Explaining the origin and nature of the human predicament, the OT prepares for Christ's coming by detailing how he is both the fulfilment of divine promises

---

Sections in this chapter were written as follows – Desmond Alexander: Old Testament Story; Jamie Grant: Old Testament Background, Old Testament Interpretation; Philip Johnston: Old Testament Theology.

given centuries earlier and the means by which the consequences of human sin will be addressed.

Recognizing that the OT story is just part of a larger meta-narrative, it is nevertheless helpful to consider its content and presentation. Undoubtedly, the books of Genesis to Kings form the backbone of the OT story. Viewed together these books are, in certain respects, like a modern novel. Read from beginning to end they provide a progressive account, with later books presupposing and building upon what has been told in the preceding sections. A significant part of the Genesis–Kings story is repeated with additions and modifications in the book of Chronicles. The author of Chronicles produces another version of the history of the Davidic dynasty with its own distinctive emphases. The OT story, which contributes to the biblical meta-narrative, must incorporate the distinctive features of both versions.

The OT story extends well beyond Kings and Chronicles, taking in the return of the Judean exiles from Babylon, the rebuilding of Jerusalem and the temple (as described in the books of Ezra and Nehemiah) and the story of Esther. These events, as we shall see, introduce a further dimension to the OT story. Finally, other books which might not be viewed as forming part of the 'historical' narrative contribute to the OT story. To varying degrees the prophetic and wisdom books, as well as the Psalms, enrich the OT part of the biblical meta-narrative, adding important elements that look forward to the coming of Jesus Christ.

While the distinctive shape of the OT story is provided largely by the so-called historical books of the Bible, we need to recognize that these books are not 'historical' in the modern sense of the term. Unlike contemporary historical works, the biblical writings are not governed by Enlightenment presuppositions regarding the relationship between God and the universe. Specifically, the biblical writers readily acknowledge the possibility of divine activity influencing the outcome of human affairs. This stands in sharp contrast to many Enlightenment thinkers who favour a mechanistic view of the universe, concluding that every event in history can be explained without recourse to divine intervention. Not surprisingly, because they work with a very different set of presuppositions, the authors of the Bible's 'historical' books frequently affirm the role of God in shaping world events. Indeed, for them human history can only be accurately comprehended when the activity of God is fully recognized. Consequently, the OT story is in large measure an account of the interface between divine and human activity, especially as it relates to God's redemptive plan for all creation.

The OT story moves through a number of distinctive stages which are clearly marked by chronological and geographical factors. While these stages provide one way of setting out the OT story, there is a continuity to the story that bridges and unites these different elements. These stages may be outlined as follows:

A. Primeval era

The opening eleven chapters of Genesis provide a brief overview of the early history of humanity from creation up to about 2000 BC. By focusing on a small number of highly significant episodes, the dominant perception in these chapters is of the deep alienation that exists between God and humanity, resulting in a world that is marred by all kinds of divisions. Yet, while divine punishment is meted out in a variety of ways, a thread of hope runs throughout the narrative that through a righteous line of Adam's descendants, associated with the descendants of first Seth (Gen. 5) and then Shem (Gen. 11), the consequences of Adam and Eve's actions will be reversed. Linear genealogies are used to establish the identity of Eve's offspring who will eventually crush the serpent's head (Gen. 3:15).

B. Patriarchal period

The line of special descendants introduced in Gen. 1 – 11 leads to Abraham. He and selected members of his immediate family dominate the rest of Genesis. Divided by genealogies, Gen. 11:27 – 50:26 falls into three main sections that focus principally on Abraham (Gen. 12 – 25), Isaac and his son Jacob (Gen. 25 – 36), and Joseph (Gen. 37 – 50).

At the start of the patriarchal period, God makes various promises to Abraham that will eventually result in two important outcomes. First, although initially childless and landless, Abraham is promised that his descendants will become a great nation. Second, through a future royal descendant of Abraham, all the nations of the earth will be divinely blessed. These promises, which are articulated by God in a variety of forms to Abraham, Isaac and Jacob, reveal that the divine redemption of humanity will be dependent upon a royal line traced from Abraham (cf. Matt. 1:1–17).

Within the patriarchal narratives the principle of primogeniture (preference for the first-born son) is often overturned, with a younger brother receiving the patriarchal blessing (cf. Gen. 27:27–29). Consequently, Genesis concludes by portraying Joseph as the heir to the royal line, which in turn will be continued through his younger son, Ephraim (Gen. 48). As 'father to Pharaoh', Joseph's administration of Egypt brings blessing to many nations when a period of famine envelops the entire region. In this he prefigures the much greater blessing associated with the special line in Genesis. Later, Joseph's lineage includes Joshua, under whose leadership the Israelites take possession of the land of Canaan.

Although Joseph is clearly presented as the one through whom the royal lineage will be initially traced, Gen. 37 – 50 draws attention to an alternative lineage linked to Judah. The insertion into the main Joseph story of Gen. 38, which focuses on Tamar's extraordinary actions in raising up an heir for Judah, gives the impression that Judah's line may yet have a role to play in the fulfilment of God's purposes. This expectation is heightened through the bizarre events associated with the birth of twin boys to Tamar. While the midwife attaches a scarlet thread to Zerah's arm in order to identify him as the first-born, it is Peres who breaks out first. As the larger OT story reveals, the line of Judah through Peres leads to King David. His dynasty is especially important as regards the fulfilment of God's promise to bless the nations of the earth.

C. The life of Moses

The books of Exodus to Deuteronomy are bound together by events that take place during the lifetime of Moses – except for Exod. 1, his birth and death frame everything recorded in these books. Within this framework, the events move geographically from Egypt, via Mount Sinai, to the eastern bank of the River Jordan in the land of Moab. Between these locations the Israelites spend periods of time wandering in the desert of the Sinai Peninsula. Chronologically, most attention is given to the relatively short period that the Israelites spent at Mount Sinai; the account of this twelve-month sojourn runs from Exod. 19 to Num. 10. In a comparable way, the book of Deuteronomy, which consists mainly of two speeches made by Moses to the people, covers a very short period of time.

The account of the Israelites' time in Egypt centres on their remarkable deliverance from bondage to Pharaoh. With Moses as his spokesperson, God challenges Pharaoh by sending a series of punitive signs and wonders. As these come with increasing severity, the Egyptians gradually acknowledge the sovereign power of the Lord (Exod. 7 – 10). Nevertheless, Pharaoh's stubborn resistance continues until God punishes the Egyptians by putting to death all their first-born males. This occasion, which requires the Israelites to distinguish their homes by sprinkling blood on the door-frames, is designated the Passover (Exod. 11 – 12). This is the decisive moment in God's deliverance of the Israelites from Egypt, and becomes the focal point for later annual celebrations as the Israelites remember their exodus from Egypt on the 14th day of the month of Abib. In Israelite thinking the Passover becomes a major paradigm for the concept of divine salvation.

While the death of the Egyptian first-born sons at last persuades Pharaoh to let the Israelites leave Egypt, a further change of heart causes him to lead out his best chariots and horsemen against the fleeing slaves. In one final display of power, God parts the waters of the Red Sea, enabling the Israelites to cross over in safety. When the Egyptians attempt to follow, God causes the waters to return, drowning the entire army.

About seventy days after the Passover, the Israelites arrive at Mount Sinai. Here, following suitable preparations, the Lord comes to the people in a theophany (divine appearance), pronouncing in their hearing the principal obligations of the covenant that he wants to make with them (Exod. 19 – 20). We know these as the Ten Commandments. Further obligations and instructions are mediated to the people through Moses before a special ceremony confirms the unique relationship established between God and the Israelites (Exod. 21 – 24).

By submitting to the Lord's authority, the Israelites, formerly slaves to Pharaoh, become servants of God. To confirm this new relationship the Lord gives Moses instructions for the manufacture of a very distinctive tent and its furnishings. Known as the tabernacle, this tent of regal design, becomes God's dwelling place, enabling him to live in the very midst of the Israelite camp. God also instructs Moses to set apart Aaron and his sons to be priests responsible for the oversight of the tabernacle and the rituals associated with it. When the tabernacle is finished God comes to dwell in it, confirming by his presence his unique relationship with the Israelites (Exod. 25 – 31, 35 – 40).

By living among them, God sanctifies the people, making them a 'holy nation'. This holy status, however, needs to be maintained in the face of various influences that make the people 'unclean'. For this reason, the book of Leviticus sets out in detail the steps necessary to promote holy living and to atone for uncleanness.

As the Israelites move on towards the promised land, their trust in God falters when they hear reports of the strength of the enemy nations facing them in Canaan. Although Caleb and Joshua speak positively about taking the land, their opinions are drowned out by the voices of others. This causes the Israelites to rebel against God. Consequently, the Israelites are condemned to remain in the Sinai wilderness for a period of forty years, until the death of all those who doubted God's power to overcome all opposition. Only Caleb and Joshua are permitted to enter the promised land (Num. 13 – 14).

At the end of forty years, Moses leads a new generation of Israelites to the eastern side of the river Jordan just north of the Dead Sea (Num. 20 – 21). In a valedictory speech making up most of Deuteronomy, Moses reminds the people of all that has happened and invites them to renew their commitment to God. Moses' lengthy speech sets out afresh the teaching or 'torah' that should guide the people as they take possession of the land of Canaan.

D. Possessing the land of Canaan

When Moses eventually dies, his place as leader is taken by Joshua, an Ephraimite. Various references to Joshua throughout Exodus to Deuteronomy indicate that he is especially well placed to assume Moses' position as national leader. Indeed, the book of Joshua subtly presents him as a second Moses. Joshua guides the Israelites into the land of Canaan, enabling them to overcome successfully various alliances of local kings (Josh. 1 – 12). While much of the land still remained outside Israelite control, by the end of Joshua's life the tribes of Ephraim and Judah are settled in the territories allocated to them. Although they still need to take possession of it, the rest of the land is allocated to the other tribes. Under Joshua, the Israelites made good progress towards occupying all of the land previously promised by God to Abraham (Josh. 13 – 24).

In contrast to the positive steps taken under Joshua, the book of Judges describes how the Israelites are attacked by surrounding nations and live under constant threat. The blame for this unwelcome transition is placed on the Israelites themselves; contrary to their covenant obligations they adopt the religious customs of the nations of Canaan and worship their gods. Consequently, God permits the Israelites' enemies to overcome them. When they cry to the Lord for help, he raises up leaders, known as judges, who bring temporary relief by repelling the oppressors and promoting justice in the land (Judg. 2).

The book of Judges, however, portrays the judges as becoming less and less effective due to the increasing spiritual and moral corruption of the Israelites. As the book's epilogue (Judg. 17 – 21) clearly demonstrates, within a few generations God's people have abandoned the covenant obligations set before them by Moses and upheld by Joshua. Significantly, Judges contains subtle criticisms that reveal how the tribe of Ephraim progressively fails to follow Joshua's example by providing positive leadership for all the Israelites (e.g. 1:29; 8:1–2; 12:1–6; 17:1–5). This has an important bearing upon the rise of the monarchy in ancient Israel.

E. The early monarchy

The books of Samuel describe the transition in ancient Israel from tribal government to monarchy, with two closely related developments. First, leadership of the nation moves from Samuel, the last of the judges, to David, the youngest of the sons of Jesse (1 Sam. 16). As the book of Ruth highlights (Ruth 4), David's family belongs to the tribe of Judah. Second, the throne of God, as symbolized by the ark of the covenant, is moved from Shiloh in the territory of Ephraim to Jerusalem, the city of David (2 Sam. 6). Neither of these transitions is straightforward. However, the eventual outcomes are highly significant. As Ps. 78 reveals, these changes are due to God's rejection of the lineage of Joseph and of Shiloh in the region of Ephraim, and to his decision instead to choose David and Jerusalem (Zion), both associated with the tribe of Judah.

By bringing the ark of the covenant to Jerusalem, David confirms his status as God's chosen king over Israel. When David subsequently desires to construct a temple for God in Jerusalem, the Lord promises him that his dynasty will last for ever (2 Sam. 7). This promise establishes between God and the Davidic dynasty a special relationship that will have an important bearing upon the future history of Israel. The construction of the temple, however, is deferred until the reign of David's son, Solomon.

While the reign of Solomon (1 Kgs 1 – 11) contains many positive features, including the building and dedication of the Jerusalem temple, his failure to adhere faithfully to the instructions for kings detailed in Deut. 17 results in divine punishment. The outcome of this is the division of Solomon's kingdom into two parts following his death (1 Kgs 12).

F. The divided kingdoms

While the reigns of David and Solomon were marked by tribal unity and national prosperity, this changes dramatically after Solomon's death about 930 BC. Ten of the twelve tribes disown Solomon's son, Rehoboam, and opt rather to be governed by Jeroboam, an Ephraimite. They form a kingdom in the north that retains the designation 'Israel'. Two tribes remain loyal to Solomon's son Rehoboam, and establish the kingdom of Judah in the south. Over the next two centuries the relationship between the two nations blows hot and cold, until the northern kingdom is decimated by the Assyrians in 72 BC. After a long siege Sargon II captures Samaria, the capital city of the northern kingdom, and deports its leading citizens to Mesopotamia.

While the book of Kings attributes the fall of the northern kingdom to God's displeasure with the people living there (2 Kgs 17), the behaviour of those in the southern kingdom is little better. In due course a similar fate befalls Judah and its capital Jerusalem. This time the invading force comes from Babylon, who become the major power after defeating the Assyrians in 612 BC.

Babylonian supremacy does not lead to the immediate destruction of Jerusalem. An invasion of Judah by the Babylonians in 598/7 BC results in some Judeans being taken off to Mesopotamia. Then about twelve years later, an ill-fated attempt by Zedekiah the king of Judah to get the support of Egypt against Babylon leads to the destruction of Jerusalem in 587/6 BC. This included the demolition of the temple and the removal of the Davidic dynasty from royal office. These dramatic events herald the start of the Babylonian exile.

G. The Babylonian exile

Like earlier Assyrian kings, the Babylonian king Nebuchadnezzar II (605–562 BC) follows a policy of relocating subjugated peoples from one part of his empire to another. As a result, many of the leading citizens of Judah are exiled to Mesopotamia. The first of these deportations may have occurred as early as 605 BC (see Dan. 1:1), with larger deportations occurring in 598/7 BC and especially 587/6 BC. These events mark the beginning of a period of extreme uncertainty for the Judean exiles as they struggle to comprehend the theological significance of their removal from the promised land, the destruction of the Jerusalem temple and the demise of the Davidic dynasty. For the author of Kings, the loss of land, temple and kingship is due to the failure of the people of Judah, especially their leaders, to keep the obligations of their covenant with the Lord (2 Kgs 22:10–17).

H. The restoration

The overthrow of the Babylonian empire by the Persians in 539 BC leads to a major reversal of fortunes for the Judean exiles. As head of the Persian empire, Cyrus facilitates the return of Jews to Jerusalem with the specific objective of rebuilding the temple. While progress towards the completion of the project is slow, temple worship eventually recommences in 516/5 BC (Ezra 1 – 6). Later, under the leadership of Ezra (from 458 BC) and Nehemiah (from 445 BC), the walls of Jerusalem are repaired, bringing greater security to the population of Judah.

While these positive developments reflect an important change in God's attitude towards his chosen people, with punishment giving way to mercy, one important element continues to be missing from the picture; a Davidic king is not restored to the throne. However, post-exilic biblical writings exhibit a clear expectation that the fulfilment of God's redemptive purposes will include the re-establishment of the Davidic dynasty. In this way the earlier divine commitment to bless all the nations of the earth through a royal descendant of Abraham will be fulfilled.

Although the OT story looks forward with anticipation to the outworking of these divinely-given expectations, they only begin to be realized with the advent of Jesus Christ. What the OT story promises, the NT story fulfils.

OLD TESTAMENT BACKGROUND

The story of Israel is a fascinating account of God's committed love for a chosen people. God's plan from the outset was to reach sinful humanity through the agency of a single people (Gen. 12:1–3). So a small Middle-Eastern nation has had a significance in world history that far outweighs its numerical size and political stature. This significance can lead us to treat Israel as a special case, beyond the norms of historical investigation. However, divine salvation actually broke into human reality – the 'really real'. Israel was an historical people, like any other, and to understand the OT we must learn something about the background of the Hebrews, the people of Israel.

A. National identity

The earliest archaeological reference to Israel as a nation is found on the Egyptian Merneptah Stele dating from c. 1210 BC, but the roots of Israel's nationhood go back much further than that. The OT points to a self-identity beginning in the prehistoric period. Israel's creation story bears clear points of contact with those of her neighbours, but is also markedly distinctive. Rather than resulting from conflict between the gods (as in Mesopotamian stories), the earth was created by the word of a personal God, who seeks relationship with those created in his image. Although the term covenant is nowhere used in the Genesis creation accounts, there are clear hints of this central OT tenet from the very beginning: the God of Israel is a covenant God, committed to his people. This is important because the idea of divine covenant shapes the formation of Israel's national identity and touches every area of her life and culture.

The implications of covenant are first seen in the calling of Abraham (Gen. 12:1–3). This begins the account of God's dealings with the patriarchs, which are foundational to the later formation of the nation Israel. The call of Abraham (early second millennium BC), is significant in that the origin of a nation lies in the obedience of an individual. Abraham enters into relationship with the covenant God. The purpose of that relationship was to bring blessing to him, to his descendants and ultimately to 'all the families of the earth' (NRSV). The choice of this one family would lead to blessing on a nation and then the whole world. Abraham's grandson Jacob (later renamed Israel) had twelve sons and from these sons the twelve tribes developed.

Exod. 1 highlights an interesting dynamic. In the opening verse 'the sons of Israel' refers to the twelve physical sons of Jacob. But when Pharaoh uses the same phrase in v. 9, he refers to a people large enough to threaten Egypt. The text indicates massive population growth, and with that comes the beginning of nationhood. It is in the events of Israel's release from slavery in Egypt, and their climactic meeting with God at Sinai (Exod. 19 – 20), that national identity is truly formed. The exodus experience came to define a nation. Further, God is now known by his personal name 'Yahweh' (usually translated in English Bibles as 'the LORD', in small capitals; cf. Exod. 3:14–15).

At Sinai the Israelites not only came to know more fully the God of their forefathers, they also received a calling to be 'a kingdom of priests and a holy nation' (Exod. 19:6). National identity was expressed in terms of divine calling. Israel was to be shaped by the ways of Yahweh (as holy) and was to be an intermediary between God and the other nations (as priests). Also significant was their calling, not only out of Egypt but also into Canaan. With the grant of land, a people group became a settled nation. The land was given as a trust to Israel, confirming their divine calling. The early chapters of Deuteronomy (4, 7, 9) make clear that Israel did not become God's 'treasured possession' because they were more powerful or righteous than other nations. Their calling was to become a light to the other nations, attracting them to the true God, Yahweh. Should Israel fail to follow this call to be God's witnesses, they too could be removed from the land.

Israel continued as a single nation through several centuries under the judges and early kings. It reached its political zenith under Solomon, but due to his unwise government and personal apostasy, inter-tribal tensions arose, leading to civil unrest and the ultimate division of Israel into two states: the larger part, still called Israel, in the north, and the smaller Judah in the south (1 Kgs 11 – 12). The formation of two nation states clearly threatened the identity of a single people with the same calling. Geographic and political factors meant that northern Israel was distanced from the Jerusalem temple, so it established alternative unauthorized worship sites. Judah maintained an official worship of Yahweh, although as a nation often strayed from true faith. Israel ultimately fell to the Assyrian empire in 722 BC, while Judah was protected by God for another century before falling to the rising superpower Babylon in 586 BC. However, the OT cites not political developments but the rejection of Yahweh as the cause of exile. Many key people from both states ultimately ended up in exile in Babylon, with only the poor remaining in the land.

Nevertheless, rather than destroying a sense of identity, the exile seemed to renew awareness of Israel's calling, resulting in the rebuilding of the temple and the restoration of Jerusalem once the exile was over. Israel remained a puppet state of one eastern power or another, but the sense of national identity remained strong, based on the call to follow the ways of Yahweh.

B. Political governance

Israel was key to God's plan to restore relationship between himself and sinful humanity and, because of this, the nation was meant to be unique. The people were not meant to follow the patterns of those who had lost the land because of their offensive acts. Israel at every level was meant to be different – from commoners to kings. The reason for Israel's uniqueness was her unique relationship with Yahweh. The covenant impacted every area of society, including political governance.

Prior to nationhood, classic ancient Near Eastern patterns of patriarchal rule governed the lives of the Abrahamic clan and their descendants. The head of the family was 'elder' (ruler) of the extended family group. Some of the patriarchal narratives demonstrate that this was not always a straightforward question of unchallenged leadership (e.g. Gen. 27), but the traditional pattern was significant for the formation of political structures within Israel. The population expansion that occurred in Egypt was to stretch these traditional paradigms, however. One son had become twelve, and the families had become tribes, yet they were still organized according to the pattern of clan eldership (Exod. 3:16; 4:29). The arrival of Moses on the scene was to significantly change authority structures amongst the Israelites. First, he himself became the divinely appointed ruler over this newborn nation (Exod. 3), a new phenomenon for Israel and in some ways a prototype of kingship. Secondly, elders were appointed on a meritocratic basis because of gifts and abilities, not simply family pecking order

(Exod. 18). The clan structure, however, continued in force throughout the wilderness years and into the early post-conquest era.

Joshua followed Moses as leader of Israel, but there was no succession beyond that second generation, which led to a breakdown of leadership. Israel still functioned as a federation of clans, each with its own land and autonomy. This worked fine in terms of local administration, but was more problematic in the face of military challenge on a national scale. The book of Judges tells of the repeated subjugation of the clans by foreign powers and of Yahweh raising up a series of leaders who focused Israelite opposition to bring a period of release. Again, however, there was no succession between these leaders, and the interim periods saw foreign nations grabbing their chance to invade or oppress Israel. Two significant features are emphasized in Judges: first, Israel's oppression in the land resulted directly from her rejection of Yahweh's rule (13:1); and, secondly, Israel's moral decline was associated with the lack of kingly leadership (21:25). The implication is that kingship would have a profound effect on the obedience of the people.

The law code in Deuteronomy contains a section addressing the key governing offices in Israel (Deut. 16:18 – 18:22). Interestingly, the law concerning judges takes priority over the law of the king, perhaps implying that justice takes ultimate precedence in a godly society. This section also defines the functions of priests, Levites and prophets within Israel. How these offices actually functioned in reality, and how closely office-bearers stuck to the Deuteronomic ideal, is far from clear. Nevertheless, this section provides for an equitable ordered society with clear division of powers and responsibilities. This included kingship, which became a reality in Israel fairly late in the day compared to other ancient Near Eastern nations.

There is much debate about whether the OT history books are pro- or anti-kingship. The account of the origins of kingship (1 Sam. 8 – 12) seems to speak both for and against the institution. Yet, since kingship was permitted in the societal order indicated in Deuteronomy, and given the pivotal, symbolic importance of Yahweh's covenant with David, it appears that monarchy was not alien to God's plan for Israel. The crucial issue regarding Israelite kingship is not whether it should have existed or not, but rather the type of kingship that Israel should have. In asking for a king 'such as all the other nations have' (1 Sam. 8:5), the people sought the wrong leadership – Israel's king should be *different* from those of the nations. They sought a strong ruler and military leader, but in covenant terms the king was only ever meant to be a vice-regent subject to the rule of Yahweh. He was to be the archetypal OT believer, to trust in God and follow his rules. Yahweh himself would protect the people. The OT history books record that when the king followed the Lord so did the people, but when he did not they did not.

Kings governed the Israelites for almost 450 years, but few of them followed their call to model Yahwistic faith for their people. Hence, after the glory years of David and Solomon, Israel and Judah often fell under the control of one or other of the superpowers. Still notionally independent, they had to pay tribute to a larger protectorate state (e.g. 2 Kgs 18:13–18). Ultimately, both king and people were removed from the land by being taken into Babylonian exile. The land grant was removed because of their rejection of Yahweh and his messengers, the prophets, who had called for repentance. Following the return to the land after exile, Israel was ruled by governors and high priests under the control of a succession of military powers (Persians, Ptolemies in Egypt, Seleucids in Syria, and Romans). It was during this time – following a series of monarchic failures prior to the exile and long years of external rule – that the expectation of a renewed Davidic king really came to the fore in the faith of Israel.

C. Religious experience

The national and political experience of Israel cannot be separated from her faith. National identity was formed in covenant with God, and all political rule in Israel was subject to his ultimate authority. The religious experience of Israel began in the patriarchal roots of nationhood (the call of Abraham) and extends through the whole history of the nation (including the exile). Everything has a 'religious' cause or effect.

From Genesis onwards, the OT highlights the call to 'walk with God'. The image is implied in Eden (Gen. 3:8) and runs like a thread through the accounts of God's dealings with his people. Abraham was called to 'walk before me faithfully and be blameless' (Gen. 17:1) and Israel as a community was called to do the same (Lev. 26:3, 12). Israel was to make a whole life response to Yahweh, giving themselves (individually and corporately) over to God. This is expressed in the central command of OT faith: to 'love [Yahweh] your God with all your heart and with all your soul and with all your strength' (Deut. 6:5).

Such devotion to God was to be demonstrated by keeping God's law (Deut. 10:13; Ps. 1); offering sacrifices for sin (Lev. 1 – 6); giving regularly to support the priests and the poor (Deut. 26); praying and fasting (both are presented as 'good practice' throughout the OT); keeping a Sabbath day of rest; and attending communal festivals of worship three times each year (Exod. 23:14–17).

However, the OT makes it abundantly clear that there is to be no separation of the religious and the secular in Israel. Following Yahweh must be formative in every area of life. It should impact family relationships, business practices, bringing up children, use of time and wealth, care for others and every area of work or leisure. This is reflected repeatedly as 'doing what is right and just' (Gen. 18:19; Prov. 21:3; Isa. 56:1). The prophet Micah sums up the essence of Israel's religious experience in this simple verse: 'And what does the LORD require of you? To act justly [or: do justice] and to love mercy and to walk humbly with your God' (Mic. 6:8).

D. Daily life and society

A snapshot of life in Israel would, of course, vary depending upon when that photograph was taken. Genesis presents the patriarchal clan as pastoral – a nomadic community with livestock (Gen. 47:1–6). Abraham and his line were tent-dwellers, who would wander with their flocks to find appropriate grazing land. Clearly Abraham was a wealthy and powerful man (note his frequent interaction with kings), yet he and his family were often confronted by the common difficulties of transient communities (Gen. 21:22–34). This type of lifestyle continued until Jacob and his clan went to live in Egypt, following a severe famine throughout the Near East (Gen. 46 – 50). There the clan grew into a nation and, for a while at least, lived as a landed people around Goshen because of Pharaoh's land grant (Gen. 47).

However, the Egyptian rulers later grew fearful of having what was effectively a foreign nation in their midst (Exod. 1). So they began a brutal programme of enforced labour and infanticide. Such atrocities were far from uncommon in the ancient Near East, where the young men of defeated nations were often taken as slave labour by the victors. The biblical accounts suggest a period of great hardship in the later years in Egypt, yet the Israelites also grew to appreciate the benefits of landed status. Following the exodus from Egypt, the return to nomadic life for forty years was clearly difficult to accept (Exod. 16:3; Num. 11:5), yet during that period the people were to learn to trust completely in Yahweh for every provision in their daily lives. This was later celebrated annually in the Feast of Tabernacles.

Life in Canaan brought great benefits, but also challenges. The Israelite community was able to enjoy the fruits of the land and the stability of settled homes. However, the great challenge of material stability was not to forget to trust in God as their provider (Deut. 6:10–25). Israel's was a predominantly agrarian society. Most people would make their living off the land, either as landowner farmers or as agricultural workers (the book of Ruth gives insight into post-conquest social life), although skilled trades of all kinds would also have been practised (stonemasonry, carpentry, etc.). The life of labourers would often be precarious, as they received their wages daily. Not working, for whatever reason, would leave a family without provision and with no social security system to fall back on. In such circumstances the nuclear family would depend on the support of the wider family and clan (Lev. 25:25–55).

Education, both spiritual and general, would normally have happened in the home (Deut. 6:6–7). The royal court in Jerusalem would have been a place where young men in training for civil service would be schooled in languages and statesmanship. As in every society, there would have been an educated class in Israel that filled the influential offices of state and religion. From the time of the early monarchy on, a standing army (as opposed to ad hoc conscription) was in place, providing a source of employment other than agriculture and the skilled trades, an option often popular amongst the poor of the land.

E. Conclusion

Israel as a nation was to be characterized by what we could call a holistic Yahwism. Every skill, gift and ability could be (and was to be) used for the glory of their covenant God (Exod. 31:1–11). This is why the OT laws address each area of human life and societal existence. One key idea of Israelite society was to live in 'fear of the LORD'. Basically, this means that Yahweh made a claim on every aspect of his people's lives, and they should respond by seeking to please God in all of life. Many times Israel strayed from the ways of her Lord. But theirs was to be a life lived – individually and corporately – in constant awareness of the presence of God, and with the deep desire to demonstrate love for him in every aspect of life.

OLD TESTAMENT THEOLOGY

A. A centre?

The NT is clearly centred on the person and work of Jesus of Nazareth. The Gospels give accounts of his life, death and resurrection, Acts and the letters spell out his significance for believers, and Revelation looks forward to his return. So the whole collection of books – and indeed Christian faith in general – has an obvious centre.

By contrast, the OT has no such centre, no single person or period around which this larger and more diverse collection of books revolves.

Various twentieth-century scholars wrestled with this issue and proposed single, dual or multiple themes as representing the core of the OT, but without reaching consensus.

A moment's reflection reveals many more contrasts between the two testaments. The NT covers a few decades, the OT several millennia. The NT presents a change of era, the OT recounts the ebb and flow of history. The NT presents one generation of a new movement, in the socio-political context of one empire; the OT covers dozens of generations, in many different socio-political contexts, countries and empires. So it is no wonder that the OT seems more diffuse, and less easy to interpret coherently.

Nevertheless, the 'problem' of no theological centre is more apparent than real. If the OT is taken on its own terms, rather than in comparison to the NT, then it clearly does have a core theme which underlies its presentation of people, events and history from one end to the other. And that theme is God and his people. Whether in the historical development from creation to the patriarchs, slavery, promised land, monarchy, exile and beyond, or in the literary diversity of law, history, poetry and prophecy, the central theme is the nature of God and of human relationship with him.

B. The Mosaic heart

For most of the OT, the Mosaic law provides the basis for this relationship between God and humanity. The foundational period in the OT is the half-century covering the exodus from Egypt and entry into Canaan, and the key body of teaching is the law of Moses originating from then. So the books of Exodus to Deuteronomy present the theological heart of the OT, the nearest equivalent to a centre. The term 'law' is often used as a handy summary of all this material, but this term can hide from view other, equally important, aspects of these books.

First, God delivered his people from slavery in Egypt, forcing their release by bringing increasingly calamitous plagues, and sealing their escape at the Sea of Reeds (traditionally called the Red Sea; Exod. 1 – 15). This event is repeatedly recalled in the Psalms and prophets, in celebration and warning. Deliverance from Egypt precedes the giving of the law at Sinai; so obedience to the law was to be a response to salvation, not the reason for it.

Secondly, God revealed himself in several ways. This occurred initially to Moses with a new name, 'Yahweh' (Exod. 3:13–14; 6:2–3). Yahweh means 'he is' (same root as 'I am'), in the sense not so much that God exists, but rather that he is present with his people. It is relational more than existential. Yahweh's presence was to be crucial to the Israelites' deliverance and vital to their faith. (Most English translations follow the ancient Jewish practice of not using the name Yahweh, but instead substituting the term LORD, in small caps. This makes the OT more accessible to many readers, though it loses the intimacy of a personal name.) God then revealed himself to the Israelites in awe-inspiring thunder, lightning, smoke, trumpet blast and earthquake (Exod. 19:16–19). This intense physical manifestation was a clear indication of God's holiness, and ample reminder that any relationship with him required a proper basis. The visible reminder of God's presence continued throughout the wilderness period as a fiery cloud over the tabernacle (Exod. 40:36–38). And God revealed himself most comprehensively in the law given to Moses, setting out the detailed requirements for holy worship and godly life.

Thirdly, God established his covenant with Israel (Exod. 19:5–6). God had already made a covenant with Abraham and his descendants (Gen. 12; 15; 17); here it is re-affirmed in new circumstances and with much more content. It is important to remember that the law is set in a covenantal context: the first section of law (Exod. 20 – 23) is actually called 'the Book of the Covenant' (24:7). The term 'covenant' simply means contract, treaty, alliance, and implies that there are obligations on both parties. It was regularly used in secular contexts for agreements between individuals or treaties between states, both in ancient Near Eastern documents and in the OT itself. And it is not just the term that is borrowed from everyday life: the very structure of Deuteronomy reflects the pattern of ancient international treaties. Israel's religion was distinctive in the ancient world in using this secular concept of mutual obligation for a people's relationship with their God. Yahweh committed himself unmistakably to Israel.

Fourthly, God gave Moses the ten commandments and the rest of the law at Sinai. This complex body of material comes both in small sections interspersed among narrative (in Exodus and Numbers) and in large coherent blocks of text (in Leviticus and Deuteronomy). Throughout there is a mixture of different types of law, sometimes described as ceremonial, civil and moral. This type of categorization is useful in helping Christians work out their implications for today: ceremonial law is largely fulfilled in Jesus Christ; civil law applies to a theocratic (i.e. God-governed) state which is no longer the case for us, even if some of the principles are still relevant; and moral or criminal law identifies activities which are still unacceptable today, even if our penalties may differ. However, the OT texts do not make these distinctions, since all the law applied to Israel. Another element of complexity is that the same laws are sometimes repeated with variations. Even the ten command-ments have two different explanations of the Sabbath law (Exod. 20:11; Deut. 5:15). This implies that the laws were passed down for generations in oral form and occasionally adapted to new circumstances. Later forms were then incorporated in the final text, without detracting from the sense of Mosaic origin – just as a modern law-code or student textbook can be emended or re-edited while retaining the name of its originator (e.g. *Gray's Anatomy*, first published in 1858, retains the same name 150 years later in its much expanded and modified 39th edition).

Fifthly, the ancient practice of sacrifice is institutionalized. While Noah and Abraham apparently built open-air altars and offered sacrifice themselves, now there is to be an enclosed portable shrine or tabernacle (later replaced by the temple), with an ordained priesthood and a regulated sacrificial system. Priests, sacrifices, people, campsite and all of life are classified on a 'holiness spectrum', ranging from holy to clean to unclean. Sin and other forms of pollution lead down the spectrum; purification and sacrifice lead back up it. Holiness has traditionally been understood as separateness, and God's otherness is certainly evident in the OT. But it also includes completeness, perfection and (for humans) consecration to God. These positive aspects complement the austerity of the traditional view, giving us a richer understanding of holiness.

Finally, the Mosaic material notes that God's interest reaches beyond Israel. They were to be 'a kingdom of priests' (Exod. 19:6): just as priests were intermediaries between ordinary Israelites and God, so the people of Israel should be intermediaries between God and other nations. Deut. 4:6–8 similarly notes that Israel's obedience to Yahweh would be a witness to the nations. Thus this theme, which stretches from Genesis (12:3) to Malachi (1:11), is also present in the heart of the OT. While it became a minor OT motif, due to Israel's disobedience, it nonetheless remains important.

C. Pre-Mosaic faith

Though 'Mosaic Yahwism' is the main and dominant form of OT religion, the Bible begins with a whole book recounting events and people before Moses. Chs. 1 – 2 give two different portrayals of creation, though both highlight the uniqueness of God and his creation of humanity as male and female. Ch. 3 presents human disobedience and resultant loss of God's immediate presence and of their potential immortality (though the link between individual sin and death is seldom noted later in the OT). In this, as in much more, the Genesis texts are distinct from other ancient creation accounts. The following chapters recount the spread of sin, leading first to the flood, and then the disruption of humanity into different language groups and the scattering of the nations. This brief section is theologically crucial, since it presents the backdrop for God's intervention through a specific family.

Chs. 12 – 50 present this divine response, through the 'patriarchal history' of Abraham, Jacob and Joseph. God makes a covenant with Abraham which will lead to innumerable descendants, national territory and worldwide blessing (12:1–3; 13:14–16). But the immediate issue was his own childlessness, and most of the patriarchal story concerns individual descendants and family survival.

Interestingly, patriarchal religion is significantly different from later Mosaic practice, lacking priests and enclosed altar, commandments and laws, Sabbath and festivals. Further, Abraham co-existed happily with his Canaanite neighbours in a way later prohibited to Israel. Also, most of the names for God in direct speech are compounds of the widespread term El (a generic term meaning 'god'), not Yahweh. The narrator often refers to Yahweh, but this probably reflects later writing, after his name became known. In fact, patriarchal religion is so different from Mosaic practice that a book title calls this early period *The Old Testament of the Old Testament* (R. W. L. Moberly, Fortress, 1992). Nevertheless, Abraham's faith was genuine, and in the NT Paul uses this to underline that the foundational aspect of OT religion was faith, not keeping the law (Rom. 4).

D. Post-Mosaic developments

1. Monarchy

Settlement in the land brought no new theological developments. On the contrary, as time progressed the Israelites slipped into ever greater apostasy, worshipping local Baal deities and adopting Canaanite practices. According to the book of Judges, they only survived because God raised up deliverer-judges who kept their enemies at bay.

The monarchy, however, brought several new elements. First there was David's capture of Jerusalem, and Solomon's construction of the temple there. So this city became the religious as well as the political capital of the nation, and came to be seen as the place of God's dwelling on earth. Secondly, for all his well-known faults, David was 'a man after [God's] own heart' (1 Sam. 13:14), and his reign was idealized in later imagination. He became the standard against which biblical historians judged successive kings (mostly negatively), and the model by which prophets presented a future deliverer. Thirdly, the king became the agent for divine blessing or the cause of divine punishment. Ps. 72 epitomizes the positive side of this theology, with the king now the protector of the vulnerable and the agent of international blessing.

2. Prophecy

Prophets were essentially intermediaries between the divine and human realms, mostly delivering God's word to the people and occasionally representing them to him. Moses fulfilled both aspects, and Abraham the second, so they could be called prophets (Deut. 18:15; Gen. 20:7). However, the term is mostly used for later figures, named and unnamed, male and female (cf. Judg. 4:4; 2 Kgs 22:14), who fulfilled this task throughout the periods of the judges and kings, the exile and beyond. The best known of these are Samuel, Nathan, Elijah, Elisha, and those with books named after them, traditionally known as classical or writing prophets.

The prophets are rightly described as 'covenant enforcers'. They reminded individual kings and the general populace of God's standards, and often proclaimed his judgment for their failure to keep them. This came to the fore in the eighth century BC, with the ministry of Amos and Hosea in northern Israel, and Isaiah and Micah in southern Judah. It is perhaps surprising that these prophets rarely use the term covenant. However, this need not mean (as some have argued) that covenant only emerged later as a theological concept, and that the Pentateuchal texts were then edited accordingly. On the contrary, the writings of these eighth-century prophets have many allusions to law and covenant, e.g. Hosea mentions half of the ten commandments in one verse (4:2), and Isa. 1:2–3 uses the language of covenant treaties (witnesses summoned, father–child relationship, the verbs 'rebel' and 'know'). Throughout, the prophets assume a relationship of mutual obligation between God and his people, and castigate the latter for failing to keep their side.

As punishment threatens and then falls, with the exile of Israel to Assyria and later of Judah to Babylon, the prophets look beyond to restoration. Even prophets who warn of imminent catastrophe give glimmers of hope. Amos urges Israel to seek God and live (Amos 5:4, 6, 14), and glimpses restoration (9:11–15). Hosea also sees beyond judgment to a return (Hos. 1:10–11). Similarly Jeremiah a century later repeatedly warns of exile, yet looks beyond it (e.g. 3:14–18). These and other passages often envisage a restored monarchy with a new King David who will shepherd the gathered flock (e.g. Isa. 11:1; Mic. 5:2; Jer. 23:5–6; Ezek. 34:23–24). They also speak of a new community, with a new relationship with God (e.g. Jer. 31, which predicts a new covenant).

This strand of prophecy moves beyond the Mosaic theology of blessing for obedience and punishment for disobedience (e.g. Lev. 26; Deut. 28), and portrays God's willingness to forgive and restore.

3. Exile and restoration

The exile was a theological catastrophe. Ps. 89 is a glorious, lengthy celebration of God's power demonstrated in creation and his love shown in covenant with David, until the dramatic change of v. 38: 'But you have rejected, you have spurned, you have been very angry ... you have renounced the covenant...'. The emotional trauma of Jerusalem's destruction is portrayed most poignantly in the book of Lamentations, five poetic laments full of pathos and sorrow, which end with barely flickering faith: 'You, LORD, reign for ever ... Restore us ... unless you have utterly rejected us...' (Lam. 5:19–22).

Some fifty years later, Cyrus defeated Babylon and the restoration began. In the early decades governor Zerubbabel and high priest Joshua are spoken of in glowing terms (Hag. 2:23; Zech. 3 – 4). Zerubbabel was a grandson of Judah's last king (1 Chr. 3:17–19), so may have seemed to fulfil the earlier prophecies. But kingship was not restored, and the province was ruled by a governor as part of the Persian empire. Indeed, another oracle addressing this context seems to 'democratize' or broaden to the whole community the Davidic covenant: 'I will make an ever-lasting covenant with you [plural], my faithful love promised to David' (Isa. 55:3). As in the past the king mediated God's blessing to the people (see D.1 above), so now the people would mediate God's blessing to the nations. God's universal purpose would be fulfilled.

Over time, the small province of Judah settled into routine under the Persians and then the Ptolemies. But persecution in the second century BC by the Seleucids led to renewed hope for political independence and national revival under a new David. This hope for restoration under a 'messiah' (literally 'anointed one') led to a proliferation of apocalyptic writing and contributed to the growth of parties within Judaism. The grandiose visions of renewal in the prophets, which had only been partly fulfilled in the return from exile, were revisited, and the Davidic figure awaited with new zeal. Jewish life and religion followed the old frame-work, but anticipated its renewal.

E. Life and death

One important aspect of OT life and faith not mentioned so far is that of life, death and the afterlife. Christians are familiar with the NT perspective of different fates after death for believers and unbelievers, and may mistakenly read this back into the OT. However, 2 Tim. 1:10 affirms that 'Christ Jesus ... brought life and immortality to light through the gospel', which implies that before then the afterlife was in the dark, or at least in the shadows. This fits with the OT evidence.

The perspective of the OT is largely limited to this present life on earth, and it repeatedly emphasizes that this is the arena for relating to God (cf. Deut. 30:15, 19). There is no other, and the OT shows little interest in death and its realm. The only post-mortem fate envisaged is the underworld, called 'Sheol' (usually translated 'grave' in TNIV), a dreary place of minimal activity whose occupants are cut off from God (Ps. 6:5). Many Israelites probably believed that everyone went to Sheol, and that relating to God would be continued by their descendants rather than themselves.

Nevertheless, there is an imbalance in the way the term Sheol is used. Passages which speak of going down to Sheol predominantly refer to the ungodly, whereas the death of the righteous is usually recounted in other terms. There are a few exceptions: Jacob, King Hezekiah, Job and a psalmist all seem to envisage Sheol (Gen. 37:35; Isa. 38:10; Job 14:13; Ps. 88:4). But they do so when in great trouble, and there is a noticeable contrast when the trouble is resolved (as in the accounts of Jacob's actual death). Further, a few psalms seem to glimpse an alternative of continued communion with God, though its form remains unspecified (Pss. 16:10; 49:15). This imbalance leaves an unresolved tension in the OT.

Finally, two eschatological passages (i.e. envisaging the future or end-time) speak of resurrection. Isa. 26:19 affirms that 'your dead will live, LORD' (but not ungodly rulers, v. 14). And Dan. 12:2 predicts: 'Multitudes ... will awake: some to everlasting life, others to shame and everlasting contempt.' These are the first rays of the hope which was developed in the NT. However, it is important to note that the concept of resurrection lies at the margins of the OT. Other books reflecting the exile and restoration maintain the traditional OT view that this life is the arena of faith. Here, as elsewhere in Israelite theology, it is the coming of Jesus which gives a new perspective.

OLD TESTAMENT INTERPRETATION

It should be clearly stated from the outset that the task of interpreting the OT is essentially no different from that of interpreting the NT. In fact, the basic principles of hermeneutics remain the same whether we are reading a passage from the Gospels or the sacrificial laws in

Leviticus. Contrary to popular opinion, there is no special, secret knowledge required for the interpretation of the OT. It is not the preserve of the learned few. The OT is much neglected today because of the misapprehension that it is beyond the grasp of the ordinary reader. Many Christians see it as being far removed from their reality and generally unintelligible, so they do not go anywhere near it. The church is *much* the poorer as a result. Without the OT, we have an incomplete picture of God, a partial comprehension of the divine plan of salvation, and a fragmentary understanding of who Jesus was and what he came to do. Simply put, we cannot really know God without the OT.

A. Bridging the gap

Key to interpreting the OT is the task of bridging the gap that exists between life in the ancient Near East at the time the OT books were written and our life now. The revelation of God in the OT was written and received in a specific context. Often we treat the OT (and the Bible in general) as a special case, as a book that is different from all others, and, of course, there is a sense in which that is absolutely right. The Bible is unique in that the living God speaks through its pages. However, we must remember that this revelation came first to a specific group of people living in the Near East centuries before the rise of the Roman Empire. It meant something first to an ancient people group known as the *ibrîm* – the Hebrews. To understand what the OT means today, we must first make the effort to understand what it meant to them in their day. This is because, with a few exceptions, the OT cannot mean something today that it could not mean then. Hence, we must ask what it *meant* then, in order to understand what it *means* now.

Several barriers to understanding need to be overcome if we are going to interpret and apply the OT properly. Primarily these are barriers of history, culture and world-view. At first glance, these barriers may seem intimidating, and place non-specialists entirely in the hands of apparent experts. However, in reality, there is a great deal that every Christian can do to overcome these challenges by careful reading of the text.

1. Read broadly

Is it possible to know how an ancient and distant people viewed the world around them? What was their 'take' on religion, family, law, education, art, recreation, commerce, politics and all the other things that come together to shape a nation's culture? How was their understanding of these matters shaped by the revelation that they gradually received, as now recorded in the OT?

In reality, learning the culture, history and mindset of the OT community is not as hard as it may seem. There is a simple key: *read the OT often and in large chunks.* The best way – the only way – to really understand the background and outlook of the ancient people of God is to take time to read their stories, to examine their history, to trace the themes and common threads that weave their way throughout all their interactions with the same God that we worship today. Part of our problem regarding OT interpretation is that we tend to atomize our Bible reading. We read short passages or even single verses, but this does not help our comprehension of the macro-themes of the OT's history, prophecy and poetry. To really grasp the significance of the OT for us today we must read the text for what it is: a story of God's amazing dealings with his people. Of course, this 'story' takes many different literary forms – narrative, law, history, poetry, philosophy – however, it is all part of one great, overarching story of God and his love for his people. Our task is to let the story captivate us, draw us in and shape us. As this process occurs, we will learn lessons of history and culture unconsciously, as if by osmosis.

2. Read inquisitively

Understanding also comes from asking questions as we read. The task of the reader is to place the text being read into *context*, because context aids understanding. For instance, when reading a passage from the prophet Isaiah, we gain deeper insight by placing his words in their historical and theological context. We should ask, 'What do we know about Judah during the reigns of Ahaz and Hezekiah?' And that question sends us to the books of Kings and Chronicles to find out more about the situations, challenges and dilemmas faced by God's people at that time. So we must read the OT broadly and inquisitively – cross-referencing, asking questions.

3. Read guide books

However much we read the text itself, there will be some issues which remain unclear without some further research. Classic novels often include an explanatory introduction, because their historical backdrop is unknown to later readers. A richer understanding of the story is opened up by this background research. The same principle applies to the OT, and pays huge dividends.

Various aids provide easy access to information that helps us grasp more fully the meaning of the OT. If you are baffled by the military manoeuvres of Dan. 11, a *Study Bible* will outline the machinations of the Ptolemies and the Seleucids in the second century BC. If you are working your way through Isaiah and get weary of all the 'woes', then an accessible *commentary* can provide insight to their context then and their application now. If you get lost in the detail of a particular biblical book and forget how it fits into the broader narrative, then *Bible guides* like this one can be very useful. There are many good aids that enable us to see both the wood and the trees.

B. Understanding genre

The next challenge – and in some ways, the greatest – is to be able to discern the essential from the peripheral. Vital to proper OT interpretation is the ability to differentiate between the indispensable, lasting truth of the text and the historical context that merely provided the setting. How do we set about this task without running the risk of 'explaining away' the plain meaning of the text?

Understanding *genre* is crucial if we are to grasp the Bible's message. The OT is not all written in simple prose. The complete text is not made up of propositional statements that are immediately clear and unambiguous. Rather, we encounter epic stories that cover many centuries with vivid ease; we find poetry that moves us to cry out in despair and to rejoice with exuberance; we are faced with philosophical deliberations that would have us question everything while retaining a vibrant faith. So we need to understand what type of text we are dealing with in order to get at the heart of its message. Straightforward statements do occur and we should treat them as such. Israel was charged to 'love the LORD your God with all your heart and with all your soul and with all your strength' (Deut. 6:5), and Christians today have every reason to accept this exhortation as our own. It is a simple truth with a very direct application in our lives (Matt. 22:37). However, this is not always the case.

We do not read English *poetry* in the same way that we read a newspaper. We expect something different in poems – pictorial language, unusual sentence structure, vivid imagery, etc. It is the same in the OT, and lessons from the poetic books are derived in a different way. Ps. 95:7 tells us that we are the 'people of his pasture, the flock under his care'. Clearly, a literal interpretation does not apply here. So we look for the essential truth that is conveyed through this literary form. Brief examination of the content of Ps. 95 shows that this verse is speaking about God's care for his people as they listen and obey. So the 'essence' is to respond in obedience to God's ways, knowing that he cares for us.

It is, perhaps, easy to acknowledge that poetry involves metaphor, and metaphor speaks indirectly rather than directly. What about the obscure *laws* that seem to dominate the OT? How are we to deal with the law of the 'goring ox', for example (Exod. 21:28–32)? Not many of us keep oxen (goring or otherwise) these days, so where does the 'didactic essence' lie in this law? If we pause for a moment, it is easy to see that this law refers to the sanctity of life and the importance of taking all reasonable action to preserve life – the responsibility lies with us to do everything we can to protect the lives of those around about us. We may not keep oxen, but we do drive cars. So the 'essence' of the law requires that we drive in a way as not to put ourselves or others at risk. This is just one example, showing that it is not really difficult to cut through the details and arrive at the essence. Ask yourself the questions, 'What is the bigger picture? Why is this law here? What does it teach?'

What about all the stories? Much of the OT is made up of lengthy *narratives* that recite the major events of Israel's history. Is this all just background, filling in the story until Christ comes? Or are we meant to learn how to live from these stories? While legal texts point to the minimum required standards, narrative passages provide us with both positive examples to emulate and negative examples to avoid. The issue of their interpretation is complicated, however, because often these stories are recorded without explicit approbation or condemnation from the narrator. So how are we to know what to think about them?

We should look for clues elsewhere – either in legal texts or in narrative passages where explicit judgment *is* passed in similar circumstances. Take the example of King Solomon. He is presented as a ruler of outstanding wisdom in 1 Kgs 1 – 11, yet at the same time the narrator subtly raises question marks. He tells us, for example, about Solomon's great wealth (10:14–21) and the requirements of his court, the fact that he accumulated chariots and horses from Egypt (4:26–29). It is well known that Solomon's many wives were ultimately a major cause of his demise and he is roundly condemned for this failure (11:9–13). But what about these other factors – what are we meant to think about them? The kingship law (Deut. 17:14–20) presents the paradigm for kingship in Israel, and that short text teaches that the king is not to accumulate for himself vast wealth or many horses or many wives. These events of Solomon's life pass without comment in 1 Kgs 1 – 11 because *we already know* what to think about them. The narrator is giving us subtle clues – great king he may be, but the warning signs are present. The narrative is telling us not to follow Solomon's example of disregarding God's word and ways, despite otherwise being greatly gifted.

So we must look for the essence of the message in the various texts that we read in the OT. Not all of the detail speaks directly to our circumstances, so we seek out the message of the broader text that speaks to every believer through all generations. Each text has a didactic purpose; our task is to ask the question, 'What is this passage trying to teach us?'

C. The Old Testament and the law

Sometimes Christians avoid the OT because they think that the law is no longer binding upon the church. Such confusion can lead to a real lack of confidence in the OT. There is one absolute point that we should always remember: When Paul writes, 'All Scripture is God-breathed and is useful for teaching, rebuking, correcting and training in righteousness' (2 Tim. 3:16), the 'Scripture' to which he refers is the OT! Is this how you view the OT *in its entirety*? God-breathed, useful for teaching, rebuking, correcting, training? Certainly, we should not allow concerns about the continuance of the law to discourage us, because it is *all* designed to teach us the ways of the Lord.

With regard to the question of the continuance of the law, the traditional understanding is probably still a very good starting point. It is helpful to think in terms of three broad categories of OT law: the ceremonial law, dealing with religious practice; the civil law, dealing with societal laws governing Israel as a theocracy in its historical setting; and the moral law, dealing with ethics for life. The OT legal sections merge these categories as all one 'law', but various parts of the NT appear to draw clear distinctions between them. For example, compare Jesus' attitude towards the moral law in Matt. 5 with the treatment of the OT ceremonial law in Heb. 10. The basic rule of thumb for Christian interpreters of the OT is that the moral law, governing ethical behaviour, continues in effect for the Christian, not as a means of salvation, but as a code – based in God's character – by which to live. By contrast, while we can learn from the civil and ceremonial laws, we are not directed by them in the same way.

Some interpreters of the Bible take a different view of the relationship between the law and the Christian. They would argue that the NT also treats the law as a single entity and therefore the separation of the law into three types is artificial. This leads to the conclusion that the law as a whole is valid for the Christian only insofar as obedience to it can flow from faith in Christ, or from the prompting of the Spirit. So some stipulations are set aside, and some are followed in a new way. This approach leads to the conclusion that the moral code indicated by the Ten Commandments continues to direct the behaviour of the Christian believer, with the possible exception of the Sabbath law, which seems to have been radically reinterpreted by Jesus. Whichever approach one takes, the net effect is similar – the moral law continues to have a profound meaning for the life of the Christian.

D. The Old Testament and Christ

Another question worth considering is, 'How should we read the OT *as Christians*?' How does the revelation of God in his Son influence our reading of the OT? When Jesus, in his conflict with the Pharisees, says, 'If you believed Moses, you would believe me, for he wrote about me' (John 5:46), just what does he mean? In what sense does the OT speak about Christ?

There seems to be a threefold sense in which the OT speaks about Christ. First, we come across occasional *prophetic* passages that point to a future individual who will transform the life of Israel and, indeed, the whole world. These passages are infrequent, but when we read them from the perspective of the life of Jesus in the Gospel accounts the correspondence is remarkable. These prophetic passages speak about two types of eschatological figure: (1) a restored Davidic king who will initiate righteous rule over all nations (Isa. 9:6–7, Mic. 5:1–5, Zech. 9:9–10); and (2) a servant figure who will suffer on behalf of Israel (Isa. 52:13 – 53:12; Zech. 12:10 – 13:1). These images provide a complex picture of this mysterious hero, who is king and servant at the same time. In OT terms alone the two images are difficult to synthesize, yet the imagery comes clearly into focus when detail is added in the Gospels.

Secondly, much of the religious and civil life in the OT Israel points towards Jesus in a *typological* sense, i.e. by presenting a typical pattern of how God works. (The OT example is called the 'type', its NT fulfilment the 'antitype'.) We read about practices which were a functioning reality within Israel, yet which also point towards a greater reality in the person of Christ. For example, the temple was an expression of divine presence on earth, the dwelling place of God amongst humanity (Ps. 26:8). Yet there is a sense in which the temple points the Christian reader to a greater reality of divine presence on earth: 'The Word became flesh and made his dwelling among us' (John 1:14). Other significant institutions of the OT also point towards a greater fulfilment in Christ: the system of sacrifices, the roles of prophet, priest, king, judge, sage, etc. However, we can only fully understand the completeness of the work of Christ when we understand the real significance of the original OT phenomena. If we do not grasp the blood-drenched solemnity of the sacrifices for sin in Leviticus on their own terms, then we cannot properly comprehend the significance of the sacrificial work of Christ in the Gospels. The OT institutions point to a greater fulfilment, but understanding the type increases our knowledge of the antitype.

Thirdly, the OT provides essential *theocentric background* to the coming of Christ. This is often referred to as 'salvation history'. The incarnation did not just happen out of the blue, there was a whole long history of God's dealings with his people throughout many generations that leads up to this ultimate revelation of his plan of salvation. Probably the majority of the OT comes into this third category – it is neither prophetic nor typological of Christ in particular, but it teaches us of the covenant God and his dealings with his people in general. In learning about God, we learn about Christ too.

So Christians will read the OT with one eye on the Gospels, but we should never be guilty of fanciful Christology. While Christ is occasionally portrayed in the OT in prophecy and typology, the vast bulk of the OT text teaches us about *God* more generally and about how we should live our lives in his presence.

D. Conclusion

How then should Christians interpret the OT? Just as we would the rest of the Bible – aware of the original cultural and historical setting, seeking the didactic essence of each passage we read, conscious of the literary genre, and looking to place each passage within the broader picture of salvation history. Most of all we should immerse ourselves in 'the Scripture' that teaches, rebukes, corrects and trains – in it we find the very words of life.

Further reading

Good general introductions to the Old Testament include:
John Drane, *Introducing the Old Testament* (Lion, 2nd edn 2000) – excellent, well-illustrated summary of Israel's story and faith.
Tremper Longman III, *Making Sense of the Old Testament: Three Crucial Questions* (Baker, 1999) – concise treatment of OT issues including God's portrayal and Christian usage.
Alec Motyer, *Introducing the Old Testament* (Crossway, 2005) – very readable guide to the various sections and themes of the OT.

Raymond Dillard and Tremper Longman III, *An Introduction to the Old Testament* (Apollos, 1995) – a more detailed standard textbook for evangelical theological study.

Good summaries of OT themes and theology include:

Alec Motyer, *Look to the Rock* (IVP, 1996) – good demonstration of how the OT leads to and is fulfilled in Christ.

Graeme Goldsworthy, *Gospel and Kingdom*, now published in *The Goldsworthy Trilogy* (Paternoster, 2000) – popular short guide, though the theme 'Kingdom of God' fits the NT better than the OT.

Philip Jenson, *The Problem of War in the Old Testament* (Grove, 2002) – best booklet discussion of this difficult subject.

3. Pentateuch

Desmond Alexander

OVERVIEW

The first five books of the Bible (Genesis, Exodus, Leviticus, Numbers and Deuteronomy) have been known collectively as the Pentateuch from at least the third century AD. The designation Pentateuch comes from the Greek term *pentateuchos* meaning 'five-volume work'. While Christians favour the term Pentateuch, Jews have traditionally preferred the title *Torah*. This is a Hebrew term meaning 'instruction', which is commonly – if inappropriately – translated as 'law'.

The five 'volumes' of Genesis to Deuteronomy narrate a remarkable story that begins with the divine creation of the earth and concludes many centuries later with the people of Israel poised on the eastern bank of the River Jordan. From here they anticipate a future across the river in the land of Canaan.

The Pentateuch falls into a number of distinctive chronological stages, which reflect to some degree its structure. Gen. 1 – 11, often designated the 'primeval history', gives a brief but important account of selected episodes in the early stages of human history. Since these events set the scene for all that follows, their significance is immense. Against this background, Gen. 12 – 50 proceeds by focusing on the lives of three men: Abraham, his grandson Jacob, and his great-grandson Joseph. The events associated with this family build around divine promises that are given to Abraham. These promises, which have various components, focus on two main ideas. One concerns the creation of a nation that will come to possess the land of Palestine (or Canaan, as it is called in the biblical text). The other is about the provision of a future king, descended from the patriarchs, who will bring God's blessing to the nations of the earth, reversing the consequences of Adam and Eve's earlier rebellion against God. These two core promises set the agenda for the meta-narrative that runs from Genesis to 2 Kings.

While Genesis concludes by recording how the descendants of Abraham, numbering about seventy, relocate to Egypt, the book of Exodus moves forward several generations to a time when the origin of the Israelites in Egypt is forgotten and Abraham's descendants, now many thousands, are subject to harsh exploitation by the Egyptian pharaoh. Through a series of divine interventions, which conclude with the Egyptian army being drowned, the Israelites are rescued from Egypt and embark upon a journey though the wilderness that brings them to Mount Sinai.

At this stage the pace of the narrative slows down considerably, and detailed attention is given to the process by which the Lord establishes a unique relationship with the Israelites. This is designed to make them into a 'holy nation'. The description of this process begins in Exod. 19 and continues throughout the book of Leviticus and into the early chapters of Numbers. It begins by setting out the covenant obligations that Israel must obey, centred on ten principles commonly known as the Ten Commandments. Following Israel's acceptance of these, the final chapters of Exodus record how the tabernacle is constructed. This unique tent with royal overtones (in its historical and cultural context) will be God's dwelling place among the Israelites. When the tent is assembled, the Lord comes to dwell within it, confirming the special relationship ratified by the covenant. By living in their midst, the Lord transforms the Israelites into a holy nation; his presence sanctifies them.

The book of Leviticus builds on this by detailing various rituals and customs that the Israelites must adopt in order to dwell safely in the presence of a holy God. With almost everything in place, the book of Numbers begins by orientating the people towards the future occupation of the land of Canaan. In due course, they leave Mount Sinai, travelling once again through the wilderness. However, progress into the promised land is halted when the people's trust in God weakens in the face of reports that emphasize the strength of the opposition awaiting them in Canaan. Unwilling to confront the nations of Canaan, the Israelites rebel against God. Consequently, God punishes them by making them spend a further forty years in the wilderness. Only after the death of the adult exodus generation is it possible for the Israelites to reconsider taking possession of the land of Canaan.

While the book of Numbers concludes with several chapters that anticipate the Israelites' future in the promised land, the entire book of Deuteronomy is built around this expectation. With the people camped on the eastern bank of the River Jordan, Moses challenges them regarding their future commitment to God. In two lengthy speeches he invites the people to reaffirm the covenant obligations first made at Mount Sinai. Since the book of Deuteronomy anticipates life in the land, a strong emphasis is placed on the importance of being faithful to the divine Torah that Moses sets out. Obedience to these instructions will bring divine blessing; disobedience will result in God's curses coming on the people.

The book of Deuteronomy concludes by reporting the death and burial of Moses in the land of Moab, outside the promised land. Although the books of Exodus to Deuteronomy are bound together by the birth and death of Moses, the fulfilment of God's promises to the patriarchs in Genesis remains incomplete. The book of Deuteronomy does not mark the end of the story. On the contrary, it merely introduces themes that are developed throughout the books of Joshua to 2 Kings.

While the Pentateuch is often perceived as being a major, self-contained section of the Bible, it is very closely linked to the books that follow. For this reason, the Pentateuch has to be viewed as part of a larger meta-narrative. To consider it simply as an entity in its own right is to fail to appreciate how the books of Genesis to Kings are designed to be understood as a continuous story. The study of the Pentateuch must take into account this connection, for without these books the story recorded in Genesis to Deuteronomy is unfinished.

GENESIS

Genesis is very much a book about beginnings, as its opening words indicate. Starting with the creation of the earth, it traces the progress of a unique family line that begins with Adam and Eve and concludes with Jacob and his twelve sons. Two features structure Genesis around this family line. First, new sections of the book are introduced by a distinctive heading or title, translated 'These are the generations of...' (AV, RSV, ESV) or 'This is the account of...' (TNIV) (2:4; 5:1 with slight variant; 6:9; 10:1; 11:10; 11:27; 25:12; 25:19; 36:1; 36:9; 37:2). These headings function like the zoom lens of a camera, focusing attention on a smaller part of the picture.

Secondly, these titles introduce three distinctive types of material:

1. narrative sections that concentrate upon an individual and his immediate family: Adam (2:4 – 4:26), Noah (6:9 – 9:29), Abraham (11:27 – 25:11), Jacob (25:19 – 35:29) and Joseph (37:2 – 50:26);

2. segmented genealogies that outline a family tree for several generations, giving basic information about characters of secondary importance (10:1–32; 25:12–18; 36:1–8; 36:9–43);

3. linear genealogies that cover ten generations but name only one ancestor in each (5:1–32; 11:10–26).

By carefully combining these different types of material the author of Genesis presents a continuous story that focuses attention on a unique line of descendants, from Adam to Noah, then to Abraham, Isaac, Jacob and Joseph. Crucially, this special family line plays a central role in the outworking of God's purposes for the whole of humanity by anticipating and preparing for the coming of a future king who will mediate God's blessing to all the nations of the earth.

Genesis opens by boldly proclaiming the supreme authority of God in creating the universe and appointing human beings as his vicegerents on earth. Yet one of the key ideas permeating the book is the disruption of the divine–human relationship. Through disobeying God and submitting to the serpent, Adam and Eve throw creation into disorder, reversing the structures instituted by God. Although they were appointed to rule over the animals (1:26, 28), Adam and Eve accede to the serpent's authority when they eat from the tree of the knowledge of good and evil (3:1–6). Their rebellious action immediately alienates them from God, with disastrous consequences for the whole of creation. While Genesis vividly describes the tragic impact of this alienation, especially in chs. 3 to 11, various divine promises hold out hope that one day God's blessing will be mediated to the whole of humanity through a descendant of the family line traced through the book. Readers need to appreciate how the early chapters of Genesis are foundational in describing the origin and nature of our human predicament. Building on this, the whole of Genesis points forward to a divinely promised resolution linked to a future descendant of the unique family line around which Genesis is centred.

The importance of the family line outlined in Genesis is highlighted in more ways than can be enumerated here, and there are interesting twists. The barrenness of the matriarchs, Sarah, Rebekah and Rachel, draws attention to God's role in continuing this special lineage. This motif is especially prominent in the Abraham story where in desperation Sarah mistakenly attempts to provide an heir through her servant Hagar. Later Abraham is tested to the extreme when commanded by

God to sacrifice the long-awaited child of promise, Isaac. This incident, however, brings the Abraham story to a dramatic climax in which God swears by himself that through a future descendant of Abraham all the nations of the earth will experience divine blessing (22:18; cf. 12:3; 18:18). Building on this, the remainder of Genesis describes how God's blessing is uniquely associated with and mediated to others through Isaac, Jacob and Joseph.

In Genesis divine blessing is often associated with the concept of first-born, as seen particularly in the story of Esau and Jacob. While Esau is prepared to sell his birthright for a bowl of stew (25:29–34), Jacob risks everything in order to gain the paternal blessing that promises to the first-born not only authority over nations and peoples but also blessing to those who bless him, echoing God's promise to Abraham (27:29; cf. 12:3). Joseph's misfortune comes due to the jealousy of his older brothers who accept neither their father's promotion of Joseph to the status of first-born nor Joseph's dreams that portray him as a king.

Although Genesis later associates the royal line with Joseph's son Ephraim (48:1–22; another instance of the first-born blessing being given to a younger brother), an alternative kingly lineage from Judah is hinted at in Gen. 38 when Perez breaks out ahead of his 'first-born' twin brother, Zerah. Isaac's blessing of his sons in Gen. 49 confirms this possibility, for future kingship is associated with Judah (49:10), although Joseph receives a comparable blessing. While Joseph's line through Ephraim initially enjoys God's favour, as evidenced by Joshua's leadership of the Israelites, in the time of Samuel the lineage of Ephraim is divinely rejected in favour of David, from the tribe of Judah (see Ps. 78:67–72). Eventually, the divine promises associated with the royal line anticipated in Genesis find their fulfilment in Jesus Christ (cf. e.g. Acts 3:25–26; Gal. 3:16). By pointing forward to the coming of a king who will reconcile humanity to God, Genesis lays the foundation upon which the rest of the Bible builds. Readers need to grasp this agenda in order to understand subsequent developments in the biblical story.

The family line in Genesis not only points forward to the coming of Jesus Christ, it also provides an insight into the nature of the promised king who will emulate fully the positive qualities observed in those who belong to this special lineage. Like Abraham, Jesus will trust and obey God. Like Joseph, he will bring salvation to many (cf. 50:20). As a 'righteous' line of seed that eventually leads to Jesus Christ, the central characters of Genesis also serve as role models for readers who wish to be Christ-like. Throughout the narrative of Genesis indications are given regarding the kind of behaviour that is pleasing to God. While attention is sometimes drawn to their moral weaknesses and their need to overcome sinful tendencies, the members of the main family line display positive qualities that set them apart from others. The contribution of Genesis to a biblical understanding of both God and humanity cannot be underestimated, for it establishes the basis and agenda for God's redemptive purposes in the world.

Genesis poses other questions, which can only be noted here without discussion. Its historical veracity has often been assessed negatively, on the grounds that no known extra-biblical sources confirm the Genesis record of the patriarchs. While this is undeniably so, we are dealing with accounts that relate to around 2000 BC and are largely concerned with the lives of a semi-nomadic family that migrated from northern Mesopotamia to the land of Canaan. Not surprisingly, archaeological investigations and extant texts are highly unlikely to provide explicit evidence about the biblical patriarchs and their families. Such limitations need to be remembered when assessing views for and against the truthfulness of the Genesis record.

Other considerations need to be taken into account when considering the historicity of the early chapters of Genesis. This is especially so as regards ch. 1, given modern theories about how the world was created. We need to appreciate that this chapter sets out to answer the question, 'Why did God do it?' not 'How did God do it?' As many biblical scholars now recognize, the entire chapter is a literary-artistic representation of creation, designed to establish the status, in relation to each other, of the objects and creatures mentioned within it. Since ch. 1 is not attempting to describe the 'how' of creation, the chapter sheds little light on the mechanism by which God created the world. We need to remember that the biblical writers want to communicate particular truths. As readers we need to attune ourselves to what these ancient authors wished to say and not impose our present-day agenda on their writings. We must not expect the biblical text to answer questions that its authors were not addressing.

EXODUS

Continuing the story of Genesis, the book of Exodus divides into three main sections on the basis of geographical location: chs. 1 – 15 are associated with Egypt, chs. 16 – 18 with the wilderness and chs. 19 – 40 with Mount Sinai. While there is a clear continuity between these sections, their contents differ markedly, producing a narrative that moves forward in distinctive stages.

Chs. 1 – 15 record the dramatic deliverance of the Israelites from slavery in Egypt, climaxing in a hymn of praise that extols God's victory over the forces of Pharaoh, the Egyptian god-king. After briefly describing the oppression of the Israelites, the book introduces Moses by recounting his birth and upbringing in the Egyptian court, his stand for the Israelites against their Egyptian slave-masters and his flight to the land of Midian. Then, forty years later, God dramatically commissions Moses to lead the Israelites out of Egypt. Through a series of 'signs and wonders' God reveals his power to the Egyptians, some of whom acknowledge this sooner than others. While Pharaoh stubbornly resists the Lord, he eventually permits the Israelites to go free after all the Egyptian first-born males are struck dead. In marked contrast, the Israelite first-born are protected by sacrificial blood on the door frames of their houses. One further futile attempt by Pharaoh to resist the Lord results in the drowning of his elite troops after the Israelites have safely crossed through the waters of the Red Sea.

Exod. 15:22 – 18:27 covers the seventy days immediately following the exodus from Egypt, when the Israelites travel through the wilderness towards Mount Sinai. Several incidents highlight the ephemeral nature of their trust in God. When confronted with shortages of water and food, they grumble against him. This contrasts sharply with God's care of them and underlines their shallow perception of the one who miraculously delivered them from slavery in Egypt.

Chs. 19 – 40 narrate what happens when the Israelites come to Mount Sinai. After suitable preparations have been made, the Israelites witness a theophany (divine appearance), during which God communicates directly to them the ten principles (Ten Commandments) upon which their future as a nation should be based. To these are added more detailed obligations, mediated through Moses. Then a solemn covenant ratification ceremony seals the special relationship which God establishes with the people (chs. 19 – 24). To finalize this process, Moses receives instructions from God for the construction of a tent or tabernacle that will become his dwelling place in the midst of the Israelite camp. By coming to live among the people, God demonstrates the reality of their unique relationship. Additionally, his presence will have a sanctifying effect upon the people; they will be a 'holy nation' because the holy God lives among them (chs. 24 – 31 and 35 – 40).

All of this, however, is placed in jeopardy by the Israelites (chs. 32 – 34). When Moses is on Mount Sinai receiving instructions for the construction of the tabernacle, the Israelites fashion a golden calf. By doing so, they breach their covenant commitment to be faithful to the Lord alone. Their action is equivalent to a bride committing adultery on her wedding night. But for God's gracious nature and the intercession of Moses, the Israelites' action would have cut short their unique relationship with God. The seriousness of the situation is underlined when Moses breaks the stone tablets containing the covenant obligations. Although a resolution is achieved, the rebellious nature of the Israelites continues to be a significant theme throughout the rest of the Pentateuch. Of the entire adult generation that leaves Egypt, only Joshua and Caleb will enter the promised land.

Running through the book of Exodus is the theme of 'knowing God'. The opening two chapters give the impression of God being somewhat remote from the plight of Abraham's descendants. Then in ch. 3 he reveals himself and his plans for the Israelites privately to Moses. By ch. 15 God has demonstrated through signs and wonders his divine power to both the Egyptians and the Israelites. They now know who the true God is. Through their wilderness experience, the people witness God's ability to provide for them in another hostile environment. Next, at Mount Sinai they see and hear him in an awe-inspiring theophany. Yet God still remains at some distance and the people are prohibited from approaching closer. Finally, Exodus concludes with God coming to inhabit the special tent that is assembled in the centre of the Israelite camp. From the beginning of Exodus to its end, God moves from being distant to being close, from being largely unknown to being intimately known.

While Exodus may be viewed as a story about the liberation of people from cruel oppression, it is essentially a story about changing masters. The Israelites, having been freed from brutal servitude to the god-king Pharaoh, the archetypical tyrant, are invited to submit to the lordship of God. They are to serve him only: the Hebrew word for 'serve' may also be translated 'worship'. The Lord is, however, a very different kind of master, as reflected in his actions and words.

Centred on the theme of knowing God better, Exodus is rich in theological concepts that later play a significant role in defining the gospel. The death of Jesus is closely linked to the Passover sacrifice which both atoned for sin and sanctified those who participated in the meal. Christians are redeemed from the power of evil through a new exodus and enter into a new covenant relationship with God. John's Gospel also contrasts the 'signs' performed in Egypt with those done by Jesus. Whereas the former were mainly punitive, the latter bring blessing: water becomes wine rather than blood; the first-born is raised to life rather than put to death. Further, arising out of this second exodus, the apostles are commissioned to construct a new dwelling place for God: the church becomes his spiritual temple. By appreciating these themes in the book of Exodus, readers may understand better their own Christian experience of God.

In spite of the centrality of the exodus experience in the life of ancient Israel, as reflected in the various festivals based upon it, modern scholarship is largely sceptical about the historical veracity of these events. This is partly due to presuppositions that discount all accounts of divine activity on earth. It is also partly due to the absence of extra-biblical records that confirm the basic details of the Israelites' departure from Egypt. However, given the limited nature of Egyptian sources for this period and the strong likelihood that Egyptians would not have wished to document their ignominious defeat by the Israelites' god, the silence of the extra-biblical sources is understandable.

LEVITICUS

Leviticus continues the account of the Israelites' sojourn at Mount Sinai in the thirteenth month after their deliverance from Egypt (cf. Exod. 40:17; Num. 1:1). Leviticus presumes from Exodus the construction of the regal tent to enable the divine king to come and reside among his people. This portable residence is placed within a fenced enclosure, designed to maintain a safe distance between the Israelites and their God. All this presupposes that imperfect human beings cannot enter into the presence of a holy God, due to their sinfulness. Against this background, Leviticus consists almost entirely of divine instructions intended to enable the Israelites to dwell safely in close proximity to God.

While these directions facilitate the creation of a new social order in which God and humanity live together in proximity, barriers still exist, preventing the Israelites from having immediate and direct access to the presence of God. The high priest alone may enter into the inner chamber of the tabernacle, the Holy of Holies, and even he is only permitted to do this once in the year, on the Day of Atonement. Although God's presence in the midst of the Israelite camp marks an important new development in reversing the alienation between deity and humanity that begins with Adam and Eve, much more has still to be accomplished before a complete reconciliation is achieved.

The divine instructions that make up about nine-tenths of Leviticus are usually addressed to Moses, with his brother Aaron occasionally included. These directions, however, are normally intended for either the ordinary Israelites (e.g. 1:2; 4:2) or the priests (e.g. 6:9; 21:1).

With the erection of the tabernacle, the priests, under the control of Aaron, take on responsibilities that are entirely new. Never before did the Israelites have a sanctuary in which God lived. Consequently, Leviticus describes the process by which the priests themselves are set apart from other Israelites in order to serve God at the tabernacle.

Fulfilling earlier instructions (Exod. 29), Aaron and his sons are consecrated (chs. 8 – 9). Leviticus then underlines the importance of obeying carefully the Lord's commands by recording how two of Aaron's sons, Nadab and Abihu, are struck dead when they offer 'unauthorized fire before the LORD, contrary to his command' (10:1).

Given the potential danger of living in God's holy presence, the opening chapters provide instructions for sacrifices designed to address human sinfulness in different ways. Five main types are listed, with various names: burnt offerings, grain or gift offerings, fellowship or peace offerings, sin or purification offerings, and guilt or reparation offerings. The instructions for each sacrifice differ, providing clues as to how they function. The burnt offering restores a broken relationship, appeasing the anger of God, i.e. it brings atonement. The fellowship or peace offering possibly celebrates the restoration of peace after having offended God. The grain offering may have been a gift intended to acknowledge God's sovereignty. The sin offering removes the ritual defilement or pollution caused by human sin. The guilt offering makes restitution for a wrongful action by compensating the injured party. These sacrifices reveal that there are different dimensions to human sin, and its consequences need to be dealt with in a variety of ways.

While the sacrifices seek to reverse the results of human wrongdoing, most of the other instructions in Leviticus are geared to encouraging behaviour that minimizes the need for atonement, purification and restitution. To understand these instructions we need to appreciate that Leviticus has a world-view based around the concepts of holiness and its antithesis, uncleanness. While Leviticus emphasizes God's power to make holy or sanctify people and objects, it also highlights the danger posed by the moral and ritual uncleanness associated with human behaviour.

Holiness is associated with wholeness, perfection and life; it derives from God and reflects his perfect nature. In marked contrast, uncleanness is linked to physical and moral imperfection, disorder, illness and death. Holiness and uncleanness are mutually exclusive. Between these two extremes exists a spectrum that moves by degrees from holy to clean to unclean. This may be illustrated spatially in terms of the layout of the Israelite camp. The tabernacle and its courtyard are holy. However, differing degrees of holiness exist within the tabernacle, reducing in intensity as one moves out from the Holy of Holies. The Israelite camp around the tabernacle is clean. The region outside the camp is unclean. Similar degrees of holiness and uncleanness are found among people. In general terms, priests are holy, Israelites are clean and non-Israelites are unclean. However, different factors could affect an individual's condition. For example, those who *touched* an animal carcass became unclean for a day; those who *carried* an animal carcass sustained greater impurity and were required to wash their clothes (11:24–25, 27–28).

Many of the instructions in Leviticus are designed to impress upon the Israelites the need to be holy. Some are largely symbolic in nature. By eating only 'clean' food, the Israelites distinguish themselves from those who are 'unclean'. Consequently, centuries later when the early church is being established God removes the distinction between clean and unclean food in order to signal that the longstanding distinction between Jew and Gentile is now abolished (Acts 10).

Other instructions emphasize the importance of being morally perfect, like God himself. Indeed, for the Israelites to enjoy a meaningful and fruitful relationship with God, they must reflect his holiness in their daily lives. For this reason, the Israelites are commanded, 'Be holy because I, the LORD your God, am holy' (19:2; cf. 11:44–45; 20:26). Leviticus instructs the people on how they may overcome uncleanness and be holy.

To the twenty-first-century Christian reader the book of Leviticus seems remote and irrelevant. God's instructions address a situation very different from that of today. Christians neither offer sacrifices nor eat only ritually clean foods. When we look deeper, however, Leviticus has much to teach us about the holy and perfect nature of God, and how human nature is inclined towards uncleanness. Leviticus also establishes a world-view out of which we come to understand better the significance of Christ's sacrificial death for us, and our calling to be holy as God is holy (cf. Heb. 12:10–14; 1 Pet. 1:15–16). Since this world-view underlies the rest of Scripture, a knowledge of Leviticus is often essential for understanding it.

NUMBERS

Picking up the story of the Israelites' stay at Mount Sinai, the book of Numbers provides a selective record of incidents that cover a period of about forty years. For almost all this time the Israelites are condemned by God to wander in the wilderness rather than enter the promised land. During this extended sojourn in the wilderness all the adult Israelites who experienced the exodus from Egypt die, apart from Joshua and Caleb.

Structurally the book of Numbers falls into three distinctive sections. Chs. 1 – 10 narrate the final preparations which the Israelites undertake prior to leaving Mount Sinai. These activities, spread over two months, are largely focused on helping the people prepare for the onward journey and the task of dispossessing the inhabitants of Canaan. This section concludes with the Israelites leaving Mount Sinai, apparently in a very positive frame of mind (10:35).

The central section, chs. 11 – 25, records various events over the next forty years. The recurring theme of these chapters is the failure of the people to trust and obey God. The main example of this occurs when ten of the twelve spies persuade the Israelites that they cannot possibly overcome the nations of Canaan. Consequently God announces that the Israelites will all die in the wilderness (chs. 13 – 14). On different occasions, arising out of rebellious behaviour, large numbers of Israelites are struck dead so that, by the start of the final section in Numbers, Joshua and Caleb are the only surviving adults of the exodus generation.

Chs. 26 – 36 concentrate on positive developments in the fortieth year that prepare the way for the new generation to enter the promised land. Framed by episodes that focus on the inheritance rights of the daughters of Zelophehad (27:1–11; 36:1–13), this section is clearly orientated towards the future occupation of the land.

The threefold structure of Numbers is reinforced by the fact that the first and third sections begin with a census of all men who are twenty years old or more (chs. 1, 26). Those listed are expected to serve in the Israelite army as it confronts the inhabitants of Canaan. However, of all those recorded in the first census, only Caleb and Joshua remained alive when the second is taken (26:64–65). This second census marks an important new stage in the narrative, confirming that God's punishment has been enacted on the disobedient exodus generation. Although chs. 11 – 25 record various incidents which involve the death of many Israelites, chs. 26 – 36 mention no deaths, not even during a battle against the Midianites (cf. 31:49).

The two censuses record the number of men of military age as 603,550 (2:32) and 601,730 (26:51), which elsewhere is rounded to 600,000 adult men (Exod. 12:37; Num. 11:21). This would give a total population of two to three million. On the one hand, it is mathematically possible that the Israelites increased rapidly during their four centuries in Egypt, and some interpreters take the figures literally. On the other, there are problems with these large numbers: since the number of firstborn males was 22,273 (3:43), the average family unit must have had 35–40 male children; nearly all the figures are exact hundreds, which is highly unlikely (and the figure for Levites is seen as exact, not approximate, 3:39–43); the wilderness stories assume a much smaller group, e.g. all could see the serpent on a pole (21:9); Israel was the smallest of peoples and would meet seven more numerous nations (Deut. 7:1, 7); and archaeology suggests population groups much smaller than these figures. For these reasons, many commentators now argue that mistakes crept into the census figures at an early stage, and that the actual number of Israelites was significantly smaller.

The positive outlook of the opening and closing sections of Numbers contrasts sharply with the very negative presentation of the Israelites in chs. 11 – 24. A variety of stories illustrate well the ungrateful and rebellious nature of the people. In ch. 11, the reason for the people's dissatisfaction with God is their craving for food. Although the Lord has provided them with manna, the Israelites yearn to return to Egypt: 'If only we had meat to eat! We remember the fish we ate in Egypt at no cost – also the cucumbers, melons, leeks, onions and garlic' (11:4–5). Their complaint is full of irony as the people forget the terrible conditions under which they had laboured as slaves in Egypt, and the fact that they are journeying towards a land 'flowing with milk and honey'. Not surprisingly, the Lord interprets their complaint as a personal rejection of him (11:20).

While the central section of Numbers is dominated by incidents that focus on the discontent and rebelliousness of the Israelites and their subsequent punishment, an element of hope is introduced towards the end of this section. This comes through the inclusion of a series of episodes that describe how Balaam, a Mesopotamian seer, is summoned by Balak, the king of Moab, to curse the Israelites. Balaam, however, is forced by God to bless them (22:12) on four separate occasions (23:7–10; 23:18–24; 24:3–9; 24:15–19). In doing so he echoes briefly the divine promises made earlier to the patriarchs in Genesis: 'Who can count the dust of Jacob' (23:10; cf. Gen. 13:16; 15:5); 'The Lord their God is with them' (23:21; cf. Gen. 17:8); 'May those who bless you be blessed and those who curse you be cursed' (24:9; cf. 23:8, 20; Gen. 12:3); 'A star will come out of Jacob; a sceptre will rise out of Israel' (24:17; cf. Gen. 17:6, 16; 49:10). In spite of punishing the exodus generation, God still intends to fulfil through the Israelites his promises to the patriarchs.

The account of the wilderness experience of the Israelites provides a solemn reminder of how prone the human heart is to rebel against God (cf. 1 Cor. 10:1–12). Numbers contains serious warnings about the need to trust God completely and avoid the temptation to grumble against his provision or distrust his ability to keep us secure. Significantly, these are the very temptations that Jesus confronts during his forty days in the wilderness. The repetitive description of the Israelites' behaviour creates a narrative that is designed to encourage the reader to trust God in the face of major obstacles. By reflecting on the experiences and responses of the Israelites, Christians may be helped to avoid failure in their own journey with God.

DEUTERONOMY

With the Israelites standing on the verge of entering the promised land, the book of Deuteronomy consists largely of two speeches delivered by the elderly statesman Moses shortly before his death. The first speech (1:6 – 4:40) reviews the Israelites' relationship with God over the previous forty years, observing what has happened to them since leaving Egypt. Stressing the disobedience of the exodus generation, Moses exhorts the present generation to love and obey the Lord wholeheartedly. His second speech (5:1 – 26:19) contains instructions which are intended to shape the future life of Israel in Canaan. Later this material is recorded on a scroll and designated the 'Book of the Law', better translated 'Book of Instruction' (31:24–26). Because Moses speaks here on his own behalf, passionately exhorting the people to obey God, Deuteronomy often reads like a sermon and differs stylistically from the rest of the Pentateuch.

At the heart of Deuteronomy is a challenge to the next generation of Israelites to embrace the covenant obligations given forty years earlier at Mount Sinai. Because of their failure to fulfil these obligations, the exodus generation died in the wilderness, outside the promised land. As Moses invites a new generation to affirm and embrace their covenant relationship with the Lord, he sets before them an important choice, a choice between 'life and death, blessings and curses' (30:19).

The renewing of the covenant between God and Israel resembles a marriage ceremony. While both parties promise allegiance to each other, the strength of the relationship depends not on the ceremony itself, but on the love and loyalty which each has for the other. For this reason, Moses emphasizes that the Israelites are to adore God with their whole being: 'Love the LORD your God with all your heart and with all your soul and with all your strength' (6:5; cf. 11:13; 13:3; 30:6). Without such devotion the covenant relationship will be meaningless. Moreover, true love will demonstrate itself in perfect obedience. What was true for the ancient Israelites remains true for today's Christian.

In ch. 27 Moses instructs the Israelites to carry out a covenant renewal ceremony after they cross over the River Jordan into the promised land. As part of this, the contents of the 'Book of the Law' are to be inscribed on large plastered stones as a public reminder of the obligations which the people must keep (27:2–8). Six tribes are to pronounce blessings from Mount Gerizim, and the other six tribes are to respond with curses from Mount Ebal (27:12–13). Obedience by the Israelites will ensure blessing in terms of material prosperity and national security; disobedience will have the opposite consequence, resulting in expulsion from the promised land.

Moses emphasizes that the Israelites must be faithful in loving God. In religious terms this means that they are not to practise idolatry; they must worship the Lord alone. Throughout Deuteronomy, Moses reinforces this point through negative warnings against bowing down to, following, serving or worshipping other gods. The Israelites also need to distance themselves from the practices of those who worship idols, otherwise they will be tempted to do likewise. Such is the danger posed by idolatry that the death penalty is imposed on anyone who practises it or entices others to do so. Modern western readers need to transpose the temptation of idolatry into their own context where 'other gods' may take very different shapes. Anything that dethrones God from his rightful position of supreme authority must be shunned.

Although Moses strongly exhorts the people to obey the covenant obligations, Deuteronomy as a whole anticipates that the Israelites will fail to keep them. In his final exhortation Moses clearly envisages a future in which the land will be devastated (29:23) and the people exiled (30:1–4). Not only do God's own words in 31:16–17 confirm this, but he proceeds to instruct Moses to teach the people a special song which will remind future generations of this (32:1–43). Anticipating this negative assessment of Israel's future, the list of blessing given in 28:1–14 is clearly overshadowed by the longer lists of curses that surround it (27:15–26; 28:15–68).

Building on the covenant initiated at Mount Sinai, Deuteronomy underlines the special relationship that exists between the Lord and the Israelites. Out of all the nations they have been chosen to be 'his people, his treasured possession' (7:6; cf. 14:2; Exod. 19:4–6). As such it is God's intention that they should be a light to other nations, reflecting the righteousness which he expects of all people. Consequently, the covenant obligations set out in Deuteronomy emphasize among other things a strong sense of brotherhood, a compassionate concern for the weaker members of society, a generous spirit and an integrity of heart that displays itself in righteous living. God desires that the Israelites should provide a positive example, but even when they fail, their punishment will be a lesson to others.

Deuteronomy underlines how true love for God expresses itself in an unswerving allegiance to him that leads to a lifestyle marked by integrity and righteousness. While the instructions outlined here were specifically intended for the people of Israel, the principles underlying them remain applicable today. Given that the Book of the Law was to instruct the Israelite king (17:14–20), it is interesting to observe how Jesus Christ frequently quoted from Deuteronomy, most notably in the context of being tempted by Satan (cf. Matt. 4:1–11).

During the past fifty or so years, the study of Deuteronomy has been enriched by the observation that its structure and contents closely resemble ancient treaties made between kings of powerful nations and the rulers of weaker, vassal states. While scholars continue to debate the extent and nature of this correspondence, these texts all formalize a special relationship between two parties, one strong and one weak, with the listing of extensive obligations and the pronouncement of blessings and curses. These observations remind us of the importance of understanding biblical texts in their original context.

COMPOSITION

Due to the prominence of Moses in the books of Exodus to Deuteronomy, it is hardly surprising that one of the earliest designations for the Pentateuch was 'the book of Moses' (Mark 12:26) or 'the Law of Moses' (Luke 24:44; cf. John 1:45). Indeed, it was even possible for the Pentateuch to be designated simply by the name 'Moses' (e.g. 2 Cor. 3:15, 'Moses is read'; cf. Luke 16:29; 24:27). While this was an obvious title for the first five books of the Bible, through time it was understood as indicating that Moses was the actual author of these books. Support for this idea also came from within the Pentateuch itself, because various references attribute the writing of blocks of material to Moses (e.g. Exod. 24:4; Deut. 31:9). However, at no point does the Pentateuch attribute to Moses the composition of all five books.

The academic study of the Pentateuch has been dominated for well over a century by a theory known as the documentary hypothesis, which was championed by the German scholar Julius Wellhausen. In his book *Prolegomena to the History of Israel* (English translation published in 1885), Wellhausen presented an entirely new way of understanding the history of Israelite religion. Rejecting the Mosaic authorship of the Pentateuch, Wellhausen borrowed from earlier studies which had pointed to the presence of four different literary styles within the Pentateuch, each associated with a different author. These four supposed authors are now known as the Yahwist, the Elohist, the Deuteronomist and the Priestly Writer.

The first two titles derive their names from the terms used for God in the Hebrew Bible. In Genesis certain passages show a preference for the divine name Yahweh (which usually gets translated into English as 'the LORD', using small capitals). Other passages use the divine name Elohim (which gets translated as 'God'). The uneven distribution of the divine names in Genesis were thought to point to different authors: one preferred the name Yahweh, while another preferred Elohim. The material assigned to the Deuteronomist, as the name suggests, is found mainly in the book of Deuteronomy. The material assigned to the Priestly Writer, much of it in Leviticus, was considered to be of special interest to priests.

While others had identified these four styles of material within the Pentateuch, Wellhausen took this a stage further and assigned to each of them a relative date of composition. He himself was cautious about giving absolute dates for all of the documents, but his position is usually represented as follows:

J   c. 840 BC
E   c. 700 BC
D   c. 623 BC
P   c. 500–450 BC

By so ordering the materials that compose the Pentateuch, Wellhausen challenged the long-standing tradition that Israelite religion was to be traced back to Moses. Rejecting a second millennium BC date for the beginning of Israelite religion, when Moses received the Torah at Mount Sinai, he argued that the true originators of Israelite religion were the prophets of the late ninth and eighth centuries BC. With them ethical monotheism began.

Wellhausen's ideas were quickly and widely assimilated by others. Only the most conservative of Jewish and Christian scholars spoke out against this, and they soon found themselves in a minority. To a large extent they became the victims of the spirit of the age. Perceived as advocates of tradition, their well-founded criticisms of Wellhausen's theory were casually dismissed or ignored. Wellhausen's approach, in marked contrast, represented a triumph for human reason over tradition. This triumph was perhaps all the greater in that it related to the Bible, the very book that for centuries had epitomized the importance of tradition based on divine revelation. Human reason now demonstrated that divine revelation was wrong.

While the documentary hypothesis crystallized by Wellhausen has dominated OT studies for the past century, support for it has diminished significantly, with more and more scholars expressing unease regarding both its methodology and its conclusions. Alternative theories have been advocated, though none has succeeded in gaining widespread acceptance. Consequently, the question of how the Pentateuch was composed remains open.

Two important factors need to be taken into account in considering how and when the Pentateuch came into being. First, the books of Genesis to Deuteronomy consist of a rich amalgam of materials that reflect different literary types. Side by side we encounter, to list but some: narratives of different lengths and complexity, genealogies of different kinds, paternal blessings, hymns, covenant obligations, laws, moral imperatives, instructions for the manufacture of cultic furnishings, and guidelines for the performance of religious activities. The variety of literary types found within the Pentateuch argues against a single author being responsible for everything. Rather, the evidence points to one or more editors taking existing materials and skilfully shaping them together according to an overall plan. As a result the Pentateuch is perhaps best viewed as a literary collage: different types of material have been brought together to produce a story that, while displaying a variety of styles, exhibits an overall coherence of plot and themes.

Second, as it now stands, the Pentateuch is closely tied to the books of Joshua to 2 Kings, forming a continuous story that moves from creation through to the sacking of Jerusalem by the Babylonians in 587 BC. The very last event recorded is the release of King Jehoiachin from prison in Babylon, which probably took place in 562 BC (2 Kgs 25:27–30). Given the interconnectedness of the books of Genesis to 2 Kings, it seems likely that all these books took their present shape shortly after 562 BC. In support of this is the lack of evidence for the existence of the Pentateuch as a five-volume work prior to the period of the exile. This seems to be confirmed indirectly by the discovery of the law book in the time of Josiah (2 Kgs 22). Had the Pentateuch already existed, the contents of the book of the law would have been widely known.

This, however, does not mean that the varied elements that make up the Pentateuch were not in existence much earlier. On the contrary, there is good reason to believe that its contents were known for some considerable time prior to 562 BC.

Speculation regarding the process of composition should not detract attention from the more important issue of understanding the message of the Pentateuch. The significance of these books should not be underestimated, since they provide the theological foundation that undergirds the whole of Scripture. Without the Pentateuch the rest of the Bible would be largely incomprehensible.

Further reading (see **Introduction** for good commentary series)

Gordon Wenham, *Exploring the Old Testament 1. The Pentateuch* (SPCK, 2003) – excellent introduction, with panels highlighting themes and points to ponder.

Desmond Alexander, *From Paradise to the Promised Land: An Introduction to the Pentateuch* (Paternoster, 2nd edn 2002) –

another well-written book, with more detail on all the issues noted above.

Victor Hamilton, *Handbook on the Pentateuch* (Baker, 2nd edn 2005) – good detailed introduction to the books and each section or chapter.

4. Historical Books

Philip Johnston

INTRODUCTION

The Historical Books discussed here are Joshua, Judges, Ruth, 1 and 2 Samuel, 1 and 2 Kings, 1 and 2 Chronicles, Ezra, Nehemiah and Esther. They recount the history of Israel from entry into the promised land under Joshua, through decline under the judges, prosperity in the early monarchy, mixed fortunes in the divided monarchy and eventual exile of both kingdoms, and on to the various returns of some Jews to Judah and their survival in the Persian empire. Between them these books cover about 1,000 years in time, and sweep across some 1,000 miles of the ancient fertile crescent, though most of the story relates to the small territory known variously as Canaan, Palestine or Israel. The story recorded covers much social and political development, but concentrates on God's perseverance with and preservation of his faltering people Israel. (Note that God is often referred to by his Hebrew name Yahweh, usually translated in English as LORD, in small capitals.)

A. Christian and Jewish orders

The order of the Historical Books in English Bibles follows the ancient translation of the Hebrew Scriptures into Greek, commonly called the Septuagint (and abbreviated as LXX). This was made in the third and second centuries BC, though our earliest complete manuscripts come from the fourth and fifth centuries AD. The translation of the Septuagint was done by Jews in the pre-Christian era, but its later preservation and the ordering of books was done by Christians. This order obviously reflects the nature of these books, since together they recount Israel's history. And it contributes to the traditional Christian division of the Old Testament into four sections: Pentateuch, History, Poetry and Prophets.

By contrast, Jewish Bibles have only three sections: Pentateuch, Prophets and Writings. The second is subdivided into the Former Prophets, with four books: Joshua, Judges, Samuel and Kings; and the Latter Prophets, also with four books: Isaiah, Jeremiah, Ezekiel and The Twelve (i.e. the 'minor prophets'). The third section, Writings, includes Ruth, Chronicles, Ezra, Nehemiah and Esther. This division highlights the fact that Joshua, Judges, Samuel and Kings have a distinctly prophetic perspective: they note many prophets who proclaim God's approval or disapproval, and the narrators themselves give similar verdicts. In particular, the man Samuel dominates the first part of 1 and 2 Samuel, while Elijah and Elisha provide a crucial counterpart to the monarchy in 1 and 2 Kings.

The other 'historical' books have different, less prophetic perspectives. Chronicles focuses more on the temple and worship, while Ezra, Nehemiah and Esther recount post-exilic reconstruction and survival. Their placement in the Writings thus has thematic reasons, though may also be due to their later composition and acceptance into the Hebrew canon. In addition, Esther and Ruth were two of the five short books (or 'scrolls'; also Song of Songs, Ecclesiastes and Lamentations), each read at an annual festival. So Jewish and Christian ordering of these books give complementary insights into their nature.

B. Historical setting

When did all this take place? Dating ancient history is a difficult exercise, and becomes increasingly hazardous the further back we go. However, there is one great help. The Mesopotamians were often keen star watchers, and they cross-referenced their historical records to eclipses, comets, etc. Modern astronomy can now give us exact dates for these celestial occurrences, and hence for much of Assyrian and Babylonian history in the first millennium BC. On its own that would be of little use. But fortunately Mesopotamian records occasionally mention battles fought in the Levant (i.e. the eastern Mediterranean lands) and also the names of various kings of Israel and Judah. As a result, we can derive reasonably accurate dates for the Hebrew monarchies back to the time of David. Historians now largely agree on these dates, within about a ten-year margin for most. The following sections use the dates given in the *New Bible Dictionary*.

As we work back to the second millennium BC, however, dating is less easy. 1 Kgs 6:1 states that Solomon started building the temple 480 years after the exodus. The temple construction began in Solomon's fourth year, 967 BC, so this dates the exodus to 1447 and the events of Joshua to 1407 onwards, i.e. the late fifteenth century BC. However, many scholars argue that the archaeological record of destruction in various Canaanite towns places the conquest more in the late thirteenth century. In this case the figure of 480 years is figurative for twelve generations, which in reality would have spanned much less time. For our purposes here, this issue only affects the length of the judges period, where there was some overlap between judges anyway (see below). The following table gives an overview, with the four most important framework dates.

Century BC	Events and people
late 15th C	Israelites enter Canaan, taking 1 Kgs 6:1 literally
late 13th C	Israelites enter Canaan, taking 1 Kgs 6:1 figuratively
10th C	David and Solomon
	931, Solomon's death, and division of kingdom into Israel and Judah
9th C	Elijah and Elisha
8th C	722, Assyrians conquer Samaria, and exile many Israelites
6th C	587, Babylonians conquer Jerusalem, and exile many Judeans
	539, Persians conquer Babylon, and allow Jews to return

C. Authorship and date

All these books are anonymous, i.e. they have no named authors, though Ezra and Nehemiah have significant sections apparently written by these two men. Authorship of each book will be dealt with in turn below, but one widespread view merits brief discussion.

Following Martin Noth (1943), many scholars think that Joshua, Judges, Samuel and Kings were put together at the time of the Babylonian exile. Some exiled Jews recorded their history as it had been handed down in various stories and official documents, partly to preserve this history now that Jerusalem and other cities had been destroyed, but mainly to explain why the exile had happened. The stories had different sources but were linked together by a common theology, which explains the diversity of style yet the similarity of interpretation across these books. Deuteronomy was seen by Noth as a historical and theological introduction, so these books are often called the 'Deuteronomistic History'.

There is some value in this approach. The early stories especially may well have been handed down orally for centuries, preserved in separate parts of the country, and not written down till much later. These books do have similar theological assessments, often using distinctive vocabulary. This theology partly reflects Deuteronomy, regardless of when the later was finalized. And there are many indications throughout the OT of later editing of earlier material.

But several aspects invite caution. First, the books are all significantly different: Joshua is positive and progressive, whereas Judges is negative and cyclical; Samuel has many detailed stories with little overt interpretation, whereas Kings has fewer and briefer stories with explicit theological assessment. This suggests that the stories have different origins, and that later editors showed great respect in preserving their different styles. Secondly, many stories seem to have been recorded early on, as shown by eye-witness-type accounts (e.g. tactics against Jericho and Ai), ancient place names (e.g. Kiriath-Arba for Hebron, Josh. 14:15), or the phrase 'to this day' (e.g. Josh. 15:63, Judg. 1:21, only valid until 2 Sam. 5). Thirdly, the theological interpretation may have been nurtured in prophetic circles right from the start, so that the eventual writer simply standardized the theological assessments of Samuel, Nathan, Elijah, Elisha and many others. In summary, while the books have a common thread, and may truly reflect Deuteronomy, this can be explained as ancient legacy as well as exilic interpretation.

JOSHUA

A. Contents

1 – 12	Invasion
1	Joshua's commission
2 – 5	Spies in Jericho, crossing Jordan, circumcision, Passover
5 – 8	Jericho and Ai, altar on Mount Ebal
9	Gibeonite deception
10 – 12	Campaigns in south and north, list of conquered kings
13 – 24	Settlement
13 – 21	Tribal allocations, cities of refuge and Levitical towns
22	Return of eastern tribes
23 – 24	Covenant renewal at Shechem

The book named after him covers the life of Joshua from the death of Moses (1:1) to that of Joshua himself (24:29). It has two quite distinct halves. Chs. 1 – 12 recount the momentous events of entry into the promised land: Joshua's commission and reassurance; crossing the Jordan; the capture of two bridgehead towns, Jericho in the rift valley and Ai in the hills; the grand covenant renewal ceremony at Mount Ebal; the mistaken treaty with the Gibeonites; and finally, in rapid overview, the campaigns in the south and the north, with lists of cities taken and kings captured. This is an all-action story, mostly positive and successful.

The second half, chs. 13 – 24, is quite different. It begins by noting 'very large areas of land to be taken over' (13:1), mostly west and north of Israel's later borders. It then proceeds to detail the allotment of the land to each tribe, noting also the cities of refuge and towns for the Levites. These lists were clearly important, though their inclusion here interrupts the story of conquest. This is resumed in ch. 22, with the return home of the fighting men from the two-and-a-half tribes allotted land east of the Jordan. They set up a commemorative altar which is misinterpreted, and civil war is only averted by their promise of perpetual allegiance to Yahweh and his sanctuary. Finally, there are two rather similar farewell speeches by Joshua, and closing burial notices.

This summary shows that Joshua has three types of material: programmatic theology (chs. 1, 23 – 24), narrative (chs. 2 – 11, 22), and lists (chs. 12 – 21). Thus the book, like many in the OT, seems to be a compilation of different sources brought together.

B. Historical setting

Unfortunately there is no unambiguous extra-biblical evidence for *any* of the characters or events of the early biblical period: the patriarchs, the Israelites in Egypt, the exodus or the conquest. This is not hard to explain. Palestine was off the beaten track, and has left very little writing from the second millennium BC. Also, the Egyptians were notoriously xenophobic, they often had Semitic slaves, and they avoided accounts of defeat. So lack of extra-biblical evidence does not mean that the biblical account is inaccurate. Indeed, many aspects of it fit their historical setting well. But it does mean that the accounts are not supported by external sources.

The main historical issue regarding the Book of Joshua is Israel's entry into Palestine. The book portrays a violent military conquest with the capture of many Canaanite towns, including three which were burned down: Jericho (6:24), Ai (8:28), and Hazor in the north (11:11). Traditionally, this conquest was dated to c. 1400 BC, but no destruction layers in Palestine cities correspond to this early date, on conventional archaeological dating. Alternatively, the conquest has been dated to c. 1200 BC, which gives at least a partial correspondence with archaeological evidence (see Introduction to this chapter). In both cases, however, the cities of Jericho and Ai remain problematic, since the archaeological evidence does not fit a conquest at either date.

These views have been challenged by some evangelical scholars in different ways. For instance, John Bimson suggested an early conquest date by realigning an even earlier destruction layer, conventionally dated at 1550, to the late 1400s. Also Bryant Wood has questioned the standard view on Jericho, arguing that the site's famous excavator Dame Kathleen Kenyon was looking for the wrong evidence in the wrong place. Their views have not generally been accepted by archaeologists. Nevertheless, they indicate some of the uncertainties on the subject and the need for further study.

In recent decades many scholars have suggested that Israel did not enter Canaan violently at all. Rather they emerged from within Palestine, as refugees from lowland Canaanite cities or as nomads who eventually settled down. These groups populated many new villages in the central hills c. 1200 BC, gradually developed a separate identity, and invented for themselves a glorious past. However, this view fails to explain how the biblical tradition arose in the first place. Also, there is some archaeological evidence that the inhabitants of these new villages already had different values, since they did not eat pigs (animals forbidden to the Israelites, Lev. 11:7).

The settlement of Israel in Palestine is probably the most complex issue in OT studies today. Nevertheless, a recent thorough assessment by evangelical scholars concludes: 'we have found nothing in the evidence considered that would invalidate the basic biblical contours'.[1]

One particular incident in Joshua has often intrigued Bible readers: 'the sun stood still and the moon stopped' for 'about a full day' to enable the Israelites to rout the southern kings (10:12–14). Various explanations have been proposed, e.g. suspension of the normal laws of the universe (though claims of scientific corroboration have never been substantiated), or highly unusual light reflection or refraction. More appropriately to the ancient context, John Walton notes that the vocabulary of theses verses reflects that of Mesopotamian celestial omen texts, and has often been misunderstood. To see both the rising sun and the setting moon at the same time on the 'wrong' day was a bad omen, so Joshua prays that his superstitious opponents will see a bad omen and lose heart before they even engage battle.[2]

C. Relevance for Christians

The Book of Joshua has many themes relevant to Christians. Centrally, it shows God fulfilling the promise made to Abraham by bringing his descendants back into the land promised to him. God does this through Joshua, whose name means 'Yahweh saves', a pithy summary of divine activity in human history. This name recurs later (e.g. for the prophet Hosea, and Israel's last king Hoshea), and of course supremely in the person better known by the name's Greek form, Jesus. The covenant God had made with his people at Sinai is reaffirmed immediately after entry, as the people gather at Mount Ebal (8:30–35, cf. Deut. 27–28), and again at the end of Joshua's life at Shechem (ch. 24). God's people are now a nation, settled in their land, in covenant relationship with him.

However, the book also poses a major challenge to Christians: the extermination of the Canaanites. This issue more than any other has led many people to reject the OT, and some to reject the whole Bible. So how can we come to terms with this command?

The first thing to notice is the terminology. This is not just any type of war. This is *herem*, variously translated as 'proscription', 'sacred ban', 'devotion to destruction'. *Herem* was a well-known concept in the ancient world: it involved complete destruction of all living beings in devotion to one's god, and sometimes consecration of precious metals to their temple. So it is a religious as well as military term. It is only used of Israel's early wars of conquest and consolidation, in Deuteronomy, Joshua and 1 Samuel. Once the land was firmly secure, warfare became simply defence.

Other passages have complementary emphases. Exodus repeatedly notes that God will 'drive out' other peoples (e.g. Exod. 23:27–30), though whether by death or banishment is unspecified. Deuteronomy allows citizens of surrendering towns to live and non-combatants of conquered towns to be spared (Deut. 20:10–15), though this only applies to distant towns. Perhaps more importantly, the Joshua accounts suggest only occasional application of the *herem*: at Jericho, Ai and some other resisting towns (6:21; 8:26; 11:12). Other texts reveal that many Canaanites were spared, though admittedly this happened because of Israel's military weakness rather than any moral compunction (Judg. 1:27–35). This attenuates the problem historically, but not theologically.

Why did God command it? There are three key elements of the biblical explanation. First, this was divine punishment on people for their sin, not their race: 'the sin of the Amorites' was now complete (Gen. 15:16). Their abhorrent practices included sacrificing their very own children to appease the gods (Deut. 12:31; 18:10). So they were to be punished for basic crimes against humanity, like the nations listed in Amos 1 – 2. Several points show this was punishment for sin, not extermination of race. On the one hand, Canaanites who trusted in Israel's God were spared, like Rahab and her family (2:11). On the other, Israelites who fell into similar sin would meet equally severe punishment, like Achan and his family (7:24–26). And any apostate Israelite town would also be subject to annihilation by *herem* (Deut. 13:12–18). Of course, these texts reflect the group solidarity of ancient times, where all in a family or clan lived or died together.

Secondly, this was prevention for Israel adopting pagan beliefs and practices (e.g. Deut. 7:3–4). God knew how strong their temptation was, and wanted to protect his people. Sadly, the incomplete conquest and the survival of many Canaanites led to exactly what God feared.

Thirdly and most importantly, most of the OT has no developed concept of life after death. So God's punishment of sin had to be seen in this life, if at all. The NT says more about judgment after death, both acquittal and punishment. So in Christian theology divine judgment is equally certain and equally severe, though no longer visible here on earth. How God will ultimately judge those who never had a chance to respond to him is his alone to decide. But the Israelite enactment of immediate judgment reminds us of the Christian doctrine of ultimate judgment.

JUDGES

A. Contents

1:1 – 3:6	Partial conquest and theological assessment
3:7 – 16:31	Oppression and deliverance: twelve judges
17 – 21	Two unattached narratives:
17 – 18	Danite idolatry and kidnap
19 – 21	Rape, murder and inter-tribal warfare

Judges tells the depressing story of Israel's gradual decline between the conquest and the monarchy. It opens positively, with a summary of territory captured (1:1–20). However, it then gives a long catalogue of failure (1:21–36), followed by a historical and religious summary of the ensuing period (2:1 – 3:6). This includes the tragic downward spiral of apostasy – oppression – judge raised up – deliverance – worse apostasy . . . (2:11–19). The opening section thus provides an overview and theological explanation of the whole period.

The second and main section (3:6 – 16:31) recounts the exploits of some twelve 'judges'. Elsewhere this term means judge in the modern sense of one who settles legal disputes, but here it implies more a hero-deliverer who became a ruler. Some clearly exercised leadership already, like the prophetess Deborah (4:4), but many were 'raised up' by God for the occasion. In any case, from what we know of characters like Jephthah and Samson, their justice was probably very rough and ready.

The third section gives two narratives outside the cycle of judges, which illustrate the near anarchy of the times. The first concerns the Danites' migration and the kidnap of a Levite priest. The second recounts horrific rape, murder, inter-tribal warfare and sponsored kidnapping. The refrain 'In those days Israel had no king' (four times), with its addition 'everyone did as they saw fit' (twice), thus suggests that the book was written in the early monarchy, when the order established by David contrasted sharply with this period's lawlessness.

There are two groups of judges, sometimes described as major and minor. The former all have stories about their exploits, the first two fairly briefly and the others at significant length. After the accounts of the first four we read that the land had peace for 40 or 80 years, which look like round figures for one or two generations. Othniel led a successful revolt against 'Cushan-Rishathaim king of Aram-Naharaim' (3:8; since Aram-Naharaim lay beyond the distant Euphrates, this king presumably reigned more locally). Ehud the left-hander assassinated King Eglon of Maob, defeated his forces, and established a long-lasting peace. Deborah the prophetess and her general Barak defeated the powerful King Jabin of Hazor and his general Sisera. Here the prose and poetry accounts in chs. 5 and 6 display some minor differences, though these can easily be explained as complementary rather than contradictory. Gideon leads a rout of the encroaching Midianites with initial humility and courage and then declines the proffered kingship, though later succumbs to pride and idolatry. On his death, one son Abimelech kills the other seventy and proclaims himself king (ch. 9). The disastrous consequences and the implicit suspicion of kingship explain the presence of this non-judge story in this section. Jephthah was illegitimate and ostracized, but later summoned to save the eastern tribes from Ammonite oppression. His military success was marred by his rash vow, fulfilled in the sacrifice of his daughter. Finally Samson, for all his dubious activities, at least kept the Philistines at bay when they were increasingly aggressive.

The 'minor' judges have only a few verses each, in three short sections. Of Shamgar we know nothing except that he 'struck down six hundred Philistines' (3:31), the only military conflict recorded for this group. The other five have brief, formulaic notices of their home town, length of judgeship (in exact rather than round figures) and notice of burial, plus the considerable progeny of three of them (10:1–5; 12:11–15). The different style and content of these brief notices suggests that the final compiler of the book combined two types of material, stories of hero-deliverers and a list of other leaders. The following table summarizes the data.

Reference	Judge (and origin)	Years of oppression and cause	Years of peace	Years of judgeship
3:7–11	Othniel (Calebite)	8, Cushan-Rishathaim	40	–
3:12–20	Ehud (Benjamin)	18, Eglon of Moab	80	–
3:31	Shamgar	Philistines	–	–
4 – 5	Deborah (? Ephraim)	20, Jabin of Hazor (with Sisera)	40	–
6 – 8	Gideon (Manasseh)	7, Midianites and Amalekites	40	–
10:1–2	Tola (Issachar)	–	–	23
10:3–5	Jair (Gilead)	–	–	22
10:6 – 12:7	Jephthah (Gilead)	18, Ammonites	–	6
12:8–10	Ibzan (Bethlehem)	–	–	7
12:11–12	Elon (Zebulun)	–	–	10
12:13–15	Abdon (Ephraim)	–	–	8
13 – 16	Samson (Dan)	40, Philistines	–	20

B. Historical setting

The figures given in Judges for years of oppression, peace and judgeship total 407 (though see above on 40 years as a round figure). If one adds suitable lengths before this for the wilderness period and for Joshua and the elders, and after this for Samuel, Saul and David, the total is clearly more than the 480 years given in 1 Kgs 6:1 for the period from the exodus to building the temple. This means that some of the judgeships must overlap. This in itself is hardly surprising, since it was a period of continued unrest, and there could be simultaneous oppressions or judgeships in the north (Issachar, Zebulun), east (Gilead) and south (Benjamin, Dan). But once overlap is admitted, there is no way of knowing its extent, so the figures in Judges cannot be used to support an early date for the exodus and conquest (see Historical Setting in Introduction to this chapter).

In his dispute with the Ammonites, Jephthah claimed that Israelites had occupied the territory for 300 years (11:26). If true, this would imply a longer period for the judges and hence an early exodus. But Jephthah may well have been exaggerating to bolster his case, or simply ignorant.

Later Israelite history testifies to continued conflict with neighbouring peoples, so the periodic invasion and oppression of the judges period fits the wider context. Unrest in Palestine in c. 1350 BC is related in letters from Canaanite city-states to the nominal overlord Egypt (excavated at El-Amarna, by the Nile). If the Israelites had already entered the land, these letters could reflect their continued attacks. Otherwise they provide general evidence of conflict in the area.

C. Relevance for Christians

A useful initial question concerns the purpose of the book within the OT. Some commentators take their cue from the closing refrain 'Israel had no king', and see it as pointing to the need for a monarch. However, while this is a clear implication from the concluding section, kingship is mostly ignored in the introduction and main section, and once even portrayed negatively (ch. 9). More central to the book is the theme of God's provision for his wayward people, raising up judges to deliver them and enable them to survive. So its overriding message is that of God's grace in response to human failure.

This theme is equally important for Christian interpretation, since it shows God's desire to rescue and restore a wayward people. This can be applied in different ways to both evangelism and the church. Further, the judges can be seen as 'types' of Christ in their role as deliverers, i.e. their activity foreshadows his. However, it is important to note that this relates to their activity, not their morality, which in some case was distinctly dubious.

As to the judges' morality, it is important to remember their times. Obviously there was little knowledge or acceptance of Mosaic law in any form, and the judges were known for military and political leadership rather than religious orthodoxy. Jephthah's foolish vow serves as a sad cautionary tale, even if we note the loyalty of father and daughter to their terribly misguided beliefs (11:30–40). And in the worst case of all, we can see Samson's faith at least in the final act of his life, even if his motives still remain mixed (16:28).

RUTH

A. Contents

The book of Ruth, set in the same period as Judges (Ruth 1:1), provides a delightful and welcome contrast to it. It tells the simple story of an ordinary family struck by tragedy, yet experiencing love and acceptance in unexpected ways. This leads eventually to new hope through marriage and a son, who became King David's grandfather.

Faced with famine, Elimelech and Naomi leave Bethlehem (which ironically means 'House of Bread') for Moab, where their two sons marry but die childless, along with Elimelech. Naomi decides to return home and her daughter-in-law Ruth determines to go too, pledging lifelong loyalty to Naomi and her god. The two women return in poverty, and Ruth the foreigner goes out to glean. She catches the eye of Boaz, who insists she stays in his fields and looks after her. On Naomi's instructions, Ruth then makes a silent approach to Boaz, who responds by redeeming Elimelech's property and marrying Ruth. On the birth of their child, Naomi ((meaning 'pleasant'), who had earlier wanted to be renamed Mara (meaning 'bitter') is again happy, while Boaz and Ruth are lavishly praised by the local women.

B. Historical setting

The book of Ruth provides various historical insights. Foremost is the portrayal of ordinary life continuing at village level, presumably in one of the calmer periods. The anarchy of Judges is complemented by the tranquillity of Ruth. Not that life was easy – famine was a frequent hazard, no doubt exacerbated by political unrest, and it led to Naomi's ten-year voluntary exile. The sojourn to Moab and intermarriage there, even by apparent God-fearers, shows that survival mattered more than any sense of ethnic or religious separateness.

The legal aspects of the book's denouement are intriguing, and involve two features of Israelite law: property redemption and marriage obligation. When someone sold their property, their next-of-kin had both the right and the moral responsibility to buy it back and keep it in the family (Lev. 25:25). Also, when a man died childless, his brother had the moral responsibility to marry his widow and give her a son; the latter would be considered legally as the dead man's son, and would inherit his property and perpetuate his name (Deut. 25:5–6). This practice, attested in many other cultures, is sometimes termed levirate marriage (from the Latin *levir*, 'brother-in-law').

The two concepts are combined here in a way not reflected in Israel's legislation. Elimelech's next-of-kin first agrees to redeem the land, accepting that this includes caring for Naomi (4:1–4). But when he realizes it also involves levirate marriage to Ruth, he declines on the grounds that it will endanger his own estate (4:5–6). He could not afford to buy land which would not become his. At this point Boaz proceeds to redeem the land and marry Ruth. But when Ruth has a son, the father is named as Boaz, not her deceased husband Kilion. While the combination and outworking of these customs did not exactly reflect Pentateuchal provision, the story shows that these customs were known and respected, though also adapted. It gives oblique but strong witness to their antiquity.

C. Relevance for Christians

Ruth is a little jewel. It sparkles like a diamond against black velvet, 'a masterfully crafted response to the politics of despair in Judges'.[3] It provides models of love and loyalty in Ruth, and of compassion and integrity in Boaz, showing how these qualities can redeem tragedy and bring hope. And it wonderfully illustrates the work of the '(next-of-kin) redeemer', or *go'el*. Even in despair, Job still knew that his redeemer would vindicate him (Job 19:25). And Christians know that their Redeemer has done so for them.

1 & 2 SAMUEL

Early tradition followed the Hebrew text in seeing 1 and 2 Samuel as a single book, as attested in the Babylonian Talmud and by church fathers Eusebius and Jerome (fourth century AD). Division into two is commonly attributed to the Septuagint translators, on the basis that the Greek text needed two scrolls whereas one had sufficed for the more compact Hebrew text. The same applies to Kings and Chronicles.

A. Contents

1 Sam. 1 – 7	Samuel as judge
1 – 3	Samuel and Eli
4 – 7	Wars with Philistines, ark captured and returned
1 Sam. 8 – 15	Samuel and Saul
8 – 12	Saul becomes king
13 – 15	Various wars, Saul rejected
1 Sam. 16 – 31	Saul and David
16 – 27	David's rise, Saul's jealousy, David a fugitive
28 – 31	Saul's final battle and death
2 Sam. 1 – 24	David
1 – 4	David's lament, civil war
5 – 10	David as king, Jerusalem as capital, ark installed, covenant, empire
11 – 12	David, Bathsheba and Uriah
13 – 20	Rape of Tamar, Absalom's rebellion, Sheba's rebellion
21 – 24	Appendix

1 & 2 Samuel record Israel's transition from a loose confederacy of tribes partially governed by occasional judges, to a united kingdom with a strong monarchy and a subservient empire. It was a remarkable political transformation in little over a century, involving enormous social, economic and religious change. Some of this is noted directly in the text, but much is simply implied. The development was initiated by popular request for a king, which Samuel interpreted as rejection of the old order, but which God granted. While the first king Saul failed the challenge, the second, David, achieved political success and became the benchmark for future kings, indeed the model for the eventual messiah.

1 Samuel opens with the annual visit of an ordinary Israelite family to the central shrine at Shiloh, giving a rare glimpse into the religious practice of ordinary Israelites. This led to the birth of Samuel, who grew up as an apprentice attendant at Shiloh, and later combined the roles of judge, priest and prophet as 'God's emergency man'.[4] Philistine expansionism marked the careers of Samuel and later Saul, but Samuel initiated spiritual and military recovery, and led Israel during an uneasy peace (ch. 7).

But the situation was unstable, and when Samuel grew old the people demanded a king. For all his qualities, Samuel himself was partly at fault in appointing his sons as judges, even though this was not a hereditary office and they were known to be corrupt. On divine prompting Samuel acceded and Saul was appointed, first anointed privately, then chosen by lot in public, and finally confirmed after exercising impromptu leadership (chs. 8 – 12). Given this succession of events, occurring in different places, and recounted in texts with different emphases, some scholars conclude that the editor merged accounts from different periods, some from the early monarchy when kingship was seen as successful (e.g. 9:1 – 10:16), and others from later centuries when it was unsuccessful and divisive (e.g. chs. 8, 12). However, it must also be noted that there was already longstanding opposition to kingship (cf. Judg. 9), and its anti-egalitarian tendencies were easily visible in neighbouring cultures.

Unfortunately, Saul did not live up to early promise, and quickly lost divine and prophetic endorsement. While his fall appears rapid, it may already be presaged by his ignoring the challenge, hinted at in his anointing, to attack the Philistines (10:5–7). In offering sacrifice and sparing Agag (chs. 13, 15) Saul oversteps his authority and begins a long and painful slide, which leads eventually to his tragic and lonely death (31:4). Meanwhile David gradually rises to be king-in-waiting.

2 Samuel opens with a brief period of civil war, after which David established first a united kingdom then a huge empire. Jerusalem became the political and religious capital, and divine approval was

encapsulated in a dynastic covenant (chs. 1 – 10). However, David's adultery with Bathsheba and murder of her husband Uriah (chs. 11 – 12) are a turning point, and the following chapters relate only family troubles and nearly fatal revolts (chs. 12 – 20). David's despicable actions affected far more than the immediate victims. The final chapters form an appendix of six elements from throughout David's reign, arranged in chiasm: atonement story, warrior list, song; song, warrior list, atonement story (21 – 24).

B. Historical setting

There is ample extra-biblical evidence that the Philistines were a group of Greek-speaking 'Sea-Peoples' who settled in south-west Palestine about 1200 BC. They ruled over five city states as a military aristocracy, and gradually assimilated with the indigenous Canaanites over the following centuries. Their possession of chariots and control of iron gave them military ascendancy over Israel for a long period. Recent excavation has revealed much about them, including the name Goliath (though from the century after the time of David's famous foe).

However, the main problem in finding archaeological corroboration for this period is the difficulty of excavating relevant sites in Jerusalem, for modern political reasons, and the ambiguity of the available evidence. Nevertheless, the existence of some stone building, including an extensive 'step structure', leads many scholars to conclude that Jerusalem underwent significant development at this time. Further, the later 'House of David' inscription found at Dan in the far north clearly shows that a Davidic kingdom stretched that far.

David's empire (2 Sam. 8) was apparently enormous, including all the neighbouring territories and stretching to the distant north, through what is now Lebanon, Syria and north-west Iraq as far as the Euphrates River. So geographically and demographically Israel became only a minority part of this. While some scholars have dismissed this as implausible, Kenneth Kitchen has shown that the eleventh to tenth centuries BC witnessed a power vacuum between the major powers of Egypt, Hittites (central Turkey) and Mesopotamia. This led to several mini-empires, including that of David and Solomon.[5]

C. Relevance for Christians

1 & 2 Samuel abound with lessons. There is the political development from confederacy to monarch to empire, under God's watchful providence, and the implication that different political systems can

work well when leaders are godly and act responsibly. Within this there is the rejection of Saul, whose rebellion hardened, and the approval of David, whose sin was confessed.

There is also the detail of many finely-told stories (the most extensive in the OT), which qualify the big picture with a more nuanced portrayal of characters and events. Close reading of the text (as rediscovered by scholars in narrative criticism) highlights these details, and reminds us of the ambiguity of some actions and the humanness of all the characters, and warns us against simplistic interpretation.

The overall picture and close reading together reveal David in his grandeur and his weakness. Above all, it shows 'a man after [God's] own heart' (1 Sam. 13:14) who regularly sought divine guidance. Despite his terrible sin and its catastrophic consequences, which the text starkly portrays, David's repentance revealed his continued faith in God. No wonder he became the standard against which future kings were assessed, and the model for the one whom a much later hymn writer called 'great David's greater son'.

1 & 2 KINGS

A. Contents

1 Kgs 1 – 11	United Kingdom: Solomon's accession and reign
1 Kgs 12 – 2 Kgs 17	Divided Kingdom:
1 Kgs 12 – 16	Schism and early kings
1 Kgs 17 – 2 Kgs 8:15	Elijah and Elisha
2 Kgs 8:16 – 17:41	Further kings, Israel's exile
2 Kgs 18 – 25	Remaining kingdom: Judah's last kings and exile

The books of Kings cover some four centuries of Israel's history, from the death of David to the death of his kingdom. It opens with David entrusting the kingdom to Solomon, who started well, constructed the temple plus various royal buildings, and led Israel in peace and prosperity (1 Kgs 4:20). But his reign was tarnished by unwelcome economic conditions for the people and his own gradual apostasy (1 Kgs 5:13–14; 11:4–6). Even so, on his death the Israelites would have accepted his son Rehoboam as king. But having known only pampered court life, Rehoboam refused their reasonable request, and the northern ten tribes separated under Jeroboam. They were then known as Israel, in distinction from Judah.

Jeroboam's first task was to create a separate political and religious life, including new temples, priests and festivals. Because of this, he is repeatedly judged to have 'caused Israel to commit sin' (e.g. 1 Kgs 15:26, 34). All Israel's subsequent kings 'did evil in the eyes of the LORD', following Jeroboam's ways. The northern kingdom was inherently unstable, with three new dynasties in its first fifty years, and another three in its last thirty. Only the dynasty of Jehu continued to the fourth generation, and then only briefly. Prophets often pronounce judgment on a dynasty (1 Kgs 14:10; 16:3; 21:21), and some scholars have suggested that they never accepted the monarchy in principle. However, their judgment is always proclaimed on certain kings in particular, not on the northern monarchy in general.

For a large middle section (1 Kgs 17:1 – 2 Kgs 8:15), the focus shifts from kings and politics to prophets and people. Dry records of battles fought and cities built give way to dramatic narratives of miraculous events. Some of these had far-reaching consequences, like the contest on Mount Carmel (1 Kgs 18), but most involved individuals or small groups. Many involved 'the sons of the prophets', who seemed to live on the margins of society, and may have descended from the companies of prophets in Samuel's time (e.g. 1 Sam. 10:5; 19:20). These stories provide intriguing glimpses into ordinary life as well as the role of prophets in ancient Israel.

Israel and Judah together went through cyclical half-century phases of political weakness and strength, with periods of strength in the mid-ninth century (under Omri and Jehoshaphat) and early eighth century (under Jeroboam II and Azariah/Uzziah). This second prosperous period led to Amos's vivid condemnation of ill-gotten and misused wealth. By the third quarter of the eighth century, Assyria was advancing westwards, and in 722 captured Samaria and exiled many Israelites, who never returned. God's assessment was that they refused to listen to 'my servants the prophets' (2 Kgs 17:13).

The Assyrians advanced further and would have conquered Judah too, but for God's intervention to save Jerusalem, in response to the prayers of Hezekiah and Isaiah (2 Kgs 18 – 19). Hezekiah enacted sweeping reforms, including removal of the 'high places'. Sadly his son Manasseh reversed all these, became Judah's worst king, and was seen as a major cause of its later exile. His grandson Josiah again enacted reform, helped by Assyria's rapid decline. But the Babylonians, the new world power, pressured Josiah's weak successors. Eventually Judah too was captured, Jerusalem and its temple were destroyed, and many of its people exiled.

So Kings ends with the tragedy of defeat and exile. God's provision of king, city and temple were all swept away. Other passages like Ps. 137 and Lamentations convey something of the emotional impact of this.

UNITED MONARCHY

1 Sam.	*Samuel*	Saul	1045–1011	
2 Sam.		David	1011–971	
	Nathan			
1 Kgs 1 – 11		Solomon	971–931	

– – – – – – – 931   schism – – – – – –   *10th century*

		JUDAH		**ISRAEL**			
12 – 14		Rehoboam	931–913	• Jeroboam	931–910		
		Abijah	913–911	Nadab	910–909		
15 – 16		Asa**	911–870	• Baasha	909–886		
				Elah	886–885		
17 – 22		Jehoshaphat**		• Omri	885–874		*9th century*
			873–870–848	Ahab	874–853	*Elijah*	
2 Kgs 1 – 8		Jehoram	853–848–841	Ahaziah	853–852		
		Ahaziah	841	Joram	852–841	*Elisha*	
9 – 13		Qn Athaliah	841–835	• Jehu	841–814		
		Joash**	835–796	Jehoahaz	814–798		
14		Amaziah*	796–767	Jehoash	798–782		
				Jeroboam II	793–782–753		
15		Azariah*	791–767–740	Zechariah	753–752	*Amos*	*8th century*
		= Uzziah		Shallum	752		
16 – 17	*Micah*	Jotham*	750–740–732	• Menahem	752–742		
		Ahaz	744–732–716	Pekahiah	742–740	*Hosea*	
18 – 20	*Isaiah*			• Pekah	740–732		Exile to
		Hezekiah**	716–687	• Hoshea	732–722	722 ⟶	**Assyria** –
21		Manasseh	696–687–642				no return
22 – 23		Amon	642–640				*7th century*
		Josiah**	640–609				
24	*Jeremiah*						
		Jehoahaz	609				
		Jehoiakim	609–597				
		Jehoiakin	597	597 ⟶			Exile to
25	*(Ezekiel)*	Zedekiah	597–587	587 ⟶			**Babylon**
	(Daniel)						Return
				539 ⟵			under
Ezra 1 – 6	*Haggai*	Zerubbabel					**Persia**
	Zechariah						
(Esther)							*5th century*
Ezra 7 – 10		*Ezra*	458–...	⟵			
Neh.		*Nehemiah*	445–...	⟵			
	Malachi						

Data simplified from *New Bible Dictionary* 3rd edn 1996, pp. 188–189.

Where three dates are given, the first gives the start of a co-regency.

Key: * = king commended in 1 & 2 Kgs ** = reforming king • = new dynasty in Israel
() = books relating to Jews in Babylon and Persia

Kings was probably written during the exile to explain how and why this tragedy had occurred. However, there is a glimmer of hope. The final paragraph shows an improved status for the exiled king Jehoiachin, a portent of the renewal to come.

B. Historical setting

1 & 2 Kings are clearly intended as history and often refer to source documents, notably the chronicles or annals of the kings of Israel or Judah. This implies that the facts could be checked, though these records are now lost (they are *not* the OT book of Chronicles). They also date each king in reference to his contemporary in the other kingdom, showing careful historical method. The figures largely concord, with allowance made for co-regencies – when a son was appointed king while his father was still alive (e.g. 2 Kgs 15:5). This, plus Mesopotamian records of unusual celestial events, allows us to give fixed dates to the whole monarchic period, as in the chart on p. 86.

There are many cross-references between biblical and ancient Near Eastern historical records. OT books frequently mention rulers of both immediate neighbours like Phoenicia (i.e. Tyre and Sidon) and Syria (often called Aram), and the more distant powers of Egypt, Assyria, Babylon and Persia. These rulers are amply attested in extra-biblical sources. Further, these sources also mention many Israelite and Judean kings, as shown in the following table.[6]

Ancient Near Eastern texts	*Date BC*	*Israelite kings mentioned*
Tel Dan stele	c. 850	David, Jehoram/Joram, Ahazaiah
Moabite stele	c. 835	(David), Omri
Shalmaneser III, Kurkh Monolith	853	Ahab
Shalmaneser III, Black Obelisk	828	Omri, Jehu
Adad-Nirari III, Calah stele	c. 800	Omri
Adad-Nirari III, Tell Al-Rimah stele	797	Joash
Tiglath-Pileser III, annals	c. 730	Omri, Menahem, Pekah, Hoshea, (Uzziah), Ahaz
Sargon II, annals	c. 720	Omri
Sennacherib's siege, three sources	c. 700	Hezekiah
Essarhadon, Prism B	c. 670	Manasseh
Ashurbanipal, Rassam Cylinder	c. 640	Manasseh
Nebuchadnezzar, ration lists	c. 570	Jehoiachin

A notable absentee from this list is Solomon. But his reign coincided with weakness of the major powers (see above), who were in no position to attack his territory or claim tribute, the usual reasons for mentioning foreign kings. Further, five years after Solomon's death, Pharaoh Shishak carried off all Jerusalem's gold and silver (1 Kgs 14:25–28). Shishak (called Shoshenq in Egyptian records) died the following year, but his son Osorkon soon dedicated vast amounts to Egyptian deities – very probably Solomon's gold.

C. Relevance for Christians

The 'prophetic' book of 1 & 2 Kings gives many big-picture lessons. God blesses obedience and punishes apostasy, though often not immediately. Divine sovereignty and human responsibility are both relevant, e.g. at the schism (1 Kgs 12), even if hard to reconcile logically. High position brings great responsibility.

Above all, Kings shows that God's assessment of value may not be ours. Politically important kings like Omri receive less space than religiously important ones like his son Ahab. Prophets pervade the book, with two receiving more attention than many monarchs. Unnamed women and children from hamlets like Zarephath and Shunem share the story with kings and emperors. And throughout the centuries, God preserves his people.

1 & 2 CHRONICLES

A. Contents and historical setting

1 Chr. 1 – 9	Genealogies and lists
1	Noah & Abraham
2 – 8	The main tribal lines, notably David's family and Levites
9	Post-exilic Jerusalemites
1 Chr. 10 – 29	David: particularly military and religious leadership (difficulties and sins omitted)
2 Chr. 1 – 9	Solomon: particularly temple construction (apostasy omitted)
2 Chr. 10 – 36	Kings of Judah: particularly reformers Hezekiah and Josiah (kings of Israel mostly omitted)

Chronicles retells the history of Israel from Adam to the exile, though only by genealogical list until the death of Saul, and only for the southern kingdom of Judah after the schism. The book has long been misunderstood, e.g. the Greek title 'Omissions' (*Paraleipomenon*) is inappropriate, since much of the history is already given in Samuel and

Kings. Rather, it is a retelling of the story of the monarchy period from a different perspective and for a different purpose.

Chronicles was written well after the exile. 1 Chr. 3:17–24 lists the descendants of Judah's penultimate king Jehoiachin to at least seven generations and possibly twelve, depending on the interpretation of v. 21. This means the book was completed at the earliest c. 400 BC. By this time the exile was long past, various groups had returned to Jerusalem under Zerubbabel, Ezra and Nehemiah (see below), and between them had established a viable if small Jewish community around a rebuilt temple and city. However, they were now firmly within the Persian empire – kingship and political independence were distant memories. So what this community needed was not an explanation of the exile (as in Kings), but encouragement from God's past provision for present circumstances.

This explains the two key features of the book, evident above in the outline. First, it concentrates on David and his line, as those through whom God worked. In consequence, it ignores Saul's reign except for his death, which is seen as judgment on his unfaithfulness (1 Chr. 10:13). It also virtually ignores the schismatic state of northern Israel: they had not been governed by a Davidic king; after conquest by Assyria they had become ethnically and religiously mixed; and in post-exilic times their descendants the Samaritans had actively opposed Jewish re-establishment.

Secondly, Chronicles concentrates on the temple and its worship, as led by priest and Levites. Hence the greater detail in the genealogy of Levi than of other tribes (1 Chr. 6). Hence the focus for Hezekiah and Josiah's reforms on purifying the temple and celebrating the Passover (unlike the focus in Kings). And hence the frequent reference to Levites throughout the book.

This also explains the glaring omissions regarding David's adultery and murder and Solomon's apostasy. The account of these kings concentrates on their preparation for and construction of the temple, with some description of David's early exploits and of Solomon's other activities. The books of Samuel and Kings were clearly known to the author of Chronicles, who copied or paraphrased significant sections, so presumably their contents were known to his community. Like any historian, the Chronicler used his source material selectively to tell a particular story. Just as histories of the British empire or of the Second World War written in, say, 1945 and 2005, would have different contents and interpretation, with complementary insights, so do the OT historical books.

B. Relevance for Christians

Chronicles has a broad vision of God's work and a strong hope for the future. Through his covenant with king and people, God provided security, peace and prosperity, and through obedience in life and worship the small Jewish community can still experience his blessing. The book has relevance for many Christians today, e.g. those with no political influence, or who long for experiences of previous generations, or who desire church renewal. And the model which Chronicles gives of fresh interpretation of the past encourages us to keep rethinking what we can learn from biblical and Christian history.

EZRA AND NEHEMIAH

The Books of Ezra and Nehemiah are closely related, since they present successive episodes of post-exilic history, and the man Ezra appears in both. Indeed, Jewish tradition sees them as a single book (as in the Talmud, Baba Bathra 15a, the earliest known Jewish list of OT books). But there are also differences. For instance, the Book of Ezra has sections in Aramaic (4:8 – 6:18; 7:12–26), including several official letters – obviously early readers were bilingual. And it has two distinct halves, the first of which recounts events long before Ezra's ministry. The Book of Nehemiah is more uniform in its style and more cohesive in its story.

A. Contents and historical setting

These books have four main stages, as shown in the following table.

Stage	Date	Reference	Event	Persian king	Dates
1.	539	Ezra 1:1 – 4:5	**'First return'**, temple started	Cyrus	550–530
				Cambyses	530–522
2.	520–516	Ezra 4:24 – 6:22	**Temple completed**	Darius I	521–486
	?	*Ezra 4:6	Local opposition	Xerxes/Ahasuerus	486–464
3.	458	Ezra 7 – 10	**'Second return' with Ezra**	Artaxerxes I	464–423
	pre-445	*Ezra 4:7–23	More opposition		
4.	445	Neh. 1 – 12	**Nehemiah to Jerusalem**		
	post-433	Neh. 13	Nehemiah's second term		

* Note that this opposition is recorded with earlier opposition, not in chronological order.

The Book of Ezra is in two distinct halves, the first of which records events before Ezra himself was even born. It opens (as Chronicles closes) with Cyrus's decree enabling Jews to return to Jerusalem to rebuild their temple. The initial leader is prince Sheshbazzar (1:8), perhaps Jehoiachin's son (the 'Shenazzar' of 1 Chr. 3:18), but he is soon replaced by Jehoiachin's grandson Zerubbabel and the high priest Jeshua. These latter lead some 50,000 returnees and initiate temple reconstruction. The altar is rebuilt and new foundations laid, to joyous if poignant celebration. But local opposition soon halts activity for nearly two decades. At this point the text inserts two examples of later opposition (4:6–23). The prophets Haggai and Zechariah then encourage resumption of work, and this time local opposition is thwarted by Darius, who rediscovers and reinforces Cyrus's earlier decree. The temple is completed four years later in 516 BC, with a memorable Passover celebration.

The book then jumps some 60 years to 458 BC (7:8). King Artaxerxes sends the learned Ezra to Jerusalem with royal authority and finance, to establish proper judicial procedure. Ezra and his large delegation were descendants of exiles, 'returning' to Jerusalem for the first time. On arrival, Ezra immediately sees the many mixed marriages as a fundamental threat to the nation's very survival. He responds with spontaneous confession and grief, leading to widespread conviction and a resolve to dissolve the marriages. This one glimpse of Ezra's ministry reveals much about his devotion to God's law. Nothing more is said of the repudiated families: some commentators assume this was a callous act, while others argue that a leader like Ezra would have ensured appropriate provision for them.

The book of Nehemiah is the story of one man used by God to protect and re-invigorate Jerusalem, and is drawn largely from his own, first-person memoirs. Like Ezra, Nehemiah was apparently a child of the diaspora, and like Mordecai he rose to high office. With support from King Artaxerxes, Nehemiah travels to Jerusalem in 445/4 BC as its new and energetic governor. He immediately challenges the city's inhabitants and galvanizes them into action. Despite increasing opposition and intimidation, the walls are rebuilt in the amazingly short period of fifty-two days (chs. 1 – 4, 6).

Other reforms proceed apace. Nehemiah vigorously attacks financial abuses, minimizes the governor's costs, reorganizes temple and defence personnel, and repopulates Jerusalem with descendants of the first returnees (chs. 5, 7, 11 – 12). Meanwhile Ezra and others read the law, and the people respond in confession and recommitment (chs. 8 – 10), and the walls are rededicated with joyful festivity, audible miles away (12:27–43).

Nehemiah returns to Artaxerxes after some 11 years, in 433 BC (13:6). He goes back to Jerusalem 'some time later' during Artaxerxes' reign (i.e. before 423 BC), discovers further abuses and sets about reform with typical vigour. These include the recurrent issue of mixed marriages, with the resultant mixed language, culture and religion. Nehemiah's response (13:25) is more physically confrontational than was Ezra's, with some effect amongst priest and Levites (13:30) but no record of wider divorce. The book ends with Nehemiah's characteristic appeal, 'Remember me with favour, my God' (13:31; cf. 5:19; 6:14; 13:14, 22). To the modern reader this may sound arrogant; for Nehemiah it may simply have reflected a sense of personal unworthiness before God and the knowledge that his good work would inevitably be compromised.

B. Relevance for Christians

The post-exilic situation was very different from the pre-exilic. Politically the Jews were now a small part of a large empire, dependent on local governors and the king. Religiously they had moved from syncretism to accepting only Yahweh, but they often became dispirited in their faith and worship. This has many parallels with the Christian era, so the post-exilic books, both prophetic and historical, have much relevance to us. They portray God's overruling in political events, through Cyrus, Darius and Artaxerxes, in conjunction with the faith and action of men like Zerubbabel, Ezra and Nehemiah. They show how unpromising situations can be turned around through faithful action, but also that apathy and inappropriate relationships often recur. And through the highs and lows, God continues to provide for his people.

ESTHER

A. Contents and historical setting

The Book of Esther tells a short story of great consequence. Historically it falls between the two halves of Ezra (see above), though it deals with Jews in the Persian capital Susa rather than in Jerusalem. Xerxes (called Ahasuerus in Hebrew) deposes his queen and chooses Esther instead. Meanwhile his chief official Haman, angered by her uncle Mordecai, plots to kill all Jews throughout the empire. So Esther reveals her identity and pleads for her people. Haman, already humiliated, is then executed in the way he intended for Mordecai, either hanged (NIV) or impaled (TNIV), and replaced by his nemesis. Subsequently the Jews are allowed to defend themselves and attack their enemies. From then on, they celebrate their survival in the new annual festival of Purim.

Esther is an exquisitely told story, whose deft characterization and subtle plot devices continue to delight today. Its annual retelling by Jews at Purim is accompanied by enthusiastic audience participation, cheering the heroes and hissing the villain. Partly because it is so well crafted, some think it is largely fictional.

Surprisingly, Persian records have no mention of the book's events or its main characters: Vashti and Esther, Haman and Mordecai. Many other aspects seem at variance with surviving records of Persian history and practice. There are no records of the empire divided into 127 satrapies, of the immutable 'law of the Medes and the Persians', of laws promulgated in all languages, or of war between Jews and their enemies. And the Greek historian Herodotus calls Xerxes' queen Amestris. As a result, for the last century most scholars have seen Esther as legendary. However, the records for this period are poor, and this alone should invite caution. Further, Vashti and Amestris are both portrayed as strong-willed; and the transcription of Persian names into Hebrew and Greek could be very different, e.g. the king's Persian name Xshayarshan became Akhashverosh in Hebrew and Xerxes in Greek! Noting other evidence, including many historically appropriate elements, Timothy Laniak argues cogently that the story should indeed be taken as historical.[7]

B. Relevance for Christians

From Luther on, many Christians have been troubled by Esther. One problem is that God is unmentioned. But this is a minor difficulty, since a trust in divine providence pervades the book, and is encapsulated in 4:14. More serious are the desire for and the acts of revenge, resulting in the death of some 76,000 (9:12–16). However, we must note three important points: the Jews acted in self-defence, within the law and without taking spoils; the number killed was not large given the number of Jewish communities scattered throughout the empire; and this is seen as justice within an OT perspective.

On a more positive note, the book of Esther reminds us of God's care for his people, his activity 'behind the scenes', his use of faithful people like Esther and Mordecai, and their willingness to stand up for the right, whatever the outcome. So while it is unlike the other historical books in some ways, e.g. its Persian location and its oblique reference to the deity, it is similar in its portrayal of God's response to his people's faith.

Notes

[1] I. Provan, V. P. Long, T. Longman III, *A Biblical History of Israel* (WJKP, 2003), p. 192.

[2] J. H. Walton, 'Joshua 10:12–15 and Mesopotamian Celestial Omen Texts', in A. R. Millard et al, eds., *Faith, Tradition, and History* (Eisenbrauns, 1994), pp. 181–190.

[3] J. G. Harris, C. A. Brown, M. S. Moore, *Joshua, Judges, Ruth*, NIBC (Paternoster, 2000), p. 300.

[4] F. F. Bruce, *Israel and the Nations* (Paternoster, 4th edn 1997), p. 11.

[5] K. A. Kitchen, *On the Reliability of the Old Testament* (Eerdmans, 2003), pp. 98–107.

[6] J. B. Pritchard, *Ancient Near Eastern Texts* (Princeton, 1969), pp. 279–294, 308, 320.

[7] L. C. Allen, T. S. Laniak, *Ezra, Nehemiah, Esther*, NIBC (Paternoster, 2003), pp. 176–182.

Further reading (see **Introduction** for good commentary series)

Philip Satterthwaite, *Exploring the Old Testament 2. The Historical Books* (SPCK, 2007) – excellent introduction, with panels highlighting themes and points to ponder.

Victor Hamilton, *Handbook on the Historical Books* (Baker, 2001) – good detailed introduction to the books and each section or chapter.

Iain Provan and others, *A Biblical History of Israel* (WJK, 2003) – the best detailed study by evangelical scholars of ancient Israel's history, affirming the OT's historical reliability.

5. Poetic Books

Tremper Longman III

JOB

The problem of suffering is one that has plagued ancient and modern people. Why do good things happen to bad people, and bad things to good people? The ancient Hebrews and those who read their sacred literature felt this problem acutely. After all, the very structure of the covenant Israel enjoyed with God would lead one to expect reward for obedience. The book of Deuteronomy is a case in point. Chs. 27 and 28 indicate that those who obey the preceding laws will be rewarded with blessing while those who disobey will be cursed. The historical narrative in Samuel–Kings uses the laws of Deuteronomy, particularly the law of centralization in Deut. 12, to justify the exile. Israel did not worship the LORD only at the place he chose, and so God turned them over to the Babylonians. The prophets, best understood as upholders of the covenant, had anticipated this judgment by warning Israel that they would be punished for their sin. And the book of Proverbs, at least in the bulk of its teaching, emphasizes good outcomes for wise behaviour and negative results for foolishness.

The book of Job grapples with the issue of retribution, and provides a corrective to overconfidence that in this life people necessarily get the reward/punishment that they deserve. However, it would be a mistake to think that retribution was the main concern of the book of Job. A key purpose of the book of Job is to proclaim that Yahweh is the only source of wisdom. This perspective may be observed by following the plot of the book.

A. *Structure and message*

The book opens and closes in prose, while the body (3:1 – 42:6) is in poetry. The prose prologue sets the scene and presents the scenario. Job is a man from Uz, indicating that he is not an Israelite. This fact, and also the description of his wealth, set the story in patriarchal times, though it was almost certainly written later, perhaps much later.

1. *The prose prologue (1:1 – 2:13)*

Job is 'blameless and upright'. We hear this important fact right at the beginning (1:1). Further, this is confirmed by none other than God himself when he points Job out to 'the Satan' (literally 'the accuser'). However, the latter uses God's evaluation as an occasion to question Job's integrity. He agrees that Job is blameless, but he throws doubt on his motivation. Job is blameless because of the rewards that come from such behaviour. Challenged in this way, God then grants permission to allow the Accuser to bring suffering into Job's life and then observe whether or not he maintains his integrity.

Job's suffering is severe and, in response to his pain, three friends come to commiserate with him. They sit in silence for seven days (2:13), and Job is the first one to break this silence with a bitter lament (ch. 3) that begins the poetic portion of the book. This lament provokes responses from the three friends: Eliphaz, Bildad and Zophar. The debate between them and Job provides the bulk of the book (4 – 31) and it has a very set pattern.

2. *The debate (3:1 – 31:40)*

The friends speak in turn, each being answered by Job before the next voices his concerns. There are three cycles of the debate, though the last is somewhat truncated, perhaps indicating that the friends are running out of steam. The section is extensive and there are three speakers, but their message is fairly repetitive. They represent a hard-and-fast view of the relationship between sin and suffering. As they observe Job's suffering, they reason that sin results in suffering, so suffering is the result of sin. As a result, the solution to Job's conundrum is quite clear: he must repent.

Job, however, has a conflicting perspective on the situation. He knows he does not deserve to suffer. While everyone sins (9:2), he has not sinned so much that he deserves such horrific suffering. He questions God's justice (9:21–24). At the end of his speeches, he says he wants God to charge him properly, so he can then meet him and justify himself (31:35–37). As we will soon see, Job gets his wish for an encounter with God, but it doesn't go the way he expects.

In a word, Job's view is really not substantially different from that of the three friends. All of them believe that consequences follow from one's deeds. The difference is that Job thinks God is unfair towards him, while the friends insist that God is fair and that Job is being punished for his sins. Eventually, the three friends run out of arguments without convincing Job.

3. Elihu's monologue (32:1 – 37:24)

Into the silence steps a man named Elihu. He is young and full of bluster, upset that the three friends, whom he had respected as wise elders, have not adequately shown Job that he is wrong. He reasons that it must not be age, but the spirit that renders a person able to discern the proper state of a situation (32:6–9). However, when all is said and done, Elihu too expresses a simple retribution theology (34:11, 25–27, 37). This explains why no one responds to Elihu and, even at the end, God does not address him.

While the debate has centered on the reasons for Job's suffering, this is not the heart of the debate. The question behind the issue of suffering is: who is wise? Both Job and the friends set themselves up as sources of wisdom and ridicule the wisdom of the other side (11:12; 12:1–3, 12; 13:12; 15:1–13). The question of who is wise is central to the book.

4. Yahweh's speeches and Job's repentance (38:1 – 42:6)

The answer to this question comes in the climax to the book with Yahweh's speeches (38:1 – 42:6). As mentioned earlier, Job desired an interview with God so he could set him straight and accuse him of unfairness. God now appears to Job, but the latter does not get the opportunity to challenge him. On the contrary, God appears to Job in the form of a whirlwind and challenges him by giving him a surprise test. God asks Job a series of questions that only the Creator could possibly answer. The questions demonstrate God's full knowledge and control of the natural order that he created and this contrasts with Job's ignorance. When so confronted, Job recognizes God's superior power and wisdom and responds with repentance. He submits himself to the almighty God of the universe.

5. The prose epilogue (42:7–17)

In the epilogue, the story comes to a happy conclusion. Job is reconciled with God and his fortune is restored. God blesses him and allows him to live a long life. Thus this book wrestles with the issue of proper retribution and concludes that God is wise.

B. Date and authorship

The book of Job is notoriously difficult to date. No author or date is specified in the book itself. The early setting of the story (see above) has led some to suggest that it is early, perhaps even the first book of the Bible to have been written. This conclusion is unlikely. Others have put forward the idea that Job is one of the last books to be included in the OT. This viewpoint too is unprovable. The language of the book is unique, but its specific characteristics have been pressed into service to demonstrate both an early and a late date. The best conclusion is to remain agnostic about its date of composition and fortunately the answer to this question does not bear on its interpretation.

C. Historicity

A similar debate surrounds the historicity of the book. It is true that the figure of Job is mentioned outside of this book (Ezek. 14:14, 20), alongside Daniel and Noah. Further, the opening of the book bears resemblance to the opening of Judg. 17 and 1 Sam. 1, two passages with fairly certain intention to communicate historical events.

Thus there appears to be a historical intention in the book. We are probably to understand Job to be a real person who lived in the past and who suffered, though this cannot be proven by reference to extra-biblical material like archaeological data. However, although the book of Job intends to be historical at least in a general sense, there are other indications that suggest that the book does not consider historical precision a high priority. For instance, the dialogues are in poetic form. Clearly people did not speak to each other in poetry, especially when they were in deep pain. Poetry elevates the book from a specific historical event to a story with universal application. The book of Job is not simply a historical chronicle; it is wisdom that should be applied to all who hear it.

D. Continuing significance

The book of Job continues its relevance today as witnessed by the fact that it is one of the best-known books of the OT. It grapples with the issue of suffering, and people suffer today as they always have. People of faith come to the book of Job and learn that not all suffering can be explained as penalty for evil behaviour. The book teaches us that we should not be quick to judge the morality of those who suffer. If we do, we might end up in the position of the three friends whom God clearly reprimands at the end of the book (42:7–9).

Christians read this book from the perspective of the cross. The NT brings us to a deeper understanding of God's dealing with the suffering in our life. In Jesus, God enters the world and endures the most horrible suffering on our behalf. Jesus Christ is the only truly innocent sufferer, the only one completely without sin. He submits himself to suffering voluntarily (unlike Job), for the benefit of others. No wonder the early church read the book of Job during Passion week.

It is not as if Christ has put an end to the suffering of his people. 2 Cor. 1:3–11 describes the church as those who receive comfort in the midst of suffering. But the hope of the NT is that Jesus suffered on our behalf and so we anticipate a glorious future (Rom. 8:18–27).

PSALMS

The book of Psalms is a collection of 150 separate poetic texts. There are indications that a few of the psalms that are now separate were originally a single composition (e.g. the refrain in Pss. 42 and 43), but, if so, we do not know the reasons why they were split.

A. Titles

Many of the psalms have brief introductions, traditionally called 'titles', that are part of the Hebrew text. These were probably added later than the composition of the psalms, but before the canonical collection was closed. It is debated whether they should be considered canonical or not. If one takes the titles as authoritative or as reliable early tradition, they inform concerning composition and function of the psalms. For instance, the titles make it obvious that psalms were sung, since they often use the labels 'song' (*shir*) and 'psalm' (*mizmor*). However, phrases that are generally taken to be tunes are unclear (e.g. 'Do Not Destroy' for Ps. 58). There are also references to instruments, and the parenthetical expression *selah* is best understood as some kind of musical direction, even though its exact meaning is unclear. Thus the psalms are songs as well as prayers.

Many titles associate certain individuals with particular psalms. The largest number of such psalms, seventy-three in total, are associated with David (known in Amos 6:5 as a great musician; see also 1 Sam. 16). The earliest attribution is Moses (Ps. 90), and then there are others such as Solomon (Ps. 72), Asaph (a temple musician at the time of David, Ps. 73), and more. Some songs clearly come from the latest period of OT history (Pss. 126; 137). So if the titles are taken to indicate authorship, which seems their intention, then the psalms were written over the long period of time from Moses to the post-exilic era. Even if the titles indicate a looser association with the named individuals, as some interpreters suggest, the psalms still come from many different writers, times and situations.

The titles also give evidence for the purpose behind certain psalms. There are a handful of historical titles that cite the occasion for composition. Ps. 51 is well known for its connection to David after Nathan the prophet confronted him following his sin with Bathsheba (2 Sam. 11). Indeed, when one reads the psalm two things are immediately apparent. First, the contents, a petition to God to forgive the psalmist's sins, is very appropriate to that historical occasion. Second, the psalmist does not refer to the specifics of the story as we know them in 1 Samuel. The request is for forgiveness from sin generally, not adultery specifically. Thus if, as is likely, the composition of the psalm was inspired by a particular experience, the psalmist intentionally avoided specific reference to that experience in order that later worshippers could use the psalm when they found themselves in a similar though not identical situation. 1 Chr. 16 pictures David handing a psalm to Asaph, the Levite in charge of music, thus providing a narrative to bolster the claim that psalmists were mindful of later users in their compositions.

Most scholars today would agree that the book of Psalms functioned as the hymn book of ancient Israel. Its primary setting was corporate, though individual use of psalms is portrayed in the OT (1 Sam. 2:1–10; Jon. 2). The label 'hymn book' is also appropriate because the church's hymns often came into existence in a similar way. 'Amazing Grace', for instance, may have been written by the author John Newton because he was moved by his own conversion, but he wrote it so that others who sang the song would marvel at their own conversions, not his.

B. Structure

One obvious difference between modern hymn books and the Psalms is their structure. While most hymnals have a topical or liturgical structure, that of the Psalms is unclear. There have been many attempts over the years to discern an underlying structure of the psalter, but these have failed to convince a majority of readers. Since a clear structure has not been observed in the past millennia, one should be suspicious of any new insight that claims to have discovered it.

While there is no apparent overall structure in terms of how one psalm moves to the next, there are still some useful observations about which there is general agreement. The first has to do with the presence of 'mini-collections' in the book. One example will suffice, the Songs of Ascent. Pss. 120 – 134 are so named in their title, probably because they were used by pilgrims as they were 'going up' to Jerusalem to celebrate one of the annual festivals. Mini-collections like the Songs of Ascent were then incorporated in the Psalter as a group.

The second observation is that there are intentional placements of psalms at the beginning and at the end of the book. Early rabbis called Ps. 1 the gatekeeper of the psalms, making an analogy between the holy physical space of the temple, where the gatekeeper kept the wicked out, and the holy textual space of the psalms, where Ps. 1 encourages the righteous and condemns the wicked. Ps. 1 also places the Torah front-and-centre, thus making a connection between Pentateuch and Psalms. After entering the literary sanctuary, readers then encounter the other psalm that forms the introduction, Ps. 2, which brings them into contact with the LORD and his anointed one. In the monarchical period, the 'anointed one' was the Davidic king, and the psalm was probably composed as a coronation or pre-battle song. But after the monarchy's demise, when the psalter was compiled, thoughts would have turned to a future messianic deliverer. There is also a clustering of praise songs at the end. Pss. 146 – 150 resound with hallelujahs, especially the last of that group. These psalms form a final doxology to end the book.

Finally, picking up on the observation made above in regard to Ps. 1 and the Torah (Pentateuch), the final canonical form of the book of Psalms is divided into five books:

Book 1: 1 – 41
Book 2: 42 – 72
Book 3: 73 – 89
Book 4: 90 – 106
Book 5: 107 – 150

Each book ends with a doxology. The idea behind this division is again to make an intentional connection between Torah and Psalms and thus support the latter's claim to authority. Though these are prayers to God, they are also God's Word.

Though one can make some general observations, the final form of the Psalter gives the general impression of a rather random order of psalms. This may be observed in terms of the different types of psalms that the book contains, to which we now turn.

C. Genre

In terms of genre, we first observe that the psalms are poems. Of course, the book is not unique in this regard. Most of the wisdom books, large sections of the prophetic books, and even some parts of the Torah (e.g. Exod. 15) and the historical books (e.g. Judg. 5) are poetic. Hebrew poetry is characterized by brevity of expression, parallelism within lines, and an intense use of imagery. In addition, poets utilized a host of other poetic conventions on a more occasional basis, e.g. acrostics, alliteration, and other types of word play and sound play. In a word, poetry is compact language, and must be read slowly and reflectively to be read well.

The Psalms are a certain type of poetry, namely lyric. Lyric poetry conveys the emotional expression of the composer. Indeed, the different categories of psalms discerned by scholars are mainly recognized by the emotional state of the poet. For illustrative purposes, we name four main categories as follows:

Hymn: These are songs of unalloyed joy (24; 98). They are songs sung when everything is going well and one wants to celebrate God. They have been called descriptive songs of praise and psalms of orientation.

Lament: These are songs of disorientation. The psalmist expresses discouragement, anger, disappointment, grief with oneself, the 'enemy', or even God himself. There are laments of the individual (77) and corporate laments (83). Interestingly, while there are exceptions (88), most laments turn at the end to some statement of praise or confidence (69).

Thanksgiving: These psalms are very similar to hymns. They often begin that way (30), but in the body of the psalm there is some recognition of previous trouble and an earlier lament to which God has responded. These psalms are psalms of new orientation.

Confidence: Ps. 23 is an excellent example of a psalm of confidence, that expresses trust in God in the midst of a struggle.

D. Theological message and continuing significance

Though the psalms are the prayers of Israel to God, they also have a theological function that is recognizable through the many images of

God that the psalmists invoke. In the psalms God is a king (47), a warrior (24), a shepherd (23), a mother (131), and so on. These metaphors throw light on the nature of God and his relationship to his people.

The book of Psalms continues to be significant in the light of the NT people of God. First, attention should be paid to the fact that the book is frequently cited in the NT, indeed second only to the book of Isaiah. This should not be surprising, since Jesus himself said that the Psalms anticipated his suffering and glorification (Luke 24:25–27, 44). Admittedly, 'Psalms' here stands for the whole third part of the Hebrew canon, but of course that includes this book. We see that Jesus' own emotional state is occasionally expressed through psalm citation (Matt. 27:45–46).

Further, Christians continue in the line of later worshippers who use the psalms to help them express their own thoughts and feelings in prayer to God when they have similar though not necessarily identical experiences. Calvin described the psalms as a 'mirror of the soul'. As worshippers read a psalm, they find themselves being read. They find words to help them express their own feelings, and the psalm, whether hymn or lament, brings them face to face with God.

PROVERBS

Proverbs is a book of wisdom similar in many ways to the wisdom literature of the broader ancient Near East, especially Egypt. The predominant style of the book is that a father instructs his son in the pursuit of wisdom and avoidance of folly.

A. The nature of wisdom

At first glance the wisdom of Proverbs seems largely and simply practical advice. The preamble of the book (1:1–7) gives the purpose of Proverbs: to give the simple-minded prudence and the wise increased wisdom, including how to avoid problems, deal with difficult people, and maximize the good things of this life (wealth, health, happiness). In other words, wisdom is a skill of living, navigating life's hardships. In many ways, wisdom is similar to the modern idea of emotional intelligence, knowing how to say and do the right thing at the right time in order to enjoy life.

This description of the wisdom of Proverbs is true as far as it goes, but it does not go far enough. Wisdom is not just a practical skill; it is more profoundly a theological idea, since it involves relationship with God.

The last verse of the preamble, often called the book's motto, makes this clear from the start:

The fear of the LORD is the beginning of knowledge,
    but fools despise wisdom and instruction. (1:7)

Thus knowledge (a synonym of wisdom, see the statement at 9:10) is not just skill, but involves a particular type of relationship with God, one characterized by godly fear, the recognition that God is the centre of the universe, not human beings.

The idea that wisdom is a theological category is also presented in the interesting figure named Woman Wisdom. While Woman Wisdom is first encountered in 1:20–33, she is extensively described in ch. 8. There we see that she accompanied God during creation (8:22–31). The implicit message here is that if one wants to know how the world works, one must have a relationship with this woman.

But what or whom does Woman Wisdom represent? The clearest evidence to answer this is found in 9:3, where the reader learns that her house is on the highest point of the city. It is common knowledge that only the deity has a house on the high place in an ancient Near Eastern city, and thus the reader should recognize that this woman is a personification of Yahweh's wisdom and ultimately stands for Yahweh himself.

With this background the reader can recognize the main purpose of the book. As mentioned, the literary form of the book is primarily a father who is encouraging his son to pursue wisdom. The book itself may be divided into two parts: the discourses of chs. 1 – 9 and the proverbs (brief observations, prohibitions, admonitions) in chs. 10 – 31. The proverb section is mostly practical advice, but must be read in light of chs. 1 – 9 in the following way.

Readers of the book of Proverbs are supposed to identify themselves with the son. The son/reader is walking on the path, a metaphor often found in the first nine chapters of the book. In ch. 9, the path takes the son past the high hill where Woman Wisdom dwells. She invites him in for a meal (9:1–6). But another voice also beckons (9:13–18). This is Woman Folly, whose house is also located on the highest point of the city. This indicates that she too stands for a deity, in this case a false god. The reader must choose with which woman (which god) to enter into an intimate relationship. Thus, at the heart of the book of Proverbs there is a fundamental religious choice. Will the son be wise and therefore godly and righteous, or foolish and therefore ungodly and wicked?

The teaching of the book spans a broad spectrum of behaviours and actions as it differentiates wise speech and actions from foolish. Some of the main topics addressed are: speech, friends and neighbours, business ethics, honesty, planning ahead, family relationships, behaviour before kings, even table manners and moderation in the use of alcohol.

B. Date and authorship

The superscription of the book associates it with King Solomon (970–930 BC), renowned for his wisdom (1 Kgs 3 – 4). While there is no good reason to dissociate Proverbs from Solomon, the internal evidence of the book indicates that others were involved in its final form. For instance, 22:17 and 24:23 mention a group simply called 'the wise'; 30:1 and 31:1 name two otherwise unknown kings named Agur and Lemuel respectively; 10:1 and 25:1 mention Solomon again, but the latter verse also ascribes a role to the 'men of king Hezekiah of Judah'. Another complicating factor is the fact that a comparison with other ancient Near Eastern texts, some coming from before Solomon (e.g. the Egyptian *Instruction of Amenemope*) shows a strong likelihood that some proverbs were adopted and adapted from non-Israelite sources. It appears that the composition of Proverbs, like that of the Psalms, took place over a long period of time, before the book came to a close and no more proverbs were added.

C. Continuing significance

The book of Proverbs retains its relevance in the Christian canon and for the Christian church. Theologically, it should be noted that Jesus Christ is revealed as the very pinnacle of God's wisdom (1 Cor. 1:30; Col. 2:3). But even more, Jesus uses language that identifies himself with Woman Wisdom (Matt. 11:18–19) and the NT writers also describe him in language closely associated with her (John 1; Col. 1:15–17). Thus when Christians read Prov. 9 they should take it as a choice between Jesus and some kind of false god.

And further, the advice that the proverbs offer is still relevant for navigating life. Principles are expressed in this book that help in marriage, society and self-understanding. However, readers need to remember two important things about the genre of 'proverb'. In the first place, a proverb states a truth which is time-conditioned: the proverb must be stated in the right circumstance to be true. In other words, the wise must read the circumstances before knowing whether to 'answer fools according to their folly' or not (compare 26:4 and 5). The time-conditioned nature of proverbs is true no matter what the language. In English, sometimes 'too many cooks spoil the broth' is appropriate, but at other times, 'many hands make light work'. In the second place, proverbs are not in the job of giving promises. If one 'start[s] children off in the way they should go' as 22:6 suggests, it is more likely, but it does not guarantee that 'when they are old they will not turn from it'. It will come true, everything else being equal, but not in all contexts.

When read properly, Proverbs is a source of great richness, presenting its readers with an image of God as a female sage. It also provides helpful advice about how to get along in the world.

ECCLESIASTES

The book of Ecclesiastes is best known for the repeated refrain that proclaims 'everything is meaningless' (Hebrew *hebel*; see 1:2; 12:8 and throughout), and for this reason the book's appropriateness for the canon has often been questioned. However, a thorough reading of the book demonstrates that 'meaninglessness' is not its final conclusion.

A good way to interpret Ecclesiastes is to note its two voices, that of 'the teacher' (Qohelet in Hebrew), who speaks in the first person ('I') in 1:12 – 12:7, and a second unnamed wisdom teacher who speaks about Qohelet in the third person ('he') in 1:1–11 and 12:8–14. The second speaker is teaching his son (12:12) by exposing him to Qohelet's thinking and then evaluating it.

A. *The message of 'the teacher'*

To understand the book of Ecclesiastes, we must first understand the logic of Qohelet's thought. In a sentence, the nub of his point is 'Life is hard and then comes death'. Death renders everything meaningless. In this regard he surveys various areas where one expects to find meaning. In turn, he examines work (3:9–13; 4:4–6), pleasure (2:1–11), relationships (4:9–12), status (4:13–16), wealth (5:8–10), even wisdom (2:12–16), and though there might be a relative advantage, say, to wisdom over folly, death is the great leveller. Two other issues plague Qohelet and lead him to the conclusion that life is meaningless. First, as a wise man he knows that it is vitally important to know the right time to say the right thing or perform the correct action. However, though God has created everything appropriate for its time, he has not let human beings in on the secret (3:1–15). Second, wisdom thinking would lead one to believe that good things happen to good people and bad things happen to bad people. However, Qohelet's observations on life lead him to conclude that life is essentially unfair (7:15–22; 8:10–15).

Qohelet does have some advice for people in the light of the fundamental meaninglessness of life: seize whatever enjoyment comes along. This attitude is often summarized by the Latin phrase *carpe diem*, 'seize the day'. These passages (2:24–26; 3:12–14; 3:22; 5:18–20; 8:15; 9:7–10) indicate that the benefit of such momentary joy is to keep from thinking about the hard realities of life.

B. The message of the book

But, as mentioned, Qohelet is not the final voice heard in the book. That role belongs to the second speaker, sometimes called the frame narrator since his words frame the long quotation from Qohelet. The prologue (1:1–11) simply introduces and sets the mood for Qohelet's dark thoughts, but the epilogue interacts with the substance of Qohelet's thought. In the first place, he tells his son that what Qohelet says is indeed true. After all, while Qohelet's perspective encompasses 'everything', it is circumscribed by the phrase 'under the sun', that is, apart from a heavenly perspective. Due to a number of allusions to the language of Gen. 2 – 3, we can say that Qohelet rightly describes the world as a function of the fall. But the frame narrator wants to point beyond an 'under the sun' perspective, and he does so in 12:13–14, where he instructs his son to 'fear God', 'keep his commandments', and expect the coming judgment.

Of course, readers ancient and modern are to take this admonition to heart and adopt this attitude in order to avoid Qohelet's pessimistic thought. In a word, the book of Ecclesiastes is an idol-buster. If one tries to make anything other than God the source of meaning in life, it will ultimately fail. Thus, fear God.

C. Date and authorship

The authorship and date of this intriguing book are matters of debate. Some believe that there is only one voice in the book, that of Qohelet who is identified with Solomon. Most scholars today would disagree, believing that the connection with Solomon is a matter of literary argument. Thus, even the name Qohelet, which literally means 'one who assembles (a group)', is a way to associate this figure with Solomon (since he summons and addresses 'the assembly', Hebrew *qahal*, in 1 Kgs 8) rather than a means of identifying the two. It is best to think of Ecclesiastes as an anonymous book. There is some evidence that the book was written late in the history of the OT.

D. Continuing significance

Christians who read the book of Ecclesiastes can also benefit from the book's function as an idol-buster, reminding them that no true meaning comes apart from God in a world suffering the effects of the fall. Rom. 8:18–27 has a fascinating association with Ecclesiastes when in v. 20 it describes how God subjected creation to 'frustration'. The Greek here is the same word as that used to translate the Hebrew *hebel* ('meaningless') in the Greek OT (the Septuagint). But here Paul tells us that God did so 'in hope' of a future redemption. That redemption, we learn in the NT, is accomplished by Jesus Christ, who subjected himself to the fallen world (Phil. 2:6–11) in order to free us from the curse (Gal. 3:13). Indeed, he does so by subjecting himself to death and defeating it on the cross (1 Cor. 15). Thus Jesus had victory over death, the issue which particularly robbed this life of significance for Qohelet. A canonical reading of Ecclesiastes encourages us that, once we make God the source of ultimate meaning in our lives, we can find enjoyment and significance in other areas such as work, money, pleasure and wisdom.

SONG OF SONGS

The Song of Songs presents the reader with passionate dialogue between an unnamed man and an unnamed woman, filled with intensely sensuous imagery. Occasionally, a chorus of women chime in to encourage, help, or learn from the couple, and once we hear from the woman's brothers (8:8–9).

The erotic nature of the language of the Song concerned early interpreters, who felt that sexuality and spirituality were at polar opposites. For them, the Song could not truly be saying what it seemed to be saying on the surface, but rather must have a deeper spiritual sense. Thus was born the allegorical interpretation of the book. The idea that matters of the spirit and matters of the body were dissonant resulted from the influence of Platonic thought on early biblical interpreters.

A. Genre

Both Jewish and Christian interpreters adopted an allegorical approach to the Song. Typical early Jewish interpretation is presented in the Targum (eventually completed AD 700–900). Here, when the woman (standing for Israel) urgently asks the man (representing Yahweh) to bring her into his bedroom (1:2–4), this allegorically describes the exodus from Egypt. Or when the woman demurs at her dark skin (1:5–6), the blackness signifies the sin and shame of the worship of the golden calf in the wilderness (Exod. 32). Christians simply adapted this interpretive strategy to their distinctive theology. In a Christian allegorical reading, the man represented Jesus Christ and the woman either the church or the individual Christian. As with Jewish interpretation, the details of the text were also thought to be allegorically significant. Cyril of Alexandria, for instance, stated that the sachet of myrrh lodged between the woman's breasts (1:13) stood for Jesus Christ who spanned the Old and the New Testaments. This interpretive tradition was passed down from generation to generation until the period of the Enlightenment.

It was especially in the nineteenth century that opinion about the genre of the Song began to change. Due to the diminishing influence of neo-Platonic ideas on theology, biblical scholars no longer felt that a book celebrating sexuality was inappropriate for the canon. The arbitrary character of allegorical interpretation was also recognized. Further, it was during the nineteenth century that the literature of the ancient Near East was rediscovered and among those treasures were love poems, especially those in Egyptian, similar in theme and imagery to the Song.

Thus, for the past century and a half interpreters have recognized that the Song was not primarily about the love between God and his people, but a celebration (and warning) of passionate love between a man and a woman.

Even so, debate remains. Does the Song tell a story (the dramatic approach) or is it a collection of love poems (the anthological approach)? The Song can be made to tell many stories, and that is problematic. There is no overarching narrative voice to guide the reader through a plot. Thus it is best to think of the Song as a love psalter, a number of different love poems, loosely united by consistency of character, occasional refrains (compare 2:6 with 8:3, and 2:7 with 3:5 and 8:4), and echoes particularly between chs. 1 and 8. It is truly a song composed of many songs, producing the most sublime song of all.

B. The message

The message of the Song is thus a celebration of love. The poem in 4:1 – 5:1 is an excellent example. This is a type of poem known as a *wasf*, an Arabic word for 'description'. In this *wasf*, the man describes the physical beauty of the woman from the head down to her 'garden', a euphemism for her most private bodily part. At the climax of the poem, she opens her previously locked garden to allow him to enter it, as the chorus chimes in their approval. Not only is the woman's body often likened to a garden, the man and the woman frequently make love in a garden-like locale, thus recalling the Garden of Eden (Gen. 2) where the man and the woman were naked and felt no shame. Thus the Song has the message of the restoration of the marriage relationship after its disruption at the Fall (in Gen. 3 Adam and Eve feel compelled to cover their nakedness).

Even so, some of its poems acknowledge there are still problems in the garden of love. In the narrative of 5:2 – 6:3, the man approaches the house where the woman lives and knocks on the door, a double-entendre suggesting sexual desire. Instead of opening the door the woman demurs, but the man persists in his attempt to enter. At this point, the woman's passion heats up and she moves to the door to open up to her lover. However, when she does, he is gone. Rather than simply giving up she goes in pursuit of him, moving through the watchmen (representative of social custom), and enlists the aid of the daughters of Jerusalem to whom she gives a passionate description (a *wasf*). Finally, they achieve union in the garden of love.

Thus, the Song is a celebration of human love. In the context of the canon where only marital love is permitted such intimacies, we are certainly right to imagine that the unnamed couple are a married couple, at least in many of the poems. Just as the Psalms give those who praise and lament words that will help them pray, so the Song gives married lovers encouragement to develop their own language of love and permission to seek physical intimacy with each other.

C. Theological significance

But there is more to the song than simply love and sex. It is also a theologically rich book when read in the context of the canon. After all, throughout the Old and New Testaments, marriage is a metaphor of the divine–human relationship. This is often expressed negatively when Israel breaks its intimate and exclusive love relationship with God, but it also has a positive expression, especially in the NT. Eph. 5:22–33 likens the relationship of Christians to Jesus to that of husband and wife.

D. Date and authorship

Not much is known for certain about the composition, authorship and date of this book. The superscription mentions Solomon, but it is debated whether this means he is the author (of all or of part), or a character, or whether it is written in the tradition of wisdom of which he is the figurehead. If it is an anthology, there is the possibility that its separate poems were composed at different times by different people on analogy with books like Psalms and Proverbs. Fortunately, the authorship of the book bears no significance for its interpretation.

LAMENTATIONS

In 587 BC the armies of Nebuchadnezzar of Babylon captured the city of Jerusalem, destroyed its temple, and exiled a large number of its inhabitants, especially its leading citizens. The devastating effect on the community was enormous and is nowhere more emotionally expressed than in the book of Lamentations. This honest book struggles with this destruction, realizing that, though Nebuchadnezzar was its human agent, the ultimate author was none other than God himself.

A. Genre, structure and style

The book as a whole is a corporate lament, generally similar to laments in the book of Psalms (e.g. Pss. 44; 60; 74; 79; 80; poems that bemoan defeat in battle). It is true that some parts of the book speak in the first person singular (3:1–21), but it is best to understand the first-person speaker here as personified Jerusalem, or in some way to stand for the community as a whole.

The book neatly divides into five parts, following the division into five chapters. The first four chapters are individual, complete acrostics, though they differ in their detail. Chs. 1 and 2, each twenty-two verses long (the number of letters in the Hebrew alphabet), are three-line acrostics, that is, the first letter of the three-line stanza begins with a successive letter of the Hebrew alphabet. Ch. 3, composed of sixty-six verses, also contains three-line stanzas, but in this case all three of the lines begin with the relevant letter (similar to the stanzas of Ps. 119). Ch. 4 has two-line stanzas, more in keeping with the style of chs. 1 and 2. Even ch. 5, which is not an acrostic, nonetheless alludes to the acrostic by having twenty-two verses.

The predominant emotional note of the book is sadness and shocked despair. However, there is a note of hope found, surprisingly, in the middle (3:19–27). After this, though, there is a return to sadness, and the book ends with an appeal to God to 'restore' his people, while expressing concern that God may have 'utterly rejected' them and be angry at them 'beyond measure' (see 5:19–22).

B. Date and authorship

Lamentations is an anonymous book, but tradition has assigned its authorship to Jeremiah. While not impossible, such a position is unlikely and in any case does not affect the interpretation of the book. The vividness of the description of the destruction of Jerusalem and the rawness of the emotional expression have led many scholars to identify the time of writing as relatively soon after the destruction of the city in 587 BC. However, some scholars dissent, claiming that the book's ancient Near Eastern background argues for a later date. The argument is as follows. First, no one seriously doubts the close generic relationship between the book of Lamentations and a number of Sumerian city-laments, e.g. the 'Lamentation over the Destruction of Sumer and Ur' and the 'Lamentation over the Destruction of Ur'. These compositions also express deep sadness and bewilderment over the divine realm's involvement in the destruction of their cities. Interestingly, some of these ancient Near Eastern texts date not to the time of destruction but to the time of rebuilding the destroyed temples. Thus some scholars date the biblical book of Lamentations closer to the time of the rebuilding of the Jerusalem temple in 520–515 BC.

In either case, the content struggles with the fact that God had abandoned his city and his people. He not only allowed the enemy to defeat them, but he had become an enemy himself (2:1–5) and had attacked and destroyed them. The theological purpose of the book is to acknowledge God's judgment against Jerusalem and to move him to intercede for and restore his people.

C. Theological message and continuing relevance

The leading theological theme of the book is certainly the divine warrior. While much of the OT pictures God as fighting on behalf of his people (the Red Sea, Exod. 14:14; Jericho, Josh. 6:16; etc.), he also attacked his own people when they disobeyed him (Ai, Josh. 7). Lamentations pictures God as divine warrior in the second sense. This attack should not have surprised the faithful in Israel. After all, in the covenant, God not only promised that he would protect faithful Israel, he also announced that he would attack and defeat them if they disobeyed the covenant (Deut. 28:15, 49–50).

But the final word is not negative. As already pointed out, there is also an expression of hope in the book (3:22–33). Here the poet voices his assurance that God does not abandon those who turn to him for help. Although Israel has sinned in the past (1:8, 14, 18; 2:14; 4:13), they appeal to him for help, expecting that he will forgive and restore.

Reading Lamentations from a NT perspective, we know that God did end the exile and returned a remnant to the land (Ezra 1 – 6). We also know that the exilic and post-exilic prophets looked forward to a future intervention of the divine warrior to free them from their oppressors (Dan. 7; Zech. 14; Mal. 4). The NT identifies Jesus as the divine warrior who defeats the forces of evil on the cross (Col. 2:13–15) and as the one who will come again in the future for the final battle against all human and spiritual enemies of God (Rev. 19:11–21).

Further reading (see **Introduction** for good commentary series)

Ernest Lucas, *Exploring the Old Testament 3. The Psalms and Wisdom Literature* (SPCK, 2003) – excellent introduction, with panels highlighting themes and points to ponder.

Daniel Estes, *Handbook on the Wisdom Books and Psalms* (Baker, 2005) – good detailed introduction to the books and each section or chapter.

Tremper Longman, *How to Read the Psalms* (IVP, 1988) – helpful and inviting exploration of the many facets of the Psalms.

Barry Webb, *Five Festal Garments* (Apollos, 2000) – Christian reflections on Ecclesiastes and the Song of Songs (as well as Ruth, Lamentations and Esther).

6. Prophets

Ernest Lucas

PROPHETS IN ANCIENT ISRAEL AND ELSEWHERE

The first mention of prophecy within Israel is the story in Num. 11:16–17, 24–30. When seventy elders were appointed to help Moses, they received some of the spirit which empowered Moses and prophesied, but they did so only on this occasion (v. 25). Moses is referred to as a prophet in Deut. 18:15, where God promises to raise up a prophet like him from among the Israelites. This has been taken to refer to both a continuing line of prophets and a final unique prophet.

Prophecy was not unique to Israel, as references to Canaanite prophets of the god Baal and goddess Asherah show (1 Kgs 18:19). The Egyptian story of Wen-amon (twelfth century BC) tells of someone in a frenzied state giving an oracle in the name of the god Amon during a sacrifice in a temple in the Phoenician city of Byblos. The eighth-century BC inscription of Zakir, king of Hamath, says he received an answer to prayer through prophetic oracles. Prophecy was not common in Mesopotamia, but excavations at Mari, a city on the Euphrates, have found seventeenth-century BC texts with oracles that were written down and sent to the king. These came from both men and women. Some were attached to the worship of the goddess Ishtar, and apparently exhibited frenzied behaviour. Others had no official office. Prophets are mentioned in seventh-century BC texts from

Assyria. Some of these prophesy in a frenzied state while others have visions or dreams.

A. The early prophets

By the time of the early Israelite monarchy prophecy seems a well-established phenomenon. The story of Saul's meeting with Samuel in 1 Sam. 9:1 – 10:13 provides a picture of it:

- It was often a group phenomenon (10:5, 10).
- Prophets were sometimes found at 'high places', the local centres of worship (9:13; 10:5, 10).
- It involved frenzied or ecstatic behaviour (10:6, 10; see also 1 Sam. 19:23–24).
- It could be stimulated by music (10:5; see also 2 Kgs 3:15).
- Prophets might give oracles of guidance for payment (9:7–8), and were often consulted (see 2 Kgs 4:23).

In this period many of the prophets lived communally. Elisha appears as the leader of such a community (2 Kgs 4:38; 6:1). The organization of the group seems to have been fairly loose. Prophets could marry, have their own homes (2 Kgs 4:1–2; 5:9) and travel around (2 Kgs 4:8).

Most of the prophets mentioned in the books of Samuel and Kings seem to be on the fringe of society and independent of its power structures. Yet some get deeply involved in politics. Two things seem to have motivated them in this. One is zeal for the defence of the worship of Yahweh, the God of Israel. This led them to oppose kings who tolerated or encouraged the worship of Baal (Elijah in 1 Kgs 18) or other foreign gods (prophets who opposed Manasseh, 2 Kgs 21:10–15). They were also nationalistic in the sense that they were concerned that Israel should be respected among the nations because Yahweh's reputation was related to theirs (1 Kgs 20:13–15). Prophets sometimes instigated revolutions, for example Ahijah of Shiloh (1 Kgs 11:26–40) and Elisha (2 Kgs 9:1–10).

There were some prophets at the centres of power. David had two court prophets, Nathan and Gad (2 Sam. 7:1–3; 24:11–12). They were not mere yes-men: Nathan fearlessly rebuked David's sins of adultery and murder (2 Sam. 12:1–15); and Micaiah courageously opposed Ahab, unlike the four hundred prophets who said what Ahab wanted to hear (1 Kgs 22:7–28).

The ethical concern evident in the books of the prophets is fore-shadowed in the earlier prophets. Two prominent examples are Nathan's rebuke of David and Elijah's rebuke of Ahab for his murder of Naboth (1 Kgs 21:20–23).

B. The later prophets

The prophetic books come from prophets active from the eighth century BC onwards. Why not until then? Several answers have been offered. Maybe the spread of writing was important. There is archaeological evidence of writing in Israel from the tenth century onwards, but it seems to become more widespread in the eighth century. Then, as we shall see, there is the fact that many of the 'writing prophets' about whom we have information came from those nearer the centres of power – unlike most of the early prophets. This begs the question why prophets should arise from that sector of society at that period and not earlier. Finally, the fact that the prophecies of doom uttered by Amos and Hosea were vindicated within a few decades, by the destruction of Samaria, must have been important. This was a shattering event for Yahweh's covenant people, and one can understand why the oracles of the prophets who foretold it would be collected, preserved and studied, to understand both why it happened and what could be learned from it.

There is very little evidence of how the books were put together. In Isa. 8:16–18 the prophet called on his disciples to preserve his warnings against appealing to Assyria, which King Ahaz had rejected, until after the disaster he had foretold. A century later Jeremiah dictated some oracles to his scribe Baruch so that he could read them in the Temple. After King Jehoiakim burned the scroll, Jeremiah dictated it again, adding other oracles (Jer. 36). These incidents may give some clue as to how and why prophetic oracles began to be written down.

The activities of the 'writing prophets' cluster around four periods: the fall of Samaria (Jonah, Amos, Hosea, Micah, Isaiah 1 – 39), the fall of Jerusalem (Zephaniah, Habakkuk, Nahum, Jeremiah, Ezekiel), the return from exile (Isaiah 40 – 66, Haggai, Zechariah) and the ministry of Ezra and Nehemiah (Obadiah, Joel, Malachi).

INTERPRETING THE PROPHETS FOR TODAY

The clustering of the 'writing prophets' in particular periods provides an important pointer to their function and to how we are to understand their message for us today. Many Christians think of the prophets primarily in terms of foretelling the future. They read them looking for predictions about the coming of Jesus, the new covenant age and the end of the world. However, less than 5% of OT prophecy describes the new covenant age, less than 2% is 'messianic' (even broadly speaking), and less than 1% concerns the end of the world. Most OT prophecy can be described as 'forth-telling', declaring to the hearers God's perspective on them and their situation, usually in terms of exposing their sinful state. So most 'foretelling' elements warn of imminent judgment, though some tell of salvation beyond judgment. This judgment and salvation involved events that lay in the prophets' near or medium-term future, but which happened long ago from our perspective. So what does most of the material in the prophetic books have to say to us? Before answering that we need to think further about the role of the prophets.

A. *The role of the prophet*

The first thing to say is that the prophets were God's ambassadors. They did not speak on their own authority but were spokesmen for the God of Israel. This is made clear by their use of the phrase 'This is what the LORD says' (1 Kgs 14:7; 2 Kgs 22:15; Jer. 31:2, 7, 15, 23). When a king sent a message to another king in the ancient Near East the messenger would read or recite the message, beginning with a 'messenger formula' such as 'This is what king X says'.

Israel had made a covenant with God at Sinai. For this reason the major part of the prophets' role was that of 'covenant enforcers'. Their forth-telling is based on Israel's covenant traditions. Their exposure of sin is rooted in the covenant law. The echo of the Ten Commandments in Hos. 4:2 is a particularly clear example, but there are many other allusions to the covenant law. Their threats of judgment are not arbitrary. The specific calamities threatened in Amos 4 are based on the curses pronounced on covenant breakers, and the promise of restoration in Amos 9:13–15 has its roots in the blessings of the covenant (Lev. 26; Deut. 28). God had also made a covenant with David (2 Sam. 7) and this is the basis of the 'messianic prophecies' of hope and restoration, such as those in Isa. 9 and 11. The better acquainted you are with Israel's covenant traditions (especially Exod. 20; Lev. 26; Deut. 4, 28), the better you will be able to understand much of what the prophets said.

As covenant enforcers, the prophets became interpreters of God's activity in the history of Israel. Before the exile in Babylon their main task was to confront their hearers with the fact that they were living in disobedience to the covenant law and to warn them that, unless they repented and changed their ways, God would visit the covenant curses upon them. After the exile, when at least some had learned the lesson it taught, the prophets brought a message of hope and restoration. The prophets interpreted key events in the history of Israel and Judah within this context: the fall of Samaria and the destruction of the kingdom of

Israel; the fall of Jerusalem and the end of the kingdom of Judah; Cyrus' capture of Babylon and his edict allowing the return of the Jews to Jerusalem; the rebuilding of the temple by Joshua and Zerubbabel; and the rebuilding of the walls of Jerusalem by Nehemiah. This means that the more you know about the historical situation within which a prophet was active (see chs. 2 and 4), the better you will be able to understand his message.

B. Prophetic speech

The prophets were primarily preachers, and the prophetic books consist mostly of the written record of originally spoken words. Most of the prophets' preaching took the form of fairly short poetic 'oracles' rather than lengthy prose sermons. The use of poetry is understandable in a culture where only a minority were literate. Poetry is highly 'patterned' speech. It uses patterns of rhythm (metre) and sound (rhyme, alliteration). Hebrew poetry also contains patterns of thought (parallelism). All this makes poetry easier to remember than prose. Poetry also makes far greater use of figurative language than does prose. This gives it its emotive power, but also gives it a 'mind-teasing' quality since the meaning of figurative imagery is not always obvious. It is important not to treat the figurative language as if it were straightforward prose. For example, the language of cosmic upheavals in Isa. 13:10, 13 might lead one to take this as talk of the end of the world. However, what follows shows that the language is figurative since it is referring to the end of the Neo-Babylonian Empire (vv. 17–19). The figurative language is used to make the point that this historical event is an epoch-changing act of God's judgment.

When reading the collections of poetic oracles in the prophetic books it is important to try to recognize the individual oracles. They may be linked together in a variety of ways, for example by theme (Jer. 23:9–24 is a collection on the theme of false prophets), or by catchwords (Isa. 1:2–3 is linked to vv. 4–6 by the catchword 'children', and vv. 7–9 to the following oracle by the catchwords 'Sodom' and 'Gomorrah'). These kinds of links often do not result in the logical flow of thought that would be expected in prose teaching. Therefore looking for that kind of flow will result in misunderstanding.

The messenger formula is a helpful indicator of the beginning of an oracle. Recognizing individual oracles is helped by an awareness of some of the common types of oracle:

- 'Woe' oracles (threats of judgment) are easy to spot because of the word 'woe' or 'ah' at the beginning (Isa. 5:8–23).

- 'Lawsuit' oracles are recognizable by the elements they contain: summoning the jury; the complaint; the defendant's response; the sentence (Mic. 6:1–8).
- The 'promise of salvation' oracle has the phrase 'do not be afraid' (Isa. 43:1–4, 5–7).
- 4 Oracles using other literary forms, such as love song (Isa. 5:1–7), number proverb (Amos 1, 2), allegory (Ezek. 17).

C. Interpreting the prophets

So, in the light of what we've said, how are we to interpret the message of the prophets for today? There is no simple method that guarantees a right interpretation, but there are a number of steps that provide a helpful way of dealing with prophetic texts. Of course the whole process should be done in prayerful reliance on the God who spoke through the prophets.

1. Begin by trying to separate out the individual oracles in a passage. Then summarize what you understand to be the main message of each oracle. Knowing something about the type of oracle you are reading will be a help.
2. If the oracle is part of a cluster, note how it is linked to those before and after it. Does the fact that it is in the cluster throw any particular light on its meaning, or emphasize some aspect of it?
3. What is the significance of the oracle in the historical context in which it was given? Some oracles can be related to a specific time or event in the prophet's life, others only to the general context.
4. Finally, consider how the message that the oracle had in its original historical context might apply to us in our context. Often this is not as difficult as it may seem. What were sins under the old covenant (personal immorality, social injustice, idolatry, hypocritical worship) are still sins under the new, though they may take different forms. Some of the more material blessings of the old covenant were related directly to Israel being a political community living in a specific land, and do not apply to the new covenant, where the emphasis is more on spiritual blessings in Christ (Eph. 1:3). Sometimes the message will point to some truth about the nature of God, or principle upon which God acts in the world, which we can then relate to our lives today.

The fact is that down the centuries Christians have found that the words of the OT prophets continue to be the living and active word of God (Isa. 55:10–11).

ISAIAH

A. Historical setting

Isaiah was active from about 740 BC until at least 700, a period of growing Assyrian power. He lived through some major crises. In 735/4 Israel and Syria invaded Judah. Against Isaiah's advice King Ahaz of Judah appealed to Assyria for help, becoming a vassal and introducing aspects of Assyrian worship into the temple (2 Kgs 16; Isa. 7 – 8, this is the setting for the Immanuel prophecy of 7:14). The kingdom of Israel was destroyed by the Assyrians in 722/1 (2 Kgs 17), becoming three provinces of its empire (cf. 9:1; Galilee, 'the Way of the Sea', 'beyond the Jordan'). When Ashdod, Edom and Moab rebelled against Assyria in 713–711, appealing to Egypt for help, Isaiah opposed Judean involvement (14:28–32; 18 – 19). He also opposed a similar revolt in 705 (30 – 31) which resulted in Sennacherib's devastating invasion. Because of the Assyrian's pride and blasphemy Isaiah prophesied the miraculous deliverance of Jerusalem (36 – 37; 2 Kgs 18 – 19).

Isa. 40 – 55 assumes a different historical setting, being addressed to the Judeans in exile in Babylon (587–539). These chapters promise that the time of deliverance is near (40:1–2). God has chosen Cyrus as the agent who will set them free to return to rebuild Jerusalem (44:24 – 45:7). Isa. 56 – 66 seems concerned with events after the return, when faithfulness to God has begun to decline.

B. The book of Isaiah

The three parts of Isaiah have other differences besides historical setting. The oracles in chs. 1 – 39 have a terse style that is different from the hymnic poetry of chs. 40 – 66. While some themes do run through the whole book (e.g. God's holiness and sovereignty), there are differences of emphasis: the remnant and the Davidic messianic hope in chs. 1 – 39; God as Creator and Redeemer in chs. 40 – 55; the new heaven and earth in chs. 56 – 66. This raises questions about the origins of the book.

Traditionally Isaiah of the eighth century has been taken as author of the whole book. There are two indications of occasions when some of his oracles were written down (8:16; 30:8). Some scholars still support this view. Others think that the differences in style, content and historical setting suggest different authors. They argue that, since the prophets generally spoke to their own generation and about the fairly near future, the book of Isaiah probably contains the words of two, three or more different prophets from different periods. Some take Isa. 8:16 as evidence of a group of disciples around Isaiah. These could have formed a 'school' that preserved his words for generations and produced later prophets who added to them. Of course, Isaiah's prophesying could have been different from the more common pattern. The debate continues (see commentaries for more details).

In recent years, even those who assume several different authors increasingly treat the book as a single volume encompassing different emphases rather than as three separate volumes. Whoever was responsible for the final form of the book has given it a measure of unity and coherence in its themes and theology.

C. Structure

1 – 12	Judah judged and redeemed
13 – 27	God's sovereignty over the nations
28 – 35	Oracles of judgment and hope (a righteous king)
36 – 39	Jerusalem saved, but the Babylonian exile prophesied
40 – 55	Return from exile promised
56 – 66	Oracles of judgment and hope (a new heaven and earth)

D. The message of Isaiah

The sovereignty, holiness and grace of God are portrayed in Isaiah's call vision (Isa. 6). They are themes that run through the whole book.

God's sovereignty is displayed in history. He uses Assyria to punish his people for their sins (10:5–19; 14:24–27) and Cyrus to deliver them from exile (44:24 – 45:7). In chs. 40 – 55 another aspect of God's sovereignty is brought out: he is the Creator of heaven and earth (40:12–26). This gives the exiles hope because Israel's Creator (through the exodus) is *the* Creator (51:9–16). A new exodus is promised (52:11–12). The proper human response to God's sovereignty is faith (7:9; 28:16; 30:15). Since God is the Creator it is appropriate that salvation is presented in terms of a new heaven and a new earth (65:17–25).

In 1 – 12 and 56 – 66 there is emphasis on the moral aspect of God's holiness, his justice and righteousness (5:16; 59:15b–17), as Isaiah exposes Judah's sins and calls for repentance (1:16–20; 56:1–2). Chs. 40 – 55 emphasize God's holiness as his 'uniqueness', with phrases like 'the first and the last', 'apart from me there is no God', 'I am he' (44:6, 8; 46:4). All other gods are worthless idols (44:6–20).

God's grace is expressed in chs. 1 – 39 in terms of the purified 'remnant' that will survive judgment (10:20–23). In chs. 40 – 56 God is spoken of as Israel's Redeemer (41:14) who will bring about the new exodus (43:1–7; 62:10–12).

Isa. 9:2–7 and 11:1–9 are classic 'messianic' passages which speak of the coming ideal ruler from the line of David. In both, righteousness and justice are marks of this ruler, a theme taken up in 32:1–8. This messianic vision falls into the background in chs. 40 – 55, where the promise to David is applied to the people as a whole (55:3) and the central human agent of God's salvation is 'the servant of the LORD'. The servant is portrayed in four 'songs' (42:1–4; 49:1–6; 50:4–9; 52:13 – 53:12). Although David can be called God's servant (Ps. 89:3), the servant in Isaiah seems more like a prophet. He is called by God to proclaim salvation, not just to Israel but to the nations. His ministry involves suffering and death, though there is a hint that death may not be the end for him. His death is spoken of as an atoning sacrifice for all. The servant is identified with Israel (49:3) and may represent the righteous remnant. Isa. 61:1–3 is often linked with the servant songs.

In the NT Jesus is seen as the Davidic Messiah, and Matt. 1:23 refers to Isa. 7:14. This gives the 'sign' a double application, first to the child born in Ahaz's day and then to Jesus. Jesus is also identified with the Suffering Servant (Matt. 12:18–21; Acts 8:32–33). He himself described his ministry in terms of 61:1–2 (Luke 4:18–19).

Isaiah's rich portrayal of the nature of God is one that should inspire the same responses today as he looked for: faith in God in the midst of the problems of life; a life in which true worship is linked with the practice of justice and righteousness; and a concern to share the message of salvation with all nations. The picture of a new heaven and new earth shows that God's saving purpose includes all his creation, not just humans, so we should be concerned about the non-human creation too.

JEREMIAH

A. Historical setting

Jeremiah was a priest from Anathoth, a town three miles north-east of Jerusalem (1:1). He may have been a descendant of Abiathar, one of David's chief priests, who was banished to Anathoth by Solomon (1 Kgs 2:26–27). Jeremiah's ministry began in the thirteenth year of Josiah (626 BC) and continued beyond the destruction of Judah and Jerusalem in 587 BC. This period included several important events: Josiah's reform (begun in 621); Josiah's death in battle with Pharaoh Neco (609); the Babylonian defeat of the Egyptians at Carchemish, which brought Judah under their control (605); the Babylonian capture of Jerusalem and the first deportation of Judeans (597); the fall of Jerusalem and the exile of many Judeans to Babylon (587); the murder of the Babylonian-appointed governor, Gedaliah, and the flight of some Judeans to Egypt, taking Jeremiah with them (39 – 44; 52; cf. 2 Kgs 22 – 25).

B. Structure

The book contains three different kinds of material, all mixed together: poetic oracles, prose sermons and prose narratives. The poetry probably comes more or less directly from Jeremiah. Most of the prose narrative tells stories about him and so was probably written by somebody else. Some of the prose sermons repeat what is said in the poetic oracles, suggesting that they are reports of Jeremiah's preaching written by someone else. In style and vocabulary the prose resembles Deuteronomy and Kings:

1 – 10	Pronouncements of judgment and calls to repent
11 – 20	The broken covenant and the prophet's laments
21 – 25	The failure of Judah's kings and prophets
26 – 29	Controversies with false prophets
30 – 33	The 'book of consolation', hope beyond judgment
34 – 36	King and people reject Jeremiah's words
37 – 45	Events before and after the fall of Jerusalem
46 – 51	Oracles against foreign nations
52	Another account of the fall of Jerusalem (cf. 2 Kgs 25)

Jeremiah's oracles include poems in which he protests to God about the pain and grief he is suffering, about how God is treating him, and he sometimes prays for punishment of his enemies (11:18–23; 12:1–6; 15:10–14, 15–21; 17:14–18; 18:18–23; 20:7–12, 14–18). They are called his 'confessions' but might better be called 'laments' since they resemble the psalms of lament.

C. Jeremiah's message

Two Hebrew words characterize Jeremiah's preaching: *sheqer* (lie, deception, delusion) and *shub* (turn, turn away, return, repent). A major theme is that Judah has lost her true identity as God's covenant people because deceit permeates her life, destroying the social fabric (9:1–6). Only genuine repentance can avert disaster (3:12–14).

Jeremiah attacks three particular forms of *sheqer*.

(1) *Idolatry*. Since entering Canaan Israel's history was one of apostasy after the Baals (2:7–8). Jeremiah uses Hosea's imagery of the unfaithful wife (3:1–5, 20) and the delinquent child (3:19, 21–22). He declares that idolatry is a delusion and calls the idols 'non-gods' (3:22–23; 16:19–20), contrasting their powerlessness to help with the power of the LORD who is the living God (10:1–16). God's power is seen in his control of other nations (46:1 – 51:64). This makes Israel's apostasy an incredible and unnatural thing (2:9–13).

(2) *A false sense of security*. This is highlighted in the 'temple sermon' (7:1–15; 26:1–24). The people believed that because the temple was the LORD's sanctuary he would never let it, the city and the nation be completely destroyed. They may have based this on the covenant traditions and the memory of the deliverance of the city from Sennacherib in 701 BC (Isa. 37; 2 Kgs 19). Jeremiah declared this attitude a delusion because they were constantly breaking the covenant law (7:4–10). Once before God had allowed his sanctuary, then at Shiloh, to be destroyed because of Israel's sinfulness (7:12–15). Worship that is not linked with obedience to God is worthless (7:21–26).

(3) *False prophecy*. Jeremiah prophesied imminent disaster unless there was repentance. He was opposed by prophets who declared that all would be well. Some of his strongest words are addressed to them (14:13–16; 23:9–40). That they could prophesy 'peace' (enjoyment of the covenant blessing) when the nation was breaking the covenant showed that they were not sent by God.

Jeremiah offers three liturgies of repentance (3:22–23; 14:7–9, 19–22), but seems pessimistic about the possibility of his hearers repenting (13:23). He does, however, have a message of hope. He promises that the exiles in Babylon will return after seventy years (24:1–10; 29:10–14; the figure may mean 'a lifetime'). Because of this hope he bought land at Anathoth despite it being useless to him (32:6–44). Though 22:28–30 might imply the end of the Davidic covenant, it refers just to Jehoiachin's descendants since elsewhere Jeremiah promises a restored Davidic monarchy (30:9) and an ideal Davidic king (23:5–6; 33:14–16).

Jeremiah's most striking word of hope is the promise of a new covenant (31:27–34; 32:37–40). The old covenant led to disaster because of the stubbornness and corruption of the human heart (7:23–24; 17:9). The new covenant promises a God-given change of heart so that each individual will know God and his law, and want to do it. Jeremiah puts an emphasis on the individual not found in the earlier prophets. He stresses the importance of the individual's heart being right before God, and calls repentance the 'circumcising' of the heart (4:1–4) – in Hebrew thought the heart is the centre of thought and the will, rather than emotion. The nation will find its God again when they seek him with all their heart (29:13–14). There are parallels between Jeremiah's preaching of repentance and Deut. 4:25–30; 30:1–6. Deut. 30:6 foreshadows the new covenant promise when it says that God will circumcise the nation's heart.

Jeremiah's exposure of *sheqer* as a corrupting force is as relevant as ever, though the particular forms it takes today in the church and in secular society may be different. For Christians the hope of the new covenant is fulfilled in Jesus (Luke 22:19–20; Heb. 8 – 9), who also fulfils the promise of a Davidic descendant (Luke 1:68–74).

LAMENTATIONS

See ch. 5 pages 111–113

EZEKIEL

A. *Historical setting*

Ezekiel was a priest who was among those deported from Judah when the Babylonians took Jerusalem in 597 BC. In 592 he had a vision which was his call to be a prophet to the exiles in Babylon (1:1–3). He was active for at least twenty-two years (29:17). The 'thirtieth year' (1:1) probably refers to his age. This was when priests were meant to enter fully into their duties (Num. 4:3). The Kebar was probably a major irrigation canal. The destruction of Jerusalem in 587 was a watershed in Ezekiel's ministry (24:2; 33:21). Before it he prophesied judgment, challenging the exiles' complacent view that it would not happen. Afterwards he brought messages of hope, deliverance and restoration. Ezekiel sometimes acted out his message and used allegories and parables.

B. *Structure*

1 – 3	Ezekiel's commissioning
4 – 7	Messages of judgment
8 – 11	A vision of Jerusalem's sin and judgment
12 – 24	The sins of Israel, Judah and Jerusalem
25 – 32	Oracles against the nations
33 – 39	Oracles of salvation
40 – 48	Vision of a renewed city, temple and land

The unity of thought in Ezekiel leads most scholars to conclude that a significant core of the book derives from the prophet, with some additions and expansions by his followers (though there is little agreement on these).

C. The message of Ezekiel

Much of Ezekiel's preaching can be related to three aspects of God's nature that are evident in his call vision: holiness, glory and sovereignty.

For Ezekiel, God's holiness is primarily his awesome 'otherness'. This colours his attack on Israel's sinfulness, which concentrates on cultic sins such as apostasy and idolatry. The worship of other gods is the central theme of chs. 8 – 11. These sins impugn the otherness of the only true God. Ezekiel presents sin as a deep-seated resistance to God. This is expressed in three horrifying recitals of Israel's history (16, 20, 23). At the heart of Israel's sin is unfaithfulness to the Sinai Covenant (5:6–12), and the punishments threatened echo the covenant curses (Lev. 26).

Hope for the future rests on the nature of God, especially his concern for his glory, his 'reputation' among the nations. In Ezekiel, God's glory is closely linked with his 'name', because his name is related to his nature as understood by people. In the past he withheld judgment to prevent his name being profaned among the nations (20:9, 14, 22). The depth of Judah's sin means that he must now risk this reputation by sending her into exile. Ezekiel is sure that God will act to restore the nation in order to vindicate his reputation (36:22–23, 32). The vision of the valley of dry bones (37:1–14) shows that this will be a miracle of divine grace and power, as does the promise in 36:22–32, which has three elements: cleansing (forgiveness), a new heart (attitude towards God), and the gift of God's Spirit (the power to obey God). This means a new covenant, as implied by the words 'you will be my people, and I will be your God' (36:28). Also the blessings promised (36:29–30) echo the blessings of the Mosaic covenant (Lev. 26). Ezekiel has little to say about the 'messianic hope', but does expect the monarchy to be restored (21:26–27; 34:24; 37:24–25).

The sovereignty of God over Israel's history is clear from the three surveys of Israel's history. Although he allows their rebellion, he is always there, free to act or refrain from acting. The oracles against the nations show his sovereignty over all nations. He wants all the nations to know that he is God and to accept him as such (20:41; 36:23).

The ultimate blessing for God's people is that he should dwell in their midst. Their sin had driven him out (11:22–23), but he would return to a repentant and purified people (37:26–28). The symbolic vision in 40 – 48 gives a picture of this.

Ezekiel's emphasis on God's awesome 'otherness' needs to be heeded today when holiness is often limited to moral purity. Grasping the larger concept enriches worship. Bringing glory to God as the prime motivation for how we live is endorsed by Paul (1 Cor. 10:31). Ezekiel's view of the deep-seatedness of human sin is also shared by Paul (Rom. 7). The 'new heart' promise lies behind 2 Cor. 3:1–6. The valley of dry bones vision, with its message of God overcoming human sinfulness and failure by his grace and power, has been a constant source of hope to God's people. Jesus' claim to be the Good Shepherd is clearly rooted in Ezek. 34, where the Sovereign LORD condemns Israel's shepherds (kings) and says he will shepherd his people.

DANIEL

A. Historical setting

Dan. 1 – 6 contains stories which cover the period from 606/5 BC (1:1) to after Cyrus' capture of Babylon in 539 (6:28), recounting the experiences of some Jewish exiles in Babylon. Darius the Mede (5:30–31) is not known in historical records, but this may be another name for Cyrus the Persian, since 6:28 can be translated 'the reign of Darius, *that is*, the reign of Cyrus'. The visions of chs. 6 – 12 focus on the persecution of the Jews by Antiochus IV in 169–165 BC. He banned Jewish religious observances. In 167 he desecrated the Jerusalem temple by erecting a statue of the god Zeus Olympius and sacrificing pigs there (11:31). The Maccabean Revolt led to the rededication of the temple in 164. Some scholars date the whole book to the sixth century. Others, while often accepting this date for the stories, date the visions and final form of the book just prior to Antiochus' persecution (see commentaries for detailed discussions).

B. Structure

Chs. 2 – 7 are in Aramaic rather than Hebrew and form a distinct section, beginning and ending with dream-visions of four world empires. Chs. 3 and 6 are about faithful Jews, while chs. 4 and 5 concern proud kings.

1	Introduction
2 – 7	Faithfulness under pagan rulers
8 – 11	Faithfulness under persecution
12	Resurrection and judgment

The stories resemble ancient stories known as 'court-tales' (the Joseph and Esther stories are other biblical examples). The visions resemble those in apocalypses, like Revelation, and contain symbolic imagery.

C. The message of Daniel

The overarching theme of Daniel is God's sovereignty over history (4:17). The surveys of history (2; 7; 11 – 12) end with the establishment of God's eternal kingdom. God is faithful to those who trust him under persecution (3; 6) and martyrdom (11:33–35). Dan. 12:1–4, the first clear promise of resurrection and judgment in the OT, gives hope to the martyrs.

The message of Daniel has often encouraged Christians facing the pressures of a pagan environment. Jesus' use of 'the Son of Man' is rooted in 7:13. Here, after judgment of the beast-like empires, a human figure represents the kingdom of God which fulfils God's original purpose for humanity (Gen. 1:26–28). Jesus inaugurated that kingdom.

HOSEA

A. Historical setting

Hosea's ministry, beginning soon after Amos', lasted at least thirty years (755–25 BC), and covered the turbulent final decades of the kingdom of Israel, where he prophesied. There is no reference in the book to the fall of Samaria in 722/1 BC. His marriage shaped his message. Most scholars think chs. 1 and 3 describe his marriage. Hos. 1:2 may indicate that he married Gomer knowing she was sexually promiscuous, or may describe her in retrospect. The third child's symbolic name (1:8–9) suggests that Hosea was not his father. Ch. 3 implies that Gomer became a prostitute, possibly in a Baal temple. Baalism was a fertility religion which involved ritual prostitution. Hosea bought her freedom and sought to restore their relationship.

B. Structure

1 – 3	Hosea's marriage, Israel's unfaithfulness
4 – 7	Sins of the people, priests and leaders
8 – 11	Apostate worship
12 – 14	Past failure, future repentance and restoration

C. The message of Hosea

Ch. 2 makes Hosea's experience a picture of the broken covenant relationship between God and Israel, summarizing the prophet's message. He concentrates on Israel's unfaithfulness to God. People were worshipping the Canaanite rain-god Baal, alongside, or instead of, the LORD. Yet the LORD is the true God of nature and fertility (2:8). Political intrigue involves seeking security from other nations, and is also unfaithfulness to God (7:8–13). Hosea urges Israel to repent and acknowledge God, showing faithfulness (4:1–3), steadfast love (6:6, TNIV 'mercy'), righteousness (10:12) and justice (12:6).

Hosea presents two profound and enduring pictures of God's love for sinners. One is the deserted husband who continues to love his wife and pays the financial and emotional cost of redeeming her and restoring the relationship (Hos. 1 – 3). The other is the parent who loves and refuses to give up on a delinquent child (11:1–11).

JOEL

A. Historical setting

Since the prophecy assumes temple worship, Joel was not prophesying during the exile. There are verbal parallels with several other prophetic books (see commentaries for details), which may indicate that Joel lived after the exile. The nation faces a crisis from a locust plague – but was this literally of locusts, or metaphoric of a military invasion?

B. Structure

1:1 – 2:17	Locust plague, the Day of the LORD and calls to repent
2:18 – 3:21	Promises of salvation
2:18–27	Plague-damage restored
2:28–32	Outpouring of the Spirit
3:1–14	Judgment of the nations
3:15–21	Judah restored

C. The message of Joel

The locust imagery asserts that God is Lord of nature as well as history, and can act in either realm for judgment and blessing. The calls to repent, implying hope of averting judgment, rest on God's character (Joel 2:13, a classic definition; see Exod. 34:6). Joel's special contribution regarding the Day of the LORD is the promise of the outpouring of the Spirit, which was fulfilled at Pentecost (Acts 2:16–21).

AMOS

A. Historical setting

Tekoa, Amos' home, was ten miles south of Jerusalem. As a sheep-breeder ('shepherd' in 1:1 means this) he probably owned land. His seasonal sideline tending sycamore fig-trees (7:14) involved travel to areas where they grew. Although he came from Judah, Amos prophesied in the northern kingdom of Israel. The visions (7:1–9) may record his call experience. Amos distanced himself from the 'professional' prophets serving at sanctuaries like Bethel (7:14).

The earthquake (1:1) happened around 760 BC. (It was still remembered centuries later; Zech. 14:5.) By then Israel and Judah had enjoyed a period of peace and prosperity due to the weakness of Egypt and Assyria.

B. Structure

1:1 – 2:16	Oracles against the nations – including Israel and Judah
3:1 – 5:17	Judgment oracles
5:18 – 6:14	Woe oracles
7:1 – 9:10	Vision reports
9:11–15	Promise of restoration

C. The message of Amos

Israel has fallen short of God's standards (7:7–8); judgment has been withheld (7:1–6), but must now fall (7:8–9; 8:1–3). These standards are the covenant demands (3:1–2). Amos alludes to covenant laws (2:4–16) and curses (4:6–12). He condemns rampant materialism, social inequality, perversion of justice, sexual immorality, and hypocritical worship. The 'Day of the LORD', when God punishes evil, will mean disaster for Israel (5:18–20). There are exhortations to repent (5:4, 6, 14–15) but the promise of restoration addresses Judah, perhaps after Israel's fall, making Amos' message relevant to Judah too.

God is sovereign over all nations, the judge of evil and upholder of good worldwide (9:7–8). His demand for social justice and righteousness applies today, as does his rejection of lavish, enthusiastic worship which ignores these demands (5:21–24).

OBADIAH

A. Historical setting

Obadiah prophesied against Edom, Judah's south-eastern neighbour. There was a history of conflict between them. Obadiah probably prophesied after 587 BC, when the Edomites joined in the Babylonian destruction of Judah (Ps. 137:7).

B. Structure

vv. 1–4	Judgment declared on Edom's pride
vv. 5–14	Edom will be destroyed for plundering Judah
vv. 15–21	The Day of the LORD: judgment for all nations and deliverance for Israel

There are many parallels between vv. 1–5 and Jer. 49:7–16. Verse 17 has links with Joel 2:32.

C. The message of Obadiah

Obadiah gave encouragement to post-exilic Judah. Edom and Judah were brothers (v. 10) since Edomites were descended from Esau the brother of Jacob, Judah's ancestor. Thus Edom's behaviour was an act of betrayal, and Obadiah strongly condemns it. Edom would be punished by the Sovereign LORD, who acts justly (v. 15). This encourages us to trust God's justice when we are badly betrayed by someone close to us.

JONAH

A. Historical setting

The book is mostly a story about a prophet, and contains only one brief oracle (3:4b). Jonah prophesied in the reign of Jeroboam II of Israel (about 760 BC; 2 Kgs 14:25), when Assyria was relatively weak. Scholars debate whether Jonah should be read as an historical narrative or as a parable. Among other features, there is hyperbole ('great' occurs fourteen times) and satire (in the portrayal of Jonah), which point to the story being told primarily as a parable conveying a message. Of course, parables may be based on actual events.

B. Structure

1	Jonah's first call: flight
2	Jonah's prayer, thanksgiving and deliverance
3	Jonah's second call: obedience
4	Jonah's prayer and argument with God

C. The message of Jonah

The enduring message of Jonah is found in its affirmations about God. He is the Creator of all (1:9) and so worthy of worship by all people, including pagan sailors and Ninevites, not just Israelites. He is compassionate and loving, ready to forgive all who repent (4:2, echoing Exod. 34:6). His loving concern even extends to the non-human creation (4:11).

MICAH

A. Historical setting

Micah came from Moresheth, a town twenty-five miles south-west of Jerusalem. The reigns during which he prophesied (1:1) spanned over fifty years, including Israel's final troubled years before its destruction in 722 BC, and Sennacherib's invasion of Judah in 701. An autobiographical note (3:8) expresses his sense of calling and inspiration. The word 'justice' in it refers to the rights and duties flowing from the Sinai covenant. Micah was zealous for the covenant. A century later his preaching was remembered as a cause of Hezekiah's reform (Jer. 26:18–19).

B. Structure

1 – 2	Samaria and Jerusalem judged – but deliverance promised
3 – 5	Jerusalem condemned – but redeemed
6 – 7	Israel proven guilty – but pardoned

Most scholars see the prophet's own words in chs. 1 – 3. Debate continues about possible additions by his followers in chs. 4 – 7, particularly 4:6–13 and 7:8–20, which may reflect the exile in Babylon. Mic. 4:1–4 is very like Isa. 2:2–4; both may quote a temple hymn.

C. The message of Micah

Mic. 6:1–8 (a 'covenant lawsuit' oracle) sums up much of the book's message. The LORD defends himself against his people's complaints, stressing his graciousness towards them and condemning dependence on religious observances without obedience to the moral demands of the covenant.

The book's message of hope concerns a 'remnant' that will survive judgment (2:12–13; 4:6–8; 5:7–9). Mic. 5:2–6 (a classic messianic text, cf. Matt. 2:4–6) promises a 'new David'. Ultimately hope rests in God's compassion and forgiveness (7:18–19).

God's 'requirement' (6:8) remains today: live by his standards ('act justly'), treat people as he does ('love mercy'), and live appropriately ('walk humbly'), aware of his presence ('with your God').

NAHUM

A. Historical setting

Nahum prophesied against Nineveh, the capital of Assyria, and so dates from before the destruction of Nineveh in 612 BC. Reference (3:8) to the fall of Thebes dates the prophecy after that event in 663 BC. The site of Nahum's home town, Elkosh, is uncertain.

B. Structure

1:1–8	God's character and power
1:9 – 2:2	God will deliver his people from oppression
2:3–13	Nineveh's destruction depicted
3:1–19	Judgment pronounced on Nineveh

C. The message of Nahum

Nahum asserts God's sovereignty over the world; though 'slow to anger' (1:3) he will eventually punish oppressors. God is 'a refuge in times of trouble' to those who trust him (1:7). This belief, not a nationalistic desire for revenge, underlies the book. Assyria is condemned for cruelty towards all nations, not just Judah.

Nahum means 'comfort' and his prophecy brings hope to God's people whenever they face oppression by seemingly invincible powers or ideologies. These will eventually fall, like Nineveh.

HABAKKUK

A. Historical setting

Hab. 1:6 suggests a date in the late seventh century, when the Babylonians were rising to power. Hab. 1:2–4 probably refers to the state of Judah in Jehoiakim's reign, when Josiah's reforms were being reversed.

B. Structure

1:1–11	Habakkuk's lament and God's response
1:12 – 2:5	Habakkuk's protest and God's response
2:6–20	Five woes against Babylon
3:1–19	Psalm of confidence in God

C. The message of Habakkuk

Habakkuk complains that God is inactive when the sinful state of society cries out for action. When God replies that he intends using the Babylonians to punish Judah, the prophet protests at his use of a wicked nation to punish a relatively righteous people. God's answer is a call to trust in him and an assurance that the Babylonians will be punished for their wickedness. Habakkuk responds with a psalm expressing confidence in God.

God's people are often perplexed by current events. Habakkuk shows how to deal with this. He commits his problem to God. When the answer is primarily a challenge to renewed faith in God's justice, he responds with an expression of trust in God to preserve him through troubled times.

ZEPHANIAH

A. Historical setting

Zephaniah is given an unusually long genealogy, possibly because the Hezekiah mentioned was the Judean king of that name. He prophesied during Josiah's reign, before the destruction of Nineveh (612 BC) and probably before Josiah's reform (621), since he condemns practices that were common before it.

B. Structure

1:1–6	Warning of judgment
1:7 – 3:8	The Day of the LORD – judgment
1:7 – 2:3	A day of wrath
2:4–15	Oracles against the nations
3:1–8	Condemnation of Jerusalem
3:9–20	The Day of the LORD – salvation

C. The message of Zephaniah

Zephaniah asserts the two-sidedness of the Day of the LORD, as both judgment and salvation. Idolatrous worship and social injustice provoke God's judgment, expressed in terms echoing the covenant curses (1:13, 15, 17–18). Beyond judgment lies salvation and blessing for 'the remnant', those who humbly trust in God and seek righteousness (2:3; 3:12–13). Both judgment and salvation are presented as universal since the LORD is the universal king.

Zephaniah asserts the kingship of the God of justice in the midst of a corrupt and oppressive society. It is therefore a call to faith and endurance to the 'remnant' in any society who 'seek first [God's] kingdom and his righteousness' (Matt. 6:33).

HAGGAI

A. Historical setting

Haggai and Zechariah 1 – 8 share a common framework of dating. Haggai's ministry coincided with Zechariah's (Ezra 5:1; 6:14). He prophesied in Jerusalem in 520 BC, early in the reign of Darius I of Persia. Eighteen years earlier Jews returned from Babylon intending to rebuild the temple. Opposition halted the work (Ezra 4:1–5). Since then they had continually postponed restarting it, concentrating on meeting their material needs.

B. Structure

The four sections are each introduced by a date.

1:1–15	An exhortation to rebuild the temple
2:1–9	An encouraging word
2:10–19	A promise of blessing
2:20–23	A messianic promise (cf. Jer. 22:24)

C. The message of Haggai

The temple was God's ordained 'means of grace' for the Judeans, a source of blessing. Its ruined state evidenced their spiritual state and caused their plight (1:10–11 echo the covenant curses). Like a dead body, it contaminated all they did (2:10–14). Any tendency to feel daunted by the task of rebuilding was met by promises of empowering, resources and blessing. Under the new covenant we have different means of grace, which we neglect to our detriment. When God gives us specific tasks to do, he will provide what we need to complete them.

Haggai gave an assurance that the covenant with David still stood and the messianic kingdom would come. Christians see this promise fulfilled in Jesus.

ZECHARIAH

A. Historical setting

Zechariah 1 – 8 shares Haggai's historical setting. Zechariah began prophesying a month before Haggai finished (1:1), and his last dated prophecy came two years later (7:1; dated 7 December 518 BC). He may be mentioned in Neh. 12:16 as a priest. The historical setting of chs. 9 – 14 is unclear.

B. Structure

Chs. 1 – 8 and 9 – 14 differ in content, style and vocabulary. Since 9:1; 12:1 and Mal. 1:1 are each headed 'prophecy' (or 'oracle', NIV), chs. 9 – 11 and 12 – 14 may be independent collections of prophetic sayings, perhaps by Zechariah's disciples. They develop the message of chs. 1 – 8.

1:1–6	Israel's past sins and God's judgment
1:7 – 6:8	Visions of encouragement
6:9–15	Joshua crowned as a symbol of the coming king
7 – 8	The covenant renewed and a call to renewed obedience
9 – 11	Salvation and judgment. The coming King
12 – 14	Final judgment and salvation. The LORD worshipped as universal King

C. The message of Zechariah

Zechariah's visions brought encouragement to those rebuilding the temple. Their main thrust is that the exile is over, Israel's past sins are cleansed and God is beginning to fulfil the promises of salvation given by the earlier prophets. Here was encouragement to persevere and complete the rebuilding.

Promises of salvation for Israel predominate in chs. 9 – 11, centred on a coming king (9:9–13). This will mean judgment on Israel's enemies (9:1–8), but also on the faithless in Israel (10:2–3; 11:4–17).

Chs. 12 – 14 tell of the final victory of God on behalf of his people. This will involve their repentance and cleansing (12:11 – 13:9). Ch. 14's symbolic imagery depicts God's final victory over evil, which establishes God's rule, with people of all nations worshipping the LORD Almighty.

Under the new covenant God is ready to forgive our past sins if we truly repent (1 John 1:9) and give us a new start in serving him. Matthew sees Jesus in the figures of the coming king (9:9–10; cf. Matt. 21:4–5) and rejected shepherd (11:12–13; 13:7; cf. Matt. 26:15, 31; 27:9). He inaugurated God's kingdom on earth. Zechariah's vision of God's final victory encourages us to persevere in the work of the kingdom.

MALACHI

A. Historical setting

'Malachi', which means 'my messenger' (the same Hebrew term occurs in 3:1), is not a name elsewhere in the OT, so here it may introduce an anonymous prophecy. It is often dated to the early fifth century BC because it mentions religious abuses which Ezra and Nehemiah dealt with later that century.

B. Structure

Malachi is a collection of 'disputes' between God and the covenant community.

1:1–5	God's love for Israel
1:6 – 2:9	God's dispute with the priests
2:10–16	Dispute about marriage and divorce
2:17 – 3:5	God's justice and judgment
3:6–12	Dispute over tithes
3:13 – 4:3	God's final judgment
4:4–6	Moses and Elijah

C. The message of Malachi

The assertion of the LORD's love for Israel assumes the covenant

(Deut. 7:7–11). The basic sin of priests and people is covenant-breaking (2:8, 10). The covenant was meant to be a living relationship like that of a child with its father (2:10), but the people had become lukewarm towards God and apathetic in worship (1:13; 3:8). The broken relationship with God led to broken relationships in society (2:14). God's love is not to be presumed upon. As the God of justice (2:17), he punishes sinners (3:13 – 4:3).

Malachi gives a fitting end to the OT, looking back to Moses, mediator of the old covenant (4:4), and forward to a future 'messenger of the covenant' (3:1), who will make God's people righteous. He will be preceded by 'the prophet Elijah' (4:5), with whom John the Baptist is later identified (Matt. 11:14; Mark 9:12–13).

Malachi's challenge not to become lukewarm towards God remains today. The risen Lord Jesus warned the church in Ephesus of judgment for abandoning its first love (Rev. 2:1–7), and called the church in Laodicea to repent of its lukewarmness (Rev. 3:14–18).

Further reading (see **Introduction** for good commentary series)

Gordon McConville, *Exploring the Old Testament 4. The Prophets* (SPCK, 2002) – excellent introduction, with panels highlighting themes and points to ponder.

Robert Chisholm, *Handbook on the Prophets* (Baker, 2002) – good detailed introduction to the books and each section or chapter.

Brent Sandy, *Plowshares and Pruning Hooks: Rethinking the Language of Biblical Prophecy and Apocalyptic* (IVP, 2002) – engaging study of prophecy's language and imagery.

John Sawyer, *Prophecy and the Biblical Prophets* (OUP, 1993) – good general scholarly survey.

7. Between the Testaments

Carl Mosser

A. *Times of great change*

Many people attempt to read the Bible like a modern book, straight through from beginning to end. Christians are sometimes encouraged to begin with the NT and then read the OT. However, the perceptive reader immediately notices that Jewish life and faith in the NT is very different from that in the OT. The obvious reason is the gap of about 400 years between the end of the OT and the beginning of the NT. A great deal happened during this time to shape Jewish society.

At the close of the OT story the Jewish homeland is a province of the Persian empire, and Aramaic is the language of diplomacy and commerce. Jews have recently begun returning from exile to rebuild Jerusalem and its temple. But when the NT story begins Persia has long ceased to be a major power. Rome is the dominant empire but Greek, not Latin, is the language of diplomacy and commerce. The Jewish homeland is a kingdom ruled by Herod the Great, an ethnic Idumean (see E and F below) placed on the throne by Rome. Jewish piety is expressed in synagogues as well as the temple. There are religious and political groups like the Pharisees, Sadducees and Samaritans, but their origins and beliefs are not explained. Knowledge of the developments that took place during the intertestamental period will greatly assist our understanding of the NT.

This chapter will give a survey of the four centuries between the testaments. For the social and literary developments of the final century or so, see New Testament Background in ch. 8.

B. From independent kingdoms to Persian province

Following Solomon's death the twelve tribes of Israel were split between two kingdoms: Israel in the north and Judah in the south. The Assyrians conquered Israel in 722 BC, exiled some inhabitants and brought in other displaced peoples to dilute their ethnic and religious identity (and reduce the likelihood of rebellion). These groups settled together and became known as the Samaritans. Though they later accepted the Jewish law, they were excluded from the Jewish people because of their mixed background.

A century later the Babylonians conquered the Assyrians, and in 605 BC Judah became their resentful vassal. Judah eventually rebelled, and in 587 BC Babylon responded by destroying Jerusalem and the temple. Many of its inhabitants were exiled to Babylonia.

The Babylonian empire was short-lived, and fell to an alliance of Persians and Medes in 539 BC. The Persian empire sought the loyalty of its inhabitants by reversing many Babylonian policies and permitting exiles to return to their homelands. They were also allowed to take the statues of their gods and other sacred items that had been removed from their national temples. A minority of the Jewish population took advantage of this policy and returned to Judah, now a Persian province called Yehud.

The biblical books of Ezra and Nehemiah recount many of the difficulties faced by several groups of returning Jewish exiles down to the late 400s. Relatively little is known about events in Judah after this time, but archaeological evidence suggests that the province eventually prospered under Persian rule. We also know that Judeans served in the Persian army. For example, documents and the remains of a Jewish temple have been discovered at Elephantine in southern Egypt. These indicate that a Jewish military garrison was stationed there to protect the south-west border of the Persian empire.

Many significant events took place under Persian rule that would have a lasting affect on Judaism. The Jerusalem temple was rebuilt, though less grand than its predecessor. It remained the central focus of Jewish piety until it was destroyed in AD 70. The priesthood came to control many secular as well as religious affairs within the province. The high priest came to rule Jerusalem as a temple city with some degree of autonomy. He was viewed as the chief representative and leader of the Jewish people around the world. Jewish identity came to be determined by descent through the mother. The study and interpretation of the law of Moses took on greater significance than it had in the pre-exilic period.

C. Alexander the Great and the spread of Hellenism

Another formative stage in the development of Judaism was ushered in by Alexander the Great's conquest of the Persian empire in 333–330 BC. Alexander sought to unify his vast domain by spreading Hellenistic (i.e. Greek) language and cultural institutions throughout his newly acquired territories. He did this primarily by founding hundreds of new cities, settling them with colonists from Greece and veterans from his army. These Hellenistic cities included an acropolis (central fortress), a market, temples dedicated to Greek deities, a theatre and a gymnasium. The gymnasium was particularly important as the primary centre for education and training in sports and combat. The goal was to train body, mind and soul in preparation for citizenship in a Greek city. Pious Jews objected to the gymnasium because athletic activities were conducted in the nude. They also objected because gymnasia were associated with homosexual activity, especially pederasty.

The Greek inhabitants of these new cities became a cultural elite. The indigenous peoples reacted in ways similar to the way people in modern non-Western countries respond to the encroachment of Western ideals and fashions. Some embraced Greek culture and language. They did so because they were either enamoured by its chic 'modernism' or because doing so provided means of social and economic advance. Others considered Hellenism a threat to their traditional way of life and resisted it as much as possible. But as these Greek cities became permanent fixtures in a region, the surrounding peoples were all affected by Hellenism to some degree, the Jews no less than others.

D. Judea under the Ptolemies and Seleucids

When Alexander died in 323 BC his massive kingdom was divided among his generals. After several wars between the generals, the non-European territories near the Mediterranean were divided between Ptolemy and Seleucus. The Ptolemaic empire was centred in Egypt. The Seleucid empire initially spread from eastern Syria to Afghanistan, but soon came to be centred in Syria and Asia Minor. Considerable numbers of Jews made their homes in both empires.

The Jewish homeland was included in territory initially assigned to Seleucus, but Ptolemy seized it in 301 BC and incorporated it into his holdings. This served as the pretext for a number of Seleucid invasions of the Ptolemaic empire. Like the Persians and Alexander, the Ptolemies granted Judea limited freedom in the administration of internal affairs, though little is known about Jewish attitudes toward them. Hellenism continued to exert influence on Jewish society generally, with many wealthy Judeans freely adopting the Greek language and aspects of Greek culture.

In 200 BC the Seleucids were finally successful in taking control of this territory. They were initially generous towards their Judean subjects because the inhabitants of Jerusalem sided with them at a crucial moment in their conflict with the Ptolemies. The Seleucid king Antiochus III even gave financial support to the temple. Little changed under his successor, Seleucus IV. However, the situation changed dramatically when Seleucus was murdered and his brother Antiochus IV 'Epiphanes' became king in 175 BC.

Though Onias III was the high priest, his brother Jason bribed the cash-strapped new king to obtain the high priesthood, and actively promoted Hellenism. As part of his agreement with Antiochus, he secured the right to establish a gymnasium in Jerusalem. This effectively re-founded Jerusalem as a Greek city. Young men from the nobility were enrolled in the gymnasium, and priests participated in its athletic competitions. Because they were conducted in the nude, participation violated Jewish law and defiled priestly purity. Greek customs were introduced on a wide scale, but they were not imposed. Individuals who chose to do so could still maintain traditional Jewish practices, and the temple remained dedicated to Yahweh. But this too would change.

After three years Jason was replaced by Menelaus, who was not even a member of the priestly family descended from Zadok (cf. 1 Kgs 2:35; Ezek. 40:46). But the only qualification Antiochus was concerned about was whether Menelaus could deliver a larger sum of money than Jason. This proved more difficult than Menelaus anticipated, and he resorted to stealing gold vessels from the temple. Meanwhile Jason waited for an opportunity to regain the office. Following a rumour that Antiochus had died, he gathered a small force and attacked Jerusalem, but was forced to withdraw. Antiochus, however, was very much alive. Hearing that Jerusalem was in rebellion, he attacked the city and massacred many inhabitants. Afterwards he entered the most holy place of the temple, guided by Menelaus himself, and pillaged its wealth.

For reasons that are not entirely clear, Antiochus then instituted a policy of forced Hellenization. Completing the transformation of Jerusalem into a Greek city, the temple was dedicated to Olympian Zeus, and a pig and other 'unclean' animals were sacrificed on the altar. The Judean people were forbidden to keep the Sabbath or festivals, or circumcise their sons, under pain of death. Once a month they were required to celebrate the king's birthday with a festival dedicated to the god Dionysus. The king's representatives went to Jewish villages and required the locals to prove their abandonment of Judaism by sacrificing a pig and eating a portion of its flesh. Many people obeyed while others resisted to the point of martyrdom. In one famous episode a mother refused to compromise even as she was forced to watch her seven sons being tortured and killed one by one (2 Maccabees 7).

E. The Maccabean revolt and Hasmonean period

Open rebellion began when the king's representatives went to the village of Modein. A priest named Mattathias refused to make the required sacrifice. When a fellow Judean stepped forward to offer it, Mattathias killed him and the king's officer. He called upon all who were zealous for the Jewish law to follow him and his sons to the hills, where they began a guerrilla war against the Seleucids. In addition to harassing Seleucid troops, they went through Jewish villages tearing down pagan altars, forcing boys to be circumcised and killing collaborators. Mattathias soon died, but his son Judah Maccabee ('the Hammer') took command of the growing army and won a string of stunning victories. In 164 BC he captured Jerusalem and rededicated the temple, an event still celebrated today in the Jewish festival of Hanukkah. Judah was succeeded by his brothers Jonathan and Simon, who managed to secure concessions from the Seleucids and finally independence.

The family of Mattathias were known as the Hasmoneans after the name of one of their ancestors. At first they ruled as high priests; later they added the title of king. John Hyrcanus (134–104 BC) expanded the nation's borders to their greatest extent since the time of Solomon. Taking advantage of weakness in the Seleucid empire, he conquered territory east of the Jordan, including several Greek cities. To the north he conquered Samaria and destroyed the rival temple on Mount Gerizim. To the south he conquered the Idumeans, descendants of ancient Edom, forcing them to submit to circumcision and convert to Judaism. The Seleucid empire continued to weaken as Rome began intervening in the eastern Mediterranean. This allowed subsequent Hasmonean rulers to expanded Judea's borders further.

In 76 BC King Alexander Janneus died, leaving the kingdom to his wife Alexandra. She was able to rule as queen but had to appoint one of her sons as high priest. She chose her eldest son Hyrcanus II because he was not politically ambitious. By contrast, his younger brother Aristobulus II was ambitious, and proclaimed himself high priest and king when his mother took ill. Alexandra did not recover, and civil war broke out between Hyrcanus and Aristobulus after her death.

Hyrcanus was initially defeated and forced to give up his power and titles. A wealthy Idumean named Antipater advised Hyrcanus to seek the support of Aretas, ruler of the south-eastern Arab kingdom of Nabatea. Antipater brokered a deal in which Aretas promised to help Hyrcanus regain the throne in exchange for territory lost to Judea in earlier wars. Hyrcanus and his Nabatean allies were able to besiege Aristobulus in Jerusalem. At the same time the Roman general Pompey arrived in the eastern Mediterranean with a commission to pacify various territories and organize provinces. Hyrcanus and Aristobulus both appealed to Pompey to intervene on their behalf. At first the Romans preferred Aristobulus, but Pompey distrusted him. Pompey committed his troops in support of Hyrcanus. Three months later in the autumn of 63 BC Aristobulus was defeated and Pompey entered Jerusalem. Pompey insisted on entering the holy place of the temple, an action that sowed seeds of distrust against the Romans among the populace. A few years later Julius Caesar returned political power to Hyrcanus, appointing him ethnarch (a title lower than king) in addition to high priest. He would be the last member of the Hasmonean dynasty to rule.

The Hellenization crisis led to several developments within Judaism during the Hasmonean period. The chief result of the attempt to forcibly Hellenize the Judean people was a backlash that solidified Jewish identity. The crisis under Antiochus IV was widely seen as divine judgment for tolerating idolatry and for neglecting the commandments of the law of Moses, and the Maccabean victory was attributed to uncompromising zealousness for the law. Afterwards monotheism was finally secured among the Jewish people once and for all. Obedience to the law in basic matters of Jewish identity such as circumcision, Sabbath-keeping and food laws became the norm.

Commandments pertaining to purity, priesthood, sacrifice and festivals were also looked at with renewed seriousness. The proper implementation of the purity laws became a particular concern among some groups because the Mosaic law indicated that the well-being of the nation was directly contingent upon purity (Deut. 23:14). Ambiguities in the biblical commandments led to debates about their proper interpretation. Combined with various political factors, these debates led to the development of distinct parties within Judaism such as the Pharisees, Sadducees and Essenes. These groups enter the historical record during the reign of John Hyrcanus and remain very influential until the destruction of the temple in AD 70.

F. Herod the Great

When Julius Caesar granted Hyrcanus II the title of ethnarch, he also recognized Antipater the Idumean as administrator of Judea. Caesar seemed to like Hyrcanus and was persuaded by him to grant Jews within the Roman empire significant rights and privileges that would later prove beneficial to the spread of the Christian movement. These included the right to meet in synagogues, gather for public meals, keep the Sabbath and pay the yearly temple tax. But Antipater was the real power behind the throne. In 47 BC he moved to secure additional power for his family by having his son Phasael appointed governor of Jerusalem and another son Herod appointed governor of Galilee. This set the stage for the end of the Hasmonean dynasty.

When the young Herod was appointed governor, Galilee was an unruly territory terrorized by a brigand named Ezekias. Herod quickly proved himself an effective (albeit harsh) leader by pacifying the region. This earned him the respect of the Galilean Jews and Romans. He served as governor of Galilee until members of Hyrcanus' court felt he was becoming too powerful. He was brought to trial before the Jewish ruling council, the Sanhedrin, but the Roman governor of Syria intervened on his behalf. Herod was then appointed as governor of the Roman territory of Coele-Syria for a term, again proving himself an effective leader.

For the next few years Herod was embroiled in the intrigues of Roman politics and various controversies in Judea. An adept politician, he outmanoeuvred his enemies and increased his power. Things nearly came to an end for him when in 40 BC Judea was invaded from the east by Rome's arch-rival, the Parthian empire. They sought to depose Hyrcanus and place his brother's son Antigonus on the throne. Hyrcanus and Herod's brother Phasael were captured by the Parthians through a ruse and Antigonus was installed as king. Herod managed to escape and eventually made his way to Rome. Sensing the need for a strong and effective ruler in Judea, the Roman Senate appointed Herod king of the Jews. With Roman support he returned to Galilee and captured it. From there he moved on Judea. In 37 BC he captured Jerusalem and beheaded Antigonus. Shortly before this Herod married Mariamne, a Hasmonean princess, to strengthen his claim to the throne.

Herod ruled as king of the Jews from 37–4 BC. In the first few years of his reign he consolidated his power by eliminating various rivals and critics. Once power was consolidated, Herod revitalized the kingdom's economy. He used his wealth to build fortresses, palaces, theatres and various civic buildings throughout his territory. He had a small coastal town rebuilt into a prominent port city and renamed it Caesarea

Maritima in honor of Caesar Augustus. Pagan temples were built under his patronage in Gentile areas both within and without his kingdom. His most notable building project, however, was a massive renovation and expansion of the temple in Jerusalem.

The final stage of Herod's reign was plagued by domestic problems. Many of these were generated by the fact that he had ten wives, each of whom wanted her son to inherit the throne. His wives and children plotted against one another and attempted to discredit their rivals. Herod's favour tended to shift between his sons, leading him to rewrite his will six times. Always known as a harsh ruler, Herod's actions became more erratic in the final years of his life. He was growing ill and was increasingly paranoid about possible plots against him. During these years Herod had numerous alleged conspirators put to death, including several of his wives and sons. It is against this background that Matthew records Herod's order to kill all the children in Bethlehem aged two and under in an attempt to eliminate a possible rival (Matt. 2:16).

When Herod died in 4 BC the Roman Senate divided his kingdom between three of his sons. Archelaus was appointed ethnarch over Samaria, Judea and Idumea. Herod Antipas was appointed tetrarch of Galilee and Perea. Philip was made tetrarch of various outlaying territories. Archelaus was promised that he would be elevated to king if he proved an effective ruler. He instead proved to be an inept and oppressive ruler hated by his subjects. This explains why Joseph and Mary were afraid to return to Judea after the death of Herod (Matt. 2:22). In a rare show of unity, in AD 6 a delegation of Jews and Samaritans complained to Caesar Augustus about Archelaus' tyranny and he was deposed. Antipas and Philip retained their territories, but those of Archelaus were placed under direct Roman rule. As a concession to the Judean people, Antipas was given the right to appoint the high priests and officiate at the annual festivals. This basic political arrangement was maintained throughout most of the NT era.

G. The rise of Jewish messianism

Judaism developed in many ways during the intertestamental period. One of the most important concerned the expectation that God would send one or more messiahs to redeem Israel.

Upon their return from exile, Jews hoped that the Davidic monarchy would soon be restored. But their homeland remained under the control of foreign powers until the Maccabean revolt. The Hasmoneans managed to free Judea from Greek rule and rededicate the temple, but did not return the high priesthood to the descendants of Onias III, the last legitimate Zadokite high priest. Nor did they re-establish the Davidic monarchy. Instead they took for themselves the titles of high priest and (later) king, which some Jews saw as usurpation and blatant violation of God's law. The same was felt about Herod's ascendancy to Israel's throne. Greek and Roman oppression contributed further to messianic hopes for a time when God would set things right by sending a righteous Davidic king and/or a priest anointed to redeem Israel from foreign oppression and internal corruption.

The roots of messianism lie in the OT, though it nowhere refers to 'the messiah' as an individual who is anointed by God to redeem Israel in the last days. The word *messiah* comes from a Hebrew term meaning 'anointed'. In the OT, priests, prophets and kings were anointed with oil as part of their installation to office (e.g. priests: Exod. 28:41; prophets: 1 Kgs 19:16; 1 Chr. 16:22; kings: 1 Sam. 10:1; 16:13). Kings were especially known as 'the LORD's anointed', though most were criticized by the prophets for their failure to rule in a godly manner. Some of the prophets express hope for a new Davidic king who would reign righteously and justly (see, e.g. Isa. 11:1–5; 32:1–2; Ezek. 34:23–24; Hos. 3:5; Amos 9:11; Mic. 5). In some texts an anointed priest is hoped for alongside this ideal king (Jer. 33:15–18; Zech. 4:14).

Three OT texts were widely interpreted in a messianic sense and played a particularly important role in the rise of messianic ideas. Gen. 49:10–11 says that the royal sceptre and ruler's staff will not depart from the tribe of Judah. This text implicitly indicted both the Hasmonean and Herodian kings as pretenders to Israel's throne. It was also understood to be a divine promise which God would fulfil by establishing one of David's descendants as king. The second important text was Num. 24:17: 'A star will come out of Jacob; a sceptre will rise out of Israel.' Many Jewish texts written near the first century interpret this prediction to refer to a messianic figure of the last days, e.g. Aramaic paraphrases which expand the line to say: 'a king shall arise out of Jacob and be anointed the messiah of Israel.' The third text was Isa. 11:1–9, where the prophet foretells of a day in which a 'shoot will come up from the stump of Jesse', an allusion to a restored Davidic monarchy. The passage describes this 'shoot' or 'branch' as a just and righteous ruler filled with the Spirit of the LORD, and goes on to associate his rule with the establishment of harmony in nature (e.g. 'the wolf will live with the lamb', v. 6) and universal knowledge of the Lord (v. 9). These and other texts came to be understood as predicting a messiah who would deliver Israel and usher in a new age of peace and righteousness.

Jewish literature written around the turn of the eras attests a variety of messianic expectations. Some of the Dead Sea Scrolls portray a priestly messiah from the house of Aaron, sometimes alongside a kingly messiah from the house of David. Most texts, however, mention only a kingly messiah. A variety of roles are attributed to the messiah(s). Inspired by the imagery of Ps. 2, he is usually depicted as a warrior who plays a decisive role in an end-time war in which unrighteous Israelites and foreign oppressors are destroyed. The messiah is always a remarkable figure, but he is not a supernatural being and he is never expected to perform miracles.

The rise of messianism in the intertestamental period prepared the way for Jesus to be proclaimed the messiah. In harmony with common expectations, the NT describes Jesus as a descendant of David anointed by God's Spirit. He is referred to with recognized messianic titles such as 'son of David', 'Branch', 'Son of Man', the 'Chosen One' and 'the Christ' (Greek for 'messiah'). Features approximating Qumran's priestly messianism are also attributed to Jesus throughout the epistle to the Hebrews. But in other ways the messianism of the NT is unique. Instead of immediately waging war against God's enemies, Jesus performs miracles, preaches and engages in religious controversy. He is killed, raised from the dead and ascends to God's right hand, from which he will return. The NT also insists that Israel's messiah did not come just to deliver righteous Israelites. He came to redeem sinners and reconcile to God people from every race, tribe and tongue. In light of pervasive Jewish attitudes towards Gentiles at the time (see New Testament Background in ch. 8), this became one of the most distinctive and controversial features of Christian messianism.

Further reading

Anthony Tomasino, *Judaism Before Jesus* (IVP, 2003) – informative retelling of the story of Israel between the testaments.

James Vanderkam, *An Introduction to Early Judaism* (Eerdmans, 2001) – useful overview of intertestamental history and literature and of early Judaism.

8. Introducing the New Testament

Ian Paul, Carl Mosser, Mark Strauss and Brian Rosner

NEW TESTAMENT STORY

A. The story of Jesus

The New Testament is the story of the coming of the promised kingdom of God in the person and work of Jesus of Nazareth. This highlights some important aspects of what the NT is and what it does:

It is primarily a story. The longest sections consist of stories: Jesus' life and teaching and the church's missionary expansion. And the more doctrinal letters are part of this story, addressing issues raised in the fledgling churches.

It is about the fulfilment of promise. The early pages of the Gospels are full of expectation, and at numerous points there is a sense of hope fulfilled, disappointed or reapplied. This finds no better expression than in John the Baptist's question (through his disciples) to Jesus: 'Are you the one who was to come, or should we expect someone else?' (Matt. 11:3).

Sections in this chapter were written as follows – Ian Paul: New Testament Story; Carl Mosser: New Testament Background; Mark Strauss: New Testament Theology; Brian Rosner: New Testament Interpretation.

It is about the kingdom of God. The expectation found in the NT concerns the coming of the just and perfect rule of God, recognized as king first by his people and then in the wider world. But this kingdom does not come in the abstract. It breaks into a world full of competing kingdoms and would-be rulers, political and personal, and inevitably comes into conflict with all of them in different ways.

It is about the person of Jesus. As typical for a rabbi in his day, Jesus gathers around him a group of followers to be with him and to learn from him. However, it is striking that time and again, it is not so much how people respond to his teaching that matters to Jesus, but rather how they respond to him. Even in the later parts of the NT, the theme of response to the person of Jesus is paramount. In the book of Revelation, the challenge for late first-century Christians is to be faithful witnesses just as Jesus was a faithful witness.

It is about the work of Jesus. The NT appeals throughout for a response to Jesus on the basis of his death and resurrection. Thus Paul could be misunderstood as teaching about the two gods 'Jesus' and 'Anastasis', the Greek word for resurrection (Acts 17:18). Paul always pointed people to what Jesus could mean to them because of what he had done for them.

It is about the particular and the cosmic. The story of what God has done in Jesus is rooted in a particular time and place. And yet the events which happened then and there constantly spill over into here and now – indeed, into every here and now there has been, since the NT claims that this person and these events have cosmic significance: 'God has made this Jesus, whom you crucified, both Lord and Messiah' (Acts 2:36).

The gap between the Old Testament and the New is sometimes called the 'silent years' – but they were far from inactive. Expectation of God's intervention in the history of his people focused around a number of issues important to different groups. God's people would have the land of Israel restored to them, free from oppressive rulers. The temple would be restored, and pure worship would be re-established, free from compromise or corruption. There would be a renewal of covenant relationship with God, and this would be marked by the presence of God with his people through the gift of the Spirit of God. As a result, the law would be kept, and the people would have no king over them but God. These diverse ideas, all rooted in OT promise, were held together in the twin ideas of 'this age', in which God's face is hidden and his people suffer oppression, and the 'age to come' brought about by God's anointed one ('messiah' in Hebrew), in which God's presence is clear and his people liberated.

B. Quiet beginnings

The story of the NT starts quietly enough, though even here there are hints of what is to come. In a troublesome corner of the great Roman empire, towards the end of the reign there of Herod the Great (probably before 4 BC), a young woman is visited by a messenger from God who brings a startling message: she will conceive miraculously and the child who is born will be the one to fulfil all these hopes. The account of Jesus' birth is given mostly from the men's perspective in Matt. 1 and 2 and mostly from the women's perspective in Luke 1 and 2. Zechariah's song (Luke 1:68–79) spells out how this Jesus will be the hope of Israel. But the threat of another king sets the paranoid and insecure Herod on a murderous frenzy as he orders the killing of boys aged two and under in the Bethlehem area (Matt. 2:16). And yet the wider significance of the coming king is already there, as the wise 'Magi' from nations to the east come and pay homage in response to the cosmic sign of the star. All this 'fulfils' the prophets (Matt. 1:22; 2:17, 23; 4:14); with vivid detail it paints in the hope sketched in outline in the former Scriptures.

C. Dramatic developments

The story moves on, jumping perhaps twenty-five or thirty years to the dramatic arrival on the public scene of John the Baptist. Here all four Gospels join the story, each bringing its own distinctive emphasis. John's cousin Jesus joins the thronging crowds in this 'repentance' movement that has drawn large crowds ('the whole Judean countryside and all the people of Jerusalem', Mark 1:5, and 'the whole region of the Jordan', Matt. 3:5). Already there is recognition that Jesus is someone special, as John hesitates to baptize him. But special though Jesus is, his ministry cannot begin without the anointing of the Holy Spirit (signified by the descent of a dove from an open heaven), the word of affirmation as the beloved Son, and the discipline of temptations in the desert.

The drama of John's ministry is matched by the drama of the beginning of Jesus' own ministry. He strides across Galilee, proclaiming in word and deed the coming of the long-awaited kingdom of God, calling people to follow him as they turn from old ways of thinking and acting, to think again (the meaning of the term translated 'repentance') and trust in God.

D. The eye-witness view

Mark depicts Jesus' ministry in particularly dramatic fashion. A typical day sees Jesus driving out demons, healing the untouchable, clashing with the religious authorities, forgiving sins and calling those on the fringes to belong to his new community. All this is accompanied by radical new teaching that redefines traditional understandings of Sabbath, family, law and spiritual reality. This teaching comes from Jesus' own authority, and is authenticated by the spiritual power of his actions (Mark 1:27). And the result is crowds pressing in from every direction, straining to hear his words, longing to feel his healing touch.

Matthew too has this double emphasis on Jesus' action and his teaching, organizing his account into five blocks of teaching interspersed with stories of Jesus' healing. Here we have a new Moses bring a new law from the mountainside (Matt. 5:1), though this time with blessings as much as commands. And yet this new teaching is not so much new set against the old, but rather a new understanding of what has always been true (Matt. 5:17).

For Luke, this combination of teaching and healing spring from Jesus' understanding of his mission – to proclaim the year of the Lord's favour prophesied in Isaiah (Luke 4:18–19), a time which would bring wholeness of understanding as well as wholeness of life. Luke sees in Jesus' ministry a distinctive concern for those without power – women in a world belonging to men, the poor in a world controlled by the wealthy, the diseased in a world acclaiming the unblemished.

John's perspective is rather different. Less concerned with chronology, he appears to be writing for those already familiar with the other Gospels, perhaps especially the Gospel of Mark. The truth about Jesus is seen in seven of his miracles, depicted as seven 'signs' – not proofs, but glimpses into the reality of who he is – starting with the changing of water into wine at Cana (John 2:1–11) and ending with the raising of Lazarus (John 11:1–44). But the truth is also seen in Jesus' claims, in this case his seven declarations that 'I am', related to the seven signs and connecting his identity with the God of Israel. He is the bread of life (6:35), the light of the world (8:12), the door for the sheep (10:7) and the good shepherd (10:11), the resurrection and the life (11:25), the way, truth and life (14:6), and the true vine (15:1). John does not record the language of the kingdom of God on Jesus' lips as do the other Gospels. Instead he records Jesus' kingdom ministry as opening the way to 'eternal life', literally, 'life of the age [to come]' of Jewish expectation.

E. The turning point

As Jesus' ministry grows in its impact, it becomes a shared ministry; Jesus commissions and sends first the twelve (Matt. 10:5–14; Mark 6:7–13; Luke 9:1–5) and then seventy-two (Luke 10:1–12) to spread the good news of the kingdom, teaching, healing and driving out demons as he has done. But a crucial moment comes when Jesus hears of the execution of John the Baptist by Herod the Great's son, Herod Antipas (Matt. 14; Mark 6). This shows clearly the personal cost of the clash between the kingdom of God and the kingdoms of men. The turning point comes at the most northerly point of this Galilean phase of his ministry. In response to Jesus' question, Peter declares Jesus' true identity as messiah (Matt. 16:16; Mark 8:29; Luke 9:20), and yet the disciples still have much to learn about what true messiahship entails. From then on, Jesus 'resolutely set out for Jerusalem' (Luke 9:51) to meet his destiny and to take the conflict with the authorities to the heart of the nation's worship, the temple. From now on, his work and teaching are done 'on the way' to the cross. Glory and agony are set alongside one another as the path that Jesus must follow – and along with him, any who want to be his followers. Even at this turning point, the overflow of Jesus' ministry to the lost sheep of the house of Israel is a blessing to those beyond God's historic people (Matt. 15:21–28; Mark 7:24–30), giving a foretaste of what is to come.

F. The finale...

Like other 'lives' of important people in the ancient world, the Gospels focus most of their attention on the time which showed above everything else the importance of and the truth about their subject. If the subject was a great general, then the focus would be on an important battle; for a politician, perhaps an important speech. For Jesus, the telling moments were the days leading up to his crucifixion and resurrection, and in particular that final week.

Jesus enters Jerusalem on a donkey, as a king coming to his people in peace, just as it has been foretold. But he finds few who welcome his reign; his cleansing of the temple and his challenge to the religious authorities upset too many vested interests. While many of the people are still entranced by his teaching, the pressure amongst their leaders mounts, until they find in Judas a way to seize Jesus and bring him to trial. Knowing what is at hand, Jesus shares a last Passover meal with his disciples. Here he makes clear the purpose of his coming; the deliverance of God comes only at a great price. He is to be a new Passover lamb, following the pattern of the OT, but this time setting God's people – and not just them, but 'many' others too (Mark 10:45; 14:24) – free from the root of all bondage, from sin that enslaves all humanity. And at this moment of greatest sacrifice, even the disciples cannot face the cost of faithfulness, and one by one they betray him in his hour of greatest need.

But as in his temptations, as through all the demands and testing of his ministry, Jesus stays true to the end, even asking for forgiveness for those torturing him (Luke 23:34). John depicts this moment of greatest humiliation and apparent defeat as in fact the moment of greatest glory (John 12:23, 28) which ends with a cry of triumph: 'It is finished!' (John 19:30). Everything has been accomplished; Jesus' mission is complete. The promised water of life flows from his broken body for the sake of a thirsty world (John 19:34). And in this moment of victory-in-defeat, the truth of it, missed by the religious leaders, is understood by foreigners. The truth of Jesus' kingship is written in all the major languages (John 19:19–20) and a Roman centurion recognizes Jesus' identity in death (Mark 15:39).

G. ... or perhaps only the beginning

But this is not, of course, the end of the story. Even the tomb of a rich man, with a stone rolled across the entrance, could not contain this king. On the first day of the week, symbolizing the beginning of the new age, the stone is rolled away and the tomb is empty. Seeing the grave clothes still laid out, as if the body had passed through them (John 20:6–7), the disciples begin to grasp the truth of what has happened. As before his death, so after his resurrection, Jesus turns the conventions of his day upside down and appears first to women, even though their testimony has no status in Jewish law. One by one, he restores his disciples, forgiving their failure and nurturing their understanding. He is the one who fulfils all the Scriptures (Luke 24:27) – not so much in satisfying isolated predictions, but in following the pattern of God's dealings with his people. God turns into redemption the moments of supreme rejection by his people, leading ultimately to restoration for those who would receive it.

H. A new chapter

Mark's Gospel leaves us with an incomplete ending, and perhaps in that an invitation to write ourselves into the story. Luke takes up the challenge, and starts by showing how Jesus continued to do all the things he had begun in his earthly ministry (Acts 1:1). Having dealt with sin and broken the power of the ruler of this age in his death and resurrection, Jesus now ascends to be with his heavenly Father so that he might release the gift of the Spirit on his followers. Just as Jesus brought the kingdom of God into people's lives by the power of the Spirit (Matt. 12:28), so the same Spirit would empower Jesus' disciples for similar kingdom ministry.

The feast of Passover, which celebrated the exodus from Egypt, was followed fifty days later by the feast of Pentecost, which celebrated the giving of the law on Mount Sinai, showing God's people how they were now to live, free from the tyranny of slavery. As Jesus' death on the cross was a new Passover, so a new Pentecost came in the gift of the Spirit (Acts 2), the new way God would shape his people for a life of freedom and witness. Peter explains how this is the climax of God's dealings with his people (Acts 2:14–39), many people come to recognize Jesus as God's anointed one and put their faith in him (Acts 2:41), and the kingdom advances forcefully (see Matt. 11:12).

But as for Jesus, so for his followers: kingdom ministry leads to persecution. The apostles perform 'signs and wonders' amongst the people, who are at once fearful and amazed (Acts 5:12), but they are then arrested and flogged (Acts 5:40). Practical pressures lead to the appointment of seven men to manage the care of the growing group of followers of 'the Way', but one of them, Stephen, is eventually stoned to death for blasphemy (Acts 6 – 7). This leads to wider persecution and many believers are scattered to other cities. But hardship leads to fruitfulness, and the scattered believers share the message about Jesus wherever they go (Acts 8:4).

I. A new mission

The desire of the dispersed believers to share the message about Jesus leads them, almost inadvertently, to talk to non-Jews who also believe (Acts 11:19–21). At the same time, Peter is given a vision from God explaining that no-one should be considered unfit to hear the message. As a result, Peter tells a God-fearing Gentile centurion called Cornelius and his household the story of what Jesus has done. He knows that the message applies to them when he sees the Holy Spirit come upon all the listeners (Acts 10:44)!

One of the leading persecutors of Jesus' followers, a Pharisee named Saul, encounters the risen Jesus on the road to Damascus when heading there to arrest believers. He immediately starts sharing the good news, first to his fellow Jews, but then also to Gentiles. Eventually he becomes one of the leaders of the church in Antioch, and is sent by them on three successive missionary journeys, establishing communities of believers throughout the area now known as Turkey and on into Greece.

Because of the numbers of Gentiles coming to faith, there is a dispute about how far Gentile believers have to follow Jewish patterns of life to be followers of Jesus, and this is largely resolved at a council in Jerusalem (Acts 15). Other issues arise in the fledgling churches, and in response to some of these issues Paul writes letters to the different communities. Some of his letters are circulating more widely and are collected, eventually being added to accounts of the life and words of Jesus as part of the apostolic teaching.

Paul's letters address questions such as:

- How can Gentile believers be sure that they do not need to become Jews to be followers of Jesus?
- Will Jesus return soon, and what will happen to those who have already died?
- What is life like when led by the Spirit?
- What is the appropriate discipline for those who are not living out a life of holiness?
- How should we conduct ourselves when we meet together?
- What has Jesus' death achieved for us?
- What pattern of living follows on from understanding what God has done for us in Jesus?

Other leaders, including Peter and John, also wrote letters addressing further questions:

- How can we live with integrity whilst suffering for our faith?
- What does it mean to follow Jesus' example?
- What are the marks of a believing community?
- How can we understand what Jesus has done from the perspective of Jewish hope?

J. A new future

The story finishes with a vision, in the book of Revelation, in which the widening circle of mission eventually reaches every corner of the earth. It is a vision of the risen Jesus, walking amongst and protecting his persecuted people, in this case in the west of modern Turkey. Despite dissent from within and pressure from without, despite natural disasters and imperial oppression, Jesus the faithful witness will keep faith with his redeemed people from every nation, and invites them to keep faith in response. Their particular situation, like all the generations to follow, is caught up in the grand vision of the renewal of the whole created order, where God will meet his people face to face when Jesus comes again. In that moment all God's promises will reach their fulfilment, the kingdom will be made manifest, the work of Jesus will have achieved its full effect, and Jesus himself will be at the centre of it all.

NEW TESTAMENT BACKGROUND

A. A time prepared

Significant changes took place throughout the Mediterranean world during the time between the testaments that prepared the world for the advent of Christianity (see ch. 7 for historical survey). For example, the empires of Alexander and his heirs established Greek as the common language of commerce, diplomacy and scholarship. This allowed people from numerous ethnic groups in and around the Roman empire to communicate with one another on an unprecedented scale. The Roman system of roads and shipping lanes allowed people to travel throughout most of the empire with relative safety. It also served as the infrastructure for a communications network that allowed geo-graphically distant persons and communities to stay in contact with one another. The new institution of the synagogue arose as an import-ant institution in Jewish communities both in Palestine and in the diaspora (Jews living outside Palestine). Each of these developments allowed the Christian message to spread quickly from Palestine to the far reaches of the empire and beyond. They also set the stage for the Jesus movement to develop into the first truly multi-ethnic religious movement.

By NT times some Gentiles (non-Jews) were becoming discontented with the implausibility of polytheism and the separation of religious and moral practices. While Gentiles worshipped at temples dedicated to various deities, they typically looked elsewhere for moral instruction, such as to philosophers. The Hellenization crisis in the second century BC (see ch. 7) increased Jewish antipathy toward Gentiles, yet also made Judaism attractive to discontented Gentiles because of its commitment to monotheism and the Mosaic law. In Judaism religious devotion and ethics were entailed by one another. Food laws and Sabbath-keeping made the Jewish way of life distinctive and gave it the appearance of wholesomeness.

Sometimes Jews outside Palestine were treated harshly for being foreigners (as were other ethnic groups). But Gentiles could be found in many cities who were attracted to the 'Jewish philosophy'. A few would convert, an act requiring circumcision. Others, known as 'God-fearers', attended synagogue and followed Jewish moral standards but did not convert due to the repulsion many Gentiles felt toward circumcision. Early Christian preachers found a receptive audience among the God-fearers. It was through them that the Christian message was able to spread into the Gentile world.

B. Early Christians and Judaism

The NT should be read as the literary product of a *Jewish* religious movement, including those few books probably written by Gentiles (e.g. Luke and Acts). This will seem counter-intuitive to modern readers accustomed to thinking of early Christianity as a new religion that quickly separated from Judaism. But it should be remembered that *Jewish* and *Christian* were not mutually exclusive categories in the first century. Moreover, Jesus and his earliest followers all lived and died as Jews. The earliest Gentile members of the Jesus movement were God-fearers who had already associated with the Jewish community. In fact, the earliest Christians were more integrated into Second Temple Jewish society than some other Jewish groups. Knowledge of this fact was forgotten because of the way in which Rabbinic Judaism and Christianity developed in polemical distinction from one another after the temple's destruction in AD 70. But it can be readily illustrated by comparing the participation of different groups in the sacrificial worship of the temple.

The Jerusalem temple served as the most visible and concrete marker of Jewish identity until its destruction. Signs warned non-Jews not to enter its sacred precincts on pain of death. Samaritans worshipped the God of Israel and accepted the Mosaic law but they were still pro-hibited from offering sacrifice in the temple because they were not considered Jews. At the same time, a few Jewish groups did not worship at the temple but nonetheless remained Jewish, for example the Qumran community responsible for the Dead Sea Scrolls who thought the temple had become defiled.

In contrast, the Jerusalem church often met in the temple courts (Acts 2:46; 3:1; 5:25). The apostle Paul was arrested while at the temple to offer a sacrifice in fulfilment of a vow (Acts 21:17–26). According to early tradition, James the brother of Jesus frequently prayed at the temple for long periods of time until he was killed in AD 62. The fact that Christians were *permitted* to worship in the temple shows that they were recognized as Jews. The fact that they *wanted* to worship at the temple shows that they thought of their faith as a form of Judaism.

In fact, the early Christians considered their faith to be the true Judaism. As far as they were concerned, the rejection of Jesus called into question the authenticity of the Judaism practised by non-Christian Jews (cf. Rev. 2:9; 3:9). According to Paul, true Jews are followers of Christ who experience the circumcision of their hearts (Rom. 2:28–29). The earliest Christians perceived no contradiction between the confession 'Christ died for our sins according to the Scriptures' (1 Cor. 15:3) and participation in the sacrificial system, at least as long as the temple stood (cf. Heb. 9:8–10). On the contrary, they were zealous to obey God's law (cf. Acts 21:20). After all, it was only natural for sinners who repented in response to the gospel to worship God in the ways ordained in his law. This is also why some initially insisted that Gentile believers had to be circumcised, keep the Sabbath and follow the food laws (cf. Acts 15:1–29).

C. Other Jewish groups

First-century Judaism was diverse. Rabbinic Judaism did not begin to emerge as normative to most Jews until the second century, a generation or two after the temple was destroyed. Prior to that several competing groups could be identified. The most prominent of these were the Pharisees, Sadducees and Essenes. These groups disagreed with one another about various political and religious issues (politics and religion were inseparable). Some of their disagreements were theological and similar to issues debated by Christians today, e.g. predestination and free will. Their most serious disagreements, though, were about issues related to ritual purity, sacrificial procedures, the dates of Jewish festivals and the rules regulating the priesthood and operation of the temple. At the centre of their disputes was the proper interpretation of the various laws found in Exodus, Leviticus, Numbers and Deuteronomy. While all Jews accepted this Mosaic law as normative, they disagreed about how to apply it because there are inconsistencies in the formulation of various commandments and ambiguity about what to do when more than one law governs a situation. For example, when a festival falls on a Sabbath, do you offer the Sabbath offering, the festival offering, or both?

The *Essenes* were the smallest of the three major groups and required members to go through a three-year initiation process. They lived communally and one branch was also celibate. They were known for praying before sunrise, taking a daily purification bath and wearing distinctive white clothes. They ate common meals in silence, regarding them as sacred. They rejected free will and believed that God had predetermined everything. The sources disagree as to whether they believed in the resurrection of the righteous dead or a disembodied afterlife as in Greek thought. Many scholars think that an offshoot of the Essenes were responsible for the famous Dead Sea scrolls discovered at Qumran. This is not certain, but there were at least some significant commonalities.

The *Sadducees* were associated with the temple and the priesthood and were prominent in the Sanhedrin, the Jewish ruling council. They disagreed with the Pharisees on many legal issues related to ritual purity, temple ceremonies and Sabbath regulations. At times, though, the political and social climate obliged them to follow Pharisaic practices. They were known for rejecting any form of predestination in favour of a robust notion of human free will. They were also known for dismissing the elaborate hierarchy of angels espoused by others and the notion of resurrection (cf. Acts 23:8). Furthermore, they appear to have disregarded the notion of an afterlife altogether. In some ways the Sadducees might strike the modern reader as 'liberal', but in fact they were conservative in that they would not accept beliefs and practices that could not be clearly established from the Torah (i.e. the Pentateuch). The later two canonical divisions of the Hebrew Bible, the Prophets and the Writings, support some of the positions rejected by the Sadducees (e.g. Dan. 12:2 on resurrection). This suggests that they did not consider these writings to be as authoritative as the Law. Deeming them innovations, they also rejected practices which the Pharisees regarded as sanctioned by authoritative oral traditions.

The *Pharisees* are the most important of the Jewish groups for understanding the NT. They play a prominent role in the Gospels and Acts, and the Apostle Paul was a Pharisee. Theologically, the Pharisees were known for their belief in the resurrection of the dead, an elaborate hierarchy of angels, the compatibility of free will and predestination, and an authoritative legal tradition. They were laymen, not priests, and had a reputation as expert interpreters of the Mosaic law. Of special concern were issues related to ritual purity, tithing and the Sabbath. Today the Pharisees are popularly associated with legalism, but the nature of Pharisaic 'legalism' is often misunderstood.

Like other Jewish groups, the Pharisees believed that they should keep the law as part of the covenant between Israel and God. They prided themselves for being experts in the law who zealously kept it. But, their zeal to keep the law was not always what it appeared to be. The Pharisees employed clever legal reasoning and drew fine distinctions to determine precisely when the various commandments had been fulfilled or broken. Positive commandments require Israelites to do certain things. The Pharisees wanted to know the minimum that had to be done in order for them to have fulfilled the commandment. Other commandments are prohibitions. The Pharisees wanted to know precisely at what point the commandment was violated, i.e. how much they could do before breaking a commandment. In this regard their motive was probably like that of young people who want to know exactly how far they can go with their boyfriend or girlfriend before doing something immoral. Determining the precise parameters of the commandments in this way allowed the Pharisees to maintain a reputation for strictly observing the law while devising self-serving ways to constrict some commandments and liberalize others.

In the Dead Sea scrolls the Pharisees are accused of being 'seekers after smooth interpretations'. This seems to be a way of saying that the legal expertise of the Pharisees was used to find loopholes and make distinctions that would make following the law easier. Jesus similarly criticized the Pharisees for using extra-biblical legal traditions and distinctions to avoid fulfilling commandments that might prove costly or difficult (see Mark 7:9–13). The heart of Pharisaic legalism was not an attempt to impose legal requirements and good works in order to merit salvation. Rather, it was the tendency to devise self-serving interpretations of the law. These interpretations could also be used to attack the reputation of opponents. This is seen in the Gospels, for example, when Jesus is repeatedly accused of violating the Sabbath (e.g. Mark 2:23–28; 3:1–6; Luke 13:10–17; John 5:9–18; 9:1–34). But not all Pharisees approached the interpretation of the law in this manner. Some genuinely desired to serve and love God. While the Pharisees are often depicted as Jesus' chief opponents, a Pharisee named Nicodemus is portrayed as a disciple (John 3:1–21) as was his friend Joseph of Arimathea (John 19:38–39), probably also a Pharisee.

It is tempting to think that the Jewish groups functioned like competing religions or modern denominations. They did not. In the first century Judaism was not primarily a religion of bounded beliefs and practices. Rather, it was an ethnicity whose identity was expressed through various foundational beliefs and practices common to the entire ethnic group. These included belief in and worship of the God of Israel, the inspiration and authority of the Mosaic law, circumcision as a mark of God's covenant with his people, the observance of the Sabbath and food laws, and the centrality of the promised land and its temple. Just how these things were understood could be the subject of intense debate and mutual denunciation. The vast majority of Jews, however, did not belong to any of the named parties and were content simply to be Jews.

A few first-century texts outside the NT mention Jesus or individual Christians. Interestingly, none identify the Christians as a distinct group alongside the Pharisees, Sadducees and Essenes. Most Jewish groups were distinguished from one another by their mutually exclusive approaches to the interpretation of the law. The Christians, however, became an identifiable group because of their conviction that Jesus is the risen and soon-to-return messiah. It was therefore possible to be both a Christian and a member of at least one of the other groups. There were, for example, a number of men in the Jerusalem church who were

Pharisees (Acts 15:5). The apostle Paul continued to identify himself as a Pharisee as well (Acts 23:6), though he no longer found it something to boast about (Phil. 3:4–7).

D. Christian Jews and Gentiles

After Jesus' ascension his followers quickly established the centre of their activities in Jerusalem. Within twenty-five years Christian communities could be found in most major cities of the eastern Mediterranean as well as Rome itself. Christianity was initially established outside Palestine by Jewish pilgrims who had travelled to Jerusalem for one of the pilgrimage festivals and heard the gospel while they were there. Acts records one instance of this happening on the day of Pentecost (Acts 2:1–41). It is likely that diaspora Jews responded to the Christian message during subsequent festivals as well, though perhaps not in such numbers as on that initial Pentecost. The Christian message was taken to new regions when these pilgrims returned to their homes.

Within a few years Christian missionaries began to take their message to Jewish communities outside Palestine. Key to their success was the synagogue. It is not known when or where the first synagogues were built (they are not mentioned in the OT), but by the first century AD they were an important institution in Jewish society. They served as a place for the Jewish community to assemble on the Sabbath for prayer and study of the Torah. The formal service included prayer, Scripture reading, exposition and a benediction. The men then had opportunity for open discussion about the text. At this time any travelling teacher who might be present could share their ideas (e.g. Acts 13:15–16). Jesus had regularly proclaimed his message in the synagogues of Galilee. Sometimes this took place as part of the formal service (Luke 4:16–21), at other times probably during the discussion period. Early missionaries utilized Jesus' technique in diaspora synagogues.

Gentile God-fearers could be found in a few Palestinian synagogues, but not in as large numbers as in diaspora synagogues. Christian missionaries often found God-fearers to be more receptive to their message than their fellow Jews. While already associated with the Jewish community, these God-fearers had not been circumcised and thus were not Jews. This gave rise to a theological problem. The natural Jewish assumption was that any Gentile would need to be circumcised and keep the Mosaic law in order to be a full member of the Christian community. The apostle Paul insisted that Gentiles did not, in fact, need to be circumcised or keep most aspects of the law in order to be equal with Jews in the church. Moreover, Paul and his associates did not confine their proclamation to the synagogues. They also shared their message with Gentiles fully immersed in pagan culture and with no prior association with Judaism or its moral standards. This served to exacerbate the theological issue and led to many pastoral problems in the churches they founded. It also served as the bridge that allowed Christianity to fully enter the Gentile world and eventually transform it.

Most of the opposition Paul faced in his ministry came from Jews, both Christians and non-Christians, who vigorously opposed his teaching that Gentiles did not need to be circumcised. To them it was highly counter-intuitive to think that God would save Gentiles *as Gentiles*. Surely, they reasoned, Gentiles had to become part of Israel to experience the benefits of Israel's God and his messiah. This controversy dominated much of Paul's ministry, and many of the central themes of his letters, such as justification by faith, are directly related to the issues involved in the debate. Eventually a meeting was held in which the apostles and elders of the mother church in Jerusalem debated the issue. They determined that OT prophecy supported Paul's basic position (Acts 15:1–30; cf. Amos 9:11–12). In theory this settled the issue for the Christian community, but Paul's teachings were still subject to misunderstanding (cf. Acts 21:17–26). Of course, opposition also continued from non-Christian Jews who did not recognize the authority of the Jerusalem council. Nonetheless, his message won the day and by the middle of the second century the majority of Christians were Gentile converts. It is then, a generation after the last books of the NT were written, that it begins to make sense to think of Christianity and Judaism (i.e. Rabbinic Judaism) as truly separate from one another.

E. Jewish literature

Roman Catholic editions of the Bible include several Jewish works not found in Protestant editions. Catholics classify these books as Deuterocanonical ('second canon') while Protestants generally refer to them as the Apocrypha ('hidden books' – see ch. 1, D.2). Among these books are pious tales of courage and virtue (Tobit, Judith), wisdom literature similar to the book of Proverbs (Ecclesiasticus, Wisdom of Solomon) and historical narratives that describe events that took place in the intertestamental period (1 & 2 Maccabees). Protestants don't consider any of these books to be Scripture, but can cherish them for their devotional value in addition to the information they convey about Second Temple Judaism.

Other Jewish works have also been preserved that help us better understand the NT. The writings of Flavius Josephus recount the history of the Jewish people with a special focus on the events leading up to the Jewish revolt against Rome. Josephus mentions several people named in the NT, including Jesus, his brother James and John the Baptist. The works of Philo of Alexandria, a Jewish philosopher, inform us about Judaism in the diaspora and, to a lesser extent, Palestine. Philo is also important because later the Church Fathers utilized his philosophical ideas in their theology. The Dead Sea scrolls were produced by a dissident group living at Qumran near the Dead Sea, mostly in the second and first centuries BC. They are especially helpful because they give us a direct window into some of the issues debated by first-century Jews in Palestine. They have also helped scholars to better appreciate the Jewishness of several NT teachings that had previously been thought to have come from Greek philosophy. Insight into first-century Jewish beliefs, practices and scriptural interpretation can also be found in the motley assortment of narratives, apocalypses, letters, wisdom literature and other texts that modern scholars have grouped together under the (only partly accurate) title of Pseudepigrapha.

F. The New Testament

The books of the NT are simultaneously Jewish, Christian and Greco-Roman literature. They describe aspects of Jewish society and clearly utilize the conceptual categories of Second Temple Judaism. They address problems particular to Christian communities and develop Jewish ideas in light of what God had done through Christ. They also employ Greek language, literary forms and rhetorical techniques. In addition, there are numerous passages in the NT that assume knowledge of ancient Jewish, Greek or Roman customs. Scholars often find that other literature produced during the same period can enlighten our understanding of the NT. Greco-Roman literature is most useful for understanding the meaning of words, grammar and rhetorical techniques. Jewish literature informs us about most of the relevant history of the period as well as Jewish beliefs, practices and attitudes. We also know that some of this other Jewish literature is alluded to in the NT. So, reading other Second Temple Jewish literature along with the NT can be especially fruitful.

The reader of the NT should keep in mind that most people in the first century were illiterate. Those who could read nearly always read aloud. When authors wrote, they were concerned about how their work would sound when it was read. In addition, the books of the NT were written specifically to be read in the churches. Modern readers can draw closer to the world of the NT if, on occasion, they listen to the text rather than read it from the page. (Audio versions are now widely available.)

And when they listen to the words read, they should be mindful to listen for what God is saying to his people through the NT – and not merely to hear it, but also to do it (Jas 1:22).

NEW TESTAMENT THEOLOGY

A. What is New Testament theology?

New Testament theology is part of *biblical theology*, which may be defined as the progressive revelation of God through particular persons and periods. Biblical theology is distinct from *systematic theology* in that the former concerns truth from the perspective of the individual biblical writers while the latter concerns the systematization of truth based on the complete revelation of God. Systematic theology is at heart a *philosophical* discipline, asking the question 'What is truth?' Biblical theology is fundamentally *historical*, asking 'What is truth from the perspective of individual authors and periods?' In this sense biblical theology focuses on the progress of revelation and the diversity of Scripture, asking 'What did Isaiah believe?' 'What did Paul believe?', etc. It then seeks an internal unity behind these authors' diverse expressions of faith.

Any systematic theology that claims to be biblical should have biblical theology as its foundation. This is because biblical theology is simply 'theology done in context'. For example, exegesis of the Pauline letters produces theological conclusions which may be developed into a 'Pauline theology'. This Pauline perspective is then compared to other biblical authors to analyse differences and similarities and integrate them into a broader NT theology. Since evangelicals affirm the ultimate unity of biblical truth, there is an assumption that the integration of the Bible's diverse expressions will result in a theology that is complementary and consistent rather than contradictory.

Based on our definition above, we can see that the goals of NT theology are threefold: (1) to discern the theological themes and emphases of each biblical author; (2) to compare and contrast these perspectives with other books and authors; and (3) to seek to integrate these theologies into a comprehensive and coherent unified theology. In our discussion of NT themes and theology below, we will first suggest a common theme of integrated theology, and will then identify some of the diverse expressions of that theme throughout the NT.

Certain limitations of NT theology should also be noted. First, the NT documents are all occasional in nature, written to address specific needs and concerns. No biblical author set out to write a systematic theology or a comprehensive statement of faith. We must therefore expect gaps in our understanding of each author's theological perspective. It is unsafe to draw conclusions based on silence, assuming what an author must or must not have believed. Similarly, all the theology of the NT is *task theology*, truth brought to bear on real-life situations. Caution must be exercised before assuming that every statement is intended to be universal in application. For example, are Paul's commands related to the role of women in 1 Tim. 2:11–15 meant to apply to the church of all time? This is a question outside the scope of biblical theology. It must be dealt with in the larger context of biblical interpretation and the present-day application of the text.

B. Salvation history

Does NT theology have a central theme from which all other categories emerge? While a variety of themes have been proposed, perhaps the most appropriate is *salvation history* – the idea that God is acting through human history to deliver his people and to bring them back into relationship with him.

Salvation history in the OT. It is impossible to comprehend the theology of the NT without the foundation laid in the OT, the Hebrew Scriptures. The OT recounts that God created a perfect universe, but this world became fallen through the rebellion and disobedience of Adam and Eve (Gen. 1 – 3). The rest of Scripture is the account of God's redemptive purpose for his creation. Through a series of covenants – with Abraham (Gen. 12, 15, 17), the nation of Israel (Exod. 19 – 31), David (2 Sam. 7), and finally a promised 'new covenant' (Jer. 31:31–34) – God gradually brings redemption to sinful humanity and restoration to his creation. (See ch. 2.)

Salvation history in the NT. NT writers assume this OT background and announce that with the coming of Jesus the Messiah, God has inaugurated the final redemption and renewal. Through Jesus' life, death and resurrection, the judgment on humanity has been reversed and the end-time resurrection has begun. God is now creating a new people of God – the church – whose mission is to proclaim the message of salvation to the whole world. All who respond in faith by confessing Jesus to be the Saviour receive salvation from their sins and a renewed relationship with God.

While this framework of salvation permeates the NT, it is expressed differently by different authors. Some of the clearest expositors of salvation history are Luke, Paul and the unknown author of Hebrews. Luke's grand scheme throughout Luke–Acts, his two-volume work, is to demonstrate that the coming of Jesus and the establishment of the church represents the fulfilment of the promises to Israel and the culmination of God's purpose for the world. For Luke, Jesus is the centrepoint of human history; 'all the Scriptures' point to him (Luke 24:27). For Paul, God's sending of his Son represents the 'fullness of time' (ESV), and leads to the redemption of God's children (Gal. 4:4–5). With Jesus, the fulfilment of the ages has come (1 Cor. 10:11). The writer to the Hebrews draws a strong dichotomy between the old and the new. While the revelation given through the prophets was partial and preparatory, the revelation through Jesus the Son of God is complete and perfect (Heb. 1:1–4). The sacrificial and atoning death of Christ on the cross is more than the fulfilment of the promises. It is the only true reality. The OT temple and sacrifices were a mere shadow for what was to come, and could never take away sins. They pointed forward to the true salvation accomplished through Jesus' high-priestly service and sacrificial death on the cross (Heb. 10:1–18).

C. Jesus Christ: God's agent of redemption

Throughout the NT Jesus is presented as God's agent of salvation. Yet different aspects of his person and work are developed by different authors. The following are some of the more important Christological categories of the NT.

Jesus the Messiah. The most common title for Jesus in the NT is *christos* ('Christ'), a Greek translation of the Hebrew *mashiach* ('Messiah'), meaning 'anointed one'. To be anointed meant to be set apart by God for a special task. In the OT period, priests, kings and prophets were anointed for service. Most commonly, 'the Lord's anointed' means Israel's king, chosen and appointed by God. By the first century AD the term was used of God's agent of end-time salvation – 'the Messiah'. First-century messianic expectations took on a variety of forms, but focused especially on the Davidic Messiah, the king from David's line who would re-gather Israel, defeat the nation's enemies, and reign in righteousness and justice in Jerusalem, the city of God.

Jesus' identity as Israel's Messiah is most prominent in the Synoptic Gospels. Matthew identifies Jesus as the royal Messiah, the son of David born in Bethlehem who fulfils the promises made to Israel. For Luke, Jesus is also the Davidic Messiah (Luke 1:32–35), but with special emphasis on the theme that Jesus is the Saviour of all people every-where. The salvation which began in Israel is now going forth to the whole world. Mark presents Jesus as a mysterious and enigmatic figure. He is the mighty Messiah and Son of God who challenges and defeats the forces of Satan. But his task is not the military conquest of Rome, as many in Israel had hoped. It is to suffer and die as a ransom payment for sins (Mark 10:45). Victory over sin and Satan comes through suffering and death.

Son of Man. All four Gospels affirm that Jesus' favourite self-designation was 'Son of Man', from a common Hebrew term for 'human being' (*ben adam*). Jesus seems to have used this as a title both to affirm his solidarity with the human race, and as a veiled allusion to Dan. 7:13–14, where an exalted messianic figure – one 'like a son of man' (i.e. having human form) – comes before God and is given authority, glory and an eternal kingdom. In the Synoptic Gospels, the title appears predominantly in three key contexts: affirming Jesus' authority on earth (Mark 2:10; 2:28), predicting his coming death (Mark 8:31; 9:31; 10:33), and describing his return in glory (Mark 13:26; 14:62).

Son of God. Closely related to the title Messiah is 'Son of God'. In the OT a variety of figures are called sons of God – from angels, to Israel as a nation, to the coming king from David's line (Pss. 2:7; 89:26; cf. 2 Sam. 7:14). In some NT contexts 'Son of God' is practically synonymous with 'Messiah'. and carries the sense of God's representative ruler (Mark 3:11; 14:61; Matt. 16:16; John 1:49). Elsewhere the title carries a deeper significance as the divine Son in unique relationship with God the Father (Matt. 11:27 // Luke 10:22; Rom. 1:3; 8:3; Gal. 4:4; Heb. 1:1–14, etc.). John presents Jesus as the divine Son who came from heaven to bring glory to the Father and eternal life to all who believe (John 3:16–18).

Second Adam. Jesus' unique role in salvation history is especially evident in his role as the second 'Adam', a portrait explicit in Paul and implicit elsewhere in the NT (cf. Luke 3:38; Heb. 2). Just as sin and death entered the world through the disobedience of one man, Adam, so forgiveness and resurrection life came through the obedient sacrifice of one man, Jesus Christ (Rom. 5:12–21; 1 Cor. 15:21–22).

High priest and once-for-all sacrifice for sins. The portrait of Jesus as eschatological high priest is the unique contribution of the author of Hebrews. Writing to a Jewish–Christian community in danger of reverting back to the social and political safety of Judaism, the author affirms the superiority of Christ and the new covenant. Jesus is a high priest according to the order of Melchizedek, a priestly order greater than the OT order of Aaron and Levi. Yet Jesus is more than a priestly mediator, offering sacrifices to God on behalf of human beings. He is also the *means* of atonement, who offers himself as a single sacrifice for sins for all time and all people. Jesus' death on the cross inaugurates the new covenant and achieves eternal salvation for those with a persevering faith.

God in human form. While Jesus is explicitly identified as 'God' in only a few passages (John 1:1; 20:28; Titus 2:13; 2 Pet. 1:1), throughout the NT divine attributes and titles are attributed to him. John's prologue presents Jesus as the pre-existent 'Word' (*logos*), who was 'with God' (i.e., distinct from the Father) and yet 'was God'. He is the creator of all things, and the 'Word made flesh' who came to earth to reveal the invisible God (1:1–18). Elsewhere in John, Jesus says that to know him is to know the Father (14:7–9), and he claims to have existed before Abraham (8:58). Here Jesus seems to be identifying himself as the 'I am', God's self-revelation to Moses in Exod. 3:14–15.

Other authors take up similar language. Hebrews describes Jesus as the creator of all things, 'the radiance of God's glory and the exact representation of his being' (Heb. 1:2–3). For Paul, Jesus is the one Lord 'through whom all things came and through whom we live' (1 Cor. 8:6). He is 'the image of the invisible God', and in him 'all the fullness of the Deity lives in bodily form' (Col. 1:15; 2:9). In Revelation Jesus is called 'the Alpha and the Omega, the First and the Last, the Beginning and the End' (Rev. 22:13; cf. 1:17; 2:8), titles elsewhere attributed to the Lord God (Rev. 1:8; 21:6; Isa. 44:6; 48:12). The title 'Lord' (Greek *kyrios*), commonly used in the Greek OT (Septuagint) to translate the divine name Yahweh, is applied to Jesus throughout the NT, often with divine connotations (e.g. 1 Pet. 3:15). Similarly, quotations referring to God in the OT are sometimes applied to Jesus (Acts 2:20–21; Rom. 10:13; Heb. 1:10). These references confirm that the early church viewed Jesus as more than God's agent or spokesperson. He is the real presence of God with his people.

D. Salvation: the goal of redemptive history

Various images and metaphors are used in the NT to describe the nature of the salvation achieved through Jesus Christ.

The kingdom of God. The Synoptic Gospels affirm that Jesus' central message concerned the coming of the 'kingdom of God'. The OT concept of God's kingdom was dynamic and multi-dimensional. It could refer to God's sovereignty over the cosmos *in the present*, or the consummation of that reign *in the future*. Jesus' proclamation of the kingdom included both dimensions. He spoke of entering the kingdom in the present, but also the final establishment of the kingdom at the end. At its heart, receiving the kingdom means submitting to God's reign – his sovereign purpose and plan for the world. It means faith in Jesus the Messiah, who is both herald and executor of God's final salvation. It also means embracing the kingdom ethic: love for God and unconditional love for human beings – even one's enemies.

Eternal life in the present. While the Synoptics speak of salvation especially with reference to the kingdom of God, John's Gospel emphasizes *eternal life*. Eternal life in John is more than a future condition; it is true spiritual life in the present. Jesus says, 'I have come that they may have life, and have it to the full' (John 10:10). While he will raise the dead to eternal life on the last day (6:40), Jesus is already the resurrection and the life, bestowing eternal life on those who believe (11:25). This is because eternal life is equivalent to *knowing God*, a relationship with the Father through the Son (17:3).

A future inheritance kept in heaven. While the Gospel of John emphasizes the present, other writers stress the future dimensions of salvation. This is especially important since the church is experiencing suffering and longs for future deliverance. Writing to persecuted believers in Asia Minor, Peter encourages perseverance and hope in 'an inheritance that can never perish, spoil or fade ... kept in heaven for you'. Through faith believers are 'shielded by God's power until the coming of the salvation that is ready to be revealed in the last time' (1 Pet. 1:3–5). The writer of Hebrews speaks of a Sabbath rest which believers must strive to enter through perseverance and enduring faith (Heb. 4:11; 10:36; 12:1–3).

Reconciliation through justification. For Paul salvation means especially reconciliation with God, the restoration of a right relationship with him (2 Cor. 5:17–21; Rom. 5:1). Though all people are sinners who fall short of God's righteous standards, God 'justifies', or declares righteous, those who have faith in Christ's atoning death on the cross. Justification is a free gift of God, bestowed on all who believe (Rom. 3:23–26). Salvation comes through identification with Christ in his life, death and resurrection. Believers are now incorporated 'in Christ', dying with him to their old life of sin and being raised with him to new resurrection life (Rom. 6:3–4). Now adopted as children of God, believers receive the Spirit of God as the seal and assurance of their future glorification (2 Cor. 1:22).

E. The Holy Spirit: God's power and presence with his people

While the OT speaks of the 'Spirit of God' primarily in the sense of the manifestation of God's power and presence, in the NT the Holy Spirit is identified more specifically as distinct from the Father and the Son. The most developed theologies of the Holy Spirit appear in Luke, John and Paul.

In Luke–Acts the Holy Spirit is associated especially with the fulfilment of prophecy, the evidence of the arrival of God's end-time of salvation. In Luke's birth narrative, the Spirit-inspired renewal of prophecy after some 400 years of silence confirms that God's final deliverance is about to arrive. Elizabeth and Zechariah are filled with the Spirit when they break into prophetic utterance (Luke 1:41, 67), and the Spirit rests upon righteous Simeon, granting guidance and revelation (2:25–27). During Jesus' public ministry, the Spirit is identified uniquely with him. In fulfilment of OT prophecy (Isa. 42:1; 61:1–2), the Messiah is 'anointed' by the Spirit at his baptism and 'filled with the Spirit' to accomplish the messianic task (Luke 3:22; 4:1, 14, 18; 10:21). Following his resurrection, Jesus ascends to the right hand of God and – as promised (Luke 24:49; Acts 1:4–5) – pours out the Spirit upon his disciples (Acts 2:16–21; Joel 2:28–32). Throughout Acts the Spirit guides and empowers the church to take the gospel to the ends of the earth.

John shares with Luke–Acts a special interest in the work of the Spirit. Here also the Spirit represents the continuing presence of Jesus in his church, guiding and directing the disciples on their mission. Yet while Luke emphasizes the role of the Spirit as sign of the new age, John presents the Spirit as *another* counsellor (paraclete), who will act in Jesus' place to mediate the presence of the Father. As Jesus imparted life, light and knowledge of the Father to the disciples, so now the Spirit will do the same thing. He will guide them into all truth, testifying to Jesus and reminding them of all he taught them (John 14:26; 15:26).

The most comprehensive theology of the Holy Spirit comes from the letters of Paul. For Paul, life 'in the Spirit' represents all that believers are and have by virtue of their reception of the salvation available through Jesus Christ. The Holy Spirit is the agent of redemption who washes, sanctifies and justifies the believer (Rom. 15:16; 1 Cor. 6:11; 12:13; 2 Thess. 2:13; Titus 3:5). He is the very presence of God (2 Cor. 3:17–18), who indwells, fills, guides, enlightens and empowers believers (Rom. 8:9–14; 15:19; 1 Cor. 2:10–14; 3:16; Gal. 3:5; 5:18). He is the bestower of spiritual gifts, providing unity and spiritual vitality to the church (1 Cor. 12:7–13; Eph. 4:3–4). He provides peace and assurance of salvation, and is the seal and guarantee of our final salvation (Rom. 8:13–16, 23; 2 Cor. 1:22; 5:5; Gal. 4:6; Eph. 1:13; 4:30). Life 'in the flesh' (fallen human life apart from God) leads to death; while life 'in the Spirit' leads to peace and life.

F. The church: the Spirit-filled community of salvation history

Throughout the NT, the community of salvation is the church, the people of God indwelt and guided by the Spirit of God in the new age of salvation. The Greek term *ekklesia* means a congregation or assembly, and in the NT usually refers to a congregation of believers in a particular place. At times, however, it carries the universal sense of believers everywhere (Matt. 16:18; Gal. 1:13; Eph. 1:22; 3:10, 21; Col. 1:18, 24). The church's task is to manifest the presence of God in the world and to take the message of salvation to all people everywhere. While this portrait of the church permeates the NT, certain themes and metaphors are emphasized by particular authors.

For Luke the church is the end-time people of God, the restored remnant of Israel together with the Gentiles who have been incorporated into the people of God. The church is established on the day of Pentecost, when Jesus, now ascended to the right hand of God, pours out the Spirit on his disciples, who then boldly proclaim the message of salvation. The church's strength and vitality comes from the power and guidance of the Spirit, and from unity based on the apostles' teaching, fellowship, breaking bread, and prayer (Acts 2:42–47). Its success and phenomenal growth confirms that this is no human endeavour, but is truly the work of God (Acts 5:39).

Paul uses a variety of metaphors for the church (temple, household, etc.), but the most important is that of the body of Christ. This metaphor emphasizes both the unity and diversity of the church. As one body filled with one Spirit and serving one Lord, the church strives together for the common goal of the gospel. Like the individual parts of a body, each member exercises unique Spirit-bestowed gifts for the common good (Rom. 12:4–8; 1 Cor. 12 – 14; Eph. 4:1–16).

Peter develops a number of metaphors for the church from OT descriptions of Israel. The church is 'a chosen people, a royal priesthood, a holy nation, God's special possession', and all this with the purpose 'that you may declare the praises of him who called you out of darkness into his wonderful light' (1 Pet. 2:9).

Baptism. Throughout the NT, incorporation into the church comes through baptism, the outward sign of an inward cleansing and renewal by the Spirit. For Paul in particular, baptism is symbolic of incorporation in Christ and identification with him in his death, burial and resurrection (Rom. 6:3–4).

The Lord's Supper. In worship the church celebrates the Lord's Supper (eucharist/communion), a rite inaugurated by Jesus on the night before his crucifixion. The Lord's Supper is a remembrance of Christ's sacrificial death on the cross and an anticipation of his return in glory. The bread represents his body, given up as a sacrifice of atonement. The wine represents his shed blood and the inauguration of the new covenant (Luke 22:17–20; 1 Cor. 11:23–26).

Leadership in the church. Leaders in the church are identified by a variety of titles: apostles, elders, overseers, deacons, pastors, etc. No specific model of church governance is established, since the NT documents are occasional in nature and were written before patterns for such offices were codified. What *is* normative throughout the NT is that church leaders must be Spirit-filled people of integrity, with a good reputation in the community and behaviour that is above reproach.

G. The goal: consummation of redemptive history

Throughout the NT, the completion of salvation history is the second coming of Christ to judge and to rule. The Synoptic Gospels identify Jesus as the Son of Man who will return on the clouds of heaven to gather the elect and to judge the wicked. Believers are called to be watchful and prepared, because they do not know the day or the hour when he will return (Matt. 24 – 25; Mark 13; Luke 17, 21). Although the Gospel of John emphasizes eternal life as a present possession, Jesus also teaches that he is going away to prepare a place for his people, and will return to gather them to himself (John 14:1–3, 28; 21:23).

Paul speaks of the return of Christ as our hope of deliverance from enemies and from the wrath of God coming against the world (1 Thess. 1:10). Christ will descend from heaven with the voice of the archangel and with the trumpet call of God. Believers who have died will be raised in glorified bodies and those who are still alive will be instantly transformed into incorruptible, immortal bodies (1 Cor. 15:50–57; 1 Thess. 4:13–18).

The book of Revelation presents the most developed description of the end-time (Greek *eschaton*, from which we get 'eschatology'). At its climax, Christ returns on a white horse with the armies of heaven. He defeats the wicked nations, binds Satan in the abyss, raises the righteous dead, and reigns on earth for a thousand years. Following the thousand years, Satan is released and instigates a final revolt against God. He is defeated and cast into the lake of fire, the 'second death'. God creates a new heaven and a new earth, and the new Jerusalem, the holy city, descends from heaven. God will dwell with his people; he will wipe every tear from their eyes; death and suffering will be no more (Rev. 19 – 21). Salvation history concludes with the restoration of all things to a relationship with the creator God. While the nature of the thousand years (the 'millennium') is debated – whether present or future, literal or figurative – the message of the book is clear: God is the sovereign Lord of all, who will right every wrong and bring history to its destined conclusion.

Throughout the NT the final state of the wicked is most commonly referred to as 'hell' or 'Gehenna' (Greek *geena*; Matt. 5:22, 29; 10:28; 18:9; 23:15, 33; etc.). Gehenna is a Latin term derived from the Hebrew *ge'hinnom*, 'Valley of Hinnom' – originally an OT place of pagan sacrifices. A variety of images are used to describe this final state: eternal fire and torment (Matt. 25:41, 46; Mark 9:43–48; Jude 7); outer darkness (Matt. 8:12); the pit or Abyss (Rev. 9:1–2, 11); the lake of fire and sulphur (Rev. 20:10); and the second death (Rev. 21:8). Interpreters are divided on whether these images are literal or figurative and, especially, what they denote. Some suggest that they depict the eternal conscious torment of the wicked. Others claim such torture would be unjust punishment for temporal sins, and that the images rather represent utter destruction – the annihilation rather than the unending torture of the wicked. In either case, the primary characteristic of hell is the agony of separation from our creator God, who is the only source of life, joy and fulfilment.

The final state of the righteous is in the presence of God (Rev. 21:3), usually referred to as 'heaven', but also with terms like 'paradise' (Luke 23:43; 2 Cor. 12:4; Rev. 2:7) and 'the new Jerusalem' (Rev. 3:12; 21:2). Heaven is described as a place (and a state) of security, rest and bliss, where believers will experience complete fellowship with the Father and the Son for all eternity. Sorrow, evil and death will be no more (John 14:2–3; 1 Thess. 4:17; Heb. 4:9–11; Rev. 21:3–4). Apart from these generalities, little is said about the details of life in the eternal state. The reason, no doubt, is that it is so qualitatively different from our own that finite minds are incapable of comprehending it. As Paul writes, 'What no eye has seen, what no ear has heard, what no human mind has conceived – these things God has prepared for those who love him' (1 Cor. 2:9).

NEW TESTAMENT INTERPRETATION

A confident and appropriate reading of any text recognizes its key features and considers its stated purposes. This is just as true of a novel, an engineering manual, a poem or a TV guide as it is of the Bible. Essentially, the NT is three things: *literature*, *history* and *theology*. These three aspects correspond to its impulses to engage, record and teach respectively. To bring us into relationship with God through Jesus Christ is its overriding purpose.

A. *The New Testament as literature*

The NT consists of three main types of literature, or genres. The Gospels and Acts are narrative, the book of Revelation is apocalyptic and the rest is letters. Subtypes appear within these, including genealogies, parables, miracles, sermons, proverbs, vice-lists, hymns and confessions. Whereas some are more straightforward than others, each has unique features that the interpreter must bear in mind. The best interpreters notice the details of the passage they are reading without losing sight of the overall thrust of the book, and they also respond to the impact of the text on our senses and emotions. Rather than merely reading to gain information, the literary nature of the NT encourages us to 'stop and smell the roses'. As good literature, the NT does not merely inform but unnerves, enthrals, inspires and transforms.

Two of the Gospels tell us their purpose. Luke wrote that Theophilus might 'know the certainty of the things' he had been taught concerning Jesus (Luke 1:4), and John 'that you may believe that Jesus is the Messiah, the Son of God, and that by believing you may have life in his name' (John 20:30–31). Thus the main purpose of the Gospels is to lead people to put their trust in Jesus as their Lord and Saviour and then to follow him in discipleship. This can be easily illustrated with reference to the Gospels' major features.

The many miracle stories in the Gospels are clues or 'signs' (John 20:30) to the identity of Jesus. They demonstrate his power over nature, evil and sickness and the extent of his dominion and authority. Our main response is not to look for similar experiences but to mimic the disciples' reaction: 'The men were amazed and asked, "What kind of man is this?"' (Matt. 8:27). Other actions of Jesus equally point to his unique identity. His entry into Jerusalem on a donkey with the adulation of the crowds (Matt. 21:1–11, etc.) stamps him as a king, but the humble beast on which he rode marks his agenda as distinct from that of military liberation.

Parables are among the Gospels' most puzzling yet alluring features. These are stories Jesus told to describe his kingdom, his return, future judgment, and how disciples should behave. They can pack a punch like a good political cartoon, as in the Good Samaritan (Luke 10:25–37), where the hero isn't the religious worker but the despised foreigner. Parables dress profound truths in memorable and provocative garb. Instead of merely stating that finding God is supremely valuable, Jesus said, 'The kingdom of heaven is like treasure hidden in a field. When a man found it, he hid it again, and then in his joy went and sold all that he had and bought that field' (Matt. 13:44).

In terms of application when reading the Gospels, an important task is to distinguish between what was unique to Jesus' context and what is exemplary for all believers. We should not expect every chapter in the Gospels to contain specific instructions for our daily lives; application is not as simple as doing what Jesus told the disciples to do. Clearly, some of the commands are situation-specific. Even within one Gospel not everything applies uniformly. For example, in Matt. 10:5–6 Jesus told the Twelve to minister only to fellow Jews, but in 28:19 they are to go to all ethnic groups. The promise in John 14:26 that the Holy Spirit will remind the disciples of everything Jesus had said to them obviously does not include us. We should also take care not to take the many figures of speech literally. The command to gouge out your eye in Matt. 5:29 is a vivid way of recommending drastic action to avoid temptation. Similarly, the call in Matt. 6:3 not to 'let your left hand know what your right hand is doing' when you give to the poor concerns the motives of seeking human praise rather than being an attack on keeping financial records.

This is not to say that the distinctiveness of Jesus' life limits its relevance. In John 3 and 4 Jesus has conversations with a religious leader and a woman on the fringes of society. If the former, Nicodemus, finds Jesus perplexing, the latter, the Samaritan woman, responds in faith and becomes a witness to her people. Such narratives invite readers to consider the great reversal of the kingdom of God, its universal appeal and the surprising nature of God's grace. To give another example, while Jesus' death and resurrection are obviously unique, his followers are called to give up their lives in imitation, dying to self-centredness (Luke 9:23).

Acts narrates the progress of the gospel from a small gathering of Jewish disciples of the earthly Jesus in Jerusalem, across formidable boundaries, to Paul's bold and unhindered preaching of the risen and ascended Jesus to Gentiles in Rome. Hence its main purpose is to report the progress of the faith and to show how this is in continuity with both the time of Jesus and the time of Israel. What God is doing through the apostles in the early church is the activity of Jesus and the Spirit, and the climax of salvation history. The consistent message to which we are still called to respond is that salvation is to be found in Jesus (e.g. Acts 4:12; 16:31).

The question for application with reference to much of Acts concerns whether what is narrated is prescriptive for the church today or merely descriptive of the early church and its experience. Like the Gospels, the narrative of Acts provides clues as to its correct appropriation. The sharing of goods in the community in 2:44–45 and 4:32–35 is a case in point. Acts records that the practice led to positive results, including the expansion of the church, but also to the judgment of Ananias and Sapphira (5:1–11). So in general, sharing of possessions is strongly commended. Should we then set up comparable communities of shared goods? Since in 6:1–7 and 11:27–30 different approaches are used to make provision for those in material need, the model of communal sharing in chs. 2 and 4 is not to be adopted in all circumstances.

Revelation, like Matt. 24 – 25, represents apocalyptic literature. Prone to major misunderstanding, such texts are not meant to be read as code for interpreting contemporary events or predicting the second coming. Rather, in this genre, past, present and future events are presented in symbolic garb to bring encouragement to God's people in difficult times. As the letters to the seven churches show, the setting of Revelation includes persecution by the emperor (2:3, 10, 13; 3:10), harassment by the synagogue (2:9; 3:9), compromise urged and practised by false teachers (2:2, 6, 14, 15, 20), and complacency related to excessive wealth (2:4–5; 3:1–3; 3:15–17). The eschatology of Revelation calls its readers to alert resistance to the seductive powers of the present age and an active obedience to a merciful God who will make all things new.

A major feature of the literary nature of the NT is its wide use of figurative language. For example, 1 Corinthians compares the church to a cultivated field in 3:5–9, a temple in 3:10–17 and a body in 12:12–27. The right approach to such metaphors is to discern the relevant comparison, and the danger is over-interpretation. In all likelihood, the author is only drawing on a small range of possible resemblances. In 1 Cor. 3:5–9, using the analogy of the church as a garden with servants, Paul points out that it makes no sense to venerate your favourite minister, because they are just serving God who assigned them their tasks (v. 5); it is God who causes the church to grow (v. 6). In comparison with God who gives the growth, church leaders are nothing (v. 7) and God, not the Corinthians, is the one who assesses the workers, giving the appropriate reward for their toil (v. 8). Metaphors carry an affective impact and create a mood and tone for the passage. They cue the reader as to how to feel as much as what to think. The base character of the image in question, with unskilled farm labourers and a common field, impresses upon the readers the unimpressive and menial nature of the work of Christian ministers and add weight to Paul's case for 'no more boasting about human leaders' (3:21).

B. The New Testament as history

1. The NT and its historical context

The NT was written two thousand years ago, in Greek. So it is foreign to most modern readers in terms of culture, customs and geography. As on London Underground platforms, we do well to 'mind the gap'. An understanding of the historical background is sometimes crucial to its interpretation and application. For instance, the words of Jesus to turn the other cheek (Matt. 5:39) are not a recommendation to put up with physical abuse, but a call not to retaliate when mistreated; a 'slap on the cheek' in the ancient world was a form of insult rather than an act of violence. Changed social conditions may also blunt the impact of the NT's teaching today. The NT's consistent advocacy of humility as a virtue was revolutionary in its day. To 'value others above yourselves' in humility (Phil. 2:3) was unheard of in a society obsessed with preserving one's status and honour and avoiding shame. Until God's Messiah took the form of a servant and was crucified, humility was thought of negatively as servility, the domain of the pitiful and weak. The more we know about life in the days of Jesus and the apostles, from washing feet to forms of travel, conditions of work to building materials, the better equipped we are to understand it accurately.

The fact that all the NT letters arise out of and are intended for specific situations makes them trickier to interpret than at first sight. Initially, they were each addressed to one Christian congregation or individual. Who wrote, to whom and to what ends, are questions that must be answered if these letters are to be read aright. As to be expected when reading someone else's mail, some imagination is required to reconstruct what is going on. In 1 Corinthians, for example, it is clear that Paul had planted the church in Corinth and that problems had arisen since his departure. The precise nature of their faults may never be known, but some sense that Paul is correcting them is needed in order to put his words in context.

The next step is to work out which commands in the letters are timeless in nature and which apply only under certain circumstances. Some statements are clearly ageless, such as Paul's conclusion that 'all have sinned and fall short of the glory of God' (Rom. 3:23), where 'all,' in the context of Rom. 1:18 – 3:20, means every human being. Sometimes, however, the rationale for a particular command does not work in other cultures. The reason Paul insists on head coverings for women in church in 1 Cor. 11 was that a covered head suggested sexual fidelity. Since in our culture a hat carries no such symbolism, we should look for other ways to be true to his instructions.

2. The NT as a historical record

The NT is not only historical in the sense that its origins lie in the distant past, it is also history in terms of its subject matter: it purports to record historical events. The Gospels, for instance, are examples of a recognized category of Greek historical writing, namely, the biography.

And most of the letters are pages from chapters in the lives of real churches.

A fair assessment of the available evidence supports the reliability of the NT documents. Obviously, the NT does not follow the conventions of modern historiography with its attention to full documentation and precise quotation. Nonetheless, what the NT depicts fits well with the chronology and geography of ancient history, and archaeology has confirmed some of the details, such as the description of the pool of Bethesda in John 5:2 and the existence of 'Pontius Pilate, Prefect of Judea'. Only a few pagan and Jewish sources refer to Jesus and the early church, but this is not surprising since Christianity was only a small movement in the context of world history at the time of its beginnings.

Some people object to reading the NT as history on the grounds that it contains accounts of Christ's miracles. Science, they say, has removed the need for appeal to the supernatural to explain things. However, if God exists then miracles cannot be excluded in principle. Whereas science operates in the realm of the predictable and repeatable, miracles are by definition unique events. Concerning the miracles of Jesus, such as those surrounding his birth, the nature miracles, exorcisms and healings, his own resurrection is the linchpin. Here the evidence has been scrutinized to the nth degree and no one has come up with a better explanation for the empty tomb and the transformation of the disciples from frightened deserters to fearless proclaimers than that he was raised from the dead by the power of God.

3. The NT and biblical history

The fact that the NT records history is something it shares in common with the OT. The OT recounts the history of Israel as the chosen people of God, from the covenant promises to Abraham, the conquest, kingship, exile and return, and the NT continues the story at a later period. Reading the NT with no knowledge of the OT would be like reading a later volume of a fiction series with no knowledge of the earlier ones. Although not impossible, it would hardly be satisfying.

Matthew opens with a genealogy that demonstrates continuity of 'Jesus the Messiah the son of David, the son of Abraham' (1:1) with the story of Israel. He gives more than sixty OT quotations, forging links between the life and death of Jesus and what God did to save his people in the past. For Matthew, the OT is a book of prophetic predictions: 'this took place to fulfil' punctuates the Gospel. More allusively, through typology (i.e. patterns or analogies in history), Jesus is depicted as a new Moses, who demands a 'higher righteousness' and a new Israel, who recapitulates the nation's history (rescued from Egypt, tempted in the wilderness, etc.), but without failure, and fulfils her destiny.

The use of the OT in the rest of the NT is no less profound. Mark describes the good news in terms of the fulfilment of Isaiah's prophecy of a new exodus (1:2–3; cf. Isa. 40:3; Mal. 3:1). OT passages and themes frequently underlie Mark's narrative. Jesus' messianic identity is made clear at his baptism in words which echo Ps. 2:7: 'you are my Son, whom I love; with you I am well pleased' (1:11). Luke emphasizes that God has bound himself to Israel with words of promise (e.g. to David, 1:30–32, 68–71, cf. 2 Sam. 7:14; to Abraham, 1:54–55, 72–73, cf. Gen. 12:1–3, etc.), which are accomplished in Jesus. Jesus is also depicted as the interpreter of Scripture himself (24:25–49), for 'everything must be fulfilled that is written about [him] in the Law of Moses, the Prophets and the Psalms'. The story of the inception and growth of the early church in Acts is likewise depicted as a continuation of biblical history.

OT antecedents also define the shape of the Messiah and his mission in John. The final revelation from God which Jesus embodies is contrasted with that received and mediated by Moses. The signs he performs, recalling the 'signs and wonders' of Moses, point to a new exodus. Jesus eclipses the great Jewish feasts and institutions which marked God's saving work in the past. As the 'light of the world' and 'living water' he fulfils the torch-lighting and water-pouring ceremonies of the feast of Tabernacles. He replaces the Jerusalem temple and, by dying during Passover week, is the ultimate Jewish Passover sacrifice. He is also seen as the long-awaited 'prophet like Moses' (6:14; 7:40; cf. Deut. 18:15).

In Paul's letters, God's dealings with Israel recorded in the OT lead to Christ who is the turning point of history. History divides into two epochs, the old age of sin, death and the Torah, and the new which eclipses it. The decisive act is the ending of Israel's exile and the restoration of God's people which has now taken place in Christ.

The other books of the NT are equally intertwined with the OT. Gathering together many of its major themes, the NT closes in Rev. 21 – 22 with a vision of a new Jerusalem and temple (21:2; 21:9 – 22:5), a new covenant (21:3–4), and even a new Israel; both the 'names of the twelve tribes of Israel' (21:12) and 'the names of the twelve apostles of the Lamb' (21:14) are found on the gates and walls of the city.

It is no accident that the two parts of Scripture are usually bound together in one 'Holy Bible'. Considering the ways in which the NT relates to the OT is one of the main tasks of biblical interpretation. In one sense the only compulsory prerequisite for NT interpretation is to have read the OT. In Matthew Jesus asks six times with reference to the OT, 'have you not read?'

C. The New Testament as theology

Although essential, neither literary nor historical analyses suffice. There is a sense in which reading the NT is *unlike* reading any other book. We read it to answer life's most fundamental questions: Who am I? Why am I here? Where is the world heading? Above all, who is God? In particular, what has he done? What are his plans for the future? Where do I fit in? Notwithstanding the historical distance and the literary unfamiliarity of the NT to modern readers, we share with the first readers the conviction that God has changed the world forever through Jesus Christ. As Peter writes: 'Though you have not seen him, you love him ... you believe in him and are filled with an inexpressible and glorious joy' (1 Pet. 1:8).

The best way to read the NT is to allow it to shape all our faith, life, worship and service. This includes everything from our private prayers to our political engagement. It can be a subversive and unsettling document, as well as comforting and reassuring. At root, the NT wants to transform all our relationships, not only with God, but also with ourselves, our families, our enemies and friends, and with society as a whole.

The task of reading the NT for all its worth is a challenging endeavour. It takes the sensitivity of a literary critic, the skills of an historian and the vision of a theologian. On the other hand, 'the word is very near you' (Deut. 30:14), especially if you heed the advice to 'smell the roses' and 'mind the gap'. Such readers will always find not only things to believe, but also reasons to trust God and ways to obey him. Ultimately Scripture is clear because God is light (1 John 1:5), Christ is the light of the world (John 8:12), and his word is like a lamp in a dark place (2 Pet. 1:19). The radiance of God is not a mystery of metaphysics but a matter of fellowship between himself and those he enlightens through his Word.

While it is true that the NT handsomely repays careful study, it can be read by anyone with profit. The biggest obstacle to right reading is not a dull mind, nor the absence of specialized knowledge, but a hard heart. As God's word to the world the message of the NT is accessible to all who come to it in faith.

Further reading

Good general introductions to the New Testament include:
John Drane, *Introducing the New Testament* (Lion, 2nd edn 1999) – excellent, well-illustrated summary of the NT's story and early Christian faith.

Don Carson and others, *Introduction to the New Testament* (Apollos, 2nd edn 2005)
  – more detailed standard textbook for evangelical theological study.
David deSilva, *Introduction to the New Testament* (Apollos, 2004)
  – another more detailed standard textbook for evangelical theological study.

Other useful books include:
Ben Witherington, *The New Testament Story* (Eerdmans, 2004) – well-presented summary of 'the story of' and 'the stories in' the NT.
Ben Witherington, *New Testament History: A Narrative Account* (Baker, 2001) – more detailed description of the history of the whole NT period.
Leon Morris, *New Testament Theology* (Zondervan, 1986) – clear presentation of the teaching of the whole NT and its individual books.
Howard Marshall, *New Testament Theology* (IVP, 2004) – good, more detailed, exposition of NT theology.

9. Gospels

Howard Marshall

Four accounts of the life of Jesus open the NT. They were the earliest such books to be written and come from people closely associated with Jesus or his first followers. Other accounts of Jesus were written later but are often legendary, and written to further the purposes of various groups generally considered heretical. They have not survived except in fragments.

THE GOSPEL OF MARK

A. The earliest Gospel

Although some early Christian scholars (such as Augustine c. AD 400) thought that Matthew was the first Gospel to be written, and some still do, the majority opinion is that Mark was the earliest writer. If he was not, it is difficult to see why Mark would have written a shorter work that leaves out much that is in Matthew. Various signs indicate that it is the earlier composition. Matthew, Mark and Luke are compositions with individual features and characteristics but also with so much material in common, often expressed in passages with the same basic structure and wording, that it is universally agreed that there is some kind of common basis behind them. That is not surprising; within the comparatively limited and closed group of followers of Jesus it is likely that one basic version of the story would quickly develop and be told with individual variations. When we compare the three Gospels, for the most part it is Mark who seems to have formed the basis for the other two writers, and the majority view is that Matthew and Luke had access to copies of Mark (or something extremely like what has been handed down to us as his work) and used it as their main source. Such a procedure is perfectly natural, especially if the tradition is correct that Mark was associated with Peter and wrote down what he remembered.

B. The storyline

Mark's Gospel begins with a scene that brings together two men. There is John, nicknamed the Baptizer, who felt called to prepare a people, currently in danger of divine judgment, to repentance and to readiness for when the Lord himself would come among them. And there is Jesus, who joins the crowds flocking to John in the desert, and indicates his personal association with them by taking part in the ceremony of washing with water. This was a symbol of consecration to God and of the way in which God would give them the gift of the Holy Spirit. But, whereas the people experienced forgiveness, Jesus experienced the Holy Spirit, and heard a heavenly voice assuring him that he was God's Son and commissioning him for his own task (1:1–13).

Thus begins a mission in which Jesus announces the arrival of God's rule over his people (the kingdom of God), and calls them to turn in their tracks and accept this good news with all its implications. He gathers a group of young men to be his companions in the task – in the social and cultural setting of Judaism it would have been unheard of and counter-productive to include young women, although Jesus certainly encouraged women also to respond to his message. And he sets out on an itinerant mission mainly in the small towns and villages of Galilee (1:14–20).

In the story as Mark tells it, there are two fairly explicit stages (1:1 – 8:30; 8:31 – 16:8), in both of which there are three interwoven strands of plot. These three storylines can be seen as the relationships of Jesus with the crowds, with the people who responded positively to him, and with those who developed hostility.

The two stages are concerned with the figure of Jesus himself. Although his own message was concerned with the coming of the kingdom of God (1:15), it was impossible to separate this from the question of his own status and role. His announcement of the kingdom was accompanied by his own remarkable deeds: he quickly acquired a reputation for healing diseases and disabilities and for other remarkable deeds. This naturally raised the question of his own role in relation to the kingdom of God. This could have been that of a prophet who simply announced what God was doing (or about to do) without actually bringing it about. But under the influence of prophetic statements in the OT many Jews believed that there would be an agent of God, the Messiah, who would act as king in God's kingdom (like the Israelite kings, especially David). The first part of Mark's Gospel is essentially the telling of a story which raises the question of Jesus' identity and gives the evidence to enable people to answer it. The readers, of course, already know what the right answer is, because they have read the opening sentences, but Mark takes us along the journey of discovery.

So Jesus spoke and acted with an impressive appearance of authority, and did his mighty works in the presence of the people, constantly moving around to fresh audiences. He did not tell people who he was, and when he referred to himself he often used the strange phrase 'Son of Man'. This reflects an Aramaic form of modest self-reference; it also reflects the reference in Dan. 7:13 to a heavenly figure who receives authority from God as the representative of his people.

From the start his activity aroused opposition because he said and did things that went against the teaching and practices of the Pharisees, who were sticklers for the minutiae of God's law as they understood it. He quickly became *persona non grata* with them, and disqualified himself for being an agent of God in their eyes. Mark records several stories of conflict between them.

At the same time there were people who responded to him positively, out of whose number he enlarged his group of companions. To this group he gave deeper insights into his teaching. The first part of the Gospel culminates in Jesus putting to them the question that was being widely discussed (8:27–30): Who am I? What do you make of me? At various points in Mark's story people under the control of evil spirits cried out that Jesus was the Son of God or the Holy One of God, but Jesus tried to silence them. Now his close companions (the disciples), led by Peter, recognized that Jesus must be the Messiah, although he could hardly be said to have acted like a traditional king.

But they were in for a greater surprise. If the first part of Mark identifies Jesus as the Messiah, the second relates a story in which he is seen to be a rejected, suffering Messiah who would give his life to set people free (10:45). The same activity of responding to the crowds continues, but the relationships with his companions and his opponents intensify. There is more teaching for the companions on two main issues when they are alone with him. The first was his repeated revelation to them that he must suffer rejection and be put to death, but would return to life (8:31; 9:31; 10:33–34). This was probably totally beyond their comprehension, for how could God's agent be overcome and defeated like that? The second was a lengthy session on what was going to happen after his departure, including the demolition of the temple and the fulfilment of the picture in Daniel of the coming of the Son of Man as God's agent on earth (ch. 13). In line with Jesus' own prophecy regarding himself, the opposition of the Jewish religious leaders came to a head in a series of verbal battles that led to the decision to get rid of him. A major part of Mark's story is thus taken up with the events leading to the trials and execution of Jesus.

Then the story, as we have it, ends quite abruptly with accounts of his burial and a subsequent visit by some of his women followers to the tomb. They found it to be empty, save for a young man who told them that Jesus had come back to life and they would see him if they returned to Galilee. (Note that 16:9–20 is missing from the oldest manuscripts of the Gospel and is written in a different style, so it was not part of the original Gospel. It is unclear whether Mark intended to conclude at v. 8, or whether the original ending has been lost.)

C. The character of the story

Such a brief sketch of the story has inevitably left out most of the detail and some of the main points as well. As Mark tells it there is a sense of movement and hurry, one of Mark's favourite words being 'immediately'. His Greek is somewhat rough and homespun, as in his frequent use of the present tense to tell the story (Matthew and Luke generally replace it by the more usual past tense). The story is a compilation of brief vignettes rather than lengthy narratives. Much of Jesus' teaching is given in the form of soundbites, brief and memorable sayings, apart from the longer stories (parables) and the two or three places where there is something more like a connected discourse (the collection of parables in ch. 4; the dialogue about aspects of the law in ch. 7; and the look into the future in ch. 13).

At the same time there is a sense of mystery and wonder conveyed by the story. There are demonic powers inhabiting human beings who recognize who Jesus really is. The things that Jesus does, both in the presence of the crowds and when alone with his companions, have a numinous quality about them, and the vocabulary of wonder and amazement is common. There is constant misunderstanding or lack of understanding, as if Jesus' identity and teaching are beyond the grasp of his hearers.

D. The evangelist

The book is anonymous, like the other Gospels, purely in the sense that the narrator does not name himself within the story. But it is hard to believe that the first readers did not know who the author was, or were unable to find this out. Our earliest information comes from Papias very early in the second century; he names the author as John Mark (known as a companion of Paul, Acts 13:5, 13; Philm. 24), an associate of Peter and dependent on him for much of his information. Despite the rigorous scrutiny of sceptical scholars, there is no solid reason to reject his statement.

Dating the Gospel is less certain. The considerable amount of space devoted to the hardships and suffering of people, culminating in the destruction of the temple in Jerusalem in AD 70 (referred to in coded language in 13:14) leads most scholars to conclude that the Gospel was written around that time, and that one purpose of the writer was to help people to understand what was going on around them in the light of what Jesus had said. Nevertheless, the primary purpose of Mark seems to have been to enable Christian believers to know the important features of the earthly life of the One whom they now knew as their heavenly Lord, and to provide them with a book that would be of great value in their evangelism.

Attempts have been made to identify the audiences and origins of the individual Gospels with specific places or Christian communities. A number of features suggest that, though Mark belonged to Jerusalem, his Gospel may have been composed and first used in Rome. The fact that it was written in Greek, not Hebrew or Aramaic, makes it unlikely that it was meant for a Jewish audience whose first language was not Greek. However, Greek was the common language of the eastern Mediterranean world, and writing in Greek would give the book a wide circulation and readership.

THE GOSPEL OF MATTHEW

A. Matthew and his predecessors

The first thing that we observe about the Gospel of Matthew is that it is considerably longer than Mark (c. 18,300 words in Greek, compared to 11,200 words). This is not due to its author being more expansive in his style, for in fact where he relates the same incidents as Mark he does so in briefer fashion. Rather, it is because he has more information to include, and the effect of his additions (together with some rewriting of the common passages) is to cast fresh light on the story of Jesus and bring out some significant new features. The generally accepted view is that Matthew has produced what is in effect a revised and augmented version of Mark.

A considerable amount of the fresh material is shared with Luke, and the symbol 'Q' is commonly used to refer to this shared material. The majority of scholars hold that Q existed as an earlier collection of (mainly) sayings of Jesus, and was utilized independently by the two evangelists. Those who postulate the existence of this earlier collection can be sure of its contents only when they are found in both Matthew and Luke. But both Gospels contain other materials peculiar to them-selves, and we cannot rule out the possibility that in each case some of this material may be items taken from Q that the other evangelist did not take over. Yet another problem is whether the basic minimum of Q material common to Matthew and Luke was taken from one compre-hensive collection of sayings (and some stories) of Jesus, or whether it came from two or more independent collections. In the absence of firm evidence a good deal of speculation is involved.

The postulation of this source (or sources) may thus seem to put a lot of uncertainty into attempts to trace the line from Jesus to the completed Gospels. There has been much scepticism regarding the reliability of the transmission of the material; some more radical critics insist that we cannot be sure that any sayings, as they stand, go back to Jesus unless they survive various tests of their authenticity. We cannot be sure (it is said) that the early Christians did not create fresh sayings and attribute them to Jesus (possibly through prophets who claimed to speak in his name), or that sayings were not substantially modified as they were handed down by word of mouth.

Over against such scepticism it is fair to make a number of points. First, the postulation of collections of sayings earlier than Matthew or Luke shows that the sayings were not invented by the evangelists but were in circulation at an earlier stage. Second, various parallels from semi-literate societies (including Middle-Eastern ones) show that, despite individual variations in telling stories, the main substance was handed down with considerable fixity, and the presence of people who had good memories for what we might call the authorized form of the tradition prevented wild deviations. Third, putting arguments of this kind together, it is fair to say that the Gospels give us an accurate picture of 'Jesus Remembered' (the title of a recent detailed defence of this view), and that the onus of proof is on those who claim that this collective memory was faulty or that it deliberately skewed the evidence.

B. Matthew's story of Jesus

Back then to Matthew! His Gospel differs from Mark at the outset by containing an account of the birth of Jesus preceded by a genealogy which links him back to Abraham (as a Jew) and to David (as the starting point of the kingly line). Alongside the genealogy of his earthly pedigree, however, there is the narrative of the conception and birth of Jesus by the Holy Spirit. This shows that he is more than a human being or even a human king, and is rightly understood as 'God with us' (chs. 1 – 2). This extended prologue thus identifies Jesus at the outset in the same way as the statement in Mark 1:1.

After this the story unfolds in a way that follows Mark fairly closely, but can be the better appreciated by noting the similarities and differences. The basic similarity is that it is the same story, virtually all of the incidents in Mark being included in it. Like Mark, it has the same two-part structure in which the companions of Jesus come to recognize him as the Messiah and then accompany him on a journey to Jerusalem. During this journey they learn that the Messiah must suffer and rise again, and then see these things actually happen (3:1 – 16:20; 16:21 – 28:20; note the parallel wording of 4:17 and 16:21). The same essential picture of Jesus emerges.

Although Matthew contains the same stories about Jesus as Mark, there is quite a bit of difference, at least in the earlier chapters, in the order of the material. This shows that, while the evangelists give the same broad picture of the historical course of his mission, many individual stories contained no means of identifying when they happened in relation to one another, or where. So the evangelists were free to arrange them topically rather than chronologically. We cannot expect a day-by-day account of what happened, and we lose nothing of significance by being unable to reconstruct one.

Second, Matthew is much fuller on the sayings and teaching of Jesus than Mark. And where Mark had relatively few connected accounts of Jesus' teaching, Matthew has several extended accounts, clearly structured round particular themes. There is no reason to doubt that Jesus gave an extended 'Sermon on the Mount' (chs. 5 – 7), perhaps repeating the same basic teaching in more than one location. Matthew's account may well incorporate sayings from a number of occasions, and the structure may be partly due to him. Compare how the teaching in 10:17–22 is found in Mark 13:9–13. Such editorial rearrangement and compilation is a fact that is there to be observed. It demonstrates that the evangelists were real authors, not simply annalists recording everything in the precise order and the original wording.

With this emphasis on Jesus' teaching, Matthew brings out more clearly a number of features:

1. The new way of life that Jesus put before his hearers, combining both the blessings that come from the kingdom of God and the demands placed upon its members (chs. 5 – 7).
2. The call to discipleship and mission that he gave them, both for when he was with them on earth and for later (ch. 10).
3. The way in which Jesus used parables to describe how the kingdom of God will grow, and how it will lead to a final consummation in which those who refuse to enter the kingdom will be excluded from its blessings and will suffer unutterable loss (ch. 13).
4. The way in which the followers of Jesus form a community (Matthew alone of the evangelists uses the word 'church') and must relate to one another in love (ch. 18).
5. The need for his followers to be faithful in service of their Master while waiting for his return (chs. 24 – 25).

Interwoven with such themes as these is the way in which the Gospel deals particularly with the attitude of Jesus to the Jewish people, warning their religious leaders against a form of religion which concentrated on trifling matters of ritual while ignoring the great issues of justice and mercy (ch. 23). Running through the Gospel is the tragedy of a people who failed to recognize the Messiah and leaders who failed in their stewardship. Matthew is the Gospel most concerned with the Jewish people, and this may well reflect something of the situation of its author and primary audience, who faced the continuing opposition of many Jews to the Christian church. At the same time it fully recognizes the calling of followers of Jesus to bring the gospel to Gentiles as well as Jews.

C. The origins of the Gospel

Early Christian tradition refers to Matthew, a follower of Jesus (9:9), as the composer of the 'logia' (oracles), and one possibility is that this notice identifies him as the writer of this Gospel. This identification makes the author of the Gospel somebody who had been in the close circle of companions of Jesus. A major difficulty is that the Gospel betrays little or no evidence of being written by somebody personally involved with Jesus. Another possibility is that these oracles were a compilation of teachings of Jesus (perhaps Q – see above on Mark). In this case the Gospel is associated with Matthew less directly, and we simply do not know who the author was. There is insufficient evidence to come to a firm decision.

Nor can a firm date or place of composition be identified. If our reasoning above is correct, it is later than Mark. There is some evidence to connect the Gospel with Antioch in the north of Syria, where there was a substantial Christian presence from an early date.

The special value of Matthew is as a more systematic collection of the teaching of Jesus. It was the most popular Gospel in the early church, if the number of early citations is any guide. Matthew gives the impression of being more of a Gospel for those who are already believers. It is much more concerned than Mark with the ongoing life of the followers of Jesus, as regards both their personal behaviour and their community life. And it is particularly focused on the situation of Christian believers who are Jews, living alongside other Jews and yet standing under the command of Jesus to make disciples from all nations. This is very much a churchy Gospel.

THE GOSPEL OF LUKE

A. *The Gospel and the book of Acts*

The third Gospel differs significantly from the two that we have already considered by the fact that it is the first volume in a two-part work. It is unclear whether Luke intended a two-volume work from the outset, or wrote the Gospel and then later decided (or was persuaded) to write a second volume telling 'what happened next'. In any case the present form and wording of the two books shows that a unified, single whole has resulted. Consequently, the Gospel and Acts each need to be read in the light of the other, and of the whole of which they are parts. Those who later created the NT chose to place Luke alongside the other Gospels and to separate off Acts so that the latter occupied the bridge position between the Gospels and the Epistles. Although the order of the Gospels varies in our earliest manuscripts, none of them keeps Luke and Acts together.

B. *The storyline*

What distinguishes this Gospel from the others? As in the case of Matthew, we appear to have a work that incorporates Mark and expands the story by numerous additions. Like Matthew this Gospel has an account of the birth of Jesus, a rather different story from that in Matthew, told more from Mary's point of view than from Joseph's. It is also interwoven with the story of John the Baptist, who had the role of preparing the people for the coming of Jesus. But it has the same function of letting the readers know the real identity of the main character (chs. 1 – 2).

Thereafter the story follows the now familiar course, keeping to the thread of Mark, but with significant sections of new material and (unlike Matthew) with two lengthy omissions of material (Mark 6:45 – 8:26; 9:42 – 10:12). This was probably sacrificed for the sake of including additional matter from Luke's other sources. (He may have been constrained by the practical consideration of how much could be included in a single scroll or codex.) Where Matthew tended to combine materials from his different sources, Luke's policy was more to alternate between them. It is not inconceivable that the material from Q and Luke's other stories and sayings were combined before Luke then incorporated this material with his revision of Mark.

The resulting Gospel tells the same story but does so in its own distinctive way. What happens is that Luke really gets going in ch. 3 (in a way that might suggest that what preceded was prologue to the main story). Where Matthew places the Sermon on the Mount up front, Luke begins with the scene in Nazareth (brought forward from its position in Mark) because it epitomizes so aptly several key themes: the role of Jesus as the bringer of good news and salvation, the opposition that he (like earlier prophets) faced, and the threat of action against him that would not prevent him from accomplishing his purpose. After this we read the same stories as in Mark and Matthew: Jesus' deliverance of people from diseases, disabilities, demonic possession and the power of sin itself, and his conflict with the Jewish religion and customs of the day. We read a shorter version of the Sermon on the Mount, with the same promises of God's goodness to those in his kingdom, the same demands for a radical ethic of love, the same appeal for self-examination and repentance, and the same choice between acceptance and rejection of his appeal for discipleship.

Luke notes how the theme of Jesus' 'departure' (i.e. his death and resurrection) already surfaces in the story of the transfiguration, following which Jesus sets himself resolutely to go to Jerusalem. But, whereas in Mark and Matthew the departure from Galilee and the arrival in Jericho en route are separated by a comparatively short piece of narrative, in Luke this is expanded to some ten chapters. Here the real interest is the teaching of Jesus to the usual three audiences (followers, crowds and opponents), always set against the foreboding background of what will happen in Jerusalem (9:51 – 19:27). Thereafter the story is again close to Mark, but is noteworthy for the fuller account of what Jesus said to his companions at the last supper (22:14–38) and for the fresh details in the account of his crucifixion. Like Matthew, Luke follows up the account of the discovery of Jesus' empty tomb with narratives of his appearances to various groups of his followers, and lays particular stress on the reality of his resurrection and the call to mission.

C. Some highlights in the Gospel

The way in which Luke handles the story brings out several significant aspects of it. These are not absent from the other Gospels, but they stand out more emphatically in Luke.

(1) Luke brings out more fully the role of Jesus as a prophet, even though this term expresses only part of his role and status as the Messiah. As Messiah he is the Son of God in a way that transcended the relationship of the previous kings of Israel to God. The term 'Son of Man' also expresses his authority as God's agent. And where Matthew and Mark use 'Lord' simply for people addressing Jesus with some respect (cf. our use of 'sir' or 'madam'), Luke also uses the term to convey Jesus' high authority as the exalted Lord, in the way which became normal in the early church (e.g. 'the Lord saw', Luke 7:13; 10:1; cf. Acts 2:36; 10:36).

(2) Again, Luke lays more stress on the role of the Holy Spirit as the empowerer of Jesus (similar to the later experience of his followers), and he draws more attention to the place of prayer in both Jesus' personal practice and his teaching.

(3) Luke's Gospel also depicts more clearly the way in which the proclamation of the kingdom of God and the accompanying mighty works of Jesus brought the benefits of salvation to marginalized people, including women and non-Jews (such as Samaritans).

(4) Finally, Luke highlights the concern of Jesus for the materially poor, and the duty of his followers to be free from love of possessions and to give generously to those in need.

For Luke the story of Christian beginnings is not confined to the story of Jesus on earth. This Gospel is summed up as being about 'all that Jesus began to do and to teach' (Acts 1:1), and it leads on to the story of how Jesus continued to work through his witnesses. Thus the account of his death and exaltation became the basis for a declaration of his roles as saviour and judge; the missions of his followers during his lifetime became the models for the wider mission of the church; and the pattern of Jesus' own life set the pattern for the way of his followers.

D. Theophilus and the author

The formal occasion for this Gospel lay in the further instruction of an otherwise unknown individual called Theophilus. He was probably a

Christian believer already, but needed a written account of what he had been taught orally. This would provide confirmation through careful historical research that made use of material handed down by those involved in the story from its beginning (1:1–4). Luke thus presents his account in a self-consciously historical kind of way. But it is highly important to note that his predecessor, Mark, and his opposite number, Matthew, evidently wrote their Gospels in the same kind of way, so much so that Luke was happy to utilize the work of the former as a major component of his own work. Mark and Matthew's works are no less historical than is Luke's.

Much attention has been given to trying to establish the particular genre or type of writing to which the Gospels belong, and there is a growing consensus (but not a universal recognition) that they are closest to the ancient kind of biography. Biographical writing could be used in the service of commending the particular virtues of a subject (or drawing attention to vices to be avoided). The Gospels partly reflect this, but are more concerned with persuading the readers to believe in Jesus or with strengthening their belief.

It is patently obvious that Theophilus would have known who was the author of the two books sent to him, even if the author is not named within the narrative. In the second volume there are passages in which the author lapses into writing in the first person plural ('we'), thereby identifying himself as a companion of Paul on some of his missionary travels. An undisputed second-century tradition has identified this companion as Luke, referred to by Paul as a physician and missionary colleague (Col. 4:14; 2 Tim. 4:11). This tradition has been questioned for various reasons. In particular, the picture of Paul presented in Acts is said to be sufficiently different from that given by Paul's own writings as to make it doubtful whether a close companion could have written thus about him. For further discussion see the section on Acts in this book. But in summary, the evidence against Luke's authorship is not compelling, and there is no good reason to reject the traditional ascription.

The circumstances of composition are obscure. The preface to the Gospel (which also covers Acts) makes clear that it is written to enable Theophilus, and people like him, to have a reliable basis for their faith. Various suggestions that the books were written to provide evidence for Paul's defence at his trial before the Emperor, or to rehabilitate him against opposition within the church, thus fall from consideration. We should take Luke at his word and see in his work a more comprehensive and more deeply researched account of Jesus and the early church than previously existed. The very fact that Luke tells the story of the early church makes his work fuller than that of any other author – there is no reason to believe that he had any predecessors in this part of his composition.

The date of the finished work clearly cannot be any earlier than the last event recorded, and there is a case that Luke brought his story up to the point at which he was writing. So he did not record the death of Paul, for example, because it had not yet happened. A date somewhat later, to allow time for the development of some perspective on the events recorded, is also possible.

THE GOSPEL OF JOHN

A. The 'different' story

To turn to John from the three Gospels that we have considered so far is to enter what appears to be new territory. There is a considerable degree of resemblance between Matthew, Mark and Luke, in that the general character of their contents, whether shared by two or more of them or peculiar to any one of them, is broadly similar. John's Gospel, however, stands somewhat apart.

It begins with a prologue that is more like a theological meditation interwoven with some historical reference (1:1–18). Its main purpose is to identify Jesus as the human incarnation of the Word of God, a phrase that might seem abstract but refers rather to a personal being sharing the nature and functions of God. Then a story begins, commencing (like the other Gospels) with the activity of John the Baptist as a witness to Jesus. As a result various people come into contact with Jesus and believe in him as the Messiah (1:19–51). The action shifts from Judea, where John was active, to Galilee, where Jesus makes an impact at a wedding (ch. 2). Then he goes to Jerusalem for the Passover, makes a demonstration in the temple (contrast the placing of such an incident at the end of his life in the other Gospels), and has a significant interview with Nicodemus and a conversation about new birth (ch. 3).

Jesus returns to Galilee via Samaria, where he has another significant scene with an individual, this time a woman. Some time afterwards he revisits Jerusalem for an unnamed festival, at which he heals a paralysed man. This incident becomes the occasion for an extended discourse by Jesus (chs. 4 – 5). Then he is back in Galilee where he feeds the large crowd who came to hear him in the desert, and again there is a lengthy dialogue (ch. 6). Although he wanted to stay in Galilee because opposition to him was mounting in Judea, he nevertheless went up to Jerusalem for another feast (Tabernacles), where his public teaching in the precincts of the temple led to further controversy, largely concerned with whether he was the Messiah (chs. 7 – 8). A blind man is healed in Jerusalem, and again the incident becomes the occasion for a series of dialogues (chs. 9 – 10).

Jesus spends some time away from Jerusalem east of the Jordan, and then returns to the neighbourhood of Jerusalem where he raises Lazarus from his tomb. The effect of this is to reinforce the determination of the Jewish authorities to do away with him (ch. 11). Once again he leaves Jerusalem but does not go far away, and then returns to ride into the city. Some Greeks attending the festival meet up with his followers (ch. 12). He gathers with his close companions for a meal at which he, the host, washes their feet. Then comes a long dialogue in which he tries to prepare them for a future time without his physical presence with them, when they will experience severe opposition but must continue to be his witnesses and will have the help of the Advocate, i.e. the Holy Spirit (chs. 13 – 16). A lengthy prayer by Jesus is recorded (ch. 17). This is followed by Jesus going to a garden where he is arrested and taken for examination before the high priest. There is a lengthier examination before the Roman governor Pilate, which issues in his condemnation to death and crucifixion (18 – 19). The story of the discovery of his tomb is told, but in this version the resurrected Jesus appears to his follower Mary in the vicinity of the tomb, and there are accounts of his appearances to his followers as a group in Jerusalem (ch. 20; cf. Luke's account). The Gospel appears to come to an end, but a further story of an appearance by the shore of Galilee is added (ch. 21).

B. Explaining the differences

This outline story is clearly different from the one found in the other Gospels, in that it has repeated visits by Jesus to Jerusalem for Jewish festivals (perfectly credible for a pious Jewish male in the light of Jewish customs), and a good deal of the action takes place there. Nevertheless, the two accounts can be slotted into each other. Jesus also acts and teaches in different ways. The list of mighty works performed by him is different (except for the feeding of the crowd and his walking on the water of Galilee), although they are of the same general kind. The way in which the mighty works often become the starting point for teaching and dialogue goes well beyond what happens in the other Gospels.

It is possible to find many individual sayings of Jesus in this Gospel that are very similar to the things he says in the other Gospels. Nevertheless, there are no examples of the parables that are so characteristic of the other three Gospels, apart from some brief similes that look like undeveloped parables. The vocabulary of John is smaller than that of the other Gospels (roughly 1,000 words, compared with 2,000 in Luke), but the principal theological terms employed are somewhat different. Where the 'kingdom of God/heaven' is a major term in the other Gospels, in John it is almost absent.

Some points that receive greater emphasis in this Gospel are:

1. There is much more open discussion of Jesus' identity. Jesus speaks about his personal relationship to God as his Son and this is challenged by his audience.

2. There are extended passages in which Jesus' significance is explained in terms of physical images like bread, a vine, the gate of a sheepfold and the shepherd with his flock, and abstract images such as resurrection, life and truth. All this goes well beyond the traditional concept of the Messiah and represents the new understanding of Jesus and his followers.

3. Correspondingly, this Gospel emphasizes the need for faith in the dual sense of believing what Jesus says and committing oneself to him.

4. The teaching of Jesus about humanity is structured by a more conspicuous dualism of light and darkness, righteousness and sin, life and death. Salvation from judgment consists positively in eternal life, and this life is essentially a personal relationship with God and Jesus expressed in terms of people being in fellowship with one another.

5. There is much fuller teaching on the role of the Holy Spirit as the Counsellor and Helper ('Advocate', TNIV) in helping the followers of Jesus after he has left them.

6. There is less emphasis on the final return of Jesus (though it is not absent) and more on his spiritual relationship with his followers here and now.

The basic storyline certainly remains the same. The earlier part of the Gospel is concerned with Jesus' identity and teaching to the people in general, and the latter part with his teaching to his committed followers. There is no difficulty in principle in holding that this writer told the story from a different angle to the other evangelists. One group of artists might paint broadly similar pictures of a particular scene, while another artist (an Impressionist perhaps) might produce something extraordinarily different which nevertheless expresses what was there all along. Hence we have the famous statement of Clement of Alexandria (c. AD 200) that 'last of all John wrote a spiritual gospel'.

Two extreme positions exist. One is that Jesus literally said and did everything recorded in all the Gospels and was capable of speaking and behaving in two rather different idioms. The other is that the Gospel of John is simply untrue and contradicts the picture gained from the other more realistic Gospels. In between there is the view that John has written a Gospel based on sources with the same level of ascertainable historical reliability as the other Gospels, but has cast it in his own unique idiom to present the true significance of Jesus.

C. The origin of the Gospel

The identity of the author is much disputed. No name is given in the Gospel itself, but there are several references to a follower for whom Jesus had a particular affection and a concluding note that he wrote the Gospel, followed by an attestation of reliability by his associates (21:24). Internal evidence suggests that he was John, the son of Zebedee, and this was the view taken in the early church. Other less plausible identifications have been made, e.g. Lazarus. It is also often argued that, while John was the authority behind the Gospel, somebody else may have written up his testimony.

The occasion for writing the Gospel of John is unknown. There have been many speculative reconstructions of a Christian community in which the material in the Gospel was gradually put together in the form that we now have, but these remain hypothetical. As with the other Gospels, John's expressed purpose should be taken seriously: to persuade people to believe in Jesus as the Messiah and Son of God (20:30–31). This purpose is broad enough to challenge non-believers and to strengthen the faith of believers by enlarging their knowledge of Jesus.

Many readers have had the same impression as Clement, that this Gospel presupposes the existence of the other three and was in fact the latest to be written. Others have argued that it was composed independently by a writer with information about Jesus (whether personal memory or community traditions) unknown to or not used by the other evangelists. In this case there is no necessary reason for dating his Gospel later than theirs. We don't know, and it doesn't really matter.

READING THE GOSPELS

What are we to do with the Gospels? One thing is clear at the outset. Over the centuries people with little or no knowledge of Christianity have read the Gospels and come to living faith in Jesus. Possibly the Gospel of John has been most used in this way. These books retain their comprehensibility and their power to change lives. Yet this basic fact should not mask the various difficulties of reading them.

First, there is the fact that the Gospels were originally written in Greek and have been translated into many other languages – just as in its own time the teaching of Jesus needed to be translated from Aramaic into Greek. But translation may need to be accompanied by some explanation, to put later readers as far as possible into the position of the original readers. They understood not only Greek, but also what kind of people were named Pharisees, or what the Jewish regulations about clean and unclean foods were, or what was meant by the phrase 'Son of Man'. Reading through the parable of the vineyard, for example, we may not get the point because we do not know that a vine or vineyard was a long-standing symbol for the Jewish people, whereas Jewish hearers would easily get the point that their rulers were failing in their responsibilities towards the 'owner' of the nation, God himself. Commentaries exist to provide readers with such basic background material. We should not be surprised that the Gospels need to be read within an interpretative community, and it is a myth that we can understand everything in them by ourselves.

One very important case of this background knowledge is that much of Jewish religious teaching was naturally taken from their Scriptures, our Old Testament. All the Gospels contain citations from the OT and other less obvious allusions to it. Matthew in particular has a series of quotations to show how the story of Jesus corresponds in important details with patterns and prophecies in the OT. It is essential to recognize when this is happening, and the use of a Bible which indicates quotations and verbal allusions is very helpful.

Second, there are some statements whose meaning was largely self-evident to those who understood the language and concepts involved. Jesus told a story about some tenant-farmers left in charge of a vineyard who failed to behave responsibly and maltreated the owner's agents. Mark comments that the Jewish leaders who heard the story 'looked for a way to arrest him because they knew he had spoken the parable against them' (Mark 12:12). They got the point!

But there were also occasions when Jesus spoke cryptically and even the people of his time were puzzled:

'I am with you for only a short time, and then I go to the one who sent me. You will look for me, but you will not find me; and where I am, you cannot come.' The Jews said to one another, 'Where does this man intend to go that we cannot find him . . . ? What did he mean when he said . . . "Where I am, you cannot come"?' (John 7:33–36).

In some cases we know the meaning because we have fuller knowledge in light of what subsequently happened, and we know that Jesus was speaking about his return to be with his Father. At other times it may not be so easy. When Jesus told one story about farming, even his closest friends could not understand what he was getting at and asked him what it meant (Mark 4:10). Jesus seems to have expected them to understand, but needed to supplement this and other such stories with an explanation (Mark 4:33–34). We might compare the way in which the Bible contains several accounts of dreams that were believed to have a meaning, but the dreamers could not get the message and had to find an interpreter. In the Gospels there are some texts that were expected to convey a clear message, and others that were meant to make people think about their significance.

And, third, there is the question of whether what Jesus says is credible and should be accepted. He said, 'I am the light of the world. Whoever follows me will never walk in darkness, but will have the light of life' (John 8:12). The Pharisees responded, 'Here you are, appearing as your own witness; your testimony is not valid' (John 8:13). Clearly they did not accept his affirmation. And throughout the Gospels there are many instances of people not believing what he said.

It has been said that 'A Gospel is more of a creed than a biography; it is a proclamation of faith.'[1] While a Gospel is partly biography, it is more like the statement 'I believe that Jesus is the Son of God', which challenges me to consider whether I could make the same affirmation. John makes this clear when he sums up what he has been doing in his Gospel:

> Jesus performed many other signs in the presence of his disciples which are not recorded in this book. But these are written that you may believe that Jesus is the Messiah, the Son of God, and that by believing you may have life in his name. (John 20:30–31)

It is because of this faith perspective that many wonder whether the evangelists were tempted consciously and unconsciously to play around with the facts and put a spin on them to make their narratives more persuasive. The question is crucially important because so much is at stake. On a humbler level a political party may aim to win an election and attempt to do so by making promises that cannot be kept. The Gospels are concerned with belief about what matters most in human life, the identity of Jesus as the Messiah and his role as the Saviour of the world – and our own Saviour. The question of truth is at stake.

There are two questions that are sometimes confused. One is whether Jesus' recorded words and actions show that he understood himself to be the Messiah. The other is whether such a self-understanding was correct. The problem may be seen by thinking of some contemporary person who is said to suffer from delusions because he claims to be the Messiah. We would need reliable evidence that he actually made these claims, but we would also need to ask whether he was in fact the Messiah. Concerning the former, we would like to have reliable evidence of what he said, for example, the testimony of trustworthy witnesses. In theory at least it should be possible to find these, although there may be many difficulties, and we might have to be content with less than absolute certainty. We might not have much difficulty in deciding that he was deluded (e.g. because he showed other signs of abnormality), but there might always be the niggling trace of doubt that maybe our judgment is mistaken and perhaps that person is actually what he claims to be.

Similarly, it is one thing to enquire historically into what lies behind the narratives in the Gospels; it is another to decide whether the narrative conveys ultimate truth. To answer the first question is a historical enquiry; to answer the second is to take a step of faith. And unfortunately it is difficult to separate the two questions from one another. Many a historian has examined the narratives on the basis of a set of beliefs that exclude the possibility of (say) a dead person being resurrected, and the result of the enquiry is therefore foreclosed in advance. Others, whose beliefs include that possibility, may too easily accept the historicity of the narratives or adopt a certain interpretation of the evidence without sufficiently careful examination. Complete objectivity is difficult, if not impossible.

This book is written from a standpoint of faith by people who have been persuaded by the kind of things written by John in his Gospel. Nevertheless, we have to tackle the historical questions in a responsible manner, in order to help people who cannot believe that things happened just as they are narrated simply because (in the words of an old hymn) 'the Bible tells me so'. An introduction to the Gospels, therefore, has to provide information that will help contemporary readers to decide whether they can trust the story. But in the end they must make their own response to that story.

USING THE GOSPELS TODAY

There are two broad types of approach to Christian use of the Gospels. One is to read the Gospels as presumably they were intended to be read, right through from start to finish, as complete works. It doesn't take that long: they are much shorter than the Oxford series of 'Very Short Guides'! What is the total impression made by the story? How do the various parts contribute to the meaning of the whole, and how do they become more comprehensible in light of the total account? The other approach is to read the Gospels in short sections and ponder their meaning closely. Each section needs close investigation to get the full effect of the details.

From an early date Christians divided up the Gospels into short sections for consecutive reading Sunday by Sunday, and thus achieved something of a compromise between the two approaches. Another type of reading consisted in weaving together the texts of the four Gospels to produce a single account (called a 'harmony') in which everything in each Gospel was included – although differences in the recording of the same incidents or sayings would tend to be ironed out in favour of one version. This type of composition is not without its value, but it is open to the obvious criticism that it flattens out the four distinct accounts of Jesus, each with their own individual artistry, into one rather bland narrative.

We have noted that the Gospels were written for slightly different audiences and situations. Mark and John are both concerned with presenting the story of Jesus in a way that will especially help not-yet believers, although they are also intended to be of value to believers. Luke is part of a larger work aimed at strengthening the faith of a believer who has so far had to reply on oral accounts, and who wanted a coherent written record of what he had heard piecemeal. And Matthew looks more like an orderly textbook for the instruction of the Christian congregation and its workers as they lead the congregation and engage in evangelism and face controversy. Each of the Gospels could be used for any of these purposes, but each has its own special angle on the story of Jesus.

Similar audiences have existed ever since then, and readers today have the same kind of needs, although their actual situations are different. Few of us today live in direct contact with Jewish groups who would question whether Jesus is the Messiah or would argue that the Messiah is still to come. In the western world few of us live in situations where religion and politics are so closely associated as in ancient Judea, although it is different for people in, say, a Moslem or Hindu setting. Many of us live in urban and global settings rather different from the rural world in which Jesus and his followers lived, although we should not underestimate the degree of 'globalization' that had already taken place. Alexander the Great had conquered much of the known world and imposed Greek language and culture upon it, and the Romans had then set up their imperial system all round the Mediterranean Sea. We have to do some transposition in order to think ourselves back into the ancient world and apply to ourselves the teaching given then. It is therefore important that we learn to recognize the basic principles of living under the rule of God taught by Jesus in ways appropriate to his first-century context, and then learn to apply these basic principles to ourselves in our different situations.

One key question is how we apply the teaching given to individuals in their personal relationships to ourselves in our social relationships: what does loving my neighbour (never mind my enemy!) mean if I am the director of a commercial company and my neighbour is the director of a business rival (Matt. 22:39)? Or how do I 'turn the other cheek' if I am a soldier engaged in a war for the defence of my country (Matt. 5:39)? And how do I act in the spirit of 'Do not judge, or you too will be judged' (Matt. 7:1) if I am a magistrate? These questions have often been ignored, despite the fact that they are of crucial importance for what people do with the major part of their time, and despite the fact that they arise in the Gospels (see Luke 3:10–14). Reading the Gospels is going to be challenging, and perhaps upsetting!

Note

[1.] J. Ashton, *Understanding the Fourth Gospel* (Oxford, Clarendon, 1991), p. 432.

Further reading (see Introduction for good commentary series)

Steve Walton and David Wenham, *Exploring the New Testament 1. The Gospels and Acts* (SPCK 2001) – excellent introduction, with panels highlighting themes and points to ponder.

Richard Burridge, *Four Gospels, One Jesus?* (SPCK, 2nd edn 2003) – lively, lucid exposition of the four portraits of Jesus.

Craig Blomberg, *Jesus and the Gospels: An Introduction and Survey* (IVP, 1997) – well-written guide to all the key points.

Craig Blomberg, *The Historical Reliability of the Gospels* (IVP, 1987) – clear, carefully reasoned defence of this important issue.

.

10. Acts

Mark Strauss

As a companion volume to the Gospel of Luke, Acts continues the story of the Christian movement from the ascension of Jesus and the coming of the Spirit on the day of Pentecost, to Paul's arrival in Rome – a period of about thirty years. While the Gospel records what Jesus 'began to do' through his life, death, resurrection and ascension, Acts records what he continues to do as the risen head of the church through the Holy Spirit he has poured out (1:1; 2:33).

A. Unity and purpose of Luke–Acts

The Gospel of Luke and the book of Acts were written by the same author. This is evident in that they are addressed to the same recipient (Theophilus), share similar style and vocabulary, have common themes and theology, and are cross-referenced ('my former book', 1:1). Yet Acts is more than just a second book written by Luke. It is the second part of a two-volume work ('Luke–Acts'). When Luke wrote the Gospel he probably already had the book of Acts in mind. The two form a *literary and theological* unity.

This conclusion has important implications for the way we approach both books. (1) Luke and Acts should be read as a single narrative. The story that begins in the first chapter of the Gospel does not come to its conclusion till the end of Acts. (2) Luke and Acts share common themes and theology which should be progressively followed through both volumes. (3) Luke and Acts were written with a common purpose.

The prologue of the Gospel, which probably serves as an introduction to both volumes, states Luke's purpose. He is writing so that Theophilus might know 'the certainty of the things you have been taught' (Luke 1:4). Luke's overall purpose is *the confirmation of the gospel*, i.e. the veracity of the gospel *message* and the gospel *messengers*. He writes to show that God's great plan of salvation has come to fulfilment in the events of Jesus' life, death, resurrection and ascension, and continues to unfold in the growth and expansion of the church.

B. Central message of Acts

How does the book of Acts fit into this broader purpose of Luke–Acts? The first chapter gives us the key to Luke's central theme. Following his resurrection and before his ascension, Jesus commands his disciples to remain in Jerusalem until they receive the Holy Spirit:

> But you will receive power when the Holy Spirit comes on you; and you will be my witnesses in Jerusalem, and in all Judea and Samaria, and to the ends of the earth (1:8).

The rest of the book tells how the church, filled and empowered by the Holy Spirit, takes the message of salvation from Jerusalem to the ends of the earth. Throughout Acts the gospel advances despite strong opposition and apparent setbacks. Persecution and imprisonment only strengthen the church (4:23–31; 5:41–42; 8:4; 12:24; 16:16–40; 28:30–31). In an ironic episode, the Pharisee Gamaliel warns the Sanhedrin that if the Christian movement is not from God, it will surely fail; but if it is from God, they will not be able to stop it (5:33–40). The unstoppable progress of the gospel confirms that the church – including both Jews and Gentiles – represents the true people of God in the new age of salvation.

C. Occasion of Acts

Luke writes at a time of increasing challenges for the church. While many Gentiles have responded positively to the gospel message, most Jews are rejecting it. This raises many questions: (1) How can Jesus be the Messiah if he died on a cross like a criminal? (2) How can the salvation have arrived if the Messiah is not reigning in Jerusalem? (3) How can Israel's promises be fulfilled if most Jews are rejecting the gospel? (4) How can the church be the people of God if it is increasingly made up of Gentiles who are uncircumcised and do not keep the OT law?

Luke's narrative provides answers to these questions. (1) Jesus is indeed the Messiah, as confirmed through signs and wonders which God performed through him (2:22; 9:22). Furthermore, Scripture predicted that the Messiah would die and rise from the dead (2:30–31; 3:18; 17:3; 26:23; Luke 24:26, 46). (2) God's great salvation has indeed arrived, as evidenced by Jesus' exaltation to the right hand of God as Messiah and Lord, and his pouring out of the Spirit of God (2:17, 33–35). (3) While many Jews are rejecting the gospel, a remnant is being saved (2:41; 4:4; 6:7; 21:20). Furthermore, this rejection was predicted in Scripture, and is part of Israel's history as a stubborn and resistant people (7:51–53; 13:40–41, 46). (4) The mission to the Gentiles was also predicted in Scripture as part of God's end-time salvation. It was not instigated by any human being, but by God himself (10 – 11:18; 13:47; 15:1–29; 28:28–29). Paul of Tarsus – the apostle to the Gentiles – is not a renegade Jew preaching against the traditions of Judaism, but is God's faithful instrument to bring salvation to the Gentiles (9:15–16; 13:46–48; 22:21; 26:20).

In addition to these Jewish challenges, the infant church is facing increasing hostility from the Gentile world. Luke seeks to show that Christians like Paul are not renegades and troublemakers, but law abiding citizens with a message of hope and salvation for the world (16:37–40; 18:12–15; 19:35–41; 22:22–29; 23:27–30; chs. 24 – 28).

D. Structure of Acts

An outline of Acts can be derived from its theme verse, 1:8. The book progresses outward geographically, from Jerusalem to Judea, to Samaria, and beyond. It climaxes in Rome, the symbolic 'ends of the earth', with Paul freely proclaiming the gospel message to Jews and Gentiles alike (28:30–31). The book also progresses ethnically, as first Jews, then Samaritans, and finally Gentiles received the message. Much of Luke's purpose is to show that the salvation of the Gentiles was all along part of God's purpose and plan.

1:1 – 8:3	The gospel to Jerusalem
8:4 – 12:25	The gospel to Judea, Samaria and Syria
13:1 – 28:31	The gospel to the ends of the earth

E. Themes and theology

1. The Holy Spirit as sign of the new age

For Luke the coming of the Spirit marks the dawn of the new age. The OT prophets predicted that in the last days God would pour out his Spirit on all humanity (2:17–21; Joel 2:28–32). Now resurrected and ascended to God's right hand, Jesus pours out the Spirit to fill, empower and guide the church (2:33). In many ways the Spirit is the leading character of Acts, referred to over sixty times. Throughout Acts reception of the Spirit marks entrance into the people of God (2:38; 8:17; 11:17; 15:8; 19:6). The Spirit fills and empowers believers (2:4; 4:8, 31; 6:3, 5; 7:55; 9:17; 11:24) and guides the progress of the gospel (8:29, 39; 10:19; 11:28; 13:2, 9; 16:6, 7; 21:4). The Spirit of God is the Spirit of Christ, his presence among his people (Acts 16:6, 7).

2. God's purpose and plan

The theme of divine sovereignty and purpose permeates Luke's narrative. God ordained not only the death and resurrection of Jesus, but also that salvation would now go to the ends of the earth. Throughout Luke, there is the overriding concern that what is happening is the work of God – the Greek term *dei*, meaning 'it is necessary', occurs forty times in Luke–Acts. Though wicked men put Jesus to death, this was God's plan, accomplishing salvation by raising him from the dead (2:23–24; cf. Luke 24:7, 26–27, 44–47; Acts 3:18; 4:28).

3. To the Jew first

Luke strongly stresses the theme of promise and fulfilment, and the continuity between the old and new covenants. Though writing from a Gentile perspective, he firmly grounds the Gospel in its Jewish roots. Jesus is the Jewish Messiah who fulfils the promises of the Hebrew Scriptures (Luke 1:32–35; 2:11; Acts 2:36). The birth narrative at the beginning of the Gospel plunges the reader into the world of first-century Judaism (Luke 1 – 2). The characters we meet represent the faithful remnant of Israel eagerly longing for the Messiah (2:25–26). In Acts the original disciples are all Jews who continue to worship in the temple and proclaim Jesus to be Messiah, the fulfilment of Israel's hopes. The salvation Jesus accomplishes is the 'consolation of Israel' (Luke 2:25), the fulfilment of the promises made to the Jewish nation (2:39). The gospel finds huge initial success in Jerusalem as thousands respond

(2:41; 4:4; 6:7; 21:20). When Paul enters a city, he preaches first to the Jews and then turns to the Gentiles. Salvation comes forth from Israel and goes first to Israel.

4. The Gentile mission

Despite this emphasis on salvation for Israel, the key theme of Acts is the outward expansion of the gospel, both geographically and ethnically. As many Jews reject the message, the church increasingly becomes a Gentile entity. Luke writes to justify the Gentile mission by showing that the mission to the Gentiles is not a departure from God's purpose for Israel, but is its fulfilment, predicted in Scripture (15:15–18). Paul, God's apostle to the Gentiles, is not unfaithful to his Jewish roots, but is fulfilling God's purpose for Israel: to be a light of revelation to the Gentiles (13:47; Isa. 49:6).

F. Authorship, date and audience

Both the Gospel and Acts have been traditionally ascribed to Luke, a physician and part-time missionary companion of the apostle Paul (Col. 4:14; 2 Tim. 4:11; Philm. 24). Col. 4:11–14 implies that Luke was a Gentile, which would fit well with the author's strong emphasis that the good news is for all people everywhere.

The tradition of Lukan authorship can be traced back to the middle of the second century, and there are no statements in the early church that would point to any other author. Considering Luke's relative obscurity in the NT, it is unlikely that a Gospel would have been attributed to him had he not been the author. There is also the internal evidence of the 'we' sections in Acts, which confirm that the author was at times a companion of Paul (16:10–17; 20:5–21; 21:1–18; 27:1 – 28:16). Though Paul had other companions (Mark, Timothy, Titus, Silas, Barnabas, etc.), when this internal evidence is placed beside the strong and unanimous external testimony, there seems no reason to doubt Luke's authorship. While authorship by Luke remains the most likely option, other scholars opt for an unknown author – perhaps drawing on sources compiled by a companion of Paul – writing in the last decade of the first century AD. In any case, it should be noted that Lukan authorship is part of church tradition rather than the inspired text. Like the other Gospels, Luke and Acts are anonymous, strictly speaking, and their inspiration and authority do not depend on the traditional view of their authorship.

The date of Acts is uncertain. Since Paul is alive and in prison in Rome at the end of Acts (about AD 60), some believe that Luke finished writing before Paul's release and later martyrdom. This would place its writing sometime around AD 60–62. The Gospel of Luke would then be dated sometime prior to this, perhaps in the late 50s.

On the other hand, if Mark was the first Gospel written (as seems likely), and was composed in the late 60s shortly before the destruction of Jerusalem (see Mark 13:14), Luke's Gospel must have come later, perhaps in the 70s or later. In this case, Luke would have had a different reason for ending his Gospel with Paul alive in Rome, perhaps to show that the gospel message was reaching 'the ends of the earth' (1:8).

Luke addresses both his books to Theophilus, who was probably the patron who sponsored their writing (1:1; Luke 1:1–4). Yet Luke clearly writes to a larger audience, probably mostly Gentile churches who are wrestling with their identity as the true people of God. Luke assures believers of the historical foundation for their faith. The coming of Jesus and the growth of his church represents the culmination of God's purpose and plan for the salvation of the world.

G. Reading Acts today

The reader of Acts should first recognize what it is *not*:

1. It is not an 'Acts of the Apostles' in the sense of a history of the twelve apostles. The Twelve appear in the early chapters and then mostly disappear from the narrative. Peter shows up again in chs. 10 – 12 and 15, but we learn nothing about the later ministries of the other eleven apostles or their ultimate fate. The second half of the book (chs. 13 – 28) mostly concerns the ministry of another apostle, Paul, rather than that of the Twelve.

2. Nor is Acts a history of the early church. While it provides an account of the church's growth in Judea, Samaria and Syria, and then through Paul's ministry into Asia Minor, Greece and Rome, these accounts are highly selective and little is said about the church's outreach into many other regions (Egypt, Libya, Arabia, Cappadocia, etc.).

3. Further, Acts is not a manual on church polity and order. Many readers come to Acts for direction on how to administer the church. Yet not everything that happens in Acts is meant to establish the pattern for the church today. Many critical issues of church order and function are barely addressed in Acts, or do not follow a consistent pattern. This includes things like church governance (rule by elders, bishops or congregation?), baptism (immersion or sprinkling? infants or believers?), the Lord's Supper (frequency of observance? spiritual significance?), the reception of the Spirit (at

conversion? following baptism? accompanied by tongue-speaking?). The point is that Luke was not intending to write a handbook on how to run the church. Rather, his purpose was to demonstrate how the church, filled and empowered by the Holy Spirit, crossed geographical and ethnic boundaries to take the good news of Jesus Christ from Jerusalem to the ends of the earth.

Acts should therefore be read for what it is: *historical narrative motivated by theological concerns*. Luke's stated purpose is historical: to give Theophilus an authoritative account of the origin of the Christian faith (Luke 1:1–4). This historical purpose continues in Acts (1:1) with the account of the growth and expansion of the church. Functioning on this level, Acts give us a (limited) glimpse of the early church and provides the historical background for the letters of Paul.

Yet Luke writes not merely as an historian, but also as an evangelist and theologian, seeking to convince his readers of the spiritual significance of these salvation-bringing events. His account is therefore selective, focusing on key persons and events which are meant to confirm that the coming of Jesus and the growth of the church represent God's purpose for the world.

What has been said above confirms the abiding relevance of the book of Acts for the church today. The book is not dry and dusty ancient history; it is *our* history and *our* heritage. Acts tells us who we are as a Christian movement and how we came into being. It reminds us what it means to be the church: a Spirit-filled and Spirit-directed body of believers whose purpose is to cross every ethnic and geographical boundary to take the message of salvation to the ends of the earth. The same Jesus Christ whose death and resurrection the early church proclaimed still reigns at God's right hand as head of his church. The same Spirit who was poured out on believers on the Day of Pentecost is still empowering and guiding the church today.

Further reading (see **Introduction** for good commentary series)

Steve Walton and David Wenham, *Exploring the New Testament 1. The Gospels and Acts* (SPCK 2001) – excellent introduction, with panels highlighting themes and points to ponder.
Craig Blomberg, *From Pentecost to Patmos: An Introduction and Survey* (IVP 2006) – well-written guide to the key issues.

11. Letters

Ian Paul, Brian Rosner and Carl Mosser

INTRODUCTION

A. Letters in the New Testament

A significant proportion of the NT – something like 40% – consists of letters. The simplest classification would be to group them as 'written by Paul' (the majority) and 'the rest'. But in fact the letters are of several types:

- Those written by one or more individuals to a church. This includes most of Paul's letters and 2 John.
- Those written by an individual to several churches as a kind of circular. This includes Galatians (written to the churches in a region), probably Ephesians, 1 and 2 Peter and Jude.
- Those written by an individual to other individuals. This includes Philemon, 1 and probably 2 Timothy, Titus and 3 John.
- Those called 'letters' but lacking some of the formal features of written letters, and apparently with a wide audience in mind. This includes Hebrews and James.

In addition, Revelation has many of the formal features of a letter, but is clearly something more, and the texts of two letters are included within Acts (in chs. 15 and 23).

Sections in this chapter were written as follows – Ian Paul: Introduction, 1 & 2 Timothy and Titus, James to Jude; Brian Rosner: Paul's letters, Romans to 2 Thessalonians, Philemon; Carl Mosser: Hebrews.

B. Letters in the ancient world

Letter writing developed in the ancient world whenever information needed to be recorded or when face-to-face communication was not possible. Letter writing only flourished under certain social and cultural conditions, notably the existence of a reliable network of communication. But for letter writing to become important, there had to be a consistent need, and this primarily arose from the administration of empires.

From as far back as the eighteenth century BC we have evidence of regular letter writing from empires in Mesopotamia. By NT times letter writing was an important part of the administration of the Roman empire, aided by the development of the road network which was first designed to allow rapid movement of troops. The Emperor Augustus had developed a postal system that allowed official letters to travel on horseback at a rate of fifty miles a day. Private letters would use the same network of roads, but would have to be carried by a slave, friend or trusted stranger going to the right destination.

C. Letter format

As today, ancient letters followed a conventional pattern and this remained constant for several centuries:
- *Opening*, containing the names of sender and recipient, a greeting, and usually some form of wish for good health.
- *Thanksgiving*, thanking the gods for some aspect of good news about the recipient.
- *Body of the letter*, with the main message to be conveyed.
- *Closing*, with final greetings, possibly from other people connected with the sender, and a final wish for good health.

The letters of the NT mostly show this conventional pattern, but often adapt and extend it.

In the *opening* the NT writers frequently add some form of self-designation. For example, Paul usually calls himself 'apostle' but sometimes 'servant' or 'prisoner'. Paul also frequently adds the names of others as co-writers. This was unusual in Greek letter writing, so we must assume that these others made a real contribution to the contents and construction of the letters.

Paul's letters in particular develop the *thanksgiving* section. His letters are regularly marked by praise for the faithfulness of the church and a reminder of God's faithfulness, and often include a report of the way Paul prays for the church. Sometimes these thanksgivings flow into the body of the letter so that it is hard to see where one finishes and the other begins. In 2 Corinthians, Ephesians and 1 Peter the (Greek) thanksgiving is replaced by a (Jewish) blessing of God. Galatians is notable for omitting the thanksgiving altogether.

The *body* of the NT letters varies widely. In 1 Corinthians we have perhaps the best example of conventional letter-like correspondence, as Paul answers questions he has been asked in a letter from Christians in Corinth (see 1 Cor. 7:1). The body of Romans appears to be a much more general statement of Paul's understanding of the gospel, in preparation for asking support for the next stage of his missionary work. But some 'letters' read much more like written sermons (e.g. Hebrews), and others consist of general exhortations (e.g. James). Throughout the body of their letters, NT authors deploy a whole range of rhetorical techniques.

The *closing* section also involves developments from the standard pattern, while still retaining the basic shape. Paul often includes (sometimes extensive) greetings from others in leadership with him. He ends with a blessing rather than a farewell, and this at times develops into a short piece of liturgy, suggesting that Paul expected his letters to be read to the community in the context of a meeting for worship.

This all shows the range of purposes that the NT letters have – something mirrored, in fact, in secular letter writing. For example, the Roman philosopher Seneca (also writing in the first century) wrote a large number of letters to a friend which were, in effect, essays on questions of ethics.

D. Significance of letters in the New Testament

We are so used to having letters in the NT – and for many Christians, some letters are the part they are most familiar with – that we might not have reflected on how unusual this is. The correspondence of an individual to another individual or small group at a particular time and place has become recognized as God's word, in some way or other, to all Christians at all times and in all places. This highlights two key issues.

First, it reminds us that these documents are *acts of communication* between people. All too often, the Bible is treated as an object to be studied which sets out certain doctrines to be believed – and the pastoral implications are somehow seen as detached and secondary. But in the NT letters we find belief expressed in the context of pastoral relationships, doctrine interleaved with the consequences for individuals and their relationships.

As a spin-off, this also reminds us how interconnected the communities of the early church were. The communications network of the Roman empire meant that the traffic of both individuals and theology flowed relatively freely between one community and another. It is now less and less sustainable to argue that there were distinct Christian communities with their rival theologies battling it out for influence in the young church.

Secondly, we need to recognize the *particular circumstances* that each letter was written for. Most of the letters are 'occasional'; that is, in contrast to stories of historical events or collections of wise sayings, or gatherings of the praise songs of God's people, letters were written for a specific purpose to address a particular situation. In reading the letters, we are wanting to hear *God* speak *to us* in the *here* and *now* through what (say) *Paul* said to the *Corinthians* in the *there* and *then*. We are eavesdropping, as it were, on the conversation of another, and we need to bear this in mind as we think about interpreting the letters, that is, as we seek to make sense of them as God's word to us.

Of course, these two factors are true to some extent for every section of the Bible and every kind of writing in it. But the letters serve to offer a particular reminder of these features, which we need to bear in mind whenever we open the Scriptures.

E. Interpreting the letters

A helpful way to approach any text of the Bible is to ask three questions: 'what?', 'why?' and 'how?' What was the author saying to the first hearers of this text? Why was this said in this way at this time? How does this relate to our own situation and speak into it? Problems arise when we move too quickly from the 'what?' to the 'how?', and the particularity of each letter makes it especially important that we reflect on all three questions.

We need to be aware that the letters were written in a particular *cultural context*. So we might read Rom. 1 differently when we realize that Paul's critique of the secular world parallels closely the kind of critique that Jews offered of Greek culture – something Paul then turns on its head in Rom. 2. It will shape our reading of 1 Cor. 11 if we know something about the assumptions made in the first century about human anatomy, and in particular the significance of hair. 1 Cor. 8 makes much more sense when we are aware of the availability of meat and its relation to pagan temple worship.

We also need to be aware of *questions of vocabulary* and the use of language. Much ink has been spilled concerning the meaning of 'head' in 1 Cor. 11:3f.; the use of 1 Tim. 2:12 will depend on what we think the unusual word 'to take authority' meant to Paul's first-century readers.

The *occasional nature* of the letters will also guard us against thinking that these are systematic guides to Christian belief and practice. If the Corinthians hadn't had problems with celebrating the Lord's Supper together, making it necessary for Paul to write a few paragraphs in 1 Cor. 11:17–34, we would know little about the importance of this in the early church, aside from the brief reference in Acts 2:42 and evidence from the second century. It is difficult to know exactly what Paul is referring to in some of the spiritual gifts he mentions in 1 Cor. 12, so we must exercise some caution in making too quick a link with modern phenomena.

An important element will be to follow the *structure* of the argument before us. Whatever the meaning of 'head' or 'because of the angels' (1 Cor. 11:10), the point of Paul's argument here is to allow women to pray and prophesy in the assembly (1 Cor. 11:5), in a context where Paul sees prophecy as the pre-eminent gift of the Spirit (1 Cor. 14:1).

It is sometimes thought that interpretation is the art of making the Bible say something different when you don't like what it appears to be saying! But really it is recognizing that what *we* think the text appears to be saying may not be what *the author* or the *first readers* would have thought it was saying. And it is what would have made sense to *them* which must have controlling influence over any responsible claim as to how it should make sense to *us*.

F. Pseudonymity

It has been suggested that some letters were written not by those to whom they have been attributed, but by others using their name (i.e. pseudonymously). The questions have been especially persistent in relation to 2 Peter, the Pastoral Letters (especially 2 Timothy) and Ephesians. Discussions on authorship can be found in the sections on these letters, but two general points are worth making.

Letter writers often used a secretary ('amanuensis') whose role could vary from simply taking down dictation, to composing under direction, to freely composing a letter under the author's general instructions. This makes the task of identifying authorship slightly different from the modern context, where we would think of an author as the person who wrote every single word.

On the other hand, the practice of writing under the name of someone else, living or dead, was a common feature in the ancient world. However, there is no evidence that it was ever thought acceptable in the Christian community, and apostolic authorship was one important criterion in determining what was included in the emerging canon that was added to the Jewish Scriptures.

PAUL'S LETTERS

Letter	Date	Origin
Galatians	Probably (a) 49 – after first missionary journey (Acts 13:2 – 14:28)	(a) Syrian Antioch or Jerusalem
	Possibly (b) 53 or 55 – during third missionary journey (Acts 18:23 – 21:17)	(b) Ephesus or Macedonia
1 Thessalonians	50–51 – during second missionary journey (Acts 15:40 – 18:22)	Corinth
2 Thessalonians	50–51 – during second missionary journey	Corinth
1 Corinthians	55–56 – during third missionary journey (Acts 18:23 – 20:3)	Ephesus
2 Corinthians	55–56 – during third missionary journey	Macedonia
Romans	57 – during third missionary journey	Corinth or Cenchrea
Ephesians	60–61 – first Roman imprisonment[1] (house arrest; Acts 28:16–31)	Rome[1]
Colossians	60–61 – first Roman imprisonment[1]	Rome[1]
Philemon	60–61 – first Roman imprisonment[1]	Rome[1]
Philippians	62 – first Roman imprisonment, near the end[1]	Rome[1]
1 Timothy	63–65 – some time after the first Roman imprisonment[2]	Philippi[2]
Titus	63–65 – some time after the first Roman imprisonment[2]	Macedonia[2]
2 Timothy	67–68 – second Roman imprisonment, near the end of Paul's life	Rome

[1] Possibly written in earlier imprisonment in 57–59 in Caesarea (Acts 23:23 – 26:32), or earlier still in 53–55 in Ephesus (Acts 19:1 – 20:1).

[2] Possibly written later, after a trip to Spain.

Destination	Contents	Issues scholars discuss
(a) Churches in south Galatia (b) Churches in north-central Asia Minor	The gospel of the grace of God	Date, origin, destination
Christians in Thessalonica	Encouragement for new Christians	
Christians in Thessalonica	Comfort for a church in distress	Author, date, relationship to 1 Thessalonians
Christians in Corinth and Achaia	Problems of a Gentile church	Chronology of Corinthian correspondence and Paul's visits
Christians in Corinth and Achaia	The heart of an apostle	Literary unity (2:14 – 7:1; chs. 8 – 9; chs. 10 – 13)
Christians in Rome	The righteousness of God revealed in the gospel	Literary unity (chs. 15 – 16)
Christians in Ephesus and surrounding region	The church of Christ	Author, date, origin, destination
Christians in Colossae and Laodicea	The supremacy of Christ	Author, date, origin, nature of heresy
Philemon and the Christians in Colossae	The dilemma of Christian slave ownership	Origin
Christians in Philippi	The joy of knowing Christ	Origin, literary unity (3:2 – 4:3)
Timothy and Christians in Ephesus	Teachers and leaders in the church	Author, date, origin, destination, nature of heresy
Titus and Christians in Crete	The grace of God and Christian living	Author, date, origin, destination, nature of heresy
Timothy and Christians in Ephesus	Encouragement to be faithful	Author, date, origin, destination, nature of heresy

ROMANS

Described by Samuel Coleridge as the most profound book in existence, of all Paul's letters Romans presents the most comprehensive exposition of his gospel. Probably no book in the NT has exerted more influence in the history of the church.

A. *Occasion and purpose*

Rome was the centre of a vast empire that encompassed all the countries around the Mediterranean Sea. With a population of around one million people, the city included a sizeable Jewish population. In the mid 50s AD there were probably several groups of Christians composed of both Jews and non-Jews meeting in different places. The greetings in ch. 16 mention a number of people and the churches that met in their homes. Reading between the lines of 14:1 – 15:13, it seems that the Roman Christian community was split between Jewish and Gentile factions.

Paul wrote Romans on his third missionary journey from Cenchrea or nearby Corinth. He had never visited the city and we do not know how the gospel first came there. Why did he write such a weighty letter to them? Three related reasons are evident. These are of a missionary, apologetic and pastoral nature.

First, Paul wrote to inform the Roman Christians of his desire to visit them on his way to Spain (15:23–24) and to enlist their interest, prayers and support. Just as Syrian Antioch was Paul's home base for his first three missionary journeys in the east, Paul apparently hoped that Rome would become a base for his missions further west. In this sense Romans is a letter of introduction in which Paul explains himself, both his message and agenda, fairly comprehensively (see 15:14–24). The letter serves this same purpose for us too, as the first in the sequence of Paul's letters in the NT.

Secondly, familiar with opposition, Paul wrote to defend both himself and his message. Romans functions as an apologia for Paul, the sort he would soon be giving in Judea when he brought the money he had been collecting from the Gentile churches to Jerusalem for the poor Jewish believers (see 15:25–33).

Thirdly, Paul had apparently heard of a split in the church between Jewish and Gentile believers. The first part of Romans presents a theology that bolsters his plea that the two groups 'accept one another' (15:7). The issue of Jew–Gentile relationships is evident throughout the letter and reaches centre stage in chs. 9 – 11.

B. Content and structure

The letter opens with a good summary of Paul's identity and task. Paul is an authoritative messenger charged to spread the good news, especially to Gentiles, about Jesus Christ, who is God's Son, promised in the OT (1:1–7). The conclusion (15:14 – 16:27) expands on Paul's role in God's plans as apostle to the Gentiles, notes that he intends to visit Rome in connection with this commission, warns against 'those who cause divisions' (16:17), greets those Paul knows who have an active part in the life of the church, and ends by praising God in terms that recall the main ideas of the letter.

In 1:16–17 Paul gives a brief statement of the gospel, which he goes on to expound in the rest of the letter. The gospel offers salvation to all, both Jews and Gentiles, is received by faith, and reveals the righteousness of God.

In the first main section, 1:18 – 3:20, Paul establishes the sinful condition of all human beings with the relentless drive of a trial lawyer. Jews and Gentiles alike are under the guilt and power of sin and deserve God's wrath. Next, in 3:21 – 4:25, Paul announces that God has done what is needed for us to be right with him through Jesus Christ and his sacrificial death. Our acceptance with God is not our own achievement and is not dependent on keeping the law; it is by faith. However, it is not contrary to the law, but rather upholds it, as the examples of Abraham and David attest.

In 5:1 – 8:39 Paul explains that the new situation of the justified person brings peace, hope, freedom and life. Believers have a sure hope of final salvation; have been set free from sin as an enslaving power and from law as a condemning power; and are indwelt by the Holy Spirit, who leads them onward to a life of righteousness.

In 9:1 – 11:36 Paul defends God against the charge of unrighteousness in the light of Israel's substantial failure to respond to the gospel and his consequent rejection of them. What of his pledge to Abraham and the patriarchs? Paul explains that, despite Israel's rejection of the righteousness of God by faith, God still remains faithful to his covenant promises.

The last major section lays out the practical implications of the righteousness of God. In 12:1 – 13:14 believers are called to obedience and faith in their daily attitudes and actions. In the light of the coming consummation of salvation they are to live in humility and love towards each other and in submission to civil authorities. Finally in 14:1 – 15:13, in what many see as the climax of the letter, Paul seeks to calm quarrels in the church by urging Jewish and Gentile believers to act responsibly towards each other in matters of social custom.

1:1–7	Opening greeting
1:8–15	Thanksgiving
1:16–17	Theme: God's righteousness revealed in the gospel
1:18 – 3:20	God's righteousness in his wrath against sinners
3:21 – 4:25	God's saving righteousness: justification by faith
5:1 – 8:39	The effects of God's righteousness: freedom and life in the Spirit
9:1 – 11:36	The rejection of God's righteousness: the problem of Jewish unbelief
12:1 – 15:13	God's righteousness in everyday life
15:14–33	Paul's past, present and future plans
16:1–27	Closing greetings

C. Reading Romans today

Romans is not an easy read. One problem can be losing the thread of Paul's argument. When reading the letter, it is always worth asking, where am I in the major divisions of the book? These are chs. 1 – 4, 5 – 8, 9 – 11, 12 – 15 and 16. Individual sections must be read in the context of the big picture. To this end, it is important to read Romans both slowly, verse by verse, and rapidly, covering whole sections and even the whole book in one sitting.

Attention to Paul's extensive use of the OT in Romans, which boasts as many as fifty quotations, is essential to appreciating the nuances of Paul's message. Key examples are Hab. 2:4 quoted in 1:17 ('The righteous will live by faith'), several psalms in 3:10–18, Gen. 15:6 in 4:3, Hos. 2:23 in 9:25 and Isa. 11:10 in 15:12.

In expounding the gospel in depth, Romans uses technical language that can be confusing. So vast are the blessings of salvation that Paul draws on terms from different realms of life, such as courts of law for justification, the temple for propitiation and family relations for reconciliation. Bible dictionaries and modern English versions provide assistance with these concepts.

For all its difficulty, the theological and practical significance of Romans is immense. There has never been written a more compelling exposition of the way of salvation, which defends the character of God at every turn, and of the nature of holiness and Christian obedience.

1 CORINTHIANS

1 Corinthians gives an insight into a church struggling to apply the lofty truths of the gospel to the problems of everyday life. It was not in fact Paul's first letter to the Corinthian Christians, nor was it his last. Paul's

relations with the Corinthian church spanned several years in the 50s AD and produced some of Paul's most profound teaching on the Christian life.

A. *Occasion and purpose*

The capital of the province of Achaia, Corinth was the seat of its governor and a major trading route between the east and west of the empire. Corinth was cosmopolitan and religiously pluralistic, accustomed to visits by impressive, travelling public speakers. It was obsessed with status, self-promotion and personal rights.

Paul laid the foundation for the church of God in Corinth on his second missionary journey, and spent eighteen months there building it up (Acts 18:1–18). Most of its members were former Gentiles (cf. 12:2: 'when you were pagans . . . ') and had turned to God from idols. Sent from Ephesus on his third missionary journey a few years later, 1 Corinthians mentions a previous letter of Paul to the church (1 Cor. 5:9–11). In it he had warned them not to associate with those who were guilty of serious sins, such as sexual immorality, greed and idolatry. Since these were the typical faults of the Gentiles, Paul was effectively exhorting them not to be conformed to the world. Unfortunately, some in the church mistook Paul to be saying they should shun not just fellow believers who behaved in such ways, but their non-Christian friends also. The book which we call 1 Corinthians is in part Paul's attempt to correct this misunderstanding. Paul was prompted to write it in response to disturbing news from the church. This included both oral reports, from Chloe's people (1:11) and from Stephanas, Fortunatus and Achaicus (16:17), and a letter from the church (7:1) consisting of a series of questions posed by the congregation.

As far as we can reconstruct the situation, after Paul had left, Apollos, and possibly Peter, visited Corinth. As well as bringing various benefits, this caused unintended problems. The congregation was now divided based on loyalty to their favourite Christian leader (1:12). Further, Paul learned that they were in considerable disarray with civil litigation between members (6:1–11), sexual immorality (5:1–13; 6:12–20), marriage problems (7:1–40) and questions concerning food offered to idols (chs. 8 – 10) and spiritual gifts (chs. 12 – 14).

The common element in all the problems in the church is that the Corinthians were 'worldly', 'acting like mere human beings' (3:3). The social values of secular Corinth had infiltrated the church. Paul's attempt to sort out the serious problems within the largely Gentile church in Corinth consists primarily of a confrontation over two particular vices: sexual immorality and idolatry.

Paul wrote 1 Corinthians to tell the church of God in Corinth that they are part of the fulfilment of the OT expectation of worldwide worship of the God of Israel. Therefore, as God's end-time temple, they must act in a manner appropriate to their pure and holy status by becoming unified, shunning pagan vices, and glorifying God as they reflect the lordship of Jesus Christ.

B. Content and structure

In 1:2 Paul refers to the Corinthians as those 'sanctified in Christ Jesus and called to be his holy people, together with all those who call on the name of our Lord Jesus Christ [literally] in every place'. The last phrase echoes Mal. 1:11, which predicts a future time when God would be worshipped by Gentiles all over the world: ' "My name will be great among the nations, from where the sun rises to where it sets. *In every place* incense and pure offerings will be brought to me, because my name will be great among the nations," says the LORD Almighty.' For Paul, the Corinthians are part of the fulfilment of God's plan to be worshipped among all the Gentiles and he wants them to help fulfil this worldwide eschatological vision by glorifying God.

In chs. 1 – 4 Paul urges the Corinthians to be united in the proclamation and service-oriented lifestyle of the cross, for they have entered the new eschatological age of salvation. There is a negative treatment of the wisdom of the world, which asserts that God has outsmarted and overpowered human powers and authorities (1:10 – 2:5), followed by a positive section that proclaims the Christ-centred wisdom of the cross (2:6 – 4:17). In 4:18 – 7:40 Paul deals primarily with issues related to sexual immorality, first in a negative treatment of its manifestations in the church in Corinth (4:18 – 6:20) and then in a positive treatment of marriage (7:1–40).

Chs. 8 – 14 deal with the issue of idolatry, beginning again with a negative treatment of its manifestations in Corinth (8:1 – 11:1) and then moving to a more positive treatment of the proper worship of the one true God (11:2 – 14:40). 1 Corinthians comes to a climax in ch. 15 with a discussion of the resurrection as it relates to the ultimate triumph of Christ over all adversaries and the final transformation of our corruptible humanity into a humanity that fully reflects God's glory. Ch. 16 closes the letter with instructions for the collection, some personal requests and Paul's final greetings.

Paul's use of the key words 'flee' and 'glory' reveal his main concerns in the letter. In concluding the negative section on sexual immorality, Paul exhorts the Corinthians to 'flee from sexual immorality' (6:18) and to 'glorify God' with their bodies (6:20, literally). In concluding the negative section on idolatry, Paul exhorts them to 'flee from idolatry' (10:14) and to do everything 'for the glory of God' (10:31).

1:1–9	Letter opening
1:10 – 2:5	Division and false wisdom of this world
2:6 – 4:3	True wisdom of the cross and the Spirit
3:5 – 4:17	Nature of Christian leadership
4:18 – 6:20	Condemnation of illicit sexual relations and greed
7:1–40	Affirmation of sexual purity in marriage and singleness
8:1 – 11:1	Condemnation of idolatrous practices
11:2 – 14:40	Affirmation of edifying worship
15:1–58	The resurrection of the body
16:1–24	Letter closing

C. Reading 1 Corinthians today

Reading Paul's letters can be like listening to one end of a telephone conversation; unfortunately we are left to guess what the party on the other end of the line is saying. Called mirror reading, this strategy is especially pertinent to the interpretation of 1 Corinthians. In each section attentive readers gain from Paul's responses some sense of what had been said and was going on in Corinth. Read this way, the letter is far from dry moral discourse, but is a vital conversation. It is possible to speculate too much about the situation in Corinth, but English versions usually give a starting point by indicating where Paul is quoting the Corinthians, as in 1:12: 'I follow Apollos'; 6:12: 'I have the right to do anything'; 7:1: 'It is good for a man not to have sexual relations with a woman'; and 8:1: 'We all possess knowledge.'

As well as supplying concrete answers to many problems which have comparable manifestations today, on subjects as diverse as preaching, sexual ethics and worship, 1 Corinthians models how to approach complex ethical problems of Christian living with the resources of the OT and the example and teaching of Jesus. Above all, it shows the importance of asking, how does the gospel of the death and resurrection of Jesus, which envelop the letter in chs. 1 and 15, teach us to live?

2 CORINTHIANS

If 1 Corinthians reveals the heart of a church, 2 Corinthians shows us the heart of an apostle. In it Paul expresses not only his anguish, distress and sorrow but also his deep desires, hopes and joys as he struggles to secure the Corinthians' sincere and pure devotion to Christ.

A. *Occasion and purpose*

Following the writing of 1 Corinthians, a number of developments took place between Paul and the church in Corinth. 2 Corinthians refers to a 'painful visit' (2:1), a tearful letter (2:4), and visits by Timothy (1:19; cf. 1 Cor. 16:10–11) and Titus (7:6–7). It also mentions Paul's own plans to visit being changed (1:15–16). Further, Paul had experienced great hardship in Ephesus (1:8–10) and had instigated a major collection of financial aid for famine-stricken believers in Jerusalem to which he hoped the Corinthians would contribute. How this all fits together in the story of the Corinthian correspondence is not entirely clear.

What is clear is that 2 Corinthians was written after some of the problems in the church had been resolved, and when visiting preachers threatened to undermine Paul and his gospel in Corinth. Paul's rivals were evidently Jewish Christian missionaries (11:22), some of whom claimed to be apostles (11:5, 13; 12:11). Apparently they disparaged Paul as being a lousy speaker (11:6) and lacking in personal presence (10:1, 10; 13:3–4). They boasted of their own eloquence and erudition (11:6), visions and revelations (12:1, 7), pure Jewish lineage (11:22) and impressive letters of recommendation (3:1). In short, they commended themselves as in every way superior to Paul (10:12). In response Paul accused them of preaching another Jesus, a different spirit and a different gospel (11:4).

In Macedonia, on his way to Corinth, Paul wrote 2 Corinthians to express his relief that the church had responded well to his 'tearful letter' and to the visit of Titus (2:6, 9, 12–14; 7:5–16), and to encourage them to reaffirm their allegiance to him and to complete their contribution to the collection for the saints in Jerusalem (8:6–7, 10–11; 9:3–5). His defence to those who accused him of personal weakness was to agree with the accusation, but to counter that in this very weakness God reveals *his* power. To prepare the church in Corinth for his upcoming visit, Paul exhorted them to examine themselves in the light of his teaching (12:14; 13:1, 5, 11) and save him from having to exercise discipline in the community when he arrived (10:2, 5–6, 11; 11:3; 12:19–21; 13:10).

B. *Content and structure*

The letter has three main sections. The main theme of chs. 1 – 7 is 'comfort in the midst of troubles' (cf. 1:4). Paul tells of his own suffering in 1:3–11, 6:4–10 and 11:23–29. Throughout we learn that suffering endured patiently deepens our appreciation of God's character, drives us to trust in God alone, leads us to identify with Jesus Christ (cf. 1:5: 'the sufferings of Christ'), is met by comfort from God and is ultimately eclipsed by eternal glory. All this leads Paul to reflect directly on death and resurrection in ch. 5, where death brings deepened fellowship with Christ and a spiritual body. The prospect of being accountable to Christ prompts the believer to seek to please the Lord in every circumstance (5:9). Other teaching in this section covers church discipline (2:5–11), the old and new covenants (3:7–18), reconciliation (5:11–21) and holiness (6:14 – 7:1).

Chs. 8 – 9 highlight several features of genuine Christian giving, as Paul encourages the Corinthians to finalize their contribution to his collection for the 'the poor among the Lord's people in Jerusalem' (Rom. 15:26). Generous giving is motivated by the example of other believers, by a desire for spiritual excellence and supremely by the example of Christ. An equal sharing of burdens and voluntary mutual sacrifice are endorsed. Christian giving is to be voluntary, enthusiastic and sensible and is an evidence of God's grace.

Finally, in chs. 10 – 13 Paul defends his authority as an apostle against the intruders from Palestine, who were 'false apostles, deceitful workmen, masquerading as apostles of Christ' (11:13). His main theme is 'strength in the midst of weakness' – paradoxically, the power of God finds its full scope and potency only in acknowledged human weakness (12:9; 13:4).

1:1–2	Opening greeting
1:3–11	Thanksgiving for Paul's deliverance
1:12 – 2:13	The rift with the congregation
2:14 – 7:1	Gospel ministry: divine power and human weakness
7:2–16	The joy of reconciliation
8:1 – 9:15	Arrangements for the collection
10:1 – 13:10	Paul's apostleship: Christ's 'fool' versus the 'super apostles'
13:11–13	Closing greetings

C. Reading 2 Corinthians today

Paul's robust response to a church in turmoil models the proper concern of a pastor for the congregation. Paul was willing 'to spend and be spent' for the benefit of his spiritual children (12:14–15). He calls them to 'open wide' their hearts to him (6:13). Indeed, throughout the letter his paternal affection for them is obvious: 'If I love you more, will you love me less?' (12:15). 2 Corinthians is punctuated by desire, compassion, joy, tears, courage, shame, anxiety, fear, sorrow and regret. This dimension of the letter can make it frustrating to interpret; it lacks the order and logic of a less emotive text like Romans. However, readers today should beware of favouring cognition over emotion and filtering out the affective elements of the letter. Feelings play an essential role in Christian faith.

Theologically, 2 Corinthians develops a profound and yet practical truth introduced in 1 Corinthians: God's power is revealed in the midst of human weakness (cf. 1 Cor. 1:17 and the power of the cross). Just as the power of God was revealed in the death of Christ, so the power of the resurrection is revealed in the ministry of those who recognize their own weakness and therefore trust in God (like Paul) and not in themselves (like the false apostles). The crucifixion of Christ appeared on the surface to be a manifestation of his weakness, but in fact it revealed God's power. Likewise the weakness of the Christian is the key to experiencing the power of God.

GALATIANS

As one of Paul's earliest letters, if not his first, Galatians provides invaluable information about the apostolic age. Written in response to a serious crisis in the church, the letter defends our full acceptance and freedom in Christ alone. Strident and even intimidating in tone, Galatians has been a cornerstone of our understanding of the gospel of the grace of God for two thousand years.

A. Occasion and purpose

While there is some debate over the destination and date of Galatians (see chart), the setting is clear. Jewish Christians had come from Jerusalem to the church that Paul had planted in central or northern 'Asia' (now Turkey). They then told Paul's Gentile converts that, in order to be accepted by God and be fully integrated into his family, they needed to be circumcised and to keep the Jewish festivals and food laws. These so-called Judaizers questioned the adequacy of Paul's gospel and his credentials as an apostle. Evidently, some in the church were buying their arguments.

This scenario can be reconstructed from clues scattered throughout the letter:

- The Galatians were Gentile believers who had gladly received Paul and his message (4:8–9, 13–15)

- They were now confused and turning to a 'different gospel' (1:6–7)
- They were considering circumcision and keeping the Mosaic law (3:2–5)
- Some visitors were trying to compel them to be circumcised (6:12–15)
- Paul warns: 'if you let yourselves be circumcised, Christ will be of no value to you' (5:2).

Paul wrote to the Galatians to call them to remain firm in the gospel message he had preached to them on three grounds: his law-free gospel is of divine origin; their experience and the Scriptures show that they have become full members of God's new people by faith in Christ and not by works of the law; and the Spirit is the true remedy to the problem of the sinful nature.

B. Content and structure

In Paul's view, the solution to the Galatian crisis is to remember what time it is. The coming of Christ has brought about a radical transformation. The promises to the Jewish forefather Abraham (3:7–8, 16–17, 29; 4:22–23), the giving of the law (3:17, 19; 4:24–25), the execution of the curse of the law in Israel's exile (3:10, 13; 4:24–25) and the prophetic promise regarding the future salvation and restoration of God's people (3:6–9) are all part of a unified historical drama which climaxes in the coming of Jesus, his death for sins and his resurrection from the dead. In Jesus Christ, God has pierced the barrier between the divine and human (1:12), heaven and earth (4:25–26), spirit and flesh (5:16–17), new and old creation (6:15). A new age has dawned in which God the Father deals with humanity as sons, not slaves (4:3–5); where humans relate to God not by law, but by faith working through love (3:23, 25; 5:6).

Related to this, Galatians trumpets the grace of God as the fundamental basis of Christian existence (1:3, 6; 2:21; 5:4; 6:18). Our standing with God rests entirely on his undeserved favour. Justification, leading to acquittal on the day of judgment, is not gained by keeping the law, by living according to a set of community standards or by performing good deeds, but is experienced now by those who simply have faith in Jesus.

Galatians is the only letter of Paul to a church that does not begin with some kind of thanksgiving. With so much at stake, Paul launches immediately into a defence of his apostleship, since his person and message are inseparable. He then defends justification by faith and Christian liberty against his opponents' attempt to impose adherence to the Mosaic law on the church.

1:1–5	Opening greeting
1:6–12	Setting: the message of the Judaizers is not the gospel of Christ
1:11 – 2:21	Autobiography: Paul's gospel and apostleship is of divine origin
3:1 – 4:31	Doctrine: justification by faith and not by works of the law
5:1 – 6:10	Practice: walk in the Spirit
6:11–18	Final plea

C. Reading Galatians today

Since Paul's opponents were basically urging Gentile believers to become Jews, many of Paul's arguments are based on the OT. He quotes Gen. 15:6 in 3:6, Gen. 12:3 in 3:8, Deut. 27:26 in 3:10, Hab. 2:4 in 3:11, Lev. 18:5 in 3:12, Deut. 21:23 in 3:13, Gen. 12:7 in 3:16, Isa. 54:1 in 4:27, Gen. 21:10 in 4:30 and Lev. 19:18 in 5:14. We need to read these in their OT contexts, along with the other texts he cites less explicitly, to appreciate the full impact of Paul's rejoinder.

Galatians answers abiding questions of fundamental importance: How do you know you are a child of God? How do we decide who else is a member of the family? How do we live out our family life? Paul's letter warns against limiting our fellowship with fellow believers because of any cultural, racial or social differences.

The letter also acknowledges that our freedom in Christ is open to abuse (5:13); rather than indulging the sinful nature we are to serve each other in love. Walking in the Spirit is put forward as the solution to gratifying 'the desires of the flesh' (5:16, literally). If the flesh is the weakness of the human nature living on the resources of this age (4:23), promoting corruption and disunity (5:19–21), life in the Spirit represents the presence and power of the age to come (4:29) with its supernatural ability to manifest love and promote good in the community (5:22–23).

EPHESIANS

Ephesians expounds the nature of Christian salvation and the character of the new life that flows from it. The letter bears many similarities to Colossians, though the latter concentrates on the person of Christ. Ephesians presents Paul's most mature thought on the church in God's purposes.

A. Occasion and purpose

Ephesus was the capital of the province of Asia (now Turkey) and a major city of the Roman Empire situated on a busy trade route. Its theatre had a seating capacity of 24,000 people. Not surprisingly, then, it became a focus of Paul's missionary labours over many years. He visited Ephesus at the end of his second missionary journey (Acts 18:18–21) and spent most of his third missionary journey there (Acts 19:1 – 20:37). According to 1 Tim. 1:3, he later appointed Timothy to oversee the work in Ephesus.

Paul wrote Ephesians from prison (3:1; 4:1; 6:20). The letter is fairly general in content and may even have been a kind of circular letter intended for several congregations in Western Asia Minor since some early manuscripts do not have 'Ephesus' as the specific destination in 1:1.

However, certain emphases in the letter do suggest some of Paul's reasons for writing. The emphasis on the unity of Jewish and Gentile Christians may well be intended to address tensions in the church. Additionally, the fact that the devil and various 'powers' are mentioned sixteen times in the letter suggests a concern to encourage believers in their struggle with pernicious spirit-forces. Acts 19 associates demonic activity with Ephesus, and archaeology has uncovered ancient Ephesus as a centre for magical practices, the Artemis cult, a variety of Phrygian mystery religions and astrological beliefs. Paul wrote Ephesians to celebrate God's mighty work of redemption, which includes the forgiveness of sins and raising up of believers, both Jews and Gentiles, to new life in the power of the Spirit.

B. Content and structure

The letter has a basic two-part structure, with chs. 4 – 6 setting out conduct appropriate to the gospel which Paul expounded in chs. 1 – 3. The transition comes in 4:1: 'I urge you to live a life worthy of the calling [to salvation] you have received.'

Ch. 1 opens with an inspiring thanksgiving for the gift of salvation, planned from eternity past and now being realized in the lives of believers. Paul then prays for the spiritual progress of his readers in light of Christ's supreme power in the universe. Ch. 2 recalls the readers' hopeless situation of death and condemnation and God's astounding deliverance. The barriers between Jews and Gentiles have now been demolished and their reconciliation through the cross has been achieved. Those who believe in Jesus are now united in one body on an equal basis. Ch. 3 explains the way in which this truth (of God bringing diverse people into one church) had been hidden for ages, but has now been made known to the Christian apostles and prophets and especially to Paul. The apostle then prays again for the readers, that they may know the love and power of God.

In 4:1–16 Paul exhorts them to express this unity through the rich variety of gifts which Christ has given to the church. The rest of chs. 4 – 6 offer practical instruction for appropriate Christian living. Most readers were former Gentiles, whose way of life before their conversion needed to be replaced by new patterns of behaviour: 'put on the new self ... in true righteousness and holiness' (4:24). The letter closes with a call to spiritual vigilance in 6:10–20.

1:1–2	Opening greeting
1:3–14	Thanksgiving for salvation in Christ
2:1–22	Reconciliation of both Jews and Gentiles to God
3:1–21	The mystery of Jews and Gentiles in one body
4:1–16	Appeal to live in unity
4:17 – 5:20	Moral exhortation: new life/new lifestyle
5:21 – 6:9	Christian relationships in the household
6:10–20	Appeal to spiritual warfare: the armour of God
6:21–24	Closing greetings

C. Reading Ephesians today

Ephesians presents a vision of the love and power of God as comprehensive as that found in Romans. A number of features stand out. The letter's teaching on reconciliation being both vertical (with God) and horizontal (with people unlike ourselves) is an important lesson to those of us in Western societies that are riven by individualism and often xenophobia.

The preponderance of 'power' language in the letter reminds us that people need not only forgiveness, but also deliverance from the evil forces that enslave them and control their destiny. Ephesians announces both God's power and Christ's supremacy over these forces, along with the believer's access to that power. We have been transplanted from one sphere of power, or 'kingdom', to another. The role of faith for obtaining God's strengthening is stressed (1:19; 3:17; 6:16) and the purpose of this power is to show love following the example of Christ (3:16–17; 5:2).

Finally, worship and praise dominate the letter. People filled with the Spirit speak to one another 'with psalms, hymns and songs from the Spirit' (5:19). This reminds us of the celebration of God's work of salvation in chs. 1 – 3. In talking about God we must avoid the trap of reducing everything to arguments and propositions. Ephesians expresses the profoundest theology in dazzled worship.

PHILIPPIANS

Although written from prison, Philippians contains some of the most encouraging passages in the NT. In it Paul writes of his passion for knowing Christ, his joy in the midst of adversity and his confidence in the face of death.

A. Occasion and purpose

Paul and Silas arrived in Philippi in Macedonia (mainland Greece) from Asia (now Turkey) on Paul's second missionary journey, having received a summons in a vision from God (Acts 16:9–10). A small but important city on a busy overland trade route, Philippi was named after Philip of Macedon, the father of Alexander the Great. It was a Roman colony with the privileges of self-government and freedom from taxation, and many of its inhabitants were proud to be Roman citizens. The account of Paul's visit in Acts 16:11–40 tells of the conversion of Lydia, an encounter with a slave girl who told fortunes, and Paul's subsequent arrest and miraculous escape from prison. The apostle and his associates made a number of visits in the years to follow.

A close relationship between Paul and the church developed, and they supported him financially. When Paul ended up in prison, probably in Rome (cf. Acts 28), they sent Epaphroditus with another gift and enquired about his welfare. Several things about the church concerned Paul. As well as facing the general hostility regularly met by Christians in the ancient world (cf. 1:29–30), the church was experiencing quarrels among prominent members (cf. 4:2) and was in danger from Judaizing Christian missionaries who, as in Galatia, held that the gospel must be supplemented by circumcision and the Jewish law. Additionally, Epaphroditus had fallen severely ill (cf. 2:25–30).

Paul wrote Philippians for a number of reasons: to inform the Philippians that his current troubles are reason to rejoice (1:12–26); to thank them for their support (1:3–7; 2:25; 4:14, 18); to urge unity (1:27–2:18; 4:2–3); to warn of threats to the church (3:2–18); to reassure them that Epaphroditus is now well (2:25–30); and to inform them of his intention to send Timothy to help them out (2:19–24).

B. Content and structure

Although addressing some serious concerns, Philippians maintains a mood of confidence and optimism based on what God is doing with respect to Paul and the church: the word 'joy' occurs sixteen times in the letter. In ch. 1, even in the midst of what seem to be tragic circumstances, Paul is upbeat and chiefly concerned with the progress of the gospel and the welfare of the church.

Ch. 2 urges meekness and unity in the church and a good witness to the world. The ground for this appeal is the example of Christ himself, whose own humiliation in becoming human and dying on the cross was vindicated by God. The magnificent hymn about Christ in 2:6–11 shows that it is not the nature of God to seize and to grasp, but rather to share and to give at great personal cost.

According to Paul in ch. 3, progress in the Christian life is not about keeping rules. Rather, it involves concerted effort toward the goal of knowing Christ (cf. 'I press on' in 3:12, 14). Likewise, Paul's warning against false teaching includes a description of holiness in terms of an ever-increasing understanding of the surpassing value of Jesus Christ.

Ch. 4 addresses directly some of those members causing problems in the church (Euodia and Syntyche), gives some general exhortations to positive Christian living, and thanks the Philippians for their financial support.

1:1–11	Opening greeting and thanksgiving
1:12–26	Paul's imprisonment and prospects for Paul and the gospel
1:27 – 2:18	Appeal for humility and unity in the church
2:19–30	Future plans for visits to Philippi
3:1 – 4:1	Warning about Judaizing missionaries
4:2–9	Encouragement to unity, prayer and Christian virtues
4:10–23	Thanks for personal gifts and closing greetings

C. Reading Philippians today

Philippians contributes much to our understanding of Christian doctrine and practice, and demonstrates the secure connection between the two. A prime example is the teaching about Jesus Christ in 2:6–11; Paul recounts that Christ renounced the privileges of deity in order to be a servant of others. Strikingly the profound truth of the incarnation is used by Paul for the practical end of urging humility and unity in the congregation (2:1–5).

At the same time, the letter contains some of the most personal reflections in the NT. In wrestling with the prospect of his own death the apostle takes a remarkably positive view. It is the gospel that imbues him with such confidence: 'to live is Christ and to die is gain' (1:21). Central to Christian experience is knowing Christ and sharing in his sufferings and resurrection (3:10).

In relation to church and society, without diminishing civic responsibility, Paul exploits the status of Philippi as a Roman colony to teach that Christians belong to a higher and more important commonwealth: since 'our citizenship is in heaven' (3:20) we are to 'live in a manner worthy of the gospel of Christ' (1:27).

COLOSSIANS

Although one of the shortest of Paul's letters, Colossians expresses more fully than his other letters what he believes about Jesus Christ. Writing in response to false teaching in Colossae, Paul offers a profound exposition of the supremacy of Christ and the completeness of the believer's new life in Christ.

A. Occasion and purpose

Colossae was a small town on a Roman road in the Lycus valley, about 100 miles/160 kms east of the provincial capital city of Ephesus. Paul had not visited Colossae (2:1), but the church was probably planted as a result of his wider ministry. Paul spent three years in Ephesus on his third missionary journey and, as Luke reports, 'all the Jews and Greeks who lived in the province of Asia heard the word of the Lord' (Acts 19:10). It was probably during this time that Epaphras, one of Paul's fellow workers, evangelized Colossae and established the church (1:7; 4:12–13).

Along with general encouragement (1:4, 6; 2:5), Colossians is sharply focused on a particular problem in the church. It appears that while in prison (4:3, 10, 18) Paul received news of dangerous teaching that had infiltrated the region. This teaching was Jewish and ritualistic in nature (2:16–17) and philosophical in approach (2:8, 18), advocating the worship of angels and harsh treatment of the body (2:18, 20–23). In Paul's view it was a denial of the sufficiency of Christ.

Paul wrote to the Colossians to provide a refutation of this false teaching and to commend a truly Christian way of life. Col. 2:6 sums up his message: 'Just as you received Christ Jesus as Lord, continue to live your lives in him.'

B. Content and structure

The letter opens with Paul's thanksgiving for the Colossian Christians and his prayer for their future. They are characterized by faith, hope and love (1:4–5), and their goal ought to be to live a life befitting the people of God.

The hymn-like description of Christ in 1:15–20 sets the tone for the rest of the letter. Two 'stanzas' proclaim him as supreme in creation, as the uncreated image of God (1:15–17), and supreme in redemption, as the first to rise from the dead and as the reconciler of the universe (1:18–20). But Christ has a unique relationship not only to God, the universe and the cross, but also to the Colossian believers (1:21–23). Anticipating his rebuttal of false teaching, 1:24 – 2:5 explains Paul's authority to teach as a servant of the church. Paul devotes all his energy to sharing the fullness of wisdom that comes from Christ.

In 2:8–23 Paul insists that all the knowledge they need is contained in Christ. Consequently, any teaching that seeks to supplement this is effectively a denial of the truth. In 3:1 – 4:6 the Colossians are told to be what they really are, those who have died to the sinful world and now live to God. Far from impractical or merely theoretical, being 'raised with Christ' (3:1) has radical implications for personal relationships and for the shape of family life.

1:1–14	Opening greeting and prayer for the Colossians
1:15–23	The pre-eminence of Christ in creation and redemption
1:24–29	Paul's ministry in Christ
2:1–5	Paul's ministry to the Colossians
2:6–7	The theme of the letter: continue in Christ
2:8–23	Attack on false teaching: the sufficiency of Christ
3:1 – 4:6	Moral exhortation: new life in Christ
4:7–18	Further news and final greetings

C. Reading Colossians today

While the 'Colossian heresy' is long gone and is not a threat to us, Paul's response to it contains numerous insights into genuine faith and spirituality, and continues to serve as a warning against substitutes. Counterfeit faiths range widely, but all foolishly underestimate Christ (2:8–9), while counterfeit spiritualities naively underestimate sin and 'lack any value in restraining sensual indulgence' (2:23). Paul's answer in both cases is to point to the sufficiency of the believer's relationship with Christ (3:3: 'your life is now hidden with Christ in God').

Colossians addresses the most profound questions of human existence and points to Christ as the answer to them all: What is God like? Why are we here? How can the world be put right? How can I be put right?

1 THESSALONIANS

One of Paul's earliest letters, 1 Thessalonians provides an insight into the deep affection Paul felt for people and the manner in which he worked with and helped young Christians. Since every chapter ends with a reference to the second coming of Christ, 1 Thessalonians also contains vital teaching on the end of the world.

A. Occasion and purpose

Paul's crossing into Europe on his second missionary journey, in answer to the call of 'a man of Macedonia' in a dream (Acts 16:6–10), was a major step forward in the progress of the gospel. The new campaign consisted of two phases, in the north and then the south of modern-day Greece. The first was in Macedonia, in the cities of Philippi and Thessalonica, and the second in the region of Achaia, where Paul visited Athens and Corinth. Trouble in Thessalonica meant that Paul had to leave in a hurry (Acts 17:1–10). Even if his initial stay was only three weeks, it was long enough for the formation of a small congregation of mainly Gentile believers ('you turned ... from idols', 1:9; cf. 2:14).

However, after Paul left, the situation in the church was one of instability. Paul had sent Timothy to strengthen them in the faith (3:2), and it seems that he wrote this letter to support Timothy's ministry and to encourage them to live a life pleasing to God (4:1). Apparently the Thessalonian believers were disturbed by opposition and by the death of some members of the church (4:13–18). They wanted to know when the Lord would arrive and how those who died would fit into the divine plan regarding the second coming.

Paul wrote this letter to encourage the Thessalonian believers not to be shaken by the opposition they were experiencing or by the death of their fellow members, but rather to be strengthened in their faith and to grow in Christian character (see Paul's prayer for them in 3:12–13). To do this he offers them some doctrinal instruction, and corrects some errors in living.

B. Content and structure

Paul reminds the Thessalonians that, having turned to God from idols, they are under his protection and are to live holy lives befitting their new status (4:3; 5:23). The Father has called them, Jesus is their Lord, and the Spirit is active in the powerful proclamation and joyful reception of the gospel that gave them new life. The letter reminds the church that they are 'in God' (1:2) and 'in Christ Jesus' (2:14; 3:8; 4:1, 16; 5:12, 18).

The warm relationship between Paul and this church is also a highlight (2:17, 20; 3:6).

The teaching about the second coming serves a pastoral rather than speculative purpose. Paul writes to reassure the Thessalonians that Jesus will certainly return, and that all believers, living and dead, will be taken up to be with the Lord forever (4:13–18). Confidence in our own resurrection rests on God having raised Jesus from the dead (4:14). The Day of the Lord will come like a thief in the night (i.e. when we least expect it). In the meantime the children of light must remain vigilant (5:1–11).

1:1–10	Opening greeting and thanksgiving
2:1–16	The apostles' ministry in Thessalonica
2:17 – 3:13	Paul's plans to revisit, and his continuing concern
4:1–12	Living to please God
4:13 – 5:11	The return of Christ
5:12–24	Life in the church
5:25–28	Closing greetings

C. Reading 1 Thessalonians today

1 Thessalonians offers comfort and encouragement to young Christians experiencing opposition to their faith, feeling the pressures of temptation to sexual immorality, or losing confidence in the future following the death of a loved one.

The two millennia since Christ first came have not altered the character of Christian hope. In the face of undeniable evil in the world, the resurrection of Jesus from the dead guarantees that the God of love and justice will ultimately triumph. Being ready for the return of Jesus (5:23–24) is a good summary of the Christian life.

2 THESSALONIANS

2 Thessalonians offers comfort to a church in distress. The letter testifies to powerful spiritual opposition to God and the gospel. God's control over the course of history, including a final victory over evil, is affirmed as an integral part of Christian faith.

A. Occasion and purpose

After receiving their first letter from Paul the Thessalonians began to panic, thinking that the countdown to the end of the world was already far advanced and that the end times were upon them. This error seems to have arisen because of the immaturity of the persecuted church and a mistaken interpretation of Paul's first letter with its references to trials and persecution (1 Thess. 1:6; 3:3–4, 7) and 'wrath' (1 Thess. 1:10; 2:16; 5:9). Further, the exhortations to be ready at all times and to be vigilant until that day (intended to encourage them to live holy lives) may have led them to neglect daily responsibilities such as work, and to devote themselves exclusively to waiting for the return of Christ (3:6–14).

These misunderstandings of his first letter came to Paul's attention while he was still in Corinth and prompted him to write 2 Thessalonians. Some scholars doubt the letter's authenticity, presuming that it is a pseudonymous work by a later Christian writer. The primary objection to Pauline authorship is the striking similarities between the two letters, thought to suggest imitation by a follower of Paul. However, the overlap between the letters is best explained by assuming that they really are by the same author, on the same subjects, to the same audience, and written one shortly after the other.

Paul wrote to tell the Thessalonians that the Day of the Lord had not yet come (2:1–12) and to encourage them to remain firm, hold fast to the teachings that Paul had passed on to them (2:15), and live orderly lives (3:6–10) worthy of their calling by God (1:11; 2:14).

B. Content and structure

If 1 Thessalonians expresses a lively hope in the imminent coming of the Lord (e.g. 1 Thess. 4:17), 2 Thessalonians counsels that the end of the world cannot happen before the Satanic opposition to God has reached a climax. Other NT texts, such as Mark 13 and Revelation, likewise stress that evil will increase before the final showdown with God. Before the day of Christ, there will be rebellion and 'the man of lawlessness' (2:3), who will exalt himself as if he were God and will deceive many (cf. Dan. 11:3–36). The identification of who or what is 'holding him back' (2:6) is beset with difficulty. It may be that God himself restrains him with the purpose of providing opportunity for the gospel to be heard everywhere. What is clear is that the glory of Christ's coming will most certainly defeat the forces of wickedness (2:1–12).

The final part of the letter addresses the practical problem of the laziness of some believers in the church. Paul appeals to his own example of hard work as a model to imitate.

1:1–22	Opening greeting, thanksgiving and prayer
2:1–12	Lawlessness will precede Christ's return
2:13–17	Exhortation to stand firm

| 3:1–16 | Exhortation to pray and work |
| 3:17–18 | Closing greetings |

C. Reading 2 Thessalonians today

Given its particular teaching about 'the man of lawlessness', 2 Thessalonians is among the most difficult of Paul's letters. As strange as this teaching on the second coming and the last days may seem to some, it brings comfort to those overwhelmed by forces hostile to God, a common experience in the twenty-first century AD. In emphasizing the sovereignty and goodness of God, 2 Thessalonians continues to bring consolation to Christian people in all kinds of distress.

1 & 2 TIMOTHY AND TITUS

The Pastoral Letters of 1 & 2 Timothy and Titus belong together and are distinctive amongst the NT letters. They are the only ones written to individuals in church leadership, and generally focus on the personal lives and activity of those leaders (or 'pastors' – hence the title 'pastoral' letters). They also have a common literary style, but one which is quite different in a number of respects from other Pauline writings. This raises sharply the question of their origin.

Of a vocabulary of 901 words in the Pastoral Letters, 335 are not found elsewhere in Paul. Every letter has its own distinctive vocabulary, but this proportion is about twice that of the other Pauline letters. The Pastorals also omit many terms that are characteristic of Paul's other writings, including 'free', 'to work', 'to preach the gospel', 'heaven', 'spiritual', 'wisdom', 'body', 'son' and 'soul'. There are a number of other points of style that differ. Further, there is a distinct lack of Paul's theological emphases, with little mention of the fatherhood of God, of being 'in Christ', or of the work of the Spirit in the believer.

If Paul is the author, then these differences are due to changes of situation for him and the churches, and his writing to individuals rather than groups of believers. But if we conclude that Paul was not the author, then there are serious problems with the integrity of these letters in the Bible – and we are also faced with the challenge that Pauline authorship was never doubted in the early church.

A. Occasion and purpose

Titus appears to have travelled with Paul for part of his missionary work, and was Paul's companion at Jerusalem during the controversy about circumcision (Gal. 2:1, 3). Later he made several visits to Corinth and reported back to Paul (2 Cor. 7:6–7, etc.).

Timothy joined Paul on his second missionary campaign (Acts 16:1–3) when Paul visited his home town of Lystra. He appears to have worked closely with Silas, and travelled with Paul to Thessalonica, Philippi and Corinth. He is listed as co-writer with Paul in the letters to the Thessalonians, Colossians, Philippians and the second to the Corinthians, and was with Paul when he wrote Romans.

2 Tim. 1:17 places Paul firmly in Rome, but in rather different circumstances from those depicted in Acts 28:30–31. Although we have no record of what happened after the end of Acts, it seems probable that Paul was released and engaged in further missionary activity. If so, then this is the most likely time for him to have written Titus and 1 Timothy. Eusebius (c. AD 300) records the tradition that Paul was again imprisoned in Rome and executed under Nero, and that he wrote 2 Timothy at that time. The personal nature of the letter accords with this. So all three letters are likely to have come from the 60s.

B. Content and structure

1 Timothy and Titus contain many practical instructions, while 2 Timothy is more like a 'testament' of Paul as he faces death. Nevertheless, there are common themes in Paul's description of the opposition facing the churches:

- A recurrent theme is of 'myths and genealogies' (1 Tim. 1:3–4; Titus 1:14; 3:9), probably esoteric interpretations of Jewish tradition.
- Related to this are various debates and arguments (2 Tim. 2:23; Titus 3:9); Paul's reference to 'knowledge' (1 Tim. 6:20) may suggest the development of a kind of rational intellectualism.
- Some were engaging in ascetic practices, i.e. abstaining from food and sexual relations, as part of a claim to spiritual superiority (1 Tim. 4:2–3).
- There was some debate about whether the resurrection of the dead had passed (2 Tim. 2:18).
- There was also moral laxity or licence (1 Tim. 1:19; 2 Tim. 3:1–9; Titus 1:15–16).

There are signs of these debates in Paul's earlier letters, especially to the Corinthians and Thessalonians. It may be that these challenges to Christian faith were growing and eventually fed into the second-century development of Gnosticism, with its emphasis on special knowledge and secret ritual.

1 Timothy

1:1 – 3:16	Teachers and leaders in the church
1:3–11	Warning against false teachers
1:12–20	Paul's testimony
2:1–15	Prayer and worship when meeting together
3:1–16	Qualifications for overseers and deacons
4:1 – 6:21	Instructions to Timothy
4:1–16	How Timothy is to respond to the threat of heresy
5:1 – 6:2	Different groups in the church
6:3–21	False teaching, love of money, and the call to godliness

2 Timothy

1:1 – 4:5	Timothy's role as leader
1:3–18	Encouragement to be faithful
2:1–13	Encouragement to be strong in the face of suffering
2:14–26	Encouragement to purity in the face of pressure
3:1–9	Warning of godlessness in the 'last days'
3:10 – 4:5	Encouragement to give mature leadership
4:6–22	Paul's personal experience and greetings

Titus

1:1–4	Opening greeting
1:5–9	Appointment of elders/overseers
1:10–16	Warnings about false teachers
2:1–15	Different groups in the church
3:1–11	Peaceful living, through God's grace
3:12–15	Closing instructions and greetings

C. Two key issues for today

1. Church order

The Pastoral Letters are the only place in the NT where there is a sense of developed church order in leadership. But there appears to be some interchangeability of terms (e.g. 'elder' and 'overseer', Titus 1:6–7) and the structure has the fluidity seen elsewhere in the NT, rather than the rigidity and hierarchy which emerged in the second century.

2. *The place of women*

1 Tim. 2:11–15 has probably caused more debate and upset than any other paragraph in the whole NT! Any credible interpretation needs to take account of the following issues of text and context:

- 'Quietness' (v. 11) has to do with demeanour and is not the same as 'silence'; 'submission' is the quality that elsewhere Paul commands of all believers to all others (Eph. 5:21).
- Inviting women to participate in worship and learn alongside men would have been a radical challenge to some first-century religious traditions.
- 'I do not permit' (v. 12) is an unusual expression, better translated 'I am not permitting', i.e. current practice rather than permanent ruling.
- The word for 'to have authority' is an odd one and used only here in the NT. In other literature it means 'taking power to oneself', often with overtones of violence.

All this needs to be read in the context of Paul's other statements about the status of men and women in Christ (such as Gal. 3:28) and his particular concern that women should participate fully in worship through praying and prophesying (1 Cor. 11:5), and through exercising spiritual gifts which are given 'to each one' (1 Cor. 12:7).

PHILEMON

The shortest and most mundane of Paul's surviving letters, Philemon is a potent illustration of the breaking down of social and cultural barriers in Christ. In it we see not only the intriguing story of an errant slave, but also the essence and power of the gospel.

A. *Occasion and purpose*

Two reconstructions of the letter's background are possible. Either Onesimus had stolen from his master Philemon and run away (18), or the two had simply fallen out and Onesimus had gone to Paul for help. In either case, once they had made contact, Paul led Onesimus to Christ (10). Philemon is also a Christian and is faced with the dilemma of Christian slave ownership.

Paul wrote to effect reconciliation between Onesimus and Philemon, by encouraging Philemon to forgive Onesimus and welcome him back as a dearly-loved Christian brother.

B. Content and structure

The letter is an example of Paul not exercising his authority coercively. The apostle forgoes his right to command (8–9), seeking instead Philemon's voluntary consent (14), and allows him the freedom to express his love as he sees fit (5, 7). Paul effectively hopes to persuade Philemon to think through the implications of there being no slave or free person in Christ (Gal. 3:28). He may even be hinting that Onesimus should be released, in order to become a colleague of Paul.

vv. 1–3	Opening greeting
vv. 4–22	Request
vv. 23–25	Closing greetings

C. Reading Philemon today

Philemon reveals Paul's attitude to the institution of slavery. Although on face value he accepts its legitimacy, his championing of the individual slave undermines the practice. Paul emphasizes Onesimus' true identity as a brother in Christ. His appeal echoes the gospel in urging Philemon to welcome his slave and give him a new status (16–17) and in offering to pay his debt in his stead (18).

HEBREWS

The thirteen chapters of the book of Hebrews form a tightly reasoned argument designed to encourage faithfulness and bolster confidence. This argument forms the NT's longest explanation of the significance of Jesus' person, ministry and death. The explanation is given in terms of priesthood, sacrifice, covenant and ritual purity, and reminds us that early Christianity was a movement within Judaism.

A. Author and origin

Hebrews nowhere identifies its author or recipients. Nonetheless, there are several things we can say about them. The Greek style of the book is eloquent and precise, and the argument rhetorically sophisticated. The author displays an intimate knowledge of the OT, and close familiarity with Jewish interpretative techniques. This points to both Greek and Jewish education. The author had long known the readers and planned to visit them soon (13:23). He knew Timothy and hoped to travel with him (13:23). This indicates that he was part of the early missionary circle which included Paul and his associates. While Hebrews nowhere claims Pauline authorship, ancient manuscripts always include Hebrews among Paul's letters. However, from ancient times readers have observed significant stylistic differences between Paul's letters and Hebrews. The differences are so great that nearly all modern scholars conclude that Paul did not write Hebrews. Who did? We don't know. We cannot be certain that the author is even a person named in the NT. Nevertheless, we can credit him for being a creative and pastorally wise theologian.

Heb. 13:24 contains greetings sent by 'those from Italy' (13:24). If this refers to Italian ex-patriots sending greetings home, then the recipients lived somewhere in Italy. However, the idiom 'those from (place name)' usually identified people living at the named location. Further, several ancient manuscripts allude to the greeting in longer versions of the letter's title, so their scribes took Italy to be the place of composition. Thus we should conclude that Hebrews was written from Italy, and in 13:24 local Italians convey their greeting to Christians elsewhere.

B. Occasion and purpose

The readers had been believers for some time (5:11–14). Heb. 2:3 implies that they had been evangelized by those who had heard Jesus in person. In the past they had endured persecution because of their confession of Christ (10:32–34). Now they found themselves facing hardship again, but this time their faithfulness waned. Some grew lax in doing good works (10:24; 13:1–3). They were perplexed that God was permitting hardship (12:3–17). Some even stopped meeting with other believers altogether (10:25). Others continued to meet, but apostasy was a foreseeable possibility which the author sought to pre-empt.

The book's preoccupation with sacrifice and priesthood would have had particular relevance for Christians living near the temple, so the traditional title 'to the Hebrews' probably refers to Christians in Palestine. Some discount the title as speculation, noting that the book's argument depends on descriptions of sacrifice and priesthood found in the Mosaic law, and that it consistently refers to the tabernacle (or tent of meeting) rather than the temple. This is thought problematic for a Palestinian destination. Recent discoveries, however, support the traditional view.

A Dead Sea letter known as 4QMMT protests against the policies of Jerusalem's leaders regarding the sacrificial cult and Levitical priesthood. This dispute centred on the proper application of OT laws originally formulated for the wilderness camp and the tabernacle. The author of 4QMMT insists that 'the temple is the place of the tent of meeting, and Jerusalem is the camp; and outside the camp is outside Jerusalem'. Thus 4QMMT defines 'tabernacle/tent of meeting', 'camp' and 'outside the camp' very specifically.

These definitions are helpful for understanding Hebrews. First, the book expresses significant concern about the law's status (7:12; 10:1), the basis in it for Jesus' priesthood and sacrifice (e.g. 5:1–10; 7:11 – 8:13; 9:15–24), and other related matters. As with 4QMMT, our author apparently referred to the tabernacle rather than the temple because for him the temple is the tabernacle.

Secondly, the book's climax refers to 'the camp' (13:11–14). This is often presumed to indicate Judaism in general, but there is no precedent for this in contemporary sources. By contrast, the definitions of 4QMMT fit the context perfectly. Jesus suffered 'outside the city gate' (13:12), i.e. outside Jerusalem. The readers are to 'go outside the camp' (13:13) because 'here we do not have an enduring city...' (13:14), i.e. earthly Jerusalem (cf. 12:22; Gal. 4:25–26), '...but we are looking for the city that is to come', i.e. the heavenly Jerusalem (cf. Rev. 21:10). The parallel structure of the passage supports identifying 'the camp' with Jerusalem, in line with 4QMMT. Corroborating this, Jerusalem is referred to elsewhere in the NT as 'the camp of God's people, the city he loves' (Rev. 20:9).

According to early traditions, the Jerusalem church received prophetic warning to leave Jerusalem before its destruction. The call to 'go outside the camp' (13:13) may be advice to obey that warning (cf. 11:13–15; 12:26–28). Even if not, 'the camp' appears to designate Jerusalem. Thus the recipients probably lived in Jerusalem before AD 70, and their concerns with sacrifice, priesthood and ritual purity were real, not theoretical.

C. Structure and genre

1:1 – 10:18	The superiority of Jesus, and exhortations for faith
1:1–4	God's revelation through his Son
1:5 – 2:18	Jesus' superiority to angels
3:1 – 4:13	Jesus' superiority to Moses and Joshua
4:14 – 10:18	Jesus' superiority as high priest and sacrifice
10:19 – 13:25	Exhortations for faithful living

Typical Greek letters begin by identifying their author and recipients. Because Hebrews does not, some interpreters suggest that it is not really a letter. Many classify it instead as a sermon, because it supposedly calls itself a 'word of exhortation' (13:22). The same Greek phrase is used in

Acts 13:15 to refer to a message Paul delivered in the synagogue at
Antioch. However, there is good reason to believe that the normal
synagogue sermon would have been completed before Paul gave his
'word of exhortation'. Further, the close association between exhortation
and prophecy in Acts and Paul's letters suggests that Paul delivered a
prophetic exhortation in Antioch (cf. Acts 4:36; 15:32; 1 Cor. 14:3, 31). So
here in Hebrews, 'the word of exhortation' may refer to a prophetic
warning the community had already received (12:25; cf. 11:7).

In any case, Heb. 1 – 12 contains a handful of features character-
istically found in the body of ancient letters. And the book clearly ends
like a letter (13:20–25), e.g. 13:24 (see above) and 13:22, where the
author uses a Greek word for 'write' (*epistello*) that often means 'write
an epistle/letter' (*epistole*). So the author apparently considered himself
to be writing an epistle.

D. Reading Hebrews today

1. Jesus' supremacy

The earliest Christians were zealous to obey God's law (cf. Acts 21:20),
and saw no tension between the gospel and the sacrificial system (cf. Acts
2:46; 3:1; 5:25; 6:13–14; 21:17–26). For the readers of Hebrews, however,
there was a tension between obeying Jesus and obeying the law. Further,
the law seemed to have more in its favour, as God's word to Israel
mediated by angels (2:2; cf. Gal. 3:19) and delivered by Moses.

The author tackles this concern head-on. The word spoken by
God's Son is superior to the word spoken by the prophets (1:1–2). Jesus
himself is superior to the angels who mediated the Law (1:3 – 2:18). He is
also superior to Moses who received the law (3:1–6). This implies
that the message first declared by Jesus (2:1–4) has greater authority
than the law. In these arguments Jesus is unhesitatingly identified with
Israel's creator God (1:2, 10; cf. 11:3), and deserves worship from the
mightiest angelic beings (1:6). In fact, he is nothing less than God (1:8).

2. Contrasting covenants

Several times Hebrews contrasts the old and new covenants. These
covenants do not represent two religions, as often assumed, but rather
the stages in God's redemptive work. They are contrasted to demonstrate
primarily two things. First, by its very nature the old covenant could not
fully sanctify the worshipper or put sin away once and for all (cf. 9:9–10).
Jesus' new covenant ministry does accomplish this (9:11–28), and the

new covenant contains better promises (8:6). Second, the old covenant was never intended to be permanent, but only applied 'until the time of the new order' when things would be set right (9:10). Now the messiah has come. The institutions of the old covenant have fulfilled their purposes, are obsolete, and will soon disappear (8:13). So Christians may leave them behind, and are no longer obligated to follow OT laws governing sacrifice, priesthood and ritual purity.

3. Examples of faithfulness

The readers faced a crisis that shook their confession of faith in Christ. God was speaking to them (cf. 12:25), but they found it difficult to obey. The author encourages them 'to imitate those who through faith and patience inherit what has been promised' (6:12). They should 'believe and [be] saved' (10:39), like 'the great cloud of witnesses' (12:1). These are the heroes of Israel's past (11:1–40) who endured hardship and death as they faithfully obeyed God. Similarly, the community's former leaders displayed faithfulness worthy of imitation (13:7). Lastly, Jesus endured much for his people. He exemplifies what it means to be a faithful son of God who obeys even in hardship (5:7–10). Jesus did this in order to bring 'many sons and daughters to glory' (2:10). As children of God destined for glory (2:17), the readers should imitate their brother's example (12:1–2; 13:12–13). We likewise should imitate the faithful obedience of the Bible's heroes, Christian leaders and, above all, Jesus himself.

JAMES

The letter of James was famously denounced by Luther as 'an epistle of straw'. Yet it remains a favourite letter of the NT for many Christians, and its call to integrity of living is strikingly relevant to both the contemporary church and contemporary society.

A. Occasion and purpose

Although English derives the author's name from Latin, his name in Greek is 'Jacob', like Israel's patriarch (Gen. 25 – 35). Of the Jacobs/Jameses mentioned in the NT, the only serious contender for authorship is James the brother of Jesus (Mark 6:3; Gal. 1:19), who became a believer after the resurrection (1 Cor. 15:7) and went on to be a leading figure in the church in Jerusalem (Acts 12:17; 15:13). One tradition says he was known as 'camel knees' because of his habit of praying in the temple!

If this authorship is correct, then the letter must have been written before AD 62, since we are told by Josephus that James was stoned to death by order of High Priest Ananus prior to the arrival of a new governor of Judea that year (Josephus *Antiquities of the Jews* 20.197–203). The lack of reference to the fall of Jerusalem in AD 70 and the assumption that the church is led by elders (5:14) both fit with this early date.

Commentators have speculated about the possible situations that the letter is addressing. But the general title and the general nature of the comments make defining the situation of the intended audience difficult – and in fact this does not affect interpretation.

The language and rhetorical style of James compares very well with other Greek literature, and this has made some question whether it could really be written by an Aramaic-speaking Jew from Galilee. However, we know of other competent writers in Greek from the region, so this is not as unlikely as it may at first sound. Other objections to James as author are based on the few references to Jesus, and on the relation between the teaching here on faith and works and the teaching of Paul – and to these we now turn.

B. Content and genre

In contrast to some of Paul's letters (especially Romans), James does not appear to present a developed argument of any kind. The most obvious division of the letter is into three sections:

1:2–27	Introduction to the letter's themes
2:1 – 5:6	Development of these themes
5:7–20	Conclusion, with final appeals

Although the themes in ch. 1 are not developed in the same order in the body of the letter, there are striking correspondences between the two sections:

1:2–27		**2:1 – 5:6**	
2–4	Endure testing with joy		
5–8	Ask God for wisdom	3:13–18	The nature of the wisdom from above
9–11	Rich and poor are equal in the face of mortality	4:13–17	Plans to prosper come to nothing in the face of mortality
12–16	Endure testing, which comes from inner desires not God	4:1–10	Disputes arise from our worldly desires

1:2–27 (*cont.*)		**2:1 – 5:6** (*cont.*)	
17–18	God the giver		
19–21	Be quick to listen, slow to speak and slow to anger	3:1–12	The powers and peril of speech
		4:11–12	Don't judge one another
22–25	Be doers of the word, not merely hearers	2:14–26	Verbal assent is worth nothing without action
26–27	True religion means helping the poor	2:1–13	Don't show favouritism to the rich
		5:1–6	Judgment on rich oppressors

Although the opening greeting styles this book as a letter, James has a distinctive feel compared to other NT letters. The main reason is that about half the verses in James have verbs in the imperative form, that is, they are commands or encouragements to do something (e.g. 'consider it pure joy', 1:2; 'don't be deceived', 1:16; 'take note of this', 1:19). Other NT letters have sections written in this style, but no other consists only of this kind of writing.

This has made some commentators argue that James is a particular kind of literature labelled *paraenesis* (Greek for 'encouragement'), which consists of collections of sayings, unconnected with one another, and without reference to a particular author or situation. However, we shall see that James does not fall so neatly into this category.

James' ethical perspective and use of practical examples and general sayings, along with the reference to 'wisdom', have suggested to some that it sits within Israel's 'wisdom' tradition, represented chiefly in the OT by Proverbs and Ecclesiastes. Despite these common features, James has more emphasis on eschatology (God's end-times judgment of all) than does other wisdom literature. And James offers a much more radical ethic in relation to wealth and poverty than we find in (for example) Proverbs.

The opening greeting 'To the twelve tribes scattered among the nations' is very general, and it is perhaps difficult to imagine this actually being sent as a letter. In comparison with Paul's letters, which have much more detailed introductions and conclusions, following the usual conventions of ancient letter writing (see section above), James looks rather sparse. But we do have examples of circular letters which have a very similar form, e.g. in the intertestamental book 1 Maccabees 10:25–45. We also know that the Pauline letters were circulated beyond the churches to which particular letters were addressed, and in the case of Ephesians we have a letter probably intended to be a circular from the beginning.

So James may well have been written as a circular letter, but with a particular focus on encouragement, drawing on Jewish wisdom traditions and elsewhere.

C. James, Jesus and Paul

There are only two references to Jesus, in 1:1 and 2:1, and these are made almost in passing. There is no reference to the major events of Jesus' life, and in particular his death and resurrection, and no reference to the Holy Spirit.

Closer inspection, however, shows that there are many links to the teaching of Jesus as recorded in the Gospels, and especially the Gospel of Matthew, which is often understood to be addressing Jewish concerns. The closest is in 5:12 ('All you need to say is a simple "Yes" or "No"') which looks like a quotation of Matt. 5:37 – but there are many other similarities in wording and theme. The ethic of James looks as though it has been closely shaped by the teaching of Jesus.

At first sight, James' statement that 'people are justified by what they do and not by faith alone' (2:24) looks like the opposite of Paul's comment in Rom. 3:28 that 'a person is justified by faith apart from observing the law'. Further, both Paul and James appeal to the example of Abraham, but apparently to prove opposite ideas. This has been one of the main reasons for the neglect of James – but it is something of a false dichotomy.

The idea that Paul is only interested in what we believe, not what we do, is at best a poor parody. For instance, the failure to act aright highlights humanity's need of God in Rom. 3; the struggle to act right in Rom. 7 is answered by the gift of the Spirit in Rom. 8; and Rom. 12 is all about how we live out in action what God has done for us in Christ. On the other hand, James is clearly not interested in action alone; for Abraham, 'his faith and his actions were working together' (2:22). James' concern is that our trust in God should be seen clearly in how we live our lives. Paul and James would agree that the problem of human sin is *both* a spiritual one (our standing before a holy God) *and* a practical one (our inability to live aright).

D. Reading James today

Perhaps a helpful key to understanding James' concerns, and putting the discussion about faith and works into context, is to notice the importance for James of integrity, wholeness or oneness. The confession of the oneness of God in Deut. 6:4 ('Hear O Israel: the LORD our God, the LORD is one') was central to Jewish belief. Although sometimes understood as emphasizing that there is only one God, it is at least as important in affirming the single nature of God. James cites this confession near the middle of his letter, at 2:19, but the idea permeates his reflection about the nature of God and the nature of discipleship.

- There is no changing in God; he is not fickle, showing a dark side one minute and light another, tempting then accusing (2:17).
- We are to treat others with integrity, rather than paying attention to their outward appearance (the Greek for 'favouritism' in 2:1, 9 means literally 'looking upon the face') and ignoring their inner reality.
- Our speech should be marked by integrity, not saying one thing at one time and another at another, letting our 'yes' be 'yes' and our 'no' be 'no'.
- We must have integrity within ourselves, so that what we believe in our hearts is matched by the actions of our lives.
- We need to live in communities of integrity, seeking together God's wisdom rather than be broken up by disputes arising from our own desires.
- We need to integrate how we see the present and how we see the future, living now in the light of the coming judgment of God.

Living in a broken world – where the church appears (in public at least) to do nothing but fight with itself, when the most persistent question about faith is whether you can believe in a good God in the face of human suffering, and when nothing hinders mission more than lack of integrity amongst believers – this is a message we need to hear more than ever.

1 PETER

Unlike the letter of James, the first letter of Peter has many more of the features of a NT letter. It also has a clearer sense of progress and developing argument, and, like many of the Pauline letters, has a general pattern of moving from exploration of theological truths to the working out of these truths in daily living.

A. Occasion and purpose

1. The apostle

The letter claims to be from Peter, 'apostle of Jesus Christ'. Although the term 'apostle' may have been applied more widely, it is usually understood in the NT to refer to the Twelve. The style of the letter borrows some elements from classical Greek, and this might be seen as odd for something written by an 'unschooled' fisherman (Acts 4:13).

However, Galilee was on a major trade route, and it would not be unusual for ordinary people to be multilingual. Moreover, the letter cites Silas (Silvanus) as Peter's *amanuensis* or letter-writing 'secretary', and from Silas' extensive travels with Paul it is clear that he was a skilled Greek speaker.

2. The dispersed

The letter is addressed to 'God's elect' who are 'scattered'. The word used here is *diaspora*, a standard term for the Jews living outside Palestine following the exile to Babylon in 587/6 BC. (Some versions translate this term 'the Dispersion'.) Along with Peter's use of the OT, this might suggest that he is addressing a primarily Jewish audience. However, the language about the believers' former way of living in 4:3 echoes typical Jewish criticism of pagan living, so Peter is in fact carrying language about the Jews over to the mixed Jewish/Gentile Christian community. (The use of 'Christian' in 4:16 is the only occurrence of the term outside Acts in the NT.) What is particularly interesting is that Peter applies the promises of God and identity of God's OT people to this mixed Christian community *without exception*. There are no promises which this community will not inherit, no aspects of identity from the OT which are not true of them.

3. Foreigners and aliens

Peter also addresses his readers as 'exiles' and 'foreigners' (1:1, 17; 2:11). In the Greek OT (the Septuagint) these words were applied to Abraham in Canaan (Gen. 26:23; 23:4) and Israel in Egypt (Gen. 15:13) and later to Judah in exile in Babylon and the Jewish community in Egypt. In the Greco-Roman world, these terms referred to resident aliens who ranked above foreign visitors and slaves, but below full citizens, and were often viewed with some suspicion. Peter is not using the term to suggest that his audience belong to this actual social class – after all, they are viewed with mistrust because of changed lifestyles, not social standing (4:4). Rather, this term shows the severe social pressures they were under, treated as strangers in their own land and paying the price for standing out as different from the surrounding culture.

4. Persecution

Pliny was governor of Pontus-Bithynia in the early second century, and took specific measures against Christians in this area. We know of this from a letter he wrote to Emperor Trajan in AD 111–112. Some of the language he uses has echoes in 1 Peter, which might suggest that our letter is of a similar date. However, Pliny talks of executing Christians, which Peter does not mention. In fact, Peter comments that the suffering of his readers is no different from what other Christians are suffering (5:9), and he uses the general Greek word for suffering (*pascho*, 12 times, more than any other NT book) rather than the word for persecution.

5. Babylon

The use of 'Babylon' as a symbol for Rome is found in a number of Jewish and Christian documents. This would be a natural association to make, especially after the destruction of Jerusalem by Rome in AD 70 – and most of the references come from this later period. If Peter, whom tradition strongly associates with Rome and who died c. AD 65, is indeed the author of this letter, this makes 5:13 one of the earliest such references.

B. Content and structure

1:1–2	Opening greeting in standard letter format
1:3–12	Praise to God ('doxology', similar to many Pauline letters)
1:13 – 2:3	Response to God's grace in holy living
2:4–10	Jesus, the living stone, and his chosen people
2:11 – 3:7	Live godly lives: everyone, slaves, wives, husbands
3:8–22	Live well together, and accept suffering
4:1–11	Live changed lives, alert and sober
4:12–19	Suffering as sharing in the suffering of Christ
5:1–11	Appeals to elders, young men, and all
5:12–14	Greetings from Peter, Silas and the church in 'Babylon'

The letter is notable for its extensive use of the OT, not only in direct quotations (usually indicated in English Bibles) but also in phrases and sayings throughout the letter. Especially notable are its references to Isa. 53, e.g. 2:22 quotes a verse, and 2:24–25 quotes three other phrases. Although this passage is not cited very frequently in the NT, it probably stands behind much of its understanding of Jesus' death, including Jesus' own predictions of his being rejected and killed (see Mark 8:31; 9:13; 10:33 and parallels), and perhaps Paul's description of Jesus dying for our sins 'according to the Scriptures' (1 Cor. 15:3).

C. Reading 1 Peter today

1. Community

1 Peter is full of very strong language about the communal identity of believers, mostly rooted in the OT but also echoing Paul (cf. 4:8–11 with Rom. 12:4–8). This is a powerful challenge to individualized ideas of 'personal' faith in Western society today, which prizes individual freedom of choice.

2. Witness

Our engagement with society will involve affirming the positive alongside bearing witness to God by living good lives (2:12) and speaking out (3:15). And we might not always realize how radical this is. The simple command to 'honour everyone' (2:17, literally) flew in the face of hierarchical Roman society, where honour was accorded in proportion to someone's power and influence. In our society, which values appearance above everything, to imitate God in not judging by outward appearance would be radical indeed.

3. Submission

In making sense of how, exactly, we 'live well' before others, we need to think carefully about the nature of the various submissions that Peter mentions.

- He words the commands carefully (cf. his distinction between *fearing* God and *honouring* the king/emperor in 2:17). Wives should 'submit' to their husbands, the word used elsewhere of the attitude all believers should have to one another (the NT never uses the word 'obey' for wives, though it does use this word for children to their parents). As in Eph. 5:22, wives should submit to *their own* husbands.
- The three commands to submit must be read in the wider context of the NT. The respect due to authorities (Rom. 13) does not ignore their potential as agents of the enemy (Rev. 13). The apparent acceptance of slave/master relationships must be held in tension with the radical equality of all in Christ. And the ordering of family relations needs to take account of the radical involvement of women in the worshipping life of the Christian community.
- How we live out the radical challenge of the gospel today in a context where there is still a legacy of respect for Christian belief, and where all have a democratic right to speak out, will be very different from

living it out as a small and threatened minority in the autocratic and hierarchical society of the first century.

4. Jesus descending to hell?

1 Pet. 3:19 ('the imprisoned spirits') and 4:6 ('gospel preached to those who are now dead') have been understood to mean that Jesus 'descended into hell' (as found in the Apostle's Creed) to preach to those who died before his coming. But there is now widespread agreement that these difficult verses do not support this interpretation. The first is best read in the context of Jewish belief about 'fallen angels' awaiting final judgment, to whom Jesus' victory is proclaimed. The second refers to those who have been evangelized but who have now died, as can be seen by the reference to the dead in the preceding verse.

2 PETER AND JUDE

2 Peter and Jude are often treated together in commentaries because of the large overlap in material between Jude and 2 Pet. 2. This in itself is not a problem; after all, there is considerable overlap between the three 'synoptic' Gospels, while Isa. 36 – 39 is reproduced almost word for word in 2 Kgs 18 – 20. But it does raise the question of the relation between the two texts. The close similarity in wording implies some literary dependence. So either both used a common source – but then more than half of Jude consists of this source, and its writer simply repeated what was written elsewhere; or Jude drew on 2 Peter – but strangely used only the middle part; or 2 Peter used Jude – the view of most commentators, supported by close study of the relevant passages.

A. Occasion and purpose

The author of Jude identifies himself as 'a servant of Jesus Christ and a brother of James' (v. 1). It was unusual to identify oneself as a brother rather than a son, so this probably relates the author to Jesus' brother James, who was prominent in the leadership of the church in Jerusalem. Like James (Jas 1:1), Jude now sees Jesus' position as 'Master and Lord' as more significant than his relation as brother, not least because, again like James, he was not a disciple during Jesus' earthly ministry (Mark 6:3).

The authorship of 2 Peter is probably the most hotly contested in NT studies. The clear claim of the letter is that it is written by the apostle Peter (see 1:1 and 3:1) and there are comments about being an eyewitness to Jesus to back this up (1:16–18). However, the style of writing appears quite different from 1 Peter; the letter incorporates Greek religious and philosophical ideas that might be surprising for a Galilean fisherman (such as 'participating in the divine nature', 1:4; and the list of virtues in 1:5–9); and the tense shifts between present and future in describing the threat of false teachers (compare 2:1–3 with 2:10–12).

So some scholars conclude that 2 Peter is a form of Jewish 'testament', where a later author writes in the name of a famous leader as if giving his last words. However, while some features of 2 Peter fit this theory, others do not. Computer linguistic analysis shows 2 Peter to be significantly closer to 1 Peter than to the rest of the NT, and there is always a danger in assuming a limited understanding for a 'simple' Galilean fisherman. So the case against Peter as author is not as strong as it might be – though puzzles, especially those concerning tense, remain.

Some claim that Jude and 2 Peter mark the beginnings of an early 'catholicism', which would make them late. However, both show expectation of Christ's return and neither show interest in sacramentalism or church offices, which argues against this.

A letter written by Jude would most naturally be dated to the 50s. If 2 Peter is written by Peter, it must be no later than the 60s; if by someone else, it must be no later than around 100, when other writings appear which seem to be dependent on it.

B. Content and structure

Jude's style of argument is evident from its structure.

1–4	Opening greeting and purpose
5–13	Six OT examples, applied to false teachers
14–16	A prophecy from 1 Enoch 1:9, applied to false teachers
17–19	A prophecy from the apostles, applied to false teachers
20–25	Closing exhortations and doxology

2 Peter includes different styles of writing, but the shape of its argument is clear.

1:1–2	Address and greeting
1:3–15	Summary of message and reason for writing
1:16–21	Apostolic witness and prophecy is from God
2:1–22	Future false teachers and God's certain judgment
3:1–10	Future scoffers and Christ's certain return
3:11–18	Exhortation to holy living and doxology

C. Reading 2 Peter and Jude today

These two letters contain some of the most obscure verses in the NT (Jude 6, 9, 14–15; 2 Pet. 2:4) and others that have caused considerable disagreement as to their interpretation (such as 2 Pet. 3:10). But there are also some key verses, not least the acknowledgment of the import-ance of Paul's writings in 2 Pet. 3:15–16. These have been perhaps the most neglected books of the NT and need to be taken seriously – but we need to be careful how we interpret and use them.

Much of the language, particularly in Jude and the parallel sections in 2 Peter, is highly polemical, and makes sharp distinctions between true and false teachers. These texts have at times been used to justify a confrontational approach to relations with other Christians, or a retreat into a 'faithful remnant' detached from others. So it is important to notice these features of the text:

- The sections about false teachers are not simply outbursts of animos-ity, but are reasoned arguments based on texts of Scripture that would have been recognized as such within first-century Judaism.
- The consistent appeal is not to separation but to a shared communal inheritance in the OT Scriptures and in the apostolic witness prior to its being formalized within the canon of the NT.
- Jude's warnings appear to be against rejecting traditional Jewish and Christian teaching on morality (i.e. 'antinomianism'). 2 Pet. 2:7–9 adds to this a focus on the security of the godly; whenever we talk of the judgment of others, we must also face the reality of judgment ourselves.
- We need to read these calls to purity of life and doctrine in the light of Jesus' ministry: both his own call to holiness and warnings of judg-ment, and his radical inclusion of the unholy and the marginalized.
- In all this, grace remains central. Jude's letter closes with an injunction to be 'merciful to those who doubt' (22) and a wonderful doxology to God, who alone guarantees our security and fashions in us his perfection. 2 Peter places a list of virtues in the context of the forgiveness of sins (1:5–9) and of receiving the inheritance God has given us (1:10–11). Moreover, many of these ideas, originally expressed in Jewish terms, are re-expressed in a way that is acces-sible to a Greek audience. Grace is always mission-hearted.

1, 2 & 3 JOHN

The three Johannine letters have a style distinct from other NT letters, and some clear connections with the Gospel of John. These connections are most evident in 1 John, though there are phrases in the other two letters that in turn connect them with 1 John.

A. *The letters and the Gospel*

It is not immediately clear that 1 John is in fact a letter. It has no mention of author or audience, no opening or closing greetings, and no obvious structure, unlike the Pauline letters. At first reading it feels rather repetitive, or at least has a circular, reflective shape to it.

There are many connections with John's Gospel both in vocabulary and ideas. Many of them are found in the opening verses, but in most cases they are repeated throughout:

- The opening of the letter talks of 'the beginning' (1:1; cf. John 1:1).
- The place of testimony to what has been seen and heard (1:2–3; cf. John 1:14).
- The ideas of light and life, closely related to one another (1:2; cf. John 1:4; 8:12).
- Eternal life (1:2; cf. John 1:4; 3:16).
- Jesus as God's son (1:7, 9–10; cf. John 1:14, 18; 5:17–18).
- Joy being made complete (1:4; cf. John 3:29; 15:11; 16:24).
- The new commandment (2:7–8; cf. John 13:34–35).
- Contrast between light and darkness (2:8–10; cf. John 1:5).
- The hostility of the world (2:15–17; cf. John 1:10–11).
- Living in the truth (2:21; 3:18–19; cf. John 3:21).
- Remaining (abiding) in God (2:24–27; cf. John 15:4–10).
- Jesus laying down his life for us (3:16; cf. John 10:11; 15:13).

By contrast, there are three areas which might set the letter apart from the Gospel. First, the letter appears still to expect the coming of Jesus in the near future (e.g. 2:28), in contrast to the 'realized eschatology' of the Gospel which suggests that the full reality of Christ has come in his death and resurrection. However, the Gospel does still retain a future perspective (e.g. John 6:39–40), and conversely the letter sees the reality of the final victory already anticipated in the present (2:13–14).

Secondly, the letter describes Jesus' death as an 'atoning sacrifice' (2:2) which rather contrasts the Gospel's idea of the Son being 'lifted up' (John 12:32–34). However, the Gospel also talks of Jesus as the sacrificial lamb (John 1:29), and both Gospel and letter refer to Jesus laying down his life.

Thirdly, the letter's references to the Holy Spirit do not match the highly personalized language of the Gospel (John 14 – 16). However, the letter does identify the 'anointing' of the Spirit as leading into truth (2:20, 27) in a way that is strikingly reminiscent of the Gospel (John 16:13).

2 & 3 John share some phraseology with 1 John: a new command, loving one another, obedience, Jesus coming in the flesh and joy being complete (2 John); and doing what is good and having true testimony (3 John). But they are more obviously written as letters, in the one case to a church, in the other to an individual church leader.

With so much overlap in vocabulary and theme, it is hard to resist the conclusion that 1 John was written by the same person who wrote John's Gospel – or at least someone who was very familiar with and influenced by the Gospel.

Papias, writing in the second century, adds a possible confusion to the question of authorship. He refers to 'elders', including John, who were disciples of the Lord, but then also refers to 'the elder John'. It is unclear whether he is referring here to one person or to two separate people. If there was a 'John the elder' as distinct from John the apostle, then he may have been the author of 2 and 3 John. And 1 John may then have been written by either of the two.

B. Content and structure

Rather than having a typical letter structure, 1 John moves in a particular shape, often making general statements from which conclusions about Christian living and behaviour are then drawn.

1:1–4	Prologue (similar to John 1:1–18)
1:5 – 2:14	We must walk in the light, obeying God's commands
2:15–17	We must not love the world
2:18–27	We have the anointing of the Spirit, to know the truth
2:28 – 3:10	As God's children, we cannot continue in sin
3:11–24	We must love each other in action, as Jesus loved us
4:1–6	Spirits from God acknowledge Jesus' incarnation
4:7–21	God's love for us prompts our love for each other
5:1–12	We overcome the world through obedience and faith
5:13–21	Conclusion: our confidence in approaching God

Like other early Christian writings, 1 John appears to be addressing concerns raised when Christian belief encountered Greek philosophical ideas, especially those that gave rise to Gnosticism in the second century. There is a strong emphasis on Jesus' true humanity, the reality of sin, and the need for practical ethical change in response to knowing God. There is also a clear focus that so-called 'special knowledge' is actually the privilege of all who follow Christ, and is in fact the open secret of transformed relationships.

2 John and 3 John are brief letters, with encouragement and warning:

2 John		3 John	
1–3	Opening greetings	1–2	Opening greetings
4–6	Love one another	3–8	Love visiting believers
7–11	Watch out for deceivers	9–12	Diotrephes and Demetrius
12–13	Closing greetings	13–14	Closing greetings

C. Reading 1, 2 & 3 John today

1 John offers us an integration between truth and love, so often separated in our modern concerns. It also holds together the work of the Spirit with the affirmation of tradition, at least in some form – again, issues which are often set against each other today. The letter at times has an inward-looking feel with its focus on loving relationships within the believing community. But alongside that is the emphasis on the importance of testimony, and a recognition that claims to know God are vacuous without the evidence of transformed relationships.

With 2 & 3 John it is important to note that the discussion of welcome occurs in the context of offering hospitality to wandering teachers. The refusal of hospitality (2 John 10–11) is not about being mean, but about being careful not to give approval to their teaching.

JUDE

See under 2 Peter.

Further reading (see **Introduction** for good commentary series)

Howard Marshall, Steven Travis and Ian Paul, *Exploring the New Testament 2. The Letters and Revelation* (SPCK 2002) – excellent introduction, with panels highlighting themes and points to ponder.

Tom Wright, *What Saint Paul Really Said* (Lion, 1997) – very readable summary of Paul's main themes across his letters.

F. F. Bruce, *Paul: Apostle of the Free Spirit* (Paternoster, 1981) – great combination of Paul's story and his teaching.

Craig Blomberg, *From Pentecost to Patmos: An Introduction and Survey* (IVP 2006) – well-written guide to the key issues.

12. Revelation

Carl Mosser

Revelation is the most misunderstood, abused and maligned book of the Bible. It is also a book of singular importance when properly understood.

A. Authorship and date

Four times the author indicates that his name is John (1:1, 4, 9; 22:8). He refers to himself as a 'servant' of God (1:1) as well as a 'brother and companion' in suffering (1:9). An angel classifies him among a group of Christian prophets (22:9), a designation consistent with John's awareness of writing a prophecy (1:3; 10:11; 22:7, 10, 18–19).

Traditionally the author has been identified with John the son of Zebedee, one of the twelve apostles. There is clear Semitic influence on the book's Greek grammar, indicating that he was a native of Palestine whose first language was Aramaic or Hebrew. This is consistent with authorship by John the son of Zebedee.

However, John was an extremely common name among Palestinian Jews, and we know that at least one other prominent first-century Christian bore the name. John the son of Zebedee became an apostle, but little in Revelation supports identifying its author with one of the apostles. He never calls himself an apostle, and gives no indication that he is among the twelve apostles written on the New Jerusalem's foundations (21:14), or is among the twenty-four enthroned elders, probably the twelve patriarchs and twelve apostles (4:4, 10; 5:8; 11:16;

19:4). So it seems unlikely that the author was John the son of Zebedee but we cannot determine his identity any more than that.

Since the second century most have thought that Revelation was written late in the reign of the emperor Domitian (AD 81–96), though some have argued for the reigns of either Nero earlier (AD 54–68) or Trajan later (AD 98–117). None of the proposals easily accounts for all the internal evidence, but a date near the end of the first century faces the fewest difficulties.

B. What is Revelation?

Misinterpreting Revelation usually begins with misunderstanding the kind of book it is. So we need to consider its genre very carefully.

1. Revelation, not revelations

Revelation is commonly but erroneously referred to as 'the Book of Revelations' (plural). This stems from the widespread assumption that it is a series of esoteric revelations about end-time events. Readers then treat its imagery and symbolism as a kind of code, and attempt to decipher it to reveal literal descriptions of the near future. For example, some have 'discovered' that the locusts with human faces, breastplates and stings in their tails (9:7–10) are really Apache attack helicopters, or that the 'mark of the beast' (13:16–17) is really a microchip placed under the skin or on product barcodes. And every few years someone claims to have deciphered the precise date of Jesus' return. But numerous predicted dates have now passed, and Jesus has yet to return.

Does the Bible really conclude with a book of cryptic revelations, undecipherable until long after it was written? The book itself refutes this view. It begins by declaring itself a 'revelation [singular] from Jesus Christ' (1:1). This revelation was written for churches in the first-century Roman province of Asia (1:11; 22:16), what today is western Turkey. Church members were told to read and listen attentively, because the time was near (1:3). So they would have had to understand the book in order to comply with it. Moreover, the author was told not to seal up the book's prophecy due to the nearness of its fulfilment (22:10). This contrasts markedly with Daniel in the OT, for whom 'the words are closed up and sealed until the time of the end' (Dan. 12:9). All this entails that Revelation's symbolism and imagery would have been meaningful to the first recipients. So the context for properly under-standing the book's message must be their historical situation, not ours. Nevertheless, as with the rest of the NT, the message of Revelation transcends the circumstances of its original readers to speak to Christians in all times.

2. Revelation the letter

After a brief prologue (1:1–3), the formal beginning of Revelation (1:4–6) is that of a typical letter. It identifies the author, John, and the recipients, the seven churches in Asia. This is followed by a wish of grace and peace, a common feature of early Christian letters. The book also concludes with a grace wish (22:21), another characteristic of early Christian letters. In this way the entire book is framed as a letter to seven churches. So it is a serious mistake to divorce chs. 1 – 3 from chs. 4 – 22, as if only the first part of the book was really intended for those named as the addressees.

John informs us about a visionary experience he had while exiled on the island of Patmos. He is instructed to record his vision and send the written scroll to the churches (1:9–11). Each church is discussed specifically (2:1 – 3:22), but the letter as a whole is addressed to all seven. This means that the visions were intended to be applied in practical ways to the specific circumstances of these churches. We must therefore take their first-century historical context seriously in the interpretation of every part of the letter.

3. Revelation the apocalypse

The book's opening line refers to 'the revelation [Greek: *apokalypsis*] from Jesus Christ' (1:1). It is not clear whether this is intended as a technical literary classification. Nonetheless, the word revelation and the book's subsequent content suggest that it should be regarded as an 'apocalypse'. Modern scholars classify a number of early Jewish and Christian texts as apocalypses, though Revelation is the only NT example.

Apocalypses centre on a first-person narrative in which a supernatural agent mediates revelatory visions to the narrator, who then records them for the benefit of others. These visions employ rich imagery, symbolism and other literary devices to communicate a transcendent perspective on human experience, especially that of the readers, and to encourage conformity to this perspective in thinking and behaviour. But the visions are *not* encoded instructions. Whereas code must be deciphered and translated into plain language to be understood, symbolic imagery is an irreducible part of the message being communicated in the apocalypse. The symbolism conveys something about reality that is otherwise impossible to articulate.

Revelation's symbolic visions are not encoded descriptions of events either. Even less are they John's attempts to describe technologies of the far distant future. Instead, the symbols would have communicated transcendent truths in a meaningful way to the immediate addressees. They were meant to give the original recipients insight into their own situation and its place in God's plan of salvation, and to inspire confidence in God's promise.

4. Revelation the prophecy

In addition to being a letter and an apocalypse, Revelation also identifies itself as a prophecy to be read in the context of Christian worship (1:3). Like OT prophetic texts, its primary purpose was not foretelling the future. Rather, as a prophecy, it contains God's rebuke of the sinful compromises of his people (e.g. 2:4–5, 14–16, 20–25; 3:1–3, 15–18) and his critique of a corrupt society's rampant injustice and immorality (see esp. 17:1–4; 18:2–24; 21:8, 27). It calls the people of God to respond in repentant obedience (cf. 22:7).

To the degree that future events are predicted, they chiefly declare two certainties. The first is the certainty of God's coming judgment against unrighteousness. The second is the certainty of his promise to make a world that reflects his untarnished goodness and glory. Both aspects encourage repentance and faithful perseverance. Those who hear the prophecy are expected to heed its warnings, and will be blessed if they do. By contrast, judgment awaits anyone who attempts to alter the prophecy and its implications, whether by subtraction or addition (22:18–19).

C. Structure

1:1–8	Prologue and epistolary introduction
1:9 – 3:22	Initial vision of Jesus and messages to the seven churches
4:1 – 5:14	Vision of heaven and the Lamb worthy to open God's scroll
6:1 – 8:5	Opening the scroll's seven seals
8:6 – 11:19	Blowing the seven trumpets
12:1 – 14:20	Conflict between the saints and the powers of evil
15:1 – 16:21	The seven bowls of plague
17:1 – 19:10	Babylon the Great and her downfall
19:11 – 20:15	The world's conquest and judgment
22:1 – 22:5	The New Jerusalem and renewal of the cosmos
22:6–21	Epilogue and epistolary closing

D. Content

Revelation opens with a prologue that describes the book and its basic purpose (1:1–3). Then comes the formal beginning of the letter (1:4–8). This epistolary introduction leads into a vision of the glorified Jesus and his messages to the churches in Ephesus, Smyrna, Pergamum, Thyatira, Sardis, Philadelphia and Laodicea (1:9 – 3:22). Each message follows the same basic pattern: address to the church's angel or messenger; Jesus' self-description drawn from the vision in ch. 1; commendation for the church's good qualities and critique for its faults; warning to heed the message; and finally promise for the victorious. Within this pattern, nothing good is said about the churches in Sardis and Laodicea, and nothing bad about those in Smyrna and Philadelphia.

Next, John is taken up to the throne room of heaven by the Spirit (4:1–11). God is on the throne, holding a sealed scroll with his decree of judgment and redemption for the world. A voice asks, 'Who is worthy to break the seals and open the scroll?' (5:2). But no one worthy is found anywhere in the created order, so John weeps (5:4). Then the Lamb of God enters and is declared worthy to open the scroll, because he shed his blood to purchase people for God from 'every tribe and language and people and nation' (5:9).

After receiving praise from every kind of created being (5:13), the Lamb proceeds to open each of the scroll's seals in turn. For the first six seals this is accompanied by momentous events: conquest (6:1–2), the removal of peace (6:3–4), famine (6:5–6), death (6:7–8), the cry of the martyrs for justice (6:9–11), an earthquake and cosmic signs of doom (6:12–14). Then, before the final seal's opening, John has two visions of groups of people, first 144,000, consisting of 12,000 from each of the twelve tribes of Israel (7:1–8), and then a vast multitude (7:9–12).

The identity of the 144,000 has often been misunderstood. They are mentioned again later, where they are identified as the human 'first-fruits' offered to God and the Lamb (14:4), and described as those who 'did not defile themselves with women', truthful and blameless (14:4–5). This does *not* intend to idealize ascetic celibacy or imply that women are somehow tainted! Rather, 'blameless' refers to the OT requirement that priests and sacrificial animals be free from physical defect, and that soldiers on duty be free from ritual impurity caused by seminal emission (Deut. 23:9–14; 1 Sam. 21:5–6). The 144,000 are a contingent of physically whole, ritually pure, morally upstanding individuals qualified to serve as warriors in a holy war. In other words, the 144,000 represent the armies from heaven that the Messiah leads to victory over the forces of evil (cf. 19:11–14).

The opening of the seventh seal is followed by a long silence and the distribution of trumpets to seven angels (8:1–5). As with the opening of each seal, the blowing of each trumpet leads to disaster on the earth (8:6 – 11:19). Prior to the seventh trumpet, John again has two visions (10:1 – 11:14). In one he eats a little scroll, and in the other he sees two witnesses who prophesy, are killed and rise up again. The seventh trumpet is then blown, leading to hymns praising God for his righteous judgments (11:15–19).

At 12:1 the book takes a new direction. John's vision shifts from God's outpoured judgment to a series of 'signs' which depict God's people in conflict with evil (12:1 – 15:4). The theme of divine judgment is picked up again with an even greater 'sign'. John sees 'seven angels with the seven last plagues' (15:1) representing 'God's wrath on the earth' (16:1). As with the plagues on Egypt in Exodus, the angels pour out the full force of God's holy anger against the wickedness embodied by Rome. We then see Rome, called 'Babylon the Great, the Mother of Prostitutes', destroyed and lamented (17:1 – 19:10).

The vision reaches its climactic section with the arrival of the rider on a white horse along with the armies of heaven (19:11–16). They prove victorious in their battle against the kings of the earth. This ushers in a millennium in which the righteous reign with Christ on the earth (20:1–6). After the thousand years Satan is released and prepares for one final battle, but fire from heaven devours his forces (20:7–10). This sets the stage for the resurrection and last judgment (20:11–15). John's vision – as well as the entire biblical drama – then reaches its climax as he sees 'a new heaven and a new earth', in which God dwells with his people for ever (21:1 – 22:5).

E. Symbolism

The imagery of Revelation is intentionally evocative and suggestive. While depicting both transcendent and earthly realities, it does not always correspond with literal events. Moreover, it often alludes to the experiences and fears of people living in the Roman Empire at the end of the first century, including popular myths, rumours and expectations. For example, it alludes to popular fears about a Parthian invasion from the east (9:13–19; 16:12), and to the contemporary myth that Nero, though long dead, would one day return (13:3; 17:8) – 'the number of the Beast', 666, is also 'the number of a man' (13:18), probably Nero. He was the 'head' of the Roman Empire that violently persecuted Christians, one of the chief sins for which Rome would be judged (cf. 16:6; 17:6; 18:24; 19:2).

This kind of imagery engages the imagination and provokes consideration of the divine judgment that awaits Rome and the world. Christians have long debated whether it also predicts specific future events. Similarly, they have long debated whether the evocative description of the saints' millennial reign on earth is meant to be fulfilled literally. These are important questions, but they should not be allowed to eclipse the book's central message. Even if this symbolism is meant to find fulfilment in future events, that is not its primary purpose. Rather, Revelation seeks to influence present behaviour by a profound vision of God, his judgment, the vindication of the righteous, and the renewal of creation.

F. Canonical function and contemporary significance

John sees himself as standing in the tradition of the OT prophets, and his prophetic commission (10:8–11) clearly recalls Ezekiel's (Ezek. 2:8 – 3:3). But he goes beyond them in declaring 'the mystery of God ... announced to his servants the prophets' (10:7). They foretold the coming Day of the Lord, while John proclaims its fulfilment in God's final judgment and re-creation of the earth. Like them, he is someone to whom the Lord reveals his secrets (cf. Amos 3:7; 1 Pet. 1:10).

Revelation is saturated with the terminology and imagery of the OT, especially the prophetic books. Yet, John never quotes any specific passages. Instead he appropriates prophecies and applies them in new ways. They provide him with building material for a prophetic vision that brings the entire prophetic tradition to a stunning climax. Regardless of their original application, John interprets their ultimate fulfilment in the events he foretells. For example, Isaiah and Jeremiah deliver a number of oracles against Babylon (Isa. 13:1 – 14:23; 21:1–10; 47; Jer. 25:12–38; 50 – 51), and John echoes these in his own oracle against Babylon (18:1 – 19:8). But whereas Isaiah's and Jeremiah's oracles were directed against the Neo-Babylonian empire, John's is directed at Rome, giving the ancient oracles new currency. This one example illustrates the way in which John's prophecy serves as the culmination of the Bible's entire prophetic tradition. His prophetic critique continues to apply whenever injustice, tyranny and wickedness are recapitulated within human history.

As the climax of biblical prophecy, Revelation also brings the biblical drama of creation and redemption to a close. It gives readers a glimpse of the reality that lies behind world history. While evil may seem unstoppable in our fallen world, this is mere appearance. Reality is found in the promise of the almighty Creator. Revelation reveals that promise by portraying the drama's final act: the enemies of the Lamb are defeated, his followers are vindicated, and the kingdom of the world becomes the kingdom of God and the Lamb. The God who created the world triumphs over evil, renews the cosmos, and comes down to dwell with humanity in the New Jerusalem. The purposes for which the cosmos and humanity were originally created are now fulfilled. The biblical drama is brought full circle.

This brings the canon of Scripture to a close with a solemn promise – God obligates himself to complete the salvation that he revealed in Jesus Christ. He binds himself to consummating the new creation begun in Jesus' resurrection and the regeneration of his followers (cf. 1 Pet. 1:3–5; 2 Cor. 5:17). This promise is intended to bolster confidence and hope in God's people, as they contend with the powers of this age.

With John we are able to penetrate heaven and see what is really going on in the world. There we see that the views of reality perpetuated by every tyrannical regime and power are false, that the façades and illusions created by evil powers like Rome are lies. We discover that the Creator has intentions for the world that transcend anything rebellious creatures might concoct for themselves. And the Creator's intentions will be fulfilled, whereas those of rebels will be brought to naught. The here-and-now can be depressing and hopeless when viewed only from within. But when seen from a transcendent perspective, it looks quite different. And this vision has a powerful effect on how one lives in the eager anticipation of the revealing of Jesus Christ.

Further reading (see **Introduction** for good commentary series)

Howard Marshall, Steven Travis and Ian Paul, *Exploring the New Testament 2. The Letters and Revelation* (SPCK, 2002) – excellent introduction, with panels highlighting themes and points to ponder.

Marvin Pate (editor), *Four Views on the Book of Revelation* (Zondervan, 1998) – good summary of different interpretations.

Richard Bauckham, *The Theology of the Book of Revelation* (CUP, 1993) – careful, readable study.

Craig Blomberg, *From Pentecost to Patmos: An Introduction and Survey* (IVP, 2006) – well-written guide to the key issues.

Reading the Bible

Suppose that you are sitting down with your Bible for the first time. How then do you best approach the job of reading it?

From start to finish

This is certainly a valid approach: begin with Genesis and work your way through to Revelation. It will give you a comprehensive idea of what is in the Bible, and you will avoid the danger of spending all your time in certain books and ignoring others. You will also be beginning where Jesus and the apostles began: the only Bible they had was the OT. A variation on this theme is to read the OT and the NT side by side, taking a chapter or two from each every day. This gives you a more varied diet.

The major problem with reading the Bible in this way is that some of the earlier books of the OT are not easy to understand, especially for new Christians. If you start at the beginning and quickly arrive at some difficult material, you may get stuck. For more established Christians, however, this method could well yield surprising and fruitful discoveries. But be aware that unless you can tackle large chunks of the Bible every day, you will take a long time to read from cover to cover.

A book at a time

Although individual Bible texts can mean a great deal to us, the authors wrote whole books, which have various themes running through them. This means that a logical way to read a Bible book is from beginning to end. In doing this we see how the author has developed the themes, and get an idea of how the readers were meant to respond. We see isolated verses and events in their wider context. As we go along, we begin to understand the sequence of the story or argument.

Some people prefer to start with the big picture and fit all the details into it; others would rather begin with the details and use them to put the picture together. If you are a big picture person, you will want to try to take in a whole book before going on to look at shorter passages and separate verses. But whatever your point of departure, remember that the parts need to be set in the context of the whole, or you may interpret them in ways that the authors never intended.

Small sections

At some point we will want to begin asking what the individual passages, sentences and words of the Bible meant to the authors, and what they mean for us. This approach means reading much shorter portions than whole books, and for this we will need some sort of plan. You can make your own, by reading to the most natural break in the story or argument, or reading one or two of the sub-sections into which many Bible translations divide the text. Most daily Bible reading notes also take you through a book by short steps.

Because you are dealing only with short sections, you have more time to ask detailed questions about the meaning of the passage. It is at this point that many of the books in the Further Reading sections will be most useful, helping you to understand the background issues, illuminating the difficult words and phrases, and applying the text to your own life. You may also like to make notes as you go along, especially if one reason for studying the Bible is to teach it to others. In your preparation you can then go back to what you have discovered yourself.

Themes

This is a more challenging method of Bible study, but it repays the effort. We may want to know what the whole Bible teaches about 'the kingdom of God', or what Paul meant by 'righteousness'. If so, we will need to look at all the major passages that deal with the theme, collecting their teaching and building up the picture for ourselves. The possibilities are numerous and varied, and a Bible dictionary or other study aid will give you some ideas and help you pursue them.

But notice the reference above to 'passages'. When studying a Bible topic it is tempting to get out a concordance and look up every verse in which the term is mentioned. Although this exercise has some value, you run the risk of seeing individual verses in isolation from their context, and so of misunderstanding them. It is much better to find the longer sections in which the subject is discussed and study these one by one. When you put their teachings together you will have a much more coherent view of the theme.

Reading for pleasure

Some people like to sit down in comfort, pick up their Bible and just read it. We can relax into the world of Scripture and simply let it speak to us. Or we can read it more slowly and prayerfully until we find it addressing our current circumstances. Often we will discover a new command or promise, or some aspect of God's purpose that strengthens or challenges us. But if you like to use this method, don't neglect to do some detailed study as well, so that it is God's voice that you hear in the Bible and not just your own!

Studying with others

Although it is good to read the Bible for yourself, it is also useful to come to it with other Christians. Some people have the gift of teaching, and can make the Bible clear to a whole group of people. In our churches we have an opportunity week by week to explore God's Word together through the ministry of our leaders. We may like to use the church Bibles or take one of our own to follow the readings and look up the references.

Another popular and helpful way of looking at the Bible is in small groups. The particular value of this approach is that, although the group leader will have prepared the study, it gives an opportunity for each person to share their understandings with the others. Also the leader is able to put right any obvious *mis*understandings!

To get the most out of a small group study, have a look at the passage and any notes beforehand, and come prepared to share what you have found, as well as to listen to others and ask questions. The best small group studies are very practical, so expect to learn together how the passage you are studying can apply to your lives.

Memorization

One well-tried way of retaining what you have read is to commit it to memory. With our convenient chapter and verse divisions, it is fairly easy for us to memorize verses from the Bible, and we can learn the references too. But as we have already seen, single verses can too easily be taken out of their context and be made to mean less – or more! – than they should. So it is often more helpful to learn chapters or passages.

In your studies you will come across sections that mean a great deal to you. Note these, reread them several times, try writing them from memory, and you will find that learning a passage is not so hard. But make sure that you have first tried to understand them and apply them to your own life. Repeating Bible passages parrot-fashion is no use at all!

Meditation

Meditation is something we can do at any time of the day, and not just in special times that we set apart. If we have spent time studying the Bible, trying to understand and apply it, and perhaps committing it to memory, then through the day, when our minds would otherwise be idle, it can come back to us. Sometimes we realize how the passages we have been reading apply to particular situations at home or at work.

But meditation is something more than just casually remembering what we have read; it is taking time to ponder it. We have worked hard to understand what it means in its setting; now we let it run through our minds. As we do so, we begin to use our imagination as well as our reason to explore the implications of the truth under review. Sometimes it is good to sit down quietly and close your eyes, shutting out the world. Some people find it helpful to jot down their thoughts as these arise.

You don't have to be very knowledgeable to meditate. You need only a Bible verse to start, and then a little mental discipline so that your mind doesn't wander. Meditation is an art, so you will find it getting easier the more you do it.

Prayer

As Christian believers we come to the Bible with faith, expectancy, and willingness to submit to God's will as he reveals it to us. That is why it is most natural to ask God for his help as we read it. This principle applies whether we study it privately, or whether we listen to its exposition in public.

Not only should we move into our Bible study with prayer; we should also move from it in the same way. We may turn the themes, promises and commands that we have read into praise, confession, petition and intercession for others. To surround our Bible study with prayer is to approach it in the right way, as God's written Word to us.

Index of Scripture References

THE COSGRAVE PARTY

A history of Cumann na nGaedheal, 1923–33

CIARA MEEHAN

The Cosgrave Party: A history of Cumann na nGaedheal, 1923–33

First published 2010
by Prism

Prism is an imprint of the Royal Irish Academy
19 Dawson Street
Dublin 2

www.ria.ie

The author and publisher are grateful to the following for permission to reproduce the documents, photographs and illustrations in this book:
National Library of Ireland; UCD Archives, School of History and Archives; Cork City and County Archives; Trinity College Library Dublin;
Getty Images; Corbis Images; Library of Congress, Washington; and Mary Evans Picture Library.

Every effort has been made to trace the copyright holders of these documents, photographs and illustrations and to ensure the accuracy of their captions.

British Library Cataloguing in Publication Data. A CIP catalogue record for this book
is available from the British Library.

Printed in Spain by Graficas Iratxe.

10 9 8 7 6 5 4 3 2 1

For my parents and in memory of my godmother, Margie Markey

W.T. Cosgrave at his desk, 1922. (Courtesy of the National Library of Ireland.)

CONTENTS

This book could not have been written without the support and input of a number of people. Professor Diarmaid Ferriter provided invaluable feedback and direction on the first draft of the manuscript. Dr John Bowman, who read parts of the text with great attention, invariably offered perceptive criticism. Dr Paul Rouse has been unfailingly generous with his time and advice throughout the duration of this project. I am also grateful to the external reader for his or her helpful observations.

I would like to acknowledge Professor Michael Laffan, who supervised the PhD thesis from which parts of this book originate, and also my examiners, Professor Mike Cronin and Dr Susannah Riordan, for their comments on that work.

Niamh Cullen, Eoin Jennings, Neil Johnston, Paul O'Brien, Kevin O'Sullivan and Patrick Walsh read sections of the book, or listened and offered suggestions—or fixed printers when they refused to work. A special word of thanks is due to Justin Dolan Stover who has generously shared ideas and sources over a long period of time, and who helped make completion of this book possible. Naturally, any errors or omissions are my own.

Mark Duncan shared his knowledge of locating photographic material. Dr Adrian Dunne and Seán Kearns assisted in the calculation of the statistics used in the final chapter. A number of politicians, both past and present, spoke to me about their perceptions of Cumann na nGaedheal and the party's legacy to Fine Gael.

I am grateful to the staff of the National Library of Ireland especially Mary Broderick, the National Archives of Ireland, Cork City and County Archives and, in particular, UCD Archives, School of History and Archives. I would also like to thank Fine Gael and Fianna Fáil for granting me permission to view the parties' papers held at those archives, Declan Costello for allowing me access to his father's papers, and the Labour Party for making the relevant annual reports available to me. I wish to acknowledge the generous grants provided by the National University of Ireland and by UCD Seed Funding towards the publication of this book.

At the Royal Irish Academy, I would like to sincerely thank Ruth Hegarty, Helena King, Fidelma Slattery, Pauric Dempsey and, in particular, my editor, Lucy Hogan. Her patience, attention to detail, support and good humour have made writing this book a most enjoyable experience.

Thanks are due to Des Brennan, Aoife Collins, Jenny Doyle, Laura O'Brien and Graham O'Neill who, over the years, have always been willing to talk about Cumann na nGaedheal and much else besides.

Finally, I would like to thank the people closest to me. I would be lost without the friendship of Cerrie Byrne, Pamela Casciani-Dawson and Aisling Corby. Their amazing patience, understanding and encouragement as the book was being put together, along with their infectious wit and constant readiness to distract me from writing, are just some of my favourite things about them. My greatest debt is to my parents, Patrick and Jennifer, whose support and generosity knows no bounds. Everything that I have achieved is due to them, and it is for that reason that this book is, in part, dedicated to them.

The Cosgrave Party

Introduction

'Cumann na nGaedheal should have a proud place in history'.[1] Such was the opinion of the *Star* in 1931, but this pride of place has not always been afforded to the party in the pages of history books and even members of Fine Gael, its natural successor, regularly overlook their antecedents. This book seeks to evaluate the party and locate its place in Irish history.

Under the leadership of W. T. Cosgrave, Cumann na nGaedheal was the government party of the third, fourth, fifth and sixth Dála during the first ten years of Free State independence. It was a decade of considerable achievement. When the government was ousted by Eamon de Valera's Fianna Fáil in 1932, the state—created in the midst of a civil war only a mere ten years previously—had been stabilised. To challenge the emerging dominance of Fianna Fáil, Cumann na nGaedheal subsequently merged with the National Centre Party and the Army Comrades Association (ACA commonly known as the 'Blueshirts') in 1933 to create the United Ireland Party: Fine Gael. This political metamorphosis has left Fine Gael unsure of its precise date of origin: 1923 or 1933? Largely neglected by both historians and its descendants, Cumann na nGaedheal has remained something of an enigma.

The Irish Parliamentary Party (IPP)'s tradition of moderate nationalism was continued by Cumann na nGaedheal. The IPP had been the voice of nationalist Ireland and under the leadership of Charles Stewart Parnell and later John Redmond, it sought to bring a degree of independence to Ireland through a Home Rule settlement. Concessions were to be won through peaceful agitation and on the floor of the British House of Commons, not by resort to physical violence. It was Redmond who came closest to achieving his party's aim when, on its third reading, the Home Rule Bill passed the Commons on 25 May 1914. The *Freeman's Journal* declared in September 1914, 'Home Rule is a reality',[2] but the outbreak of the First World War resulted in the legislation being placed on the statute books until peace was restored. As the war that most people predicted would end by Christmas dragged on, the Irish Party—formed to deliver Home Rule to Ireland—was left without a purpose and went into decline. It suffered also because of the 1916 Rising, the conscription crisis and leadership problems, and was subsequently routed by Sinn Féin—which became the new voice of nationalist Ireland—at the 1918 general election. Most of the leading Cumann na nGaedheal figures were drawn from the ranks of this, the third Sinn Féin party. Broadly Republican in its outlook, it set up the first Dáil. On the occasion of its inaugural meeting, two policemen were killed at Soloheadbeg, Co. Tipperary, and although the ambush had not been approved by the Dáil or the IRA's General Head Quarters, it is retrospectively seen as the start of the War of Independence.

The spilling of blood that was central to winning national independence continued following the departure of the British. Many of those who had stood shoulder to shoulder—brothers, sisters, cousins and friends—against the enemy subsequently found themselves on opposing sides. Winston Churchill, who had been on the British negotiating team, would later describe the Treaty, signed on 6 December 1921, as 'a great pact and symbol of peace between the British and Irish peoples after 700 years of reciprocal maltreatment and misunderstanding'.[3] On the Irish side, however, the agreement split the Cabinet, subsequently Sinn Féin, and finally the country. A new native government sought to restore peace from chaos. Most political parties are created to win power through electoral success, but Cumann na nGaedheal—born into the blood of this fratricidal conflict—was built by men already exercising power. A party of government for most of its existence, it is the only party in the Irish system to have been created after coming into government. Irish politics has witnessed the birth and demise of a multitude of parties, but few spent most of their political life in power as Cumann na nGaedheal did.

The death of Arthur Griffith on 12 August 1922 and that ten days later of Michael Collins denied Cumann na nGaedheal of its natural leaders, and their place was taken by the widely respected W.T. Cosgrave, who had fought in 1916 but who had then taken a step back from the military campaign to serve as minister for local government in the revolutionary Dáil.[4] There was a strong Irish-Ireland dimension to his first Cabinet: Eoin MacNeill, minister for education; Joseph McGrath, minister for industry and commerce; Richard Mulcahy, minister for defence; Ernest Blythe, minister for finance; and J.J. Walsh, postmaster general. Those who supported Irish–Ireland—an expression of cultural nationalism—were largely influenced by Douglas Hyde and his 1892 essay, 'The necessity for de-anglicising Ireland', in which he placed an emphasis on fostering Irish culture, language and literature. Supporters of the movement were committed to Gaelic–Ireland. In contrast to them, there was a more conservative element, sometimes suspected of having imperial sympathies and coming from the Redmondite tradition: Patrick Hogan, minister for agriculture; and Kevin O'Higgins, minister for home affairs and a supporter of Griffith's proposal of a dual monarchy, based on the Austro-Hungarian model. Support for the Treaty was the glue that held Cumann na nGaedheal together. More importantly, the party based its legitimacy on that settlement so that endorsement of it was not merely a party line. In 1927 de Valera would conveniently reinterpret his 1922/3 definition of the Oath.[5] In contrast, Cumann na nGaedheal was never willing to change its strict interpretation of the Treaty for political gain. The party, the settlement and the state were synonymous and an attack against one was considered an attack against all. Thus any perceived threats to the stability and security of the state—from either the extremists or even Free State elements—were responded to decisively.

The amateur nature of Cumann na nGaedheal was a consequence, not just of its unusual birth, but also of the composition of Dáil Éireann. Anti-Treaty Sinn Féin applied its policy of abstention from Westminster to the Dáil after independence. This resulted in the government being assured an in-built majority for as long as the abstentionist tactic remained in place and complacency consequently set in. Cumann na nGaedheal did not pursue votes assiduously and its instincts were rarely populist. The disregard for its grass-root supporters is reflected in the scale of anguished correspondence from frustrated party workers. However, 1927 was to be an important turning point, not just for the Irish party system, but also for the development of Cumann na nGaedheal. Having decided that the Oath was merely an empty formula, de Valera led his Fianna Fáil deputies—who had also continued the policy of abstention after the party's founding the previous year—into the Dáil. The parliament was immediately transformed and Cumann na nGaedheal was no longer assured of its unchallenged position. Consequently the party approached the September 1927 election with an energy that had been noticeably absent from its previous campaigns.

By that stage, McGrath, Mulcahy, MacNeill—and soon Walsh—had left the government. There was a definite shift towards the right and as the party began to absorb the remnants of William Redmond's National League Party—a short-lived entity that attempted to appeal to supporters of the old IPP—and ex-Unionists like Bryan Cooper, it was alleged that Cumann na nGaedheal had completely rejected Irish-Ireland. Fianna Fáil, playing the green card, keenly emphasized Cumann na nGaedheal's refusal to remove the Oath, as well as the involvement of government representatives at imperial conferences. Although the latter produced the legislation that would later allow de Valera to dismantle the Treaty, participation at the time was mocked as complicity with the old enemy. Cumann na nGaedheal had been unable to satisfy the lofty aspirations of Sinn Féin's revolution, but it had secured the state, before passing it to de Valera who seemed to promise much. Ironically, Cumann na nGaedheal's greatest achievement was arguably the creation of stability and an environment in which de Valera could work to undermine the settlement that the party was created to defend.

The creation of Fine Gael has since posed a problem for commemoration. When did Fine Gael actually come into existence—in 1923, under the guise of Cumann na nGaedheal, or in 1933, as a new party distinct from the old pro-Treaty organisation? The Cumann na nGaedheal period has not always been keenly emphasized by party members due to the negativity that surrounds it. Of course, if Fine Gael were to deny its Cumann na nGaedheal parentage, the alternative would be to accept the controversial Eoin O'Duffy—the man indelibly linked with the Blueshirts—as the party's founding father. The merger in 1933 certainly brought with it new traditions: the National Centre Party and even the tradition of the old Irish Parliamentary Party as represented by James Dillon. However, the line of continuity, although distorted, cannot be denied. Policy remained virtually unchanged, and although new personalities emerged, some—most notably Frank MacDermot, leader of the National Centre Party—disappeared just as quickly. Rather than a new party being established, there was a real sense of the new elements being *accommodated* within an existing structure. Donal O'Sullivan was undeniably accurate when he observed that 'new Fine Gael was but old Cumann na nGaedheal writ small',[6] and as such 1923 should be considered the party's date of origin.

Brian Hayes—the then Fine Gael leader in the Seanad—observed to the Ireland Institute in 2003 how remarkable it was that despite Cumann na nGaedheal's pivotal role in establishing Irish democracy, very little has been written about its leading figures. He expressed the view that what had been written, painted an 'unfair and unsympathetic historiography of the period'.[7] Certainly this has largely been the case as much of the focus has been on Cumann na nGaedheal's failures and shortcomings. The party's history lacks the same appeal as that of the revolutionary period or the rise of Fianna Fáil. Cosgrave and his colleagues undertook the work of building the Free State, which was essential but not 'glamorous'. Although father and son are the focus of Stephen Collins's *The Cosgrave legacy*,[8] the work makes no claim to be an exhaustive biography of the first president of the Executive Council. Anthony J. Jordan's *W.T. Cosgrave: founder of modern Ireland* appeared in 2006.[9] Its brief treatment of some of the pivotal events of Cosgrave's governments and lack of in-depth primary-source research makes the work problematic, as does the fact that it does not deal with Cosgrave's career in opposition. Compare this then with the attraction to Michael Collins. The entry of his name into any keyword search of a library database will produce an extensive list of titles. Collins, 31 when he died, was assassinated in an ambush in his native west Cork during the Civil War. Cosgrave passed away quietly at 85, having succumbed to old age; his memory was not sealed by a bloody death. As Michael Laffan put it, in Ireland it was useful to die a violent death, as less attention has been given to those who died in their beds.[10] Collins is inextricably associated with the glory of the revolutionary period, while the history of the Cumann na nGaedheal period lacks that same appeal.

The signing of the Treaty, the subsequent debates and ensuing Civil War; the establishment of Fianna Fáil and its entry into the Dáil; the transfer of power in 1932: these are the defining features of the historiography of the Free State. But it is the rise of Eamon de Valera's party which features most heavily and, to its detriment, Cumann na nGaedheal has been in its shadow. This is despite the fact that the papers of virtually all of the leading figures are available, many of which were deposited at University College Dublin (UCD) Archives before those of the Fianna Fáil personalities. The only existing study is John M. Regan's *The Irish counter-revolution*,[11] which has a narrow focus on Cumann na nGaedheal's role in consolidating the Irish revolution. In keeping with the historiography of the period, the tone of the book is quite negative and achievements—including the Shannon Scheme—are dealt with swiftly, while other important aspects of the party—such as its innovative approach to electioneering—are overlooked, but, the focus of Regan's book is different to that of this work.

To fully understand Cumann na nGaedheal, it is necessary to define the nature of the party in its own right. While outlining the party's mistakes in power, this book documents its achievements and attempts to deliver a more balanced judgement than has previously been offered. A new picture of the party—typically dismissed as amateur and lacking ingenuity—is elucidated. Through an exploration of its electioneering techniques, which have never previously been the subject of academic investigation, a professional side emerges (although what a party does once it is in power is of more importance). The common view that Cumann na nGaedheal collapsed in the late 1920s and early 1930s because of the rise of Fianna Fáil is also contested. The government certainly lost the 1932 election because it lacked any clear policy for the future and was burnt-out by that stage, whereas de Valera's party had energy and seemed to have a strategy for dealing with the economic crisis. Nonetheless, while Cumann na nGaedheal's results between 1927 and 1933 show a decline, particularly compared to Fianna Fáil's improving performance, the crucial point is that its votes were lost to the other, smaller parties and not to its main rival.

In the proceeding pages, the true complexity and, at times, contradictory nature of Cumann na nGaedheal is revealed. The internal politics of a party struggling with ideological tensions and personality clashes, while simultaneously running a government and building a state, are examined. It is shown how Cumann na nGaedheal helped to consolidate the tradition of constitutional nationalism and how that commitment later made it easier for the party to disengage from the Blueshirts. This book aims to establish how the founders of the state not only lost power, but also spent such a long period in the political wilderness, never actually returning to the government benches in their original form. Reflecting on the change of power in 1932, J.H. Thomas, the British dominions secretary, would tell the House of Commons that there were many people in Ireland who had risked their lives for the Treaty.[12] Cumann na nGaedheal ministers had given their talents, and in the case of Kevin O'Higgins, his life, to create and ensure the stability of the new state based on the strictest interpretation of the Treaty. The smooth transfer of power was testament to their commitment. This book brings together separate strands of evidence from party and personal papers, newspapers and secondary sources to offer a re-appraisal of Cumann na nGaedheal, and to determine its place in this history of the independent Irish state.

1921–1923

W.T. Cosgrave, date unknown. (George Grantham Bain Collection, Prints & Photographs Division, Library of Congress, LC-DIG-ggbain-36549.)

Above: Crowds of people on Downing Street, London, pray for an end to the violence in Ireland, 1921. (© Hulton-Deutsch Collection/CORBIS.) Below: Free State Government meeting, including Joseph McGrath, Hugh Kennedy, W.T. Cosgrave, Ernest Blythe and Kevin O'Higgins, *c.* 1922. (Courtesy of the National Library of Ireland.)

Richard Mulcahy, c. 1922. (Courtesy of the National Library of Ireland.)

Eoin MacNeill, date unknown. (George Grantham Bain Collection, Prints & Photographs Division, Library of Congress, LC-DIG-ggbain-36708.)

Right: 'Comic Cosgrave. Jester in chief to the Freak State. As seen in the empire' attributed to Countess Markievicz, c.1922. (Courtesy of the National Library of Ireland.)

JESTER   IN   CHIEF   TO   THE   FREAK   STATE.

AS   SEEN   IN   THE   EMPIRE.

Comic Cosgrave tells us that it is a short step from the bar to a Judge's chair.   We ask him was it a big jump from behind the bar to the President's chair?

President Arthur Griffith en route to Sligo, August 1922. (Courtesy of the National Library of Ireland.)

Michael Collins (with Kevin O'Higgins to the far right in the background) outside the pro-cathedral in Dublin at the funeral of Arthur Griffith, 16 August 1922. (© Hulton archive/Getty Images.)

Above: General Eoin O'Duffy laying a wreath on Michael Collins's grave in Glasnevin Cemetery, 28 August 1922. (Courtesy of the National Library of Ireland.) Below: The newly formed Garda Síochána on parade at the Depot, Phoenix Park, 18 January 1923. (Courtesy of the National Library of Ireland.)

.1.
Life after Collins

[W.T.] Cosgrave is a man with a sense of humour, with the wit and smartness of repartee that is typical of Dublin. One cannot fall out with him … There is really no outstanding man in this ministry; none that can be regarded as a popular hero, and perhaps this is just the very best for Ireland at present. [Kevin] O'Higgins is probably the ablest, but he can be very bitter and somewhat unscrupulous, I think. Most of them are suffering from overwork. [General Richard] Mulcahy in many ways is the finest type, a product of Gaelic League ideas. And of course, in intellect, Eoin MacNeill towers over all. But, none is a popular hero.[1]

Liam de Róiste's 1922 assessment of his colleagues captures the essence of the Cumann na nGaedheal government: a Cabinet of men who were honest and hard-working, but who eschewed popularity in the interests of the work they considered essential. De Róiste was a co-founder of the Cork branch of Sinn Féin and TD for Cork Borough, who spoke his mind freely and who wrote critically within the privacy of own his diaries, which paint an intimate portrait of the time. His observations also reveal a frustration felt by the organisation in general towards the government, a feeling that they were ignored or even resented. This often strained relationship was a consequence of Cumann na nGaedheal's unusual birth. Born in the midst of the bloodshed of a civil war, the party was created to support a government already in power, and in the decade that followed the relationship between the two bodies was far from harmonious. Aside from the dislocation between the élite and the grass roots, Cumann na nGaedheal as a party was one of uneasy alliances. When the Labour leader, Thomas Johnson, argued that it was really a 'coalition of elements which happen to have been fused into a political party without any other coherent principle than to maintain the Treaty',[2] he succinctly defined not only the nature of the party, but also one of its primary difficulties. Divided on such important issues as an economic policy, internal tensions caused rifts that sometimes played themselves out in public.

Idealists with their feet on the ground

The 1921 Anglo–Irish Treaty that would bring members together and act as a binding force was to define the party. That Cumann na nGaedheal continued to reference the settlement as part of its campaign from the opposition benches as late as the 1933 election, is testament to the level of the party's commitment, while also serving as a reminder to voters of the legitimacy of the state and the party that had created it.

Those deputies who had supported the Treaty during the Dáil debates did not defend it as an ideal. Kevin O'Higgins, the future minister for home affairs, acknowledged that better terms would have been desirable, but appealed to his colleagues not to waste time debating irrelevancies. He wondered how they would defeat the British Army and Navy to secure more agreeable terms.[3] In contrast, Countess Constance Markievicz probably spoke for the majority of those who opposed the agreement when she asserted that 'we are idealists believing in and loving Ireland'.[4] So too did Sean Etchingham when he spoke of defaming men in their graves.[5] This type of high rhetoric had previously been commented on by the *Irish Times* special correspondent who observed of a speech earlier in 1921 by de Valera that he 'soared into the realms of pure theory and lofty idealism'.[6] But, while the pro-Treatyites were not completely above referencing the dead themselves, they tended to deal far more with solid fact and the immediacy of the situation which faced them. Arthur Griffith, for example, could tell the Dáil that:

> We have brought back the flag; we have brought back
> the evacuation of Ireland after 700 years by British troops
> and the formation of an Irish army. We have brought back
> to Ireland equality with England, equality with all nations
> which form that Commonwealth, and an equal voice in
> the direction of foreign affairs in peace and war.[7]

Despite this, the expectations of what the revolution and an independent government could deliver were inflated. Likening the hopes of the Republicans to that of a man who projects his image of an ideal onto a woman, only to be disappointed that she does not match his desires, de Róiste noted that the 'abstract being' was 'not at all the same as his subjective ideal'. 'Why grown men, knowing this cause of life, should be willing to die for an *illusory* ideal, is difficult of comprehension: while greater ideals, that are not illusions, based as they are upon eternal verities, can be sought after.'[8] The pro-Treaty wing of Sinn Féin, rechristened Cumann na nGaedheal, sought to implement those practicalities, and from them build a new state. As 1922 drew to a close, O'Higgins wrote to his cousin Tom about the situation in Ireland; the burden, which had been tough, was growing lighter, but it had to be shouldered or the country would have gone 'down to a deeper depth than it ever reached'. Apportioning blame to the 'long fellow' (de Valera), somewhat prophetically he expressed the view that their duty seemed clear: 'push along' and take what was coming to them afterwards. He concluded with the view that 'even idealists have a duty to keep their feet on the ground and take stock of facts, particularly if the destinies of a country happen to be in their charge'.[9]

When Winston Churchill sent his condolences to the provisional government on the deaths of Arthur Griffith and Michael Collins, he also reassured the leaders of the new Irish state 'of the confidence which is felt by the British government that the Treaty position will be faithfully and resolutely maintained'. He went on to say that in Cosgrave and O'Higgins were men whose word was their bond. In response to Churchill's message, the provisional government affirmed that they would 'take up the same task with the same determination and confidence [as Griffith and Collins]'.[10] The Treaty, while not ideal, was therefore an agreement to be upheld; Cumann na nGaedheal would stand by it for the duration of the party's existence. The settlement was Cumann na nGaedheal's raison d'être. Criticising the agreement was tantamount to criticising the government; any faults found in it reflected upon the ministers and their policies. Towards the end of 1923 Eoin MacNeill advised a joint meeting of the party's standing committee and Executive Council that every opportunity should be seized to 'rub in' the sovereign status of the Free State, to ensure that it would be clearly recognised as an equal with Britain.[11] References to the Treaty more than ten years after the signing, however, gave the impression that the party was static, had failed to move with the times, and was incapable of formulating new policies.

That Cumann na nGaedheal provided an umbrella under which the pro-Treatyites could converge weakened and compromised the party. The first notable, though relatively minor, split resulted over the army 'mutiny' in 1924. Despite attempts by Cosgrave to heal the rift, Joseph McGrath's ephemeral national group, consisting of nine deputies in total, ultimately resigned its membership of the government party. Following the collapse of the Boundary Commission and the subsequent agreement reached at Chequers, Pádraig Ó Máille and William Magennis, together with a supporter from the Dáil and the Senate,[12] left Cosgrave's party to form the short-lived Clann Éireann. J. J. Walsh, minister for posts and telegraphs, was also to leave very publicly over policy matters in 1927. (These disagreements are explored more fully in the following chapters.) The fact that internal struggles and eventual splits occurred not over power but over basic policy, highlighted the conflicting views in the party, while also tacitly suggesting that Cosgrave's position as leader went undisputed. Furthermore, the disagreements became more noticeable and pronounced as the Treaty settlement became more secure with the passage of time. Without that common cause for the party to unite behind, the cracks began to show as deputies began to consider finer policy points beyond the central plank of their platform.

The formation of Cumann na nGaedheal

At the 1922 pact election, Michael Collins and Eamon de Valera had tried to replicate the second Dáil by offering the voters panels of pro- and anti-Treaty Sinn Féin candidates in an attempt to heal the split and avoid further conflict. That Labour, the Farmers' Party and several independents also went forward in a contest conducted under proportional representation (PR) naturally frustrated their plans. The result was an overwhelming victory for those who supported the Treaty, with the consequence that the complexion of the third Dáil, abstention aside, was very different to that of its Republican predecessor. In the aftermath of the election, a joint meeting of the general and election committee 'agreed unanimously that the Treaty was still paramount and that the committee should carry on as a pro-Treaty party'.[13]

A special meeting of that committee was held on 7 September 1922 to discuss the formation of a new political party. Ernest Blythe 'urged the need for a party in parliament that would specifically seek to carry on the national cause to completion under the Free State'. He advocated the name 'National Party', and suggested that in its relationship with the government, it be modelled on the British Liberal Party (which was to be practically wiped out at the 1924 general election). Pádraig Ó Máille—deputy for Galway—suggested instead 'Cumann Sonais Éireann'. A subcommittee was subsequently appointed to draft the objects of the new party; it consisted of Diarmuid Fawsitt, Sean Milroy, Walter Cole, James O'Dwyer and F. J. Allen, with Séamus Hughes acting as secretary. Richard Mulcahy felt, however, that the objects could not be defined with deserved justice in the present climate, and considered the timing unsuitable for launching a political organisation of any kind.[14] Some other members of the party shared his scepticism,[15] although the extent of such concerns is not clear.

A private conference was held at 5 Parnell Square, the new pro-Treaty headquarters, on 7 December 1922 with the view to launching the organisation. It was there that Cumann na nGaedheal, in the presence of 38 TDs and 58 constituency delegates, was inaugurated. It aimed 'to carry on the national tradition, and to utilise the powers of government in the hands of the Irish people as well as other forms of public activity for the fullest development of the nation's heritage, political, cultural and economic'.[16] There was no media fanfare to mark the birth of this new party. Instead, the following day's newspapers reported the assassination of General Seán Hales, a pro-Treaty deputy who represented Cork. Having left the Ormond Hotel, on Dublin's north side, to return to the adjourned meeting, he was in a sidecar with Pádraig Ó Máille when they were approached by six men who fired at them; Ó Máille was wounded, but not fatally. An IRA activist once in charge of the Bandon Battalion and who had earned the name 'Buckshot' while in Frongoch internment camp,[17] Hales had been regarded an extremist before voting in favour of the Treaty, which his brother Tom rejected. The killing came one day after the IRA army council issued a threat to the Dáil that members who voted in favour of the Public Safety Act—which established military courts with the power to impose the death penalty—would be targeted. Had the tragedy not occurred, the outcome of the Parnell Square meeting would not have been emphasized anyway. Those in attendance had agreed to proceed without any immediate attempt at publicity.[18]

Several names, emphasizing either the nation or the idea of Irish nationality, had been outlined in a circular on 10 October 1922: An Cumann Náisiúnta, People's League, Cumann na nGaedheal, Cumann Saoirse na hÉireann, Cumann an tSaorstáit, Páirtí Náisiúnta, and United Irishmen. They were discussed more fully at the 7 December meeting. The first of the names initially appeared on the party's draft objects and constitution before it was proposed by Alderman Monahan, seconded by W.J. Ryan and subsequently decided by nineteen votes to sixteen to change it to Cumann na nGaedheal.[19] The chosen name, meaning the organisation or party of the Irish, was clearly a nod to the concept behind the naming of Sinn Féin ('Ourselves Alone').

Cosgrave envisioned Cumann na nGaedheal as a party of 'nation-builders, who would rear the new Ireland in the light of the old ideals'.[20]

As it was not practicable to retain the name Sinn Féin, it is evident from the list of alternatives that there was an effort to create a title that would identify the party with those 'old ideals', thus legitimising it. An Irish name also created a connection with Ireland's Gaelic past. The chosen name strongly echoed Cumann Lúthchleas Gael, the Irish appellation of the GAA, which was the strongest element of the cultural nationalist movement. It should also be remembered that the organisation founded in 1900 by Griffith—which, in 1907, merged with the National Council (formed in 1903 as a protest body against a visit by Edward VII to Dublin) and the Dungannon Clubs (founded in 1905 by Bulmer Hobson and Denis McCullough with the aim of promoting nationalism) to create Sinn Féin —was also called Cumann na nGaedheal. It, too, was an umbrella group, aiming to promote and preserve Ireland's Gaelic identity. The new Cumann na nGaedheal would remind voters of the continuity, albeit with a philosophy rather than with the parent party itself. As Michael Laffan has observed, 'the party saw itself less as the successor of the pre-treaty Sinn Féin than of the pro-treaty faction in the split which had divided the movement'.[21]

Some members recognised the benefits that could be gained from claiming continuity with revolutionary Sinn Féin. However, the suggestion that the pro-Treatyites might simply take over the machinery of the fractured party rather than launch a new organisation was rejected at the conference on 7 December.[22] There was a sense among many of those involved in creating the new organisation that, based on the acceptance of the terms of the Treaty, it must separate itself from old Sinn Féin and, more particularly, from the recently fractured Sinn Féin. Canon William O'Kennedy and Commandant Patrick Brennan had proposed that 'the Sinn Féin organisation should be captured and kept', but the motion was lost by 'a large majority'.[23]

There was a practical requirement to this need, grounded not just in the politics but also in the finances of the day. The new government was charged with building a state in the aftermath of a struggle for independence and a civil war, and, as is discussed in the following chapter, the financial burden of destruction inevitably compromised any possibility of making the lofty aspirations of Sinn Féin's revolution a reality. As Mike Cronin put it in his aptly entitled article, 'Golden dreams, harsh realities', 'it was in the sphere of economics that the division between dream and reality was thrown into starkest relief'.[24] Recovery would not occur overnight. Liam de Róiste colourfully reflected on this in late 1924 when he observed that 'we are paying for the "night out" of our fratricidal strife; the sickness of the "morning after" is still there: heartache, headache, depression, empty pockets'.[25]

The date for a convention to officially launch Cumann na nGaedheal was originally set as 20 March 1923, but this was postponed until 27 April.[26] A meeting was held in advance to discuss policy matters that would be dealt with in the new Dáil to help put the party's programme into effect. The three ministers present outlined the areas they considered necessary to address in government. Cosgrave deemed the boundary agreement and its associated financial implications to be of paramount importance; Mulcahy wished to see unemployment and education targeted, while James Burke identified the payment of tariffs.[27] Their selections were interesting. It was inevitable that the Boundary Commission would be raised, but the other choices, with the benefit of hindsight, are striking. In terms of education, Mulcahy spoke of the necessity of implementing Eoin MacNeill's proposal for eight first-rate primary schools for Irish-speaking districts; he was later to preside over the ill-fated Gaeltacht Commission, which was instituted by the government. The Cabinet would subsequently sabotage the report issued by the commission.[28] On the point of tackling unemployment, within the year Patrick McGilligan was to make the controversial remark that it was 'no function of government to provide work for anybody'.[29] He would later clarify his statement as meaning 'direct employment',[30] but by that stage the damage was done. What was particularly interesting, however, was Burke's decision to place tariffs on the agenda, given the deep divisions within the party on the subject of economics.

The cost of joining the new party was set at 1s per year, while branches were asked to pay a minimum affiliation fee of £2.[31] Membership itself was rather ambiguous. It was open to every citizen over eighteen years of age, who accepted the programme of Cumann na nGaedheal, and who adhered to the principle of majority rule.[32] In 1923, when this was enshrined in the party's constitution, supporting 'majority rule' was synonymous with supporting the Treaty, thus reaffirming the point that Cumann na nGaedheal's legitimacy as a functioning party rested on acceptance of the Treaty settlement.

Cosgrave believed that the broad qualification for membership gave the party 'a great advantage over rival political organisations'.[33] Clause 3 of the draft constitution had received opposition from some cumainn, with the consequence that it was remodelled so that the party would include all those who accepted its programme.[34] Indeed, in the formative stages, there were several discussions as to how applications from former Unionists in particular should be treated.[35] The response was invariably the same: all sections were welcome. Cumann na nGaedheal's acceptance of such members was part of the government's broader strategy of negating the traditional argument that the minority in an independent Ireland would be discriminated against. That the Unionist community in the Free State generally responded was an important step forward and a move away from the sectarianism that had characterised the Home Rule era.[36] But, this policy was to prove problematic for Cumann na nGaedheal, which was accused by its more 'green' opponents of being west-British and of turning its back on Irish-Ireland. In fact, elements within the party itself became uneasy as Cumann na nGaedheal shifted further towards the right.[37]

Between 1922 and 1937, only seven women were elected to Dáil Éireann.[38] There were no female pro-Treaty members in the third Dáil (1922–3), and between 1923 and 1933, Cumann na nGaedheal had only two female deputies. Margaret Collins-O'Driscoll—sister of Michael Collins—represented Dublin North during that period, but lost her seat at the 1933 general election, while Mary Reynolds was elected in 1932 to her husband's seat in Sligo-Leitrim. (Patrick Reynolds was shot dead during the campaign for that election and polling was delayed as a result; his wife was co-opted onto the party ticket.)[39] A third woman, Bridget Redmond, would take the seat of her late husband, William Redmond (son of the former leader of the IPP), at the 1933 election. Reynolds made no contribution to proceedings during the life of the seventh Dáil, but Collins-O'Driscoll was somewhat active. During her political career, she made a total of 82 interventions, which is a respectable figure given that she was not on the front bench, and her contributions were not simply limited to parliamentary questions. On occasion, this marginalisation of women in politics was reflected in government legislation regarding the role of women in society, most notably with the introduction of the 1927 Juries Act, which sought to exempt women from jury service.

Financing

During the campaign for the 1933 general election, Sydney Minch, the incumbent for Kildare, would declare that 'our party represents no class nor creed'.[40] However, Cumann na nGaedheal—and indeed Fine

Gael—has traditionally been seen as the party of the middle classes, farmers and big business; this was an impression that it did little to dispel. Rather, it impeded its own vision of an all-embracing party through its attitude to organisation and finance. There was a conscious effort on the part of Cumann na nGaedheal to identify influential figures in society with whom connections could be forged. Through them, members hoped to grow the party's support base, while at the same time improve its finances. Arthur Cox of the legal firm by the same name was an important benefactor of the party, although this was never publicised,[41] and when he was approached to stand in the 1927 Dublin County by-election, he declined. Butler and Briscoe Stockbrokers were targeted as potential financiers in December 1923, while it was decided also that Bank of Ireland would be approached for a subscription.[42] At a meeting on 16 December 1924, it was agreed that P.J. Egan—TD for Laois-Offaly and a member of the party's organising committee—would form a committee of businessmen to approach 'big concerns' for funding. Various different groups were identified, including members of the stock exchange, the medical and legal professions, and the Licensed Vintners Association. The banks were to be approached separately.[43] The matter was followed up at a meeting on 20 January 1925, where it was reported that Egan had circularised those in the commercial sector. J.J. Walsh was deputed to approach the independent senator James Joseph Parkinson—bloodstock breeder, veterinary surgeon and company director—about using his influence. It was also decided to send a letter to the Irish Banks' Standing Committee asking for contributions.[44] However, not all produced dividends. O'Hanlon reported poor progress from the solicitors, while Jameson's Distillery as a firm, not wanting to become involved in politics, declined to subscribe.[45] This particular push for finances coincided with preparations for the forthcoming 1925 by-elections, which were to effectively constitute a mini-general election.[46] The approach typified the party's attitude, and would also set the template for Fine Gael.

In 1927 a scorned Liam de Róiste—who had been denied a place on the party ticket for the second general election of that year—would tell the organisation, 'you have run after the men of money. Continue to do so'.[47] For Cumann na nGaedheal, there was a symbiotic relationship between recruitment and finance. Those who were selected were expected to contribute to or even fully finance their own campaigns; assistance from headquarters was minimal and the responsibility was instead placed on the individual constituencies. This largely explains the choice of many of the Cumann na nGaedheal's candidates: they could generally afford to run their campaigns. However, the practice of adding such people to the ticket bred resentment that men with money were often chosen in favour of other, willing and perhaps more suitable candidates.

One hundred and twenty-seven Cumann na nGaedheal TDs were elected between 1923 and 1933, with the farming community being the single biggest supplier of representatives and the majority of those farmers had large holdings. Two deputies, Bridget Redmond and Bryan Cooper, are listed on the Oireachtas members' database as landowners in their own right. The other main areas from which deputies originated were the merchant and the legal professions. There were no less than seven company directors elected during this period. Other forms of previous employment included teachers, doctors, newspaper writers and editors, builders, and vintners. The background of many of those who stood and were elected reinforced public perceptions of the party. But while Fianna Fáil also had doctors and solicitors among its ranks, many of that party's deputies had simply been ordinary workers. The socio-economic composition of Cosgrave's party proved divisive when contrasted with de Valera's, and served also to alienate an important demographic. Many of the Cumann na nGaedheal deputies represented the class despised by those of the Rising generation: the landowners and businessmen, people associated in the popular mind with the empire. A clear indication of support from and appeal to the upper classes could be seen in the content of *An Saorstát*, the newspaper published by the government between February and November 1922. Aside from political announcements, expensive luxuries such as motor cars and fur coats were advertised on its pages.[48] The party's white-collar complexion had no appeal to the ordinary voter. As campaigns became increasingly more negative in tone—an occurrence that most political scientists agree results in reduced voter participation—the electoral turn-out in the Free State, shown in Table 1 below, actually grew steadily as the first decade of independent government progressed. By continuing its abstentionist policy post-independence, Sinn Féin held no appeal for those interested in practical politics, but with Fianna Fáil finally entering the political arena in 1927, the ordinary voter to whom Cumann na nGaedheal did not appeal, was drawn from the armchair to the polling station.

TABLE 1—Electoral turnout, general elections, 1922-1933[49]	
Year	Turnout
1922	60.27%
1923	59.05%
1927 (June)	66.26%
1927 (September)	67.75%
1932	75.30%
1933	80.41%

Although the organisation could count among its supporters promi-nent men of society, Cumann na nGaedheal itself was not affluent. Reports and the minutes of various meetings expose the financial dif-ficulties facing the party. It was recorded on 29 June 1923, for example, that 5,400 individual appeals had been posted to that date and included many of the party's prominent supporters, of whom very few had re-sponded. In all, the response to the appeal for the organising fund was 'meagre'.[50] What makes the figures received in that instance all the more disappointing was the fact that the appeal coincided with an elec-tion period, the time when party support is most naturally at its highest.

Organisation

Ronan Fanning has noted that '*having* power they did not ... conceive of their party as an instrument for *winning* power'.[51] At the meeting on 7 December it had been decided not to immediately employ or-ganisers, but instead to rely on 'loyal elements everywhere to start the cumainn before sending out organisers'.[52] TDs and prominent party members were expected to embrace this work energetically and to use their local influence.[53] In mid-February 1923 Seamus Dolan—a TD for the then Leitrim-Roscommon North constituency, actively in-volved in forming the new party—requested information from government deputies as to what steps they were taking to have their constituencies organised.[54] It was envisioned that by 20 March, the date originally set for the inaugural party convention, every con-stituency would be 'thoroughly organised'.[55] Throughout the month of February, it was clear that definite efforts were being made to build a branch structure, with the focus initially on Dublin. From March the rest of the country, including Northern Ireland, was also considered. It was reported on 9 March that two cumainn had formed and affiliated in the North, although their location was not specified.[56] Louth, Kildare, Wicklow, Wexford, Waterford, Limerick, Clare and Galway were all listed in the minutes as places where cumainn were either being formed or where branches had been affiliated. Although the other counties are not named specifically, it would seem that attempts were being made to organise nationwide. The greatest effort to grow the branches naturally coincided with the run-up to elections, and the establishment of new ones was frequently reported in the provincial newspapers. Patrick Ryan was appointed chief organiser on 1 June 1923 with a salary of £10 per week until after the general election of that year.[57] Despite his efforts and those of his sub-organisers, discussed more fully in Chapter 2, he described in his report on 6 July how his organisers had found that people were 'very slow' in joining, and when meetings were called to form cumainn only seven or eight people attended.[58] While potential members could not have foreseen the difficulties at that stage, the poor relationship between the parliamentary party and the grass roots would later undoubtedly have made many reluctant to join.

Although on its formation Cosgrave emphasized that the new organisation was not being created simply to keep the government in power,[59] Cumann na nGaedheal was a typical top-down party. That the government existed before the party was a huge complication. The dislocation between the grass roots and the TDs meant that the organisation was not particularly effective. This had a lasting impact.

From the outset, members had been keen to ensure that Cumann na nGaedheal would be a properly functioning party and not just a government. Seán Ó Muirthile 'wanted a political organisation rather than a party', while Daniel MacCarthy—the legendary Sinn Féin organiser—went so far as to suggest that the 'party should control the government'.[60] Séamus Hughes's circular relating to the inaugural meeting recorded how 'several speakers made it clear that the organisation was not being formed merely to support the government'.[61] Due to Cumann na nGaedheal's unusual birth, however, the party structure had difficulties evolving, and the members' sense of frustration comes across clearly in letters, private diaries and minutes of meetings. From the outset, a strong element felt that they were dictated to by the élite. De Róiste recorded in his diary how a meeting of the pro-Treaty party on 28 August 1922 'developed thus—we were a government party and we were to support the government as a rigid party', while at a subsequent meeting Patrick MacCartan is alleged to have wondered, 'what is the use of criticism, everything is arranged?'[62] This early sense of resignation from a party member outside the inner circle prevailed over the following decade; the feeling that the organisation had little input in policy formation merely grew as the years passed.

There were early attempts to establish a relationship between the different bodies that constituted Cumann na nGaedheal, with members of the parliamentary party and even the Cabinet promoting a close relationship. At a special meeting of the standing committee on 27 November 1923, Eoin MacNeill had urged close co-operation between the party and the government.[63] This preceded a conference between the committee and the Executive Council on 3 December to discuss how better co-ordination between the organisation, the party and the government could be achieved. However, the matter was not resolved in these formative years, and what persisted over the following decade was a growing frustration that the organisation was being ignored and marginalised. The Dublin North Constituency Committee, which was particularly vocal on the matter, requested a further convention in early 1924 to define and clarify the relationship between the bodies.[64] This became a special concern at times when unpopular decisions were made or legislation was passing through the house. On 13 May 1924 P.F. McIntyre of the Dublin North branch proposed that:

> in future when legislation is intended on matters that stir popular feeling, a real effort be made to sound the public through the organisation as to what views are held on controversial points, and if the government have to adopt unpopular measures under pressure of necessity that an adequate explanation be furnished through the TDs to their constituency committees of the reasons for such measures.[65]

The standing committee also considered the matter at its meeting seventeen days later, where Pádraig Ó Máille complained that policy was 'usually presented to them ready-made by the Executive Council, to be accepted or rejected'.[66]

The continued sense of annoyance was, however, blatantly clear from a series of correspondence later that year between Séamus

Hughes, on behalf of the standing committee, and Ernest Blythe, the minister for finance. Referring to the cut in the old-age pension, Hughes dealt not just with the impact on the country, but also the effect on party supporters. In one letter, he outlined for the minister the implications in Mayo North, where there was a by-election pending; their organiser was forced to leave the constituency because he was assailed for the government's actions by those who had grievances.[67] Previously, he had explained how the standing committee was 'at a loss to know' whether the government had taken into consideration the consequences of Blythe's actions.[68]

In a frank memorandum on 16 October 1924, the standing committee further expressed the view that the organisation's influence on policy and the power to affect change had been 'negligible, if not, nil', and went on to speak of the 'insulation of the Executive Council from the currents of thought of its supporters'.[69] The views of the grass roots were paralleled in some of the regional newspapers. In a memorandum to the minister for external affairs, Desmond FitzGerald, Seán Lester, the director of publicity at the Publicity Bureau, reported how some newspapers were editorialising that the government did not sufficiently consider local views.[70] In making unpopular but often necessary decisions, the government alienated various sections of society, and the arrogance with which it often pressed forward with its policies also alienated the grass roots.

W.T. Cosgrave

Had Michael Collins and Arthur Griffith lived, they might have stabilised the party in its early years. Although circumstance had taken Griffith down a political route, he was more comfortable with the life of a journalist. Nonetheless, while not a natural politician, his ability to conceptualise large ideas into communicable articles and pamphlets would have served the government well in its quest to sell its decisions to the voters. In Collins—a man who understood the needs of the local constituency, but who had the charisma to excite a national assembly—there was an obvious leader. Many of those involved in the independence struggle would, at some point, have come into contact with him. His close proximity to the fighting, more so than that of his colleagues, was such that he was respected, if begrudgingly, by many on the other side, and it has been said that with his death, any possibility of healing the divide was lost. His personality was such that he would have provided Cumann na nGaedheal with a more charismatic rival to de Valera, while his exceptional organisational abilities might have resulted in the creation of a more professional party machine. In the absence of Griffith and Collins, the mantel of responsibility passed to W.T. Cosgrave.

Despite his obvious conservatism—the *Irish Times* even described him as having a 'thoroughly conservative face'[71]—and the fact that many of his middle-class contemporaries would have joined the Irish Parliamentary Party, Cosgrave was associated with Sinn Féin from the outset. Having attended the inaugural meeting of the Sinn Féin council at the Rotunda in 1905, he became an active member. The following year, he set up his local branch and was the driving force in shaping its organisation. Although he twice declined membership of the IRB,[72] when the Irish Volunteers were formed in November 1913, Cosgrave was on the platform for the meeting—a sign of his importance in the nationalist movement. During the Easter Rising he fought at the South Dublin Union under the command of Eamonn Ceannt and was sentenced to death, but had his penalty commuted. When Sinn Féin began to embrace politics in 1917, Cosgrave stood on the Sinn Féin ticket for the Kilkenny City by-election in August 1917 and secured for the party its fourth successive triumph in the by-elections of that year; he subsequently won a seat in Kilkenny North at the 1918 general election.

In 1922 the *Irish Times* deemed him to be the 'most capable man in the new Irish Parliament'.[73] Certainly he was not without ability. Cosgrave had experience of practical politics long before Sinn Féin made the transition in 1917–18. He had been a councillor for Usher's Quay since 1909 and also the chairman of Dublin Corporation's finance committee from 1915; one British observer considered him to have been the 'most honest and efficient member' of that committee.[74] His own modest background and familiarity with the poorer parts of Dublin City influenced his attitude as a councillor. He proved to be an active and dedicated representative, concerned particularly with housing, an area that required much reform. In 1911, for example, there were 118,000 Dubliners living in just over 5,000 tenement homes, 1,500 of which had been deemed unfit for human habitation.[75] Cosgrave played a key role in shaping housing policy and what is now known as Ceannt Fort in Kilmainham—started in 1917—serves as lasting evidence of his influence on the corporation's decision to build social housing estates. It is believed that Cosgrave's reputation for being a reforming politician helped to save his life after 1916 when he was granted a reprieve.[76]

Due to his vast experience, he was appointed minister for local government in the first Dáil. Like all of the other ministries, his also operated under very difficult circumstances and Cosgrave was often on the run. Additionally, there was some resistance to his policies—such as the collection of rates—in parts of the country.[77] Nonetheless, his work has been praised and his department is considered to have been one of the most successful of that period. He garnered support for Sinn Féin on the councils so that the county and most borough councils in the 26 counties recognised his department almost a year before the truce and a year-and-a-half before the Treaty.[78] Most significantly, he succeeded in securing the payment of rates to his department rather than to the British. All of this was important in legitimising the Dáil, particularly in the eyes of foreign onlookers. By mid-1920 it was reported that southern Unionists—'even if their compliance was often induced through fear'—were impressed by the efforts at local government.[79] On the day that the Free State officially came into existence, Ernest Blythe reflected on aspects of the progress made by Cosgrave's department between 1920 and 1921: 'in all but three counties the workhouses were abolished, county homes and county hospitals were substituted and outdoor relief was replaced by a system of home help'.[80]

When the Civil War began, Collins shifted his attention to the fighting and in his absence—perhaps a prophetic precursor—Cosgrave took on the role of chair of the provisional government. With the deaths of Griffith and Collins within ten days of each other, the Cabinet gathered to select a new leader. Cosgrave was the natural choice to succeed the Free State's lost leaders, although both Eoin MacNeill and Richard Mulcahy were approached by some supporters. General Mulcahy—proposed by Kevin O'Higgins—would have ensured the loyalty of the army and continuity with Collins, but a uniformed leader would have hindered the creation of a normal political situation, while MacNeill was not acceptable as a leader after 1916.[81] At the time of Griffith's death, O'Higgins was rumoured to have been mentioned by some in Dublin as a possible successor.[82] However, the transcript of a conversation between Mulcahy and Michael Hayes in the 1960s suggests that he was not a contender to succeed Collins, and Hayes went so far as to surmise that even O'Higgins himself did not consider it a possibility at that point. Ultimately there was no leadership contest and Hayes later recalled that the meeting had been 'quite harmonious, that there was no objection to Cosgrave',[83] while Ernest Blythe believed the selection was a 'foregone conclusion'.[84] Cosgrave officially became president of the Executive Council on 9 September 1922 and inherited Collins's Cabinet. Of his front bench, with the exception of O'Higgins, who had been his assistant at the Department of Local Government, he was the only politician with practical experience.

To use Brian Farrell's classification, W.T. Cosgrave was chairman of his Cabinet; this was particularly reflected in his approach to forming his first ministry when he consulted with the other ministers.[85] Looking back in 1971, Ernest Blythe recalled how Cosgrave never hurried a decision around the Cabinet table, allowing ministers the necessary time to voice their views, but that once he reached a conclusion, it was usually accepted by the rest of the Cabinet.[86] Cosgrave was particularly good in his role. His Cabinet was composed of men of talent and he allowed his ministers the flexibility necessary to pursue their own projects. But Cumann na nGaedheal was also a disparate coalition of interests that contained strong personalities like Kevin O'Higgins and J.J. Walsh, and Cosgrave played an important role as a mediator between the various groups in his party. Even when Walsh quit Cumann na nGaedheal in 1927, his departure—as well as the resignations of 1925—did not affect the government's stability. Correspondence and contemporary commentary at this time frequently referred to the dominant groups within the party. Cosgrave is often mentioned as an affable or good-humoured figure, but never really discussed in the manner of someone forcefully asserting himself. While this demonstrates his chairman-style approach to leadership, it also reflects his careful judgement in not allying himself to any one group. On the occasion of Cosgrave's death, John A. Costello spoke of how Cosgrave had been a 'driver driving a team of high-spirited horses'.[87]

Although he played the role of chairman, Cosgrave never relinquished control of his Cabinet. This was particularly the case during the army mutiny, an event in his career that is often dismissed as one of his low points. As discussed in the following chapter, Cosgrave—even when physically absent through illness—still had a presence during the crisis and insisted that all decisions were passed by him before official announcements were made. When necessary, Cosgrave asserted his authority. As Ronan Fanning has pointed out, Cosgrave's 'handling of the divorce issue shows that, if so inclined,

he was quite capable of retaining power in his own hands'.[88]
Additionally, when he called the 1932 election early, he appears to
have acted unilaterally and in the same manner as de Valera when
the Fianna Fáil leader announced the 1933 snap election. He had
also displayed his leadership skills early on. The assassination of Seán
Hales fuelled fears of further assassinations of deputies and consequently many of the rural TDs left Dublin. Had this been allowed,
the political system would have been seriously compromised.
Cosgrave is alleged to have reacted decisively and sent members of
the secret service to retrieve the unnerved deputies, whom he then
met individually and persuaded to remain in Dublin.[89]

By the late 1920s Cumann na nGaedheal was generally known as
the 'Cosgrave party'.[90] This label, used by both the national and provincial press, reflected the attitude of ministers towards their leader. This
may simply have been due to the fact that a more attractive alternative
was not available. O'Higgins was not a popular figure publicly and the
same held true of his relationship with many of his colleagues. But for
many, Cosgrave was 'the boss'.[91] For some, like Desmond FitzGerald,
their support was particularly strong;[92] although overall there was at
least a general loose loyalty.

Among the British there was a certain degree of respect for the
president; he was certainly more favourable than the gun-wielding
Collins or the extremist de Valera. Samuel Hoare, the British
Conservative, reporting on the position of the provisional government, felt that Cosgrave, because of his practical experience, would
be more likely to overcome the difficulties of getting an administrative
structure to operate 'than Collins with his cinema and star turning at-
titudinizing'.[93] Criticism of Collins was shared by Major Whittaker,
who believed that 'he [Collins] had not sufficient statesmanship to
survive even in Ireland'. He was more flattering of Cosgrave, to whose
'desire to avoid rhetoric and be a real minister' during his time in local
government, he made specific reference.[94]

Cosgrave was a man of government, interested in exercising power
rather than concerned with its trappings. His commitment to the stability of the state and the issue of law and order is beyond question.
Although these matters predominantly influenced his policy-making,
his religion—he was a devout Catholic—at times guided his decisions.
He was disinclined to make lengthy speeches, and he regularly delivered succinct, pointed contributions to the Dáil. His quiet sense of

humour often revealed itself in the chamber. Michael Hayes, who served as Ceann Comhairle for almost a decade, became so familiar with those deputies who regularly participated in proceedings that he could predict the manner in which they would respond on most subjects. He was never able to do so with Cosgrave, whose contributions varied from the quiet to the passionate.[95] He was a well-liked and well-respected member of Leinster House, and it was often said that his absence from a funeral was like dying without the rites of the church.[96] He was an unassuming leader and, on his death, his modesty was one of his praised characteristics. Speaking in the Seanad, William Stanford recalled him to be a 'great man—all the greater for being a quiet, unpretentious man'.[97]

Commenting on the dejected Fine Gael party in the 1990s, Olivia O'Leary remarked that 'it is a real sign of a party in free fall when it becomes a serial leader-killer'.[98] Yet after the devastating general election of June 1927, which returned Cumann na nGaedheal's worst performance during its decade in power, Cosgrave's leadership was never challenged. Perhaps this is because Kevin O'Higgins—the man most likely to contest the position—was assassinated shortly afterwards. Had he survived, J.J. Lee suggests, 'it is not inconceivable that he would have contested Cosgrave's faltering leadership in the 1930s'.[99] Had O'Higgins lived, a heave might have occurred. Speculation is pointless—neither of his biographers has dwelt on the subject[100]—although his uneasy relationship with many of his Cabinet colleagues would suggest that he would not have been a popular choice. While O'Higgins had aspirations, other members never really displayed any such inclinations, but that is not to suggest that Cumann na nGaedheal was devoid of men of talent after O'Higgins's murder. Patrick McGilligan was one of the most able ministers around the Cabinet table, while Richard Mulcahy had already been considered for the leadership in 1922. With the Civil War firmly ended and normality restored, Mulcahy could have replaced Cosgrave as Cumann na nGaedheal's fortunes began to wane. He certainly had the potential, as evidenced by the fact that he succeeded Cosgrave as leader of Fine Gael on the latter's retirement in 1944, and were it not for the inclusion of Clann na Poblachta, Mulcahy would have become Taoiseach of the first inter-party government four years later.

However, if some were unsure of Cosgrave's leadership,[101] it was never challenged and he continued to lead Cumann na nGaedheal until the party's transformation into Fine Gael, before handing over the leadership to Eoin O'Duffy, who was easily a more appealing alternative. In doing so—because he believed it to be in the best interests of the party—he showed the same qualities of character that he had displayed during his ten years in government. In many respects, his actions mirrored those of Arthur Griffith who three times stood aside in the best interests of the party that he had founded. In opposition, he continued to hold his party together and the minutes clearly reveal a conscious effort to encourage his fellow deputies to continue actively participating in the Dáil proceedings and in the life of the party. With O'Duffy's departure in September 1934, Cosgrave returned to the helm, where he stayed until his retirement in 1944. In response to the announcement, Daniel Morrissey, Patrick McGilligan and James Fitzgerald-Kenney were among those who urged him to reconsider.[102] His decision to step back from public life, John A. Murphy argues, was 'another setback' for Fine Gael. 'With his departure from the front bench there died the interest of those who had remained in active politics only out of affection and respect for Cosgrave'.[103] Although Fine Gael has at times shown itself reluctant to acknowledge its Cumann na nGaedheal parentage,[104] Michael Marsh and Michael Gallagher in their extensive survey of party membership conducted in 1999, found that its adherents rated Cosgrave as the second best Taoiseach whom the country has ever had.[105]

Eunan O'Halpin, Cosgrave's biographer for the *Dictionary of Irish biography*, has commented on the unfavourable comparisons that are often drawn between Cosgrave and Collins or O'Higgins, with the result that he is often portrayed as being too fiscally conservative, too deferential to the Catholic Church, and generally lacking a modern outlook. 'In such interpretations', O'Halpin points out, 'Cosgrave held on to the leadership of pro-Treaty opinion for over two decades largely by luck', but, as he further contends, it was Seán Lemass, on the occasion of Cosgrave's death, who offered the more fair assessment.[106] During his time in power, as Brian Farrell has observed, Cosgrave 'survived more frequent and serious cabinet crises than any of his successors in office'.[107] (His *Chairman or chief* was published in 1971 and thus the turbulent political and economic climate of the 1980s lay a decade in the future. Nonetheless, he makes a valid point.) Cosgrave, although not nearly as charismatic as de Valera, did command the respect of his colleagues, and during his time as leader, particularly that as president of the Executive Council, he had shown an ability to bring his party with him.

.2.
'Standing amidst the ruins':
1923-7

Kevin O'Higgins made the now familiar observation towards the end of 1924 that 'the provisional government was simply eight young men in the City Hall standing amidst the ruins of one administration, with the foundations of another not yet laid, and with wild men screaming through the keyhole'.[1] Standing amidst those ruins, Cumann na nGaedheal was faced with the challenge of building a state, stabilising democracy, and making hard and unpopular decisions at government level. What it did in those early years, is remembered mostly in negative terms. The government showed an innate ability to make tough decisions, even if those decisions would be to the detriment of its electoral performance. Through its failure, or refusal, to court popularity, the party alienated various sections of society. This often caused a groundswell of opposition, which in June 1927 resulted in a devastating electoral reverse. But more than anything, the executions of Rory O'Connor, Liam Mellows, Joseph McKelvey and Dick Barrett—which made the front page of the *New York Times*[2]—together with 73 other Republican prisoners, cast a long shadow. And yet, in those formative years, the government achieved much. The Garda Síochána, an unarmed police force, was created before the Civil War was brought to an end; the great Shannon electrification scheme was launched; the party defended the tradition of constitutional nationalism from threats not only from Republicans, but also from some Free State elements; entry into the League of Nations helped to emphasize the Free State's status abroad; while concessions extracted at the 1926 Imperial Conference further advanced Irish sovereignty. That all of this was achieved in the immediate aftermath of a civil war was remarkable.

State before party

Cumann na nGaedheal placed the interests of the state before its own needs; however, this policy of relegating organisation to a distant second on its list of priorities was not immediately problematic due to the party's artificial majority in the Dáil and a generally sympathetic press. At the time when preparations were being made for the formal formation of a pro-Treaty party, *An Saorstát*—the newspaper of those supporting the settlement—was nearing the end of its short existence. A subcommittee, which operated between April and November 1922, oversaw its publication, and the minutes of the meetings reveal the difficulties encountered by those involved in keeping the paper afloat.

Mismanagement and poor control of finances were the biggest problems. Despite a determined effort to improve the running of the paper, by 19 June the advisability of continuing publication was being discussed. Arthur Griffith—who remained a journalist at heart[3]—attended that particular meeting and, unsurprisingly, thought it 'absolutely necessary that it should continue'. Previously, on 14 May, those in attendance had agreed that it 'was never really an official organ as its direction was never kept in touch with the policy of the party' and questioned its continued existence. The paper struggled on for a while longer—its problems never resolved—before eventually being wound up with the edition of 11 November 1922. Despite its demise, the members of the subcommittee felt press propaganda was important and urged the executive to continue active propaganda through the Dublin and provincial papers. The establishment of a Press Bureau—considered to be 'particularly urgent'—was also advocated.[4] This bureau was reported to be in 'working order' on 1 December 1922.[5]

Had Griffith lived, his journalistic skills would have been an invaluable asset to Cumann na nGaedheal. Favouring the power of the pen over that of the sword, he made an important contribution to the nationalist cause through his newspapers, of which he had an impressive résumé of titles: *United Irishman*, *Sinn Féin*, *Éire*, *Scissors and Paste*, and *Nationality*. Each of these was a response to the suppression of its predecessor, and through them, he advanced his views. A party paper may have been established under his editorial guidance; in his absence, Cumann na nGaedheal felt no sense of urgency. Both sides of the Treaty divide had realised the importance of newspapers early on, and the government even exerted influence on certain publications to the extent that some felt it necessary to defend their independence.[6] But because the national newspapers and the majority of the provincial press supported the government—ensuring column inches for its policies and speakers—there was no pressing need for Cumann na nGaedheal to establish its own.

The complacency that the party showed in relation to creating its own newspaper was repeated in other aspects of party organisation. There was, however, a clear effort on the part of Patrick Ryan to organise the party for the 1923 general election. He had been appointed chief organiser on 1 June 1923 with a salary of £10 per week until after that year's election.[7] His weekly reports listed the appointment of organisers to constituencies across the country. Those found to be unsuitable were usually replaced immediately. Where it was not possible to establish cumainn, Ryan instructed organisers to set up committees to undertake election work.[8] Recognising the importance of including the organisation outside Dublin, he also appointed provincial organisers, in addition to those already working in the constituencies. Seán Cagney was placed in charge of Munster, while Connacht was made the responsibility of William Burke. Through these men, Ryan expected to be in 'closer touch' with the various constituencies.[9]

However, the standing committee received little assistance in its endeavours from the government ministers. They had no appetite for door-to-door canvassing, speaking at church gate platforms in the wet and cold, or appealing for funds.[10] Liam de Róiste—writing of how he hated and despised electioneering and public meetings—corroborated this assessment.[11] In 1922 the anti-Treatyites confirmed that they would not take their seats in the new Dáil, and as long as the Republicans continued their policy of abstention, Cumann na nGaedheal was free from any form of serious opposition in parliament. There was no sense of urgency among members of the parliamentary party, therefore, to promote their policies or to engage with the voters. During the campaign, Cosgrave flew from Ennis to Carlow to fulfil his programme of meetings.[12] This was the first occasion on which an aeroplane was used in an election in the Free State. It was, however, for practical purposes rather than as part of a country-wide electioneering plan; not until 1929 would a plane be used for such purposes.[13]

Frank Aiken had called a cease fire on 30 April 1923, and the Irregular forces were subsequently ordered to dump arms on 24 May. That the election was held in August 1923 inevitably meant that the Civil War and its associated problems—the Treaty controversy, assassination and execution—would dominate the hustings. There was much heckling at meetings of both sides. The theme of the government's campaign would set the tone for its decade in power. Eoin MacNeill told one audience that his government had restored order to the country, but could not continue to do so unless the people's support was forthcoming on polling day.[14] Some of the leaflets used by the party were plain but striking. The stark image of petrol can, a revolver and a pepper shaker superimposed against a black-and-white background with the title 'Arguments against the Treaty', was arguably one of the most effective.[15]

Naturally Cumann na nGaedheal candidates were questioned about the executions and their legality on the campaign trail. Cosgrave informed interrupters at Eyre Square that no prisoners were shot without first giving notice that execution would be the penalty for those found in arms against the state. When asked how that could be reconciled with the execution of Rory O'Connor, he replied that no notice had been given to Seán Hales and Pádraig Ó Máille who were 'shot in the back by cowards who dared not face them in the front'. He declared that his party was willing to submit to a jury of the electorate for a verdict on what they had done during the past twelve months.[16]

The general election of 1923 was the first one in Irish history at which every constituency was contested. The level of interest was high, with nineteen interests declaring and in total 375 candidates stood for the 153 available seats.[17] Republicans took 25% of the vote, mostly in poorer areas and where there was still a strong IRA presence.[18] Cumann na nGaedheal received 39% of the vote, which translated into 63 seats. In fifteen of the thirty constituencies, Cumann na nGaedheal secured its highest ever share of first preferences for the decade between 1923 and 1933. Michael Gallagher has described that election as having been the party's 'high watermark'.[19] The obvious implication with such a term is that everything thereafter was mediocre. Certainly Cumann na nGaedheal's later performances were not sufficient to allow it to repeat or exceed the 1923 levels, but it would be incorrect to suggest that the party was in a constant state of decline thereafter. In September 1927 the party came within a fraction of the 1923 figures, while at by-elections it also performed well.

In the aftermath of the general election, the party's general council turned its attention to the pending local elections. It believed that 'work and construction and sound administration' rather than national politics, which were a matter for elections to the Dáil, should domi-nate the locals.[20] There was a practical concern that if the Treaty was the dominant issue, the resulting boards would be paralysed.[21] This attitude was in keeping with the practice of putting nation above party, but in practical terms, it did not make good political sense. Active service can establish a politician's reputation—Cosgrave, more than anyone else, in Cumann na nGaedheal should have been aware of that fact—and Fianna Fáil was very active on the ground. Capturing the local councils would be a stepping-stone towards national government. Not until it became Fine Gael did Cumann na nGaedheal attach any real importance to contesting such elections.

Four days after polling in the 1923 general election, all but two of the party's organisers were dismissed.[22] This was despite the fact that local elections were looming and that the standing committee, at the same meeting that the redundancies were announced, decided to instruct all cumainn and election committees to make preparations.[23] Although he did not refer to them specifically, the implications of the organisers' absences were apparent from Diarmuid O'Hegarty's circular to the members of the Executive Council on 24 October. He reported that 'Cumann na nGaedheal is not as active as would be desirable', and informed them that the anti-Treatyites intended to prevent civil administration from functioning by capturing the local councils. He also observed that wherever the government party was active, the Irregulars were losing ground, but where the contrary was the case they were gaining ground.[24] The party's stance was unique, making it the only one of the three main parties to downplay the importance of local elections. It was reported in April that Labour had begun preparations for its campaign.[25] Cumann na nGaedheal's intransigence showed both the amateur nature and complacency of the party.

A social and moral consciousness

Reflecting on those early years, Ernest Blythe suggested that Cumann na nGaedheal's achievement was in getting 'things going'.[26] The statute books for the first couple of years of independence are a testament to a flurry of activity and progress. In 1924 alone, the government guided 62 measures through the Oireachtas, a record unrivalled by its successors.[27] Focus was placed on introducing legislation that not only sought to strengthen the structures of the state, but also aimed at increasing efficiency. The 1923 Civil Service Commission, which was followed up with the 1926 Local Appointments Commission, resulted in the creation of a new meritocratic system. Similarly the 1925 Local Government Act provided for an Appointments Commission designed to eliminate a perceived culture of corruption regarding the selection procedure for local bodies. The 1924 Ministers and Secretaries Bill aimed to define the nature of each government department. It was a necessary part of what Cosgrave referred to during the second stage as the 'building up of a state machine',[28] and by giving the offices a clear remit, their structures were strengthened. However, many of these administrative changes were not popular, particularly since more than 98% of the civil service consisted of those who had transferred from service under the British.[29] Much was naturally made of this by the Republicans.

Sinn Féin invited the Labour leaders to draft the Democratic Programme of the first Dáil as a 'sop for standing aside'.[30] But Sinn Féin had 'neither the means nor the intention of implementing' the social and economic policies set out in the document.[31] Conservatism was also to prevail in independent Ireland, although this was characteristic of economic thinking at the time. There was also a genuine restriction to what Cumann na nGaedheal could achieve due to a lack of available finance. The Easter Rising and War of Independence had been fought wholly on Irish soil and the cost of the destruction of infrastructure, businesses and housing compromised the new government's budgets. Early Free State estimates set the cost of the Civil War at £50 million,[32] and only after 1926–7 did compensation cease to 'rank among the five heaviest charges on expenditure'.[33] As Margaret O'Callaghan succinctly put it, '[Pádraig] Pearse's clarity of vision was a luxury the nation could no longer afford'.[34]

As minister for finance (9 September–6 December 1922), Cosgrave introduced the Local Authorities Destructive Bill, which placed responsibility for covering the costs of destruction on county councils and corporations. There had been several questions raised in the Dáil regarding the government's intentions before Cosgrave broached the issue on 22 September 1922. It was decided that a date would be determined from which the authorities would assume all liability. There was a law-and-order dimension to this decision. Cosgrave explained, 'unless there is an attempt made by all sections of the community for restoring normal conditions in the country it is obviously useless for us to try and go on with the business of the Dáil'.[35] Local authorities, not wishing to incur further debt, could possibly work to ensure that Irregular activity was kept in check. The legislation was thus part of a broader strategy of securing the stability of the state.

After the cost of destruction, one of biggest drains on the Free State's finances was pensions, which in 1922/3 accounted for £3.3 million of the £20 million expenditure.[36] The Department of Finance actually proposed a reduction of 2s in the old-age pension,[37] but the government opted instead for a 1s cut, which still caused outrage. In a profile of the minister for finance written in the 1970s, Michael McInerney commented that 'it was … a most conservative regime, and in that context, therefore, Mr [Ernest] Blythe's cut of one shilling in the old-age pension does not, perhaps, seem all that surprising'.[38] In his paper on the political economy of the old-age pension, Cormac Ó Gráda noted that, in the wake of the costly Civil War, 'not only did the pension absorb a big slice of government revenue, but both expenditure and revenue in the new Ireland were very high by contemporary European standards'. It was also the equivalent of a large portion of today's welfare spending. Thus, in his commitment to the economy, Blythe's decision was warranted but, as Ó Gráda further pointed out, 'his claim that the fall in the cost of living justified a cut in the pension carries less conviction'. The index had risen from 100 in July 1914 to 185 in June 1922, but by July 1924 it had dropped back to only 183.[39] The cut should also be seen in the context of an impending national loan. Given difficulties in raising finance from the banks, the government was keen to launch a national loan and saw a commitment to sound finance as essential to the success of this project. The cuts announced in November 1923 were an indication of its commitment in this regard.[40]

Blythe later restored the cuts made in 1924, but the reduction has gone into Irish folklore and haunted not just Cumann na nGaedheal but also its successor.[41] The minister continuously faced questioning about his actions during the campaign for the June 1927 general election. He told one audience that 'if taxation begins to show an increased yield, if there is a return to economic conditions of prosperity, the [old-age] pensions ought to be restored to their former level, but only when these conditions are going to be maintained'. Nor would he restore the shilling only to remove it again after the election. 'I am not out for a "stunt" of that kind to get votes. I will tell the truth, and if I am not elected on an honest policy I don't want to be elected at all'.[42]

Despite his honourable statements, Blythe was once more subject to fierce criticism after his budget, which included a reduction in income tax, was unveiled. The minister was charged with favouring the wealthy. Fianna Fáil's Michael O'Cleary claimed that the government was pandering to the rich;[43] similarly Labour's William O'Brien described Blythe's efforts as having produced a 'rich man's budget'.[44] His party colleague, Daniel Morrissey, observed that 'it was a remarkable coincidence that the amount of money "economised" as a result of the reduction in the old age pensions was exactly equivalent to the amount paid by the state to relieve income tax by a shilling in the pound'.[45] While at a meeting of the party in Drogheda, David Hall asserted that 'a reduction of income tax was not going to do the working man much good'.[46] Ó Gráda has suggested that Cumann na nGaedheal's 'handling of the pension issue presaged its ultimate downfall in 1932'.[47] It certainly compounded the perception that Cumann na nGaedheal was the party of the middle classes and of big business.

The conservatism which characterised Cumann na nGaedheal's fiscal legislation also extended to its views on moral issues. One of the most commonly quoted expressions of Unionist opposition to Home Rule was the notion that such a government would result in 'Rome Rule'. Cumann na nGaedheal attempted to negate the concept, both as a party and as a government. As already discussed in Chapter 1, membership of the party was open to people of all backgrounds, and ex-Unionists certainly expressed interest in joining. In government, Cumann na nGaedheal encouraged this minority community to participate in the political system; sixteen of Cosgrave's appointments to the Senate were Unionists and among them was Lord Glenavy—the second-last lord chancellor of Ireland—who served as Cathaoirleach until 1928. However, religion could not always be escaped and it occasionally crept into policy-making. Cosgrave was a devout Catholic; he regularly attended Mass, made numerous trips to the Vatican during the course of his life, and, in keeping with general practice at the time, he said the rosary at his home most evenings. However, while he sought guidance from the Church on issues of a moral nature, he was prepared to diverge on matters that affected security, and ultimately the stability of the state remained the foremost consideration for him and his government. This contrast was most clearly evident in his interaction with the Church in the early 1920s regarding the government's treatment of Republicans—discussed below—and his handling of the divorce issue, the latter of which appeared to vindicate the 'Rome Rule' accusation.

Prior to independence, a divorce could be obtained in Ireland by seeking a private bill in the House of Lords once a decree of judicial separation had been passed by the High Courts in Dublin. However, the procedure was not dealt with in the 1922 Constitution and Hugh Kennedy, the attorney general, approached Cosgrave about the matter to clarify the new state's position. He himself was 'strongly of [the] opinion that we should make provision for those who approve of that sort of thing', and although Cosgrave was opposed, Kennedy did not see how they could 'prejudice the position of the minority in this country by depriving them of this little luxury'.[48]

The government was forced to address the issue after three applications for leave to introduce divorce bills were presented to the Private Bill Office in 1924. The standing orders were suspended to prevent them coming before the Dáil, and early in 1925 Cosgrave introduced a motion that would prevent applications for divorce in the Free State. For the *Irish Times*, the central issue was not the 'undesirability of divorce', but rather the 'citizen's right to that freedom of conscience, which is guaranteed by the Constitution of the Free State, as it is guaranteed by all the other Constitutions of the Empire'. The paper considered the Dáil's decision to be a breach of Article 8 of the Constitution, which guaranteed the right of 'freedom of conscience' to every citizen.[49] Similarly when the motion was sent to the Senate, its chairman, Lord Glenavy, refused to accept it and ruled it out of order on the grounds that it was a direct violation of the Constitution. However, in supporting Cosgrave's resolution—which was accepted without a division in the house—the Dáil effectively deemed divorce to be outside the remit of the article.

During the debate on Cosgrave's motion, independent deputy William Thrift declared that the resolution would further widen the gap between North and South. This was echoed in the Senate by its most outspoken critic on this subject. W.B. Yeats warned, 'If you show that this country, Southern Ireland, is going to be governed by Catholic ideas and by Catholic ideas alone, you will never get the North'. He went on to point out that the minority community considered the measure to be 'grossly oppressive'.[50] Despite Cumann na nGaedheal's declared policy of including the minority within the functioning life in the Free State, the divorce case was a quintessential example of the overriding influence of Cosgrave's devotional commitment. The president had privately sought guidance and advice from his close friend, Archbishop Edward Byrne, who advised him that the Church 'could not even sanction divorce for non-Catholics for the reason that all persons who had been baptised are members of the church and under its jurisdiction'.[51] Collectively the bishops declared that 'it would be altogether unworthy of an Irish legislative body to sanction the concession of such divorce, no matter who the petitioners may be'.[52] Although Cosgrave had the support of the majority in both the Dáil and Senate, it was ultimately his personal decision, based on consultation with the bishops, that divorce would no longer be available to residents of the Free State. This conservatism was not confined to Cumann na nGaedheal. As John Whyte succinctly put it, 'Mr Cosgrave refused to legalise divorce; Mr de Valera made it unconstitutional. Mr Cosgrave's government forbade propaganda for the use of contraceptives; Mr de Valera's banned their sale or import'.[53]

The government's view of morality also found expression in legislation regarding censorship and licensing laws. The Committee of Inquiry on Evil Literature was set up in 1926 and the 1929 Censorship of Publications Act was a direct result. The first Intoxicating Liquor Bill was introduced by Kevin O'Higgins in 1924 and it was intended to address opening hours, licensing, clubs, illicit distillation and methylated spirits. The second—introduced in 1927—also addressed opening hours and additionally sought to reduce the number of licenses. The second was the more far-reaching of the two and had serious electoral implications for Cumann na nGaedheal, discussed later in this chapter, at the general election of June 1927.

As Diarmaid Ferriter has pointed out, lesser known efforts to preserve the moral nature of Irish society included the suppression of the Carrigan Committee Report.[54] The report was uncomfortable reading for a government attempting to construct a particular image of independent Ireland—that of a moral, virtuous nation. In 1930, James Fitzgerald-Kenney—successor to Kevin O'Higgins as minister for justice following O'Higgins's assassination—appointed a committee chaired by William Carrigan to consider amendments to the 1880 and 1885 Criminal Law Amendment Acts and possible legislation regarding juvenile prostitution. The committee was particularly influenced by the advice of the Garda Commissioner, Eoin O'Duffy, who was willing to play a part in 'refining the regulation of social behaviour' so that the Free State would be 'not only a safe but a virtuous place'.[55] O'Duffy's submission included cases of indecent assault, rape, homosexuality and incest. Between 1927 and 1929 more than one-third of prosecutions involved offences against girls under the age of thirteen.[56] The suppression of the report was part of an effort to perpetuate the myth of a virtuous society in independent Ireland. As Finola Kennedy has pointed out, a memorandum from the Department of Justice advised that it 'might not be wise to give currency to the damaging allegations made … regarding the standard of morality in the country'.[57] Both Cumann na nGaedheal and Fianna Fáil were guilty of burying the report. James Geoghegan became minister with the change of government in 1932 and he delivered a fourteen-page memorandum to the Cabinet recommending that the report should not be published, while his successor in the eighth Dáil, Patrick Ruttledge, chaired a new committee of deputies that examined the report and their recommendations fell short of Carrigan's.[58]

In 1932 the author Signe Toksvig, wife of critic Francis Hackett, would record in her diary how she and her husband were 'hoping not so much [that] Fianna [Fáil] would get in as that holy Willie's gang would be booted out'.[59] But the conservative nature of the Cumann na nGaedheal government was not simply the product of tight finances or a religious devotion; it was also a continuation of an attitude that had prevailed in the revolutionary period. As Michael Laffan has noted, 'the Irish Volunteers, Sinn Féin, the Dáil cabinet and the IRA were rebels and revolutionaries but they were not radicals. With few exceptions they had no interest in digging down to the roots of Irish society'. Under Cumann na nGaedheal, the 'old habit of postponing social change was maintained intact'.[60]

The party of law and order

The restoration of law and order was a pressing concern for Cosgrave's government, which used several measures to secure the state including, the shutting down of the Sinn Féin courts, reform of the police and the army, and the more extreme step of symbolic executions. With the exception of ordering the executions, much of the law-and-order legislation was piloted by Kevin O'Higgins. On 29 June 1920 the first Dáil had approved the resolutions that 'the establishment of Courts of Justice and Equity be decreed' and that 'the Ministry be empowered when they deem fit to establish courts having criminal jurisdiction'.[61] The Sinn Féin courts quickly replaced the British court system, but with the outbreak of civil war, the provisional government moved to close them down as they were largely presided over by anti-Treaty judges. In doing so, the government was forced to rescind the original Dáil decree that had created the courts and, as Mary Kotsonouris has noted, 'that was the antithesis of the promise invested in self-government'. George Gavan Duffy resigned in protest.[62] In a letter to the editors of the Irish newspapers, Gavan Duffy argued that it was a 'very dangerous attack upon the first principles of our freedom and democracy'.[63] As Kotsonouris discusses in more detail in her book on the winding-up of the Dáil courts, the decision to permanently close them created a legalistic nightmare as several cases before them had not been concluded. But, in the context of July 1922, the provisional government, 'in danger and in panic' felt that it did not have an alternative.[64] O'Higgins subsequently set up a judicial commission to deal with the pending cases.

The assassination of Seán Hales in December 1922 prompted the government to retaliate the following day with the execution of four Republican prisoners, each representing a province of Ireland, notionally for a crime they could not have committed. This extreme measure was outside the law as all four of the men had been imprisoned in Mountjoy since July of that year, but it serves as an example of the lengths to which a party seemingly wedded to the principals of law and order was willing to go in order to secure the state. That the Catholic Church did not publicly condemn or even comment on the executions of O'Connor, Mellows, McKelvey and Barrett was interpreted by Republicans as complicity. Moreover, as Patrick Murray has noted, the pastoral letter of October 1922—which condemned Irregular activity—was freely suggested by Republican apologists to be a 'licence to kill Republicans'. In a letter to his wife, Seán T. O'Kelly wondered 'would they have dared to execute only for the Pastoral'.[65]

However, the pastoral letter was never intended to sanction the government's actions. In fact, Archbishop Byrne had privately petitioned the government against the executions, and considered them to be 'not only unwise but entirely unjustifiable from the moral point of view'.[66] Republicans were also unaware that the archbishop made a representation on behalf of the 8,000 anti-Treaty prisoners who were on hunger strike by October 1923. His appeal to Cosgrave that the government take a more lenient view was dismissed by the president, who replied that his government 'could not give way on it'.[67] O'Higgins declared in the Dáil that if the state was to function properly then it had to assert its 'right to arrest and detain' its citizens.[68] On the issue of law and order, Cumann na nGaedheal had a clear policy that did not require guidance from the Church and demonstrated that, when necessary, the government was capable of taking an independent line.

Although there were no further assassinations of elected representatives until 1927, Republican outrages—including an attack on Cosgrave's home and the murder of O'Higgins's father after he tried to stop Irregulars from burning his house—continued. The military courts continued to order executions, but none were government ordered. The government's swift and strong response to Irregular activity ensured victory by May 1923. However, the actions of the Free State Army were at times questionable during the campaign to secure the state, and the incident at Ballyseedy, Co. Kerry, where Republican prisoners were tied to a mine before it was detonated resulted in a particularly bitter legacy. But while the government had been willing to act outside the law in response to Hales's murder, it was not an action that would become policy. As a consequence of the atrocity at Ballyseedy, a Council of Defence consisting of Cosgrave, McGrath, O'Higgins and Mulcahy was established to inquire into the administration of the military, to recommend the removal of officers above the rank of major general, and to exercise supervision over strategy.[69] As normal conditions returned, O'Higgins replaced extraordinary legislation with the permanent Treasonable and Seditious Offences Act in 1925. While some opponents feared that the legislation might provoke a return to violence, O'Higgins felt it necessary to provide the state with legal instruments for dealing, if necessary, with a still present illegal army.

In early 1922 the Civic Guard later known as the Garda Síochána was created to replace the Royal Irish Constabulary (RIC), disbanded under the terms of the Treaty. The Dublin Metropolitan Police (DMP), which had never been deployed against the revolutionaries during the independence struggle, continued in existence and was later subsumed into the Garda Síochána. Michael Collins also created a special branch, based at Oriel House. Composed of recruits from Collins's hit-men, the group gained a notorious reputation—it was believed that they were responsible for the brutal murder of Seán Lemass's brother, Noel[70]—and it was disbanded in November 1923 as the attitude of its members did not fit with the ethos of the new state.

The Civic Guard formally came into existence on 22 February 1922 and by 25 September 1922 it had 1,500 officers and unlisted men.[71] As John McCarthy has noted, the force was able to gain popular confidence because it largely remained outside the Civil War conflict and was used primarily to protect railways and bridges.[72] The majority of its early members were ex-IRA, but a small number of former RIC also signed up. The presence of the latter provoked anti-Treaty IRA veterans who forcibly seized a small, temporary depot in Kildare on

24 April 1922. The consequence was a decision that the police force should not carry arms, and therefore the Civic Guard became an unarmed force.[73]

One British commentator suggested that the provisional government was 'quite right in emphasizing the civil character of the Civic Guard by not giving them rifles. The greater the contrast between the Free State and the British regime, the less dangerous will be the charge that the Free State government is really the British government under another name'.[74] The RIC—arguing that an absence of arms would result in a fall-off of IRA raids on barracks—had previously requested to disarm, but the British government had declined.[75] Furthermore, being unarmed would have relieved them of the charge of being legitimate targets; this unwritten rule was largely adhered to regarding the Garda Síochána.

Legislation was introduced in May 1924 to give permanency to the Garda Síochána, and in June to allow the government to regulate the Dublin Metropolitan Police force, with the ultimate aim of merging the two bodies at a later stage. This was ultimately brought about following a lack of communication between the DMP and the local Gardaí in relation to the killing of a Garda in Co. Wicklow by two bank robbers. When required, the armed DMP, rather than the army, would serve to reinforce the unarmed Gardaí.[76]

The establishment of an unarmed police force was a courageous decision, taken in the midst of a civil war in which one member of the government party would be shot dead and another wounded. However, it was a necessary decision, required to ensure the establishment of normalcy in the state, and to remove the gun from everyday life. As Tom Garvin explains, British rule had been unpopular partially because it was British, but also because it was armed and untrusting. The Free State did not make the same mistake.[77] Viewed along with the government's response to the army mutiny, the establishment of this force was part of a broader strategy of ensuring democratic, civilian rule.

Eoin O'Duffy was appointed commissioner of the new force on 11 September 1922. His first task was to tackle discipline. As Fearghal McGarry has shown, he quickly weeded out unsuitable and inadequate elements.[78] The gardaí co-existed with the Dublin Metropolitan Police until 1925, when the two bodies were merged. Although the Garda Síochána was not without its difficulties, reorganisation of that body proved far less problematic than the army.

The army mutiny

On 4 December 1923, Richard Mulcahy, minister for defence, circulated a memorandum to the Cabinet outlining a scheme for the
reorganisation of ex-IRA members into a state army.[79] By the end of
the hostilities, the army had swollen to 55,000 unlisted men and 3,300
officers,[80] far more than was necessary—or financially acceptable—
since peace had been restored. The Irish Republican Army Organisation
(IRAO), or members of the old IRA, considered themselves the heirs
and protectors of Collins's legacy. They established themselves in late
1922 as a group, the IRAO, within the ranks of the army. Major General
Liam Tobin and Colonel Charles Dalton—men described by Ronan
Fanning as being 'fanatically loyal to the Big Fellow'[81]—were president
and secretary of the IRAO's executive council. Membership of this
group was limited to officers with the proper 'past and present outlook
from a national point of view'.[82] As members of this group faced demobilisation, they became increasingly concerned about the retention
and promotion of British officers in preference to former Volunteers,
and also believed the IRB to have a controlling influence over the army.
Tobin believed Mulcahy was using that group to undermine the 'old
Republican position'.[83] The internal workings of a military dispute—
dismissed by O'Higgins as a conflict between two letters of the
alphabet—have been established by Maryann Valiulis;[84] it is the political
implications for Cumann na nGaedheal which are of relevance here.

Tobin and Dalton presented the Cabinet with an ultimatum on 6
March 1924 and requested a reply by the tenth of the month. They
issued two demands: that the army council (including the minister for
defence, Richard Mulcahy) be removed, and that army demobilisation
and reorganisation be suspended. They explained that the IRA had only
ever accepted the Treaty as the means by which to secure a Republican
government; an argument they had been making for the past two
years. It was felt that their intention was incongruous with the aims
and objectives of the Cumann na nGaedheal government.[85] Cosgrave's
administration had been clear from the outset that it was only willing
to govern within the framework of the Treaty; while greater autonomy
would be achieved over time—mostly through participation at imperial conferences—progress would be piecemeal. There was a strong
grass-roots element within the party, and indeed, given the level of
confidence displayed by Dalton and Tobin, within the army that also

subscribed to Collins's view. But, while accepted in theory, this was generally not shared in practice at Cabinet level. For ministers, freedom had already been achieved under the terms of the Treaty; their day-to-day activities at Leinster House were testament to that. The minister for industry and commerce, Joseph McGrath, however, was of an Irish-Ireland background and was uneasy with Cumann na nGaedheal's appearance as being sympathetic to the British. In him, the IRAO, perhaps inevitably, found a supporter. Although speculative, it could be argued that J. J. Walsh—close to McGrath in opinion— might also have been a sympathiser, but as postmaster general, his was neither an important nor influential voice in the government.

At the Cabinet meeting held the day after the letter was received, it was decided that Tobin and Dalton were to be arrested. Joseph McGrath tendered his resignation in a show of protest or a demonstration of support. Eoin O'Duffy was subsequently drafted in to take control of the army. As is clear from Cabinet minutes, he was anxious to clarify the exact nature of his new role. When it later became apparent that he held no authority over the army council, the Executive Council also made him inspector-general of the defence forces.[86] The Cabinet's reaction, appointing, as it were, the chief-of-police over the head of its own commander-in-chief has been deemed 'curious'.[87] However, given the circumstances, it was necessary to create a position superior to that of minister for defence.[88] The Cabinet also recognised that a neutral appointment was necessary to exact loyalty from the army.[89] As is clear from his submission to the inquiry set up to investigate the affair, O'Higgins felt that Mulcahy—whom he had once supported as a successor to Griffith and Collins—had not sufficiently engaged with the Irregulars and other threats.[90] At the Cabinet meeting on 19 March, it was agreed that Mulcahy be asked to resign. Cosgrave was not present at this meeting, but the proposal was communicated to and approved by him. However, Mulcahy pre-empted his colleagues and tendered his resignation first.

Much has been made of Cosgrave's temporary absence during the crisis. The exact nature of the illness, which confined him to bed during one of the biggest crises to threaten the state he strove to secure, remains unknown. John Regan has concluded that the president was sent to his bed by O'Higgins rather than illness; the minister for justice's biographers have neither confirmed nor denied this, but have remained silent on the subject. Regan has argued that in the period between 12 and 25 March, Cosgrave was 'incommunicado, refusing to see anyone or even answer the telephone at his home',[91] while Ronan Fanning has noted that one of O'Higgins's letters suggests that he had been unable to gain access to Cosgrave.[92] Whatever the illness, however, it was severe enough only to prevent him from attending five Cabinet meetings, which occurred over four consecutive days: 18–21 March (there was a morning and afternoon meeting on 19 March). Though typically dry and vague, there is a strong sense in the minutes that Cosgrave's presence could be felt nonetheless: memos and letters from him were read aloud.[93] It would also seem that all decisions had to be approved by him before any announcements or final judgements were undertaken; Hayes and Blythe remained adamant in later life that all final decisions were made by Cosgrave.[94] Additionally, the minutes clearly show that during this time, he received visits to his home from ministers.[95] Moreover, according to the attendance record, Cosgrave was present at the meetings on 12, 14 and 15 March, and returned after his absence on the twenty-fourth of the month.[96] Even if he was not available for consultation outside Leinster House, his Cabinet colleagues would have had ample opportunity to consult with him at these meetings.

That O'Higgins had ambition cannot be denied. Mrs Cosgrave believed that he wanted her husband to resign also.[97] Hers was hardly the only mind that thoughts of a leadership struggle would have crossed. A glimpse, perhaps, of his ambition can be witnessed in a draft statement prepared for the press on the occasion of Mulcahy's resignation at a meeting from which Cosgrave was absent: 'The president has decided, subject to the approval of Dáil Éireann, to take up the duties of the Ministry of Defence. During the illness of the President, the Vice-President will act for him in that Ministry'.[98]

Having been submitted to Cosgrave at his home, and with the approval of O'Higgins and MacNeill, the statement was amended and the final line omitted before publication. The practical side of Cosgrave's absence meant that O'Higgins would have to take up the duties—he affirmed this to the Dáil on 20 March[99]—but the omission of that fact in the official statement to the press was symbolic: Cosgrave was not giving his public blessing to O'Higgins as his anointed successor at a later date. Many years later, General Michael Costello claimed that McGrath was in Cosgrave's confidence at the time. The president desired that a situation be produced which would result in O'Higgins's resignation from the government.[100] If true, this would certainly cast Cosgrave in new light. However, Costello was reflecting on events—with the benefit of hindsight—more than twenty years after their occurrence. Additionally, Maurice Moynihan's report on the interview was only written up ten days after their conversation. McGrath and O'Higgins certainly had their differences, but that the former was willing to sacrifice his career to force the latter off the political stage is questionable.

However, one thing is clear: Cosgrave never relinquished control of his Cabinet. Under his leadership, stability and normality had been restored in the aftermath of the Civil War. After a period of prolonged crisis, normality has a definite appeal; Cosgrave offered that. The one member of Cabinet who might have welcomed Cosgrave's departure was J.J. Walsh, but, as he had an uneasy relationship with O'Higgins, he would not have favoured the vice-president as an alternative. Thus, lacking support within the Cabinet, O'Higgins did not act. Had he done so, he could have destroyed the party. Though depicted as the unobtrusive chairman, Cosgrave held that government together. De Róiste suggested that if Cosgrave were to resign, the government party would split up and possibly the Cumann na nGaedheal organisation also.[101] Although this was only one man's opinion, it holds a great deal of truth.

The army mutiny not only highlighted the conflicting views within Cumann na nGaedheal, but also drew attention, once more, to the party's problematic structuring. Séamus Hughes, the secretary of the party's standing committee, had written to each member of the new national group about their decision to decline a meeting aimed at discussing their differences of opinion. McGrath's response was disparaging. He not only drew a distinction between the two bodies— 'our grounds of disagreement are based on dissent from the policy of the Executive Government and scarcely concern the Standing committee of Cumann na nGaedheal'—but he also emphasized the limited influence of the group that Hughes chaired. McGrath's accusation that the standing committee had neither the inclination nor the power to influence decisions over the executive was not unique.[102] Hughes rejected the accusation as being 'unnecessarily offensive'.[103] However, McGrath's letter was telling: it revealed the mindset of a former minister and an attitude prevalent among those at the Cabinet table towards those outside the inner circle.

The government's response led ostensibly by Kevin O'Higgins was typical of its reaction to any threat to the state. As O'Higgins himself put it, law and order had to triumph over anarchy.[104] Mulcahy's resignation was crucial to the conditions being established. By presenting the mutiny as a criticism of a specific government policy pursued by Mulcahy, Cosgrave was attempting to maintain the appearance of a strong, unified state.[105] In 1923, Mulcahy and the military had led Michael Collins's funeral procession, the politicians followed behind. The army mutiny showed that the government was the foremost authority in the state. Civilian control had been firmly established and it was a triumph for the democratic structures of the fledgling state. It also showed, as Alvin Jackson has noted, that 'some of the Free State ministers were at least as steely in their idealism as the most unyielding of their republican opponents'.[106]

For Cumann na nGaedheal itself, the event also began the process of shifting the party further towards the right. With Mulcahy and McGrath out of the Cabinet, and MacNeill soon to depart also, the conservative within the party now dominated. As explored in more detail in Chapter 5, this transformation continued as the 1920s progressed and served to further alienate much of the grass roots from the parliamentary party. If indeed O'Higgins purposely used the army mutiny as the occasion to change the complexion of Cumann na nGaedheal,[107] then Michael Hayes was correct in his retrospective observation that O'Higgins in 1924 went a long way to ruin the party.[108] But this is an unfair assessment as the government had always been composed of pragmatic politicians. Certainly, the later dominance of a conservative and pro-Commonwealth attitude would be thrown into sharp relief by Fianna Fáil's rhetoric, much to the party's detriment. But Cumann na nGaedheal had been conservative from its outset, and it never displayed any willingness to govern outside the terms of the Treaty. With the introduction of the Statute of Westminster in 1931, the government would consider measures to expand sovereignty, but not at the price of needlessly upsetting the British.[109] Although that legislation arrived on the eve of Cumann na nGaedheal's departure from office, based on the government's initial attitude, had it been available at an earlier date it is unlikely that the Treaty would have been dismantled.

Cosgrave had attempted, unsuccessfully, to heal the rift that had emerged within his party, but the decision of Joseph McGrath and eight other Cumann na nGaedheal deputies to resign their seats and form the national group prompted what was essentially a mini-general-election in March 1925. The party faced into the campaigns with the usual problems. A meeting of the standing committee on 10 October 1924, once more flagged financing, a popular policy for the organisation and government support as prerequisites for success.[110] That these were continuously stressed was a clear indication that they were not easily forthcoming. Of the nine by-elections that occurred, Cumann na nGaedheal recaptured seven of the seats. However, as Fearghal McGarry pointed out, the results should not be interpreted as a show of popular enthusiasm for the party.[111] The Sinn Féin candidates had failed to capitalise on and translate discontent into electoral success.

Identity-building and image projection

As has already been established, reconstruction and consolidation preoccupied the government in the second, third and early part of the fourth Dála. Cumann na nGaedheal was also concerned with identity-building and image projection, and it was anxious to send a clear message to international observers that the Free State was a fully functioning, independent, successful state. This desire found expression in events like the establishment of 2RN, the Tailteann games, membership of the League of Nations and the great Shannon electrification scheme. Moreover, contrary to the accusations of those involved with the army mutiny, the Free State did advance Irish sovereignty—albeit at a pace slower than some of Collins's supporters demanded—through participation at the League and also the imperial conferences.

The Dublin broadcasting station, 2RN—the origins of which have been expertly detailed by Richard Pine[112]—was the first of its kind in the Free State, although 2BE had been broadcasting in Belfast since 1924. The BBC, which had been established in 1922, was used as the model, not just in terms of organisation but also ideology. The creation was not without its difficulties. The Dáil committee created to consider the establishment of a broadcasting station was embroiled in controversy due to alleged links between one of its members, Darrell Figgis, and a private interest, Andrew Belton, lobbying for the licence. Later, the appointment of Séamus Hughes—former Cumann na nGaedheal general secretary—as announcer, caused much whispering.

Test broadcasts began in November 1925 and on 1 January 1926 the radio station made its inaugural broadcast, with the first sports' broadcast being made in August of that year. In officially opening 2RN,

Douglas Hyde expressed his hope that the station would act as a unifying agent for the diaspora.[113] As Pine pointed out, the fact that the station could be picked up in part of Britain gave confidence to the claim that an '"Irish voice" could send a cultural message to both Irish people abroad and to those who were as yet unaware of Irishness'.[114]

Programming was 'predominantly cultural and social, only marginally political, and determinedly non-ideological'.[115] Essentially, the emphasis was on Gaelic culture. Irish radio remained impartial at election time and the first party-political broadcasts were not made until 1954. But the Irish experience was not unique. In BBC radio's early days it was forbidden to broadcast political, religious or industrial controversy and although the BBC was told by the government in 1928 that an experiment ought to be made in the direction of greater latitude, the restrictions that were put in place seriously hampered the proposed experiment. The rules were not swept away until 1956,[116] two years after it had happened in Ireland. Pine has observed that in its early programming, there was no extensive indication of Cosgrave's programme of nation-building,[117] but 2RN in itself was arguably an emblem of that policy. To quote John Horgan, it was a 'badge of independence'.[118]

The staging of the Tailteann Games—an Irish version of the Olympics—was an important event in helping to shape the image of the Free State that Cumann na nGaedheal was attempting to create. The games were originally scheduled for August 1922, but the occupation of the Four Courts by the Irregulars and the subsequent outbreak of the Civil War in April frustrated those plans. Almost one year after the end of the fighting, J.J. Walsh proposed to the Cabinet that the games be revived later that year and, after some discussion, they were eventually set for August. At the time when the games were held, much of the capital had yet to be rebuilt after the fighting of the independence struggle and Civil War. The financial burden of those years limited the government's spending power, and yet, in a year which saw Ernest Blythe's budget introduce a reduction in the old-age pension, Cumann na nGaedheal sanctioned the games. But the event was an important investment in image-building. Projects such as the Tailteann Games, and later the Eucharistic Congress and the An Tóstal festivals of the 1950s were state-funded in an effort to move beyond remembrance, and to instead promote the reality of a functioning, independent country.[119]

The games—traditionally a celebration of Queen Tailté—were reputedly last held on the eve of the Anglo–Norman intervention of 1169. Holding them in independent Ireland served as a reminder of pre-colonial times and of Ireland's unique cultural heritage. Speaking at the opening ceremony in Croke Park on 2 August to an estimated audience of 20,000, J.J. Walsh—director of organisation for the games—declared that 'this island of ours is not a colony, but the home of a race of a historical lineage unsurpassed elsewhere'.[120] He felt that festival would have 'satisfied [foreign visitors] that the people of Ireland were capable of one common great effort to re-establish this old nation once again on its feet'.[121] Addressing 300 distinguished visitors at the opening banquet at Dublin's Metropole Hotel, W.B. Yeats welcomed them to an Ireland celebrating its 'coming of age'.[122]

The drive, ambition and organisational abilities that Walsh had earlier displayed in his association with the GAA—the Cork organisation of which he had rebuilt as county chairman in 1907—were replicated in his role as organiser. The GAA itself played a major role in organising the sixteen-day event, bringing the organisation closer to the government.[123] More than 5,000 competitors took part in the games for 1,000 medals across 25 different categories. The participating diaspora came mostly from New Zealand, Australia, Canada and South Africa. However, not all were of Irish birth or descent; Johnny Weissmuller—a hugely successful American swimmer born in Romania, who would later play the title role in twelve *Tarzan* films—competed in the swimming competitions held in Dublin Zoo's pond. The presence of such international stars, many of whom had competed in and won medals at the 1924 Olympics in Paris, helped draw the tens of thousands of visitors who watched the games. There was more to the event than just sport; there were competitions for painting, poetry, literature and Irish dancing, among others. It seems rather fitting that Seán Keating—the artist who, as discussed below, would later brilliantly capture the progress and modernity of the new state in his *Night's candles are burnt out*—was the winner of the painting competition.

The games were intended to provide an opportunity to forget bloodshed and division, to allow Irishmen to 'join hands in celebration'.[124] A journalist for *Irish Ireland* remarked how they could help the Irish people to 'realise the unity of the Irish race, to cast their minds back to an early time when there were giants in those days and so to realise that the political issues … dividing Irishmen are minor things not worthy of the shedding of tears much less of blood'.[125] Walsh hoped that through cultural unity, the political divide would be overcome. As the preparations for the games were being made, de Valera and other leading Republicans were still in prison. He called on his supporters to boycott the games, and rumours began to circulate that the Irregulars would attack infrastructure in an effort to hamper the event. Walsh feared for the success of the games, and twice wrote to Cosgrave urging the release of the prisoners. But although de Valera was freed, the boycott was never lifted, and while some Republicans did attend, they never officially endorsed the state-sponsored event.

Despite the fact that the Tailteann Games did not manage to transcend the Civil War divide, the event was heralded as a success by the international press, which had been monitoring the competitions. *The Times*, *New York Times* and *Sydney Morning Herald* had all covered the event, and through the pages of those newspapers a message was sent to the international community that the fledgling Free State was functioning successfully and producing something positive so soon after fratricidal strife. The *Irish Times* surmised that the games may have constituted the 'most important psychological moment in the history of the Free State'.[126] As scheduled, the games were staged again in 1928, but were not as successful. By that point, as Mike Cronin has observed, it was clear that the political value of the event was questionable and no government minister attended the opening ceremony.[127] The games were never held again after 1932,[128] although the decision by the newly elected Fianna Fáil government to end them was 'as much an act of political rejection as it was a statement of financial frugality'.[129]

Membership of the League of Nations

As Cumann na nGaedheal considered the terms of the Treaty sacrosanct, international affairs was the only medium available through which the Free State's sovereignty could be further advanced. The benefits of the state's status were appreciated by the *Irish Times*, which suggested that 'the imperial connection offered prospects of international influence that never could have been attained by an independent Republic'.[130] In the realm of external affairs, the government had much success: membership of the League of Nations, registering the Treaty as an international agreement, the appointment of Irish ambassadors, the introduction of Free State passports, and guarantees extracted at the imperial conferences. Although Cumann na nGaedheal made great strides towards securing international recognition of the new state, the removed nature of the achievements was such that they had little impact on the ordinary voter. Nonetheless, they were important in establishing the Free State's reputation abroad and were central to the government's broader strategy of image and identity-building. As Bolton Waller—a researcher at the North-Eastern Boundary Bureau—put it, admission to the League of Nations would result in Ireland ceasing to be a name, and instead the country would become a 'reality and a force in world affairs'.[131] However, it should be noted that not until 1926 did the Free State begin to press for Commonwealth reform, prior to which its main concern was with domestic and international benefits and—in relation to the League—its obligations.[132]

The League was on the Free State agenda almost from the outset. Even before the constitutional foundation of the new state was fully in place, Michael MacWhite spoke to Eric Drummond, the League's first secretary general, about the possibility of gaining entry.[133] George Gavan Duffy, minister for foreign affairs in the provisional government, pursued the matter but until the Constitution was passed, no advances could be made. He again raised the matter at the first meeting of the third Dáil, describing membership as a 'matter of the most urgent importance'.[134] He subsequently moved a motion on 14 September—which was deferred owing to the government's assurance that the matter was being considered—calling for an application to be made.[135] However four days later, the new minister for external affairs, Desmond FitzGerald, explained that the government would not yet be pursuing membership. Guiding the new state's Constitution through the Oireachtas was its main priority.[136] David Lloyd George had earlier affirmed to Arthur Griffith that Britain was ready to support the Free State's claim to a place in the League once the Constitution came into effect.[137] The government also had to contend with ongoing Irregular activity and it was generally felt that the domestic situation needed to be controlled before foreign policy could be considered. In promoting the Free State abroad, it was essential that a particular image of the country be carefully presented.

As the Free State forces asserted their control, the Department of External Affairs began preparing an application. The official request was made through Michael MacWhite on 17 April 1923—less than a fortnight before Frank Aiken called a cease fire—and it was the first formal diplomatic act undertaken by an Irish representative abroad. But support was not unanimous and it was certainly not widely heralded as a historic step for the new state. The editor of the *Irish Times*, although ultimately supportive of membership in the longer term, argued that the timing was wrong and that the annual subscription cost of £10,000 was too great a burden for a state struggling to recover from a costly campaign for independence.[138] A resolution proposed by the Earl of Wicklow was passed in the Senate recording the conviction that the government should not take steps to commit the Free State to membership of the League without the sanction of the Oireachtas. Misgivings were based on the expense involved and the necessity of settling domestic matters first.[139] There was consternation when it was revealed that the government had made a formal application without first consulting with members of the two houses.

Although the government could justifiably argue in favour of delaying membership until the Constitution had been passed and the Civil War contained, there was urgency in making the application. Membership was considered, as Waller explained, 'one of the tests of attainment of full self-government and of complete nationhood'. Abstention would result in the harmful presumption that there was 'some flaw in Ireland's title to membership, as being too small or still too much under English control'.[140] The benefits of membership were outlined for the Cabinet in memorandums from Waller and Kevin O'Shiel, director of the North-Eastern Boundary Bureau. At the time that membership was being considered the Boundary Commission also ranked high on the government's agenda, and so it was inevitable that the former would be considered in light of the latter. The League was seen as a potential forum for resolving disputes with Britain, particularly the boundary question. Writing to each member of the Executive Council, O'Shiel stressed it as essential that the government exploit every avenue available through the Treaty to consolidate and solidify the Free State's international status, thus giving a 'strong international complexion' to the boundary dispute. If the Free State was a member, should the commission's findings be considered unsatisfactory, the matter could be brought to the attention of the League.[141] Furthermore, in the event that the commission did not deliver a united Ireland, an appeal could be made on behalf of the nationalist minority to the League, which had already placed certain minorities in European countries under its special protection.[142] It was also felt that participation would throw into stark relief the status of Northern Ireland,[143] feeding into the popular notion at the time that its size inhibited its ability to function as a separate state. The possibility of promoting international trade was also identified as a benefit of membership.[144]

In September 1923 the Free State was granted entry to the League of Nations and for many the occasion was seen as proof of Michael Collins's stepping-stone theory. As Liam de Róiste put it, 'Four years ago it would have seemed a mighty thing to have Ireland recognised among the nations as a separate nation. Today it is in the natural course as flowing from the Treaty'.[145] The diplomatic correspondent of the *Irish Times* recorded the event under the headline of 'Landmark in history: equality in empire partnership', and went on to observe how the Free State's entry was among those 'moments at Geneva that constitute a definite landmark in the history of some nations, and in a lesser degree, of the League of Nations itself'.[146] The Free State was the first of the Commonwealth countries to establish a permanent delegation in Geneva.[147]

The delegation that travelled to Geneva included Cosgrave, MacNeill, FitzGerald, Hugh Kennedy, Osmonde Esmonde and a non-governmental representative, Marquis MacSwiney of the Royal Irish Academy, accompanied by Kevin O'Shiel and Michael MacWhite. Departing from Dún Laoghaire in August, their journey was the first occasion on which Irish passports were used, although they were not yet available to the general public.[148] From 1924 the Free State issued its own passports—to the objection of Britain—but it continued to collaborate with the passport control system which the British had developed as 'a shield against espionage and Bolshevik subversion throughout the Empire'. The operational aspects of Anglo–Irish passport control functioned effectively and efficiently so that the presence of a British liaison officer in Dublin was never required.[149]

The delegates were welcomed to the fourth assembly of the League with applause and a standing ovation from the other members, as well as from the diplomatic, press and public galleries.[150] Cosgrave initially addressed the assembly in Irish before continuing his speech in English. In describing Ireland as 'one of the oldest and yet one of the youngest nations',[151] he spoke in language that would be replicated by Jack Lynch half a century later when Ireland joined the EEC.[152] Cosgrave presented Free State membership as a natural continuation of a long-standing relationship, stressing the concept that although Ireland was on the edge of Europe geographically, historically it had always been at the heart of Europe.

> Ireland, in ancient times linked by bonds of culture and of friendly intercourse with every nation to which the ambit of travel could carry her far-venturing missionaries and men of learning has today formally, yet none the less practically, entered into a new bond of union with her sister nations, great and small, who are represented in this magnificent world-concourse.[153]

He also emphasized the international nature of the Treaty settlement, a status that was a crucial qualification for registering the agreement with the League.

Domestic politics could not be escaped even on the international stage. Hannah Sheehy-Skeffington and Mary MacSwiney presented themselves, protesting against the Free State's admission as the delegates did not represent the republic. Eoin MacNeill wrote in exasperation to his wife Agnes about the 'madness' of those who sent 'two women to prevent the representatives of other nations from recognising Ireland as their equal'.[154] But despite the protestations of the Republicans, the Free State's status, as Cosgrave explained, had been 'defined'.[155] E.M. Stephens, secretary at the North-Eastern Boundary Bureau, felt that 'the moral effect which joining the League of Nations has produced in this country far exceeds anything that was anticipated'.[156] Participation in a foreign organisation would have been of little interest to many ordinary voters, but Stephens was certainly right in contending that membership was a vindication that the Treaty did secure international recognition of the Free State as separate and independent.[157] A very positive image was projected through the pages of the international press. The *Journal des Débats* considered the entry to be a 'notable event' and wished the Free State well for the future,[158] while the *New York Times* recorded how no new member ever had a warmer greeting.[159] The newspaper also reported on Cosgrave's return to Dublin, noting how citizens, accompanied by military, police and civilian bands, crowded Dublin's streets decorated with flags and bunting to welcome him back.[160]

As it was incumbent upon members to register all international treaties since the League came into existence in 1920, speculation as to Free State's intention regarding the Anglo–Irish Treaty began in the immediate aftermath of the accession. When the application to join the League was being prepared, Lionel Curtis of the Colonial Office had contacted Cosgrave to establish what attitude would be most helpful on their part to assist in the process.[161] But the British were not as forthcoming when it came to registering the Treaty because of the implications it would have for dominion status. The rumours circulating in the press created a sense of urgency for Cosgrave's government. Writing to Kevin O'Shiel in Geneva, Stephens communicated how the feeling in Dublin was that failure to register the Treaty would imply that Britain had successfully prevented it.[162] Such an interpretation would have been a devastating blow to Cumann na nGaedheal's image-building project. Although Alfred O'Rahilly was not alone in urging Cosgrave to immediately register the Treaty,[163] the general consensus among those advising the government was to proceed cautiously. Joseph Walshe, secretary at the Department of External Affairs, outlined that a rejection of the application would prove more harmful than inaction, while John O'Byrne, the attorney general, advised that an application should only be made after careful enquiry to establish if the British could legitimately object on the grounds that the Treaty was a domestic and not an international agreement. Caution was necessary because the legitimacy of the Free State was based on the Treaty. Registration would solidify the state and strengthen the government, but a rejection of the application would have devastating consequences.

Just as the Boundary Commission would later defy the expectations of the Free State government, the uncertain status of the Treaty must have troubled the Cabinet and undermined confidence in the settlement. FitzGerald wrote to each member of the Executive Council that 'if England decided to resist the registration of the Treaty she could succeed in preventing it', and asked his colleagues if they thought that attempts should be made to establish Britain's attitude. A handwritten note from Cosgrave at the bottom of FitzGerald's memorandum shows that the president favoured registering the Treaty without preliminaries.[164] Given the sensitivity of the situation, it was decided that registration would be applied for, but FitzGerald emphasized that it was to be done 'quietly and unostentatiously', without any publicity.[165] Michael MacWhite subsequently presented the Treaty for registration to the Secretariat on 4 July, but not until four days later did Timothy Healy, the governor general, write to J.H. Thomas in the Colonial Office to inform him that the Free State had complied with Article 18 of the League's covenant and had deposited the Treaty for registration.[166]

Despite Britain's disapproval, the League of Nations offered no objection to registration which duly occurred on 11 July 1924. It was, as Michael Kennedy has noted, the culmination of a comprehensive two-year policy aimed at cementing the 1921 Treaty, the basis of the Free State, into international law.[167] The British continued their non-recognition after the fact, but the stance was immaterial. In a letter to Walshe, MacWhite suggested that in wider circles it was felt that the British had tried to 'strike a blow at the prestige of the League and of the Saorstát at the same time'.[168] He later relayed how the League's general secretary had revealed to him in confidence the view that the British Foreign Office had taken a most extraordinary step as the objection was without grounds.[169]

Britain's objection to registering the Treaty should be seen within the context of its attitude towards the dominions within the League. In a memorandum, O'Shiel explained how efforts had been made—with much success—to have all Commonwealth states act and vote together. There was a fear that the Free State might develop its own line.[170] But the Free State was not obliging. As Gerard Keown has observed, 'every time the Irish voted against British interest, or ignored a joint Commonwealth position, they further illustrated their independence'.[171]

Membership of the League of Nations established the Free State on the international stage and affirmed Irish sovereignty. However, the achievement did not translate into votes for the government as successes in the realm of foreign affairs did not have the same appeal as the notion of advancing towards the republic on the home front. Moreover, as Seán Lester identified, the cost of reporting on activity at the League made Irish newspapers reluctant to provide much coverage and as such there was a loss of great propaganda opportunities.[172] Desmond FitzGerald also bemoaned the lack of coverage from the domestic press corps. 'If we had a proper press we should have had good publicity, but though the *Irish Times* quotes their "own correspondent" no such person exists'. He noted with pleasure, however, that the foreign papers had 'done well by us and from the point of view of prestige that matters much more'.[173] The Free State's performance at the League was lacklustre up to 1925, but from the following year, members began to play a much more prominent role and the Seventh Assembly proved to be a turning point.[174]

On the same day that the Treaty was registered with the League, T.A. Smiddy—professor of economics at University College Cork (UCC)—was appointed the Free State's envoy to Washington. Canada had previously been granted permission to appoint its own representative, but had not followed through so the Free State became the first of the dominions to secure diplomatic accreditation in its own right making the appointment a wider historic event. The Colonial Office provided assistance in securing the appointment, although it was not always in a hurry to advance the application. It was agreed that the British would approach the Americans on behalf of the Free State. All matters pertaining exclusively to the Free State would be conducted as such, but areas where this was not the case were to be settled between the Free State and British ambassadors, and, failing that, with recourse to the respective governments.

The credentials that had been proposed for Canada were supplied to FitzGerald, but he objected to them on three grounds: that the king's title used the term 'United Kingdom of Great Britain and Ireland', that the phrase 'attach him to our Embassy' had been included, and that there was a counter-signature from the British secretary for state. The latter was particularly important to have removed, as inclusion could have implied that the king could only act on the advice of London ministers. FitzGerald was assured that steps were under way to change the king's title, while the other two objectionable aspects were not included in the letter of credence sent by the British.[175] Like so much of the Free State's foreign policy, Smiddy's appointment, as Dermot Keogh put it, 'did not cause bonfires to be lit on every hillside, but it was a significant achievement'.[176]

Investment in the future: the Shannon Scheme

In April 1924, only three months after being elected to the Dáil, Patrick McGilligan took a seat at the Cabinet table to replace Joseph McGrath as the minister for industry and commerce. McGilligan had joined Sinn Féin in 1917, but as a believer in Arthur Griffith's policy of non-violent resistance, he had played no part in the military activities of the independence struggle. During his time at University College Dublin (UCD) where he attained, among other qualifications, a law degree, he had forged a friendship with Kevin O'Higgins, to whom he acted as private secretary when O'Higgins became minister for home affairs in September 1922. The following year he was appointed secretary to James MacNeill, the Irish High Commissioner in London, and he also filled in for Eoin MacNeill—absent through his commitments at the Department of Education—at the 1923 Imperial Conference.[177] Later that year, he was invited to contest the National University constituency and he stood successfully on the Cumann na nGaedheal ticket. When he joined the Cabinet less than one year later, the sharp-minded new minister brought great energy and creativity to the industry and commerce portfolio, and he proved himself to be one of the most innovative of Cosgrave's ministers. He certainly challenged Cumann na nGaedheal's conservative image with his plans to harness the River Shannon. The manner in which he responded to the early challenges that threatened to impede progress, and indeed the project itself, revealed radicalism not usually associated with that government. The Shannon Scheme was, perhaps, in the words of Terence Brown, 'the most socially revolutionary venture of an unadventurous decade'.[178]

The Fiscal Committee appointed by the government in 1923 identified the absence of natural resources as a significant barrier to industrial power. The 1924 World Power Conference showed just how poorly serviced the Free State was. Due to a lack of availability of electrical energy, the Free State consumed just 16kwh annually, compared to 60kwh in Denmark, 147kwh in France and 790kwh in Switzerland.[179] The aim of the Shannon Scheme was the electrification of the whole Free State, to supply cheap electricity not just to the towns, but also to the rural population.[180] The idea was the brainchild of Thomas McLaughlin, who began developing the concept in 1922 in Germany while he was working for Siemens-Schuckert. He was only 25 at the time. While in Berlin, he visited a number of power plants, either under construction or already in operation. Reading introduced him to similar operations in Sweden, Switzerland, Italy, France, Canada and the United States. 'The more I heard of the national power of other countries, the more I realised the necessity of developing our own national resources, be they coal or peat or water power', he recalled in 1938.[181]

McLaughlin was fortunate in having a ready-made audience for his proposal due to his personal friendships with several of the Cabinet ministers, many of whom had been fellow students at UCD. Through William Magennis—an independent deputy for the National University constituency—McLaughlin was introduced to Cosgrave on 28 December 1923, who originally turned down the proposal but did not dismiss the idea altogether. Two further meetings were held on 26 January and 8 February 1924, at which McLaughlin was accompanied by Herr Wallem, the senior director of Siemens. At a meeting of the Executive Council on 26 February the government agreed conditions upon which the proposal could be advanced. Siemens was required to submit a detailed scheme for the distribution of electricity throughout the Free State; the scheme would have to be commercially viable, offering a reasonable return on investment; and the report, which had to be prepared by 1 September 1924, was to be examined by experts of European standing.[182]

When McGilligan became minister, he moved to set up a board within his department to advise on the scheme and related matters, and he himself displayed a great deal of energy in his commitment to understanding the electrical industry abroad. As Maurice Manning and Moore McDowell in their history of the Electricity Supply Board (ESB) have noted, the McGilligan papers show a stream of papers and reports received, and correspondence sent by the minister in mid-1924 to companies in Norway, South Africa, Belgium and Czechoslovakia. He was also influenced by developments in the US and rural electrification in France.[183]

Once the Siemens report was received, it was submitted to a panel of four experts: Dr Waldermar Borgquist, second-in-command at the Swedish State Electricity System; Professors Eugen Meyer-Peter and Rohn from Zurich; and Dr Thomas Norberg Schulz, the director of the Norwegian state electricity system.[184] The project was not put to tender. Rather it was agreed that if the panel of four Continental experts was satisfied the plan submitted by Siemens would 'distribute from the Shannon power in sufficient quantity at an economic price and at a minimum capital cost for the whole Free State', then the company would be awarded the project.[185] This duly happened in December 1924, but the lack of an open competition had attracted much criticism. After the government had announced its intention in April, the *Irish Times* conducted interviews with electrical engineers and those with an interest in hydro-electrical energy. Among those who criticised the government's closed policy was the manager of the Lucan Electric Railway Company; the president of the Electricity Supply Association of Ireland; and the chairman of the Dublin Corporation Electric Lighting Committee; who argued that America, Canada, Switzerland and Scandinavia had reached a higher standard of production than Germany.[186] Protests were also made by the directors of the Anna Liffey Power Development Company and the directors of the Liffey Syndicate about the 'secretive' nature of the agreement between the government and Siemens.[187] Such responses were hardly surprising as those involved had a vested interest. In response to the criticism of the Institute of Civil Engineers that a monopoly was being created, McGilligan replied that Siemens was the only company to assert that a scheme the size of the Shannon project was practicable.[188]

McGilligan outlined the scheme to the Dáil on 19 December and he addressed one of the main criticisms of the plan. The concept of harnessing a river for cheap electrical power was not the problem; the issue was the scale of the project. The Liffey was touted as a more reasonable size, and to this end four private bills were put before a Dáil committee in 1924.[189] The argument was also made that the biggest demand for supply would come from the greater Dublin area. However, as McGilligan explained, the River Liffey was too small and it would only supply Dublin.[190] The Siemens report had made it clear that the company conceived the scheme as something much greater than a Dublin-centred project. Making reference to the 'hardship of the farmer's life', the report observed how electricity was 'the remedy abroad'.[191] The other concern was that the project was being undertaken by a German company. At a time when unemployment was high, it was felt that the contract should have gone to an Irish company. However, Thomas Johnson of the Labour Party welcomed the proposals,[192] seeing the scheme as a partial solution to the unemployment problem. When work began, a fresh controversy would emerge over the rate of pay for certain workers.

De Valera was opposed to the notion of harnessing the Shannon, favouring instead the Liffey Scheme. The press was also initially sceptical. The *Irish Times* decided that it had 'no prospect of success', while the *Irish Independent* felt that £5 million was a huge amount of taxpayers' money to invest, regardless of how important the enterprise might be. The paper later advised the government to 'drop the whole thing' for the time being.[193] But in counties like Limerick—where the benefits of a large-scale project would be immediate in terms of providing employment for those willing to travel to the bordering county of Clare—there was obvious enthusiasm. The scheme would not only 'revolutionise' industry and commerce in the Free State, but also open up a 'future of immense progress and prosperity' for Limerick.[194]

When the banks initially refused the capital for the venture, McGilligan threatened to nationalise them, while the conservative Department of Finance and its cautious secretary, Joseph Brennan, were by-passed to ensure that the project became a reality. Brennan, who had an uneasy relationship with Ernest Blythe, kept a close eye on expenses and he was reluctant to sanction the necessary investment. Consequently, the decision to proceed with the scheme—the biggest economic decision of the decade—was taken without reference to the Department of Finance.[195] McGilligan publicly announced on 22 February 1925 that his department was moving forward with the plans, confident that there would be no financial difficulty.[196] The Shannon Electricity Bill became law on 4 July 1925.

Labour had endorsed the scheme because of the potential for employment and naturally the party paid close attention to the pay and conditions of those hired, particularly the unskilled labourers. These became the subject of controversy, with the former being pushed so hard by Labour that one government supporter observed how the matter had assumed 'almost the proportion of a national issue'.[197] The subject received ample column inches in the *Voice of Labour*. During construction, Siemens issued the *Progress on the Shannon* bulletin. More than being a record of how the project was developing, the monthly publication was an exercise in public relations. The early editions in particular spoke of attractive working and living conditions at the Ardnacrusha camp. In addition to the basics of bedding and washing facilities, medical and social needs, including a doctor, a cinema and wireless, were provided for also.[198] The reality was somewhat different. The *Voice of Labour* reported that the Irish workers were living in hovels, pigsties, barns and stables.[199] Such reports are borne out in more detail in Michael McCarthy's social histories of the scheme.[200] McGilligan, who had been robust in his defence of the conditions, was forced to reconsider some of his views after visiting the camp in July 1926. These concerns persisted at a low level, but overall, the completion of the Shannon Scheme was a triumph for the Free State, for

Cumann na nGaedheal and for the concept of nation-building.

The Shannon Scheme was a symbol of the government's investment in the future, an act of faith urgently required after the 'psychological demoralisation' caused by the recent Civil War.[201] It was, in Andy Bielenberg's words, 'the flagship of nation-building and economic modernisation'.[202] In outlining the scheme to the Dáil, McGilligan had set it within that context:

> I would put it one way and one way only: that just as there was political freedom achieved a certain number of years ago, if this scheme be carried out we have got to a point where economic freedom, without which political freedom matters very little, may be brought appreciably nearer.[203]

The state promoted the image in a number of ways. Ardnacrusha became a tourist attraction and advertisements were run encouraging people to 'Visit the Shannon works!' and to 'See this mighty project in the making'.[204] Seán Keating's paintings also proved to be an important part of the government's 'legitimising process'.[205] After the Civil War, Keating focused on capturing the development of the new state, and several of his paintings were later acquired by the ESB. From 1926 Keating sketched and painted at the Ardnacrusha site, recording such subject matters as the railway network, the preparation of food for workers, and various engineering details.[206] What the Shannon Scheme meant for the Free State's development and what Cumann na nGaedheal was attempting to achieve—aside from a cheap supply of electricity—is best summed up in his 1928/9 *Night's candles are burnt out*. The painting contrasts old Ireland and the new state to show progress, modernity, and even triumph. Central to the painting are the figures of the businessman and the gunman, with the former looking disdainfully at the latter, who is no longer relevant. Old Ireland, represented by the skeleton, is strung up. Prominent on the horizon is the imposing shape of the Shannon Scheme: the sign of a dynamic, energetic and technological new Ireland. In the words of the art historian, Brian Kennedy, it is 'an independence picture'.[207]

The Electricity Supply Board was set up on McLaughlin's advice, and he was appointed its first managing director. It was the first state-sponsored body set up under the Cumann na nGaedheal government, but its inception ran contrary to the demands of the time, which advocated private enterprise. The government had initially considered the possibility of the private sector.[208] When the opportunity was presented abroad, United States' companies, for example, felt that such a large undertaking could not be successfully operated in Ireland.[209] Additionally, allowing a foreign interest to control an important domestic matter could not be reconciled with Cumann na nGaedheal's image-projection strategy of the Free State as an independent nation.

The Shannon Scheme was completed on 29 October 1929 at a cost of £8 million, and by 1937 the Ardnacrusha power station supplied 87% of the demand in Ireland.[210] It was the greatest engineering operation ever undertaken in Ireland and it was an important symbol of modernity and progress for the fledgling state. Its construction coincided with a time of technological, social and cultural modernisation on the international stage and the scheme thus allowed the Free State to claim its place as part of that movement. The *Star* spoke of the 'triumphant success over all obstacles for Mr McGilligan, his department, and the first government of an Irish Free State'.[211] However, because of the massive overspend on its budget the scheme was subject to criticism during the 1932 election campaign.[212] Nonetheless, it helped to improve the Free State's reputation abroad, where in America, for example, the project had been monitored as evidenced by a piece in the Californian *Oakland Tribune* early in 1930 on the enormous benefits to be gained from electrification.[213]

The Shannon Scheme was one of Cumann na nGaedheal's greatest achievements. The ultimate tribute to Patrick McGilligan's vision came in July 2002 when the project received two prestigious international prizes: the Milestone and Landmark awards, both of which acknowledge the contribution of engineering projects to society. The Milestone Award recognised the scale of the project and the template it set for large-scale electrification schemes worldwide. Other winners include colour television and the space shuttle, while the Eiffel Tower is among those feats of engineering appreciated by Landmark.[214] It is hard to appreciate that a scheme, which has been bestowed such an honour, was the subject of controversy and criticism at the time of its inception.

The Northern Ireland question had found little expression during the Treaty debates, partly due to the faith that was placed in Article 12 of the Treaty, although indifference almost certainly played a role also. Article 12 provided for a Boundary Commission if the North opted to secede from the Free State and it was widely believed in nationalist circles that it would offer a solution to the problem of Partition. Correspondence in December 1921 between Barry Egan—a member of Cork Corporation and later Cumann na nGaedheal deputy whose family business was William Egan & Sons jewellers—and B.C. Waller reflected this view. Waller believed that the settlement would make Ulster 'come in freely in a few years, if not at once', while Egan believed it would happen more 'speedily and freely' than most people imagined.[215] With the exception of Arthur Balfour and Winston Churchill, it has been pointed out that, no senior British politician envisaged Northern Ireland remaining within the empire with the remainder outside.[216] And, as Kevin Matthews outlined in his excellent study of the impact of the boundary question on British politics, there was a genuine desire that—as Stanley Baldwin told James Craig—the Irish question should not be revived in the House of Commons.[217]

Waller later worked as a researcher at the North-Eastern Boundary Bureau between 1922 and 1926. The Bureau was created under the direction of Kevin O'Shiel—adviser to Michael Collins on Northern Affairs and assistant legal adviser to the Provisional and Free State governments, 1922–3[218]—to carry out research in preparation for the Free State's case. It consisted of three departments: a research division and central office, a publicity division, and a north-eastern local division.[219]

As expected, Northern Ireland did not join the Free State, but the Boundary Commission was not immediately invoked and O'Shiel expressed the view that it would be 'nothing short of folly' for the government to press the issue.[220] The considerations at the time of the Free State's application for League membership were also relevant in relation to the commission. As O'Shiel explained in April 1923:

> To have raised the Boundary issue any time within the
> past six months would have been utter folly and would
> have played directly into the hands of Craig and his

'Standing amidst the ruins'

The Cosgrave Party

British Tory allies. Happily the forces of the government have prevailed against the forces of disorder, and the chaotic revolt against the people may not safely be said to be in its death agony. With the near advent of peace and the prospect of the restoration and solid entrenchment of the reign of law, the opportune moment for dealing with this issue will have arrived.[221]

The Northern government also refused to send a delegate to the Boundary Commission, which was considered to be 'in conflict with ethical justice and public right', and the fact that the six-county state had received legal existence before the Treaty had been signed was emphasized.[222] On 10 May 1924 the governor of Northern Ireland gave due notice that the government had declined to appoint a representative.[223] This forced the introduction of legislation allowing the British government to make an appointment on the North's behalf. J.R. Fisher, editor of the *Northern Whig*, was duly chosen, and he was joined by Eoin MacNeill as the Free State's representative and Richard Feetham, a South African Supreme Court judge, as the chairman. From an early stage, the Free State had taken the standpoint that the commission was 'an international boundary commission between two distinct and co-equal governments of Saorstát Éireann and Great Britain'.[224]

Two years before the commission officially began its work, the minimum and maximum that the Free State hoped to achieve was decided based on research carried out and recommendations made by the North-Eastern Boundary Bureau. If granted, the maximum demand would have given 'all Ireland save the County Antrim, the extreme North-East corner of the County Derry, portion of North and Middle County Armagh (exclusive of Armagh City) and all the County Down save the North and Middle portions'. However O'Shiel admitted that such a grant could only be supported with one, unsustainable argument, that is, the wishes of the inhabitants. The minimum territory that the Free State expected was 'a considerable slice of County Derry, including Derry City, nearly all County Tyrone, save a small quadrangle bordering on the Lough shore, the southern portion of County Armagh and the Southern portion of the County Down, including the Borough of Newry and all the County Fermanagh'.[225]

It would seem that Kevin O'Higgins had little faith in the commission, explaining that he did not believe it to be 'a piece of constructive statesmanship'.[226] However many years later, J.J. Walsh succinctly summed up the nationalist orthodox view of the presumed outcome at the time. In his memoirs he recalled how it was thought that 'Tyrone and Fermanagh, South Down and South Armagh, as well as Derry City, would opt for inclusion in the Free State. Such a transfer would have cut the northern enclave in half and, in all probability, terminated its separate existence'.[227] A memorandum in the files of the Department of the Taoiseach shows how it was felt that:

> Co. Tyrone is, in the opinion of those who are conversant with the position in the six counties, the key to the question of whether the excluded shall remain in the Free State or vote itself out. If we retain Tyrone we automatically retain Fermanagh ... This would render the administration of Fermanagh from the Belfast Parliament practically impossible if Belfast lost Tyrone. With these two counties out, the position of the other four would be too precarious financially and economically to enable them to remain out of the Free State.[228]

It was generally hoped by the nationalist community that the Northern state would be so significantly reduced that it would be rendered ineffective, causing it to collapse and join the Free State out of necessity. However, those who supported this view overlooked the existence of comparable functioning countries like Luxembourg, which was smaller in area than County Antrim and had a population of only two-thirds that of Belfast, but it was still granted entry to the League of Nations in 1920.[229] Moreover, in setting out the commission's position, Richard Feetham—who chaired the three-man committee—made it clear that the aim was not to 'reconstitute the two territories, but to settle the boundaries between them'. Consequently, it would not be making drastic changes that would destroy the identity of Northern Ireland or make it impossible for it to continue as a separate state.[230] Thus before the commission had even started its work, the hopes of the Free State had been compromised. Nonetheless, as Margaret O'Callaghan convincingly argued, the tendency to see the period through the lens of the Troubles in Northern Ireland has resulted in a narrative which suggests an inevitability about the outcome. It is, however, important, she argued:

{63}

for historians, at least, to realise that the first Free State government took the boundary commission seriously, that its outcome to them was not a foregone conclusion, and that the elaborate case that the North Eastern Boundary Bureau constructed, on the basis of extensive research and consultation, was serious.[231]

Those nationalists concerned with the commission's work did not envisage a transfer of land from the Free State to Northern Ireland. However, a leak—which has been attributed to Fisher[232]—to the Tory *Morning Post* on 7 November 1925 revealed that such a transfer would take place. Eoin MacNeill, as the Free State representative, has sometimes been denounced for his handling of the commission and his lack of dialogue with the Free State government,[233] but it had been agreed that the representatives would not consult with their governments. Although the Free State would have gained land, the loss of part of eastern Donegal caused outrage. On 19 November MacNeill informed a meeting of the commission of his intention to tender his resignation. However, his departure did not negate the findings of the commission, which still considered him a member and had also continued its investigations. The remaining members expected 'shortly to be in a position to deliver the award'.[234]

Because the findings could still be implemented, hurried talks between Cosgrave, Stanley Baldwin and James Craig were held at Chequers on the weekend of 28 and 29 November. Maps showing the alterations—which varied slightly from those reported in the *Morning Post*—were delivered on the Saturday, although the Free State representatives refused to view them. Effectively the boundary was to be shortened by 51 miles; 183,290 acres were to transfer to the Free State and 49,242 to Northern Ireland.[235] The Free State representatives informed Baldwin that if the award had to be formally accepted, they would put it before the electorate, 'though they would not be able to commend it'. However, such a course of action would result in the defeat of the government and its replacement with 'people of no experience', the result of which would be 'chaos in Ireland'.[236] A memorandum from Seamus Dolan, Michael Tierney and J.J. Walsh, which had been sent to the government in the period between MacNeill's resignation and the talks, advocated the rejection of the commission's findings and any amendment to the Treaty that would result in the existing border being retained. Effectively, the party was searching for a solution that would relieve it from 'the necessity of accepting by explicit act a boundary which no nationalist believes to be justly in fulfilment of Article 12'.[237] Tom Jones, assistant secretary to the British Cabinet summarised Cosgrave's views in his diary: 'adoption of [the] boundary commission report would resurrect heat and hate which had been dwindling'.[238]

Article 5 of the Treaty—Free State liability for the service of the United Kingdom's public debt and towards the payment of war pensions—was discussed on the Sunday. O'Higgins requested that the Free State be released from the obligation as the announcement of such would act as a type of 'life-buoy … when the first great wave of opposition rolled over them'.[239] Kevin Matthews pointed out that waiving of Article 5 was introduced to the talks at this stage because Craig, who joined the discussions on the Sunday, made clear that concessions to the Northern nationalists would not be made by his government. Consequently, the Free State representatives turned to Article 5 as a '"safety valve" to channel outrage over the impending deal'.[240]

Agreement was ultimately reached that the findings in the commission's report would be suppressed and the boundary would consequently remain unchanged. Initially the British proposed only a moratorium on the payments required under Article 5, but this was eventually waived in the Articles of Agreement of 3 December 1925. It was an important concession for the Free State, and would later act as a source of propaganda for Cumann na nGaedheal during the strained economic climate in which the 1932 general election would be conducted.[241] However, as with many of its successes, there was a downside. The 'secret financial agreement', as it became known, was held up as yet another example of collusion between Cosgrave's government and the British. Moreover, the concession itself proved contentious. While Eoin MacNeill felt that if they had pushed hard enough, remission of land annuities could also have been secured,[242] Fianna Fáil would later take the view that the annuities came under the heading 'national debt', thus releasing the Free State from its obligations. The government disagreed and it was largely on that point of difference that Fianna Fáil attracted floating voters in 1932.[243]

In the aftermath of the talks Pádraig Ó Máille and William Magennis, along with two other supporters, left Cumann na nGaedheal to form Clann Éireann. 'In my opinion we were badly let down over the settlement arrived at in London', Ó Máille had written to Liam de Róiste.[244] Coming so soon after the resignations prompted by the army crisis, Cumann na nGaedheal's unity appeared to be seriously compromised. However, all political parties suffer losses and Cosgrave's party was big enough to continue. Furthermore, the Republican policy of abstention meant that the departures did not leave the government in a vulnerable position.

Although Partition had been confirmed by the 1920 Act, Cumann na nGaedheal 'had to take responsibility for the dashing of the excessive expectations many nationalists had invested in the Boundary Commission'.[245] Feetham remarked that 'the instrument in which the Free State trusted had broken in their hands',[246] thus undermining the Treaty and consequently Cumann na nGaedheal. That the commission, which was the culmination of three years' research and preparation by the Free State, did not deliver a solution to the problem of Partition was a blow to Cumann na nGaedheal's policy of image projection as it appeared to contradict Michael Collins's interpretation. Too much faith had been placed on the 'spirit' of Article 12. Speaking at a robust meeting of the party's general council, Blythe acknowledged that the article had been a failure but refused to concede that the Treaty was also. A resolution had been proposed by J.A. O'Connell of Sligo and seconded by T.P. Dowdall of Cork that under no circumstances should the government consent to the 'alienation of any part of the 26 counties'. Father Malachi Brennan, a Roscommon-based member of the party's general council, accused the government, in contrast with James Craig, of being too reasonable and also made the radical suggestion that the Treaty had been violated and so abstentionist TDs should be admitted to the Dáil without the qualification of taking the Oath. Unnamed speakers urged against adopting the resolution, as to do so would have resulted in a damaging public expression of a lack of faith in the government.[247] The exchange suggested that, despite Cumann na nGaedheal's conservative appearance, there were elements within the party that still favoured a more radical approach; this had already been seen during the army crisis.

The Free State had, according to Craig, lived in a fool's paradise.[248] De Valera actually complimented MacNeill on his handling of the situation, viewing his resignation to be the only redeeming feature; 'no Irishman could be allowed to put his signature to an instrument which meant the partition of his country'.[249] While the failure of the Boundary

Commission could be presented as the Free State's unwillingness to accept Partition—a partition that had already existed since 1920—the government was instead associated with the dashing of nationalist expectations. The seriousness of the situation was such that, as Liam de Róiste noted in his diary, 'as political crises go in countries, this one is of importance enough in Ireland to cause a general election in the Saorstát'.[250] The situation did not force an immediate election, however, so that June 1927 was the first opportunity that the electorate had to register their views on the government's handling of the situation. The natural corollary of the commission's failure was, of course, that Partition was a recurring theme discussed on election platforms.

During the campaign historical responsibility for Partition was attributed to various parties, but naturally, liability was evaded. Speaking in Cork, William Redmond claimed that the government 'had failed to protect the people's interests in their negotiations with England, just as they had failed to stand by the border nationalists in the North'.[251] Senator John McLaughlin levelled the accusation at the National League that its predecessor, the Irish Parliamentary Party, was responsible for Partition. 'It was in 1914', he argued, 'when the Irish Party held the most effective parliamentary weapon ever held by any party—the balance of power—when they were masters of the situation, that partition took root ... Six years later Mr Dillon's concessions of four counties blossomed into the tree of permanent partition of six counties'.[252] Redmond retorted in Wexford that the 1920 Government of Ireland Act—which had laid the constitutional foundations for a separate state—'was brought about largely, if not mainly, through the absence from Westminster of Mr O'Higgins and his friends'.[253] As late as 1968 Fianna Fáil's Martin Corry remarked of the party's successor, Fine Gael, that 'the partition rope is around their necks'.[254]

For Eoin MacNeill, the Boundary Commission was to be the graveyard of his political career. Although having resigned from the Cabinet in 1925, he did not bow out of politics entirely until two years later. If at a private level MacNeill recognised that his part in the commission damaged his electoral chances, he did not admit it publicly. His choice of constituency to contest hints at his uncertainty about being re-elected. In 1923, even before the boundary debacle, he had not managed to make a dent in de Valera's vote,[255] and so with the apparent dip in his popularity levels, Clare never entered the equation in June. His decision to stand only for the National University was undoubtedly a strategic move, made in the hope that the conservative NUI electors would be sympathetic.

As the tallymen's counts came in, however, it was evident that MacNeill was fighting for his political life. He lost his seat to the independent Republican, Arthur Clery, by just three votes. Given the complexities of the counting method required by the proportional-representation system, a demand for a recount would have been viable. But MacNeill never requested one. In his pre-election statement, he had sought 'the verdict of the electors'.[256] Their response had not been an overwhelming rebuff, but even if a recount did direct the outcome in his favour by a few votes, the result would not have been an over-whelming endorsement either. MacNeill had received his verdict. No surprise was registered that he had been defeated—the *Sunday Independent* had sardonically predicted that he would 'bite the dust'[257]—but astonishment was widespread as to who had claimed the former minister's seat.[258] The *Irish Times* commented that Cumann na nGaedheal could take some solace from the fact that the newly elected 'republican of the starkest brand' endorsed the policy of abstention.[259]

However, the result, although at variance with the trend in the rest of the Free State, was troubling. While victory with a margin of three votes did not indicate a strong cohort of Republican supporters, the fact that a candidate of Clery's pedigree could make an advance in a constituency of typically conservative voters was an indication that no constituency was unassailable. Cumann na nGaedheal would have to become more alert and engaged. Before the election, John Busteed, the director of UCC's bureau of economic research, high-lighted not only an absence of interest in the election by graduate voters caused by lack of contact with their representatives, but also a sense of dissatisfaction with the government. He suggested that if there were a 'reasonably strong good Republican candidate', he would receive support.[260]

Further advances in Irish sovereignty: 1926 Imperial Conference and a kingdom of Ireland

In the aftermath of the commission's collapse, the Free State pushed ahead with the notion of nation-building in the international arena and Kevin O'Higgins, in particular, sought to find an alternative solution to Partition. The 1923 Imperial Conference had been a learning exercise for the Free State representatives, but as David Harkness pointed out, 'they were never to be so quiescent again'.[261] As earlier discussed, Free State representatives abroad adopted a more radical approach from 1926 and concerned themselves with developing dominion rights rather than simply fulfilling obligations.[262] By that stage the Civil War was firmly over, normality had been restored and various state-building projects were under way. With domestic matters largely under control, the government could consider a more proactive foreign policy.

The next imperial conference opened on 19 October 1926 and the Free State delegates played a leading role. Robert Smyllie of the *Irish Times* suggested that nine-tenths of the points urged by the Free State were encapsulated in the report that came out of the conference.[263] Cosgrave was initially in attendance, but it was Kevin O'Higgins and Desmond FitzGerald who saw the negotiations through. A close working relationship, which proved very effective, was struck between the Irish, Canadians and South Africans. O'Higgins had not believed that the British definition of dominion status could produce a lasting settlement, as Ireland had been coerced into a 'free' association with the Commonwealth and could not, therefore, be considered truly equal'.[264] The question of the international status of the dominions was on the agenda for the conference and during the proceedings, the Irish delegates pushed for equality, arguing it would allow for better co-operation in international affairs.

This agenda built on a memorandum prepared by General Jan Smuts, the South African prime minister, for a 1921 conference that had not taken place. Smuts had argued that it was 'imperatively necessary that equality of statehood should in practice be carried out to the full extent of bringing about an equality of status between the British and Dominion governments as co-ordinate governments of the king'. To carry out the change, he proposed that the dominions should no longer be placed under the colonial office or any other British department; that the dominion governments should have direct access to the king; and that the governor general should become a viceroy solely representing the sovereign in his dominion and not also the British government. Smuts also advocated the establishment of a dominions committee composed of the prime ministers to oversee matters previously tended to by the colonial office.[265] L.S. Amery was anxious to keep the proposals off the agenda at the 1926 conference, but Smuts's successor, General J.B.M. Hertzog, was determined that a full statement of dominion equality, which would clearly set out the international character of the dominions for the world, be achieved.[266] New Zealand and Australia—'content and passive'[267]—were largely unsympathetic, while a constitutional crisis in Canada meant that Mackenzie King—a leading voice at the 1923 conference—arrived unprepared, although he did want the role of governor general clarified. O'Higgins played a leading role in achieving the aims laid down by Smuts and subsequently by Hertzog, which were in harmony with those envisaged by the Free State. If the Irish delegates achieved most it was because it was they who knew best where they wanted to go.[268]

The 'Existing anomalies in the British Commonwealth of Nations' memorandum prepared by the Free State delegates echoed Smuts's views. It too made reference to the 'fundamental right' of each dominion to advise the king, and to the dual-role of the governor general, whom, it was proposed, should act exclusively as the representative of the king and not the British government as well. Reference was made also to legislative authority and the continued usage of royal titles that pre-dated the birth of the Free State.[269] Arguing in favour of equality during the conference, the Free State asserted that co-operation in international affairs could be better achieved among the Commonwealth members.[270]

The Balfour Declaration defined the relationship between Britain and the dominions as 'autonomous communities within the British empire, equal in status, in no way subordinate one to another in any aspect of their domestic or external affairs, though united by a common allegiance to the crown, and freely associated as members of the British Commonwealth of Nations'. This recognition was a vindication of Cumann na nGaedheal's strategy of pursuing sovereignty through membership of the Commonwealth. As the *Irish Times* put it, 'at the Imperial Conference the Irish Free State secured a status which membership of the League of Nations could not give'.[271] The governor general was acknowledged to be a dominion representative of the crown, and legislation passed by Westminster applying to a dominion could only be passed with the consent of the dominion concerned. A notable success for the Free State came in the form of a comma. The king's title was amended so as to clearly separate the two countries: 'George V, by the Grace of God, of Great Britain, Ireland and the British Dominions beyond the Seas, King, Defender of the Faith, Emperor of India'.[272] This was a personal triumph for O'Higgins who had effectively negotiated the change alone with Amery. Writing to his wife during the conference, O'Higgins had been self-congratulatory and expressed the view—rightly, as it turned out in his lifetime at least—that 'this is by far the most important Imperial conference which has yet been held and we can claim to have left our mark all over its proceedings'.[273] O'Higgins had a particular responsibility for the advancements that were secured in 1926 and as a consequence of the role he played, the *Irish Times* suggested, he had 'made a name for himself'.[274] From the Free State's perspective, the appeal to the Privy Council was arguably the only outstanding issue yet to be resolved at an imperial conference.

In the aftermath of the conference, O'Higgins turned his attention to addressing the problem of Partition—in an address to students at Oxford University, he had affirmed that unification would not be 'lightly abandoned'[275]—and he sought a solution within the framework of the Commonwealth. The placing of a comma in the king's title prompted O'Higgins to contemplate a kingdom of Britain and Ireland. For his inspiration, he drew on Arthur Griffith's *The resurrection of Hungary: a parallel for Ireland*. Influenced by the Austro–Hungarian model, Griffith had propagated his ideas for a dual monarchy. Written in the context of the debate on the Third Home Rule Bill, it advocated victory through passive resistance rather than physical force. Griffith argued that Hungary had never once sent a party to fight for Home Rule in parliament, but had, nonetheless, 'forced Austria to her knees and wrung from her unwilling hands the free constitution that had made the potent Hungary we see today'.[276] With Griffith's idea as the premise of his proposal, O'Higgins approached Leo Amery, the secretary of state for dominion affairs, with the idea of a kingdom of Ireland: the island of Ireland, independent of Britain, but with the British monarch as the dual head of state. In relation to the obvious obstacles, Amery recalled that:

> He [O'Higgins] was not himself a fanatic about Gaelic; he thought they would readily restore the King's head once Ireland was a Kingdom again, and though he felt that the Union Jack was still regarded by most of his people as a party emblem, he saw no difficulty in dropping the Sinn Féin flag and having a new flag with, say, a harp and crown on a blue ground. He also suggested that, as part of the bargain, they would be only too

willing to accept as Viceroy Lord Londonderry or
anyone else who commended himself to the North.[277]

Clearly O'Higgins understood that the Unionists' deep attachment
to Great Britain and its symbols would have to be accommodated if
there was to be any possibility of attracting them into a union. Just
two months before his death, O'Higgins expressed a view that has
often been repeated in the decades since:

> By building up the resources of the country, increasing
> efficiency in administration, and reducing taxation until
> the people of the six counties came to an appreciation
> of the fact that it would be in their own interest to be
> part and parcel of the Free State [unification could be
> achieved].[278]

Amery was broadly sympathetic to O'Higgins's proposal, although
he expressed concern for the fundamental unity of the crown. He also
reported that Edward Carson had 'not been at all unsympathetic but had
doubted whether it was not a little too early to broach the question'.[279]
Amery suggested that O'Higgins's proposal was partially the
product of concern about the Free State's future once 'the present
government finally exhausts its popularity', and suggested that 'a union
of Ireland may make any return to power of the extremist faction impossible'.[280] If Amery's contention was correct—and it seems likely
that it was part of O'Higgins's plan—then the proposal for a kingdom
of Ireland could also be read as a type of election manifesto. The
concept obviously jarred with Republican rhetoric, but the 1925 by-
elections had confirmed that Sinn Féin was a spent political force.
Although Cumann na nGaedheal knew that a republic was not achiev-
able, a united Ireland would arguably have been enough to satisfy all
but the most extreme Republicans. IRA activity troubled O'Higgins,
and a united Ireland offered the possibility of cutting away ground
from their campaign. During the 1926 Imperial Conference, he wrote
to his wife, 'if only people at home had a true sense of their interests
they would seize the opportunity of next year's election to steam-roll
the irregular elements and go full steam ahead for a united Ireland and
a dual monarchy'.[281] Nicholas Mansergh has argued that O'Higgins
was probably alone in his readiness to contemplate a dual monarchy
to advance Irish interests,[282] but given these circumstances, there is a

possibility that it might have been accepted by the voters. However, O'Higgins never had the opportunity to put the idea before the electorate. Six months short of the June 1927 general election in the Free State, the British Cabinet firmly rejected the concept and Stanley Baldwin pronounced that 'nothing more was likely to be heard' of it.[283] The idea represented the last attempt by Cumann na nGaedheal to find a practicable solution to the question of Partition.

Authors of their own misfortune

In the lead up the general election of June 1927, the government did little to court popularity through its defeat of the Town Tenants Bill, the sabotaging of its own Gaeltacht Commission report, the harsh licensing laws that Kevin O'Higgins had attempted to push through the Dáil, and barbed criticisms by J.J. Walsh of civil servants in his own department made on the back of accusations of jobbery. These actions all raised questions about Cumann na nGaedheal's character and reinforced Fianna Fáil's case that, for example, the party had turned its back on Irish-Ireland or that the government was indifferent to the plight of the less well-off.

Town tenants

Cumann na nGaedheal's considerable achievements in the international arena had little electoral benefit for the party at home as voters were more concerned with domestic, day-to-day issues. In April 1924 William Redmond had introduced a bill designed to 'improve the position of tenants of certain houses, shops and other buildings in Saorstát Éireann',[284] but it was narrowly defeated by six votes on 4 June. Undeterred he presented another Town Tenants Bill, modelled on his 1924 proposals, to the Dáil in 1926. The bill was perceived as aiming to '[accomplish] for town tenants what successive land acts had accomplished for tenant farmers'.[285] In introducing this legislation, Redmond sought to capitalise on the sense of continuity between the National Party and the old Irish Parliamentary Party, which had championed the cause of tenant farmers in the nineteenth century. His second attempt was also destined to be defeated. The government could not be seen to reject reform of tenants' rights outright, so it attempted to minimise the probable fall out. For some time rumours had been rife that the government was considering introducing a Town Tenants

{73}

Commission. The decision had been taken at a meeting of the Executive Council on 19 January 1927, only days before Redmond's bill met its fate.[286] The opposition, quite rightly, deemed the commission to be a smokescreen—a gesture loaded with intent. Seán Lyons appeared to pinpoint the government's intention. The independent deputy from Longford-Westmeath inquired, no doubt rhetorically, 'if the appointment of this Commission by the government is really for the purpose of defeating the Bill?'[287]

Redmond's bill was undoubtedly flawed. Landlords retained the right to increase rents and, tenants, it was argued, would not belittle themselves by taking them to court.[288] Bryan Cooper also dealt the bill a fatal blow when he inquired if those employees whose work required constant movement and relocation were to be tied down for ten years to pay rent for a house in which they could not live.[289] Redmond attempted to defend his legislation by drawing attention to the clause which exempted tenants who were in the employ of their landlord. That provision had earlier been shown to be defective for not all workers resided in a property owned by their employers.

When the division was taken on 27 January, the motion was declared lost by 41 votes to 29. While independents could be found on either side of the lobby, Labour and the Farmers' Party gave their undivided support to the National League initiative. The very day that the bill was defeated a preliminary meeting of the new commission was held. The timing was crucial and was by no means a coincidence. The commencement of the commission's work was intended to overshadow the defeat of the bill. Undoubtedly that was a pre-emptive step taken by Cumann na nGaedheal to counter the expected fallout caused by an outright rejection minus any concessions. Two and a half years had passed since the defeat of Redmond's first proposal, yet in that time the government had made no solid effort to tackle the problem of rent-burdened town tenants. O'Higgins's argument that the government had not been inactive was unpersuasive. His claim that he had been engaged in vetting men for the committee positions for the preceding three months failed to offer any insight into how the other two years had been spent. In unapologetically stating that 'the executive council cannot see any urgency in this matter',[290] he exposed the government's true sentiments. The heightened and sudden importance of the matter was clearly a product of a pending general election and a vindication of Redmond's allegation that the launch of the

{74}

government's new strategy was merely 'political playacting on the eve of the election'.[291]

Legislative reform demands an assessment of the status quo and the question of who had a vested interest in maintaining the system as it was must be posed. The rejection of the bill, as had been demanded by big builders, implied that the government was unconcerned with the troubles of rent-burdened tenants.[292] Individual deputies within Cumann na nGaedheal foresaw the fallout that would be created and attempted to detach themselves. The absence of all three Galway deputies from the vote was more than coincidental. The whip had been applied for the vote, so absenting themselves from the division was the closest the men could come to dissociating themselves from the inevitable defeat of Redmond's bill. They may not have voted in favour of it, but at least they were not seen as voting against it either. Although the bill's shortcomings had been exposed, the fact that it was seen amongst tenants as proof of the National League's readiness to protect their interests, netted a body of support for the party.

Gaeltacht Commission

Arthur Griffith had once declared that every Irishman who learned the Irish language was filing a declaration of independence on behalf of his country.[293] Josu Mezo has argued that, despite Cumann na nGaedheal's emphasis on state-building and the acquisition of international respect, it did not forget its interest in the revival of the Irish language.[294] On the formation of the party, the need for creating first-rate primary schools in Irish-speaking districts had been flagged as a matter of importance.[295] A memorandum from the Department of Finance in December 1924 acknowledged the 'unquestionable' importance of preserving the Gaeltacht but pointed out that such a programme would be 'difficult to devise'. A commission to investigate the matter was recommended and the Gaeltacht Commission, chaired by Richard Mulcahy, was instituted the following year. Its aim was to define what constituted an Irish-speaking area, to improve economic conditions within this area, and also to promote the use of the language in administrative and education facilities.[296] Despite the fact that Ernest Blythe—a language enthusiast—presided over finance, the department panicked at the proposals made in the commission's report.[297] In the *Free State Handbook*, published in 1932, A. Ó Brolcháin, the secretary at the Department of Lands and Fisheries, would argue that the preservation of the Irish language was essential in attaching people to Irish soil and stemming the tide of emigration.[298] As Margaret O'Callaghan has pointed out, 'for the idea of Ireland to retain its symbolic potency the concept of a distinctive culture, unique to the island, was vital. The language was viewed as an essential wellspring of that culture'.[299] Furthermore, as Oliver MacDonagh has noted, commitment to language revival counteracted the claim of the Republicans that they were the 'sole custodians of true nationalism'.[300]

The Department of Finance, however, was concerned about the implications of the Commission's report, which included free secondary education. Restricting the recommendations to the Gaeltacht could prove problematic, particularly if lobbying began to extend the same rights to the rest of the Free State.[301] Having reviewed the report, a letter was sent from Cosgrave's office to Mulcahy:

> If, as a result of the work of the commission, means can
> be found, within the limits of the country's resources,
> to arrest the decline in the Irish speaking population and
> to preserve the language in unbroken continuity as the
> traditional language of the Irish home, then I am sure
> that the members of the Commission will feel that their
> labours have met with ample recompense.[302]

As Diarmaid Ferriter has stated, the problem of secondary school attendance and the absence of a follow on to university in the Gaeltacht areas was not due, as the commission suggested, to the use of the English language, but rather because of the interference of economic realities. Children left school after their primary education to work.[303] Cosgrave pledged that administrative arrangements to make the care of schemes for the Gaeltacht the responsibility of a single parliamentary head would be put in place after the June election.[304] Not until 1956, however, under the auspices of the second inter-party government, was a Department of the Gaeltacht established.

The government's rejection of the Gaeltacht Commission's findings because of the financial implications was in keeping with the conservative fiscal attitude that dominated its policy formation, and it resulted in a general feeling in the affected areas that the Cosgrave administration was unsympathetic to their problems. Donegal was the quintessential example. A Gaeltacht area, it was also classed as a congested district and was deemed to be among those counties with the worst housing conditions. The constituency's representatives were called upon in early 1927 to resign if 'the united demand for immediate remedial action' for the Gaeltacht was ignored or if any attempt was made to 'shelve the question'.[305] A meeting of the Donegal branch of Cumann na nGaedheal affirmed that support would be withheld pending the formulation of an acceptable policy on the Gaeltacht.[306] Individual outgoing deputies were to pay the price for the collective decision made by the government. Three Cumann na nGaedheal candidates were elected at the June election, but two of the party's incumbents—Patrick McFadden and Patrick McGoldrick—were defeated. This could be deemed a practical protest: Michael Óg McFadden and Hugh Law, elected in their stead, were not associated with what voters identified as apathy on the part of the government representatives. The rejection of the Gaeltacht report raised questions about Cumann na nGaedheal's commitment to the revival of the Irish language, and strengthened the argument of its opponents that Irish-Ireland ideals had been abandoned by Cosgrave's party.

Intoxicating liquor: O'Higgins's moral crusade

In introducing his Intoxicating Liquor Bill, Kevin O'Higgins explained to the Dáil that there were 'too many licences, that the trade is overcrowded, that the competition within it is too intense'.[307] The aim of the minister for justice's bill was to 'amend and in part consolidate the law relating to the sale of intoxicating liquor, to enable the number of licences for the sale of intoxicating liquor to be reduced by the abolition from time to time of certain such licences, and to amend the law relating to the registration of clubs'.[308] There was a low-level recognition of the need for an overhaul of the licensing laws, but the only real cross-party agreement reached was on the necessity of reducing the number of licensed houses. In Castletownbere, Co. Cork, for example, there were just 40 houses, of which 24 had licenses.[309] The general trading hours for summer that O'Higgins envisaged were 10.00 a.m. to 10.00 p.m. in centres with a population in excess of 5,000 people, in winter they were to be modified to 9.00 a.m. opening and 9.00 p.m. closing. Sunday trading was to be abolished. The only exceptions to this rule were the centres of Dublin, Cork,

Limerick and Waterford, which could trade between 2.00 and 5.00 p.m. on Sundays. In all cases public houses were to close during the week between 2.30 and 3.30 p.m.[310]

Even if O'Higgins had 'grossly miscalculated' the effectiveness of the licensed trade as a lobby,[311] his moral crusade was yet another example of Cumann na nGaedheal's tendency to place the country's welfare above the party's interests. The *Northern Standard* praised the government for displaying 'a strong sense of duty'.[312] From the moment that the bill was tabled observers predicted a 'great clash between the government and the trade'.[313] Temperance groups welcomed the legislation, although they became disillusioned as the bill was diluted. Nonetheless, disgruntled pioneers were not a match for scorned vintners, who reacted strongly to the proposals.[314] O'Higgins is once said to have confessed that 'the publicans of Ireland were far harder to deal with than the Republicans'.[315]

Like David Lloyd George, who once yielded to a 'howling mob', the *Irish Independent* claimed, 'there is confidence that Mr O'Higgins can also be compelled to yield'.[316] The public outcry provoked by the proposed Intoxicating Liquor Bill influenced O'Higgins's government colleagues to take pre-emptive steps. Despite the minister's conviction that his proposals were morally sound, back-benchers in particular were uneasy. No doubt many feared for their seat at the next general election. Pressure was brought to bear on O'Higgins and at one party meeting he was forced to abandon the principle of automatic endorsement of licenses.[317]

The *Connacht Tribune* predicted that such concessions would assuage the sensitivities of the licensed trade and reported that tension in the government party had 'relaxed considerably'. It was also expected that O'Higgins's truncated bill would dissuade the trade from formally interfering in the June 1927 election.[318] Such a prediction was without foundation. During the debates on the bill, the National League had presented itself as the one defender of the licensed trade within the Dáil. On 13 April a meeting of the Licensed Grocers' and Vintners' Protection Association of Ireland was held in Dublin. A resolution, which was tantamount to a reprieve for the government, was agreed. The decision was taken 'not to ally themselves with, or support, financially or otherwise, any political party until they [had] received instructions from the executive'.[319] Warner Moss drew attention to this resolution, and observed that 'the trade won its battle',[320] but he failed to acknowledge that the decision was reversed. The association later adopted a resolution pledging support to nominees of Redmond's party in the belief that those candidates would be 'fair and friendly to the just and legitimate claims' of the trade.[321]

The National League came into existence in September 1926 and lasted until 1931. Led by William Redmond and Thomas O'Donnell, it was most associated with the former, prompting O'Higgins to caustically remark that 'an attempt to form a political party around a surname' would not succeed.[322] The National League was dismissed by Warner Moss—a contemporary political observer—as 'a party of malcontents representing nothing fundamental in Irish political divisions'.[323] But, the party did play an important, if short-lived, role in the political system. It offered an alternative to voters who were discontent with Cumann na nGaedheal but not yet ready to vote for Fianna Fáil, which, through its policy of abstention, remained on the margins of constitutional politics. The continuity with John Redmond's party would have attracted the majority of the old IPP supporters and also the ex-servicemen who were loosely supporting Cumann na nGaedheal. Cosgrave's party had already recognised the potency of the Redmond name, and had unsuccessfully attempted to recruit him for the 1923 election.[324] His influence in Wexford, for example, was so strong that attempts to establish a cumann there in March 1923 had failed.[325] The emergence of the National League thus posed a threat to Cumann na nGaedheal at the June 1927 election, particularly as it identified itself with the casualties of recent government legislation.

J.J. Walsh's criticisms

Through its legislative reform and perceived air of indifference, the government was growing increasingly unpopular. The minister for posts and telegraphs did little to ease hostilities. J.J. Walsh had already won a bitterly fought dispute with post office employees during the first months of independence.[326] When he stood before his fellow deputies in May 1927 and made a damning indictment of civil servants in his own department, he violated tradition.[327] The level of discontent caused by his statements manifested itself in a resolution, passed by the annual conference of the Post Workers' Union, calling upon the government to remove the minister from his office.[328]

Walsh had promoted three men from outside the Dublin postal district to senior positions. The promotions were called into question because one of the men was Walsh's brother, another was his private secretary and the third was a man who, according to Labour's William Norton, had 'no record of able service'. Accused of 'favouritism',[329] the minister was unapologetic about his appointments. He delivered a severe criticism of the Dublin postal district, describing it as 'the one black spot on the Irish postal service for the last thirty years'. He referred to a 'spirit of indiscipline' and claimed that he had to force men to give 'the last ounce of their effort'. He had been forced to make appointments from outside the district, he explained, because of his lack of confidence in the 'ability of the existing command to tackle that situation'.[330] This denunciation naturally incensed the men at whom it was aimed. The fact also that Walsh had made the comments in the Dáil, where the men he disparaged could not respond, was infuriating. One postal worker, speaking on behalf of his colleagues, felt that the entire staff had been 'maligned in order to justify certain promotions'. The black spot that Walsh had spoken of, the workers believed, had been a product of his own doing, created through his appointment of men simply because they had not taken part in the bitter strike of 1922.[331] The situation worsened when those who had proposed, seconded and supported the motion urging Walsh's dismissal were suspended indefinitely.[332]

Despite the public outcry and the calls for the minister's removal, when Cosgrave appointed his ministers for the fifth Dáil, Walsh returned to the posts and telegraphs portfolio. On election day, the infamous remarks appeared to have a negligible impact on Walsh's performance: he once again topped the poll. That the minister was a candidate for a Cork borough, however, meant that his personal vote could not be affected by the actions of the Dublin postal workers. His colleagues in Dublin—where Cumann na nGaedheal lost a total of three seats—were more vulnerable to a protest vote.

'A stupid, ungrateful people'? June 1927 election

The general election of June 1927 left Cumann na nGaedheal in a minority government. Seats were won and lost by margins as narrow as three votes following a campaign that was punctuated by the government's alienation of various sectors of society. The collapse of the Boundary Commission had undermined support for the government, causing an indeterminable number of voters to support alternative constitutional candidates. A myriad of contentious issues—the Treaty, the Oath and Partition—which dogged the 1920s, continued to trouble the party, but as has already been shown, Cumann na nGaedheal was also the author of its own misfortune. One witty voter summed up the feelings of the electorate for the *Mayo News*:

I'll reduce the old age pensions by another paltry bob,

To all the friends who love me most I'll give a cosy job,

I'll send your sons and daughters in thousands o'er the sea,

This land will be a hunting ground when I'm a grand TD.[333]

On polling day the electorate delivered its verdict and registered a protest vote.

In 1926 O'Higgins had warned an audience in Cork 'against the danger of the country frittering away its strength by dividing its support among a number of parties', and he told his listeners that 'there was … one thing more important than a strong opposition and that was a stable government'.[334] In keeping with this theme, Cumann na nGaedheal argued from various rostrums during the campaign for the June 1927 election that party multiplicity would lead to governmental instability. The party attempted to project itself as the only viable government. Naturally that image was challenged by the opposition who dubbed Cumann na nGaedheal's argument 'nonsensical, arrogant and impudent'.[335] A coalition could acquire the reins of government and be successful, it was claimed. An editorial in the *Roscommon Messenger* reinforced this argument. 'A very few short years ago they [Cosgrave's party] were utterly devoid of experience, and if they have done the work as well as they have claim to have done, then there is nothing to be said against inexperience'.[336] This was certainly a convincing counter-claim to the government's assertion, although it is important to remember that the president of the Executive Council, at least, had had much experience of politics at local level.

Cumann na nGaedheal reached its nadir when the number of competing parties was at its highest.[337] Eight parties, including the independents, put forward 377 candidates for the June election. Since 1923 the political arena had been enlarged to include Clann Éireann, the National League and Fianna Fáil. Additionally, a host of candidates representing an assortment of interest groups ran under the various banners of Independent Labour,[338] Independent Republican,[339] the National League for the Blind,[340] Town Tenants,[341] Independent Business,[342] the Irish Women's Citizens' Association,[343] Protectionist Farmers,[344] and Independent Farmers.[345] Of all the parties contesting the election, however, only Cumann na nGaedheal and Fianna Fáil put forward enough candidates, who, if elected, would allow them to form a single party government.

The persistent discussion of multiple-party government and the role of small parties in the contest inevitably resulted in an appraisal of the electoral system. PR had been incorporated into the 1922 Free State constitution in Article 26 and although the precise form was not stated, the presumption was that it would be proportional representation by means of the single transferable vote (STV). The Electoral Act, 1923, clarified this ambiguity and provided for PR-STV.[346] PR was scrutinised on the pages of regional and national newspapers and in several speeches by members of the government party. Speculation was rife that the June election would be the last under the existing method; an article in the *Sunday Independent* carried the title 'The last PR election?'[347] At a meeting of his party in May, Cosgrave had announced that during the next term in office an overhaul of the voting process would be examined.[348] Desmond FitzGerald, minister for defence, gave a more definite statement on the future of PR when he told an audience in Mallow, Co. Cork, the following month that 'the system would have to be done away with'.[349] On those occasions when the abolition of proportional representation has been threatened, the exponents of change tend to be those who stand to benefit the most. Cumann na nGaedheal's authority was jeopardised in June 1927 by the presence of a multitude of competing parties. To alter the voting system would be to pre-empt all future threats. That Cumann na nGaedheal considered this suggests a cunning side to the party that is rarely evident. It also reinforces what would be more noticeable at the second election of 1927: when the party's position was threatened, it would respond to the challenge.[350] At a meeting of the Donegal branch of Cumann na nGaedheal, Francis Gallagher provided a pithy insight into the government psyche, confirming their tactics for self-preservation. Although he claimed that the removal of the PR system would make campaigning easier, he unapologetically acknowledged that it would also 'do away with small parties'.[351]

Ernest Blythe remained opposed to PR throughout his life, convinced that stability could not be achieved through it. In early 1927 he had penned an alternative to the existing procedure. His voluminous proposal, a little long-winded and at times complicated, was set out in a seven-page memorandum entitled 'Suggested new electoral system', and was circulated among the Cabinet. His proposal made provisions for party leaders in a weak position, effectively giving them two opportunities to be elected. The power of the small party was also dealt with. He argued that it was unlikely that a minority party would win a majority of seats but even if it did somehow succeed 'it would still be faced with an opposition of 40 members out of a House of 150'.[352] Reform had also been on the mind of Séamus Bourke. In a circular to the Executive Council towards the end of 1926, the minister for local government and public health had proposed that 'the Dáil should be elected according to a modified system, which will secure uniform representation in the matter of quotas, will make every vote fully effective, and at the same time prevent a majority being unrepresented by the accident of a "split vote"'.[353] His proposed modifications were discussed at a meeting of the Executive Council almost two months later, but were not approved.[354]

In a strongly worded letter to Frank MacDermot, O'Higgins bemoaned the presence of the small parties at the election. 'Had Redmond and the farmers played a different game', he resentfully lamented, 'we could have reduced de Valera to 30 seats'. In blaming the small groups for the blow dealt to Cumann na nGaedheal's total share of the votes, he colourfully summed up his party's arrogance:

> It is an irony that right wing elements here ... have gone near to destroying the Treaty! All these wretched little parties vigorously sawing the bough they are sitting on is a sight to make angels weep and devils grin. They haven't sawed it through, but they have weakened it perilously. They have strewn the road ahead with nails and stones and one would think that our feet were bloody enough from what lies behind.[355]

However, in this private letter—never intended for publication so that the electorate could cast a critical eye over the content—O'Higgins had also revealed a genuine dimension to Cumann na nGaedheal's anxiety. There was a very real concern among its members that the weakening of the constitutional side would allow for the breakthrough of the Republicans: a doomsday scenario for the preservation of the Anglo–Irish Agreement. However, despite the obvious interest within Cumann na nGaedheal in changing the voting system, reform ceased to be a major concern after the summer months. Simply put, the close proximity of the June and September elections reduced the coffers of all the parties, but particularly hard-hit were the smaller parties. Consequently, the level of competing interest at the second election of 1927 was drastically reduced.

Although Cumann na nGaedheal lost a substantial number of seats in June, the proportional representation system had actually afforded the party five 'bonus' seats.[356] With a first preference share of 27.45%,[357] the party was entitled to 42 seats but actually secured 47. Without those five extra seats, Cosgrave's government would have been in a parliamentary minority of fourteen rather than nine. As will be seen in the next chapter, even with the government's full voting strength, a motion of no confidence was defeated only by a mysterious disappearance and subsequently by the casting vote of the Ceann Comhairle. A deficit of fourteen seats would have been disastrous and would have guaranteed the government's collapse. Cumann na nGaedheal would almost certainly have won more seats under the straight vote, but in the absence of such a system, PR had been a blessing in disguise. (Of course, the government could not have known this at the time of the election.)

In a revealing and openly honest letter written to MacDermot one month before the election, O'Higgins confirmed an awareness that the government would take a hit in the polling booths. 'Some of the most useful deputies in the Dáil will have a hard fight to get back', he had admitted.[358] The principal beneficiary of the government losses in June 1927 was Labour, followed closely by the National League and the independents. Warner Moss maintained that, although it was these parties 'that really came off with the honours', their gains were the product of a protest vote. Both Labour and the National League, he noted, 'had criticised the government severely, and though Labour had a programme pleasing to socialist economists, the country was not presented with any clear picture of what Labour intended as an alternative to the government. The people voted for nothing positive'.[359] Although the *Irish Statesman* asserted that 'the success of Labour was the brightest spot in the election',[360] June 1927 did not presage a growth in the party's strength. In fact, Labour did not equal its performance again until 1965.[361]

The smaller parties gained because the body politic was not yet ready to cast its vote en masse for Fianna Fáil. This was reflected in the fact that Fianna Fáil's seat gains came primarily from Sinn Féin; also an indication, as the editor of the *Dublin Evening Mail* put it, that 'the country is tired of the futile attitude of the extremists'.[362] The Treaty was still a live issue and proved to be the main cleavage within the electorate. Indeed Fianna Fáil had made the Treaty and its contentious Oath the central tenet of its electoral agenda. This resulted in political commentators depicting the election as a battle between the constitutional parties and the anti-Treaty Republicans. The *Irish Times*'s coverage of the results incorporated a comparison of the percentage polled by the two groups in each constituency and concluded that 'for every Free Stater who has voted for the Republic, two have voted for the Treaty'.[363] Similarly, the *Irish Independent* included a table comparing support for the Treaty in 1923 with 1927.[364] The *Irish Times* captured the mood succinctly when it commented that if the government party had to lose seats, it should lose them to men who would be 'loyal to the Free State's constitution'.[365] What Richard Sinnott observed of the 1923 election is equally true of June 1927: 'Cumann na nGaedheal had a lot of competition within the area of its own principal appeal, that is, for the pro-Treaty vote'.[366] If the electorate could not vote for the pro-Treaty government they would vote for the pro-Treaty opposition. Fianna Fáil policy was not yet strong enough to stretch beyond the party's aversion to the Treaty.

The Farmers' Party should have been an obvious beneficiary of the government's losses, but this was not to be. The party had, in fact, approached Cumann na nGaedheal of its own accord about the prospect of a merger.[367] The potential was considerable for both sides. Both vied for the attention and the votes of the farming community; through fusion those votes would be consolidated. The deputies of the old Farmers' Party would have been able to speak on behalf of those they represented with a far stronger voice, while the benefits of being in power could not be denied. Cumann na nGaedheal's strength would also be enhanced. As Michael Gallagher has noted, 'at all four elections the party was weak in constituencies with a high proportion of farm labourers'.[368] To bring the official Farmers' Party into the ranks of Cumann na nGaedheal meant potentially bringing those votes also.

Senator Michael O'Hanlon and Denis Gorey met with Cosgrave, O'Higgins and Patrick Hogan to negotiate a coalition agreement. It was reported that they found themselves in substantial agreement on most things.[369] But, while the Farmers' Party was broadly in favour, divisions were rife within the Farmers' Union, with many sections resolute in their opposition to the move. A congress was held on 20 April and sat for a mammoth thirteen hours. The proceedings finally concluded after a 'substantial majority' rejected the proposed fusion.[370] Gorey resigned the leadership and his membership of the Farmers' Party, and successfully contested the June election on the Cumann na nGaedheal ticket. Martin Egan, chairman of Galway County Council, remarked at a meeting in support of the Cumann na nGaedheal candidates that 'the farmers of Ireland were incapable of organising themselves as a successful and efficient lobby united under one leadership'.[371] The various proposed or considered mergers, which all ended in failure, pointed to the fissiparous nature of both the elected representatives and the union; a feature that was reinforced by the defection of the party leader to Cumann na nGaedheal. The divisions served only to further weaken an already declining party. The protest vote should have borne fruit for a constitutional party like the Farmers'. Although the suggestion proved futile, however, the fact that they had been willing to throw in their lot with Cumann na nGaedheal robbed them of a convincing role as an opposition party and consequently as a viable alternative. Not until the formation of Fine Gael in 1933 would the Farmers' Party, by then reinvented as the National Centre Party, and Cumann na nGaedheal speak with one united voice.

The results of the election were far from conclusive. Fianna Fáil returned the same number of seats held by the Republicans before the split, while Sinn Féin was reduced to irrelevance. The already declining Farmers' Party had refused a pre-election merger and made few gains. The real winners were Labour and the National League, and, to a lesser extent, the independents. Despite offering no real alternative, they made substantial, albeit temporary, gains at the expense of Cosgrave's party. Cumann na nGaedheal's performance was dismal. The rate of decrease in its share of first preference votes in most constituencies was sizeable; the vote in Dublin, for example, dropped by almost one-quarter. Compared with the 1923 result, the party had gained a paltry single seat but ceded a sizeable total of seventeen. Of the 153 seats in the Dáil, Cumann na nGaedheal commanded only 46 (excluding that of the Ceann Comhairle); a razor thin majority of only two over de Valera's abstentionist party. 'The elections have been rather a disappointment all round', wrote Richard Mulcahy.[372] His uncle, John Slattery, was less diplomatic: 'The general public in Ireland are a stupid, ungrateful people'.[373] The result left Cosgrave's party only 13% ahead of de Valera's, and with less votes than Fianna Fáil and Sinn Féin combined.[374] Even if Fianna Fáil did not enter the Dáil, Cumann na nGaedheal was still in a parliamentary minority of nine.

Terence de Vere White argues that the disappointing June 1927 result was evidence that Cumann na nGaedheal was disintegrating.[375] However, statistics can be deceiving. Cumann na nGaedheal had certainly suffered an electoral reverse, but the plain statistics do not come with a footnote explaining that an exceptionally high number of competing parties had fragmented the vote. Not until the general election of 2002 was the 1927 figure for competing interests surpassed.[376] June 1927 should thus be considered an anomaly among the electoral contests between 1923 and 1933.

Cosgrave's last words to the electorate had been a warning: 'If we go back only 50 strong I cannot form a government. Who will supply it? My advice to you is to think very seriously before you dispense with our services'.[377] Listeners to 2RN were informed that 'Cumann na nGaedheal would not form a government either alone or in coalition'. Initially neither Cosgrave nor O'Higgins confirmed or rejected the authenticity of the claim. Two days later, however, the radio station announced that the broadcast was based, not on a communiqué from the party, but from general research carried out by the station's news correspondent. According to Maurice Gorham, however, the radio station was repeating J. J. Walsh's personal views.[378] Just after the broadcast, Liam de Róiste made a similar observation in his diary.[379]

The matter was finally settled on 23 June when it seemed that Cumann na nGaedheal was preparing to occupy the opposition benches. A morose Cosgrave informed the fifth Dáil that he did not seek office, but would accept the position of president only if the opposition were unable to form an alternative. Some reporters speculated that Cosgrave was seeking an endorsement from the Dáil, perhaps hoping that a deputy from outside his party would nominate him for president.[380] Naturally this did not happen. The Labour Party opposed his nomination en bloc, but with the endorsement of 68 deputies, the 22 votes against were immaterial. Fianna Fáil TDs had refused to take the Oath and thus played no part in the election. Cosgrave and his party formed the government for the third successive time, but the outcome of the election had left them in a precarious position. If at any time a controversial issue came before the house, the whips would need a vice-like grip on the deputies. As will be seen in the next chapter, absolute attendance at divisions was of paramount importance, especially when the fate of the government rested on the outcome.

.3.
'Helmsman lost':
the murder of Kevin O'Higgins

A potentially disastrous event for the future of the state occurred on 10 July 1927. Kevin O'Higgins, the vice-president and minister for justice, was assassinated as he walked alone to Mass. The crime sent shock waves through the country. By the time of his death, relative stability had been achieved in the state; not since the killing of Seán Hales had a deputy been targeted, while fighting in general had ceased to be part of everyday life. O'Higgins's murder therefore signalled to many a reversion to Civil War conditions and there was a general feeling that the whole process of state-building had been regressed four years. As O'Higgins was considered to be a pillar of the state, a fear was consequently prevalent that his murder might result in the collapse of the state. A poem submitted to the *Donegal Democrat* depicted Cosgrave 'alone on the ship with his helmsman lost', and posed the question 'can he guide me alright?'[1] The answer was yes. The Cumann na nGaedheal government moved quickly to introduce legislation designed to eliminate the threat from the extremists and to transform the party system, ensuring full participation.

Far-reaching legislation

The introduction of legislation designed to force the hands of Fianna Fáil deputies was a self-sacrificing measure, intended to strengthen the party system and, thereby, the state. It was very much in keeping with Cumann na nGaedheal's commitment to uphold the tradition of constitutional nationalism. Cognisant of the fact that if Fianna Fáil fully participated in the political system, it would achieve power quite quickly, Cosgrave's government nonetheless sought to bring the party from the opposing side of the Civil War into the system. The effects were immediately apparent as Labour and the National League joined with Fianna Fáil in a combined effort to bring the government down through a motion of no confidence. Cosgrave's administration was saved from ignominious defeat only by the mysterious disappearance of a National League deputy and the subsequent casting vote of the Ceann Comhairle.

The infighting in Cumann na nGaedheal was temporarily shelved as the party showed a united front. The cross-party outrage at O'Higgins's assassination also had the potential to the cause a temporary realignment of the parties, and the Labour leader Thomas Johnson approached the government with an offer of support from the opposition benches. He put it to Michael Hayes that with 'FitzGerald and O'Sullivan ill, Cosgrave, McGilligan, Hogan worn out, the ministry was very weak without O'Higgins'.[2] However, despite the fact that the government now found itself in a distinctly intractable situation, a national coalition was not created. Cosgrave's party chose instead to strengthen the government's position through the introduction of tough legislation. This was to blow apart the unity created through mutual abhorrence of the atrocious crime, and was also to result in a seismic change in the political landscape. A Public Safety Bill and two bills designed to amend the electoral laws and the Constitution were brought before the Dáil. The Labour Party, once prepared to join Cumann na nGaedheal in a coalition, now found itself firmly in the role of opposition again. The party refused to sanction what Senator John O'Farrell deemed to be 'repressive legislation of almost unexampled severity, unequalled even in the worst days of foreign rule'.[3] The National League and several independents expressed similar views as the bill made its second passage through the Dáil. Although the Farmers' Party was opposed to certain sections, Cosgrave could count on its continued support, but only because the party, in the words of Patrick Baxter, did 'not see the alternative'.[4]

Labour opposed the legislation for economic reasons also, but it was by no means the only worried group. A survey of regional newspapers shows that national interests took precedence over political sentiment. The *Irishman*, *Roscommon Messenger* and *Donegal Democrat*, all traditionally critical of Cumann na nGaedheal, each expressed concern for tourism, the next national loan and investment in industry.[5] It was a widely acknowledged fact that a new national loan would need to be floated, and since political stability has a knock-on effect on the economics of a country, concerns were voiced that if too much emphasis was placed on lawlessness and instability, then the possibility of raising a loan at favourable rates could be hampered. Even the usually supportive *Irish Times* asserted that the government's legislation would have to be reconciled with 'economic progress and the upkeep of the nation's credit'.[6] It would seem that the perceived threat to the state did have a negative impact on the country's capacity to borrow as the Free State loan dropped by 5% on the Dublin stock exchange the day after O'Higgins's murder.[7]

The Public Safety Bill contained, Cosgrave asserted, 'the minimum powers which the Executive feels are necessary to cope with the present situation'.[8] The bill provided for military courts with the power to enforce the death penalty, and treason, murder or the unlawful possession of a fire-arm was punishable by death. (Incidentally, the Public Safety Bill was neither the first time nor the last that Cumann na nGaedheal would incorporate clauses to eliminate treason. The Treasonable Offences Act had come into effect in 1925, while Section 28 (1) of the Medical Practitioners Act of 1927 provided for erasure from the register. Similar sections would later be included in the 1928 Dentists Act, and the Veterinary Surgeons Act of 1931.[9] Additionally, one only has to read Cabinet minutes to see the long lists of state employees dismissed for treason.) Random searches of persons were also introduced under the Public Safety Bill. Any individual found to be in possession of documents relating to illegal associations was to be arrested and such documents taken as proof of membership, unless proved contrary.

Eamon de Valera had immediately denounced O'Higgins's murder, deeming it to be 'inexcusable from any standpoint', and added that it was a 'crime that cuts at the roots of representative government'.[10] The assassination had been carried out by three IRA men—Archie Doyle, Bill Gannon and Timothy Coughlan—who had acted on their own initiative. Although Fianna Fáil condemned the assassination and was in no way linked to the minister's death, the remaining two bills of the package were nonetheless aimed directly at de Valera's party. Patrick Hogan, minister for lands and agriculture, explained why. 'I am not saying for a moment that they knew of [the plan to assassinate O'Higgins] or that they would have approved of it at this stage, but to say that there is no connection is absolutely wrong.' He continued, 'what is the object of that party? What is the object of the gunmen? Their object [that is, to undermine the state and the Constitution] is the same even though they may not be allies now'.[11]

The Constitution (Amendment No. 6) Bill made the initiative to remove the Oath by petition—signatures for which Fianna Fáil had begun collecting on 1 July—the exclusive privilege of attending members of the Oireachtas. Under the Electoral Amendment (No. 2) Bill, candidates when nominated to stand had to agree that if elected, they would take the Oath. Those candidates who failed to fulfil this requirement within two months of being elected would automatically lose their seats. Such legislation, to quote Donal O'Sullivan, placed Fianna Fáil in a 'cruel dilemma'.[12] That Cumann na nGaedheal took such a strong stand on imposing the Oath was due to its integral place in the Treaty. In the government's eyes, the whole legitimacy of the state, not to mention Cumann na nGaedheal itself, was based on that agreement and it could not be dismantled.

Through its response to O'Higgins's assassination, the Cosgrave administration effectively signed the government's death warrant. Seán MacEntee acknowledged that the electoral amendment bill had been the catalyst for Fianna Fáil's decision to take its seats, as the party had been left with no other option.[13] Ernest Blythe later admitted that Cumann na nGaedheal had to 'face the reality that if [Fianna Fáil did enter the Dáil] it would ultimately succeed to power'.[14] It was on balance, however, more important to have de Valera's party inside the Dáil rather than outside the fold of constitutional politics. Cosgrave in particular knew from his experience in the revolutionary Dáil that separate political systems would only compete with and eventually destroy the legitimate government. If his government was to be defeated, then the preference was for political rather than military defeat, and so Cumann na nGaedheal placed the nation above party interests.

Maurice Manning summed up the legislation by stating that its purpose was to 'force Fianna Fáil out of electoral politics or into the Dáil'.[15] But the legislation extended beyond simply forcing the hands of the Fianna Fáil deputies, making it necessary to draw a distinction between the Republican groupings which Cumann na nGaedheal targeted. The government made no secret of the fact that the electoral amendment bill was aimed at Fianna Fáil but vigorously denied that it was designed to suppress that party, while at the same time acknowledging that the purpose of the public safety bill was to eliminate the threat from the extremists.

An imagined danger?

Cosgrave issued an emotive statement from Government Buildings venerating O'Higgins but warning that the actions of his murderers would not be tolerated. 'The Irish people may rest assured that the assassin's bullet will not succeed in terrorising this country.' Although O'Higgins had 'trodden the path blazed by Griffith and Collins, even unto death', Cosgrave promised that 'there are, and will be, men ... ready to step into his place'.[16] His murder—'the killing of the symbol of law and order in the Cosgrave government'[17]—suggested to the Cabinet (and the *Irish Times*)[18] that there were unremitting threats to the new state. In his address to the Dáil during the second stage of the Public Safety Bill, Cosgrave outlined various dangers emanating from the Civil War and persisting thereafter. The government thus interpreted the murder of Kevin O'Higgins as a direct challenge to the political stability, and as John Marcus O'Sullivan, the minister for education, put it, O'Higgins's killing had been 'an attempt to assassinate the state'.[19] Cumann na nGaedheal symbolically placed the murder within the context of the Civil War when the memory of Kevin O'Higgins was committed to the Cenotaph on Leinster Lawn. The Cenotaph, which had been unveiled to the press on 11 August 1923, commemorated Arthur Griffith and Michael Collins. As Anne Dolan has observed, 'the association of O'Higgins with this monument to civil war confirmed his death as an act of civil war'.[20]

Many deputies believed that the reprehensible deed caused the government to panic and introduce a package of unconsidered legislation, but Cosgrave and his colleagues refuted the accusations. 'We regard the bill as moderate. It is not panicky,' Cosgrave explained to the Dáil.[21] When Ernest Blythe told the House that 'the state is not going to be overthrown by assassination',[22] he was not so much expressing a considered opinion, but instead warning that further activity similar to that of 10 July would not be tolerated. It was John O'Hanlon, an independent deputy from Cavan, who best captured the views of the opposition when he asserted that 'they drafted [the bill] at Booterstown—they did not draft it in the Dáil'.[23]

By July 1927, the Cosgrave government had effectively secured the state, despite threats not only from the Republicans, but also from some Free State elements, most notably during the army 'mutiny'. An attempt to overthrow the Treaty settlement by armed force had been put down, while the events of the army crisis reinforced that nobody was bigger than the state. Constitutional nationalism had become the established order of the day. For that reason, it is hardly surprising that several newspapers shared the view of the *Sligo Champion*'s editor that 'the danger is more imaginary than real'.[24] Government deputies, however, saw a genuine threat to that which they had dedicated their time and energies—and for which Kevin O'Higgins had given his life—to fostering. Furthermore, the legitimacy of the party rested on the successful implementation of the Treaty settlement and the construction of a stable state. Although the opposition found fault with it, the strong response was inevitable. According to the *Irishman*, the organ of the Labour Party, 'the assassins themselves will be flattered, rather than frightened, for they will think they have struck panic into the government'.[25] Certainly the extremists had manoeuvred themselves away from the peripheries and onto the political agenda—for a heinous crime, they had been rewarded with recognition—but they had in no way strengthened their position. The *Irishman* accused the government of mishandling the situation. 'What was needed was to show that this lamentable crime had failed, and must fail, to shake the stability of the state, that it was an isolated and despairing attempt by a few individuals who had abandoned hope of winning support from the mass of the people.'[26] However, through the government's handling of the situation, not only had the state emerged unshaken, but in fact it emerged even stronger than before. The threats of the extremists ceased to loom large, and a stronger political system was created through Fianna Fáil's full participation.

A self-sacrificing measure?

Had Cumann na nGaedheal been motivated by a desire to suppress Fianna Fáil or an acknowledgement that normality could only be truly restored once de Valera's party was within the political system? On its formation in May 1926 Fianna Fáil also subscribed to the policy of abstention. However, de Valera and his supporters had split from Sinn Féin in the belief that a new departure in their politics was required, but Cumann na nGaedheal's legislation threatened to recast Fianna Fáil in the Sinn Féin mould. By describing the controversial Oath as an 'empty formula' and arguing that 'the signing of it implies no contractual obligation,' de Valera's adroit manoeuvring created a loop-hole that allowed his deputies to present themselves at the office of the clerk and to subsequently take their seats.

Fianna Fáil's decision to abandon the self-destructive policy of abstention gave the party a patina of acceptability and contributed to the party's legitimisation. Many senior members of the government party would have been consciously aware that it was Sinn Féin's constitutional activity and handling of the conscription crisis in 1918 that had given that party its degree of respectability. With such a past precedent, Cumann na nGaedheal might have been attempting to pre-empt Fianna Fáil's transformation in the public eye, thus eliminating its most powerful threat. After the disappointing June election and even with the Republicans' continued policy of abstention, the Cosgrave administration was in a parliamentary minority. Desmond Ryan concluded that the Oath had 'only [been] retained as a barrier against de Valera'.[27] In an effort to preserve its tenuous majority, Cumann na nGaedheal could therefore be charged with pursing a policy designed to eliminate any serious opposition.

According to William O'Brien, when Gerald Boland met Thomas Johnson, he expressed the view that Fianna Fáil 'would be wiped out unless they entered the Dáil'.[28] Patrick Hogan, in dismissing claims that the bills were designed to break the strength of Fianna Fáil, vigorously argued that the political extinction of that party would bring 'no grist to the mill of the party to which' he belonged.[29] Although with time it would become increasingly difficult to distinguish between the two parties, in the 1920s supporters of Cumann na nGaedheal and Fianna Fáil subscribed to a markedly different political philosophy, and it was unlikely that there would have been an extensive transfer of loyalty if either party were to die a political death. That said, Cumann na nGaedheal would still have benefited from the absence of Fianna Fáil opposition.

It would therefore seem that the motivation behind the electoral and constitutional amendment bills was high-minded. Certainly Cosgrave *publicly* welcomed the move of de Valera and his deputies into the realm of constitutional politics, heralding it to be 'the best thing that has happened during the last five years'.[30] He reaffirmed this view in an interview with Frederick Kuhn of the *New York Times* in August 1928.[31] Robert Smyllie, however, is said to have reminisced in later years that Cosgrave had reacted with shock when he told him that de Valera was to take the Oath.[32] This does not satisfy the argument, however, that Cosgrave had never intended the act to bring Fianna Fáil into the Dáil. Cosgrave had clearly acknowledged the importance of having a large section of the electorate represented; he considered full participation in the Dáil vital to the development and stability of the state. As Frank Munger noted, it was 'a gamble with high stakes, for the injury to Ireland might have been very great if the convinced Republicans had been driven out of politics and into the IRA',[33] but it was a gamble that nonetheless paid off.

During the second reading of the Electoral Amendment (No. 2) Bill, Labour's William Davin expressed the view that 'the policy of abstention was going to kill the abstentionists'.[34] During the campaign for the general election of June 1927, Fianna Fáil had bought extensive advertising space in both the national and regional newspapers, and from the *Irish Independent* to the *Connacht Tribune*, advertisements had appeared with the perplexing slogan 'Fianna Fáil is going in'.[35] The meaning was left to voters to interpret, but it caused considerable confusion. The dénouement of their election slogan became apparent when Fianna Fáil deputies indicated their intention to enter the Dáil, albeit without first taking the Oath. Unsurprisingly when the deputies presented themselves at the Dáil they were refused admission to the chamber for failure to fulfil the necessary requirements. If Cumann na nGaedheal was serious about eliminating its opposition, surely a policy of wait and see would have been effective. The slogan would hardly have had the same effect on the electorate twice.

Essentially the government was concerned with ensuring that the body politic was actively represented in the Dáil by all of its elected members, in which case, the amendment to the electoral laws was an effective policy. The abstentionists had been discussed at meetings of the executive organising committee on 13 and 20 January 1925. A referendum on the 46 seats in question had been suggested, although the executive was opposed to the idea. At the second meeting it was agreed that Cosgrave should 'discourage the idea of a referendum and that, prior to next general election, measures to cope with the abstentionist policy should form part of the ministerial programme'.[36] By ruling out a referendum that would have provided only a short-term solution, in favour of resolving the problem in the long-term, Cumann na nGaedheal confirmed its commitment to stabilising the party system and by extension the state. Fianna Fáil's decision to take the Oath and enter the Dáil was immediately recognised as signalling 'the dawn of a new phase in Irish politics',[37] and the result was the emergence of a two-party system. The party's U-turn in policy played a massive role in securing the stability of the state, and, according to Peter Mair, it was 'arguably the most crucial single event in creating the party system as it exists today'.[38]

An IRA statement printed in the *Nation* implied that the murder of the vice-president provided the government with the smokescreen necessary to introduce legislation already under consideration. 'The repressive legislation must have been contemplated before the shooting of Mr O'Higgins,' it was claimed, 'as a document captured from the British Secret Service shows that the growing strength of the IRA was causing anxiety in London, and that the Free State authorities were being urged to take steps to meet the situation.'[39] If the claims of the IRA were valid, the captured correspondence would appear to cast doubts over Cumann na nGaedheal's noble intentions. However, the IRA, and not Fianna Fáil, was the intended target in the alleged document and, as already mentioned, Cumann na nGaedheal did not deny that the aim of the Public Safety Bill was to eliminate the extremists. The document, taken with the meetings about a potential referendum, thus provides further evidence that the stability of the state was an ongoing concern for Cumann na nGaedheal and that the Public Safety Bill was not necessarily a knee-jerk reaction to the assassination, as suggested by opposition politicians. The fact that plans to tackle the problem were being considered at this stage, indicate that O'Higgins's assassination was the occasion but not the cause for the introduction of new legislation.

It would appear, therefore, that Cumann na nGaedheal acted selflessly and in the interests of the state. When it came to public well-being, the government had a near-transparent attitude and was predisposed to eschew popularity (almost invariably failing to court it on the eve of elections). It showed an innate ability to make tough decisions, even if they would have negative consequences for the party's electoral fortunes. Earlier that year Bryan Cooper had remarked of Kevin O'Higgins, 'I am certain that if he woke up some morning and found that he was popular, he would examine his conscience'.[40] Cooper's assessment could easily have been the dictum of the Cumann na nGaedheal leadership. Cosgrave succinctly, and probably genuinely, summed up his party's attitude when he publicly asserted in August 1927 that 'the country is more important than any political party'.[41] Undeniably, Cumann na nGaedheal's gamble, together with Fianna Fáil's momentous decision, strengthened the democratic structures of the Free State. It is the party's most enduring legacy.

Fianna Fáil's entry into the Dáil posed an important challenge to Cumann na nGaedheal's authority. The Republicans previous failure to take their seats had meant that Cumann na nGaedheal's dominance within the Dáil was entirely incommensurate with its popularity among the electorate. Prior to Fianna Fáil's entry, the opposition had offered no credible threat to the administration. The *Irish Times* now predicted that 'the condition of affairs in the Dáil will be so unstable that a general election will become inevitable within a comparatively short space of time'.[42] The calculated deeds of the opposition provided the first portentous sign that the cogs of the election machine would soon begin to turn again

The repercussions of Fianna Fáil's momentous decision to take its seats were immediately apparent when a challenge of grandiose proportions was mounted. On 16 August 1927 a motion of no confidence was tabled, although it came not from Fianna Fáil, but from the party that had occupied the main opposition benches since 1922. Labour leader, Thomas Johnson, seconded by his colleague Hugh Colohan, moved 'that the Executive Council has ceased to retain the support of the majority in Dáil Éireann'.[43] This, of course, was not the first time that a constitutional challenge to the government had been launched; McGrath had moved a similar motion in 1924 during the army crisis.

The government, the opposition and the press all shared the common view that the Cumann na nGaedheal administration was destined to fall.[44] Johnson was so confident that his motion would be carried that he did not deem it necessary to recall T.J. O'Connell, who was abroad attending a teachers' conference. In an interview with Arthur Mitchell, O'Connell later revealed how he had received a telegram from his party leader offering him the education portfolio in the new government.[45] If O'Connell and therefore Johnson's full party had been present, the absence of John Jinks from the division, discussed below, would have been irrelevant.

More than two decades later, Michael Hayes, who was the speaker of the House, narrated to Jim Dooge[46] the events that took place on the morning of the motion. Cosgrave apparently called a meeting with the army generals and informed them that by the following day there would be a new government, to whom they were expected to be loyal. Reportedly, this caused disquiet among the generals, who were unwilling to serve under a man against whom they had fought during the Civil War. Cosgrave reminded them that the Civil War had been fought to uphold the wishes of the majority, and if the majority decided that Cumann na nGaedheal should quit government, then that decision would also have to be upheld. During this time, Desmond FitzGerald had been ill and Cosgrave temporarily held the defence portfolio. After the September general election, Cosgrave once more appointed FitzGerald minister for defence, intimating that he was unsure how much time Cumann na nGaedheal had left but that Fianna Fáil would inevitably come to power. A change was needed in the attitude of the army and, Cosgrave allegedly believed that FitzGerald was the only person capable of implementing reform.[47]

If Hayes's and later Dooge's recollection of events is correct, then Cosgrave was clearly expecting and preparing to lose power from as early as 1927. In an interview for Brian Reynolds's PhD thesis, Ernest Blythe admitted that 'even President Cosgrave acknowledged at a meeting of the Executive Council that a defeat on the motion was almost assured'.[48] Bill Severn stated that Cosgrave actually threw a farewell party for his staff,[49] although he did not provide a source for his claim. The undocumented nature of such suggestions reflects the clouded nature of the events and the hearsay that they provoked.

A Fianna Fáil, Labour and National League coalition seemed the most obvious alternative to the existing government and several meetings took place between key Labour and Fianna Fáil personnel.[50] A lack of cohesion in the arguments put forward by the opposition parties during the debate would suggest, however, that no joint strategy had been agreed. Labour proposed the motion on economic grounds, while the National League supported it as a type of practical protest against the Public Safety Act. Like Labour, economic considerations were also the mainstay of the Farmers' Party's arguments, but, unlike Johnson's party, it opposed the motion. The eclectic mix of views as to why the motion should be carried was an indicator of the varying opinions that would exist within the proposed coalition, making it an uneasy alliance.

While Fianna Fáil had decided unanimously at a party meeting on 12 August to support the motion,[51] during the debate the party remained remarkably silent. John Marcus O'Sullivan referred to them as 'the 44 silent deputies opposite'[52] and David O'Gorman inquired 'are they afraid or ashamed to speak?'[53] The debate started just after three o'clock, yet the voice of Fianna Fáil was not heard until nearly two hours later, when the expelled deputy, Patrick Belton, offered a one-line interjection for which the Ceann Comhairle admonished him.[54] The party did not officially contribute until after six o'clock when Seán T. O'Kelly made a brief speech in Irish. He informed the chamber that 'it is better for Ireland's cause for us not to go into argument today ... but everyone will understand that we do not think here that it is right for the government to continue in office'.[55]

The National League was experiencing internal difficulties and its resolve to vote against the government apparently lagged behind that of Fianna Fáil and Labour. Vincent Rice was to resign in protest at his leader's pledge to support the motion, which had been given without prior consultation with the party. When the division was taken after the debate, John Jinks of the National League, as discussed below, mysteriously disappeared, thus granting the government a reprieve. Moss asserts that the series of correspondence which took place between Redmond and Jinks in the page of the *Irish Times* after the debacle showed how 'Redmond was trying to force an unwilling band of followers into a policy of supporting Johnson'.[56] Jinks had written: 'on the recent issue of the proposed alliance between Fianna Fáil, Labour and the National League, I was not, to my great surprise, consulted before action (improper action) was taken by you in favour of the proposed pact'.[57] Redmond's unilateral action had, of course, been the reason for Vincent Rice's resignation.

On 13 August Redmond issued a statement dispelling rumours of dissent within the ranks, and stated that his party had 'arrived at a definite decision', which was unanimous.[58] The previous day he had written to Johnson, however, admitting that there was 'a good deal of uneasiness'. Members of the National League were concerned that the new coalition should not place 'Labour in the saddle or Fianna Fáil in effective control and pulling the strings'.[59] This idea of de Valera's party as the puppet master was a dominant theme in Cumann na nGaedheal's response. Later that day, Redmond corresponded again with Johnson, this time forwarding a resolution that had been proposed by William Coburn and seconded by Jinks in which the party pledged to support the motion. Despite a subsequent exchange of letters between the leaders of Labour and the National League relating to the composition of the government, it appeared that William Redmond's party was prepared to give its undivided support to Johnson's motion. The correspondence between Redmond and Johnson clearly showed uneasiness on the part of the National League and its leader. In fact, the day before the debate, Redmond wrote again to Johnson asking for assurances, and the Labour leader's reply showed that his patience was wearing thin.[60] A meeting held at two o'clock on 16 August affirmed that Redmond's party would act together.[61] Later to the chagrin of Redmond, Jinks's reticence at that meeting caused his leader to enter the chamber confident that his deputies, with the exception of Rice, would vote en bloc. Rice, who had not signed the pledge to sit, act and vote with the party when chosen as a candidate for the June election, would cross the floor and vote with the government.

When the debate got under way, an alternative government that included Fianna Fáil was not proposed. However, the Labour and National League coalition would inevitably be in thrall to its silent partner on the opposition benches. This featured heavily during the debate. Patrick Baxter of the Farmers' Party enquired if Fianna Fáil would be 'the power behind the throne?', while his party colleague, David O'Gorman, suggested that the government would be 'mere puppets, with deputy de Valera pulling the strings'.[62] This concept was later the subject of a Cumann na nGaedheal election poster entitled the 'Fianna Fallacy Puppet Show', which depicted Redmond and Johnson as Punch and Judy, and de Valera as the puppet master. If Fianna Fáil was to be the real power behind the scenes, deputies opposing the motion asked how could such a government function. There was, very obviously, one major point on which the parties diverged. During the five-hour debate, Johnson affirmed that Labour would 'maintain the Treaty and the Constitution',[63] while Redmond confirmed that his party was 'absolutely wedded to the fundamentals of the Anglo–Irish settlement'.[64]

The extent to which the National League held the balance of power became embarrassingly evident when the motion was put to the house. The Leas-Ceann Comhairle, James Dolan, expressed his belief that it had been carried. Patrick McGilligan challenged a division from the government benches but when that division was taken, the National League was nonplussed to find that its Sligo-Leitrim TD, John Jinks, who had been seated behind his leader throughout the debate, was no longer in attendance. He was allegedly seen at the telegram office in the porch of the Dáil writing that Cosgrave would win by two votes.[65] Such a report was probably apocryphal, but his mysterious disappearance under such ambiguous circumstances—for which there have been many and varied explanations[66]—left the house evenly divided with 71 votes supporting the motion and 71 opposed. The casting vote thus fell to Michael Hayes, the Ceann Comhairle, who appropriately voted with the government. The motion was thus declared lost, sparing the government a humiliating defeat.

Although Redmond's party held the balance of power, in retrospect, the independent deputies were the real power brokers. Even with the undivided support of the National League, victory by only a slender majority was anticipated. Such a tight margin did not allow for absences or defections (as the Jinks incident showed), although the Labour Party had believed that even with anticipated defections, the government would be brought down by two or three votes.[67] Several independents, such as Alfie Byrne, were critical of the government at times and although Labour did not explicitly name Byrne, Johnson's party believed that two of those independents would back the motion. In an article written five days after the event for the *Observer*, Stephen Gwynn suggested that independent deputies Gilbert Hewson, Alfie Byrne and Michael Brennan, who was a former Cumann na nGaedheal deputy, had been expected to vote with the opposition.[68]

In his papers on the 1927 crisis, William O'Brien notes that 'very strenuous canvassing had been done over the weekend and several of them [the independents] we thought might act with us and whom we might put into ministries … were all turned against us'.[69] The phraseology of the report of the Labour national executive for 1927–8 seems to confirm that there had been some discussion between the party and the independents in question, and that perhaps even a pledge of support had been made. 'What menaces of promises were held out by the government or others to these deputies, between Friday and Monday, is not known.'[70]

Enniskerry had played host to a political tryst of the Labour leaders on 13 August. Confident of victory, the configuration of the next government Cabinet was the subject for discussion. William O'Brien explained how they had encountered the editor of the *Irish Times*.[71] In what amounted to an incredible scoop, the newspaper printed the proposed Cabinet in its entirety the following day. O'Brien learnt many years later that Smyllie had discovered bits of torn paper in the trash where the meeting had taken place and spent the remainder of the day piecing them together.[72] Both Bryan Cooper and John O'Hanlon had been given portfolios in an obvious effort to entice the independents to support the motion.

When the division was taken, however, Patrick Belton, the expelled Fianna Fáil deputy who continued to represent Dublin County as an independent Republican, and Daniel Corkery of Cork North were the only independents who endorsed the motion. Support was otherwise not forthcoming because the independent deputies were essentially constitutionalists. Of the sixteen elected at the June general election, Arthur Clery and Daniel Corkery were then the only independent Republicans (but as Clery was an abstentionist, he was irrelevant to the debate). Additionally, elections tend to induce a feeling of trepidation among independent deputies who have neither the luxury of a support network nor the finances generally associated with party membership. Indeed, the close proximity of the June and September elections was to drain the coffers of the smaller parties and independents, and neither repeated their impressive June performances. Arthur Mitchell suggests that Johnson's nationality was a further factor that influenced certain independents not to support the motion.[73] For example, John O'Hanlon—who appeared on the potential Cabinet list—declared that 'I am an Irishman, and I cannot possibly give my vote to put at the head of this State an Englishman', while Jasper Wolfe explained that he did not believe that the Free State was 'so bereft of intelligence' that they could not have an 'Ireland governed by Irishmen'.[74] The acrimonious nature of such comments was reminiscent of Arthur Griffith's 'damned Englishman' remark to Erskine Childers during the Treaty debates.[75]

The people's motion of no confidence?

Although Cosgrave's administration had been rescued from defeat and the House adjourned until October, the party did not have time to relax and consider the future as two pending by-elections presented a further challenge. The murder of Kevin O'Higgins and the death of Fianna Fáil's Countess Markievicz five days later created vacancies in Dublin County and Dublin South respectively. Already in a precarious position and demoralised by the attack on its power, Cumann na nGaedheal considered the elections to be of paramount importance. In many ways, the two by-elections were tantamount to a people's motion of confidence. Moreover, if Fianna Fáil were to retain the seat held by Countess Markievicz as well as gaining one in Dublin County, then the balance within the Dáil would once again be altered and the fate of the government would yet again lie in the hands of the opposition. Although a victory in Dublin County would only give the party one additional seat, Fianna Fáil's position within the Dáil would nonetheless be strengthened while pushing Cumann na nGaedheal further into minority government. The chances of bringing the government down with a second no confidence motion would thus be greatly increased. The whips would have to be firmly applied and complete attendance would become a necessity, especially in the event of the opposition choosing to withdraw pairing. Working under such circumstances would have placed a great strain on the government.

The people of Dublin South and County were once again asked to cast their votes just over two months after the general election. As Labour and the other small parties opted out of both constituencies, the electoral battle, which took place on 24 August, was waged directly between the government candidates and the Republicans. The potential Cumann na nGaedheal candidates had been deliberated on at a meeting of the standing committee on 27 July chaired by J.J. Walsh. In relation to Dublin County it was decided that a subcommittee should interview Arthur Cox about the possibility of standing, while it was agreed that Thomas Hennessy would be the best candidate for Dublin South.[76] Gearóid O'Sullivan, however, stood as the government candidate in Dublin County after Cox refused permission for his name to be put forward. The *Irish Times* speculated that if O'Sullivan were successful, the former member of the army council would receive the justice portfolio.[77] James Fitzgerald-Kenney, however, was named as O'Higgins's successor. Standing on the Fianna Fáil ticket was Robert Brennan in Dublin County, while Robert Briscoe hoped to retain the Fianna Fáil seat in Dublin South. Sinn

Féin put forward Kathleen Lynn in Dublin County and Charles Murphy in Dublin South, both of whom had first entered the Dáil in 1923 but had lost their seats at the June election.

Cognisant of the seriousness of the outcome, Cumann na nGaedheal's campaign was strong and energetic. The organisation of the nascent Fianna Fáil Party was not yet greater than that of its political rival, causing the *Evening Herald* to note that although Cumann na nGaedheal's campaign machine was working 'briskly and efficiently', Fianna Fáil's was 'not so much in evidence'.[78]

The unremitting themes of the 1920s yet again made their presence felt during the by-election campaigns. Peace, stability and prosperity, as well as the Treaty, were among the main issues of the campaign. However, the fact that polling day was designated to occur eight days after the no confidence debate meant that the motion was the most salient issue on the hustings and both sides naturally attempted to use the issue to their own advantage. Fianna Fáil claimed that the government was unrepresentative of the people as it had been kept in office by 'the Independent Unionist vote', while Cumann na nGaedheal's Finian Lynch argued that the motion struck at the stability of the country.[79] While 'stability' was part of Cumann na nGaedheal's traditional vocabulary, in this instance it could also be read as a tacit reference to the economy. Such remarks were potentially designed to appeal to the Labour supporters who did not have a candidate of their own but for many of whom the economy was an important issue.

The no confidence motion was clearly on the mind of numerous constituents as they went to the polls. A slip of paper found in one of the Dublin County ballot boxes read 'may God protect us from all creeping insects such as bugs and fleas, the leaders of Labour and National League'.[80] The circumstances that had created the vacancy in Dublin County provided the government party with a 'safe seat', making victory a foregone conclusion. The outcome of Dublin South was far less predictable, for although Fianna Fáil was traditionally weak in the Dublin constituencies, a high-profile member of the party's ranks had once held the now vacant seat. But the Labour-led, National League- and Fianna Fáil-supported no-confidence motion created a back-lash against Fianna Fáil that was electorally fatal. The Dublin electorate cast their votes overwhelmingly in favour of the government candidates. Hennessey and O'Sullivan polled spectacularly, with both of their first preference totals exceeding those of Fianna Fáil and Sinn Féin combined. Based on the seemingly exhortatory by-election results, Cosgrave advised Timothy Healy to dissolve the fifth Dáil and the parties braced themselves for a controversially timed second general election of the year.

A closer examination of the by-election results suggests, however, that the results were less impressive than first suggested. Robert Briscoe pointed out that in 1923 the government party had defeated the Republicans in those two constituencies by over 10,000 first preferences.[81] While O'Sullivan's performance in Dublin County was spectacular—a victorious margin of 22,508 first preferences over the combined Republican showing—it was to be expected. A display of sympathy for the murdered vice-president at the polls would have been strongest in his own constituency. In contrast, Hennessy won by a much slimmer margin of 4,377 votes. Nonetheless, it was a strong margin, particularly since the party was not defending an existing seat. Furthermore, as the following chapters will show, the results from both the general election of September 1927 and the by-elections that occurred during the life of the sixth Dáil confirm that Cumann na nGaedheal was not on a downward slide.

After O'Higgins

The most fitting tribute to O'Higgins, who had given his time and ultimately his life to secure the stability of the state, is the fact that the modern party system resulted from his death. The government was accused in 1927 of exaggerating the threat and was criticised for giving the extremists recognition by introducing knee-jerk legislation, but for the government party the threat was very real and dealing with the extremists was essential to protect the state.

'If he had lived,' Donal O'Sullivan remarked, 'it is certain that the subsequent history of his country would have been very different'.[82] His tribute to O'Higgins raises not only the question of what consequences the assassination had for the Irish Free State, but also what affect his death had on Cumann na nGaedheal. How the Free State might have developed had O'Higgins lived is merely conjecture and for that reason remains unresolved, but the impact on his party can be better determined by assessing his position within Cumann na nGaedheal and determining the importance of his role.

Educated at UCD, O'Higgins was an intellectual. Although he became involved with Sinn Féin, he—even more so than Cosgrave—might have been expected to join the Irish Parliamentary Party. His family was certainly well-connected as both of his parents were identified with the 'Bantry Band' faction of the party (so called because of their roots in that part of Cork), but he was, in the words of his most recent biographer, a 'republican dissenter in a parliamentary family'.[83] Although he did not fight in 1916, O'Higgins was an active member of Sinn Féin and won a seat for the party in Queen's County (Laois) at the 1918 general election. As already discussed in Chapter 1, he worked alongside Cosgrave in the successful Department of Local Government, and it would seem that the sometimes strained relationship that was later identifiable in the Free State government was evident at this time also. When Cosgrave—seemingly on Collins's advice—went on the run, O'Higgins was left to take over the running of the department, but apparently felt that Cosgrave had disappeared of his own accord and had left him to shoulder the responsibility.[84]

As also mentioned in Chapter 1, O'Higgins's name appears to have been rumoured as a possible successor at the time of Griffith's death, although Michael Hayes doubted that O'Higgins would have considered himself in such a role at that time. However, that he had ambition cannot be denied, but while respected, he was not necessarily popular with his colleagues. Although the 1924 army crisis had removed Mulcahy—his great opponent—from the Cabinet,[85] the remaining ministers, with the possible exception of his close friend Patrick Hogan, may not have been enthusiastic about his leadership. Although he was also close to Desmond FitzGerald, FitzGerald was completely loyal to Cosgrave. Nonetheless, there was a common perception that O'Higgins was waiting in the wings, possibly to prise power from Cosgrave if necessary. The idea was satirised by the *Nation* newspaper in 1925, which carried a cartoon depicting O'Higgins fleeing with 'state control' as represented by Cosgrave's pet dog.[86] When the general election of June 1927 produced inconclusive results, and Cumann na nGaedheal was not returned with the 50 seats Cosgrave had claimed were needed to form a government, he informed the Dáil that he was only prepared to accept the office of president if the opposition could not offer a workable alternative. Again it was the *Nation* that referred to the possible leader-in-waiting when it suggested that the position might be filled by another member of Cosgrave's own party, noting that 'there's always Kevin and his ambitions to be considered'.[87] That the *Nation* was a Republican publication probably accounts for its mischievous musings, but speculation was not confined to its pages. Just months before O'Higgins was assassinated, the *Connacht Tribune* had reported that rumours were 'again current of differences between him [Cosgrave] and his principal lieutenant'.[88]

Given O'Higgins's uncompromising personality, he would certainly have offered a different style of leadership than Cosgrave. It is unlikely that he would have allowed ministers the same degree of freedom that Cosgrave did, and tensions may have increased in the government. Michael Hayes later recollected that O'Higgins had difficulty understanding some of those who sat at the Cabinet table with him.[89] However, the government might also have become more driven under his leadership; indeed one of the reasons why O'Higgins clashed with Cosgrave was because he favoured a more direct approach than his leader. Calton Younger has argued that it was O'Higgins's handling of the army crisis which allowed him to emerge as the strong man of the Cabinet. But, as Brian Farrell pointed out, if that simple judgement is accepted, then Cosgrave's political survival after O'Higgins's death needs explanation.[90]

The assassination removed from the Cabinet one of the most able, determined and talented of Cosgrave's ministers. He was widely seen as the strong man of the government, while some of his opponents considered him an Irish Mussolini. O'Higgins was the minister most closely associated with the Civil War executions, despite the fact that he was the last member of the Cabinet to reluctantly sign off on them; Rory O'Connor had after all been the best man at his wedding fourteen months previously. His hard-line reputation increased over the following years as a result of the uncompromising approach that he took on a number of matters. He was one of the driving forces in the government and many of the major policy initiatives came from his ministries. Because of the necessity to stabilise the Free State, his role as minister for home affairs (later justice), placed him at the forefront of political life. During the third and fourth Dála, he piloted several important measures—guiding the Constitution through the Dáil; overseeing the establishment of the Garda Síochána; and the introduction of legislation aimed at restoring peace—that were vital to

the creation and development of the new state. From his contributions to the Treaty debates, O'Higgins marked himself out as a
pragmatist. Although he realised the limitations of the Treaty settlement, he was enough of a realist to recognise that it provided the
most practical means for legitimately advancing Irish sovereignty.
Along with Arthur Griffith and Éamonn Duggan, he had negotiated
with the British on the terms of the Constitution. In defending it in
the Dáil, he used arguments similar to that deployed in his defence
of the Treaty; he referred again to British naval strength.[91] He believed
in working within the Commonwealth and he played a leading role
at the imperial conference which prompted the Balfour Declaration
that Commonwealth members were co-equal. Although not well-re-
ceived, his idea for a kingdom of Ireland showed not only his
pragmatism, but also confirmed that he was a man of big ideas and
who was conscious that only through compromise could a united
Ireland be achieved.

Some of the more controversial legislation that he introduced—
Intoxicating Liquor Acts, censorship, divorce, a ban on female
jurors—addressed the morality of the nation. This was partially a
product of his background—O'Higgins had expressed a wish at the
age of fifteen to become a priest and had later attended St Patrick's
College, Maynooth, although he ultimately did not enter the priesthood—but it was also very much in keeping with the character of the
state that Cumann na nGaedheal was building. However, as Diarmaid
Ferriter has pointed out, 'not all [politicians] were able or willing to
reconcile their private behaviour with the sexual ethos of the new Free
State'.[92] Despite being a devout Catholic and family man, O'Higgins,
for example, frequently addressed his wife as 'pet lamb' in correspondence, but was infatuated with Hazel Lavery.

Rarely did he bow to pressure, and although there was some
success by the trade and his own colleagues in influencing him to
moderate his liquor legislation, he was generally uncompromising.
The result of this, combined with his often aloof personality and
abrupt manner, meant that he was not particularly popular. But, in
the early years of the Free State, a politician of O'Higgins's mentality
was essential. Had he been popular, it would have suggested that he
had not made the difficult choices that were essential for building
the new state. O'Higgins's death inevitably struck a blow at the heart
of Cumann na nGaedheal. The party lost one of its strongest elec-

toral performers and a politician of great intellectual capacity with an unrelenting work ethic. However, his death did not signal the demise of Cumann na nGaedheal. With Fianna Fáil's entry into the Dáil one of the single biggest threats to political stability had been removed. Cumann na nGaedheal thus survived—in Cosgrave's words—the death of 'a colleague, loyal, steadfast, of rare ability'[93] because the challenges that O'Higgins had faced down were no longer present in the Free State after 1927. Furthermore, the Cabinet was not devoid of men of talent, and in terms of foreign policy, McGilligan—whom O'Higgins had brought into the Cabinet—proved just as capable and successful at imperial conferences as O'Higgins had been.

.4.
Making history:
winning the September 1927 election

The September 1927 election marked a significant stage in Cumann na nGaedheal's development. A more energetic and professional style of electioneering replaced a previously lax approach. This was in response to the challenge laid down by Fianna Fáil. That party's decision to enter the Dáil had exposed Cumann na nGaedheal's artificial majority, while the outcome of the August no-confidence motion highlighted the precarious position in which the devastating June election had left the government. By fully participating in the political system, Fianna Fáil had transformed itself in the eyes of many floating or previously inactive voters, placing Cumann na nGaedheal's role as the governing party under serious threat. The panic that this induced galvanised the party, stirring it from its complacency. The transformation it underwent was noted by many commentators across the Free State, and the provincial press credited Cumann na nGaedheal with an active, intense and efficient campaign for the second election of the year.[1]

As the two elections of 1927 were merely three months apart, many of the leading issues in June were to resurface, but it was ultimately the political turmoil, which had characterised the summer months that was to dominate the agenda. Labour and the National League did not repeat their June performances. Like many protest votes, the results from June were not so much an affirmation of support for alternative candidates but rather an expression of discontent with the government. The outcome of June could be described as a temporary displacement of Cumann na nGaedheal's votes, which were returned in September, thus undoing the impact of the disappointing election three months earlier. Furthermore, the results negated the mistaken premise that Cumann na nGaedheal was a party in terminal decline

Timing

The timing of the election was controversial. When, after the no-confidence motion, Cosgrave adjourned the House until October, he had done so on the basis that if the government party candidates were defeated at the Dublin by-elections, the Dáil would reconvene within a week. Labour argued that it was an implied undertaking that if the government candidates were victorious, the Dáil would reassemble as scheduled on 11 October.[2] Yet within hours of the results being confirmed, Cosgrave had gone to the governor general as required to request dissolution of the Dáil. The opposition interpreted this as an attempt to hamper their chances, and Daniel Morrissey went as far as to liken Cosgrave's actions to those of a dictator.[3] Protests aside, both Labour and Fianna Fáil naturally stressed that that they were ready and capable of fighting a campaign. Although de Valera described the decision as 'sharp practice', Fianna Fáil was nonetheless prepared, Seán Lemass affirmed, for the forthcoming battle.[4]

In a detailed statement issued to the press, Cosgrave explained his actions. The statement was arranged into two sections, the first of which outlined the reasons for the dissolution, while the second gave an account of what a defeat of the government might mean. There was, however, no startling revelation to be found in the explanation. Justification was based on the events of the summer: the opposition alliance; the government's need for a 'margin of safety'; the country's need for stability and responsible government; and the results of the by-elections. Similarly Cosgrave's predictions for the future if his administration was defeated had a definite ring of familiarity: chaos, instability; the Treaty threatened and borrowing abilities hampered.

The decision had certainly caught both the country and the opposition parties by surprise, as well as the rank-and-file members of Cumann na nGaedheal; one regional newspaper called it 'a bombshell'.[5] Numerous reports suggested that members of Cosgrave's own Cabinet had not even been informed.[6] Liam de Róiste suggested that J. J. Walsh—who, by his own admission, believed the election to be unnecessary[7]—was perhaps among those ministers absent when the president resolved to go to the polls.[8] Labour's Richard Corish also suggested that Walsh was not consulted, nor was Patrick Hogan.[9]

At the time of the election, the state was less than five years old. Although many British practices had been retained, there was no agreed method for calling elections. The Constitution merely required that the government still retained the confidence of the majority of the Dáil before the governor general could dissolve it. In Britain, the procedure was becoming more defined so that, by 1923 when the Conservative Party leader, Stanley Baldwin, requested a dissolution, it was recognised that it was the prime minister's decision to go to the polls, although some leaders did consult the 'heavyweights' among their Cabinet.[10] In this respect, Cosgrave's decision was not unusual. That he allegedly consulted and arrived at a conclusion with Blythe and McGilligan was hardly surprising.[11] This triumvirate—deemed the 'three big Mussolinis' by Corish—held the most important positions in the Cabinet: president; vice president, and finance; and industry and commerce respectively. Nor was it startling that Walsh was not among the president's personal confidants. Aside from the posts and telegraphs portfolio only recently being elevated from the position of an extern department, the office was a political backwater. Additionally, Walsh, as was commonly known, was at odds with the party and this ruled him out as a sounding board. Hogan's Department of Agriculture was also a recent promotion from an extern position, although it is more surprising that he was not consulted considering that Cosgrave had singled him out for mention as somebody he had sought advice from when forming his first Cabinet.[12] If Cosgrave did indeed act independently, it serves as an example of his ability to take control and lead his party. In fact, his actions are no different to those of de Valera when, in 1933, the Fianna Fáil leader announced a snap election that even caught members of his own party by surprise. On this occasion, at least, instead of being the chairman that Brian Farrell has concluded him to be, Cosgrave had played the role of chief.

But Cosgrave's acumen must be questioned. Did the president misread the political barometer? Dublin County and Dublin South were considered pre-eminent constituencies by the party, but it was a mistake to interpret results there as an indicator of popular opinion across the Free State. The handsome August by-elections results did not presage a sweeping government victory. Yet, as mentioned above, in his statement to the press explaining the dissolution, Cosgrave had displayed confidence that the results were a reasonably accurate reflection of popular sentiment, although there was arguably an element of propaganda to such a declaration. Nonetheless, the results were illusory: a sympathy vote following the brutal assassination of Kevin O'Higgins in July could not be sustained indefinitely. Furthermore, the Dublin constituencies had a high concentration of ex-Unionist voters who were not to be found in the same strength in other constituencies. That their loyalties lay almost invariably with Cumann na nGaedheal meant that the results did not reflect an accurate cross-section of typical voters.

However, Cosgrave did not have any real alternative. Although victory in the two by-elections meant his party had retained a seat and gained a further one, his government would have had to work in an atmosphere of uncertainty that was not conducive to productivity. His position was weak, and there can be no doubt that the Cumann na nGaedheal leader was acutely aware of that fact; the unyielding references to discipline in the party's minute books being ample testament. Thus, rather than simply interpreting his statement as yet another familiar proclamation, it could be seen as the work of a shrewd politician. By emphasizing the apparently promising by-election results, Cosgrave sought to build on the momentum and to deflect attention away from the administration's weak position. This was for the benefit of the general voter, but it was also designed to convince the financial world that his government was sound and stable. As Cosgrave himself explained, a second national loan had to be issued in November;[13] the successful flotation of which was vital to the completion of the Shannon Scheme. Additionally, as *The Times* suggested, the timing was psychologically clever for a further reason. Many voters were disgusted by de Valera's recent reversal on the Oath, and Cumann na nGaedheal stood to gain.[14]

A new departure in campaigning

According to most accounts from various parts of the country, the party organisation was working well.[15] There was one unsurprising and unrepresentative exception. The editor of the *Roscommon Herald* declared that the government organisation was 'very slow in coming into line'.[16] Once again Roscommon was riven by internal party strife, and it is likely that the *Herald*'s editor had taken the dissension in his own county to be an indicator of what was happening throughout the country. Just as the Strokestown convention had descended into farce in June, September was no different. No less than three conventions were held, all of which produced contrasting resolutions! The *Roscommon Herald* consequently reported that the splits and rumours had created so much interest that many people were taking as much interest in the results of the convention as they would on an ordinary count day.[17]

But the Roscommon debacle was very much the exception. With Fianna Fáil clearly waiting in the wings, Cosgrave's party rose to the challenge and the September campaign marked a transformation in Cumann na nGaedheal's approach to electioneering. Over the next five years, the party would show itself to be innovative and professional; its advertisement campaign for September 1927 was held up in Britain as a model to be replicated; the party exploited the then novel use of aeroplanes to drop leaflets over a by-election constituency in 1929; while it introduced yet another first in Irish electioneering in 1933 when a 'talking film' of W.T. Cosgrave was brought to and shown in various parts of the Free State by cinema vans.[18] There can be no doubt that Cumann na nGaedheal's style of electioneering was both inventive and impressive.

David Farrell has noted that with few exceptions, there has been little evidence given of the way political campaigns were run before the 'modern' era.[19] His own article is one of the few exceptions. While a vast body of literature exists on electioneering in both Britain and America, the subject only became the focus for attention in Ireland in the 1970s when the *Ireland at the polls* and later the *How Ireland voted* series was published. These publications deal with the 'modern' era, generally accepted to have begun with Fianna Fáil's 1977 campaign. There has been little study of the 'pre-modern' era, the category into which Cumann na nGaedheal's campaigns fit. The tendency to talk about Fianna Fáil's 'legendary' machine obscures the fact that in the late 1920s and into the early 1930s, Cumann na nGaedheal showed itself to be innovative, and even somewhat 'modern' in its techniques. Fianna Fáil certainly had the more superior grass-roots network, but it was W.T. Cosgrave's party which took the lead and, beginning with the September 1927 campaign, set the precedent for many election-eering methods. The party has never received due recognition for this.

Posters and a host of advertisements appeared in both national and regional newspapers on a scale never before witnessed. Although Fianna Fáil was also very active, it was Cumann na nGaedheal's adver-tisements which dominated the newspapers. This was orchestrated on the party's behalf by the press advertising agency O'Kennedy-Brindley Ltd.[20] It was the first occasion that the professional services of an ad-vertising agency were enlisted on this scale by a political party in Ireland, and it mirrored the trend in Britain, where the Conservative Party was then working with the Holford-Bottomley agency.[21] Brian O'Kennedy was noted by the *Irish Times* to be 'one of the best known men in advertising circles in Ireland'.[22] The company, which was later bought over by the advertising giants Saatchi & Saatchi, would in time become associated with Fianna Fáil, and few realise that it was first employed by Cumann na nGaedheal.

The real significance of the association was how quickly the cam-paign was rolled out. The daily newspapers reported the sudden dissolution of the two-month old fifth Dáil on 25 August 1927. On that same day, Cumann na nGaedheal consulted with the agency, and by the following day the government party had opened a carefully crafted and co-ordinated campaign in every morning newspaper. The 'Help the government to finish the job' advertisement was used to launch the campaign and it provided the key-note for several of the other advertisements. According to O'Kennedy's report, about 300 advertisements appeared, including seven full-pages and no less than 126 half-pages or equivalent spaces. Not a single advertisement was repeated,[23] such was the variety of what was produced.

Twenty of those advertisements were reproduced by the agency in a portfolio to preserve a record of a campaign that O'Kennedy declared had made 'advertising history'. In his introduction, he noted that 'nothing more remarkable in political propaganda has ever been attempted in Great Britain and Ireland'.[24] It was a claim that he could make with some confidence because prior to 1959, due to Section 63 of the Representation of the People Act, political advertising did not feature in general election campaigns in Britain.[25] The Liberals had used newspaper advertisements to promote their policies for the 1929 campaign, but press advertising only began in earnest in Britain in 1979.[26]

Much of what O'Kennedy-Brindley produced could be best described as 'attack advertising'. Rather than shifting the focus back to the running of the country, it nurtured an unrelenting media interest in the tumultuous events of the preceding two months. This added a new dimension to Cumann na nGaedheal's stock criticisms. Although the party had historically tended to emphasize its opponents shortcomings rather than its own platform, this tendency became much more explicit in the September campaign.

Twenty of the innumerable advertisements were reproduced in the portfolio to illustrate the range of the campaign, and the selection was representative of the overall style of the 300 that had been used. Only five were positive. Two had both positive and negative qualities, with the emphasis more on the latter, while thirteen were distinctly negative. The dichotomy of stability and chaos provided the theme for the campaign. As already seen, the Fianna Fáil deputies had taken their seats, having decided that the Oath was nothing more than an empty formula. Cosgrave's party assailed de Valera's for this reinterpretation: 'They took the oath to save their party—they would not take it in 1922 to save the country from Civil War' was the caption of one advertisement.[27] This was repeated on campaign platforms throughout the country. Ernest Blythe echoed the theme at a meeting in Cavan when he accused de Valera of taking the Oath to 'save his own position in the political limelight'.[28] In emphasizing de Valera's U-turn, Cumann na nGaedheal sought to contrast Fianna Fáil's political opportunism with its own honourable defence of the Treaty. Cumann na nGaedheal could be trusted, was the message. This was repeated in many of the regional newspapers, although the events of the summer, rather than Cumann na nGaedheal's propaganda is likely to have caused certain shifts in attitude. For example, the *Waterford Standard*, usually critical of the government party, wondered what all the bother was about five years previously if the Oath was in fact merely an empty political formula. The *Sligo Champion* accused Fianna Fáil of blowing 'hot and cold'.[29] Although sections of the press faulted de Valera's party for the delay in taking the Oath, most also welcomed the move.[30]

The campaign even attracted some attention outside Ireland. An increased emphasis by all of the parties on door-to-door canvassing had been widely reported,[31] while Fianna Fáil and Cumann na nGaedheal had both advertised extensively in the press. Professor James Pollock of the University of Michigan observed in the pages of the *American Political Science Review* in 1928 that as far as political activity was concerned, the election had 'eclipsed all others. Never had the Irish people been so continuously bombarded with oral and written propaganda'.[32] It was the government party's style of campaign in particular that received praise. *Advertisers Weekly*—the principal British journal of organised advertising at the time—devoted a special article to the campaign, which it described as 'marking a new trend in political advertising'.[33] On the basis of what his agency had done for Cumann na nGaedheal, Brian O'Kennedy was invited to address a conference at the Publicity Club of London. The well-attended event, held on 9 May 1928, aimed to offer fresh ideas in advance of the forthcoming British general election, and focus was placed on techniques used in Ireland, particularly those of Cumann na nGaedheal.[34]

Events of the summer

The events of the summer shaped the campaign rhetoric for the September election. Numerous voters certainly shared the prevalent belief that Kevin O'Higgins's assassination signalled a reversion to Civil War conditions, while the no-confidence motion indicated to the electorate the full implications of their June protest vote. A reduced government had almost been toppled by the parties that many voters had supported as constitutional alternatives to Cumann na nGaedheal and which were now seen as being in league with the anti-Treaty Fianna Fáil. Unsurprisingly, therefore, the Treaty once more became the pivotal issue in the election.

There can be no doubt but O'Higgins's murder ensured a sympathy vote for Cumann na nGaedheal. On polling day the party asked the Meath electorate to consider on which side the 'murderers of Kevin O'Higgins' would vote,[35] but it was not always so blunt. A medallion in remembrance of O'Higgins was to take its place next to those of the Free State's other lost leaders on the Cenotaph on Leinster Lawn. As Anne Dolan has pointed out, the ceremony—which took place three and a half weeks before the September election—was 'yet another party political broadcast: a plea for a sympathy vote, an indictment of an opposition tainted with the common cause of the dead minister's killers'. The following year, O'Higgins's medallion was 'uncovered, but not unveiled'. Cumann na nGaedheal had, nonetheless, marked him out as another member of the party willing to make the type of sacrifice that the Republicans monopolised.[36]

In the immediate aftermath of O'Higgins's death, Liam de Róiste had speculated that

> many of those who wanted Cumann na nGaedheal defeated did not realise the consequences of weakening the government. They may be wiser now. It is hard to say. But this effect is already apparent. There is a hardening of opinion towards upholding the state; a hardening of opinion against neo-republicans.[37]

The editor of the *Donegal Democrat* confirmed de Róiste's assessment of public attitudes. At the June election a wave of opposition to the government had emerged in Donegal, resulting in the loss of a seat. Three months later, while acknowledging that its journalists had frequently criticised the government for its failures, the *Donegal Vindicator* appealed for support for Cumann na nGaedheal.[38] The party saw its share of first preferences rise there by just over 10%, due to the absence of the National League (11.29% in June), and possibly also a slight loss by the Farmers.[39] In explaining the perceptible difference in the tone of his newspaper, the editor of the *Donegal Vindicator* expressed what the crux of the issue was for most voters:

'we realise, and wish to make our readers realise, that this election is more vital than any that has preceded it. The Treaty is actually at stake now'.[40] With advertisements declaring 'The Treaty … is threatened',[41] and asking, 'Is the Treaty to be maintained or not?',[42] the government reinforced such concerns.

The menace of clandestine political arrangements was also a persistent thread in the rhetoric of Cumann an nGaedheal's campaign. The proceedings of 16 August and the subsequent events, examined in the previous chapter, were pointed to as the quintessential example of the danger of such agreements. Cosgrave's party argued that Labour and the National League had betrayed the voters by engaging in the opposition alliance, and clearly many agreed as the protagonists of the debate were punished for what was seen as a betrayal of their supporters. In Dublin County, Thomas Johnson paid a heavy price for tabling the motion; the Labour leader lost his seat. One voter in Kildare succinctly summed up the attitude of numerous voters when he wrote:

> Electors scorn the Redmond clan
>
> Who backed the guns and petrol can;
>
> Tom Johnson let the workers down
>
> To dress himself in president's gown;
>
> But the Cosgrave bunch will never fail.
>
> Up Cosgrave! Cumann na nGaedheal.[43]

This was a theme drawn on by many of the regional newspapers, most particularly in Waterford. There, in the traditional heartland of the National League's support base, William Redmond was the subject of virulent criticism. 'By attempting a coalition with a people avowedly out to destroy the constitution', Redmond, a confirmed constitutionalist, had alienated a great mass of those formerly favourable to him. It was observed that many of those who had cast their vote for him at the last election felt that he had betrayed their trust. The *Waterford Standard* predicted that the National League would be smashed at the polls, but that the memory of his father—John Redmond—might be enough to save him.[44] The speculation proved accurate. Redmond, undoubtedly rescued by his family name, survived the National League cull that saw all but one other of his colleagues—James Coburn—defeated. Yet despite topping the poll once more, his personal vote was marginally down, and in areas that lay outside of his bailiwick, it was reported that he received 'scarcely any first preferences'.[45]

Proportional representation and party competition

The events of the summer, taken with Cumann na nGaedheal's energetic campaign, contributed to the party's resurgence of strength. One of the notable aspects of the second election was the decrease in the number of competing parties and candidates, and this was a further factor in Cumann na nGaedheal's recovery. Many of the 'offending' small parties were no longer in existence or chose not to contest the election, while those that did, put forward fewer candidates. The proximity of the two elections had diluted party coffers and, consequently, 'simplified the party system'.[46] Neither the ephemeral Clann Éireann, wiped out in June, nor Sinn Féin, rendered futile by its own abstentionist policies, made an appearance at the polls. The Farmers' Party and the National League both put forward fewer candidates, as did Labour, which, despite a good performance, had been impecunious even in June. Two hundred and sixty-five candidates contested the September election,[47] marking a decrease of 112 since June. Cumann na nGaedheal put forward eight less, giving the party a total of 89. Fianna Fáil was the only party to increase the number of candidates on its ticket, albeit by only one.[48]

Aside from a depleted field reducing the probability of split voting, it also minimised the voters' choices. Shaun Bowler and David Farrell in their essay on American elections note that

> with the presence of more than two parties, voters do not have to line up on one side of a partisan fence or the other. Even though US voters may not like everything 'their' party does, the only alternative can easily seem a much worse choice. In a multi-party setting defections from one's 'own' party may well be much easier by virtue of the presence of many other parties.[49]

In the June election the high number of candidates had fragmented the vote of Cumann na nGaedheal in particular. The government had consequently contemplated abolishing proportional representation in an attempt to counter the threat posed by the presence of the smaller parties. In September the issue was never discussed in any serious manner by Cumann na nGaedheal as a party, although Blythe did personally raise the subject on a number of occasions. Speaking in Castleblaney, Co. Monaghan, for example, he told his audience that that the government proposed to alter proportional representation.[50] But in light of the silence of other deputies on the subject, this appears to have been an unrepresentative statement, reflective of Blythe's own personal beliefs rather than those of his party. The obvious effect of the much-reduced political arena in September was that the voters had fewer alternatives. Deprived of the luxury of vast choices, the electorate thus had to cast their votes in an election that was virtually a straight contest between Cumann na nGaedheal and Fianna Fáil. This political reality prompted the *Irish Statesman* to remark that 'the country is, we are convinced, taking but little interest in any except the government party and Fianna Fáil which challenges it'.[51]

Cosgrave's party gained from losses incurred by the Farmers, Independents, Labour and the National League, while Fianna Fáil acquired, with the exception of Dublin North, the remainder of Sinn Féin's seats and also benefited from Labour's losses. Despite its threats, Cumann na nGaedheal never altered the electoral system nor did it ever come as close to doing so as the Fianna Fáil government would in its failed 1959 and 1968 referendums to replace PR with the straight vote system. As was the case in June, the electoral system had again afforded Cumann na nGaedheal 'bonus' seats. With 38.65% of the vote,[52] the party was entitled to 59 seats but actually secured 62.

The Cumann na nGaedheal–Farmers' Party voting pact

The Farmers' Party once more opted out of opposition. As was the case prior to the June election, it decided not to merge with Cumann na nGaedheal for the September contest. While it went into the election as an independent party, however, the leadership called on its supporters to give their remaining preferences to Cumann na nGaedheal. The government party made a similar request, and in the local newspapers of certain constituencies even included the Farmers' candidates on their campaign advertisements,[53] but the Farmers did not reciprocate on the few that it printed. However, the actual benefits of a pact designed to encourage voters to support both parties had negligible effects, particularly because Farmers' candidates did not top the polls. They were either elected or eliminated towards the closing stages of the count—this was in contrast to the general performance of Cumann na nGaedheal—meaning that often there were no government party candidates available to whom they could transfer votes. The real advantage for the government party was in the message that the pact sent out. By endorsing the Cumann na nGaedheal candidates, the Farmers' Party had officially sanctioned their credentials. The results clearly indicated that a significant number of supporters cast their votes for the larger of the two parties, thus boosting Cumann na nGaedheal's share of the vote.

Despite Longford-Westmeath being one of Cumann na nGaedheal's traditionally weaker constituencies, the party's share of first preferences rose modestly; the figure roughly corresponded with the loss incurred by the Farmers' Party, the executive of which had pledged its support to the government party.[54] Although the collective loss of the 'others' was not significant (1.99%), the category included Patrick McKenna—an erstwhile member of the Farmers' Party, who had resigned over the Cumann na nGaedheal-Farmers voting arrangement—who probably split the farming vote. The incumbent, Hugh Garahan, was defeated to the advantage of Cosgrave's party.

In Cork East also, the Farmers' Party suffered somewhat from its pact with Cumann na nGaedheal. During a meeting addressed by Cosgrave, Brooke Brasier and David O'Gorman had joined the government platform where Brasier appealed for support not just for his party but also for Cumann na nGaedheal.[55] In that constituency, the number of first preferences received by Cumann na nGaedheal rose by almost 20%. The gains were due to the losses suffered by the Farmers and the 'others'.[56] In June this category had included John Daly, now affiliated with Cumann na nGaedheal. He brought to the party an increased body of support that allowed him to retain his seat and thus boost Cumann na nGaedheal's share of seats in the constituency. However, as Daly's surplus was distributed on the eighth count, his bundles had become 'contaminated'[57] and so it is impossible to determine if his supporters voted for the entire ticket.

In Cork North, Cosgrave's party increased its share of first preferences by a spectacular 18.4%, at least half of which came from the Farmers' Party. During the election campaign, both parties had canvassed on the same platform at a number of meetings.[58] The government party candidate was Daniel O'Leary, a vintner and farmer. He was reported as being 'very well known' and having 'a big measure of popularity in the greater part of the constituency'.[59] The remainder of Cumann na nGaedheal's gain was made as a result of the independents' collective decrease of 38.09%; a sizeable portion of this also went to Fianna Fáil, with whom Daniel Corkery—an independent Republican in June—was now affiliated. A split in the Labour vote due to the appearance of an independent Labour candidate resulted in the loss of the party's only seat in the constituency to Cumann na nGaedheal.

The greatest benefit of the alliance for Cumann na nGaedheal was in those constituencies, such as Galway, that the Farmers did not contest. But Meath was the quintessential example of where the pact really did pay dividends. The Farmers' Party actually stepped aside for Cumann na nGaedheal. The Meath Farmers' Union, despite having fielded a candidate in the general election in June, decided not to contest the forthcoming election. Financial constraints were undoubtedly a major factor in the decision, although this was not publicly acknowledged. Instead the party explained that it had bowed out of the election so that the chances of the government party might be enhanced. Cumann na nGaedheal consequently ran two candidates instead of one, as had originally been intended. Éamonn Duggan's running mate was to be 'acceptable to both parties', and although standing officially on the Cumann na nGaedheal ticket, he would be 'a sort of joint candidate'.[60] The strategy proved fruitful. The Farmers' Party had had a strong showing in June and its decision to stand aside in favour of and to back Cumann na nGaedheal was unquestionably responsible for a substantial portion of the party's impressive increase of almost 22%; the remainder can largely be attributed to the National League's loss.[61] Labour lost about one-tenth of its vote; Fianna Fáil made a similar gain.[62] Cumann na nGaedheal's increased share of the vote secured Duggan's re-election and allowed his running mate Arthur Matthews to claim a seat from Labour. Despite his party's mantra that coalitions did not work, Cosgrave found himself back in power after the election but dependent more than ever on the support of the Farmers' Party. This did not earn them a seat at the Cabinet table but—as a token gesture to ensure their continuing support—Michael Heffernan was appointed parliamentary secretary to Ernest Blythe at Posts and Telegraphs. (Blythe took up the portfolio, in addition to Finance, following J. J. Walsh's departure from the political scene, discussed below).

The results

Cumann na nGaedheal did not achieve the comfortable majority that the party desired. The results were indecisive, and it was hardly surprising to find newspapers reporting the outcome under the heading 'as we were'.[63] Nonetheless, they were reassuring: from a modest increase in Roscommon to a substantial gain in Laois-Offaly, every single constituency recovered from the dismal June performance. Moreover, the first preference vote in thirteen of the constituencies exceeded those achieved in 1923, deemed by Michael Gallagher to be the party's high watermark.[64] Although sixteen constituencies did not equal or surpass the party's 1923 share of first preferences,[65] the rate of decrease was principally minor. Nine of the constituencies dropped by less than 5%; the result in Clare, for example, came within 0.22% of the 1923 figure. The party's share of first preferences in Cavan and Wicklow fell by less than 10%, while Cork West, Dublin North, Mayo South and Roscommon all decreased by somewhat similar figures.[66]

Monaghan was the notable exception. The party peaked in strength in that constituency in 1923, thereafter the party's performance was at best erratic and at worst, in terminal decline. Despite improving on June's result in September, Cumann na nGaedheal's vote had dropped precipitously.[67] The party's share was now just over 15% below the 1923 figure, and although Ernest Blythe continued to secure election until his defeat in 1933, the party never recovered enough to regain a second seat. By the time of the 1933 election, the executive considered it superfluous for Blythe to even have a running mate, and by 1944, when James Dillon stood as an independent following his resignation from Fine Gael two years previously, the party had ceased to officially contest the constituency.

Internal disunion

Despite the impressive campaign run by Cumann na nGaedheal and the somewhat reassuring results achieved, the September election had also exposed in a very public manner the internal disunion that plagued the party. The rumour mill had suggested that fifteen or sixteen unnamed deputies were becoming increasingly uneasy in the party and were preparing to cross the floor.[68] However, these claims must be considered with the caveat that opposition deputies had circulated them. The editor of the *Mayo News* also advanced a similar argument,[69] although he may have been influenced by the rumours. While one must be cautious not to place too much emphasis on a single regional newspaper, an entry after the election in the diary of Liam de Róiste—generally an informed, if slighted observer—was akin to that of the *Mayo News* and the opposition deputies. He suggested that if some of the rank-and-file members of Cumann na nGaedheal were strong willed enough, they might break away unless the leadership accepted their ideas.[70] The sudden resignation of the minister for posts and telegraphs, J. J. Walsh, appeared to give credence to the rumours.

Maryann Valiulis has commented that 'after 1925 open dissension within the party seems to have abated ... certainly the events of the next few years—the assassination of Kevin O'Higgins and the entry of de Valera and Fianna Fáil into the Dáil had a chilling effect on dissent'.[71] Within the party, however, one senior politician was uneasy about the economic policies being pursued. Cumann na nGaedheal consisted of both free traders and those who favoured protection, epitomised in Patrick Hogan and J. J. Walsh respectively. Jeffrey Prager, echoing Valiulis, argues that 'focusing on the external Republican danger' after O'Higgins's assassination provided the 'opportunity to heal internal wounds' created by the economic debate.[72] Certainly, as discussed in the previous chapter, the party had put its differences aside and united in the aftermath of O'Higgins's death. However, the crisis potentially delayed J. J. Walsh's departure, but could not prevent it.

Walsh fully subscribed to Arthur Griffith's economic beliefs. In 1910 Griffith had expressed the view that 'if Irishmen studied economics as the people of other countries do in the right of their own interests, all Ireland would be vehemently protectionist'.[73] However, as Richard Davis has noted, Griffith was 'a propagandist, not an objective student of economic theory',[74] and that theory collided with reality when it came to the practical administration of the new state. The government did not have a doctrinaire attitude on free trade and protection, rather circumstances dictated policy.[75] Although Cosgrave explained that his government's policy was 'frankly protectionist', he also stated that it had 'no intention of imposing indiscriminate tariffs',[76] and Fianna Fáil was criticised for its 'whole-hog' approach to protection. Those tariffs that were introduced by the government were applied to existing industries that showed potential for growth.[77]

Through its reluctance to introduce tariffs and by claiming, for example, that they were simply 'taxes under another name',[78] Cumann na nGaedheal left many confused as to where the party stood on protection. This lack of a clear policy contrasted greatly with Fianna Fáil, and was to the government's detriment during the economic crisis at the time of the 1932 general election.

Walsh's main opponent to protection in the Cabinet was Patrick Hogan, the minister for lands and agriculture. According to de Róiste, Walsh was also opposed on the matter definitely by O'Higgins, and probably by Cosgrave and McGilligan.[79] The government placed an emphasis on agriculture—described by Blythe as 'the backbone of the economic life of the nation'[80]—arguing that its success would have a positive knock-on effect for the rest of the economy. Hogan believed this would be hindered by protection.[81] Nonetheless, the 1926 Tariff Commission Act established a commission to examine tariffs, but it posed no serious threat to Hogan's plans. Although the commission was formally appointed in 1927, it took the pressure of changing international circumstances for the government to appoint it on a permanent basis.[82] As Brian Girvin explains, there is little evidence of widespread sympathy for protection in 1927 as a departure from recently achieved stability would have been viewed with suspicion, thus accounting in a large measure for the success of conservative strategies.[83] While Eoin MacNeill would report that 120 new factories were established and employment had noticeably increased,[84] the commission 'discharged its duties carefully, meticulously and—according to protectionists—appalling slowly'.[85] Cumann na nGaedheal's lukewarm experiment with tariffs brought disappointing results for new business and employment.[86] This strategic folly, as Walsh believed it to be, was ultimately the catalyst for his resignation, discussed below, prompting certain commentators to assert that it was 'the Fianna Fáil policy of high protection' that 'allured Mr Walsh from his association with Cumann na nGaedheal'.[87]

While de Valera's government would pursue a widespread policy of protectionism, Jonathan Haughton has wondered 'whether a policy of more selective protection, perhaps along the lines favoured by Taiwan or South Korea, might not have proven more valuable'.[88] Although it had become apparent by the 1950s that the hopes which had been placed on the policy of protection were not realised,[89] Fine Gael—Cumann na nGaedheal's heir—announced its conversion to tariffs in the 1930s. This reflected a growing global trend.

In tendering his resignation, Walsh wrote simultaneously to Cosgrave and the press outlining the reasons for his decision. The letter was a broadside denunciation of his party. Given that the minister perceived the work of the Tariff Commission to have been proceeding at a glacial pace, it was unsurprising that he cited the economics debate as the first solid reason for his departure. Walsh explained that 'rather than cause a rift in the party', he had 'reluctantly agreed to give the tariff commission a trial' but found that it had 'dallied'. The support of 'ranchers and importers' caused, he believed, a new 'orientation' in the party, whereby Griffith's economic teachings would be further ignored. Walsh believed that the situation called for 'a vigorous and sweeping economic change'. He additionally expressed the view that 'those chunks of territory deliberately torn from us in the Treaty of 1922' should be returned. He explained that while he had 'accepted the Treaty with great reluctance', he could not reconcile himself to the payment of land annuities.[90] In an undated statement, probably from late 1947 or early 1948 (based on a reply), Walsh once more affirmed how difficult he had found deciding for or against the Treaty.[91] During the Treaty debates, he admitted that the retention of the three ports (Cobh, Berehaven and Lough Swilly) was something that he found difficult to accept, but he also recognised that supporting the Treaty would open Ireland up to the whole world.[92]

In his aptly named memoirs, *Recollections of a rebel*, Walsh suggested that the party's mishandling of the Boundary Commission initiated a process of demise. The 'abandonment of protection for native industries' was deemed the second factor that displaced Cumann na nGaedheal. 'To many of us,' he concluded, 'it was clear that it only needed time to kill Cumann na nGael [*sic*].'[93] His views must be read with caution, however, as he ultimately resigned from the party because of its preference for free trade. By placing his former party's alleged demise in the context of the economic debate, Walsh was attempting to vindicate his own stance.

Cosgrave drafted various responses to Walsh's resignation. Each displayed his anger at the manner in which his minister had resigned. In the version dated 6 September, he expressed his resentment at Walsh's failure to contact him before leaving Ireland and for sending the letter to his office and the newspapers simultaneously.[94] The final draft that Walsh received was toned down, but again Cosgrave displayed his displeasure and wrote, 'I had not the honour of seeing your letter to me until 48 hours after reading it in the press'.[95]

Blythe responded to Walsh in the press in a dismissive and disparaging letter. He subtly questioned Walsh's honour by pointing out that, although he was 'alone in his opposition' to the proposal on tariffs, the minister nonetheless supported the proposal in the Dáil, rather than leave the party. Walsh's criticism of the land annuities perplexed Blythe, who observed that Walsh had never raised the subject with his colleagues, 'even in the most casual way'. In response to the criticism of the Boundary Commission, he quoted Walsh's claim that it was 'the greatest Irish triumph since the time of Brian Boru'.[96] Indeed, de Róiste had recorded in his diary a private meeting of a small group of Cumann na nGaedheal politicians and supporters in Cork, where Walsh had defended the settlement. 'He had made up his own mind on it, he (Walsh) said'.[97] Blythe also attempted to portray Walsh as politically weak or even indifferent to the issues about which he claimed to be passionate. He argued that if Walsh had desired 'a serious discussion', he would have postponed his Continental trip to debate the issues 'face to face with the electors'.[98] Overall Blythe's response was intended to minimise the impact of the content of the resignation letter by showing Walsh to be hypocritical and irresponsible.

Walsh's actions were certainly unbecoming of the chairman of the party's standing committee, and as a former director of elections he was not so politically obtuse as to be unaware of the fallout that would occur. His decision to quit politics in such a sudden manner caused resentment in his constituency. The *Irish Statesman* encapsulated the feeling of numerous voters when it remarked that 'constituents have a right to expect something more than a curt telegram on the eve of a critical fight unaccompanied by even a formal expression of regret'.[99] The people of Cork, the *Enniscorthy Guardian* reported, were not so much angered by his retirement but rather 'by the discourteous manner in which he withdrew without giving a word of explanation to the electors'.[100] However, Walsh was initially pilloried for his behaviour primarily in papers *outside* of Cork. The local journalists did not appear to be as quick to criticise, usually wishing him a speedy recovery from his supposed illness or lamenting the loss of their minister.[101] Only when the truth was revealed following the publication of his resignation letter did the press turn. 'The regret which so many people in Cork and elsewhere share at the loss of health which caused Mr J. J. Walsh to seek rest … will not, however, extend to approving the manner in which he severed his connection with his old colleagues.'[102]

In his *Recollections*, Walsh showed no compunction for his behaviour, and revealed a feeling that was undoubtedly prevalent among many of the Cumann na nGaedheal élite: 'I resented having to depend on the public for a livelihood.'[103] Michael Hayes would later comment on how 'J. J. often said to me … that he only had £1,700 a year and that if he was a free man in business he would make £17,000 … Whether J. J. was mathematically right or not I don't know, but he certainly made an excellent living in business'.[104] This, coupled with Walsh's growing sense of disillusionment with his party, was the striking feature of the fifth chapter of his autobiography. Such a combination provided the basis for his own explanation as to why when the autumn election of 1927 was announced, he was determined 'to get out and stay out'.[105] Despite his scathing criticisms and the equally damning replies made by the party, relations were perhaps not permanently soured. In 1950 he was photographed at the Vatican along with W. T. and son Liam.[106]

Naturally the opposition, and in particular, Fianna Fáil made much capital out of the situation. Pádraig Ó Máille—also a Cumann na nGaedheal defector—claimed that he had adopted his position because of Walsh's departure from the government, which he (Ó Máille) attributed to the party's drift towards imperialism.[107] Walsh's sudden departure received special attention on one of the most commonly printed advertisements used by de Valera's party. With a caption that could easily have been found on a Cumann na nGaedheal poster, it asked the electors to 'vote Fianna Fáil and maintain the people's peace'.[108] In using this type of language, de Valera's party attempted to appeal to wavering voters. Such a challenge forced Cumann na nGaedheal, as already discussed, to reconsider its attitude towards campaigning.

There was a feeling among sections of the press that Cumann na nGaedheal would be almost thankful for Walsh's resignation.[109] An editorial in the *Irish Times*, which described Walsh as being 'an erratic administrator, a stormy politician, and a dangerous economist', suggested that the government's prospects would be improved by his departure.[110] Similarly the *Irish Independent* asserted that 'the ministry is well rid of a colleague whose mercurial temperament and erratic judgement have never been a source of strength to it'.[111] Nonetheless, no matter how controversial Walsh was, his skills would be missed. He is credited with rebuilding and developing the Free State's telephone and telegraph series, and he was involved in the establishment of the 2RN radio station. More importantly, having taken over the organisation of the party, his ability had prompted one journalist to remark that he had proved himself 'a wizard in the art'.[112]

His resignation letter had appeared in the *Irish Times* and *Irish Independent* on 6 September, but until its publication, there was general confusion about his position in relation to the forthcoming election. The media, having spotted Walsh's absence from the campaign trail, pressed the government for an explanation. Although rumours abounded as to the meaning of his absence, the Cumann na nGaedheal organisation in Cork initially rejected speculation that Walsh had parted company from the party. Ill health was quickly cited as the reason for the minister's absence. The electors were assured that, while it was unlikely that he would return in time to partake in a strenuous campaign, his name would nonetheless be found on the ballot papers on 15 September. The story proved to be a poorly attempted cover-up.

In his resignation letter, Walsh explained that before leaving Ireland, he had informed Barry Egan—chairman of the Cork executive—that he would not enter the fray. Egan, however, delayed in communicating this information. An entry in de Róiste's diary for 13 September 1927 recorded a meeting of the Cork executive that had taken place on 31 August. He suspected that Egan 'knew then, and even before' that Walsh would not stand, but 'he would not tell the executive definitely'.[113] Consequently it was decided to allow Walsh's name to go forward. Since he left Ireland on 26 August, his intentions must have been known to Egan in advance of the meeting. Nonetheless, Egan issued a statement on 1 September stating that Walsh was on a prolonged holiday due to ill health and that the rumours about his future were merely the product of a 'mean campaign of misrepresentation'.[114] According to de Róiste's diary entry for 6 September he himself made enquiries on 29 August and found that the resignation was final. One must therefore question why he did not press Egan to clarify the situation at the meeting on 31 August.[115]

Egan's motivation is difficult to comprehend and his papers, which are in the possession of Cork City and County Archives, unfortunately shed no light on the matter. Although there are at least two letters to Walsh they do not relate to the subject of his resignation. Egan certainly shared his colleague's views on protectionism,[116] and so one would naturally expect him to have been among Walsh's confidants. With the exception of a copy of his resignation letter, Walsh's own papers, shelved at the same archives, are also quiet on the subject. Egan's unwillingness to divulge the details of Walsh's intentions may possibly have been an exercise in damage limitation and a weak attempt to preserve some semblance of a united party. Instead he inflamed an already sensitive situation, emphasized the internal disunion within the party, and fuelled speculation about Walsh's motivations for quitting. Egan should have communicated to the Cabinet any information he had, so that an effective strategy could have been formulated. The controversy was containable. If the party had been adequately informed, pre-emptive steps could have been taken, and rather than telling the press that Walsh was taking a break for health reasons, a different style of statement could have been released clarifying the situation. Walsh's actions could have been projected as being singular and unrepresentative, thus preserving the image of united party. The press would have still pursued the story anyway, and Walsh's letter would inevitably have been printed. The situation was certainly unavoidable, but the damage could have been limited.

Instead, the handling of the Walsh situation left the party looking foolish, unprofessional, incompetent, and out of touch even with its own members. The party played into the hands of the opposition and gave Fianna Fáil in particular ammunition with which to further target Cumann na nGaedheal's alleged imperialist tendencies. The conflicting reports also ensured that the sensation made headlines in newspapers for much longer than the story had needed. Moreover, the event exposed a fundamental flaw in the organisation of Cumann na nGaedheal. The lack of dialogue between the local organisation and the parliamentary party was a quintessential example of how divorced the Cumann na nGaedheal élite was from its grass roots. As already discussed in the Chapter 1, there was a wide gulf between the grass roots, the parliamentary party and the leadership structure. Cork was not an exception.

A further blow to the party came when brothers, J.C. and T.P. Dowdall severed their association with Cumann na nGaedheal in favour of Fianna Fáil; T.P. later stood and was elected on the Fianna Fáil ticket at the 1932 general election. The brothers were prominent among a group of industrialists who dominated the Cork Industrial

Development Authority (IDA).[117] Given their profile and Walsh's recent departure, a picture was emerging of a local party in tatters; it suggested that there existed within the party dissent which could not be neutralised. Cork, it appeared, was becoming a hotbed of discontent.

Walsh's decision to quit politics was not impulsive, nor was his disagreement with the party a recent development, but rather the secession was the apogee of a protracted policy battle. The political correspondent of the *Irish Independent* claimed that in July and also twelve months previously, Walsh had intimated to him his desire to retire.[118] In July 1926 Liam de Róiste had warned Walsh against breaking his connection with Cumann na nGaedheal.[119] Recording a meeting in Cobh in early 1927, he noted that '*once more* J.J. is on the breaking point with the government'; '*once more*, I advised him, for his own sake, not to break with Cumann na nGaedheal' (italics added).[120]

Certain commentators suggested that Walsh would defect to Fianna Fáil.[121] De Róiste once commented that Walsh often spoke in a manner similar to that of Eamon de Valera and Mary MacSwiney.[122] For example, in his speeches during the Tailteann Games there was a definite resonance of Republican rhetoric. On one occasion the minister declared that 'they were telling the world over that in Ireland ... not withstanding their trials and difficulties in recent times, they had once again got on their feet and were marching on to that glory which awaited their people'.[123] Given his commitment to Irish-Ireland, he certainly appeared to have much in common with Fianna Fáil, but although Walsh openly supported de Valera's party for the 1932 general election, there was never any solid evidence to suggest that he formed a formal association.

Although he had at times shown himself to be a troublesome minister, Walsh was, nonetheless, one of the party's strongest performers and almost invariably topped the polls on each occasion. It had been suggested by one party activist in the constituency that support for Cumann na nGaedheal in the Cork borough was really support for J.J. Walsh. A strong replacement was needed to retain the seat and to quell the obvious dissent that was growing, and consequently it was decided that Cosgrave should contest Cork Borough in addition to Carlow-Kilkenny. He was marketed by Liam Burke—Cumann na nGaedheal's energetic director of elections—as 'Cork's greatest candidate'.[124] The party's decision to parachute the president into Walsh's constituency rather than add a local activist to the ticket implied that there was not an alternative candidate available for nomination, but also showed the importance the executive attached to the constituency. Again, Liam de Róiste's diary suggested otherwise, but his musings must be read cautiously as he was clearly wounded by the decision to run Cosgrave, despite the fact that he was keen to stand and indicated his wish to the president during a private meeting. De Róiste was bypassed, however, and attributed the decision to a 'new orientation' in the party.[125] He shared Walsh's view that Cumann na nGaedheal had gone over to the ex-Unionists and had turned its back on Irish-Ireland ideals. Certainly, as discussed in the following chapter, the party was moving further towards the right, but de Róiste lacked Cosgrave's appeal and he certainly did not have a convincing electoral record nor had he shown any real commitment to active politics. He had represented Cork Borough from 1919 until the general election of 1923, which he chose not to contest, but he later conceded in May 1926 that it had been a 'great mistake' on his part to retire from the Dáil.[126] His attempt to re-enter the political fray for the June 1927 election was unsuccessful; he was eliminated and his votes were distributed on the seventh count. The party was simply not confident in his candidacy.

Within the county of Cork, Cumann na nGaedheal was never particularly strong, with varying degrees of success within the four constituencies. To obviate the loss of what had been considered a safe seat, it was essential that the party had a sound candidate with a strong appeal. There is a certain degree of prestige associated with being represented by a minister and as the Cork Borough constituents had lost one minister, many voters, and in particular, supporters of the government party, were probably anxious to be represented by another. A candidate of Cosgrave's stature was particularly appealing, especially in light of his record in Carlow-Kilkenny. Carlow was home to the sugar factory, which provided local employment opportunities and suggested that the president's constituency was looked after. As the authors of *The personal vote* have noted, 'recollections of something special done for the district generally have at least a marginally significant effect on the vote'.[127]

Despite a relatively brief campaign in his new constituency, Cosgrave topped the poll in a spectacular fashion (and performed similarly in Carlow-Kilkenny also). With two seats, but only one vote in the Dáil, Cosgrave had to choose a constituency to represent and opted for Cork Borough, which he continued to represent until his retirement in 1944. His decision to relinquish his traditional seat in Carlow-Kilkenny was taken in order to ensure that a breakdown of support did not occur in the Cork borough.

J.J. Walsh's resignation not only drew attention to the party's internal dissenting voices, but also exposed the disconnection between the grass-roots organisation and the party élite. In many ways, the episode was a microcosm of Cumann na nGaedheal's difficulties, which were to persist in the following years. Although the event exposed the amateur side of the party, the September election had also shown that Cumann na nGaedheal was capable of professionalism. During the life of the sixth Dáil, ideological tensions within the party continued as the economic debate intensified against the backdrop of a changing world economic climate. The government continued to extol the virtues of the Treaty, while offering little guidance on how the state might recover from the depression gripping Europe. There is no doubt that ministers were both mentally and physically tired, but the emphasis in the historiography of the period 1927 to 1932 on Cumann na nGaedheal's problems and failures has meant that achievements are largely forgotten: the Shannon electrification scheme was completed and proved hugely successful; W.T. Cosgrave addressed one chamber of the American congress in 1928; and Patrick McGilligan played a leading role at the imperial conference that produced the important 1931 Statute of Westminster. For the party, like many of its long-term investments in foreign affairs, the latter came too late to be of any great benefit to Cumann na nGaedheal. The Dublin correspondent of the *Kerryman* suggested that 'in more favourable world circumstances', the achievements of the government would have stood out 'with brilliancy'.[128] Those achievements—as well as the difficulties—are discussed more fully in the following chapter.

{138}

.5.

The slow decline, 1927-32

The perception of Cumann na nGaedheal's last administration is that the government 'ran out of steam',[1] and the continued references to the virtues of the Treaty settlement certainly contributed to the impression that the government was bankrupt of policy. The fact that it actually resigned in 1930, and then reversed this decision, indicated that it was in a state of flux. Having recovered from the shock of Fianna Fáil's entry into the Dáil and back on the government benches, the parliamentary party became largely complacent, while there was discontent among the grass-roots members, who were unhappy about the direction in which the party was moving. Cosgrave's last administration certainly lacked the drama of the early years in the Free State, but it was not without its achievements. The Shannon Scheme was completed at this time,[2] Cosgrave had been given the honour of addressing the US Congress, and the Free State delegates had played an important role at the imperial conference that delivered the far-reaching Statute of Westminster. These made a positive contribution to the country's image of an independent, thriving state.

The reunification of Sinn Féin?

By the time of the September 1927 election, the Irish-Ireland complexion of Cumann na nGaedheal was no longer apparent at government level. The army mutiny had caused the departure of Joe McGrath and Richard Mulcahy, while Eoin MacNeill had lost his seat at the June 1927 election and J. J. Walsh had just resigned. As Cumann na nGaedheal was an uneasy alliance born of acceptance of the Treaty, many conflicting opinions were represented within the party. There were those who interpreted the Treaty as providing the framework within which the new state could be built, while others subscribed to Michael Collins's view that the Treaty provided the freedom to achieve freedom. Almost immediately, there was a sense that Cumann na nGaedheal was not Irish-Ireland enough in its outlook and the party's overzealous defence of the Treaty settlement gave the impression that it was anxious to please Britain. As the 1920s progressed Cumann na nGaedheal, already an uneasy alliance, became an uneasy coalition as it welcomed new, conservative members to its ranks. The entry of former members of the Farmers' Party and, more particularly, the National League, as well as several independents provided Fianna Fáil—and critics within Cumann na nGaedheal—with seeming evidence of the party's imperialistic proclivities and abandonment of

Irish-Ireland ideals. Independent deputies Bryan Cooper, John Daly and Myles Keogh had affiliated with the party for the September 1927 election. All three represented the educated and wealthy elements of society. Daly was a vintner, while Keogh was a practising physician and surgeon. Cooper proved particularly controversial. He was both a landowner and an ex-Unionist, and, as the opposition reminded voters, he had also been a censor during the war. Vincent Rice, formerly of the National League and a lawyer, later joined the party and was the Cumann na nGaedheal candidate for the Dublin North by-election of 3 April 1928. With the inclusion of these conservative elements, Cumann na nGaedheal moved further towards the right. This shift left many—particularly those in the grass roots who were attracted to Cumann na nGaedheal believing it would deliver on Michael Collins's aspirations—uncertain about the direction in which the party was moving. Liam de Róiste captured this in his diary when he observed Cumann na nGaedheal to be a 'composite party', with one section favouring the 'moneyed and big farmer interests', and another section closer to Fianna Fáil in an Irish-Ireland policy.[3]

By 1927, although few people would still have thought of the party in those terms, the Sinn Féin split had entered its fifth year. During and after the September campaign, there was much talk about the old party reuniting. The *New York Times* reported that the idea was being 're-echoed from Tipperary to Donegal', and suggested that the ambiguous results from the second 1927 general election may 'prove to have been inspired by an unconscious political prescience'. Unclear results, the paper suggested, may thrust the two parties back together and force them to communicate. The paper also predicted that 'in the future … whether near or distant, a realignment of the parties is inevitable', and it referred to the elements within the government party that were sympathetic to de Valera's policies.[4]

A general election following so closely on the turmoil of the summer of 1927 had produced a feeling of electoral fatigue among the voters. Although the notion of moving beyond the internecine struggle and eliminating the Civil War cleavage from politics was prevalent, it was certainly not a novel concept. In 1924, for example, a Cork journalist had observed that the Irish people had grown weary of 'political squabbles' that lead to nothing.[5] Several candidates, like Joseph X. Murphy, stood in September 1927 on the platform of infusing new blood into the Dáil. From the front-page of the *Irish*

Statesman, Murphy had argued—successfully—that it was time to 'get out of the rut of politics'.[6]

In relation to the general public, many would probably have welcomed the move; though others would have been indifferent. A cartoon found in one of the Dublin North ballot boxes depicted de Valera working in tandem with Cosgrave and carried the caption 'this is what we want'.[7] Sections of the press certainly favoured the idea of fusion.[8] The *Longford Leader* deemed reunion a 'probability', while the *Nationalist and Leinster Times* went as far as to suggest that talks were actually under way.[9] Members of the two parties did comment on the suggestion, but no official talks were ever held. The envisioned reunion took two forms: either Cumann na nGaedheal and Fianna Fáil would merge, or, a realignment based on economic policies would occur.

The initiative for conciliation had its roots in Cork. It was there that Cosgrave explained how he was 'anxious for peace, anxious for reconciliation', and where he outlined the necessary preconditions:

> voluntary submission to the will of the people. The balancing of the national budget. A single, disciplined army, subject to the control of parliament. An efficient police force. The collection of all arms in the possession of persons not authorised by the state. An independent judiciary. Entrance by merit to the civil service. No truce with crime of any sort. Peace at home and abroad. The fulfilment of all pledges, national and international.[10]

In order to reverse the political bifurcation of the old Sinn Féin party, certain stumbling blocks had to be overcome. There were, very obviously, fundamental policy differences, which were highlighted once more during the campaign for the September election. In Castleblaney, Blythe had declared that if he could turn the Free State into a republic tomorrow, he 'would not lift a finger to do it', but would work with all his might against it. He reminded voters that the Free State had 'all the powers and liberties' necessary for the upbuilding of the country.[11] In comparison, Fianna Fáil's Eamon Donnelly was reported by Blythe as having admitted that he was 'out to smash the Treaty'.[12] Reunification was certainly not in Tom Mullins's vocabulary when he spoke at a Fianna Fáil meeting in west Cork. He declared that his party would 'smash' Cumann na nGaedheal or they would be wiped out by their rivals.[13] Clearly, in his view, there was not room for both parties to coexist.

It is perhaps understandable that reunification was considered an option because, as Patrick Maume pointed out in a remark made about Arthur Clery but equally applicable to the wider community, 'until 1921 Clery's entire life was lived in a society which strongly felt that all nationalists should be united in a single party'.[14] But how viable was the suggested reunion? It is possible that among the grass roots of the two parties there might have been broad support for such a reunification. Liam de Róiste, for example, was among those to whom a type of reunion was not unthinkable.[15] Within the actual parliamentary parties, however, and especially among the Cabinet and shadow Cabinet, opposition would have been at its greatest. Fianna Fáil's Seán T. O'Kelly made his debut full-length speech during Cosgrave's nomination for president of the sixth Dáil. He made reference to sitting alongside Cosgrave in the revolutionary Dáil and the ideals that that they had shared, which Cosgrave had subsequently abandoned. He also spoke of the 77 dead.[16] The speech demonstrated, as Michael McLoughlin observed, the bitterness of politics and the depth of the splits caused by the Civil War.[17] There existed a deep distrust between the front benches of the two parties and, as Joseph M. Curran put it, 'the bloodshed in 1922 flowed like a river between them'.[18]

Insuperable obstacles blocked the path to reconciliation. As discussed in Chapter 1, attempts had been made to fuse Sinn Féin at the 1922 pact election. They ultimately failed, and, as Michael Laffan pointed out, any prospects for reunification had virtually disappeared by that stage.[19] De Valera was identified by the *Midland Tribune* as the major barrier to reunification, but it was conceded that there was not the 'remotest possibility' of Fianna Fáil dispensing with his leadership. To his supporters, he always remained 'The Chief'.[20] But even if Fianna Fáil had been willing to make such an immense sacrifice for the sake of reunion, Cosgrave would not have been acceptable as leader. By the change of government in 1932, de Valera explained that the two men were not on speaking terms,[21] and when the Second World War started, a national government—not unlike those that were generally being formed in Europe at the time—was declined by the Fianna Fáil leader.[22] It did not help, of course, that Cosgrave was still the leader of Fine Gael at that time.

Some conciliatory speeches responding to Cosgrave's were made. The most important came from Seán T. O'Kelly and Seán Lemass. O'Kelly welcomed the gesture, expressing the view that he hoped to see a reunification of the Republican movement within five years.[23] Lemass also indicated that such an act was possible:

{144}

I don't know what spirit moved him to speak these words but those words speak the policy of Fianna Fáil. We are prepared to forgive—though it may be difficult to forget—and to make the will of the people prevail and be supreme and to work out a peaceful alteration of the Treaty. If he wants a political truce with Fianna Fáil he can have it tomorrow. We can make a condition also, and that condition is that all repressive legislation shall cease and that there are no artificial barriers placed in the nation's path.[24]

Similarly Frank Fahy explained in Loughrea how 'they were willing to forget and forgive everything said or done against them in the last six years'. His party, however, would not 'swallow Cumann na nGaedheal principles'. If Cumann na nGaedheal wanted unity, the party would have to 'accommodate themselves' to Fianna Fáil's views.[25] Therefore, although elements on both sides were speaking in conciliatory tones, it was patently obvious that each party, Fianna Fáil perhaps more so than Cumann na nGaedheal, was only willing to consider reunion on their own terms. When the sixth Dáil met, Cosgrave was proposed as president and the Fianna Fáil deputies voted en bloc against his nomination. The development of the two-party system continued as Fianna Fáil and Cumann na nGaedheal drifted even further apart.

While reconciliation never made the transition from rhetoric to reality, elements within Cumann na nGaedheal remained uneasy about the direction in which the party was moving. The problem of the party's composition became closely bound to its economic policy. For many, Hogan was the biggest problem in the Cabinet. He was certainly despised by Walsh, who felt that the government, under Hogan's influence, was 'determined that England should be its bosom friend and its fellow Irishmen its enemies'.[26] Walsh believed that Cumann na nGaedheal, through resistance to Fianna Fáil had become an unnatural coalition that should split into its component parts for the better of the country.[27]

Land annuities

Through its campaign against the payment of land annuities, Fianna Fáil —arguing that Cumann na nGaedheal was subservient to Britain—

{145}

won much support. For Cosgrave's government, payment of annuities was not merely a matter of obligation but also one of honour. 'To repudiate the land annuities, as Fianna Fáil proposed to do, would be dishonest and calamitous to the credit of the Saorstát and every Irish citizen'.[28] It was an unpopular stance. The tripartite agreement of 1925 had not released the Free State from its obligation to pay the annuities, and continued payment was subsequently confirmed in the ultimate financial settlement of 19 March 1926, signed by Ernest Blythe and Winston Churchill, then chancellor of the exchequer. The settlement was really 'a tidying-up operation', which essentially confirmed earlier decisions between 1922 and 1925 and embodied them in a 'more formal, more conclusive' agreement.[29] The opposition argued that the tripartite agreement *had* released the government from its obligation to pay the annuities, as they were part of the public debt at the time of the Treaty. The attorney general, John A. Costello, countered that claim by arguing that 'any items which would constitute national or public debt would be found set forth' in the British financial accounts or the returns of the national debt. He subsequently pointed out that 'land stock is not to be found in any such accounts'.[30]

The problem with abolishing payment of land annuities lay in the fact that those annuities 'constituted the only real title to land in Ireland. If they were affected, or worse still abolished, all Irish rural property relationships would be thrown into disarray'.[31] For the government, however, the issue of annuities went beyond titles even; the national credit rating rested on payment, it was argued. Cosgrave's government was acutely aware of the damage that could be done to the Free State's financial reputation if the annuities were withheld. Costello dismissed the claims that the payment of annuities was illegal and that they were being used by the British government to ease the British taxpayer as being 'fallacious arguments'. He warned that unless such claims were adamantly refuted, 'the credit of the state [would] be seriously prejudiced'.[32] During the Carlow-Kilkenny by-election campaign in 1927, Blythe had warned that if the payments were not made 'no government of this state will ever be able to borrow a penny piece again, because our action in the case of the land annuities would have disgraced us and ruined our credit all over the world'. Cosgrave reiterated the point.[33]

As previously discussed, J. J. Walsh publicly announced his rigid opposition to the payment of the annuities, but his appeared to be the sole dissenting voice in the Cabinet. In 1929 representations were made

{146}

behind the scenes to ministers advocating the request for a moratorium of payments for five years. Later it was propounded that an entire cessation would be easier to achieve than a suspension. The proposal was transmitted through Diarmuid O'Hegarty to the Cabinet from Henry J. Moloney, KC. He set out an eight-point case, based mainly around the worsening agricultural conditions, as to why the Free State deserved a suspension of payments.[34] The Cabinet was weary of such proposals, which did not receive any degree of strong support from the ministers. Cosgrave, for example, dismissed it as 'a badly devised political stunt'.[35] O'Hegarty, who had detected two glaring difficulties, noted that:

> the interest for that five years would have to be borrowed and added to capital with the result that either the period of repayment would have to be extended or the annuity increased. The more important objection is however that the difficulty of inducing a person to recommence paying his debts after five years backsliding seems to me to be almost insurmountable and I fear that the net result would be that the last condition would be worse than the first. If we had a five-year moratorium all annuities would become un-collectable during that period.[36]

Moloney wrote again to O'Hegarty urging for an entire break on payments. He explained that he had consulted 'a friend' on the issue, who thought 'it would be easier to get the whole concession than to get a fractional one'.[37] Although Moloney never named him, O'Hegarty had earlier suspected that the person in question was Joseph Devlin. The proposals amounted to nothing, however, as the Cosgrave government refused to back down from what it considered its moral obligation.

In the Dáil, representations were made on behalf of those who were struggling to pay their annuities.[38] The Labour TD for Donegal, Archie Cassidy, outlined the harsh reality of the situation. He told the chamber that 'the small farmers are in a state of poverty, and many of them are unable to provide three meals a day for their families, much less pay their land annuities'. Correspondence between the Tipperary South Riding Committee of Agriculture and the government, which took place over three years, was just one example that explicitly demonstrated the worsening situation for many farmers at the time.

In late May 1929 Laurence Ryan, secretary of the committee, wrote to Diarmuid O'Hegarty, the secretary of the Executive Council, regarding a resolution passed by a meeting of the County Council where it had been agreed that the Free State should retain land annuities and help to derate agricultural land.[39] In December 1931 Ryan transmitted a further resolution, this time to Cosgrave's own secretary, Éamonn Duggan. The motion, which was passed unanimously, called for a revision in the payment of land annuities due to 'the depression in agriculture and the very serious reduction in the farmers' income'. It was a pressing issue that needed to be addressed in order to 'save these farmers and the country generally from bankruptcy'.[40] In early July 1932 Ryan again corresponded with O'Hegarty, although by that stage Cumann na nGaedheal was occupying the opposition benches. On that occasion, he requested a moratorium for two or three years, citing 'the very serious depression in our agricultural industry' as the reason.[41] The file from the Department of the Taoiseach contains no further correspondence and one can only speculate with reasonable certainty that the request was not granted. A convention held by the Irish Grain Growers' Association and the Farmers' Protection Association also highlighted the difficulties facing Irish farmers. The *Waterford News* reported that 'after a lengthy discussion the convention was unanimous on the following points: (1) that the farmers are not in a position to pay either annuities, rents or rates; (2) that immediate relief must be given'.[42]

For a myriad of owner occupants, payment proved to be a burdensome requirement and many no doubt hoped that Fianna Fáil's pledged refusal to pay Britain would mean that no land annuities would have to be paid at all. That was not the case. Fianna Fáil favoured the continued collection of the annuities but advocated that the money would be retained in the Free State; during de Valera's first term in office, the Department of Finance recognised the need for the continued payment of the annuities: 'With regard to the proposal to completely remit all purchase annuities, the problem of legal title on land must necessarily arise. The land is vested in the tenant under various land purchase acts and this vesting carries with it the statutory obligation to pay annuities'.[43] However, what D.G. Boyce observed of de Valera's time in power was equally true of his stance in opposition: his hostility to payment of the annuities was 'a policy at once popular and exhilarating for his supporters, since it combined the rhetoric of ancient wrongs with immediate tangible benefit for the Irish farmer'.[44]

{148}

Fianna Fáil's Eamon Cooney had argued in the Dáil that the annuities were being paid to 'the descendants of Cromwellian planters';[45] a similar sentiment was expressed in a *Catechism of land annuities*, penned by Colonel Maurice Moore. The pamphlet, which was brought before the attention of the Fianna Fáil national executive for consideration, posed a series of questions and provided answers that essentially encapsulated the party's arguments. He wrote that annuities were 'paid to the British government instead of the rent formerly paid to landlords' because 'Queen Elizabeth, King William and Cromwell confiscated the lands, [drove] the owners into the bogs and mountains and divided the land among the soldiers and adventurers'. Such activity, he commented, 'was robbery and plunder and was carried out by massacre and oppression. Cromwell pensioned his soldiers with Irish confiscated land. The people are still paying these pensions with rent'.[46]

Although the campaign against annuities did not originate with Fianna Fáil, it was appropriated by the party, which promptly advanced it further than Labour or the socialists ever had the potential to do. Outside the Dáil, opposition had been organised by left-wing Republicans, most notably Peadar O'Donnell, one time editor of *An Phoblacht* and author of *There will be another day*. Texts of his meetings were transmitted to various superintendents' offices and subsequently obtained by the Cabinet. His aim, he had told a small gathering at Kinsale, was 'to organise all persons paying land annuities for the purpose of resisting the collection of these annuities' and he advocated the use of constitutional methods.[47] When asked at a later meeting if he encouraged non-payment, he is reputed to have replied that 'he would not tell a man to do anything for which he was not prepared to take the consequences' and added that 'he would not say to any individual "do not pay your rent"'.[48]

There is evidence to suggest that some tenants believed that was precisely what O'Donnell urged. Patrick Hogan wrote to E. Herlihy of the collection branch of the Land Commission regarding an encounter with O'Donnell. That particular branch had been experiencing difficulties in Dungloe, Co. Donegal, as certain tenants had refused to pay their annuities, and, as a result, they had been imprisoned. The consequences of their actions caused O'Donnell to rethink his strategy, as his language of agitation had provoked them. According to Hogan, 'he was now anxious to get these people out of jail and to get them to start paying their annuities and arrears again'.[49] Hogan broached the possibility of an arrangement with the various governmental departments.

James Fitzgerald-Kenney was in favour, writing 'my view is that it might be useful at this stage if O'Donnell did anything which could amount to publicly renouncing his former attitude in regard to Land Commission annuities, hence, I think the matter should be considered'.[50] It would certainly have been a great moral coup for the government if one of the great opponents to annuities changed his position, yet according to a handwritten comment on a letter from Hogan to O'Hegarty the negotiations had been dropped.[51] No explanation was provided. Even if O'Donnell had been prepared to retract his stance, however, there was, as already noted, a much more influential force at work. From 1928 Fianna Fáil had made the issue its own.[52] It would feature heavily in the campaign for the 1932 election.

External affairs and the pursuit of Irish sovereignty

While Cumann na nGaedheal was being criticised at home for being too complicit in its relationship with Britain, on the international stage, its delegates were sending a clear statement to the world that the Free State was independent, while also successfully pushing the boundaries of Commonwealth membership.

During the latter half of Cumann na nGaedheal's decade in power, there were several other occasions on which Free State representatives confirmed their independent status. A somewhat accidental demonstration came with the delay in the Kellogg-Briand Pact—which saw its signatories condemn recourse to war for the solution of international controversies—becoming operational because Cosgrave's government—unlike the other consenting dominions—had been unable to secure an earlier approval. Writing to L.S. Amery in late January 1929, McGilligan explained that the Dáil and Senate were not due to meet again until 20 February so that ratification was not possible before the twenty-first. It was Free State policy not to ratify international agreements, save those of an administrative nature, without the assent of the Oireachtas.[53]

It is clear from Joseph Walshe's correspondence that there was pressure on the Free State to break with its usual procedure,[54] but it stood firm. In a later dispatch from McGilligan to Amery, the external affairs minister made the point that:

> the mere appearance of intervention, or shadow of intervention, by one of His Majesty's governments between the Sovereign and his other governments would

destroy the very basis of the democratic institutions upon which the British Commonwealth of Nations is founded.[55]

In response to the suggestion that there should be uniformity in the approach taken by Commonwealth members in ratifying such treaties, McGilligan pointed out such a requirement would be 'directly opposed to the principle of co-equality and free association'.[56] As Harkness has noted, 'the effect [of the delay] was to highlight Dominion freedom and individuality'.[57] The Free State's decision to ratify the pact also reflected its 'growing stature in international relations' and signature was an attempt to maximise its position in the League of Nations.[58]

The Free State, after an unspectacular start, became particularly active at the League from 1926 onwards and in 1929 it began to consider contesting Canada's soon-to-be-vacant seat on the League's council; the canvass began in earnest early the following year.[59] Seán Lester advocated 'a continuous and energetic, and concerted movement from every angle abroad—O'Kelly, Binchy, Bewley, MacWhite as well as Geneva—co-ordinated by headquarters'.[60] Those states generally unreceptive to the Free State argued that by replacing Canada, the Irish delegates would be turning the seat into a Commonwealth seat. However, support was forthcoming from the Latin American states, the Little Entente of Czechoslovakia, Romania and Yugoslavia, and elements of the Scandinavian groupings.[61] Significantly for the Free State's agenda at home, the candidacy was deemed to be independent rather than aligned to the dominions. In a letter to Gerald O'Kelly de Gallagh regarding the process of notifying other members of the Free State's intention to contest the seat, Seán Murphy, assistant secretary at the Department of External Affairs, encouraged him to point out that since entering the League, the Free State had taken an independent attitude.[62] McGilligan had also stressed that the Free State was not part of the British empire group, which consisted of Great Britain and Northern Ireland.[63] In a close-run contest the Free State triumphed. As Michael Kennedy has noted, 'the election victory was a symbol of the success of Irish League policy since 1926. It marked the state's elevation to a higher plane of League activity'.[64] The Irish members certainly exuded a degree of confidence; Desmond FitzGerald wrote to his wife Mabel how it was 'so obvious that as a delegation we are head and shoulders over the others'.[65]

Outside Europe, the Free State's reputation received a boost in America through a visit from Cosgrave, accompanied by Desmond FitzGerald, Diarmuid O'Hegarty and Joseph Walshe, in January 1928. It was an important propaganda tour—recorded by O'Kennedy-Brindley[66]—designed to affirm the Free State's self-sufficient, independent status. The *Irish Times* predicted that Cosgrave's speeches would 'convince every rational American that the Free State is as free as Canada', noting that 'the fullness of Canada's freedom is known to all Americans'.[67] On every possibly occasion, Cosgrave took the opportunity to explain how the nascent Free State had overcome great adversity to develop into a functioning and thriving state. His trip was also highly significant as it marked the first occasion on which the head of a recognised Irish government had visited the United States. He arrived to a gushing review from the *New York Times* which explained how a 'new Ireland with new responsibilities, hopes and duties' had been created under his leadership, and that the achievement was 'as difficult and brilliant as that of any contemporary statesman of Europe'.[68]

The *Homeric* arrived in New York two days behind schedule as severe weather conditions had hampered the journey, with the consequence that Cosgrave's already packed two-week schedule became even more demanding. Having passed customs, the Irish delegation spent two hours in New York at a reception hosted by the mayor before proceeding on to Chicago. A bizarre measure of how Cosgrave was received was offered by the *New York Times*, which observed that 'there were more silk hats than ever turned out for any previous visitor, and Chicago has been host to kings and queens and movie stars'.[69] Speaking to the press, probably with the Shannon Scheme in mind, he explained how Ireland had 'turned the corner' and that 'political peace' had resulted in a 'heartening and stimulating' period of industrial progress.[70] That evening, Cosgrave gave an address which was broadcast on radio to the Irish Fellowship Club in which he elaborated on the Free State's positive evolution. He spoke of Ireland's 700-year struggle for independence, in the wake of which 'very young' and 'almost inexperienced' men had the task of 'setting our house in order'. In establishing the difficulties of achieving independence and the reality of building a new state, Cosgrave went on to show how his government guided the Free State through the process and the majority of his speech emphasized the developments and achievements—industry, agriculture, the Irish language, small debt, peaceful conditions—that had taken place since 1921/2. He sent a clear message that the Free State was a 'sovereign state with all the powers, duties and responsibilities inherent in sovereignty'.[71]

Washington was the next stop, where Cosgrave visited the tomb of the state's namesake. On 25 January, he became the first Irish political leader to address the House of Representatives since Parnell in 1880. In the course of his speech, he again thanked the American people for their support for Ireland's campaign for independence. He also gave a short address to the Senate, in which he explained that he was returning Benjamin Franklin's visit 150 years previously.[72] During his four-day stay in Washington, Cosgrave was also conferred with an honorary doctor of laws degree by the Catholic University. From Washington the delegation travelled on to Philadelphia for a very short visit, but their original delay in arriving in America meant that Boston had to be crossed off the schedule.

On their journey to Ottawa, Cosgrave and his colleagues were lucky to escape harm after the special train in which they were travelling derailed, killing the driver and leaving three others injured. In all of its coverage of Cosgrave's trip, the New York Times wrote in glowing terms. Writing, for example, on the reception that the president received in Ottawa, the paper opined that 'seldom, if ever, has there been held a gathering more representative of the whole Dominion from coast to coast. Political friend and foe found common ground in extending to the President of the Irish Free State their felicitations'.[73]

As Cosgrave was being officially received, de Valera was also in America being cheered on by Republican supporters. In an address to the American Association for the Recognition of the Irish Republic on 28 January, he disputed Cosgrave's assertions, which he condemned as 'English-Cosgrave propaganda'—that Ireland was free, prosperous and contented.[74] When asked at a press conference if he would pay de Valera a visit, Cosgrave is alleged to have replied in his typical style, 'I see no reason why the head of the government should call on one of his citizens'.[75] Despite the positive press coverage, Cosgrave was not universally warmly received and while he was in New York the police commissioner had made preparations to prevent demonstrations from Republicans.[76]

In 1923 Lindsay Crawford—the Free State trade representative in New York—had suggested that Ireland would 'stand better at Washington by keeping out of the League'.[77] However, the Free State had, by the time of Cosgrave's visit, largely proved itself on the international stage and if diplomatic relations had been damaged, it was certainly not obvious in January 1928. The propaganda value of Cosgrave's American trip was enormous. Not only was he given an open and far-reaching forum, that included radio, to outline the development of the Free State, but the press coverage also assisted in building the image that the Cumann na nGaedheal government strove to project.

As discussed in Chapter 2, the Free State had achieved many of its aims at the 1926 imperial conference, but there was still the outstanding matter of the Privy Council in London which had the power to overrule the finding of any Irish court. In framing the Constitution of the Free State, there had been an attempt to expunge the appeal and Article 65 declared decisions of the Supreme Court to be 'final and conclusive' and not 'capable of being reviewed by any other court, tribunal or authority whatsoever'. However, this contravened the terms of the Treaty and in the final version an addendum was added to what became Article 66, 'Provided that nothing in this constitution shall impair the right of any person to petition His Majesty for special leave to appeal from the Supreme Court to His Majesty in Council of the right of His Majesty to grant such leave'.[78]

The appeal to the Privy Council had been included to act as a safeguard for the Unionist minority resident in the new state. However, the Cosgrave government was particularly careful to ensure that that community was not discriminated against, to the point that the administration was accused of bias. This would be clearly seen in the case of Letitia Dunbar-Harrison, discussed in Chapter 6.[79] The appeal had rarely been utilised, but its very existence compromised the Free State's judicial sovereignty. Cosgrave's government was not in a position to amend the legislation due to the ambiguity surrounding the legal foundation of the 1922 Constitution. The Free State argued that the Constitution had been created by an act of the Dáil and could therefore be amended through another act, whereas the British took the view that it was an act of their parliament that had brought the Constitution into existence and as such the Free State had no power to tamper with it.

The Free State delegates thus came to the 1930 imperial conference with a clear objective of what they wanted discussed: the Privy Council; the right of direct access to the king by all his governments; the position of Commonwealth members regarding Treaty-making; and communication between his majesty's governments other than the British government and foreign governments.[80] As long as the machinery of external relations was centred on Britain, to outsiders the Commonwealth remained an 'organic unit'.[81] The British refused to remove the appeal to the Privy Council, much to the Free State's annoyance. The Free State also brought to the conference a proposed Nationality Bill, which was a formal expression of a long-standing objective of emphasizing the difference between British and Irish citizenship. The delegates were largely successful in their aim, but some ambiguity remained about the nationality of a foreign woman who married an Irish man.[82]

Overall the conference at the time was a frustrating one which left many issues unresolved, most notably the *inter se* nature of treaties. Britain's refusal to amend its interpretation resulted in the unacceptable position that the dominions could not conduct treaties among themselves, and also invalidated the claim that the 1921 Treaty was an international document.[83] When the conference ended, no agreement had been reached on its status.

If the conference itself was disappointing, the Free State could take solace in the Statute of Westminster the following year. With its passage, Patrick McGilligan claimed that, 'the imperial system "which it took centuries to build" was finally demolished'.[84] The statute was the legal definition of Balfour Declaration secured at the 1926 imperial conference. The implications for the Free State in particular were immediately apparent: no British law could furthermore be extended to the dominions without their consent, but more importantly the dominions had the right to amend or repeal both existing and future legislation relevant to them passed by the British parliament.

The statute was not without its opposition in Britain where many forecast that the 1921 settlement would be dismantled as a consequence. Winston Churchill was particularly anxious about the future of the agreement to which he had signed his name. In a defence worthy of the Republicans, he invoked the dead generations as reasons to why the Treaty should not be revised:

> The Irishmen whom we faced knew that they took their lives in their hands for their part, and nearly all of them have given their lives for the fulfilment of the Treaty obligations ... The names of Arthur Griffith, Michael Collins, and, though he was not a signatory of the Agreement, Kevin O' Higgins ought not to fade from our memories, because they gave their lives for the

maintenance of the instrument called the Irish Treaty or the Articles of Agreement.[85]

By using the names of men prominently associated with the Free State to defend against further concessions, Churchill cannot have helped Cumann na nGaedheal's position. However, the Statute of Westminster would not have been unpalatable to Griffith, Collins or O'Higgins, who all saw the Treaty as a vehicle through which independence could be advanced. In fact, McGilligan paid special tribute to O'Higgins, describing the statute as being 'the end now achieved to the work which the then Vice-President of this state started in 1926'.[86]

A solution to the problem, as some British saw it, was a possible amendment to the statute that would exempt the Irish Free State Constitution Act, 1922, from its terms.[87] This was disastrous for the Irish government. Cumann na nGaedheal had repeatedly argued that the Treaty had changed the nature of the British–Irish relationship. And, as Kevin O'Higgins had once explained, the settlement was seen as 'the basis for rapid and far-reaching constitutional development'.[88] Griffith and Collins had given their word when they signed the agreement, and their successors in the pro-Treaty party were determined to uphold that. However, it now seemed that the British did not feel as honour-bound, and that the Balfour Declaration was little more than empty rhetoric. McGilligan expressed this view in a letter to Thomas, pointing out that any such amendment would strike at the 'whole basis of goodwill and free co-operation' on which the Treaty was founded.[89]

However, the amendment moved by Colonel John Gretton was defeated on 24 November. A second attempt at an amendment was led by Lord Danesfort. Arguably, the British were not as concerned with the intentions of Cumann na nGaedheal—the party, after all, based its legitimacy on the Treaty settlement—but rather with what would happen if Fianna Fáil came to power. Since its entry to the Dáil, de Valera's party had marked itself out as a government-in-waiting and this cannot have escaped the notice of the British.

How the government responded to the Statute of Westminster was indicative of its attitude. The government was not willing to needlessly tamper with the Treaty, even if doing so meant cutting away the ground from beneath Fianna Fáil and so there were never any plans to remove the Oath. However, at a meeting of the Cabinet on 3 March 1931 it was agreed that already prepared legislation to abolish the controversial appeal to the Privy Council be circulated in advance of the following meeting.[90] Legislation was drafted in preparation to amend the Constitution on the point of appeal to the Privy Council. Even in that, the government was careful not to upset the British. Provoking a reaction was not on the agenda.

The Statute of Westminster was Cumann na nGaedheal's crowning achievement in foreign policy. The Treatyites had been vindicated: freedom could be achieved within the capacity of Commonwealth membership.[91] But it also proved to be something of a burden. Despite the opportunity it provided the Free State to amend existing British legislation, it also afforded the government's harshest critics with propaganda. Once more, the party's willingness to work within the Commonwealth was pointed to as proof of its desire to please Britain. Within the realm of external affairs there was nowhere left for the party to go and the next logical step was outside the Treaty, which clearly was not an option. The change of government in 1932 was therefore timely. Free from the cumbersome obligation that had burdened Cumann na nGaedheal, Fianna Fáil continued the process—although not intentionally—of vindicating Michael Collins's stepping-stone theory as de Valera set about dismantling the Treaty. It was Cumann na nGaedheal's 'creative diplomatic action' that contributed to his success.[92]

The statute was not the only achievement of 1931. At the time of the 1930 conference the Free State had argued against the use of British seals, noting that 'the exercise of the powers of the sovereign is controlled through a system of state seals',[93] but no agreement had been reached. In its aftermath, however, the government communicated to the British their intention to use the 'Great seal of the Irish Free State' to authenticate a Treaty of Commerce and Navigation with Portugal.[94] In the negotiations that followed, the British eventually consented. The government had won the right to by-pass the British Foreign Office in signing treaties with foreign states.[95]

In less than one decade, Free State representatives had achieved a strong and impressive record in international affairs. Much had been done to advance Irish sovereignty through diplomatic means and to establish the Free State on the international stage as a nation in its own right rather than a colony or dependent on Britain. However, as Alvin Jackson explains, 'impressive though these diplomatic triumphs were, they did not permit the Cumann na nGaedheal ministers to claim the high ground of nationalist morality and integrity'.[96]

Law and order

The government's response to the murder of Kevin O'Higgins in 1927 had intended to eliminate the threat of extremists and as the country returned to peace the following year the Public Safety Act was repealed. However, the government was soon forced to consider further action when the IRA appeared to grow in strength from 1929 and again Cumann na nGaedheal took a strong stance on law and order. The Juries Protection Act, 1929 was introduced as a response to the intimidation of jurors. In introducing the bill, James Fitzgerald-Kenney made reference to two jurors—Messrs White and Armstrong—who had been attacked and in the case of the latter fatally wounded.[97] There had also been a worrying growth in the number of acquittals at trials, despite often overwhelming evidence against the accused. This was extremely disheartening for the Gardaí who found themselves rendered somewhat ineffective by virtue of the fact that in many instances arrests would not be followed up with a conviction. The legislation sought to protect those on the panel for political trials by providing them with anonymity and also by setting a nine to three majority as the requirement for a conviction so that it was impossible to know which way a person voted.[98] But there were obvious flaws. While the names of jurors were not supplied, in the absence of private sessions, there was nothing to prevent them from being visually identified and protection outside of the courts was not feasible. Such were the concerns for jurors that Kevin O'Higgins had already disbarred women from participating.[99] While this was interpreted as a chauvinistic attitude that women should not be exposed to often unsettling discussions, there was naturally an element of concern for their safety. The campaign to intimidate jurors continued, however, as clearly shown in a report summarising Irregular activity between January and September 1931.[100] While the minister for defence had staunchly defended the act in the Dáil during its renewal, he conceded in the Senate that it had not caused the demise of the IRA as intended.

A report sent to the Department of Justice by Eoin O'Duffy on 27 July 1931 commented on illegal drilling in various parts of the country and noted that his men were in a 'hopeless position'. The case of John O'Mahony—a former Sinn Féin TD who had publicly encouraged drilling during an oration at Kilbride Cemetery, Co. Meath—was among those cited as an example of open defiance of the government.

That arrests were proving ineffective, prompted the suggestion of two alternatives: unchecked crime or reprisals.[101] A report drawing such conclusions was bound to alarm a government utterly wedded to the principle of constitutional behaviour.

On 20 March 1931 Superintendent John Curtin of the CID was shot dead by the IRA, which unashamedly rationalised his killing in *An Phoblacht*. Three months later, an extensive arms-dump was discovered at Killakee, Co. Dublin, but rather than view it as a blow, the IRA merely dismissed the find, explaining that there were plenty more. In what was intended to be the Republicans' rival to the Griffith-Collins-O'Higgins commemoration, a parade to Bodenstown was organised. Rather than risk banning it outright only for the IRA to defy the order, Fitzgerald-Kenney used the 1925 Treasonable Offences Act to prevent Great Southern Railways from providing special trains to bring rural members to Dublin, but despite the minister's best efforts, there was still a large attendance. Republicans had secured a fleet of buses as an alternative.[102] Interspersed in the crowd was a large military presence, a sign that the government was taking the parade seriously, but also that it was willing to enforce its authority if required. *An Phoblacht* deemed the event a triumph, and encouraged its readers to 'energetically and relentlessly' push forward.[103] Although the newspaper claimed that the government was now in a state of panic, Cumann na nGaedheal was, in fact, preparing to act. The shooting dead of John Ryan, a witness in an illegal-drilling case in south Tipperary who had been warned by the IRA to leave the country,[104] the following month increased the sense of urgency. This was a prominent theme in Fitzgerald-Kenney's speech on 9 August when he announced the introduction of new public safety measures.[105]

The combination of flattering articles on Russia in *An Phoblacht* and the setting up of Saor Éire in autumn 1931 was enough to convince the government of links between the IRA and communism. This new threat added a further dimension to the government's speeches as a 'Red scare' came into play.[106] Planning for the Public Safety Act and discussions of its merits were held in tandem with rumours of and preparations for an election. The IRA took a policy of passive resistance to the new legislation, thus cutting ground away from Cumann na nGaedheal's argument that the organisation was a grave threat to the stability of the state. The IRA's silence was a tactical move, designed to assist Fianna Fáil which is confirmed by the fact that it resumed its activities the month after the

1932 election. By June of that year *An Phoblacht* had declared that 'they [Cumann na nGaedheal] must be attacked and squelched'.[107]

A party in decline?

As the life of the sixth Dáil was drawing to a close, a worrying trend had developed within Cumann na nGaedheal. There was a general malaise among back-bench deputies, who frequently absented themselves from the Dáil. As a consequence, Cumann na nGaedheal developed an almost obsessive concern with attendance. However, the important question of why deputies were not active was never asked, and instead focus was placed on methods to bring them back into the Dáil chamber. As minutes of the parliamentary party are not available prior to November 1929, one can but speculate that discipline was perhaps a pressing issue then also. Between March 1930 and July 1931, the issue of attendance and voting in divisions was discussed at no less than eleven meetings and on two occasions, the party attempted to take extreme steps to keep its deputies in line. On 25 June 1931 a resolution was unanimously passed declaring that 'any member voting against any measure introduced by a minister will be automatically expelled from the party, except he previously obtains permission in writing from the party committee and the minister concerned'.[108] The following month another resolution was proposed, aimed at amending the above quote with 'which has been submitted to and approved of by the party', but it failed to pass.[109] That the party was anxious to ensure full attendance on the government benches was understandable as the September general election had returned Cumann na nGaedheal with so narrow a majority that the support of the Farmers' Party had become an imperative.

Seven by-elections occurred during the life of the sixth Dáil. While the Cumann na nGaedheal vote did slip, the party was certainly not disintegrating. The first in the series was held in the president's traditional constituency of Carlow-Kilkenny on 3 November 1927. As Cosgrave had won two seats at the September general election, the newly re-elected government actually had a majority of five seats since the president could not vote twice. Denis Gorey sought to retain the seat for Cumann na nGaedheal. Cosgrave was the party's trump card in appealing to the electorate, and, as director of elections, Liam Burke ran the campaign as a personal vote for the president. 'Vote for Gorey and support president Cosgrave' was the slogan used throughout the campaign.[110] The 'support Cosgrave' theme had another dimension, however. The inconclusive September 1927 results meant that strict attendance at the Dáil was a necessity. At a meeting in Hackettstown, Co. Carlow, Ernest Blythe told his audience that if Gorey were defeated it would be practically impossible for Cosgrave to carry on.[111] Additionally, as the editor of the *Kilkenny People* pointed out, the loss of a traditional Cumann na nGaedheal seat to Fianna Fáil would 'materially and perhaps fatally damage the prestige of the government'.[112] Gorey's victory by a very slender margin could be seen as a drop off in support for the party. It is important to remember, however, that Cosgrave's vote was largely a personal one. It would have been an unreasonable expectation that Gorey—a relative newcomer to the party—perform to the same standard.

The following two by-elections, both occurring in Dublin North within a year of each other, were quiet campaigns. Although the necessity for the first—James Larkin had been declared an undischarged bankrupt, thus contravening the 1923 Electoral Act[113]—produced some interesting and lively debate, the campaign itself was lacklustre. Cumann na nGaedheal was victorious, but the margin was not significant. The second by-election in the constituency also proved to be an arid political battle and found little expression in the newspapers. The parties simply went through the motions. One event, however, that did add some life to the proceedings took place on polling day, 14 March 1929, and was engineered on behalf of Cumann na nGaedheal by O'Kennedy-Brindley for the party's candidate, Thomas O'Higgins. A dispensary doctor, he had been involved with the Irish Volunteers and had served in the army medical service, but, more importantly, he was a brother of the murdered Kevin O'Higgins.

The *Offaly Independent* would later proclaim it 'electioneering history' when a Clann-na-Poblachta-sponsored plane flew from one end of the country to the other during the 1948 general election. Kevin Rafter, in his study of the party, comments 'whether or not this was history is not clear', and he draws attention to the fact that a Fianna Fáil plane was also in use.[114] The fact that a plane toured the *length of the country* was certainly a new development, but neither the Clann nor Fianna Fáil were the first to requisition an aeroplane for electioneering purposes. A private aeroplane owned by a member of the Irish Aero Club, along with the services of Colonel James Fitzmaurice, was commissioned for some last minute campaigning in support of the Cumann na nGaedheal candidate on election day. Fitzmaurice was a former commandant of the air corps and was one of the three-man crew who undertook the first flight from Europe to North America on board the Bremen aeroplane the previous year. His flight in 1929 was far less extensive, although in terms of electioneering history, was nonetheless important. His path concentrated on the constituency of Dublin North and thousands of handbills requesting support for O'Higgins were dropped from the plane at intervals during the day. Cumann na nGaedheal had set another precedent.

It was also a masterstroke. The *Evening Herald* reported that thousands of these handbills dropped to the streets and the plane's movements were followed with great interest by the public.[115] The plane and its falling literature would have generated interest or at least curiosity, and therefore discussion about the event and the people involved. The novel technique would also have ensured that a myriad of people, who might not otherwise have read them, came into contact with O'Higgins's handbills that now littered the streets. There is no guarantee that the content was actually read by those who picked them up, if indeed they were picked up. However, the stunt would, at the very least, have ensured numerous people would have gone into the voting booths with O'Higgins's name in mind. At a time when party affiliation and photographs were not supplied on ballot papers, name recognition was hugely important. Again, Cumann na nGaedheal was the winner, but the margin of victory still was not significant. Only 151 votes separated O'Higgins from his Fianna Fáil rival. That Thomas was a brother of Kevin O'Higgins undoubtedly helped—this had been emphasized during the campaign—but, one must also wonder if some of those 151 votes could be attributed to people who had been swayed by his literature that had fallen from the sky.

The result of the next by-election, held in Leitrim-Sligo in June 1929, was in stark contrast to the preceding elections for a number of reasons. Despite receiving little press coverage, Cumann na nGaedheal ran a convincing campaign that resulted in its candidate securing victory with a sizeable margin over his Fianna Fáil rival. Moreover, Cumann na nGaedheal captured a Fianna Fáil seat. The by-election had been prompted by the death of Seamus Holt, a widely respected figure with strong Republican links. Eamon Donnelly, who also had strong links to the Republican movement, was selected to stand for Fianna Fáil.

When Donnelly was first announced as the Fianna Fáil candidate, the details of his credentials were printed in the *Leitrim Observer* and thereafter the paper's readership was continuously reminded of his background.[116] In contrast to the general trend in newspapers at the time, Cumann na nGaedheal did not dominate the print. The party's candidate was General Seán MacEoin. Although described as 'a popular hero',[117] the paper never reported on his selection in the way that it did Donnelly's. He was simply acknowledged to be the government candidate and nothing was said of his status. This disregard for Cumann na nGaedheal was not an isolated incident. The coverage of the campaign trail was highly unbalanced and the attention given to the government party could best be described as sparse. In fact the editorial line of the paper was undoubtedly weighted in favour of Fianna Fáil.

One of the striking features of the contest was the identity of the speakers. It appears from the newspaper coverage that Donnelly actually spoke very little. Both de Valera and Cosgrave were present in the constituency at various times. However, the level of Cosgrave's contribution is hard to gauge given the virtual disregard of Cumann na nGaedheal. It would seem that Donnelly's voters were addressed rarely by the candidate for whom they were being asked to vote and more by his party leader, ably supported by Seán T. O'Kelly.

Cumann na nGaedheal secured victory with a strong margin of 4,000 votes. It was a significant achievement. The party had captured a seat from Fianna Fáil. Furthermore, the margin of victory was greater in Leitrim-Sligo than in those by-elections during the sixth Dáil—the contest in Dublin County on 9 December 1930 being the exception—when Cumann na nGaedheal had been victorious in retaining a party seat. If the government had run out of steam, then the party was still very much alive.

Although the next by-election, which occurred in Longford-Westmeath, broke the party's unbeaten run, there was nothing startling about the campaign. Fianna Fáil retained its seat. De Valera believed that the election marked the 'turning of the tide'.[118] Fianna Fáil was certainly on the move; the party had scored its first by-election victory since the Sinn Féin split. Furthermore, the contest in Longford-Westmeath was the first occasion since the mid-1920s that the party's vote exceeded Cumann na nGaedheal's in a by-election,[119] but Fianna Fáil was yet to capture a seat in a by-election from Cumann na nGaedheal. In contrast, the government party had not only retained all of its seats in every by-election of the sixth Dáil, but it had also gained one of Fianna Fáil's.

Later that year, Cumann na nGaedheal secured a massive victory in Dublin County. The party's candidate polled more than double the votes of Fianna Fáil; while spectacular, the result should not be overstated, however, as the party had naturally strong support in the Dublin constituencies. Nonetheless, it is further evidence that Cumann na nGaedheal was doing more than simply clinging on. The final by-election occurred in Kildare in June 1931, caused by the death of Labour's Hugh Colohan. The date is of great significance; it was the first to occur since the effects of the Great Depression had really made their presence felt in the Free State. With hindsight, the contest in many ways mirrored what would happen in 1932 (although the parties could not have recognised that at the time). Cumann na nGaedheal adhered to its traditional election message and emphasized ten years of achievements. Fianna Fáil, with its message for the future, captured the Labour seat.

Lemass had told an audience in Athy that the message sent forth from Kildare would have a 'very great influence on the result' of the next general election.[120] That the constituency of Kildare was important enough to influence the entire Free State election was highly questionable, but the tone of the by-election had provided some suggestion as to how the general election would be fought. Had Cumann na nGaedheal paid closer attention, the party might have realised that its traditional election message had become outdated in a changed economic climate where the importance of the Treaty paled in comparison to the everyday needs of the voters. The Fianna Fáil campaign and result in Kildare also suggested that the party had served its apprenticeship and was soon to become master of the House. However, the seven by-elections clearly demonstrate that before the downturn in the world economy hit the Free State, Cumann na nGaedheal was performing well. That it was in decline from 1927, as John A. Murphy has argued, was simply not the case.[121]

.6.

Falling into the Great Depression

At the time of the 1932 general election, *The Times* was able to report that Cosgrave's administration was 'one of the oldest in Europe'.[1] It seems a remarkable claim, given that the Free State was only one decade old, but many of the new states that had emerged in the inter-war period disappeared just as quickly. The Cumann na nGaedheal government, however, had ensured the stability of the state to the point that the transfer of power in 1932 from the winners to the losers of the Civil War was both peaceful and smooth. By the time of the election, the political and economic climate had changed considerably. Fianna Fáil deputies, having taken their seats before the last election, had legitimised themselves in the eyes of the electorate and during the sixth Dáil they proved that they were capable of working within the political system. The threat of the IRA had again been dealt with through another Public Safety Act, while the organisation's self-imposed inactivity during the 1932 campaign meant that Cumann na nGaedheal's accusation that Fianna Fáil was closely associated with a group actively engaged in illegal activity rang hollow. Although Saor Éire—a communist organisation—was painted as posing a new threat, there was arguably a much greater issue at stake for the ordinary voter. People were more concerned with the implications of the Wall Street Crash and consequent global recession. The Red scare and the constitutional debate—to which few ordinary voters would have paid close attention anyway—gave way to bread-and-butter issues.

Attack campaigning and an emphasis on law and order in September 1927 had worked against the backdrop of revulsion at O'Higgins's assassination, but negative campaigning would not be as affective in 1932. By focusing on past achievements and attacking Fianna Fáil, Cumann na nGaedheal's campaign was far more problematic for what it had failed to say than what it actually said. The party's silence on a strategy for coping with the downturn in the global economy was in stark contrast with Fianna Fáil's approach. De Valera's party was not offering a particularly detailed explanation as to what it would do, but the fact that it was screaming from its advertisements that it had a strategy was enough to grab the attention of the voters.[2] A more defined policy would come once the party was in power.

Timing of the election

Cosgrave called the election eight months early. Although it need not have taken place until October, there were several factors which, when combined, convinced him to go to the polls at the start of 1932. The element of surprise that a snap election brings is always attractive to governments, but in this instance it was unlikely that the government would have caught its main opposition off guard. The date for the election was discussed at a meeting of the Fianna Fáil parliamentary party on 3 November 1931, although persistent rumours regarding an early election had been noted in July.[3] As far back as November 1928 Seán Lemass and Gerard Boland had written to every Fianna Fáil deputy about the possibility of an election the following year, and encouraged members to prepare for it from that day forward.[4] Similarly during the Kildare by-election of June 1931, Lemass expressed his belief that the government was planning an early election.[5] Thus given the hearsay of an election since 1928, of which Cumann na nGaedheal was clearly aware, the element of surprise could not have been a major motivation.

The possible reasons for the early election divide into two categories: self-motivation and the interests of the state. In the first instance, it has been noted that the government wished to utilise the prevailing atmosphere of the Red scare to give Cumann na nGaedheal new ground on which to attack Fianna Fáil.[6] Certainly, this was a dominant theme in the party's campaign speeches and literature. Labour's William Davin also claimed that the decision was motivated by economic concerns. He argued that the government rushed the election because it was 'fearful of the consequences which might befall' the party if it were held after the next budget.[7] Indeed a memorandum from J. J. McElligott confirmed that the prospective deficit for 1932/3 would be so large that it would require a change of policy on the part of the government.[8] However, while the early election might have had an element of self-preservation, it was unlikely that the government was simply attempting to avoid the judgement of the voters. After all, it had repeatedly shown itself to be unconcerned by the weight of popular opinion. Moreover, at a meeting of the parliamentary party on 5 November 1931, it was noted that the Executive Council felt that an early election would be inadvisable until 'economic and other difficulties' had been dealt with.[9] Although Cosgrave faced into the 1932 election almost certain of defeat, the party would not have been simply prepared to step aside for Fianna Fáil. Nonetheless, during its decade in power, Cumann na nGaedheal continuously put the nation before the party and this attitude could again be identified in the remaining reasons as to why Cosgrave went to the polls early.

Dublin had the honour of hosting the thirty-first Eucharistic Congress in June. The highlight was the Mass at the Phoenix Park, celebrated in front of one million people, which turned out to be the single biggest gathering in the country since Daniel O'Connell's monster meeting at Tara in 1843.[10] Despite the extensive press opportunities that the event would afford the government of the day, Cosgrave, a devout Catholic, did not want the occasion politicised, nor did he want international visitors seeing the Free State in the midst of an election campaign and all of its associated bitterness. The forthcoming imperial economic conference, to be held at Ottawa in August, also had to be considered. Such was its importance that whatever Free State representatives attended needed a clear mandate from the electorate as it would be that government which would be responsible for overseeing and implementing the decisions reached.

The Depression

The parallels between British Labour and Cumann na nGaedheal at this time were striking. By 1922 Labour had entered a period of considerable achievement, which ended in defeat and demoralisation.[11] Having returned to power in 1929, Ramsay MacDonald's minority government operated within the constraints of a global economic depression and consequently suffered defeat at the 1931 general election. Just as Labour viewed that election with pessimism, so too did Cumann na nGaedheal face 1932 with a feeling of trepidation. The difference was that Cosgrave's entire front bench survived intact, while Labour's leadership was practically wiped out. With Cumann na nGaedheal in mind, the Dublin correspondent of the *Wicklow People* noted how Labour had suffered because of the economic crisis for which it was 'probably … not much to blame'.[12]

Having been in power for almost a decade, Cumann na nGaedheal felt that 'the danger lies not in the length of years, but the shortness of memories'.[13] To explain the government's defeat to be a result of the electorate overlooking the past or tiring of hearing the same hollow rhetoric, however, is to only partially consider the reasons that it occurred. The Wall Street Crash of October 1929 caused ripples far beyond American shores. Prior to 1929 the strain on Europe to repay its foreign debts was great, but after Black Thursday—the single worst day of the market collapse—it became virtually impossible. 'It was a vicious spiral of falling prices, surplus stock and rising debts which spelled potential bankruptcy for families and countries alike.'[14] At the time Barry Egan wrote that 'history can give no parallel to the dangerous position of the world today', and described the global economy as 'groaning under taxation'.[15]

However, according to Mary E. Daly, Irish income actually rose in marked contrast to most European countries between 1929 and 1931.[16] But 1931 was a turning point for the global economy; by then it was no longer possible to disguise the magnitude of the crisis.[17] Although not immediately felt, the effects of the Depression gripping Europe were eventually experienced in the Free State. 'Our country did not escape', the editor of the *People* noted, 'but fortunately it was not affected as badly as others'.[18] The export of livestock was to dramatically drop from £18 million in 1931 to £7 million by 1933.[19] However, the tripartite agreement reached at Chequers following Eoin MacNeill's resignation from the Boundary Commission had relieved the Free State of its obligation to contribute to the British national debt.[20] Realising the propaganda benefit of that agreement in the current strained economic climate, Cumann na nGaedheal issued election advertisements with the succinct headings 'We have no war debt!' and 'Our national credit is sound!'[21]

These positives were negated, however, by the persistent unemployment problem. According to Cumann na nGaedheal, the number of persons registered as unemployed at the labour exchange had fallen from 41,399 in 1922 to 21,427 in 1931.[22] But these levels were at odds with those cited by Labour, which in late 1927 challenged the accuracy of the labour-exchange figures,[23] and put the estimated total at a much higher figure of 80,000.[24] In its election statement, the party's judgement of the government's attitude towards the workers and the poor was bluntly expressed in the single line: 'the present ministry has failed'.[25] Similarly Eamon de Valera deemed the government's record on unemployment to be one of 'complete impotence and failure'.[26] During its decade in power, Cumann na nGaedheal had not believed in solving the problem through the creation of employment in the public sector. Its policy instead focused on short-term unemployment insurance, the provision of relief work and support through the Poor Law system.[27] A Committee on Unemployment chaired by Vincent Rice, Cumann na nGaedheal deputy for Dublin South, had been established in 1927 and among its suggestions was a house-building programme, but little came of its recommendations.[28]

Just as the party had done during the Kildare by-election campaign of June 1931,[29] Cumann na nGaedheal rejected criticisms by pointing out that unemployment was not a uniquely Irish experience. In Britain, for example, there were 1.5 million unemployed in January 1930, that figure rose each month until, by the end of the year, it had reached 2.7 million. By July of the following year the total number of unemployed stood at 2.8 million.[30] Cumann na nGaedheal quoted the words of an 'eminent Catholic authority on sociology in the University of Washington' who observed that 'one American in three is either destitute or facing destitution this winter'.[31] But this did not pacify the opposition benches. Labour's William Norton dryly observed that 'it was an insult to their intelligence to say they ought to be hungry because there was hunger in China or America'.[32] Later that year Barry Egan wrote to Thomas Buckley in San Francisco explaining that 'our unemployment problem is a comparatively small one', but also acknowledged that it was 'serious enough'.[33] As the election approached, Cumann na nGaedheal continued to evade outlining an intelligible policy for tackling unemployment. Section 38 of the party's election handbook for speakers was entitled 'Solving the unemployment problem', but the only statement that could be classed as forward-looking, read: 'a tremendous amount of reconstruction work has *still to be undertaken*, which in the hands of a stable government, whose credit is good, can be carried out in such a way as to afford further relief for the workers' (italics added).[34]

The government was accused of making 'no effort to offer a solution'.[35] Fianna Fáil communicated its solution in distinctly protectionist language: employing Irish people in Ireland, growing food, and making clothes and implements.[36] While less vague than what Cumann na nGaedheal was suggesting, it was not an in-depth solution and unemployment did not even figure in the party's election statement. However, responsibility for solving problems lies with the government. Governments have and will continue to be blamed for situations beyond their control. Between 1948 and 1957, for example, the government changed every three years largely due to the economic difficulties facing Ireland. Each government was forced to take drastic action, which subsequently eroded the party's popularity at the polls.[37] The same could be identified in the early 1980s, when there were three elections in eighteen months.

Reflecting in 1982 on Cumann na nGaedheal's final administration, the then Taoiseach, Charles Haughey, contended that 'there had been much talk of book-keeping and accounting but no real grasp of what the country needed'.[38] His assertion is certainly harsh, although hardly surprising given that he was the Fianna Fáil leader. But when viewed in a wider context, Cumann na nGaedheal's handling of the situation was not unique. The response of governments across the globe to the Wall Street Crash has since been the source of controversy. Unemployment was not directly tackled, as it was felt to do so might increase government spending, and by extension debt, which would only exacerbate the problem.[39] Between 1929 and 1930, spending to promote employment was rejected so as to avoid unnecessary strain on national budgets and the credibility of the exchange rate.[40] Although, as Robert Blake has noted, there were alternative policies which might have solved or at least softened unemployment but the British Conservatives, for example, did not engage with the problem for the reasons already discussed.[41] Thus Cumann na nGaedheal's approach was largely in keeping with European norms, but for those directly affected by the downturn at the time, how Cumann na nGaedheal compared with other governments was irrelevant.

It is hardly surprising that the unemployment question was a major talking point given that an election was pending. Unfortunately for Cumann na nGaedheal's prospects, such criticisms were not wholly the product of the forthcoming electoral contest, aimed at winning votes. Only one month into the life of the sixth Dáil, Daniel Morrissey—a member of the Labour Party who subsequently stood on the Cumann na nGaedheal ticket in 1933—had moved 'that the measures hitherto adopted by the government for the relief of unemployment are insufficient and ought to be extended immediately'.[42] (Morrissey moved a similar motion in the seventh Dáil. That it was brought just one month after de Valera came to power, when the government was only settling in, meant that it was an implicit criticism of the Cumann na nGaedheal administration's handling of the unemployment question.)[43] As Cormac Ó Gráda has pointed out, between the mid-1920s and mid-1940s, there was only a minimal rise in real wages, and the policies of the Cumann na nGaedheal government are likely to have increased the gap between rich and poor.[44]

The Irish newspapers, with the obvious exception of Fianna Fáil paper, the *Irish Press*, sanguinely predicted, and in many cases hoped for a slim victory for the government party. Cosgrave, however, had anticipated Fianna Fáil's rise to power from as early as 1927 and he faced the 1932 general election with a degree of certainty that his party was facing defeat at the polls.[45] Consequently, he urged the British to accept a new Irish leader. Through the Irish high commissioner in London,

Cosgrave communicated to King George V that 'from all points of view it would be most unwise for the British government to adopt too aggressive an attitude or iron hand methods towards a government made up of the Fianna Fáil party'.[46] As he prepared to hand over the reins of power to his main rival, there must have been a tragic element of truth in Desmond Ryan's caustic remark that perhaps Cosgrave 'felt like comparing himself to Brian Boru, who had fallen but saved his kingdom'.[47]

Policy

Some confusion surrounds the identity of those responsible for creating Cumann na nGaedheal's 1932 campaign. The contemporary political scientist Warner Moss, who followed the campaign closely, recorded in his book that the party dispensed with the services of O'Kennedy-Brindley and that headquarters' staff instead ran the campaign themselves, confident that they had learned from the professionals.[48] In contrast, Hugh Oram in his history of advertising in Ireland, asserted that the 1932 campaign was handled by the same agency as in September 1927.[49] However, as Margaret O'Carroll in her recent examination of Cumann na nGaedheal's posters for 1932 points out, the existence of posters attributed to McConnell's Advertising Service appears to contradict Oram's observation. Although the company has no recollection or record of having printed them, the name does clearly appear at the bottom of a collection of prints.[50] Party minutes offer no insight.

Cumann na nGaedheal appeared devoid of policy at the time of the 1932 general election. The party's promises, if they could be classified as such, leaned heavily on past performances and promised a continuation. The absence of parliamentary party minutes between 17 December 1931 and 8 March 1932 makes it difficult, but not impossible to get a definite idea of what dominated the party's agenda in the run up to the election. Indeed, prior to December references to the election are rare, with party discipline instead dominating the discussion. However, recurring themes can be identified in the election literature. While the unremitting references to the past bordered on obsession, the lack of clarity on the future spoke volumes. This was explicitly clear from the party's election handbook, *Fighting points for Cumann na nGaedheal speakers and workers* (which could be considered an early form of the 'war book'[51]—a collation of expert deliberations on strategies used in US elections). The party's response to the accusation of having no policy was both evasive and rooted in the past. As pointed out in the handbook, '[Lemass] says we have given no indication of our own policy. Our policy and our record are written clearly across the bright face of a reconstructed Ireland'.[52] During the Treaty debates it had been the anti-Treatyites who had clung to the past, prompting Michael Collins to state 'I don't think it is fair to be quoting them [dead men] against us'.[53] In contrast, as Eoin O'Duffy demonstrated, the pro-Treaty side looked to the future when he asserted 'we have now our destinies in our own hands … Let us, in God's name, go ahead and build the Irish nation'.[54] By 1932, although Cumann na nGaedheal was still concerned with state-building, these roles had virtually been reversed. The party's mindset was still very much rooted in the early 1920s, but this was hardly surprising as it based its legitimacy on the Treaty settlement.

At the time that Fianna Fáil was emphasizing protectionism more so than ever, the world trend was towards such polices.[55] L.S. Amery recalled how the House of Commons met in February 1932 to 'close an era'. The principal of free trade that had dominated British national economic policy since the repeal of the Corn Laws was to be abandoned.[56] The Free State inevitably followed Britain's lead, but this had the unfortunate consequence of giving the impression that the government either took its cue from the former mother country or that it was mimicking Fianna Fáil policies. William Norton argued that Cumann na nGaedheal had no settled policy 'but appeared to drift helplessly before every economic wind that blew in other countries'.[57] The consequence of that perception was that the electorate was unsure of where Cumann na nGaedheal stood on protectionism. Although the party's election handbook declared that Cosgrave's government was not a free-trade government,[58] the fact that his administration was so reluctant to embrace tariffs suggested otherwise. This created a confused situation for voters, and further suggested that Cumann na nGaedheal had no clear policies.

Fianna Fáil produced the first formal Irish political manifesto as late as 1977,[59] while prior to that leaders' addresses and party statements were early versions of the modern manifesto. Although not nearly as extensive as today's documents, which often run to tens of pages, party statements are nonetheless an important source of information. In 1932 there was, unsurprisingly, a perceptible difference in those issued by the two main parties. The government's second sentence referred to oppression—a subject that re-emerged further on in the statement. Memory was cast as far back as the nineteenth century and reflected on the Famine. In contrast Fianna Fáil's immediately opened with the party's plans for the future, although given that unemployment was such a pressing issue at the time of the election, it is surprising not to find the subject represented directly. When the party's statement is placed beside that of Cumann na nGaedheal's, the appeal of Fianna Fáil becomes more obvious. As Michael Gallagher has noted, Fianna Fáil only appeared radical when compared with the very conservative Cumann na nGaedheal.[60]

Table 1.1 in Appendix 1 is modelled on a chart relating to UK and US manifestos produced by Ian Budge and Dennis J. Farlie, and it has been adapted to compare the Cumann na nGaedheal and Fianna Fáil statements of 1932.[61] The government party's contained a total of 43 sentences, 30 of which fitted into particular groups; while Fianna Fáil's was also the same length, 37 of the sentences contained issues that could be categorised.

As is demonstrably clear from this table, both parties had assembled statements with very different focuses. Fianna Fáil allocated only three sentences to historical-related issues, as compared with Cumann na nGaedheal's considerable seventeen and a half sentences. As most of these dealt with the Treaty settlement, the figure is hardly surprising, but the constant references to the Treaty ten years down the line served only to reinforce the static image that Cumann na nGaedheal was portraying. What was perhaps more surprising was that of those seventeen and a half references to the past, eight fell into the category of 'freedom, national history and sense of destiny', while Fianna Fáil—the Soldiers of Destiny—did not have a corresponding category. Although as John Bowman has pointed out, de Valera deliberately placed little emphasis on Partition during the campaign.[62]

The other major focus of the government's statement was the denunciation of its opposition, a topic that occupied eleven and a half sentences. This is paralleled in the party's election handbook for speakers and workers, the index of which contained a section entitled 'points against Fianna Fáil' that contained 25 subheadings and accounted for a startling 31% of the handbook's themes. In contrast, Fianna Fáil's statement made only two references to its rival, focusing instead on the welfare and running of the country. The retention of land annuities in the state treasury was the second objective in the party's eight-point programme. As already highlighted in the last chapter, farmers were struggling to meet their payments, and many—wrongly—hoped that

Fianna Fáil's policy would mean an end to their obligation. A host of other issues, ranging from social fairness, justice and equality, to a reduction in government spending, were dealt with in the statement.[63] Essentially what Fianna Fáil was offering was a dynamic and appealing package that appeared to promise future prosperity, while the government party seemingly offered no panacea for the country's ills.

The Red scare and the politics of fear

In the lead up to February 1932 the party increased its warnings about the future of the state and this can be attributed to its tacit awareness of impending defeat. A quintessential example of the party's campaign style was demonstrated in an advertisement that read: 'A vote for the government party is a vote for national sanity. A vote for Fianna Fáil is a vote for national suicide'.[64] Party literature insisted that the election of Fianna Fáil would result in the stability of the state created by the government being swept away by the tide of anarchy. References were made to 'sporadic revolution, irreligion, poverty and chaos'.[65] These apocalyptic warnings of Fianna Fáil's rise to power were designed to keep a check on the body politic.

However, Fianna Fáil's entry into the Dáil in 1927 had meant that the threat to the state was subsequently sitting directly across from the government in the main opposition benches and participating in the constitutional process. An early parallel to Cumann na nGaedheal's loss of its raison d'être after de Valera began to dismantle the Treaty can thus be identified. As Cumann na nGaedheal depicted itself as the defender of peace and stability the need to find another target thus manifested itself in the Red scare. There had, after all, been a lapse in IRA activity, thus undermining Cumann na nGaedheal's traditional warnings to the electorate.[66]

Alfie Byrne, lord mayor of Dublin, appealed to the voters, asserting that a defeat for the government would be a boost for communism.[67] One of the government's election posters read: 'We want no Reds here! Keep their colour off your flag! Vote for Cumann na nGaedheal'. Keogh points out that although Cumann na nGaedheal 'did not implicate Fianna Fáil directly in a left-wing plot to subvert the state … there was a strong emphasis on the "slightly constitutional" and "crypto-socialist" tradition of de Valera and his followers'.[68] Every opportunity was taken to exploit associations. For example, when Charlotte Despard appeared on a platform erected across from one occupied by government party candidates, Desmond FitzGerald took the opportunity to inform listeners that she was a member of the executive of Soviet Russia and of the Communist Party, which were 'seeking to establish anarchy in conflict with the teaching of the Catholic Church'. Moreover, he pointed out that she had appeared on a platform with de Valera the previous Thursday night.[69] In 1930, along with Hanna Sheehy-Skeffington, Sheila Downey and Helena Molony, Despard had undertaken an extensive tour of the Soviet Union, where the group was deeply influenced by what they saw.[70] Downey and Molony were both members of the Saor Éire national executive.[71]

A letter from an unidentified member of the Army Comrades Association claimed that communism was all the more dangerous because it wore a 'Republican mask'.[72] Fianna Fáil was, however, resolute that it had 'no leaning towards communism and no belief in communistic doctrines',[73] but the party was not as quick to fully close the door on Sinn Féin and the IRA. Lemass told Peadar O'Donnell, leader of the communist Saor Éire, 'Don't you see that we stand to gain from your organisation so long as we cannot be accused of starting the turmoil?'[74] As de Valera was privy to the memorandum sent by the government to each of the bishops, he held a pre-emptive meeting with Cardinal Joseph MacRory in Maynooth at which the Fianna Fáil leader firmly asserted that his party had no connections with communism. In this way, he detached the party from the controversy, ensuring that it would be in no way implicated in the denunciation that the religious would make.[75]

A campaign, whether negative or positive, is only effective if the voter is willing to accept the message.[76] Tony Schwartz, the creator of the much-celebrated, negative 'Daisy' advertisement,[77] remarked that 'commercials that attempt to tell the listener something are inherently not as effective as those that attach to something that is already in him'. In other words, unless an advertisement targets an existing concern or deploys a message that is not only believable but also acceptable, then it is often rendered ineffective.[78] This is also true of print media. Cumann na nGaedheal's pronouncements on the threat of communism were not wholly the product of the politics of fear; rather the Free State was following the church's line on communism in the late 1920s following Joseph Stalin's attack on religion. James Hogan would claim in 1935 that even after making allowances for exaggeration, one could not deny the existence of a 'well-organised and growing Communist movement in Ireland'.[79] But the Red scare tactics, as they were deployed in 1932, failed to boost support for the party because the electorate either did not believe the threat to be credible or felt that there were more immediate pressing concerns.

Unable to identify a Fianna Fáil-communist link, Cumann na nGaedheal looked at how the 'slightly constitutional' side of the party could be exploited. A selection of party members' statements, which would suit the government agenda, was chosen and catalogued mainly in Section 62 of *Fighting points*. The aim was to show that Fianna Fáil rhetoric had been 'an encouragement to the gunmen'.[80] Dan Breen was quoted as having said: 'Killing is a hard thing … we would kill again'.[81] De Valera, the party claimed, had the 'capacity for attracting and encouraging the mob'.[82] The party also attempted to exploit the speech made by the Fianna Fáil leader in which he spoke of wading through the blood of Irishmen. 'Even as late as December 6th, 1931', Cumann na nGaedheal claimed, 'he was being emotional about "Irishmen who might be inclined to follow in the footsteps of Irishmen of the past and try to get freedom by force"'.[83] Posters were produced that explicitly linked Fianna Fáil with gunmen, but one in particular took the alleged connection too far. The 'shadow of the gunman' showed the silhouette of an armed figure lurking threateningly over a house. 'Keep it from your home. Vote Cumann na nGaedheal' was the message. Some of the party's own members even refused to hang these sinister posters on their premises.[84] This type of marketing has what is described as the 'boomerang effect', whereby the propaganda 'hurts rather helps the sponsors'.[85]

A Cumann na nGaedheal candidate, Patrick Reynolds, was shot dead two days before polling day in Leitrim after he accused Joseph Leddy of canvassing against him and threatened to have Leddy's police pension stopped. Leddy—who was actually a party supporter—had assured Reynolds of his first preference vote after Reynolds attempted to strike him. A fight ensued, although onlookers managed to separate the two men, but as Reynolds returned to his car, he repeated the threat of having Leddy's pension withdrawn. Leddy followed him with his gun and in the altercation that followed, Reynolds was fatally wounded.[86] As the shooting was the product of a heated argument and not an attack against the state, and since the victim was not high-profile, the tragic event did not produce a sympathy vote for the party. It did, however, feed into the menace of the gunman propaganda spread by Cumann na nGaedheal, which was further fuelled by unsubstantiated reports that another party candidate was fired at the following day. The London *Daily Herald* reported that 'gunman terror' was sweeping the Free State.[87] Cumann na nGaedheal's polling day message continued the theme. Instead of taking it as an opportunity to remind voters of the issues, the party launched yet another stinging attack on its main opposition and the entire front page of the *Irish Times* bore an advertisement with the caption: 'The gunmen and communists are voting for Fianna Fáil today. How are you voting?'[88]

Cartoons ridiculing the government began to appear in the *Irish Press* in response to Cumann na nGaedheal's campaign style. One such cartoon depicted amused ex-Unionists—the anti-Fianna Fáil posters in the background—reflecting on the election results. The legend below the cartoon read 'Mr Cosgrave has not been returned, but our money has been well spent. As you will see, it has been employed by Cumann na nGaedheal to defame the natives far better than we used to do it'.[89] Fianna Fáil could thus be equally as inventive as its opposition, although such cartoons were not an integral part of the party's strategy. Nor were they as menacing in their tone as some of Cumann na nGaedheal's more extreme propaganda.

By depicting a doomsday scenario if Fianna Fáil took office, the government intended to scare voters into loyalty. However as the research carried out by the authors of an article in *American Political Science Review* indicates, negative advertising has little affect on party supporters, since the message offers no reason to vote for the candidate.[90] Rather, negative advertising presents the indecisive voters with reasons why the opposition is an unsuitable choice, but does not offer any explanation as to why the candidate in question is preferable. The government's remarks, packed with tired expressions, would no longer prove effective in a changed climate. In 1932 Fianna Fáil did not boost its vote by undermining Cumann na nGaedheal's support base, but rather de Valera's party proved more adept at attracting the floating voters, mainly due to the appealing, if somewhat vague, promises being made.

Response to accusations of west-Britainism

Ronan Fanning has argued that Cumann na nGaedheal resorted to the Red scare because the party was 'unable to trump the green card'.[91] But there were some attempts by the party to cut ground away from Fianna Fáil's patriotic platform. For the first time, the majority of its newspaper advertisements bore the party name superimposed on the tricolour. This was arguably an attempt to re-establish Cumann na nGaedheal's nationalist credentials and to detach the party from its alleged reputation for imperialism.[92]

Cumann na nGaedheal made little attempt to publicise its contributions to the imperial conferences which delivered the Statute of
Westminster. The party's near-silence on the achievement can be interpreted as a further attempt to distance itself from the imperialist
reputation attributed to it by Fianna Fáil. The dilemma for Cosgrave's
government was that such important and significant gains had little electoral benefit, for as Fanning has observed, they could be represented by
their opponents 'as but a tainted product of over-friendliness with, if not
subservience to, the British'.[93] It is hardly surprising, therefore, that it
was William Redmond who finally made reference to the issue when—
in language similar to the old Irish Party's defence of the Third Home
Rule Bill—he argued that the statute should have satisfied any 'sensible
patriotic nationalist'.[94] The benefits were not lost on many informed observers. More than one editorial of the *Roscommon Messenger*, a paper so
often critical of the government, praised the merits of the statute.[95] Yet
this success in the international arena, though great, was of little electoral
value. Jackson notes that 'the crowning glory of the party's diplomatic
offensive within the Commonwealth—the Statute of Westminster—
came too late, and was in any case an insufficiently dramatic national
achievement to be of any electoral use'.[96] In a different climate, the
achievement might have wielded a more significant electoral benefit, but
bread-and-butter issues rather than the evolution of the British–Irish relationship were of a more current relevance to the ordinary voter.

The family name and the popular vote

Given that Fianna Fáil was clearly a party on the move, a veritable government-in-waiting, one would have predicted the defection of more
ambitious politicians to a party where new chances were emerging. Yet
Cumann na nGaedheal, instead of losing deputies, actually absorbed five
new members into its ranks in the period immediately preceding the
election. They were, Michael Heffernan, Michael Jordan, John White,
Michael Brennan and William Redmond. On closer inspection, however,
it is unsurprising that when choosing a new affiliation, they joined
Cumann na nGaedheal. Michael Heffernan, Michael Jordan and John
White were all former members of the Farmers' Party. In fact, Heffernan
had been appointed secretary to the minister for posts and telegraphs by
Cumann na nGaedheal following the September 1927 general election.
The maverick Michael Brennan was simply rejoining the party of which
he had once been a member,[97] while William Redmond was without a

party following the disintegration of the National League. Of all the new affiliations, Redmond's was undoubtedly the most beneficial. Although Warner Moss is certainly correct in asserting that Fianna Fáil used Thomas O'Donnell, co-founder of the National League, and James Cosgrave, a former follower, to offset Redmond's membership of Cumann na nGaedheal,[98] he overlooked the immediate and real electoral benefit for Cumann na nGaedheal that resulted from Redmond's addition. For the first time since the birth of the Free State, the party captured a second seat in the Waterford constituency. The increase of almost 29% in first preferences was undeniably due to William Redmond's presence on the ticket, his first preference share in September 1927 having accounted for just over 20%. The propaganda value aside, de Valera's counterbalance to Redmond proved worthless in an electoral sense. James Cosgrave never contested a constituency, while O'Donnell was eliminated and his votes distributed on the sixth count for Dublin County. With only 961 votes, his elimination had no effect on Fianna Fáil's performance in that constituency; two candidates had already been elected by that stage, and no further seats were won.

It was of course his family name and not the Cumann na nGaedheal membership which propelled Captain Redmond into the seventh Dáil. In any case, it was not until the 1965 general election that the affiliation of candidates was even listed on ballot papers.[99] The absence of a listed affiliation prior to this resulted in a higher recognition of names among the electorate.[100] Richard Mulcahy had been aware of the power of the family name when, in May 1927 (at which time Redmond was the leader of the National League), he objected to 'people sticking out for family names such as de Valera or Redmond'.[101] Despite Mulcahy's protestations, Cumann na nGaedheal was not above appealing to the popular vote. Eugene Davy, a well-known international rugby player, was selected to contest Dublin South. Davy—possibly intended to be a sweeper to attract votes which would be passed on to his running mates through transfers, although Cosgrave later claimed that he had felt sure Davy would be elected—held on until the eleventh count, when he was eliminated. His nomination serves as an early example of how parties frequently co-opt distinguished personalities to stand as candidates for electoral gain.

Author of its own misfortune

Just as it was prior to June 1927, the party was yet again to be the author of its own misfortune. The government alienated large sections of the electorate by increasing taxation while at the same time reducing salaries and was also seen to interfere with free speech. Cumann na nGaedheal's political sensitivity, in the words of Tom Garvin, was 'weakened to the extent that it seems to have had a death-wish in the period 1932–3'.[102]

Increased taxation and wage cuts

The government's position on the handling of the country's finances was clear: Cosgrave had previously told the Dáil that Cumann na nGaedheal stood for 'a balanced Budget'.[103] With no elasticity in that rigid approach, solutions had to be found to remedy the deficit that threatened Ernest Blythe's budget. James J. McElligott, secretary of the Department of Finance, ruled out increased taxation, explaining that an increase at any time would be 'psychologically bad', but that the extent required to cover the prospective deficit in 1932/3 would be 'disastrous'. He therefore ruled out a tax increase, unless it was for a limited period. As an alternative, he proposed 'drastic economies' in national expenditure, which he deemed 'not only possible but justifiable'.[104]

In his memorandum McElligott offered four possible alternatives, the second of which is the most pertinent. It proposed the adjustment of pay and pensions for gardaí, teachers and the army, as well as old-age pensions, national health and unemployment insurance and various grants-in-aid, taking into consideration the cost of living.[105] Contrary to McElligott's suggestion, in his supplementary budget Blythe introduced a 4d increase per gallon on petrol and 6d increase on income tax, which consequently brought it to 3s 6d in the pound. He justified the Finance (Increase of Income Tax) Bill, introduced to the Dáil on 6 November 1931, by stating that it would significantly contribute to closing the gap that had appeared in the budget.[106]

In his definitive history of the Department of Finance, Ronan Fanning has observed that Blythe chose to ignore the advice proffered by his departmental secretary because of the effect that such tough measures would have on a government preparing to fight an election.[107] However Cumann na nGaedheal generally showed no propensity to shape its policies around electoral implications, and ultimately the government only postponed rather than rejected the implementation of McElligott's proposal. In a move that inevitably antagonised the electorate, the government later prepared to reduce the wages of the teachers and the civic guards. As a consequence, a statement that Blythe had made in the Dáil was resurrected in which he had said that the government did not intend to modify the pay or allowance of civic guards, assuring them that they did not need to fear anything in the future.[108] However, when Blythe made that statement in 1929, he could not have foreseen the massive downturn in the global economy, especially since the Wall Street Crash did not truly affect the Free State until 1931.

Cosgrave attempted to appeal to the rational side of those affected. Although they would feel the immediate effects of the sacrifice, if it was not imposed, the alternative was a bankrupt state, he reasoned. Cosgrave was obviously the first leader of independent Ireland to encounter economic depression and his response has since been mirrored in that of his successors on comparable occasions. Effectively he was urging the people to bear the cuts in the interests of the nation, just as Charles Haughey would later call on them to tighten their belts and more recently, as Brian Cowen has urged them to do their patriotic duty. Cosgrave had identified the insurmountable problem that the immediate sacrifice required by legislation, which is unpopular in the short-term, invariably obscures the long-term benefits.

While the civic guards and the teaching profession had a shared reaction to the cuts, their approach contrasted greatly. Both groups were naturally appalled, but one stood united while the other split. The Gardaí presented a strong, unified front and were resolute in their opposition. 'A prominent Garda official' described the Garda Síochána as 'the poorest paid force in the English speaking world'.[109] A statement in the *Garda Review* outlined their pay history under the Free State. A reduction of £26 per annum in 1924 was followed up with a further cut of £7 in 1929.[110] Despite these previous deductions, the Department of Finance recommended a further decrease of 5%, which would result in an annual saving of £76,000.[111] Meetings of protest were held in south Carlow, north Co. Dublin, Carrick-on-Shannon, Bray, Limerick, Dundalk, Wexford, Kilkenny, Longford and Westmeath, among other areas. A target of £5,000 to be raised was set and, according to the Garda representatives, would show that they were 'united, determined and organised'.[112] In contrast, the teachers appeared to be betrayed by their representative who accepted the 5% pay decrease. Although they no longer had to contribute to the pension fund, they were outraged, and in a letter to the *Irish Press*, David J. Kelliher, Thomas R. Ryder and Seán Sweeney outlined how the 'grand surrender' did not represent the feelings of teachers throughout the country.[113]

Ban on married, female teachers

Having already antagonised the teachers, the government further provoked the profession. On 1 January 1932 the secretary of the Irish National Teachers' Organisation (INTO) received a communication from the Department of Education stating that female national-school teachers, including junior assistant mistresses, who qualified on or after 1 April 1932 would cease to be eligible for recognition in any capacity in national schools once married. T.J. O'Connell—INTO general secretary, as well as Labour TD—described the announcement as having 'come like a bolt from the blue', adding that 'we have not had any discussion about the matter'.[114]

The headmaster of a non-Catholic school welcomed the move, telling the *Irish Press* that he felt there were too many female teachers and as a result men often found it difficult securing positions. He added that 'he had always been of the opinion that it was too much for women to teach and to look after a family at the same time'.[115] But, a prominent member of the INTO argued that the state would lose rather than gain as a result of the decision. The average age for a woman to marry, he pointed out, was 30, by which stage she would be receiving a wage of about £250. The young teacher who would replace the married woman would earn about £150. Although money would be saved by paying the lower rate, the level of experience would be incomparable. He went on to point out that the savings of about £100 made on salaries would have to go on training the new teacher and as a result there was no substantial beneficial gain to offset the loss.[116]

The INTO framed its opposition to the proposal under the following headings, as outlined by O'Connell:

❖ The regulation would be unconstitutional.
❖ It would make for inefficiency.
❖ It would involve the state in extra expense.
❖ Married women are especially suitable as teachers
    of young children.
❖ Parents favour married women teachers.
❖ There is no demand for such a regulation.
❖ The regulation will mean fewer marriages.
❖ The arguments for the regulation are devoid of substance.[117]

These points were raised at a meeting on 27 May 1932 with the new Fianna Fáil minister for education, Thomas Derrig. Although Cumann na nGaedheal had been swept from power since the ban was imposed, the issues raised with Derrig were nonetheless reflective of the feelings of the teachers' organisation when the party was still in power. Myrtle Hill notes that 'whether under Cumann na nGaedheal or Fianna Fáil, women's role in the Free State was characterised as domestic and familial'.[118] The rule eventually became operative on 27 May 1932, three months after the government defeat at the polls, and was not rescinded until July 1958. And so it was Fianna Fáil who banned married women from continuing in the teaching profession, but as the rule had been a Cumann na nGaedheal initiative and since the voters could not have foretold the results of the February election, it was Cumann na nGaedheal that suffered at the polls.

Letitia Dunbar-Harrison

Cumann na nGaedheal promoted itself as a party inclusive and representative of all sections of society, irrespective of creed. It was also anxious to ensure that the minority groups had a voice. The Letitia Dunbar-Harrison case brought the party into conflict with the church. Dunbar-Harrison was a non-Irish-speaking Protestant and a graduate of Trinity College Dublin who was appointed to the position of county librarian in Mayo following her victory in an open competition. Her selection caused consternation in a county that was, as Moss notes, 'partly Gaelic speaking and almost solidly Catholic'.[119] Her selection was not approved of by the bishops or local priests,[120] and the library committee and the county council refused to sanction the appointment. The government, however, stood by her and dissolved the council.

The situation, which was exploited by de Valera's party, was uncomfortable for the government, which had always promoted the inclusion of Protestants in the new state, but which repeatedly had to defend itself from charges of being west-British as a consequence. As the county was finally balanced between the two main parties, the chairman of the county council, who was also a Cumann na nGaedheal TD, felt obliged to criticise his own party in the Dáil for its decision to dissolve the council.[121] Ultimately Cosgrave agreed to transfer her and to allow the council to resume functioning; the agreement was kept confidential.[122] As embarrassing as the situation was, however, the incident had no real knock-on effect in the county, which was split into two constituencies.

In what was a straight fight in Mayo North, Cumann na nGaedheal lost 8.59% of its vote directly to Fianna Fáil. The 6.72% increase in Fianna Fáil's vote in Mayo South was a combination of Cumann na nGaedheal and Labour losses. Anthony Jordan wrongly claims that Fianna Fáil won five seats.[123] The reality was that the increases in votes did not translate into seat gains; rather both parties retained the seats that they had won in September 1927. While the impact on Cumann na nGaedheal in Mayo was not significant, the government standing beside a Protestant in the face of criticism from the church was of great propaganda value to Fianna Fáil, which again emphasized what Fianna Fáil cited as Cumann na nGaedheal's imperialist tendencies.

Transport

Mobilisation is a key factor in successful electioneering. Transport was a dominant feature of the election, considered noteworthy by the press. The fleets of motor cars were deemed to be the 'big feature' of the Dublin election at least.[124] At the bottom of its advertisements, Cumann na nGaedheal had called on its supporters to lend their cars to the party on polling day. The party, however, fell foul of an unpopular decision. Legislation regulating buses led bus owners to take revenge. Those owners registered a 'practical protest' by lending many of the smaller buses to Fianna Fáil instead of the government party.[125]

The increase in the cost of petrol under the Finance (Increase of Income Tax) Bill was a further incentive for owners to take action. During the debate on the second stage of the bill, Fianna Fáil's Séamus Moore had warned that the tax would destroy a number of businesses.[126] Moore's warning was borne out in the *Waterford News* on 20 November. Michael Furniss, the secretary of the Nobad Bus Company, announced that the Waterford to Dungarvan route, one of its more popular services, had been abandoned due to the price hikes, which had meant an annual increase of £1,400 on petrol alone.[127] The case of Nobad was not isolated. The more that Cumann na nGaedheal legislated, the bigger the group of discontented voters grew.

The *Irish Press*, treatment of prisoners and the government's reaction

A further example of the government's poor judgement can be identified in its reaction to editorials published in the *Irish Press* on 22, 24 and 29 December 1931 and 9 January 1932. Frank Gallagher had written the series of editorials in response to circulating rumours in parts of the country that prisoners were being assaulted.[128] The matter had also been brought to the attention of Fianna Fáil TDs by Seán Lemass and Gerald Boland in a circular requesting that deputies raise issues of maltreatment reported to them by members of the local cumainn in the Dáil. If the government's response during question time was not considered satisfactory, then the subject was to be raised again in the adjournment.[129] During the sixth Dáil, at least 39 questions were raised alleging dubious Garda activity. In many instances, deputies felt that the questions they raised were not adequately dealt with, thus implying a flippant attitude on the part of the government, and so many of those cases were later discussed in more detail in adjournment debates. There is not a single volume of the debates during the life of the sixth Dáil that does not call Garda activity into question or record instances of alleged ill-treatment of prisoners.

When the government summonsed Frank Gallagher before a military tribunal on charges of seditious libel, it made a grave error. A propensity for rash, heavy-handed decisions seemed to be confirmed, while also suggesting that the government was attempting to obstruct free speech. Furthermore, the date of the trial was disastrous as it opened only a fortnight before the election, thus ensuring a sympathy vote for Fianna Fáil.

The tribunal, due to start on 19 January 1932, was adjourned until 25 January and proved to be one of the longest of its kind on record at the time.[130] Cecil Lavery, opening the prosecution, asserted that a 'deliberate attack' had been made on the entire Garda force. Moreover, the government had been implicated through allegations that its methods of administering the law were deliberately brutal and unconstitutional.[131] The court sat for eleven days and over 55 witnesses were called. The president of the tribunal concluded that:

> we are satisfied that the true interpretation of these articles is to impute that the Executive government were party in a conspiracy to a system of beating prisoners arrested under the provisions of the Constitution Amendment (No.17) Act. This suggestion is entirely without foundation.[132]

The defendant was convicted on all counts. The Irish Press Ltd and Frank Gallagher were each fined £100, and costs were not allowed.

Counsel for the defence ensured that the government's seemingly heavy-handed response was emphasized: 'for the last 31 years there had not been a prosecution for seditious libel in this country, and they [the people] were not so innocent of what had been going on for that period'.[133]

At the same time that Gallagher was penning his articles, however, an incident had occurred that appeared to confirm the rumours of abuse. On 2 January 1932 practically the entire front page of the *Leitrim Observer* covered the death of James Vaugh, a well-known, local Republican leader who had died on Christmas Day after a week's illness.[134] Like most Republican funerals, his was a lavish affair, 'his comrades marching four deep behind the coffin, which was draped with the tricolour'.[135] The findings of an inquest and the results of a post-mortem[136]—carried out by an independent doctor, P.F. Doorly—eventually concluded that Vaugh had died from influenza, measles and congestion of the lung.[137] According to his father, however, the deceased had already had measles as a child. What was of even more importance to determining the cause of death was the fact that allegations had been made of ill-treatment while in recent custody following arrest under the Constitution Amendment Act.

For Fianna Fáil, the inquest provided an excellent propaganda opportunity. The emergence of the details of the Vaugh case had coincided with the publication of Frank Gallagher's controversial articles and his subsequent appearance before the military tribunal. Furthermore, that the chairman of the local Cumann na nGaedheal organisation became mired in the case directly implicated the party in the controversy. When the jury at the inquest assembled for a second meeting, Joseph O'Connor, solicitor for the family, requested that it be discharged because Bernard McGovern—secretary of the local Cumann na nGaedheal branch—was accused of having intimidated Bartley O'Brien, one of the key witnesses. Within an hour, a fresh jury had been empanelled.[138] It was hardly surprising, therefore, that during Gallagher's trial, the state prosecution had been insistent in denying any government conspiracy to cover up alleged Garda misconduct.

Judgement was reserved in Gallagher's seditious libel trial until after the election which meant that the electorate had cast its vote before the outcome was announced. That the articles were found to be groundless did not matter as the damage had been done. Similarly, although ultimately Vaugh's death was not determined to have been caused by maltreatment received in custody nor was it considered to have accelerated the decline in his health, the case served to further undermine a diminishing public confidence in the Garda Síochána and reinforced the perception that Cumann na nGaedheal—thanks to McGovern's meddling—was prepared to interfere with free speech. It was no longer a case of failing to court popularity; the government was now engaging in what Alvin Jackson has termed 'electoral wrist slashing'.[139] As Sean Edmonds noted, during the election campaign Fianna Fáil 'spread the kind of propaganda that had been so effective against the British in 1917–19': imperialism, mistreatment of Republican prisoners, imprisonment without trial and emigration.[140]

Why 1932?

Either Cumann na nGaedheal's unwillingness or inability to court popularity was again apparent in 1932 and yet that strategy had never betrayed the party before; so then why did it in 1932? As the author of a guide to winning elections explains, campaigns and their environment are ever changing; success comes from adaptability and innovation.[141] Fianna Fáil's Seamus Moore, speaking in Wicklow, stated that 'no one would be foolish as to blame the government for the great fall in prices which was worldwide but they were very much to be blamed for adopting the position that no government action was necessary in the face of the depression'.[142] Although Cumann na nGaedheal's approach differed little from other European governments, the crisis had burst onto the Irish scene in an election year.

75.3% of the electorate voted. 44.47% of that vote went to Fianna Fáil, while Cumann na nGaedheal received 35.28%.[143] That the change of government was smooth and uneventful was testimony to the stability that had been created. Frank Munger, in his study of the event, observed that 'the transition of 1932 had been predetermined in 1927 when de Valera agreed to play the game according to the government's rules … What 1927 began, 1932 confirmed'.[144]

Nineteen constituencies did not equal or surpass Cumann na nGaedheal's 1923 share of first preferences.[145] The gap between the share of first preferences of those constituencies that did not improve on the 1923 results in 1932 was much wider than the September 1927 figures. Almost equally, however, the difference in terms of those constituencies that did improve between the percentage of first preferences in 1932 was far greater than those of September 1927.[146]

Given the substantial increases, it would be erroneous to suggest that Cumann na nGaedheal was in terminal decline the year that the party fell from power. However, as Richard Rose and Thomas Mackie point out, 'elections are won and lost by relatively small shifts in votes'. For example, a 0.9% decrease in their vote in 1976 brought to an end an extraordinarily long stint of 44 years of virtuously continuous control of government by the Swedish Social Democrats.[147]

As already noted, the fortunes of British Labour and Cumann na nGaedheal were similar. 'Labour was beaten because of its recent record in office, because it lacked clear policies ... and because their opponents were more attractive to a country desperate for economic improvement.'[148] Less than a year later, contemporary commentators would say the same about Cumann na nGaedheal. Martin Harrop has noted that marketing a political party has more in common with marketing a service than a product; 'services are sold on trust—the belief that the supplier will offer future satisfaction'.[149] Cumann na nGaedheal's unbalanced policy statement and its handling of the economic crisis did not make the party an appealing service-provider. The great energy that Cosgrave's party devoted to pointing out why the electorate should not vote for Fianna Fáil was not matched by a dynamic statement, explaining why the people should vote for Cumann na nGaedheal. While Fianna Fáil—unlike those parties participating in the national government in Britain—had not yet had a chance in power, the party's programme appeared to offer solutions, even if they were not clearly defined.

Cumann na nGaedheal might have been defeated but it had not been routed. Nevertheless, the gains made by Fianna Fáil were a vindication of the party's policies. As de Valera succinctly put it, 'we have had a battle at the polls and our policy has won over theirs'.[150] While Cumann na nGaedheal's political epitaph should have read, 'this party worked with the interests of the people at heart', it more likely would have read 'this party was out of touch with the needs of the people'. Both have an element of truth, but while de Valera's untested party could boast 'Fianna Fáil has a plan',[151] Cumann na nGaedheal was judged by the pessimism of the final administration over which it had presided. Ultimately the people voted for the future, not the past. The party lasted for another nineteen months before attempting to inject new life and purpose by undergoing a political metamorphosis into Fine Gael. But despite being demoralised, Cosgrave and his front bench offered Fianna Fáil an active opposition.

.7.

Transformation, 1932–3

Having never experienced life in opposition, making the transition in 1932 can only have come as a shock to Cumann na nGaedheal. Many deputies took refuge in the notion that Fianna Fáil was unfit for government and that the party would soon be called upon to rescue the state, again. As the collapse of de Valera's administration seemed less likely with the passage of time, the back benches slowly lost interest. There was, however, a clear attempt on the part of Cosgrave and his front-bench colleagues to offer Fianna Fáil a vigorous opposition. Contrary to the usual depictions in the historiography of the period, the party was not demoralised to the point of ineffective opposition. Moreover, when the 1933 election was called—despite its unexpected nature—Cumann na nGaedheal responded with an energetic and fresh campaign. Given the suddenness of the dissolution, the new note struck by the party cannot have been an overnight development. While Cumann na nGaedheal showed no keenness to reacquaint itself with the ordinary voter via a more active branch structure, some of the lessons of 1932—the downfalls of negative campaigning and the necessity for a clearly defined policy—had been learned. Nonetheless, the party found itself on the opposition benches once again. Before the election was called, there had been discussion about the formation of a new national party to rival the dominance of Fianna Fáil. However, the dialogue between members of Cumann na nGaedheal and the Centre Party had not been encouraging until de Valera disarmed politicians, banned the annual Griffith–Collins–O'Higgins commemorative parade and proclaimed the National Guard. The Blueshirts had been the intended targets of these actions, which raised concerns about democracy. The Fianna Fáil leader offered the necessary incentive required to bring about a realignment of the opposition, making Eoin O'Duffy's movement the 'midwife' which brought the United Ireland Party: Fine Gael into being.[1]

Life on the opposition benches

By the time that Cumann na nGaedheal retired to the opposition benches, it had lost touch with the people and members of the parliamentary party were both mentally and physically drained. Kevin O'Higgins had once believed that if de Valera came to power, his government would be short-lived, destroyed by incompetence.[2] Contemporary commentator Warner Moss observed in the aftermath of the 1932 election that 'the conservatives … feel confident that stupid blunders and a revulsion of feeling will deliver their government back to them in a much mangled condition'. (He also suggested that 'a few improvements they did not possess the power to initiate' would also have been made.)[3] Indeed, two months after Fianna Fáil officially took power, Barry Egan predicted in a letter to Liam Burke that there would be a mixture of success and collapse in the new government's programme: success would come as a result of the groundwork laid by the Cumann na nGaedheal administrations, while the failures would be down to the 'stupidity and ignorance' of the Fianna Fáil deputies.[4] He had previously written to Burke expressing the view that after Fianna Fáil had ruined the country, it would once again be Cumann na nGaedheal's responsibility to take up the task of building a sound economy.[5] As the short seventh Dáil progressed and Fianna Fáil defied such expectations, disillusionment set in.

Opposition provided the party with the opportunity to recuperate, but Cumann na nGaedheal members only became more dejected. Such was their appearance that William Norton commented on 'the despondency' displayed by the opposition front bench.[6] While it is difficult to determine the tone of the main opposition's speeches from the Dáil debates, the party's minutes, although often dry and succinct, tellingly comment on the mood. Poor attendance was a recurring issue. As earlier minutes show, attendance in the House was a concern that Cumann na nGaedheal had brought with it when the party crossed the floor, but there was a distinct difference between the concerns expressed in government and in opposition. On 28 March 1930—the first meeting of the parliamentary party to take place following the government's Dáil defeat on the Old Age Pensions Bill—it was decided that future absence without cause would result in expulsion;[7] there is no stated record of this having ever occurred.

In opposition, absenteeism was treated more seriously because deputies were simply not turning up for routine divisions and debates. Thus, an attendance committee, consisting of Michael Davis, The O'Mahony, Margaret Collins-O'Driscoll and Thomas Finlay, was established at a meeting of the party on 27 October 1932. It was also decided that P.S. Doyle, the chief whip, would write to each deputy requesting continued attendance.[8] However, this did not solve the problem, and on 5 April 1933 it was ordered that an attendance book, which had to be signed daily, be kept in the whip's office.[9] These types of direct measures to curb absences clearly indicate that demoralisation had set in; deputies simply no longer saw the point of turning up as they had nothing to lose by being absent. This attitude continued, and is likely to have strengthened, after Cumann na nGaedheal's second successive defeat at the 1933 election. In February, May and June 1934 attention was once again drawn to inactivity in the Dáil and Cosgrave was recorded as having expressed his 'regret' that members were not giving the 'desired attention' to Dáil work.[10]

Furthermore, for the first time the minutes revealed that concerns about attendance extended beyond the Dáil to the actual meetings of the parliamentary party itself. Such a concern had never been recorded in the minutes during Cumann na nGaedheal's time in power. On 28 April 1932 Cosgrave actually had to stress the importance of attending the party's weekly meeting. The very fact that deputies were now absenting themselves, not just from debates, but also even from party meetings further confirms that apathy born of disillusionment had taken hold. This, in part, explains Fine Gael's prolonged stay in the political wilderness. A disciplined government built upon party unity can only be defeated by an equally disciplined opposition, constantly alert should an election be called.[11]

Cumann na nGaedheal has been criticised for its lacklustre performance in opposition, but what Robert Blake wrote of the British Conservative Party is equally true of Cumann na nGaedheal. By 1924 the Conservatives had not been in opposition for nearly ten years and ministers had the benefit of assistance from civil servants and other official sources of help. Once in opposition, that was denied to them and a shadow Cabinet was consequently formed.[12] Cumann na nGaedheal put similar arrangements in place to ensure an effective or, at the very least, an informed opposition. Cosgrave suggested the formation of committees in the areas of finance, external affairs, industry and commerce, local government, the board of works, education, agriculture, justice, defence, lands and fisheries, and posts and telegraphs. Each of these reflected a Cabinet portfolio and although not stated, every committee would have had a nominated spokesman acting as a shadow minister. The members of these committees were never named in the party minutes, but clearly front bench deputies continued to focus on the areas for which they had been responsible in office. Finance was naturally Ernest Blythe's domain; Patrick McGilligan dominated discussions not just on tariffs and industry and commerce, but also on external affairs. Finian Lynch, Daniel McMenamin and

Martin Roddy frequently contributed to the subject of lands and fisheries. Essentially Cosgrave had ordered the formation of a structured opposition. Out of its traditional role as a government, Cumann na nGaedheal could clearly function as a party.

Brian Maye has described Cumann na nGaedheal's performance as having been that of 'an entrenched opposition, proposing nothing and attacking everything',[13] but such an assessment is very much dependent on defining the role of the opposition. Winston Churchill, for example, believed its job was to 'attack the government' rather than propose policies as if it were a 'government in exile'.[14] As Churchill was a contemporary of the Cumann na nGaedheal politicians, it is hardly surprising that his views were not incongruous with those of the party. During the nine-month life of the seventh Dáil, few motions originated from the main opposition benches, two of which came from Cosgrave. On 15 November 1932, he moved a motion of censure and the following day, he proposed a suspension in the collection of land annuities.[15] The second was undoubtedly the more constructive of the proposals, although it jarred with the position that the party had taken in government. Earlier that month, P.S. Doyle had sought to introduce a bill to amend the punishment in the existing law for offences relating to solicitation.[16]

While Cosgrave would later bemoan the fact that, as Fine Gael, the party did not make adequate use of question time, during the seventh Dáil, Cumann na nGaedheal was particularly active. 63% of the party's 57 deputies participated in question time. Of those 36 TDs, some were naturally more active than others. The issues they raised were of both a national and local character and they ranged from questions about the Edenderry Mills in Offaly[17] to the committee's report on the Criminal Law Amendment Act.[18] However, it is not enough for a party to dominate question time for it to be deemed an effective opposition. Charles Stewart Parnell and the obstructionists had after all dominated the proceedings of the House of Commons with rambling speeches—although their motive had been greatly different—but that alone does not constitute an effective opposition.

Michael Gallagher has noted that, although the parliament passes virtually all government legislation, the opposition has a choice as to how that should be followed up: should the opposition accept the government's decisions, or act as a check, exposing mistakes?[19] Cumann na nGaedheal clearly chose the second option. The party was certainly active and going about the job of opposition in an appropriate manner, but just how effective was it? On several occasions, it moved various amendments to government legislation, but they were never adopted. That was hardly surprising given that politics in the Free State was highly polarised around the Civil War, making it extremely unlikely that Cumann na nGaedheal would have succeeded in winning over the back-benchers to support their cause. Effective opposition, in terms of influencing the government, was therefore virtually impossible.

There is a clear difference between proactive and reactive opposition, and Cumann na nGaedheal was certainly in the second category, but how typical was this type of role? Fianna Fáil spent almost five years in opposition from the time that the party entered the Dáil to its achievement of power. The party's performance in the short-lived fifth Dáil, which it had only joined midway through, was unspectacular. As already dealt with in Chapter 3, its contributions to the 1927 motion of no confidence had been minimal. However, by the sixth Dáil, the party had become comfortable in its role and had easily surpassed Labour as the main opposition. Just as Cumann na nGaedheal would later be in opposition, Fianna Fáil was exceedingly active during question time and also moved various amendments to government proposals. The party proposed fresh legislation too. For example, in October 1927 de Valera was granted leave to introduce the Public Safety (Repeal) Bill.[20] In February 1928 Lemass proposed the replacement of the Tariff Commission, which he deemed to be 'unsuitable'.[21] Later the following year he seconded James Ryan's proposal to set up a wheat control board.[22] Also in 1929, de Valera moved to have tariffs imposed on 'all imported flour, save flour admitted under special licence for biscuit manufacture'.[23] On 12 June 1932, both Frank Fahy and Martin Corry sought leave to introduce bills: the former dealt with the humane slaughter of animals, while the latter was intended to amend the existing land acts.[24] These are just some of the numerous examples that reflect Fianna Fáil's activity during its time on the opposition benches.

As already stated, Brian Maye is among those who have criticised Cumann na nGaedheal's style of opposition. It has been observed of biographies and histories of British politicians that they predominantly deal with how those politicians *felt*, but what they actually *did* on a day-to-day basis at the House of Commons is almost completely undescribed.[25] The same is largely true of Irish politicians. Two collaborative articles offered an insight into the daily proceedings of the Commons, while Irish Taoisigh received the same systematic analysis in a 2006 *Political Studies* article.[26]

To date there has been no systematic treatment of daily parliamentary activity by any leader of the opposition. The methodology from the three articles has been applied here to compare and contrast the activity of de Valera and Lemass with that of Cosgrave and McGilligan. De Valera and Cosgrave have naturally been chosen as they were their respective party leaders and in government, were both president of the Executive Council. Lemass and McGilligan both held the position of minister and shadow minister for industry and commerce. They have been chosen because of the influential role they played in their respective parties. Admittedly, de Valera's and Cosgrave's levels of contribution are not representative of the parties that they led. But, as there is no precedent for analysing activity beyond that of a party leader, it is only possible to compare and contrast the activity of those particular individuals when in government and in opposition, thus McGilligan and Lemass have been included to shed more light.

Spacing scores provide a very basic indication of how often leaders intervene in the proceedings with an interjection, question or speech. The sixth Dáil was in session for 315 parliamentary days. As de Valera intervened on 210 days, there were on average 1.5 days between each intervention. In the case of Cosgrave, the seventh Dáil sat for a total of 69 days, of which he intervened on 52 days giving an average of 1.3 days between each intervention.[27] Interestingly, the level of participation in opposition by both leaders roughly corresponds to the degree of activity while in office. Robert Elgie and John Stapleton found that during Cosgrave's decade in power, there were 1.17 days between any type of intervention, while de Valera's recorded figure was 1.98.[28] Thus, in the most general of terms, Cosgrave was more active than de Valera, albeit only very slightly, both in government and in opposition. There were 1.3 days between each of McGilligan's interventions in opposition, while Lemass was only slightly more active with 1.1 days between his. In very general terms, therefore, the levels of activity for all four concerned were quite similar.

Of more value are standardised scores, designed to capture variations in interventions. They provide a more detailed picture of parliamentary participation through the separate figures they supply to represent each activity, while adjusted average scores compensate for the different time frames.[29] The length of the sixth and seventh Dála was considerably different, with the former lasting nearly five years and the latter expiring after only nine months. Tables detailing this activity can be found in Appendix 2. The adjusted average scores, in general, correspond with the findings from the spacing scores to indicate that Cosgrave was more active in opposition than de Valera. Although de Valera made more speeches on a yearly basis, Cosgrave generally intervened more in debates. Similarly the Cumann na nGaedheal leader responded more often to items of business. In 'Leaders, politics and institutional change', the authors note that, although important, it is not enough to simply make a speech, as to do so does not fully constitute participating in proceedings. The more normal expectation is that speakers will listen to opposing views then usually respond to them in some small way.[30] The collective figure for the 'motions or proposed legislation' category reveals that the Fianna Fáil leader certainly proposed more than his Cumann na nGaedheal counterpart. However, this is an unfair assessment as the figures provided for Cosgrave are for a single year's parliamentary activity, as compared to the five analysed for de Valera. When taken on a yearly basis, 1927 was the only year in which de Valera's level of contribution to this category exceeded Cosgrave's. The adjusted averages for Lemass and McGilligan also generally agree with the spacing scores, and bear distinct similarities to those of de Valera and Cosgrave too. Lemass made more speeches per year than McGilligan, although McGilligan was far more active in responding to items of business. The number of interventions made and questions asked by both men roughly correspond.

The activity for 1927 for both de Valera and Lemass was entirely below average.[31] This can be excused by Fianna Fáil's recent decision to enter the Dáil and the initial preference of its deputies to observe proceedings. However, 1930 also recorded an entirely negative participation by de Valera, which is not as easily explained, particularly as that was the year that Cumann na nGaedheal was defeated in a routine division in the Dáil and one would have expected the Fianna Fáil leader to have applied extra pressure on the president. Rather de Valera was more inactive in 1930 than in any other year of the sixth Dáil and his level of participation was also below that of Cosgrave's in 1932. While Lemass also scored in negative figures for certain activities, he was more active than his leader.

Elgie's and Stapleton's standardised scores for government leaders in the years 1923 to 2002 are presented on a graph that shows the level of activity of the heads of successive Irish governments.[32] There is a fundamental problem with the graph; although the X-axis is labelled 'years', the number of bars in the chart exceeds 79, which are the number of years in the study. However, the authors do note that 1923 and 1924 were 'the two most active years on record so far'[33] and this certainly corresponds with their graph. As the anomalies appear to lie in the later years, one can therefore argue with reasonably certainty that Cosgrave was more active than de Valera in government. Only in (what appears to be) 1929 did his level of participation drop below average, where it remained until he left office. In contrast, not a single year of any of de Valera's administrations is recorded in positive figures. As no previous research has been carried out on the performance of deputies other than leaders, it is not possible to draw definite comparisons between the activity of Lemass and McGilligan in opposition and in government.

In general terms both parties conducted life on the opposition benches in a similar manner, and, contrary to accepted views, Cumann na nGaedheal was not demoralised and weakened to the point of inadequate opposition. The Treaty remained a central plank of the party's platform. Although some party deputies, like Margaret Collins-O'Driscoll, criticised the government during the debate on the removal of the Oath for wasting the house's time when more important issues could be discussed,[34] it seemed that the Treaty remained one of Cumann na nGaedheal's main priorities.

Commitment to the Treaty

As already noted in Chapter 6, the Statute of Westminster came too late to be of any electoral benefit to Cumann na nGaedheal, but de Valera was able to avail of that legislation in order to remove the Oath and frame his 1937 Constitution. When he began to dismantle the Treaty, Cumann na nGaedheal was naturally defensive. The contributions to the debate on the removal of the Oath, for example, were particularly telling about the party's mindset. Although John Marcus O'Sullivan was referring to the Free State in general, he, no doubt, had Cumann na nGaedheal in mind when he expressed the view that 'we are bound by a Treaty'.[35] It was this type of language that penetrated the contributions made by Cumann na nGaedheal deputies and the word 'honour' made frequent appearances.[36] It was not only during the debate on the removal of the Oath, however, that the party emphasized its allegiance to the Treaty. When Cosgrave moved a motion of censure in late 1932 on the government's failure to secure a satisfactory solution to its dispute with the British that was damaging the agricultural industry and export trade, he asserted that by breaking the 'pledged words' of Griffith, Collins and the Irish people, it brought 'discredit on the honour and reputation' of the state.[37] During the course of the debate, he displayed an almost protective, parental attitude.

By the time that the 1933 election was called, the Treaty had long since ceased to be of any electoral benefit to the party that endorsed it. However, Cumann na nGaedheal was not in a position to abandon it because, as already discussed, the Treaty was not a policy line, it was the party's raison d'être. The timing of the Statute of Westminster, therefore, is a moot point because it is unlikely that Cumann na nGaedheal would have revised the Treaty settlement to the same extent as Fianna Fáil. De Valera was able to do what Cumann na nGaedheal could not, because he was not honour-bound by the terms of the agreement. Men like Patrick McGilligan, but, more particularly, John A. Costello—who would later declare a republic and take Ireland out of the Commonwealth during his time as Taoiseach of the first inter-party government—might not have felt as similarly bound as their colleagues. Costello later told Michael McInerney that the achievement of a republic had been his aim from about 1926.[38] Nonetheless, a volte-face for Cumann na nGaedheal would not have moved the political system forward, as Fianna Fáil's entry into the Dáil had. There were no positive knock-on effects to be gained. Furthermore, if Cumann na nGaedheal had reversed its position on the Treaty, its leaders would have forfeited their credibility. The debates of the seventh Dáil thus reveal a near-desperation on the part of the party to uphold its reason for existing.

The 1933 general election

The dissolution of the seventh Dáil took the country by surprise. When de Valera asserted that he needed to be sure that his party had the full support of the electorate to carry out its programme for government, he also implied that he needed a majority in government to ensure his programme. Gerald Boland suggested that Fianna Fáil members were not 'office seekers', but rather the party had 'a mission'.[39] It was language worthy of Cumann na nGaedheal. There were certainly differences between Labour and Fianna Fáil regarding the salaries of lower-paid civil servants; a one-party government would not have to satisfy a junior partner. One further and perhaps deciding motivation in calling an early election was the suggestion that a new national party to rival Fianna Fáil should be formed. Dissolution of the Dáil afforded the opportunity to interrupt the negotiations, forcing those involved—the National Centre Party and Cumann na nGaedheal—to refocus their energies on the election. At this early stage, however, Frank MacDermot, the Centre Party's leader, was extremely reluctant to join Cumann na nGaedheal in a formal association, although he did urge his party's supporters not to vote Fianna Fáil. However, the very presence of the Centre Party moved votes away from Cumann na nGaedheal and this was to Fianna Fáil's benefit when it came to the final seat count.

As already established in the previous chapter, there were striking similarities between the final months of the British Labour Party and those of Cumann na nGaedheal. The lack of a clearly defined short-term policy has been identified as a serious weakness in Labour's 1931 campaign;[40] the same was true of that by Cumann na nGaedheal in 1932. Labour's election statement opened with an account of the country's ills, and then moved on to criticising the national government and outlining its failures. A section was dedicated to the achievements of Labour in power. Under the heading 'We must plan or perish', the reader was informed that the party was seeking a majority based on a 'coherent and definite programme'.[41] The document contained such headings as 'Tariffs no cure' and 'Efficiency in government', but the details of the promised programme were never set out. Rather than being a blueprint for action, Labour's document contained vague promises.[42] On the subject of India, for example, referring to the Round Table Conference summoned by the government in 1930, the vague promise was given that, if returned to power, Labour would leave 'no stone unturned to bring the conference to a successful issue'.[43] As the table comparing the Fianna Fáil and Cumann na nGaedheal statements in Chapter 6 has already shown, the latter was so preoccupied with the past and with denouncing its rival that future policy appeared to be forgotten.

By entitling one of its first advertisements, 'This is what Cosgrave will do',[44] Cumann na nGaedheal immediately established a new tone in its campaigning. For the 1933 election an emphasis on future policy contrasted greatly with the approach taken the previous year. References to the past, and in particular the Treaty, were still frequent, but the party was now attempting to offer a programme for government. The nine bulleted points, which provided the central focus of that particular advertisement, set out the party's policies. Point six stated Cosgrave would provide 'work instead of doles'—a statement that was difficult to reconcile with McGilligan's 1924 assertion that 'it is no function of government to provide work for anybody'.[45] According to point seven, Cosgrave would take 'millions off the present mountain of taxation'. Although an admirable sentiment, nowhere in the advertisement was it explained how that might be achieved. Maintenance of the existing rates for old age pensions and other benefits was guaranteed in point nine, and one must wonder if the party felt some embarrassment in making such a claim following Blythe's notorious cut. Heading the list had been the definite statement that 'He will end the disastrous Economic War with Great Britain', which was followed up with the assertion that Cosgrave would end and win the war in three days. 'Three' was emphasized in bold text, but while providing a concise time frame, no explanation was offered as to how a settlement could be effected so speedily. Though vague, this statement had much in common with the concept behind de Valera's 1932 'Fianna Fáil has a plan'. The perception of having a strategy could prove just as effective as an in-depth explanation. That modern manifestos are issued with a brief synopsis is testament to the fact that the general voter does not read lengthy documents. From the outset the party's attitude to the 1933 campaign gave the impression that Cumann na nGaedheal had matured and had recognised the importance of adapting to changing circumstances.

One area where that willingness to adapt was particularly evident was in the party's approach to electioneering. By hiring an advertising agency in 1927, Cumann na nGaedheal had already shown itself willing to undertake new methods of extending party publicity and a readiness to try innovations which might improve its chances. Despite a lapse in 1932, this was resumed at the 1933 election when the party, clearly influenced by campaign developments in the international arena, once more showed a willingness to try new techniques in an attempt to attract new voters.

Paul Smith has noted that film arrived when the conditions of politics were being drastically changed in Europe through the coming of manhood suffrage and the beginnings of mass political participation.[46] In 1918 men over 21 and women over 30 gained the vote causing the electorate in Ireland to expand from 700,000 in 1910 to just less than 2 million in 1918. The voting age for women was later lowered to 21 in 1923, thus expanding the electorate even further. This enlarged audience placed new demands on politicians and, in an age before television, film effectively became a means for mass communication. 2RN, the Irish radio station, had come into existence in 1926, but as has already established, it was non-political in its programming and it was certainly not a tool for electioneering.[47] The first party-political broadcasts were not made until the mid-1950s. Incidentally, Seán MacBride was denied permission by the Department of the Taoiseach to make a political broadcast in 1948 on the grounds that radio was not to be used for the purposes of 'party controversy'.[48] Without the hope of getting airtime on radio, the election film was a realistic response to existing circumstances. Irish television after all lay almost three decades in the future (1961). The advent of sound in the 1930s, made the films even more effective. Not only did they allow politicians to reach audiences on a much wider scale, but they also proved effective in providing the illiterate voter with information otherwise 'locked away' in print media. Film was an attempt to come to terms with the need for political education.

Viewed in a global context, the development can be widely identified. The Russian Bolsheviks had used cinema trains and cinema vans in the early 1920s.[49] In 1932, Hitler used ten short sound films that showed speeches of leading Nazis and mobile vans were used to screen them at open-air meetings. He captured their effectiveness in *Mein Kampf* when he observed how 'many will more readily accept a pictorial presentation than read an article of any length'.[50] In terms of America this technique was not as relevant due to the presence of other tools for mass communication. Radio there was free from the type of restrictions that had been placed on 2RN in the Free State and even the BBC in Britain. In its decision to use film, Cumann na nGaedheal was most probably influenced by the British Conservatives, which first used cinema vans in 1925 and remained the only party in Britain to do so until 1939. By 1929 it had assembled a fleet that toured the country and had even bought the patent on the sound-system used in the vans.[51] Feeling that the Labour Party had a distinct advantage with the popular press, film was believed to be one of the most potent and effective methods of publicity at the Conservative's disposal.[52] For the 1933 general election, Cumann na nGaedheal

{204}

adopted this emerging new technique, and, as far as Irish electioneering was concerned, the party took the lead once more.

Cosgrave made a twenty-minute speech on film, which was recorded by Messrs Lethbrige and Green. While Clann na Poblachta has been credited with the first political propaganda film in Ireland, it was not the first general film. Cosgrave's film was the first time in Irish political history that a 'talkie' had been requisitioned to aid electioneering.[53] 'Applause please', wrote an *Irish Independent* journalist who noted that behind the film lay a remarkable story of 'ingenuity and hustle' that reflected the 'greatest credit' on all concerned.[54] Alfie Byrne, the lord mayor of Dublin, also made an election film,[55] although his was recorded after Cumann na nGaedheal's and showings would have been confined to his constituency of Dublin North.

The film was recorded at the Imperial Hotel in Waterford. Michael Hayes, the former Ceann Comhairle, introduced Cosgrave who then made a vigorous speech lasting close to twenty minutes. Assuming the pose that has become traditional in such political films and, later, party political broadcasts, he sat behind a desk from where he spoke into a microphone. The projected image was very much controlled. By looking straight into the camera to address the viewers, a feeling of intimacy would have been created. There were a number of friendly interruptions from an imaginary audience, giving him an opportunity to reply to his critics, free from the type of heckling common at public meetings.

The film was to be shown from a specially constructed van that would travel to those parts of the Free State, in particular the rural areas, which Cosgrave was unable to visit personally on his two-week tour of the constituencies. It was noted with interest that the registration of the van was ZZ 1916.[56] The film was also shown in parts of Dublin, and reports indicated that it 'aroused considerable interest'.[57] Films were a way of reaching not only the converted, but more importantly the unconverted. Given the novel nature of the idea, aside from spreading the party's policies into areas otherwise not accessed, the showing of a film would undoubtedly have generated more interest than an ordinary meeting. They also communicated Cumann na nGaedheal's message to the illiterate or near-illiterate voters in a way that was not possible through printed material.

The use of film for campaigning coincided with the growth of cinema. By 1930 there were 265 cinema houses on the island of Ireland.[58] As Terence Brown has noted, 1930s Ireland was a decade of 'enthusiastic discovery of celluloid dreams from California' in village halls and city cinemas.[59] Although Cosgrave was unlikely to have been the most entertaining of performers, the novelty of a free showing ensured large audiences. Where a candidate was present, the evening's speaker could then take over an audience already captured. As T.J. Hollins explained in his study of the use of film in British elections, 'the cinema van's original function was not just to propagandise, but to also act as a crowd-puller for what would then become an ordinary, if unusually large, political meeting'.[60] The occasion of the film's first showing was described in a somewhat dramatic, even romantic manner. The *Irish Independent* reported, 'at 4.30 p.m. yesterday a plane flew over Howth, and a little later landed at Baldonnel aerodrome. It brought a film which was shown three hours later, under the moon-light sky, at a Cumann na nGaedheal meeting in Howth'.[61] The *Irish Times* recorded it a great success, observing that 'people around the meeting place were able to remain at the windows of their homes and see and hear the speakers without any difficulty'.[62]

We can only surmise as to how Cosgrave performed on film as there is no known surviving copy of the reel, although it is probable that the former president came across as quite stiff. When television arrived politicians often found it difficult to adapt to cameras, and the image that they projected in the early years tended to be one of un-certainty. Additionally in the absence of a contemporary survey of audience response, we cannot know the impact or influence that it had on voters. The film did show, however, the party's ingenuity at election time and its willingness to adapt; something for which its successor has often been criticised for failing to do and for which Cumann na nGaedheal has not received due credit. Nonetheless, the power of the film should not be overstated. Fianna Fáil's organisational efficiency ultimately trumped Cumann na nGaedheal's electioneering ingenuity.

This apparent professionalism inevitably raises the question: why then was the party not more successful? However, there is no basic correlation between propaganda and votes, and other influences and conditions must be considered.[63] Although the party was certainly more imaginative in its electioneering, as has already been established, Cumann na nGaedheal did not have a network to match Fianna Fáil's grass roots. If life on the opposition benches inspired Cumann na nGaedheal to reassess its style of election campaigning, it did not compel the party to reacquaint itself with the ordinary voter.

A letter to Liam Burke, written in the aftermath of the 1932 election, criticised the party's hierarchy. The eleven Cork-based signatories claimed that they were 'far more in touch with the man in the street, in the Borough, than any of the local executive'. The letter also pointed out that there was no branch in the city, and only a few in the county, of which only one was active.[64] If the local executive was out of touch with the Cork people, then the national executive would have been even further removed. Barry Egan was privy to this letter and forewarned Burke of its contents, in the letter he also confirmed that the local organisation was 'very defective'.[65] It was unlikely that this poor relationship was unique to Cork. The papers of Séamus Fitzgerald—Fianna Fáil activist and later TD for Cork—reveal that organisational difficulties in the county were not unique to Cumann na nGaedheal. He had noted that as far the Fianna Fáil cumann was concerned headquarters in Dublin was 'non-existent' and that the constituency had never received a direction from them. It was felt that the problem extended beyond east Cork.[66] While one statement cannot be taken as representative of Fianna Fáil's organisation in general, Fitzgerald's observations did reflect the Dublin-centred outlook of political parties at this time.

Cumann na nGaedheal fielded 85 candidates for the election; a decrease of 16 since 1932 and the lowest figure for the period 1923 to 1933. This was not an indication, however, that the party was experiencing difficulties attracting candidates. Rather, Cosgrave had written a letter to all of the constituencies that was to be read aloud at every selection convention. Except where there were special circumstances, no more than one extra candidate above the number returned at the previous election was to be selected. Perhaps with his own dissolution in mind, he claimed that de Valera's snap election was a sign that the Fianna Fáil leader felt the ground slipping from under him.[67] But, Cosgrave's instruction was telling. A strategy focused on retaining existing seats and keeping the number of candidates low to reduce the risk of splitting the vote, indicated that the party was on the defensive.

Cosgrave's considered approach was not adhered to in some constituencies. With the benefit of hindsight it can be seen that in Carlow-Kilkenny, despite having nearly two quotas, only one of the party's three candidates was elected; in Dublin South, even with close to four quotas, only three of the five candidates were successful. The outcome was similar in Donegal, Laois-Offaly, Leitrim-Sligo and

Waterford. In each of these cases, had the number of candidates been confined to outgoing deputies or even reduced, the party might potentially have won an extra six seats. The inclusion of extra candidates in Carlow-Kilkenny, Laois-Offaly and Leitrim-Sligo may have been due, however, to the need to nominate candidates from each of the counties that formed the constituencies.

The National Centre Party

The 1933 election had much in common with that of June 1927. Cumann na nGaedheal had then lost votes to the National League, as well as other pro-Treaty candidates. The same pattern was identifiable in 1933, but on this occasion, the party's share of the vote was undermined by the presence of the new National Centre Party—formerly the National Farmers' and Ratepayers' League—led by Frank MacDermot. This new farmers' party sought to disperse the 'bitter memories' of the Civil War and to promote good feeling between all classes.[68] John Coakley has noted that agrarian parties not just in Ireland tended to change their names to 'Centre Party' to widen its appeal.[69] This was particularly relevant to MacDermot's party. Although it described itself as being above Civil War politics, the party was essentially pro-Treaty in its outlook and its composition. There were seven planks to the Centre Party's policy, and the first three in particular—agricultural interests, overseas markets and expenditure—were very similar to those of Cumann na nGaedheal.[70] So too was the style of language used in some of the party's advertisements, one of which asked 'all who put country before party to support us'.[71] As both parties shared a near-identical political philosophy, it therefore appealed to voters on the same ground as Cumann na nGaedheal. The only real difference between them—to the benefit of the Centre Party—was that MacDermot's group was not tainted by ten years of conservative government as Cosgrave's was. It was to this new party, rather than Fianna Fáil, that Cumann na nGaedheal primarily lost votes in 1933.

While the Centre Party could have been a natural ally of Cumann na nGaedheal, in the absence of a voting arrangement, it ate into the party's vote. Although Cosgrave's party called on its supporters to give their subsequent preferences to MacDermot's, the gesture was reciprocated only after some of the Centre Party's meetings were disrupted. On 17 January MacDermot had advised voters to give their lower preferences to the Cumann na nGaedheal candidates,[72] but an advertisement that appeared in the *Roscommon Herald* urged the party's supporters to 'give their next preferences to candidates who are not members of the Fianna Fáil and Labour Parties'.[73] Although this narrowed the field to Cumann na nGaedheal and the independents, it was not an explicit endorsement of Cumann na nGaedheal. At a local level some branches did express their support. A meeting of the Bunninadden, Co. Sligo, branch of the Farmers' and Ratepayers' League, for example, passed a resolution pledging support to the Cumann na nGaedheal candidates, because if that party was not elected, then there would be 'no hope' for the farmers.[74] But despite the occasional utterance of support for Cumann na nGaedheal, the Centre Party ran an independent campaign and never made its endorsement of Cosgrave's team of candidates official by putting it in writing. This was a careful ploy to ensure that the party's separate identity was maintained as MacDermot would have been very much aware of how the previous Farmers' Party had suffered for its close relationship with Cumann na nGaedheal.

Even without the presence of the Centre Party, it is unlikely that Cumann na nGaedheal would have matched Fianna Fáil's performance, but the party's share of votes would undoubtedly have been higher. A quintessential example of this can be identified in the Waterford results. There, the party's share of the vote dropped by 12.01% from the 1932 figure. This decrease can be attributed firstly to the loss of William Redmond, who had died on 17 April 1932, and secondly, to the surprise entry into the field of a Farmers' Party candidate. John Kiersey lost his seat in what was a significant blow to a party that had an otherwise precarious performance history in the constituency.[75] By then Cumann na nGaedheal had clearly recognised the electoral value of the Redmond name and co-opted Bridget, William's wife, to retain the party's seat, which she duly did until her own death in May 1952. But the *Waterford News* quite rightly pointed out that her victory was due to her surname and not her party affiliation,[76] although her status as a landowner ensured that she blended into the membership of Cumann na nGaedheal.

Cumann na nGaedheal appears to have underestimated the appeal of the new party. An article in the *Donegal Vindicator* noted that there was 'much optimism in the Cumann na nGaedheal camp. Their hopes are based on the changing view of the farmer electors, who have almost all turned against the government as a result of the economic conflict with Britain'.[77] The results refuted the presumption that discontented farmers would switch their support to Cumann na nGaedheal. In addition to having its share of the vote undermined in a host of constituencies by the Centre Party, Cumann na nGaedheal also lost a total of seven seats.[78] Cork North was the only constituency where Cosgrave's party was unaffected by the appearance of MacDermot's.

Maurice Manning has noted that MacDermot's party had little time to prepare for the election, and was incapable of matching the spending budgets of the two big parties.[79] But the Centre Party was by far the most professional of the farmers' parties to have yet emerged and the nascent organisation showed more signs of early professionalism than the previous Farmers' Party. In the constituency of Longford-Westmeath, for example, the Centre Party ran two candidates, one from each county. In Longford, advertisements were printed asking the voters to give Belton their first preference, and Fagan their second. On the same day, the reverse was asked of the electorate in Westmeath.[80] The party's vote-management strategy paid off, and Fagan was duly elected. The party's organisation was also lauded in the pages of the *Westmeath Examiner*, which suggested that 'now is the time for them to keep on, and when opportunity again offers they can make their full strength felt'.[81] The paper's editor had earlier observed MacDermot to be an excellent organiser.[82] William Rice Kent's decision to stand for the party in Cork East was a mild indication that the party was being taken more seriously than its predecessor. Kent had been elected on the Fianna Fáil ticket in September 1927, but was now 'satisfied to sign the pledge as the Farmers' candidate'.[83]

The issues

Fianna Fáil persisted with its propaganda that Cumann na nGaedheal was west-British, while an article in the *Mayo News* claimed that the central question in the election was 'Ireland or England?'[84] This was the attitude of many commentators,[85] and a theme that Cumann na nGaedheal was eager to refute. Michael Mansfield—a Fianna Fáil candidate for Waterford—told one audience that the 'West Briton forces' were uniting against Fianna Fáil.[86] During the Treaty debates, Kevin O'Higgins had commented that the terms of the agreement would allow the Irish people to walk into the empire with their heads up.[87] Playing on this remark, a song submitted to the *Waterford News* emphasized Cumann na nGaedheal's links with the Commonwealth. The fifth verse claimed:

Oh! Shame upon those traitors!

Their day is almost done;

Fianna Fáil sends out the call

To keep them on the run!

For we have the young men with us,

Who are ready now to swear

That we'll never join the Empire

With our heads up in the air![88]

In response, Cumann na nGaedheal continuously pointed to the absence of any reference to the republic in Fianna Fáil's campaign. As Senator John McLaughlin put it at his party's convention in Letterkenny, 'the poor old Republic had shrunk beneath the horizon'.[89] However, as was the case in 1932, Fianna Fáil focused on the more immediate issues. Interestingly Cumann na nGaedheal again attempted to reconnect with its nationalist background and the fact that Cosgrave had fought in the Easter Rising was mentioned on several platforms.[90] This was something that had not been generally emphasized in the past.

A minor thread in Fianna Fáil's campaign was the issue of the Senate, which the party linked to its west-Britain propaganda. If returned to office, de Valera planned to abolish or, at the very least, reform the upper house; he followed through on this and abolished the Senate in 1936, although his 1937 Constitution provided for a new upper house, the Seanad. The Senate was viewed with suspicion by Republicans because of its composition; there were no revolutionaries from the 1916 to 1921 period among its members, while the chairman, Lord Glenavy, was a former lord chancellor of Ireland.[91] The upper house had also defeated the Fianna Fáil government's bill to remove the Oath, delaying its passage into law, and this act of defiance further deepened Fianna Fáil's antipathy.[92]

At the centre of the 'Ireland versus Britain' theme was the payment of land annuities. As detailed in Chapter 5, Cumann na nGaedheal had been implacably opposed to the proposal of a moratorium while in government, but now that the party was in opposition it actually proposed a suspension of payment. In a sensational speech in Naas, Cosgrave explained that as farmers were unable to pay more than half of what they had been paying, he would collect no more from them.[93] Cosgrave emphasized that his party's revised stance was not merely a vote-getting stunt, but because of his party's usually inflexible stance on issues, it was inevitably interpreted as a sign of desperation. The editor of the (anti-Cumann na nGaedheal) *Mayo News* likened Cosgrave to the 'drowning man', who would grasp at anything to save him from the wrath of the people he had wronged.[94]

Cosgrave's statement was followed up with the 'No land annuities till November 1934' advertisement.[95] In response, de Valera's party produced an advertisement that claimed 'Fianna Fáil was right all the time'.[96] The Cumann na nGaedheal leader had presented his party's main opposition with the invaluable propaganda claim that 'Even Mr Wm. Cosgrave ... admits it NOW!' The *Roscommon Herald*—another anti-Cumann na nGaedheal paper—in its round up of the news used the heading 'Cosgrave borrows Fianna Fáil plans'.[97] Regardless of whether Cumann na nGaedheal's eyes had been genuinely opened to the difficult position the farmers found themselves in, there was a certain hollowness to the proposal. The *Daily Express* seemed to capture the thoughts of many by describing the announcement as 'a bold and dramatic bid for power'.[98]

De Valera described Cosgrave as being 'on the run, very much trying to catch up',[99] and there certainly appeared to be a degree of accuracy to his claim. Opening Fianna Fáil's campaign in Dublin, he had announced that the government would reduce all land annuities by half,[100] and this was subsequently reaffirmed through the publication of an advertisement displaying a similar title.[101] That Cosgrave made his speech in Naas only *after* de Valera's announcement, suggested that the party felt pressured to offer some tangible concessions. The *Irish Independent* on 4 January had carried an article entitled 'Cosgrave states his policy', which included an unspecified reduction in the payment of annuities. However, this was conspicuously absent on the 'This is what Cosgrave will do' advertisement that appeared in the regional newspapers nearly ten days later.[102] In order to ensure publication, the advertisement would have to have been created and submitted to the papers earlier in the week, and thus pre-dated the Naas announcement of 13 January. Moreover, the *Irish Independent* contended that the policy outlined at Naas had been agreed at a party meeting only the previous morning. Unfortunately the minutes of the parliamentary party do not offer any further insight as they only recorded meeting in January was that of a special gathering at the start of the month to discuss the lord mayor's proposal regarding the formation of a new party. Cumann na nGaedheal had proposed in the Dáil the previous November that the collection of annuities should be suspended for the duration of the Economic War, but that was not the same as advocating a 50% reduction in the sum due. Cosgrave's speech created a confused situation. It signalled that a reduction of the land annuities and a delay in payment was not part of Cumann na nGaedheal's original plan, but rather it was prompted by Fianna Fáil.

Speaking in Cavan, Cosgrave responded to the accusation that Cumann na nGaedheal should have settled the question of annuities before leaving office. 'Eighteen months ago Great Britain was not in a very safe financial position,' he explained. 'Today Britain was in a much sounder financial position than she was at that time'.[103] While this argument is plausible, the fact remains that the farmers who could not afford to pay in 1933, thus prompting Cosgrave's announcement, had been in the same position eighteen months earlier. As already discussed, a collection of correspondence relating to a suspension of payment in the files of the Department of the Taoiseach confirms that the problem had been brought to the government's attention.[104] Cumann na nGaedheal's change in attitude left it open to the charge that the party was actually more concerned with Britain than the Irish people, thus reinforcing the Fianna Fáil claim that it was a pro- or west-British party.

De Valera's decision to retain the annuities in the Free State prompted an economic war—described by Cormac Ó Gráda as a 'silly political wrangle'[105]—with Britain, discussion of which dominated the 1933 campaign. The attitude of the two main parties towards the dispute was telling about each group's relationship with Britain. Cumann na nGaedheal considered it a dispute, and the party's language was couched in terms of negotiating a fair settlement. In contrast, Fianna Fáil viewed the Economic War as exactly that: something to be fought and won. Senator Seán McEllin expressed this viewpoint in an interview in which he talked about seeing the 'economic war to victory'.[106] Throughout Cumann na nGaedheal's campaign there was a constant emphasis on a very definite timetable of three days to settle the dispute. One advertisement reminded voters that the new Dáil was to meet on Wednesday, 8 February, and if they returned a Cosgrave government they could expect an end to the war by the following Saturday.[107] The three-day time frame was bold and ambitious, but it led some caustic observers to remark that any war could be settled in three days through 'surrender'.[108] That Cumann na nGaedheal was proposing a moratorium in the payment of annuities until 1934 indicated that the party viewed victory in the Economic War very differently to Fianna Fáil. Payment of land annuities would continue under a Cumann na nGaedheal government, albeit with a possible temporary suspension. That the party's attitude had changed when it crossed the floor of the Dáil together with the talk of settling the economic dispute, however, served only to cloud Cumann na nGaedheal's policy. This gave the impression that it had been hastily put together on the campaign trail.

The results

Cumann na nGaedheal had few direct seat losses to Fianna Fáil. In fact, not until the 1938 general election did Fianna Fáil attract votes away from Fine Gael in any significant manner.[109] However, the results in the National University confirmed what 1932 had suggested: the pendulum was beginning to swing. Of all the constituencies, the National University arguably acted as the best barometer by which to judge the political climate. Notoriously conservative, it had traditionally been one of Cumann na nGaedheal's strongest constituencies. Although the party still secured a strong percentage of the votes there, its strength had weakened considerably since the high point that had been reached in September 1927. That Republican candidates had become serious contenders from June 1927 had been a portentous sign. The inroad had been confirmed in 1932 when Fianna Fáil claimed a seat from Cumann na nGaedheal, and was reaffirmed in 1933 when de Valera's party took two seats to control the constituency. As the *Mayo News* noted, the National University gave a 'fitting lead to the country'.[110]

Nonetheless Fianna Fáil candidates unseated Cumann na nGaedheal incumbents in only three constituencies: Galway, Dublin South and the National University. The latter two were traditional Cumann na nGaedheal constituencies, and the defeats there were an indication that there was a waning of support for Cosgrave's party. Although the *Northern Standard* reported that Fianna Fáil had also gained a seat in Donegal,[111] it is more probable that the Centre Party was actually the beneficiary of Cumann na nGaedheal's seat loss there. Among the fifteen outgoing Cumann na nGaedheal deputies who lost their seats were some of the party's bigger and better known names: Margaret Collins-O'Driscoll, Michael Hayes, Denis Gorey, and finally, the most well known figure among the defeated, Ernest Blythe. Although ten of Fianna Fáil's incumbents failed to retain their seats, there were no big name casualties among the party's losses. In three constituencies—Cork North, Waterford and Wexford—Cumann na nGaedheal exceeded its 1923 figures but, while encouraging, the results should not be overstated. In 1923 all three had had a low base level—the lowest of all the constituencies—and consequently any increase on those figures was more easily achieved than elsewhere.

The outcome gave de Valera the majority he sought, albeit by only one seat, although at that stage Labour was unlikely to unite with the other opposition parties against Fianna Fáil. Seventy-seven deputies had been elected on the Fianna Fáil ticket, which was the precise number of Republicans who had been executed by the Free State government in the formative years. In his maiden speech, Seán T. O'Kelly took the opportunity to affirm that Fianna Fáil would attempt to 'vindicate them and honour their memory' by 'standing up for the cause' for which they had given their lives.[112] Conveniently overlooked, however, was the fact that 'the seventy-seven dead Republicans had lost their lives because of their fight against the same parliament in which seventy-seven Fianna Fáil deputies now sat'.[113]

The United Ireland Party: Fine Gael

The 1933 election had distracted attention away from the possibility of the formation of a new political party. From the earliest stage Alfie Byrne, the lord mayor of Dublin and legendary independent deputy, played an instrumental role in forging the notion of a new national party, but the genesis of the idea must be attributed to Senator Arthur Vincent. He had written to the press before the 1933 election suggesting a joining of power of Cumann na nGaedheal and the Farmers' Party. Echoing his letter at a speech in Killarney, Vincent explained how he was 'utterly opposed to the methods of procedure adopted by the Fianna Fáil party'. Predicting bad times ahead, he expressed the view that 'every thinking man who is not wedded to the Fianna Fáil party, must gird up his loins and seriously consider what he himself is going to do and whom he is going to follow, for the people must have a leader and an organisation'. Although Vincent admired Frank MacDermot, he felt that the Centre Party was not sufficiently broad enough to offer the type of challenge necessary. Nor was Cumann na nGaedheal on its own likely to be effective. Therefore he proposed a 'real national party, membership of which will dissipate all old time ideas of class and religions and generate a spirit of optimism and endeavour'. He concluded by saying:

> For God's sake at this New Year, let us pull ourselves together, discard our foolish suspicions and hatreds, determine to look after our individual interests and to safeguard the welfare of the country as a whole, not only by collective endeavour but by personal service. To achieve this, a new party is essential.[114]

Byrne echoed these sentiments, and issued his Mansion House call. He argued that unless a national party was created, then the next election would once again return a Fianna Fáil government, but as a result of united action somewhere between 80 and 90 seats could be secured.[115] Cosgrave communicated to Byrne a resolution adopted by the Cumann na nGaedheal standing committee, as well as the party's members in both the Dáil and the Senate, in which the proposal of the lord mayor was welcomed as 'sound and kindly', and he expressed the hope that all elements concerned would 'co-operate in giving effect to it'.[116]

However, Frank MacDermot was reported as having stated that the proposal was 'as great a surprise to him as it was to the public', and added that he would not be a party to any proposal which sought to 'perpetuate the hatreds of the civil war'.[117] He was resolute that the sacrifice of his party's identity and independence would not be good for the country.[118] While he retained these views right up to the formation of the United Ireland Party, he did become more flexible. The uneasiness with the proposed merger was understandable. During the first decade of independence the original Farmers' Party had been weak and alliance with Cumann na nGaedheal had served only to benefit the senior party, while the junior one lost both its identity and its seats. There had been discussions of a voting pact with Cumann na nGaedheal for the 1933 general election, but as already seen, a joint platform was resisted. Although Cumann na nGaedheal advertisements encouraged its supporters to continue their preferences for the Centre Party at that election, the move was not reciprocated. 1933 could be seen as the first major electoral breakthrough for a farmers' party, and although MacDermot's group did not have enough seats to make a difference to the formation of the government, it had certainly made its presence felt. As one contemporary commentator noted, 'the position of the farmer is now receiving unaccustomed attention'.[119]

All counties within the Free State, with the exception of Galway, were represented at the Centre Party convention at the Mansion House that would eventually approve the merger. There was some low level opposition. William Rice Kent, a deputy from Cork East, spoke against the move, although he did not oppose the motion that would ultimately affirm the decision. He later told an *Irish Independent* journalist that he would continue to sit in the Dáil and vote with members of the Centre Party, but that his actions there would be dictated by the interests of the farmers he represented and not the whip.[120] Cavan and Wexford were the only two represented counties that abstained from endorsing the resolution that approved the merger.

The early negotiations between Cumann na nGaedheal and the National Centre Party in 1933 highlighted how the relationship between the old government party and the Farmers' Party representatives had changed, and also reflected the extent to which Cumann na nGaedheal's strength had been compromised. Maurice Manning in his biography of James Dillon notes that in the period after Byrne's Mansion House call, 'for Cumann na nGaedheal ... to merge as equals with a party which did not as yet exist, with an inexperienced and somewhat bizarre leader, and which in some constituencies at least had been hostile to Cumann na nGaedheal, was unthinkable'.[121] But the results of the 1933 election had meant that Cosgrave's party was no longer in a position to offer only a parliamentary secretary-style gesture. In fact the lengths to which Cosgrave and his colleagues went to ensure that the merger definitely occurred revealed the weakness of the Cumann na nGaedheal bargaining position.

As already established, with 11 of its 26 candidates elected, the Centre Party was very much the up-and-coming party of the 1933 election. In his letter calling for the merger, Senator Vincent had commented on how the party had 'life, virility and that indescribable something which makes things go'.[122] In contrast, Cosgrave's party had twice been defeated in the space of twelve months and there was no prospect of resurgence in strength or a return to power. Prophecies of Fianna Fáil's failure as a government had proved to be false, and within Cumann na nGaedheal there was an ever growing sense of disillusionment. Again to refer to Vincent's letter, the party despite its men of ability was no longer a capable living entity. In order to make the transition from opposition to government, the new party's prospects would be better if it contained two reasonably sound parties, rather than an apparently failing one continuing on its own under a new name. Motivated either by its convictions or the lure of office, Cumann na nGaedheal thus took the necessary steps to strengthen its position. Of course, without the Blueshirts, but more particularly de Valera's response to the movement, the merger is unlikely to have occurred.

Disturbances at public meetings had been a feature of the 1933 campaign. Cumann na nGaedheal speakers were the primary target, but the Centre Party had also been affected. It was in this atmosphere that the ACA, under the leadership of T.F. O'Higgins (brother of Kevin), was set up to provide protection and ensure free speech. The Laois-Offaly TD

> did not view the ACA as a political body in its own right. His concern was always Cumann na nGaedheal first, the ACA came second. What he could evidently see was the ACA as a body which could protect Cumann na nGaedheal from the excesses of Communists, the IRA and Fianna Fáil, allowing the party to function unhindered.[123]

Referring to the disturbance at a meeting in Trim, Cosgrave heavily criticised the newly returned government:

> The ACA, or the National Guard, at the time had to create peace out of chaos, which they did. The officers of this State, or the Government of the State, failed to do their duty and an organisation like that came along, and where there had been chaos, helped to contribute to restore peace and order and stability, in the country whereas the Ministry neglected its duty and did not provide sufficient force to preserve order.[124]

The history of the movement and its leader has been expertly examined by Maurice Manning, Mike Cronin and Fearghal McGarry. It is the role of the Blueshirts in prompting the political metamorphosis of Cumann na nGaedheal into Fine Gael which is of relevance here.

Its original objective was to look after the interests of ex-Free State Army Men,[125] and, according to an unsigned letter in Barry Egan's papers, its objectives were claimed to be 'unimpeachably constitutional'.[126] On 20 July 1933 the ACA became the National Guard, and Eoin O'Duffy took over as leader from T.F. O'Higgins. He stressed the continued commitment to constitutionalism. While he was in charge, he would ensure that the organisation was kept within the law, and that illegalities would not be tolerated. In taking the pledge of the National Guard, members swore 'not [to] become or remain a member of any secret society whatsoever'.[127] But despite the proclamations and assurances that the Blueshirts would operate within the parameters of constitutionality, Fianna Fáil responded to the organisation in a manner similar to how the Cosgrave government had handled the threat posed by the IRA. When de Valera resurrected Cumann na nGaedheal's Public Safety Act in August 1933, the *Irish Times* would comment on Fianna Fáil's hypocrisy in using legislation which it had 'assailed with the utmost scorn and fury' at the time of its introduction.[128] Before that, however, O'Sullivan, Blythe and McGilligan—all prominent members of the National Guard—were among those whose licences to possess firearms were revoked on the weekend of 29 and 30 July. In a statement to an *Irish Times* journalist, Blythe explained how he resisted handing over the government-owned revolver that he had carried since the assassination of O'Higgins in 1927. Having left office, he was without the military guard who had protected him while he was a minister; he thus offered to apply for a licence for a privately owned revolver and would then surrender his other fire-arm. A license to hold any fire-arm, however, was revoked on the grounds that it was not deemed necessary. In response, Blythe declared that he had 'no intention of voluntarily making myself a defenceless target at the behest of Mr de Valera or any of his colleagues, acknowledged or unacknowledged'.[129]

Throughout early August the government moved rapidly to disarm members of the National Guard. Fire-arm collection resumed on 1 August and continued the following day, while the Garda presence at government buildings was stepped up on the fourth.[130] Amidst the acrimonious atmosphere in Leinster House and the now often volatile environment at public meetings, O'Duffy continued with his plans, albeit a scaled-back version, for the annual Griffith–Collins–O'Higgins commemorative parade. The government responded on 22 August by reintroducing the controversial Article 2A of the Constitution, banned the parade and proclaimed the National Guard to be illegal. The implications of this were appreciated by the *Irish Times*, which commented that the decision 'may prove to have been a happy turning point in the Free State's fortunes if it brings Cumann na nGaedheal, the Centre Party and General O'Duffy's civic supporters together in a wholehearted effort to win the next general election and to end the economic war'.[131] Indeed, de Valera's government had provided the impetus required to move forward the Cumann na nGaedheal–Centre Party talks that had been ongoing haltingly.

At the talks chaired by Senator Thomas Westropp-Bennett in June, Cosgrave and Hogan had discussed the possibility with MacDermot and Dillon. The Cumann na nGaedheal leader later reported that, although both sides agreed that it was 'time to find a common purpose and a common platform', little advance was made at that meeting.[132] The talks which eventually produced the fusion were widened in August to also include MacEoin, O'Higgins, Mulcahy and Tierney, as well as Patrick Baxter, Charles Fagan and Timothy O'Donovan of the Centre Party. By that stage there was a new sense of urgency to the opposition uniting and on 24 August, O'Duffy was approached about the possibility of the Blueshirts joining a new political organisation under his leadership. He had previously rejected any such notion, but now, as Maurice Manning has noted, 'his organisation was isolated and outside the law, and unless some new and strong allies could be found, its future looked bleak'.[133] Despite some dissenting voices, the proposal was approved by the executive of the National Guard on 8 September.

In his study of Canadian party names, John Coakley noted that 'if they are unsuccessful [parties] may abandon the old name and adopt a new one, symbolically putting failure to death'.[134] Changing the name of a party implies a fresh start, a new beginning. MacDermot was determined that any fusion would not result in the loss of his party's identity and the *Anglo-Celt* reported that negotiations between the two parties had stalled on this point.[135] He asserted that 'the people want a new party, and not an old one as alternative to Fianna Fáil'.[136] The new party was, therefore, inevitably going to be christened with a new name. It was originally called 'The United Ireland Party: Fine Gael', or simply the 'United Ireland Party'. This was to appease the Centre Party in general and MacDermot in particular, who had suggested 'United Ireland' at the first conversation in connection with the proposals and he had 'held to it throughout'.[137] His choice was not simply about ensuring that the larger party's name was replaced; it also sent a clear message about the new party's agenda. As he reminded the delegates at his party's convention on 8 September, 'you all know what a fanatic I am on the subject of a united Ireland'.[138] It is hardly surprising therefore, that the reunification of Ireland was the first point in the new party's manifesto.

Within months the subtitle of 'Fine Gael', which had been suggested by Cumann na nGaedheal's Michael Tierney,[139] was in common usage. Given MacDermot's insistence on calling the party United Ireland, the speed at which it was replaced by the parliamentary party is surprising. Minutes are headed 'United Ireland Party meeting' from 27 September 1933 until 15 March 1934, at which point they are merely marked 'party meeting'. The term 'Fine Gael' was in usage from 21 March 1934, but not consistently as 'United Ireland' still made appearances until (and including) 26 April 1934; it also made a small number of appearances in the 1960s. Tierney's suggestion not only had more of an appeal, but it rolled off the tongue more easily. The name also represented continuity with Cumann na nGaedheal: the organisation of the Irish had become the family of the Irish.

At that critical juncture in the party's history, Eoin O'Duffy and not Cosgrave was selected as leader. As the man O'Higgins is alleged to have instructed 'continue on the same lines', O'Duffy implied continuity. Energetic and charismatic, he appeared to be a Collins-type figure, and consequently he excited the party in a way that Cosgrave was not capable of doing. However, as O'Duffy was not a TD, Cosgrave would continue to lead the party in Dáil Éireann. While Cosgrave commented to the press, after the official formation of Fine Gael, that 'I have the maximum of confidence in the leader',[140] the relationship between the two men was uneasy. O'Duffy dismissed reports of a difference, stating 'there could be no split where there was no unity'.[141]

Cosgrave did not appeal to the Centre Party or the Blueshirts, while even some members of Cumann na nGaedheal had their doubts too. When he did return to the helm following O'Duffy's resignation the following year, Michael Tierney would write to Frank MacDermot that 'the return of Cosgrave to the leadership of the party quite blasts all chances of beating Dev in any measurable time'.[142] Despite the opposition, as leader of the bigger party had he asserted himself, Cosgrave would still have been in a strong enough position to retain the leadership, but to do so would have destroyed the merger. In keeping with the attitude he had displayed in his previous ten years of leadership, Cosgrave put the party and the state above personal interest and made unity a key theme in his pronouncements on the formation of United Ireland. He spoke of how 'divided counsels and divided parties' had been responsible for the election of so many Fianna Fáil deputies. 'Divided forces cannot win a political battle,' he told supporters.[143] And so, for the sake of the country, he stepped aside, because only through a fusion of the opposition could the state be rescued from what he perceived to be the ruinous policies of Fianna Fáil. Cosgrave was also enough of a pragmatist to realise that stepping aside for a non-TD, meant that he would continue as leader of the parliamentary party within the Dáil. When O'Duffy resigned on 21 September 1934, Cosgrave was selected to return to the helm at the following year's Ard Fheis.[144]

There were to be six vice-presidents. Cosgrave was accompanied by James Dillon, Frank MacDermot, Peter Nugent, James Hogan and Michael Tierney. The last three were not Dáil deputies, and although Nugent was the son of an ex-MP, Tierney was the only former TD among them. Cosgrave, MacDermot and O'Duffy were also to each nominate six people to the national executive, bringing it to a total of 25 members. Cosgrave's nominees were from his former front bench: Ernest Blythe, Richard Mulcahy, James Fitzgerald-Kenney, John Marcus O'Sullivan and Daniel Morrissey, as well as John A. Costello, attorney general during the Cumann na nGaedheal administrations. The restriction on the number he could appoint led to some high profile absences, most notably that of Patrick McGilligan. MacDermot chose Patrick Baxter, Robert Hogan, Frederick Barton, Richard Curran, Edward Cussen and E.R. Richards-Orpen. Of these, only Baxter had experience of politics at a national level. (Frederick Barton was the brother of Robert Barton, a signatory of the Anglo–Irish Treaty.) O'Duffy appointed Charles Conroy, Commandant Edward Cronin, Captain Pádraig Quinn, Seán T. Ruane and Colonel Jerry Ryan.[145] Like MacDermot's group, O'Duffy's had little experience of practical politics.

The new party's manifesto was issued to the press following the formation of United Ireland on 8 September. It opened with the party's belief in voluntary reunion of the island, followed by the people's right to decide for themselves their own constitutional status. It went on to criticise the Fianna Fáil government. It also outlined what the party aimed to do for farmers and workers. MacDermot's influence on the manifesto could be clearly identified in point six: 'United Ireland looking to the future, while rooted in the best traditions of the past, will stand for the wiping out of party animosities arising either from the Anglo–Irish war or from civil conflict'. A more detailed 25-point policy programme was presented on 11 November 1933, in advance of the 1934 Ard Fheis at which the programme was to be submitted. It gave a clearer idea of the areas that United Ireland would target, and how it planned to effect change. The topics covered ranged from abolition of proportional representation to the maintenance of free speech. The party aimed to encourage Irish industry by every effective means, including the retention and imposition of tariffs where justified by the results. Constant attention was to be paid to agricultural organisation and marketing, in recognition that agriculture was the fundamental industry of the country. A reconstruction loan of at least £2 million was to be made available for agricultural purposes. A ministry of housing was to be established, and steps taken to ensure that the problem of abolishing slums and unsanitary dwellings would be met with the same thoroughness and determination as would a direct threat to the lives of the people. Attention was to be paid to the Gaeltacht to preserve the language and raise the general conditions there; duty for this was to be discharged to a Gaeltacht Committee under the control of a Gaeltacht Commissioner, appointed by, but independent of the Dáil. The policy of the United Ireland Party in most respects thus represented a definite line of continuity with Cumann na nGaedheal, but there were also some obvious contradictions: some of these could be interpreted as an attempt to rectify previous wrongs or missed opportunities.

The announcement that the opposition parties of Cumann na nGaedheal and the Centre Party, together with the Blueshirts, were to form a new political party was met with scepticism. An editorial in the *Irish Press* observed, 'it has no policy and three leaders',[146] while Labour leader William Norton claimed that 'the new move was an attempt to put old wine in new bottles, but neither the new political label nor the colour of the bottle would make the wine any more palatable than it had been'.[147] Unsurprisingly, MacDermot constantly resisted the concept of continuity and he made it clear from the outset that he held no allegiance to Cosgrave's original party. However for many, Fine Gael was simply Cumann na nGaedheal by another name. Within one year of the transformation, Michael Tierney believed that 'to all intents and purposes, it [Fine Gael] has become Cumann na nGaedheal all over again'.[148] His observation was not unique. The following year Seán Lemass remarked, 'Cumann na nGaedheal is dead, but the spirit lives on in the men of today', while J.J. Collins felt that 'the Fine Gael party would like to forget that they were the Cumann na nGaedheal party up to 1932'.[149] The line of continuity cannot be denied. Certainly new personalities had joined the party and there had been some signs of a shift in policy. However the mark of a successful party and its capacity for long-term survival is its ability to redefine its policies and ideo-logues. De Valera had clearly recognised this in 1927 when he revised his position on the Oath to advance Fianna Fáil. As Cumann na nGaedheal, the party had been unable to change the main planks of its platform because it based its legitimacy on the Treaty, but as Fine Gael it was effectively freed from the burden of adhering to the settlement as de Valera began to dismantle the agreement. Moreover, as 1933 sig-nified a fresh start, the party was not explicitly tied to previous policies.

The United Ireland Party: Fine Gael caused a necessary realign-ment of the opposition parties and proved to be an important milestone in the development of the Irish party system. It was in-tended to offer a convincing challenge to Fianna Fáil and under the new leadership of General Eoin O'Duffy—a charismatic figure who contrasted with the conservative W.T. Cosgrave—it showed early promise. However, despite the inclusion of new elements, Fine Gael was a clear continuity of Cumann na nGaedheal and as a consequence it inherited many of the party's problems, most notably the lack of a proper grass-roots organisation. Consequently, to draw on Andrew Thorpe's observation of Labour's destiny in 1930s Britain, Fine Gael's place on the opposition benches seemed a certainty.[150]

Fine Gael's reluctance to emphasize the continuity is understand-able.[151] There have been 1,121 references to Cumann na nGaedheal in the Dáil and Seanad combined since the party went out of existence in its original form. Although not all have been negative, the party has generally been used as an unflattering point of reference. Ernest Blythe's pension cut has featured heavily,[152] although, as leader of Fine Gael, Enda Kenny twice managed to use it to his benefit to warn the incumbent government of the danger of cuts in social spending.[153] Other recurring topics include the reduction of teachers' salaries,[154] alleged patronage,[155] responsibility for Partition,[156] unemployment,[157] and a neglect of social services,[158] among other political sins. But ref-erence to the Blueshirts—almost invariably associated in the mind of many with the fascist movements that swept southern and central Europe at the time—remains the most common method to taunt members of Fine Gael. However, Cumann na nGaedheal's and later Fine Gael's commitment to constitutional nationalism meant that when O'Duffy's speeches began to show signs of extremism, the party could disengage. Cumann na nGaedheal's legacy is not the Blueshirts, but rather an unyielding commitment to building and upholding the struc-tures of the state and for that it deserves a 'proud place in history'.

" ARGUMENTS "

AGAINST THE TREATY

IRISH LABOUR, IRISH PAPER, IRISH INK.

Cumann na nGaedheal pro-Treaty leaflet used in the general election campaign, 1923.

Right: An election poster for Cumann na nGaedheal referring to Eamon de Valera's 'We will wade through the blood of our fellow Irishmen' speech made in Killarney is covered by one for Fianna Fail in the general election campaign, 1923.
(© Mary Evans Picture Library.)

Below: Captains of the American and Irish hurling teams, W. Finn and J. Humphreys, shake hands at the Tailteann Games, 3 August 1924. The final result was Ireland 5-2, America 1-3. (Courtesy of the National Library of Ireland.)

Irish protesters carrying signs in Boston during Richard Mulcahy's visit, 19 October 1925. (© Bettmann/CORBIS.)

W.B. Yeats and other dignitaries at the funeral of Kevin O'Higgins, 13 July 1927.
(Courtesy of the National Library of Ireland.)

NATIONAL HUMOROUS JOURNAL OF IRELAND

DUBLIN OPINION

Vol. VI. No. 68.
OCTOBER, 1927.

PRICE
THREEPENCE.

TO BRING THE TWO LEADERS TOGETHER,
FOLD ALONG THE DOTTED LINE.

Cover of the *Dublin Opinion* (1927) vol. 68 depicting the divide between Cosgrave and de Valera.
(Courtesy of the National Library of Ireland.)

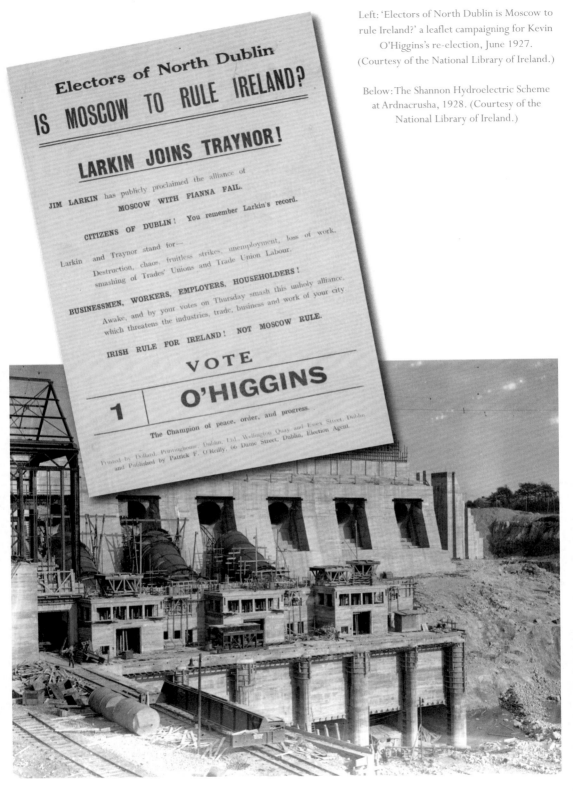

Left: 'Electors of North Dublin is Moscow to rule Ireland?' a leaflet campaigning for Kevin O'Higgins's re-election, June 1927. (Courtesy of the National Library of Ireland.)

Below: The Shannon Hydroelectric Scheme at Ardnacrusha, 1928. (Courtesy of the National Library of Ireland.)

Electors of North Dublin

IS MOSCOW TO RULE IRELAND?

LARKIN JOINS TRAYNOR!

JIM LARKIN has publicly proclaimed the alliance of
MOSCOW WITH FIANNA FAIL.

CITIZENS OF DUBLIN! You remember Larkin's record.

Larkin and Traynor stand for—
Destruction, chaos, fruitless strikes, unemployment, loss of work, smashing of Trades' Unions and Trade Union Labour.

BUSINESSMEN, WORKERS, EMPLOYERS, HOUSEHOLDERS!
Awake, and by your votes on Thursday smash this unholy alliance, which threatens the industries, trade, business and work of your city.

IRISH RULE FOR IRELAND! NOT MOSCOW RULE.

VOTE

| 1 | **O'HIGGINS** |

The Champion of peace, order, and progress.

Printed by Tollard, Printinghouse, Dublin, Ltd., Wellington Quay and Essex Street, Dublin, and Published by Patrick F. O'Reilly, 66 Dame Street, Dublin, Election Agent.

UCD Archives, Mulcahy Papers, P7a/172. 'Don't vote for party puppets',
Cumann na nGaedheal general election poster, 1932. (Courtesy of UCD Archives, School of History and Archives.)

Photograph from an article in the 21 January 1933 edition of the *Illustrated London News* covering campaigning for the general election in the Free State. The original caption read 'A talking-film of Mr Cosgrave, used in his election campaign, which made a favourable impression on electors in several parts of the Free State; the sound-reproduction being excellent'.

(© Mary Evans Picture Library.)

Appendix 1

Issues & areas of policy	Cumann na nGaedheal		Fianna Fáil	
Table 1.1—Percentage of Cumann na nGaedheal and Fianna Fáil statements devoted to issues and areas of policy, 1932	No. of sentences	Percentage of total	No. of sentences	Percentage of total
The Treaty	2	4.65%	2	4.65%
International relations & co-operation	3½	8.13%	2	4.65%
Preservation of traditions / cultural development	2½	5.81%	1	2.32%
Freedom / national history & destiny	8	18.6%	-	-
Unity / Partition	1½	3.48%	2	4.65%
Taxation / land annuities & other repayments	-	-	8	18.6%
Agriculture	-	-	2½	5.81%
Industry	-	-	3	6.97%
The economy (general)	1	2.32%	½	1.16%
Protectionism	-	-	2	4.65%
Trade	-	-	2	4.65%
Government spending	-	-	3	6.97%
Social fairness, justice & equality	-	-	6	13.95%
Communism (denunciation of)	-	-	1	2.32%
The opposition	11½	26.74%	2	4.65%
Total	30		37	

Appendix 2

The adjusted averages for Eamon de Valera and W.T. Cosgrave are outlined in Table 2.1; those for Seán Lemass and Patrick McGilligan are given in Table 2.2. The corresponding standardised scores are displayed in Figures 2.1 and 2.2.[*]

Table 2.1—Adjusted average scores of activity of de Valera and Cosgrave in days per year, 1927–1932						
	EAMON DE VALERA					W.T. COSGRAVE
YEAR	1927	1928	1929	1930	1931	1932
Average no. of speeches	24.89	34.54	27.81	11.93	35.12	16.70
Average no. of interventions	39.11	27.95	25.97	5.42	28.10	38.96
Average no. of questions asked	7.11	5.14	8.35	2.17	2.34	0.93
Average no. of responses to business items	3.56	1.47	2.78	0	3.90	11.13
Average no. of motions or proposed legislation	3.36	1.47	0.93	0	0.78	1.86

TABLE 2.2—Adjusted average scores of activity of Lemass and McGilligan in days per year, 1927-32						
	SEÁN LEMASS					PATRICK McGILLIGAN
YEAR	1927	1928	1929	1930	1931	1932
Average no. of speeches	42.67	45.61	46.38	45.56	40.59	38.96
Average no. of interventions	24.89	43.4	35.25	39.05	42.93	33.39
Average no. of questions asked	28.44	15.45	12.06	21.69	14.05	14.84
Average no. of responses to business items	3.56	2.21	3.71	5.42	7.02	11.13
Average no. of motions or proposed legislation	0	0.74	0	1.08	1.56	0

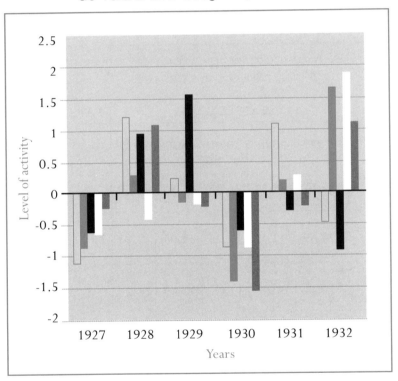

FIG. 2.1—Standardised scores in opposition for
de Valera and Cosgrave, 1927–32

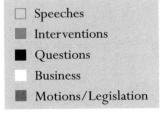

☐ Speeches
▦ Interventions
■ Questions
☐ Business
▦ Motions/Legislation

FIG. 2.2—Standardised scores in opposition for
Lemass and McGilligan, 1927–32

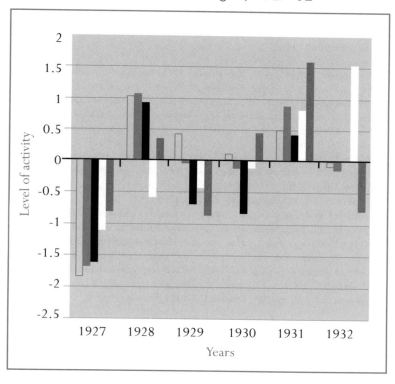

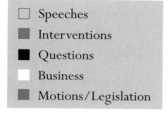

Speeches

Interventions

Questions

Business

Motions/Legislation

*I am grateful to Dr Adrian Dunne of the
UCD School of Mathematical Sciences and
also to Seán Kearns, researcher at InQuest,
for their assistance in helping to calculate
these figures.

Endnotes

INTRODUCTION

[1] *Star*, December 1931.

[2] *Freeman's Journal*, 20 September 1914.

[3] *Hansard*, vol. 259, col. 1192, 20 November 1931 (Winston Churchill).

[4] For a discussion of Cosgrave's leadership skills, see Chapter 1, 16–22.

[5] For a discussion of how de Valera later decided that the controversial Oath was an empty formula so that his Fianna Fáil deputies could gain access to the Dáil, see Chapter 3, 96.

[6] Donal O'Sullivan, *The Irish Free State and its Senate: a study in contemporary politics* (London, 1950), 474.

[7] Address by Brian Hayes on 'Ireland, Republicanism and Fine Gael' to the Ireland Institute, 10 April 2003. See: www.finegael.ie/news/index.cfm/type/details/nkey/22835 (last accessed 1 June 2010).

[8] Stephen Collins. *The Cosgrave legacy* (Dublin, 1996).

[9] Anthony J. Jordan, *W.T. Cosgrave, 1880–1965: founder of modern Ireland* (Dublin, 2006).

[10] Michael Laffan, 'Illustrious corpses: nationalist funerals in independent Ireland', unpublished conference paper, 'The politics of dead bodies' conference, University College Dublin, 10 March 2006.

[11] John M. Regan, *The Irish counter-revolution: Treatyite politics and sentiment in independent Ireland* (Dublin, 1999).

[12] *Hansard*, vol. 262, col. 935, 1 March 1932 (J.H. Thomas).

CHAPTER 1

[1] Cork City and County Archives (CCCA), de Róiste Papers (U271)/A/46, Diary entry, 25 October 1922.

[2] *Dáil debates*, vol. 20, col. 1675, 16 August 1927 (Thomas Johnson).

[3] *Dáil debates*, vol. 3, cols 42–3, 19 December 1921 (Kevin O'Higgins).

[4] *Dáil debates*, vol. 3, col. 186, 3 January 1922 (Countess Markievicz).

[5] *Dáil debates*, vol. 3, col. 54, 20 December 1921 (Sean Etchingham).

[6] *Irish Times*, 17 August 1921.

[7] *Dáil debates*, vol. 3, col. 21, 19 December 1921 (Arthur Griffith).

[8] CCCA, U271/A/46, Diary entry, 19 August 1922.

[9] University College Dublin Archives (UCDA), Papers of Kevin O'Higgins (P197)/108, Kevin O'Higgins to Tom O'Higgins, 30 December 1922.

[10] National Archives of Ireland (NAI), Department of the Taoiseach (DT), S1637, Correspondence between Churchill and members of the provisional government, November 1922.

[11] UCDA, Cumann na nGaedheal and Fine Gael Party minute books (P39/MIN)/1, Eoin MacNeill at conference of standing committee with Executive Council, 3 December 1923.

[12] Article 12 of the Free State Constitution referred to the 'Senate' as one of the bodies of the Oireachtas—although 'Seanad' was noted as an alternate term, Senate was the preferred usage. The term Seanad, and not Senate, was used in de Valera's 1937 Constitution. Therefore in this book, Senate will be used to denote the upper house of the Oireachtas from the foundation of the state and Seanad to denote the body post 1937.

[13] UCDA, P39/MIN/1, Joint meeting of the general and election committee, 29 August 1922.

[14] UCDA, Papers of Richard Mulcahy (P7)/B/325, Richard Mulcahy to Daniel McCarthy, 12 October 1922. In the letter, Mulcahy refers to their earlier conversation about the matter.

[15] UCDA, P7/B/325, J.J. O'Meara to Richard Mulcahy, 5 December 1922. O'Meara also indicated that W.J. Ryan, a Glasnevin-based member and fellow delegate to the conference on 7 December to discuss a new organisation, shared their reservations.

[16] UCDA, P7/B/325, Circular containing objects and programme, 21 December 1922.

[17] CCCA, Papers of Séamus Breathnach, unsorted, observations, [1922?].

[18] UCDA, P7/B/325, Circular from Séamus Hughes, 21 December 1922.

[19] UCDA, P39/MIN/1, Parliamentary conference, 7 December 1922.

[20] UCDA, P7/B/325, Circular from Séamus Hughes, 21 December 1922.

[21] Michael Laffan, The resurrection of Ireland: the Sinn Féin Party, 1916–1923 (Cambridge, 1999), 422.

[22] UCDA, P7/B/325, Circular from Séamus Hughes, 21 December 1922.

[23] UCDA, P39/MIN/1, Parliamentary conference, 7 December 1922.

[24] Mike Cronin, 'Golden dreams, harsh realities: economics and informal empire in the Irish Free State', in Mike Cronin and John M. Regan (eds), Ireland: the politics of independence, 1922–49 (Basingstoke, 2000), 144.

[25] CCCA, U271/A/52, Diary entry, 11 December 1924.

[26] UCDA, P7/B/325, Circular from Seamus Dolan, 6 March 1923.

[27] UCDA, P7/B/325, Meeting, 18 April 1923.

[28] See Chapter 2, 75–7.

[29] Quoted in J.J. Lee, Ireland 1912–1985: politics and society (Cambridge, 1989), 127.

[30] CCCA, U271/A/52, Diary entry, 6 December 1924.

[31] UCDA, P7/B/325, Memorandum on Cumann na nGaedheal provisional constitution, 23 December 1922.

[32] UCDA, Papers of Ernest Blythe (P24)/615, Objects, programme and memorandum, c. 1923.

[33] William T. Cosgrave, Policy of the Cumann na nGaedheal Party (Dublin, 1927), 1.

[34] UCDA, P39/MIN/1, Meeting of provisional general council, 2 February 1923.

[35] UCDA, P39/MIN/1, Meeting of provisional general council, 2 February 1923; Minutes of Cumann na nGaedheal meeting, 9 March 1923.

[36] Alvin Jackson, Ireland 1798–1998: politics and war (Oxford, 1999), 277–8.

[37] See Chapter 5, 141–51.

[38] Maedhbh McNamara and Paschal Mooney, *Women in parliament: Ireland 1918–2000* (Dublin, 2000), 17.

[39] For further information on the murder, see Chapter 6, 178.

[40] *Kildare Observer*, 7 January 1933.

[41] In a letter on 21 April 1927, Kevin O'Higgins thanked Cox for a £100 donation and promised that he would see to it that anonymity would be secured. UCDA, P197/111.

[42] UCDA, P39/MIN/1, Meeting of standing committee, 18 December 1923.

[43] UCDA, P39/MIN/1, Meeting of Cumann na nGaedheal Party, 16 December 1924.

[44] UCDA, P39/MIN/1, Meeting of the executive organising committee, 20 January 1925.

[45] UCDA, P39/MIN/1, Meeting of the executive organising committee, 6 February 1925.

[46] See Chapter 2, 43–4.

[47] CCCA, U271/A/55, Diary entry, 13 September 1927.

[48] John Horgan, *Irish media: a critical history since 1922* (London, 2001), 7.

[49] Michael Gallagher, *Irish elections 1922–44: results and analysis* (Limerick, 1993), 45, 84, 115, 147, 176.

[50] UCDA, P39/MIN/1, Finance report, 29 June 1923.

[51] Ronan Fanning, *Independent Ireland* (Dublin, 1983), 101.

[52] UCDA, P39/MIN/1, Parliamentary conference, 7 December 1922.

[53] CCCA, Papers of Barry Egan (U404)/2, Circular from Seamus Dolan, 3 May 1923.

[54] UCDA, P7/B/325, Seamus Dolan to each deputy, 15 February 1923.

[55] UCDA, P7/B/325, Circular from Seamus Dolan, 15 February 1923.

[56] UCDA, P39/MIN/1, Meeting of Cumann na nGaedheal Party, 9 March 1923.

[57] UCDA, P39/MIN/1, Meeting of Cumann na nGaedheal Party, 1 June 1923.

[58] UCDA, P39/MIN/1, Organiser's report, 6 July 1923.

[59] UCDA, P39/MIN/1, Parliamentary conference, 7 December 1922.

[60] UCDA, P39/MIN/1, Special meeting of the general and election committee, 3 October 1922.

[61] UCDA, P7/B/325, Circular from Séamus Hughes, 21 December 1922.

[62] CCCA, U271/A/46, Diary entries, 28 August 1922 and 8 September 1923.

[63] UCDA, P39/MIN/1, Special meeting of standing committee, 27 November 1923.

[64] UCDA, P39/MIN/1, Meeting of standing committee, 17 April 1924.

[65] UCDA, P39/MIN/1, Meeting of Ard Comhairle, 13 May 1924.

[66] UCDA, P39/MIN/1, Meeting of standing committee, 30 May 1924.

[67] UCDA, P24/453, Séamus Hughes to Ernest Blythe, 22 September 1924.

[68] UCDA, P24/453, Séamus Hughes to Ernest Blythe, 17 September 1924.

[69] UCDA, Papers of Desmond and Mable FitzGerald (P80)/1101, Statement on views of standing committee relative to the political aspect of the present situation, 16 October 1924.

[70] UCDA, P80/372, Seán Lester to Desmond FitzGerald, 8 December 1924.

[71] *Irish Times*, 9 September 1922.

[72] Eunan O'Halpin, 'William Thomas Cosgrave', in James McGuire and James Quinn (eds), *Dictionary of Irish biography* (Cambridge, 2009), 881.

[73] *Irish Times*, 9 September 1922.

[74] The National Archives (TNA), Public Records Office (PRO), Cabinet minutes (CAB), 24/139, Report by Samuel Hoare on the position of the Irish provisional government, circulated by the secretary of state for the colonies, 21 September 1922.

[75] Diarmaid Ferriter, *The transformation of Ireland, 1900–2000* (Dublin, 2005), 52–3.

[76] Collins, *The Cosgrave legacy*, 7.

[77] See Tom Garvin, *1922: the birth of Irish democracy* (Dublin, 1996), 67–96.

[78] Garvin, *1922*, 72.

[79] Diarmaid Ferriter, *'Lovers of liberty'? Local government in 20th century Ireland* (Dublin, 2001), 54.

[80] Quoted in Garvin, *1922*, 83.

[81] Brian Farrell, *Chairman or chief? The role of Taoiseach in Irish government* (Dublin, 1971), 18.

[82] CCCA, U271/A/46, Diary entry, 21 August 1922.

[83] UCDA, Papers of Michael Hayes (P53)/304, Draft of book on foundation of the Free State by Michael Hayes, n.d.

[84] Interview with Brian Reynolds, quoted in Brian A. Reynolds, *William T. Cosgrave and the foundation of the Irish Free State, 1922–25: an analysis of the rise to power of William T. Cosgrave and his leadership in creating a structure of government in the Irish Free State* (Kilkenny, 1998), 39.

[85] Farrell, *Chairman or chief?*, 19.

[86] Interview with Ernest Blythe, 29 June 1971, quoted in Reynolds, *William T. Cosgrave*, 54.

[87] *Dáil debates*, vol. 218, col. 1841, 17 November 1965 (John A. Costello).

[88] Fanning, *Independent Ireland*, 63.

[89] Collins, *The Cosgrave legacy*, 38.

[90] Michael Gallagher, *Political parties in the Republic of Ireland* (Manchester, 1985), 41.

[91] Collins, *The Cosgrave legacy*, 43.

[92] Interview by author with Garret FitzGerald, 21 June 2006.

[93] TNA, PRO, CAB 24/139, Report by Samuel Hoare on the position of the Irish provisional government, circulated by the secretary of state for the colonies, 21 September 1922.

[94] TNA, PRO, CAB 24/139, Report by Major Whittaker on the situation in Ireland, circulated by the secretary of state for the colonies, 19 September 1922.

[95] Interview with Jim Dooge, 22 January 2010.

[96] Interview with Jim Dooge, 22 January 2010.

[97] *Seanad debates*, vol. 60, col. 517, 24 November 1965 (William Stanford).

[98] Olivia O'Leary, *Politicians and other animals* (Dublin, 2004), 22.

[99] Lee, *Ireland 1912–1985*, 154.

[100] Terence de Vere White, *Kevin O'Higgins* (London, 1968); John P. McCarthy, *Kevin O'Higgins: builder of the Irish Free State* (Dublin, 2006).

[101] Michael Tierney, in particular, wrote of his displeasure when Cosgrave returned to the leadership after O'Duffy's resignation. See Chapter 7, 221.

[102] UCDA, P39/MIN/4, Fine Gael Party meeting, 18 January 1944.

[103] John A. Murphy, 'The Irish party system', in Kevin B. Nowlan and T. Desmond Williams (eds), *Ireland in the war years and after, 1939–51* (Dublin, 1969), 153.

[104] See Ciara Meehan, 'Fine Gael's uncomfortable history: the legacy of Cumann na nGaedheal', *Éire-Ireland*, 43 (3&4) (fall/winter 2009), 253–66

[105] The best Taoiseach according to this survey being Garret FitzGerald, see Michael Gallagher and Michael Marsh, *Days of blue loyalty: the politics of membership of the Fine Gael party* (Dublin, 2002), 200.

[106] O'Halpin, 'William Thomas Cosgrave', 885; Lemass paid tribute to the 'privations and the sacrifices which he [Cosgrave] endured so that national freedom might be ours'; his capacity for leadership in government; his dignity in opposition; and his willingness to give counsel on matters of national interest when in retirement; see *Dáil Debates*, vol. 218, col. 1839, 17 November 1965.

[107] Farrell, *Chairman or chief?*, 25.

CHAPTER 2

[1] UCDA, Papers of Eoin MacNeill (LA1)/F/305, Address by Kevin O'Higgins to the Irish Society, Oxford University, 31 October 1924.

[2] New York Times, 9 December 1922.

[3] Michael Laffan, 'Arthur Griffith', in James McGuire and James Quinn (eds), Dictionary of Irish biography (Cambridge, 2009), 278.

[4] UCDA, P39/MIN/1, Meeting of newspaper subcommittee, 30 October 1922.

[5] UCDA, P39/MIN/1, Meeting of general election committee, 1 December 1922.

[6] Horgan, Irish media, 8.

[7] UCDA, P39/MIN/1, Meeting of the party, 1 June 1923.

[8] UCDA, P39/MIN/1, Organiser's report, 26 July 1923.

[9] UCDA, P39/MIN/1, Organiser's report, 3 August 1923

[10] Thomas J. Morrissey, A man called Hughes: the life and times of Seamus Hughes, 1881–1943 (Dublin, 1991), 169.

[11] CCCA, U271/A/49, Diary entry, 10 June 1923.

[12] The flight caused much controversy as it was a military plane involved. Thomas Johnson enquired if military planes would be made available to all the parties for electioneering purposes, but was told that Cosgrave had used the plane in a 'presidential work' capacity—Irish Times, 25 August 1923.

[13] For a discussion of Cumann na nGaedheal's use of an aeroplane for electioneering in the Dublin North by-election of 1929 see Chapter 5, 161–2.

[14] Irish Times, 16 August 1923.

[15] CCCA, U271/Dáil material/k, collection of pro-Treaty leaflets, 1923.

[16] Irish Times, 16 July 1923.

[17] Cornelius O'Leary, Irish elections, 1918–1977: parties, voters and proportional representation (Dublin, 1979), 17.

[18] Tom Garvin, Judging Lemass: the measure of the man (Dublin, 2009), 143.

[19] Gallagher, Political parties, 42.

[20] UCDA, P39/MIN/1, Meeting of general council, 4 March 1924

[21] Regan, The Irish counter-revolution 1921–1936, 250

[22] UCDA, P39/MIN/1, Meeting of standing committee, 31 August 1923.

[23] UCDA, P39/MIN/1, Meeting of standing committee, 31 August 1923.

[24] UCDA, LA1/F/252, Diarmuid O'Hegarty to Executive Council, 24 October 1923.

[25] CCCA, U271/A/48, Diary entry, 14 April 1923.

[26] Ernest Blythe interview, programme one, Seven ages documentary series, 2000.

[27] O'Halpin, 'William Thomas Cosgrave', 883.

[28] Dáil debates, vol. 5, col. 920, 16 November 1923 (W.T. Cosgrave).

[29] Fanning, Independent Ireland, 61.

[30] Niamh Puirséil, The Irish Labour Party 1922–73 (Dublin, 2007), 8.

[31] Brian Farrell quoted in Puirséil, The Irish Labour Party, 9.

[32] Garvin, 1922, 174.

[33] Fanning, Independent Ireland, 39.

[34] Margaret O'Callaghan, 'Language, nationality and cultural identity in the Irish Free State, 1922–7: the Irish Statesman and the Catholic Bulletin reappraised', Irish Historical Studies 14 (94) (November 1984), 227.

[35] Dáil debates, vol. 1, cols 596–7, 22 September 1922 (W.T. Cosgrave).

[36] Mel Cousins, The birth of social welfare in Ireland, 1922–52 (Dublin, 2003), 31.

[37] Ronan Fanning, The Irish Department of Finance 1922–1958 (Dublin, 1978), 111.

[38] Michael McInerney, 'Ernest Blythe: a political profile', *Irish Times*, 3 January 1975.

[39] Cormac Ó Gráda, 'The political economy of the old age pension: Ireland *c.* 1908–1940', *Centre for economic research: working paper series* (September 2000), 28.

[40] Cousins, *The birth of social welfare*, 32.

[41] Blythe's cut was included in a collection of 'political gaffes' compiled in 2006—Shane Coleman, *Foot in mouth: famous Irish political gaffes* (Dublin, 2006), 117–20. The cut also featured in an edition of *The Phoenix*'s satirical 'Diary of a Nortsoide Taoiseach' in which 'Bertie Ahern' fictitiously wrote, 'we were still mentionin' it on de doorstep at de last election': *The Phoenix* 22 (7) (April 2004), 27.

[42] *Irish Independent*, 2 May 1927.

[43] *Derry People*, 14 May 1927.

[44] *Clonmel Chronicle*, 11 May 1927.

[45] *Clonmel Chronicle*, 11 May 1927.

[46] *Drogheda Independent*, 7 May 1927.

[47] Ó Gráda, 'The political economy of the old age pension', 35.

[48] Quoted in Fanning, *Independent Ireland*, 54.

[49] *Irish Times*, 12 February 1925.

[50] *Senate debates*, vol. 5, cols 436 and 443, 11 June 1925 (W.B. Yeats).

[51] Quoted in Dermot Keogh, *The Vatican, the bishops and Irish politics, 1919–1939* (Cork, 1986), 128.

[52] Quoted in Keogh, *The Vatican, the bishops and Irish politics*, 128.

[53] Quoted in Bill Kissane, *Explaining Irish democracy* (Dublin, 2002), 211.

[54] Diarmaid Ferriter, *Occasions of sin: sex and society in modern Ireland* (London, 2009), 102.

[55] Mark Finnane, 'The Carrigan Committee, 1930–31', *Irish Historical Studies* 32 (128) (November 2001), 520–1.

[56] Finnane, 'The Carrigan Committee', 532.

[57] Finola Kennedy, 'The suppression of the Carrigan Report: a historical perspective on child abuse', *Studies* 89 (356) (winter 2000), 356.

[58] Kennedy, 'The suppression of the Carrigan Report', 356 and 358.

[59] Toksvig and Hackett were resident in Ireland between 1926 and 1937. Quoted in Ferriter, *Occasions of sin*, 107.

[60] Michael Laffan, '"Labour must wait": Ireland's conservative revolution', in Patrick J. Corish (ed.), *Radicals, rebels and establishments: papers read before the Irish conference of historians* (Belfast, 1985), 203 and 219.

[61] *Dáil debates*, vol. 1, col. 178, 29 June 1920.

[62] Mary Kotsonouris, *The winding-up of the Dáil courts, 1922–1925: an obvious duty* (Dublin, 2004), 23.

[63] Quoted in Regan, *The Irish counter-revolution*, 96.

[64] Kotsonouris, *The winding-up of the Dáil courts*, 190.

[65] Patrick Murray, *Oracles of God: the Roman Catholic Church and Irish politics, 1922–37* (Dublin, 2000), 83.

[66] Quoted in Murray, *Oracles of God*, 85.

[67] Quoted in Keogh, *The Vatican, the bishops and Irish politics*, 124.

[68] McCarthy, *Kevin O'Higgins*, 100.

[69] McCarthy, *Kevin O'Higgins*, 98

[70] Garvin, *Judging Lemass*, 37.

[71] *Dáil debates*, vol. 1, cols 643–4, 25 September 1922 (Kevin O'Higgins).

[72] McCarthy, *Kevin O'Higgins*, 91.

[73] Garvin, *1922*, 114.

[74] TNA, PRO, CAB 24/139, Report by Samuel Hoare on the position of the Irish provisional government, circulated by the secretary of state for the colonies, 21 September 1922.

[75] Garvin, *1922*, 111.

[76] McCarthy, *Kevin O'Higgins*, 169–70.

[77] Garvin, *1922*, 121.

[78] Fearghal McGarry, *Eoin O'Duffy: a self-made hero* (Oxford, 2005), 117–18.

[79] NAI, DT, G2/3, Meeting of the Executive Council, 4 December 1923.

[80] Lee, *Ireland 1912–1985*, 96.

[81] Ronan Fanning, *Independent Ireland*, 44.

[82] Maryann Valiulis, *Almost a rebellion: the Irish Army mutiny of 1924* (Cork, 1985), 35.

[83] UCDA, P7/B/195, Interview between Cosgrave, Mulcahy and IRAO, 25 June 1923.

[84] Valiulis, *Almost a rebellion,* 27–50.

[85] NAI, DT, G2/3, Tobin and Dalton to Cosgrave, 6 March 1924.

[86] Jeffrey Prager, *Building democracy in Ireland: political order and cultural integration in a newly independent nation* (Cambridge, 1986), 117.

[87] Lee, *Ireland 1912–1985*, 186.

[88] Prager, *Building democracy*, 108.

[89] NAI, DT, G2/3, Meeting of the Executive Council, 19 March 1924.

[90] UCDA, P7/C/21, Kevin O'Higgins to Committee of Inquiry into army mutiny, 12 May 1924.

[91] Regan, *The Irish counter-revolution*, 186.

[92] Fanning, *Independent Ireland*, 50.

[93] This occurred on 18 and 21 March 1924.

[94] Interviews with Ernest Blythe and Michael Hayes, 29 June and 16 July 1971, quoted in Reynolds, *William T. Cosgrave*, 84.

[95] According to the minutes for the morning meeting of 19 March, 'at the termination of the meeting, the Minister for Education and the Minister for Finance communicated these decisions [regarding the resignation of the minister for defence and the proposal to place Eoin O'Duffy in complete control of the army] *in person* to the President, who signified his approval'. Again, the minutes for the afternoon meeting of the same day recorded how the 'statement [that Cosgrave would temporarily take up the ministry of defence] was subsequently submitted to the President *in his home*' (italics added).

[96] Regan incorrectly cites 25 March as the date of Cosgrave's return, *The Irish counter-revolution*, 188.

[97] Risteárd Mulcahy, *My father, the general: Richard Mulcahy and the military history of the revolution* (Dublin, 2009), 170

[98] NAI, DT, G2/3, Meeting of Executive Council, 19 March 1924.

[99] *Dáil debates*, vol. 6, col. 2243, 20 March 1924 (Kevin O'Higgins).

[100] NAI, DT, S5478b, Confidential report, 22 December 1948.

[101] CCCA, U271/A/52, Diary entry, 18 November 1924.

[102] UCDA, P80/1110, Joseph McGrath to Séamus Hughes, 25 June 1924; see also Chapter 1.

[103] UCDA, P80/1110, Séamus Hughes to Joseph McGrath, 7 July 1924.

[104] UCDA, P7/b/96, Memorandum by O'Higgins, January 1923.

[105] Prager, *Building democracy*, 113.

[106] Jackson, *Ireland 1798–1998*, 279.

[107] See Regan, *The Irish counter-revolution*, 244–76.

[108] UCDA, P53/304, Draft of a book on the foundation of the Free State by Michael Hayes, n.d.

[109] See Chapter 5, 156–7. The government was preparing legislation to remove the right of appeal to the Privy Council, but the Oath was not to be tampered with. The statute came too close to Cumann na nGaedheal's defeat for the government to have made use of it, but its initial response reflected the party's attitude towards the Treaty and its relationship with Britain.

[110] UCDA, P39/MIN/1, Meeting of the standing committee, 10 October 1924.

[111] McGarry, *Eoin O'Duffy*, 139.

[112] Richard Pine, *2RN and the origins of Irish radio* (Dublin, 2002).

[113] A recording of Hyde's speech, which was made in Irish, is available from the on-line RTÉ archive at www.rte.ie/laweb/brc/brc_1920s.html (1 June 2010).

[114] Pine, *2RN*, 147.

[115] Pine, *2RN*, 145.

[116] Peter Hardiman Scott, 'The development of an approach to the presentation of political and current affairs on television: the experience of the BBC', in M.J. Clark (ed.), *Politics and the media: film and television for the political scientist and historian* (Oxford, 1979), 4.

[117] Pine, *2RN*, 8.

[118] Horgan, *Irish media*, 14.

[119] Mike Cronin, 'Projecting the nation through sport and culture: Ireland, Aonach Tailteann and the Irish Free State, 1924–32', *Journal of Contemporary History* 38 (3) (July 2003), 395–411.

[120] Quoted in *Irish Times*, 4 August 1924.

[121] CCCA, Papers of J.J. Walsh (U355)/2, Unidentified newspaper clipping, n.d.

[122] Quoted in *Irish Times*, 4 August 1924.

[123] Ferriter, *Transformation of Ireland 1900–2000*, 355.

[124] Peter Somerville-Large, *Irish voices: fifty years of Irish life, 1916–1966* (London, 1999), 86.

[125] CCCA, U355/2, Collection of newspaper clippings, *Irish Ireland*, 25 August 1924.

[126] *Irish Times*, 4 August 1924.

[127] Cronin, 'Projecting the nation through sport and culture', 408.

[128] While a version of the Tailteann Games has been held annually in modern times, these games are not considered to be the successors of those of the 1920s.

[129] Cronin, 'Projecting the nation through sport and culture', 410.

[130] *Irish Times*, 12 July 1927.

[131] Memorandum by Bolton Waller, 24 March 1923 in Ronan Fanning, Michael Kennedy, Dermot Keogh and Eunan O'Halpin (eds), *Documents on Irish foreign policy* (DIFP), *volume ii, 1923–1926* (Dublin, 2000), 75.

[132] Michael Kennedy, *Ireland and the League of Nations, 1919–1946: international relations, diplomacy and politics* (Dublin, 1996), 55.

[133] Kennedy, *Ireland and the League of Nations*, 21.

[134] *Dáil debates*, vol. 1, col. 30, 9 September 1922 (George Gavan Duffy).

[135] *Dáil debates*, vol.1, col. 265, 14 September 1922 (George Gavan Duffy).

[136] *Dáil debates*, vol. 1, cols 394–5, 18 September 1922 (Desmond FitzGerald).

[137] Cited in Kennedy, *Ireland and the League of Nations*, 21.

[138] *Irish Times*, 20 April 1923.

[139] *Senate debates*, vol. 1, col. 980, 19 April 1923.

[140] Memorandum, 24 March 1923, in Fanning *et al.*, DIFP, vol. ii, 75.

[141] O'Shiel to each member of the Executive Council, 14 March 1923, in Fanning *et al.*, DIFP, vol. ii, 72.

[142] O'Shiel to each member of the Executive Council, 29 March 1923, in Fanning *et al.*, DIFP, vol. ii, 79.

[143] O'Shiel to each member of the Executive Council, 29 March 1923, in Fanning *et al.*, DIFP, vol. ii, 79.

[144] Memorandum from B.C. Waller, 24 March 1923, in Fanning *et al.*, DIFP, vol. ii, 76.

[145] CCCA, U271/A/49, Diary entry, 13 September 1923.

[146] *Irish Times*, 11 September 1923.

[147] Dermot Keogh, *Twentieth century Ireland: nation and state* (Dublin, 1994), 49.

[148] *Irish Times*, 30 August 1923.

[149] Eunan O'Halpin, '"Weird prophecies": British intelligence and Anglo–Irish relations, 1932–3', in Michael Kennedy and Joseph Morrison Skelly (eds), *Irish foreign policy, 1919–66: from independence to internationalism* (Dublin, 2004), 64.

[150] Report of the Irish delegation, September 1923, in Fanning *et al.*, DIFP, vol. ii, 176.

[151] NAI, DT, S3332, Speech by W.T. Cosgrave, 10 September 1923.

[152] At the signing of the Acts of Accession, Lynch explained that 'Ireland is the youngest of the states represented here, however we are one of the oldest nations of Europe'.

[153] NAI, DT, S3332, Speech by W.T. Cosgrave, 10 September 1923.

[154] UCDA, LA1/G/219, Eoin MacNeill to Agnes MacNeill, 17 September 1923.

[155] 'Our freedom is recognised by the nations of the world. Our status is defined'. Quoted in *Irish Independent*, 11 September 1923.

[156] E.M. Stephens to Kevin O'Shiel, 17 September 1923, in Fanning *et al.*, DIFP, vol. ii, 160.

[157] E.M. Stephens to Kevin O'Shiel, 17 September 1923, in Fanning *et al.*, DIFP, vol. ii, 160.

[158] Quoted in *Irish Times*, 12 September 1923.

[159] *New York Times*, 11 September 1923.

[160] *New York Times*, 15 September 1923.

[161] NAI, DT, G2/2, Minutes of Executive Council meeting, 21 April 1923.

[162] E.M. Stephens to Kevin O'Shiel, 17 September 1923, in Fanning *et al.*, DIFP, vol. ii, 160.

[163] Alfred O'Rahilly to W.T. Cosgrave, 19 June 1924, in Fanning *et al.*, DIFP, vol. ii, 307.

[164] Memorandum from Desmond FitzGerald, 26 June 1924, in Fanning *et al.*, DIFP, vol. ii, 311.

[165] Desmond FitzGerald to Michael MacWhite, 1 July 1924, in Fanning *et al.*, DIFP, vol. ii, 312.

[166] NAI, DT, S3328, Timothy Healy to J.H. Thomas, 8 July 1924.

[167] Kennedy, *Ireland and the League of Nations*, 53.

[168] Michael MacWhite to Joseph P. Walshe, 18 December 1924, in Fanning *et al.*, DIFP, vol. ii, 386.

[169] Michael MacWhite to Joseph P. Walshe, 23 December 1924, in Fanning *et al.*, DIFP, vol. ii, 387.

[170] Memorandum by Kevin O'Shiel, September 1923, in Fanning *et al.*, DIFP, vol. ii, 183.

[171] Gerard Keown, 'Taking the world stage: creating an Irish foreign policy in the 1920s', in Michael Kennedy and Joseph Morrison Skelly (eds), *Irish foreign policy 1919–1966: from independence to internationalism* (Dublin, 2000), 29.

[172] Seán Lester to W.T. Cosgrave and Joseph P. Walshe, 20 August 1924, in Fanning *et al.*, DIFP, vol. ii, 338.

[173] UCDA, P80/1407, Desmond FitzGerald to Mabel FitzGerald [1926?]

[174] Kennedy, *Ireland and the League of Nations*, 72 and 91. In 1929 the Free State decided to announce its candidacy for one of the non-permanent seats on the League's council and was successful. See Chapter 5, 151.

[175] Desmond FitzGerald to Senator N.A. Belcourt, 13 August 1924, in Fanning *et al.*, DIFP, vol. ii, 336.

[176] Dermot Keogh, *Ireland and Europe 1919–1948* (Dublin, 1988), 24.

[177] Brian Maye, *Fine Gael, 1923–1987: a general history with biographical sketches of leading members* (Dublin, 1993), 314–15.

[178] Terence Brown, *Ireland: a social and cultural history 1922–2002* (London, 2004), 250.

[179] Denis Gwynn, *The Irish Free State* (London, 1928), 327–8.

[180] UCDA, Papers of Patrick McGilligan (P35)/148, Unsigned policy document, n.d.

[181] Brendan Delany, 'McLaughlin, the genesis of the Shannon Scheme and the ESB', in Andy Bielenberg (ed.), *The Shannon Scheme and the electrification of the Irish Free State: an inspirational milestone* (Dublin, 2002), 12–14.

[182] Maurice Manning and Moore McDowell, *Electricity supply in Ireland: the history of the ESB* (Dublin, 1984), 21–3.

[183] Manning and McDowell, *Electricity supply in Ireland*, 24–5.

[184] Manning and McDowell, *Electricity supply in Ireland*, 27.

[185] *Dáil debates*, vol. 6, col. 2730, 2 April 1924 (W.T. Cosgrave)

[186] *Irish Times*, 15 March 1924.

[187] *Irish Times*, 10 April 1924 and 3 May 1924.

[188] Quoted in the *Irish Times*, 28 April 1924.

[189] Delany, 'McLaughlin, the genesis of the Shannon Scheme and the ESB', 16.

[190] *Dáil debates*, vol. 9, col. 2817, 19 December 1924 (Patrick McGilligan).

[191] Quoted in Michael Shiel, *The quiet revolution: the electrification of rural Ireland* (Dublin, 2003), 16.

[192] *Dáil debates*, vol. 9, cols 2840–1, 19 December 1924 (Thomas Johnson).

[193] *Irish Times*, 20 December 1924; *Irish Independent*, 24 August 1929 and 6 January 1925.

[194] *Limerick Leader,* 14 February 1925.

[195] Fanning, *Department of Finance*, 185.

[196] *Irish Times*, 23 February 1925.

[197] CCCA, U271/A/54, Diary entry, 23 November 1925.

[198] UCDA, P80/513, Monthly bulletins, 1926–1929.

[199] *Voice of Labour*, 10 July 1926.

[200] Michael McCarthy, 'How the Shannon Scheme workers lived', in Andy Bielenberg (ed.), *The Shannon Scheme and the electrification of the Irish Free State* (Dublin, 2002), 48–72; *High tension: life on the Shannon Scheme* (Dublin, 2004).

[201] Manning and McDowell, *Electricity supply in Ireland*, 18.

[202] Andy Bielenberg, 'Seán Keating, the Shannon Scheme and the art of state-building', in Andy Bielenberg (ed.), *The Shannon Scheme and the electrification of the Irish Free State* (Dublin, 2002), 125.

[203] *Dáil debates*, vol. 9, col. 2856, 19 December 1924 (Patrick McGilligan).

[204] Advertisement reproduced in *75 years of ESB advertising* brochure (Dublin, 2002), 2.

[205] Bielenberg, 'Seán Keating, the Shannon Scheme', 125.

[206] Bielenberg, 'Seán Keating, the Shannon Scheme', 128–9.

[207] Brian Kennedy commenting on *Night's candles are burnt out* for the first programme in the 2000 RTÉ *Seven ages* documentary series.

[208] UCDA, P35/66, Memorandum on ESB control, n.d.

[209] Brian Girvin, *Between two worlds: politics and economy in independent Ireland* (Dublin, 1989), 44.

[210] Ferriter, *Transformation of Ireland*, 316.

[211] *Star*, 13 July 1929.

[212] See, for example, Gerald Boland in the *Roscommon Messenger*, 21 November 1931; *People*, 2 January 1932.

[213] *Oakland Tribune*, 28 January 1930, quoted in *Electrical Mail*, 75th souvenir edition, 2002.

[214] *Irish Times*, 30 July 2002.

[215] CCCA, U404/3, B.C. Waller to Barry Egan, 9 December 1921, and Egan to Waller, 23 December 1921.

[216] Margaret O'Callaghan, 'Old parchment and water: the Boundary Commission on 1925 and the copper fastening of the Irish border', *Búllan: An Irish Studies Journal* 4 (2) (winter 1999/spring 2000), 31.

[217] Kevin Matthews, *Fatal influence: the impact of Ireland on British politics, 1920–1925* (Dublin, 2004), 6.

[218] Fanning *et al.*, DIFP, vol. ii, xxiv.

[219] Memorandum on the organisation of the North-Eastern Boundary Bureau, 14 October 1922, Fanning *et al.*, DIFP, vol. ii, 7–12.

[220] Memorandum, 10 February 1923, Fanning *et al.*, DIFP, vol. ii, 46.

[221] Confidential memorandum, 21 April 1923, Fanning *et al.*, DIFP, vol. ii, 93.

[222] TNA, PRO, CAB 24/162, Historical outline of the Ulster boundary by the government of Northern Ireland, 9 October 1923.

[223] TNA, PRO, CAB 24/167, Abercon to Arthur Henderson at the Home Department, 10 May 1924.

[224] Memorandum from Kevin O'Shiel to each member of the Executive Council, 17 May 1923, Fanning *et al.*, DIFP, vol. ii, 115.

[225] Memorandum, 17 May 1923, Fanning *et al.*, DIFP, vol. ii, 116.

[226] UCDA, P197/110, Kevin O'Higgins to Patrick McCartan, 12 September 1924.

[227] J.J. Walsh, *Recollections of a rebel* (Tralee, 1944), 69.

[228] NAI, DT, S2925, Memorandum, 3 August 1922.

[229] Michael Laffan, *The partition of Ireland 1911–1925* (Dundalk, 1983), 67–8.

[230] TNA, PRO, CAB 24/174, Richard Feetham to Stanley Baldwin, 7 December 1925.

[231] O'Callaghan, 'Old parchment and water', 31.

[232] Geoffrey J. Hand, 'MacNeill and the Boundary Commission', in F.X. Martin and F.J. Byrne (eds), *The scholar revolutionary: Eoin MacNeill, 1867–1945, and the making of new Ireland* (Cork, 1973), 251.

[233] See de Vere White, *Kevin O'Higgins*, 206, and Denis Gwynn, *The history of Partition 1912–25* (Dublin, 1950), 232–3.

[234] TNA, PRO, CAB 24/175, F.B. Bourdillion, secretary to the commission, to the Executive Council, 24 November 1925.

[235] TNA, PRO, CAB 23/51, Notes on proceedings of meetings between the prime minister and representative of the Irish Free State and the prime minister of Northern Ireland, 30 November 1925.

[236] TNA, PRO, CAB 23/51, Notes on proceedings of meetings between the prime minister and representative of the Irish Free State and the prime minister of Northern Ireland, 30 November 1925.

[237] UCDA, Papers of Michael Tierney (LA30)/317, Memorandum, n.d.

[238] Quoted in O'Callaghan, 'Old parchment and water', 32.

[239] TNA, PRO, CAB 23/51, Notes on proceedings of meetings between the prime minister and representative of the Irish Free State and the prime minister of Northern Ireland, 30 November 1925.

[240] Matthews, *Fatal influence*, 229.

[241] See Chapter 6, 170.

[242] Lee, *Ireland 1912–1985*, 145.

[243] See Chapter 5, 145–50.

[244] CCCA, U271/Dáil material/i, Pádraic[Pádraig] Ó Máille to Liam de Róiste, 4 December 1925.

[245] Richard Sinnott, *Irish voters decide: voting behaviour in elections and referendums since 1918* (Manchester, 1994), 43.

[246] Quoted in Hand, 'MacNeill and the Boundary Commission', 262.

[247] UCDA, P39/MIN/ 1, Meeting of general council, 1 December 1925.

[248] Enda Staunton, 'The Boundary Commission debacle, 1925: aftermath and implications', *History Ireland* 4 (2) (summer 1996), 44.

[249] Quoted in John Bowman, *De Valera and the Ulster question, 1917–1973* (Oxford, 1982), 91.

[250] CCCA, U271/A/54, Diary entry, 23 November 1925.

[251] *Irish Independent*, 2 May 1927.

[252] *Irish Independent*, 7 May 1927.

[253] *Irish Times*, 8 June 1927.

[254] *Dáil debates*, vol. 236, col. 2225, 6 November 1968 (Martin Corry).

[255] Kieran Sheedy, *The Clare elections* (Dun Laoghaire, 1993), 358.

[256] See *Irish Independent*, 20 May 1927.

[257] *Sunday Independent*, 5 June 1927.

[258] Arthur Clery had been a judge in the first Republican courts. After the split in 1926, he had retained good relations with both Sinn Féin and Fianna Fáil but chose to continue in political life without an official affiliation.

[259] *Irish Times*, 17 June 1927.

[260] UCDA, LA30/319, John Busteed to D.A. Binchy, 19 May 1927.

[261] D.W. Harkness, *The restless dominion: the Irish Free State and the British Commonwealth of Nations, 1921–31* (New York, 1970), 45.

[262] See Chapter 5, 151.

[263] Harkness, *Restless dominion*, 95.

[264] Donal Lowry, 'New Ireland, old empire and the outside world, 1922–49: the strange evolution of a "dictionary republic"', in Mike Cronin and John M. Regan (eds), *Ireland: the politics of independence, 1922–49* (London, 2000), 169.

[265] Jean van der Poel (ed.), *Selections from the Smuts papers* (7 vols, Cambridge, 1966–73), vol. 5, 73.

[266] Harkness, *Restless dominion*, 84.

[267] Harkness, *Restless dominion*, 98.

[268] Harkness, *Restless dominion*, 98.

[269] UCDA, P35/184, Memorandum, 2 November 1926.

[270] Harkness, *Restless dominion*, 94.

[271] *Irish Times*, 12 July 1927.

[272] UCDA, P80/960, Bill to alter royal style and titles, 9 March 1927.

[273] Quoted in McCarthy, *Kevin O'Higgins*, 235.

[274] Quoted in McCarthy, *Kevin O'Higgins*, 235.

[275] UCDA, LA1/F/305, Address by Kevin O'Higgins to the Irish Society, Oxford University, 31 October 1924.

[276] Arthur Griffith, *The resurrection of Hungary: a parallel for Ireland* (Dublin, 1918, 3rd edn), xvii.

[277] TNA, PRO, CAB 24/182, L.S. Amery memorandum on the proposed creation of a kingdom of Ireland, 13 December 1926.

[278] Quoted in the *Irish Times*, 16 May 1927.

[279] TNA, PRO, CAB 24/182, L.S. Amery memorandum on the proposed creation of a kingdom of Ireland, 13 December 1926.

[280] TNA, PRO, CAB 24/182, L.S. Amery memorandum on the proposed creation of a kingdom of Ireland, 13 December 1926.

[281] Quoted in McCarthy, *Kevin O'Higgins*, 238.

[282] Nicholas Mansergh, *The unresolved question* (Yale, 1991), 273.

[283] Quoted in McCarthy, *Kevin O'Higgins*, 241.

[284] *Dáil debates*, vol. 6, col. 2985, 9 April 1924 (William Redmond).

[285] *Sligo-Leitrim Liberator*, 30 April 1927.

[286] NAI, DT, G2/5, Minutes of the second Executive Council, 19 January 1927.

[287] *Dáil debates*, vol. 18, col. 3, 25 January 1927 (Seán Lyons).

[288] *Dáil debates*, vol. 18, cols 201–02, 26 January 1927 (Seán Lyons).

[289] *Dáil debates*, vol. 18, cols 207–08, 26 January 1927 (Bryan Cooper).

[290] *Dáil debates*, vol. 18, col. 190, 26 January 1927 (Kevin O'Higgins).

[291] *Dáil debates*, vol. 18, col. 190, 26 January 1927 (Kevin O'Higgins).

[292] Albert D. Bolton had written to the editor of the *Irish Independent* that 'the effect of the Bill would be to frighten every penny of available capital away from building operations'. *Irish Independent*, 26 January 1927.

[293] *Sinn Féin*, 16 April 1910.

[294] Josu Mezo, 'Nationalist political elites and language in Ireland, 1922–1937', in Justo G. Beramendi, Ramón Máiz and Xosé M. Núñez (eds), *Nationalism in Europe: past and present* (2 vols, Santiago de Compostela, 1994), vol. 2, 220.

[295] See Chapter 1, 9.

[296] NAI, DT, S3717, Memo from Ernest Blythe to each member of the Executive Council, 16 December 1924.

[297] Lee, *Ireland 1912–1985*, 134.

[298] A. Ó Brolcháin, 'The economic problem of the Gaeltacht', in Bulmer Hobson (ed.), *Saorstát Éireann: Irish Free State official handbook* (Dublin, 1932), 134.

[299] O'Callaghan, 'Language, nationality and cultural identity', 229.

[300] Oliver MacDonagh, *States of mind: a study of Anglo-Irish conflict, 1780–1980* (London, 1983), 117.

[301] Lee, *Ireland 1912–1985*, 134–5.

[302] NAI, DT, S3717, Cosgrave to Mulcahy, August 1926.

[303] Ferriter, *Transformation of Ireland*, 352.

[304] Cosgrave speaking at the Cumann na nGaedheal convention, quoted in *Derry People*, 14 May 1927.

[305] *Derry People*, 8 January 1927.

[306] *Donegal Democrat*, 2 April 1927.

[307] *Dáil debates*, vol. 18, col. 523, 16 February 1927 (Kevin O'Higgins).

[308] *Dáil debates*, vol. 18, col. 314, 8 February 1927 (Kevin O'Higgins).

[309] *Midland Tribune*, 11 June 1927.

[310] *Clare Champion*, 4 June 1927.

[311] Regan, *The Irish counter-revolution*, 271.

[312] *Northern Standard*, 11 February 1927.

[313] *Irish Independent*, 8 February 1927.

[314] One of the major problems that the traders had with the proposals was the compensation clause. The burden of recompensing traders whose licenses were rescinded was to fall on the shoulders of the remaining licensees.

[315] De Vere White, *Kevin O'Higgins*, 172.

[316] *Irish Independent*, 8 February 1927.

[317] *Offaly Chronicle*, 17 February 1927.

[318] *Connacht Tribune*, 26 February 1927.

[319] *Irish Times*, 14 April 1927 and *Clonmel Chronicle*, 16 April 1927.

[320] Warner Moss, *Political parties in the Irish Free State* (New York, 1933), 142.

[321] *Dundalk Democrat*, 28 May 1927 and *Roscommon Messenger*, 4 June 1927.

[322] *Irish Times*, 18 March 1927.

[323] Moss, *Political parties*, 27.

[324] UCDA, P39/MIN/1, Meeting of Cumann na nGaedheal Party, 29 March 1923.

[325] UCDA, P39/MIN/1, Meeting of Cumann na nGaedheal Party, 9 March 1923.

[326] During this time, he dismissed strikers and hired new recruits. Patrick Maume, 'James Joseph Walsh', in James McGuire and James Quinn (eds), *Dictionary of Irish biography* (Cambridge, 2009), 738.

[327] Moss, *Political parties*, 143.

[328] *Irish Independent*, 19 May 1927.

[329] *Dáil debates*, vol. 19, col. 2042, 4 May 1927 (William Norton).

[330] *Dáil debates*, vol. 19, col. 2144, 4 May 1927 (J.J. Walsh).

[331] *Irish Independent*, 19 May 1927.

[332] At meeting of the Executive Council, Ernest Blythe was authorised to investigate the matter and to make a recommendation. No further reference is made to the subject in the minutes. NAI, DT, G2/5, Minutes of the second Executive Council, 19 May 1927. The suspension of those involved was reported in the *Clonmel Chronicle*, 21 May 1927 and the *Offaly Chronicle*, 26 May 1927.

[333] *Mayo News*, 4 June 1927.

[334] *Irish Independent*, 7 October 1926.

[335] William Redmond quoted in the *Roscommon Messenger*, 16 April 1927.

[336] *Roscommon Messenger*, 19 March 1927.

[337] Cornelius O'Leary, *The Irish Republic and its experiment with proportional representation* (Notre Dame, 1961), 50.

[338] Edmond Carey (Cork East), Daniel Hinchin (Cork North), Cornelius Donovan (Cork West) and Matthew Murphy (Limerick).

[339] Daniel Corkery (Cork North), Michael O'Mullane (Dublin South) and Dan Breen (Tipperary).

[340] John P. Neary (Dublin North) and Denis Byrne (Dublin County).

[341] William Larkin (Dublin North).

[342] John Good (Dublin County) and Matthew Quilinan (Limerick).

[343] Mary Guinness (Dublin County).

[344] John J. Bergin (Kildare) and Richard Hipwell (Laois-Offaly).

345 George Henderson (Kildare) and Robert Belton (Longford-Westmeath).

346 Richard Sinnott, 'The electoral system', in John Coakley and Michael Gallagher (eds), *Politics in the Republic of Ireland* (Dublin, 1993, 2nd edn), 69.

347 *Sunday Independent*, 12 June 1927.

348 *Irish Independent*, 11 May 1927.

349 *Irish Independent*, 3 June 1927.

350 The decision of the Fianna Fáil deputies to take the Oath in August 1927 struck panic in Cumann na nGaedheal, particularly after the government barely survived a motion of no confidence. Consequently, the party's attitude towards the September general election was more energetic than was previously the case. The government's willingness to consider changing the voting system because of the composition of the June election was an earlier example of Cumann na nGaedheal's self-preservation instinct.

351 *Donegal Democrat*, 2 April 1927.

352 NAI, DT, S3766, Memorandum, January 1927.

353 NAI, DT, S3766, Memorandum, 16 October 1926.

354 NAI, DT, G2/5, Minutes of the second Executive Council, 2 December 1926.

355 NAI, Papers of Frank MacDermot (1065)/1/2, Kevin O'Higgins to Frank MacDermot, 17 June 1927.

356 The equation for calculating a party's proportionate share of votes is 'the percentage of [a party's] seats minus its percentage of first preference votes'. See John Coakley, 'The election and the party system', in Michael Gallagher, Michael Marsh and Paul Mitchell (eds), *How Ireland voted 2002* (Basingstoke, 2002), 233.

357 Gallagher, *Irish elections, 1922–44*, 84.

358 NAI, 1065/1/1, Kevin O'Higgins to Frank MacDermot, 18 May 1927.

359 Moss, *Political parties*, 157.

360 *Irish Statesman*, 18 June 1927.

361 Arthur Mitchell, *Labour in Irish politics, 1890–1930: the Irish Labour movement in an age of revolution* (Dublin, 1974), 249.

362 *Dublin Evening Mail*, 13 June 1927.

363 *Irish Times*, 14 June 1927.

364 *Irish Independent*, 14 June 1927.

365 *Irish Times*, 11 June 1927.

366 Sinnott, *Irish voters decide*, 98.

367 UCDA, P39/MIN/1, Meeting of the standing committee, 1 April 1927

368 Michael Gallagher, *Electoral support for Irish political parties, 1927–1973* (London, 1976), 30.

369 *Irish Independent*, 7 May 1927

370 *Western People* and *Roscommon Messenger*, 23 April 1927.

371 *Galway Observer*, 12 March 1927.

372 UCDA, P7/b/66, Richard Mulcahy to Patrick Mulcahy, 17 June 1927.

373 UCDA, P7/b/15, John Slattery to Richard Mulcahy, 16 July 1927.

374 Sinnott, *Irish voters decide*, 98.

375 De Vere White, *Kevin O'Higgins*, 234.

376 Coakley, 'The election and the party system', 231.

377 *Irish Independent*, 9 June 1927.

378 Maurice Gorham, *Forty years of Irish broadcasting* (Dublin, 1967), 46.

379 CCCA, U271/A/54, Diary entry, 21 June 1927.

380 *Mayo News*, 18 June 1927 and *Nation*, 25 June 1927.

CHAPTER 3

[1] *Donegal Democrat*, 20 August 1927.

[2] National Library of Ireland (NLI), Johnson Papers, MS. 17162, Report with notes on meeting with President Cosgrave after the assassination of O'Higgins, 12 July 1927.

[3] *Thirty-third annual report of Irish Labour Party and Trade Union Congress* (Dublin, 1927), 44.

[4] *Dáil debates*, vol. 20, col. 868, 26 July 1927 (Patrick Baxter).

[5] *Irishman*, 16 July 1927; *Roscommon Messenger*, 30 July 1927; *Donegal Democrat*, 16 July 1927.

[6] *Irish Times*, 1 August 1927.

[7] *Northern Standard*, 12 August 1927.

[8] *Dáil debates*, vol. 20, col. 839, 26 July 1927 (W.T. Cosgrave).

[9] For the full text of the legislation see www.irishstatutebook.ie (1 June 2010).

[10] *Irish Independent*, 12 July 1927.

[11] *Dáil debates*, vol. 20, col. 1000, 27 July 1927 (Patrick Hogan).

[12] O'Sullivan, *The Irish Free State and its senate*, 216.

[13] *Irish Times*, 15 August 1927.

[14] McInerney, 'Ernest Blythe: a political profile'.

[15] Maurice Manning, *Irish political parties: an introduction* (Dublin, 1972), 13.

[16] Quoted in *Irish Independent*, 11 July 1927.

[17] Prager, *Building democracy in Ireland*, 167.

[18] 'The Public Safety Bill, at least was a necessary safeguard against the remnants of desperate lawlessness which, as the murder of Mr O'Higgins showed, survives in some unknown, but most sinister form', *Irish Times*, 1 August 1927.

[19] *Dáil debates*, vol. 20, col. 952, 27 July 1927 (John Marcus O'Sullivan).

[20] Anne Dolan, *Commemorating the Irish Civil War: history and memory, 1923–2000* (Cambridge, 2003), 37.

[21] *Dáil debates*, vol. 20, col. 842, 26 July 1927 (W.T. Cosgrave).

[22] *Dáil debates*, vol. 20, col. 856, 26 July 1927 (Ernest Blythe).

[23] *Dáil debates*, vol. 20, col. 894, 26 July 1927 (John O'Hanlon).

[24] *Sligo Champion, Southern Star, Clare Champion*, and *Mayo News*, 30 July 1927.

[25] *Irishman*, 23 July 1927.

[26] *Irishman*, 30 July 1927.

[27] Desmond Ryan, *Unique dictator: a study of Eamon de Valera* (London, 1936), 234.

[28] NLI, O'Brien Papers, MS. 15706 (7), Diary entry, 1 August 1927 and MS. 14704 (7), Observations on the 1927 political crisis and Enniskerry affair, n.d.

[29] *Dáil debates*, vol. 20, col. 877, 26 July 1927 (Patrick Hogan).

[30] *Irish Times*, 12 August 1927.

[31] Maurice Manning, 'The *New York Times* and Irish politics in the 1920s', *Études Irlandaises* 9 (1984), 225.

[32] Collins, *The Cosgrave legacy*, 50.

[33] Frank Munger, *The legitimacy of opposition: the change of government in Ireland in 1932* (Beverley Hills, CA, 1975), 21.

[34] *Dáil debates*, vol. 20, col. 1083, 28 July 1927 (William Davin).

[35] *Irish Independent*, 3 June 1927 and *Connacht Tribune*, 4 June 1927.

[36] UCDA, P39/MIN/1, Meeting of the executive organising committee, 20 January 1925.

[37] *Longford Leader*, 10 September 1927.

[38] Peter Mair, *The changing Irish party system* (London, 1987), 15.

[39] *Nation*, 6 August 1927.

40 *Dáil debates*, vol. 19, col. 436, 29 March 1927 (Bryan Cooper).

41 *Limerick Chronicle*, 13 August 1927.

42 *Irish Times*, 11 August 1927.

43 *Dáil debates*, vol. 20, col. 1670, 16 August 1927 (Thomas Johnson).

44 See for example, *Evening Herald*, 11 August 1927; *Irish Independent*, 12 August 1927; *Irish Times*, 15 August 1927; *Kerry People*, 13 August 1927; *Roscommon Herald*, 13 August 1927; *Sligo Champion*, 20 August 1927.

45 Mitchell, *Labour in Irish politics*, 261.

46 Jim Dooge joined Fine Gael in 1947. His grandfather, John P. Dooge, was a Cumann na nGaedheal and later Fine Gael county councillor until 1942, while his aunt had worked as a secretary to Ernest Blythe. He had strong friendships with Michael Hayes, Richard Mulcahy and Seán MacEoin.

47 Interview with Jim Dooge, 22 January 2010. This appears to be corroborated in the memoirs of Desmond FitzGerald's son, Garret. However, Garret FitzGerald's knowledge of the event comes not from his father, but rather from Dooge.

48 Brian A. Reynolds, 'The formation and development of Fianna Fáil, 1926-1933', unpublished PhD thesis, Trinity College Dublin, 1976, 127.

49 Bill Severn, *Irish statesman and rebel: the two lives of Eamon de Valera* (Whitstable, 1971), 142.

50 NLI, O'Brien Papers, MS. 15706 (7), Diary entries, 1, 6, 8 and 12 August 1927.

51 UCDA, Records of the Fianna Fáil Party (P176)/442, Minutes of the parliamentary party, 12 August 1927.

52 *Dáil debates*, vol. 20, col. 1716, 16 August 1927 (John Marcus O'Sullivan).

53 *Dáil debates*, vol. 20, col. 1729, 16 August 1927 (David O'Gorman).

54 *Dáil debates*, vol. 20, col. 1695, 16 August 1927 (Patrick Belton).

55 *Dáil debates*, vol. 20, col.1723, 16 August 1927 (Seán T. O'Kelly); translation provided by Michael Laffan.

56 Moss, *Political parties in the Irish Free State*, 168.

57 *Free Press*, 27 August 1927.

58 *Irish Times*, 13 August 1927.

59 NLI, Johnson Papers, MS. 17165, William Redmond to Thomas Johnson, 12 August 1927.

60 NLI, Johnson Papers, MS. 17165, William Redmond to Thomas Johnson, 15 August 1927.

61 NLI, Johnson Papers, MS. 17165, William Redmond to Thomas Johnson, 17 August 1927.

62 *Dáil debates*, vol. 20, col. 1729, 16 August 1927 (David O'Gorman).

63 *Dáil debates*, vol. 20, col. 1676, 16 August 1927 (Thomas Johnson).

64 *Dáil debates*, vol. 20, col. 1686, 16 August 1927 (William Redmond).

65 NLI, O'Brien Papers, MS. 15704 (7), Observations on the 1927 political crisis and Enniskerry affair, n.d.

66 Commenting after the defeat, Redmond suspected that Jinks had been '"spirited away" as a result of methods of a century back', *Irish Times*, 17 August 1927. Bryan Cooper was later placed at the centre of that theory as the man responsible for mischievously plying Jinks with alcohol before shutting him away or placing him on the train back to Sligo. Another story claimed that Jinks—again most likely under the influence of alcohol—was spotted in front of Nelson's pillar on O'Connell Street looking for inspiration. For a discussion of the various theories see C.S. Andrews, *Man of no property* (Dublin, 1982), 81.

67 *Thirty-fourth annual report of Irish Labour Party and Trade Union Congress* (Dublin, 1928), 25.

68 NLI, Johnson Papers, MS. 17160 (iii), *Observer*, 21 August 1927.

69 NLI, O'Brien Papers, MS. 15704 (7), Observations on the 1927 political crisis and Enniskerry affair, n.d.

[70] *Thirty-fourth annual report of Irish Labour Party and Trade Union Congress*, 25.

[71] O'Brien seems to have been confused in his notes as wrongly cited Robert Smyllie as the editor of the *Irish Times*. The editor at the time was John Healy, who was succeeded by Smyllie in 1934.

[72] NLI, O'Brien Papers, MS. 15704 (7), Observations on the 1927 political crisis and Enniskerry affair, n.d.

[73] Mitchell, *Labour in Irish politics*, 265.

[74] *Dáil debates*, vol. 20, cols 1700 and 1725, 16 August 1927 (John O'Hanlon and Jasper Wolfe).

[75] *Dáil debates*, vol. T, col. 416, 10 January 1922 (Arthur Griffith).

[76] UCDA, P39/MIN/1, Meeting of the standing committee, 27 July 1927.

[77] *Irish Times*, 9 August 1927.

[78] *Evening Herald*, 24 August 1927.

[79] *Evening Herald*, 17 and 18 August 1927.

[80] *Evening Herald*, 26 August 1927.

[81] *Evening Herald*, 25 August 1927.

[82] O'Sullivan, *The Irish Free State*, 196.

[83] McCarthy, *Kevin O'Higgins*, 1.

[84] Collins, *The Cosgrave legacy*, 20–1.

[85] See Chapter 2, 39–44.

[86] *Nation*, 19 February 1925.

[87] *Nation*, 25 June 1927.

[88] *Connacht Tribune*, 19 February 1927.

[89] UCDA, P53/304, Draft of book on foundation of the Free State by Michael Hayes, n.d.

[90] Farrell, *Chairman or chief?*, 24.

[91] *Dáil debates*, vol. 1, col. 571, 21 September 1922 (Kevin O'Higgins). For a discussion of his arguments during the Treaty debates see Chapter 1, 4.

[92] Ferriter, *Occasions of sin*, 109.

[93] *Dáil debates*, vol. 20, col. 757, 12 July 1927 (W.T. Cosgrave).

CHAPTER 4

[1] See for example, *Limerick Chronicle, Kilkenny Journal*, 3 September 1927; *Drogheda Independent*, 24 September 1927.

[2] *Thirty-fourth annual report of Irish Labour Party and Trade Union Congress*, 26.

[3] *Limerick Leader*, 27 August 1927; *Midland Tribune*, 10 September 1927.

[4] *Cork Examiner*, 26 August 1927; *Derry People*, 3 September 1927.

[5] *Leitrim Leader*, 27 August 1927.

[6] See for example, *Roscommon Messenger, Midland Tribune, Leitrim Observer* and *Westmeath Examiner*, 3 September 1927.

[7] NAI, DT, S5470, Walsh's resignation letter, 2 September 1927.

[8] CCCA, U271/A/55, Diary entry, 20 August 1927.

[9] *Echo*, 10 September 1927.

[10] Dennis Kavanagh, 'The timing of elections: the British case', in Ian Crewe and Martin Harrop (eds), *Political communications: the general election of 1987* (Cambridge, 1989), 5.

[11] *Echo*, 10 September 1927.

[12] *Dáil debates*, vol. 4, col. 48, 20 September 1923 (W.T. Cosgrave).

[13] See Cosgrave's statement, *Meath Chronicle*, 3 September 1927.

14 *The Times*, 27 August 1927.

15 See for example, *Offaly Chronicle*, 1 September 1927; *Drogheda Independent*, 3 and 17 Sept. 1927; *Connacht Tribune*, 17 September 1927.

16 *Roscommon Herald*, 3 September 1927.

17 *Roscommon Herald*, 10 September 1927.

18 For further discussion of these innovations, see Chapter 5, 161–2 and Chapter 7, 203–06.

19 David M. Farrell, 'Before campaigns were "modern": Irish electioneering in times past', in Tom Garvin, Maurice Manning and Richard Sinnott (eds), *Dissecting Irish politics: essays in honour of Brian Farrell* (Dublin, 2004), 180. Farrell's article contains an interesting chart on page 179 that details the three phases of electioneering: pre-modern, modern and postmodern.

20 The firm was Dublin-based, with offices at 53 and 54 Lower O'Connell Street.

21 Richard Cockett, 'The party, publicity, and the media', in Anthony Seldon and Stuart Bell (eds), *Conservative century: the Conservative Party since 1900* (Oxford, 1994), 556.

22 *Irish Times*, 16 February 1927, 5. O'Kennedy was the managing director of the agency. His co-director was Thomas Brindley, the head of the well-known printing firm, Brindley and Son of Eustace Street. The company was also associated with Messrs W. and S. Crawford in Britain and therefore benefited from the experience of a leading London agency.

23 Brian O'Kennedy, *Making history: the story of a remarkable campaign* (Dublin, 1927).

24 O'Kennedy, *Making history*.

25 Section 63 provides that no person other than the candidate's duly authorised agent may incur election expenses. It was feared that a display of national posters in a constituency might be regarded an election expense and be chargeable to the local candidate. Although a 1952 court case somewhat alleviated the concerns about postering, parties remained uncertain about the legality of press advertising and abstained from it until 1979. See Dennis Kavanagh, *Election campaigning: the new marketing of politics* (Oxford, 1995), 11.

26 Martin Harrop, 'Political marketing', *Parliamentary Affairs* 43 (2) (1990), 287.

27 O'Kennedy, *Making history*, 5; *Cork Examiner*, 3 September 1927.

28 *New Ross Standard*, 2 September 1927.

29 *Waterford Standard*, 13 August 1927 and *Sligo Champion*, 3 September 1927.

30 See for example, *Cork County Eagle* and *Westmeath Examiner*, 27 August 1927.

31 See for example, *Longford Leader*, 3 September 1927; *Limerick Chronicle*, 8 September 1927; *Midland Tribune* and *Leitrim Observer* 10 September 1927.

32 James K. Pollock, 'The Irish Free State elections of September 1927', *The American Political Science Review* 22 (1) (February 1928), 156.

33 Quoted in O'Kennedy, *Making history*, 1.

34 *Irish Times*, 12 May 1928.

35 Cumann na nGaedheal advertisement, *Meath Chronicle*, 17 September 1927.

36 Dolan, *Commemorating the Irish Civil War*, 35–7.

37 CCCA, U271/A/55, Diary entry, 14 July 1927.

38 *Donegal Vindicator*, 10 September 1927.

39 Gallagher, *Irish elections 1922–44*, 99.

40 *Donegal Vindicator*, 10 September 1927.

41 *Clare Champion*, 3 September 1927.

42 *Kilkenny Journal*, 10 September 1927.

43 *Kildare Observer*, 24 September 1927.

[44] *Waterford Standard*, 27 August 1927.

[45] *Waterford Standard*, 17 September 1927. Redmond's personal vote fell by 3.7%.

[46] O'Leary, *The Irish Republic*, 23.

[47] Gallagher, *Irish elections*, 121.

[48] Gallagher, *Irish elections*, 121.

[49] Shaun Bowler and David M. Farrell, 'Party loyalties in complex settings: STV and party identification', *Political Studies* 39 (2) (1991), 353.

[50] *Anglo-Celt*, 17 September 1927.

[51] *Irish Statesman*, 10 September 1927.

[52] Gallagher, *Irish elections*, 115.

[53] See for example, *Anglo-Celt*, 10 September 1927 and *Waterford Standard*, 14 September 1927.

[54] *Longford Leader*, 3 September 1927. Cumann na nGaedheal increased its share of the vote by 6.96%, while the Farmers' Party lost 5.5%.

[55] *Cork County Eagle*, 10 September 1927.

[56] The Farmers' Party lost 3.33%, while the 'others' were down 23.12%.

[57] Richard Sinnott observes that a candidate's transfers after the second count must be analysed with caution as they include transfers from other parties, and are therefore not pure party X votes. He points out that 'contamination occurs where some or all of the votes credited to a particular candidate, whose votes are being redistributed originally belonged to a party other than the party of the candidate in question'. Sinnott, *Irish voters decide*, 204 and 207.

[58] *Cork Examiner*, 8 September 1927.

[59] *Realt A'deiscirt*, 10 September 1927.

[60] *Drogheda Independent*, 3 September 1927.

[61] The Farmers' Party had accounted for 13.5% of the first preferences cast in Meath in June 1927.

[62] The percentage change was as follows: National League down 9.01%; Labour down 10.45%; Fianna Fáil up 9.91%. For the full figures see Gallagher, *Irish elections*, 108.

[63] *Dundalk Democrat*, 24 September 1927.

[64] Cork Borough, Cork East, Cork North, Donegal, Dublin County, Galway, Kerry, Kildare, Laois-Offaly, Longford-Westmeath, Meath, the National University and Waterford.

[65] Leitrim-Sligo, Roscommon, Mayo North, Mayo South, Cavan, Monaghan, Louth, Dublin North, Dublin South, Wicklow, Wexford, Carlow-Kilkenny, Cork West, Limerick, Tipperary and Clare.

[66] The rate of decrease for Cork West, Dublin North, Mayo South, and Roscommon was 12.79%, 12.08%, 10.36% and 10.16% respectively.

[67] Cumann na nGaedheal's second worst performance in June 1927 was recorded in Monaghan.

[68] L.J. Duffy quoted in *Kilkenny Journal*, 17 September 1927.

[69] *Mayo News*, 24 September 1927.

[70] CCCA, U271/A/55, Diary entry, 21 September 1927.

[71] Maryann Gialanella Valiulis, 'After the revolution: the formative years of Cumann na nGaedheal', in Audrey S. Eyler and Robert F. Garrat (eds), *The uses of the past: essays on Irish culture* (Newark, DE, 1988), 141.

[72] Prager, *Building democracy in Ireland*, 167.

[73] *Sinn Féin*, 12 March 1910.

[74] Richard Davis, *Arthur Griffith and non-violent Sinn Féin* (Kerry, 1974), 127.

[75] James Meenan, 'From free trade to self sufficiency', in Francis McManus (ed.), *The years of the great test, 1926–39* (Dublin, 1967), 69.

[76] *Cork Examiner*, 8 September 1927.

[77] Meenan, 'From free trade to self-sufficiency', 70.

[78] Cumann na nGaedheal, *Fighting points for Cumann na nGaedheal speakers and workers: general election 1932* (Dublin, 1932), 51.

[79] CCCA, U271/A/54, Diary entry, 14 May 1926.

[80] UCDA, P24/505, Election address to the voters of Monaghan, 24 August 1927.

[81] Fanning, *Independent Ireland*, 74.

[82] Lee, *Ireland 1912–1985*, 120.

[83] Girvin, *Between two worlds*, 46.

[84] Eoin MacNeill, 'Ten years of the Irish Free State', *Foreign Affairs* 10 (1) (1932), 242.

[85] Meenan, 'From free trade to self-sufficiency', 70.

[86] Cormac Ó Gráda, *Ireland: a new economic history, 1780–1939* (Oxford, 1995), 396.

[87] *Irish Statesman*, 10 September 1927.

[88] Jonathan Haughton, 'The historical background', in J.W. O'Hagan (ed.), *The economy of Ireland: policy and performance of a small European country* (Dublin, 1995, 5th edn), 32.

[89] F.P. Ruane, 'Review of industrial policies', in J.W. O'Hagan (ed.), *The economy of Ireland: policy and performance* (Dublin, 1981, 3rd edn), 291.

[90] NAI, DT, S5470, Walsh's resignation letter, 2 September 1927, *Irish Independent*, 6 September 1927; *Realt A'deiscirt*, 10 September 1927.

[91] CCCA, U355/6, Statement by J.J. Walsh, n.d.

[92] *Dáil debates*, vol. 3, col. 187, 3 January 1922 (J.J. Walsh).

[93] Walsh, *Recollections*, 68, 70–1.

[94] NAI, DT, S5470, Draft responses to Walsh's resignation letter, September 1927.

[95] CCCA, U355/6, Cosgrave to Walsh, 7 September 1927.

[96] NAI, DT, S5470, Blythe's response to Walsh's resignation, September 1927; *Kilkenny Journal, Anglo-Celt* and *Cork Weekly Examiner*, 10 September 1927.

[97] CCCA, U271/A/54, Diary entry, 6 December 1925.

[98] NAI, DT, S5470, Blythe's response to Walsh's resignation, September 1927.

[99] *Irish Statesman*, 10 September 1927.

[100] *Enniscorthy Guardian*, 10 September 1927.

[101] See for example, *Cork Examiner*, 30 and 31 August 1927.

[102] *Cork Examiner*, 6 September 1927.

[103] Walsh, *Recollections*, 68.

[104] UCDA, P53/304, Draft of book on foundation of the Free State by Michael Hayes, n.d.

[105] Walsh, *Recollections*, 72.

[106] See photographic collection in Collins, *The Cosgrave legacy*.

[107] *Cork Weekly Examiner*, 10 September 1927.

[108] *Sligo Champion*, 3 September 1927; *Drogheda Independent, Meath Chronicle, Connacht Tribune, Limerick Leader* and *Leitrim Observer*, 10 September 1927.

[109] See Chapter 2, 79–80.

[110] *Irish Times*, 5 September 1927.

[111] *Irish Independent*, 5 September 1927.

[112] *Irish Times*, 13 March 1925.

[113] CCCA, U271/A/55, Diary entry, 13 September 1927.

[114] *Irish Times*, 1 September 1927.

[115] CCCA, U271/A/55, Diary entry, 6 September 1927.

[116] In July 1927 *The Crystal* carried a feature on Egan. The author, Eoin O'Mahony, noted how 'he has come out as a strong protectionist in the ranks of Cumann na nGaedheal'. CCCA, U404, *The Crystal* 2 (7) (July, 1927).

[117] Patrick Maume, *D.P. Moran* (Dublin, 1995), 14.

[118] *Irish Independent*, 29 August 1927.

[119] CCCA, U271/A/54, Diary entry, 25 July 1926.

[120] CCCA, U271/A/54, Diary entry, 19 February 1927.

[121] *Midland Tribune*, 27 August 1927; *Derry People*, 10 September 1927.

[122] CCCA, U271/A/54, Diary entry, 19 February 1927.

[123] *Freeman's Journal*, 18 August 1924.

[124] See Cumann na nGaedheal election advertisement, *Cork Examiner*, 14 September 1927.

[125] CCCA, U271/A/55, Diary entry, 13 September 1927.

[126] CCCA, U271/A/54, Diary entry, 14 May 1926.

[127] Bruce Cain, John Ferejohn and Morris Fiorina, *The personal vote: constituency service and electoral independence* (Cambridge, 1987), 175.

[128] *Kerryman*, 5 December 1931.

CHAPTER 5

[1] Pauric Travers, *Eamon de Valera* (Dundalk, 1994), 26.

[2] This has already been examined in Chapter 2, 54–60.

[3] CCCA, U271/A/55, Diary entry, 21 September 1927.

[4] *New York Times*, 25 September 1927.

[5] *Cork Examiner*, 18 February 1924.

[6] *Irish Statesman*, 10 September 1927.

[7] *Evening Herald*, 16 September 1927.

[8] *Midland Tribune*, 10 September 1927; *Leitrim Observer*, 17 September 1927; *Evening Herald*, 19 September 1927; *Nationalist and Leinster Times*, 24 September 1927; *Leader*, 24 September 1927.

[9] *Longford Leader*, 24 September 1927 and *Nationalist and Leinster Times*, 1 October 1927.

[10] *Cork Examiner*, 17 September 1927.

[11] *Anglo-Celt*, 17 September 1927.

[12] *Anglo-Celt*, 17 September 1927.

[13] *Realt A'deiscirt*, 3 September 1927.

[14] Patrick Maume, 'Nationalism and Partition: the political thought of Arthur Clery,' *Irish Historical Studies* 13 (122) (November 1998), 237.

[15] CCCA, U271/A/55, Diary entry, 30 August 1927.

[16] *Dáil debates*, vol. 21, cols 21 and 24, 11 October 1927 (Seán T O'Kelly).

[17] Michael McLoughlin, *Great Irish speeches of the twentieth century* (Dublin, 1996), 139.

[18] Joseph M. Curran, 'Ireland since 1916', *Éire-Ireland* 1 (3) (fall 1966), 18.

[19] Laffan, *The resurrection of Ireland*, 398.

[20] Bowman, *De Valera and the Ulster question*, 2.

[21] Somerville-Large, *Irish voices*, 146.

[22] Robert Fisk, *In time of war: Ireland, Ulster, and the price of neutrality, 1939–45* (London, 1983), 138.

[23] Quoted in the *New York Times*, 12 September 1927.

[24] *Irish Times*, 12 September 1927.

[25] *Clare Champion*, 17 September 1927.

26 CCCA, U271/Dáil Material/i, J.J. Walsh to Liam de Róiste, 8 September 1927.

27 Quoted in *Free Press*, 17 September 1927.

28 Cumann na nGaedheal, *Fighting points, 1932*, 21.

29 Fanning, *The Irish Department of Finance*, 168.

30 NAI, DT, S8333, Memorandum on land annuities by John A. Costello attached to letter from Diarmuid O'Hegarty to each minister, 3 February 1932.

31 Paul Bew, Ellen Hazelkorn, and Henry Patterson, *The dynamics of Irish politics* (London, 1989), 45.

32 NAI, DT, S8333, Memorandum to all the ministers from John A. Costello, 7 December 1931.

33 *Irish Times*, 2 November 1927.

34 NAI, DT, S8337, Henry J. Moloney to Diarmuid O'Hegarty, 14 January 1929.

35 NAI, DT, S8337, W.T. Cosgrave's notes on Moloney's proposals, n.d.

36 NAI, DT, S8337, Diarmuid O'Hegarty to John A. Costello and each minister, 19 January 1929.

37 NAI, DT, S8337, Henry J. Moloney to Diarmuid O'Hegarty, 6 February 1929.

38 *Dáil debates*, vol. 21, col. 437, 26 October 1927 (Archie Cassidy).

39 NAI, DT, S8335, Laurence Ryan to Diarmuid O'Hegarty, 30 May 1929.

40 NAI, DT, S8335, Laurence Ryan to Éamonn Duggan, 18 December 1931.

41 NAI, DT, S8335, Laurence Ryan to Diarmuid O'Hegarty, 1 July 1932.

42 *Waterford News*, 6 November 1931.

43 Bew *et al.*, *The dynamics of Irish politics*, 45.

44 D.G. Boyce, *The Irish question and British politics* (London, 1996, 2nd edn), 85.

45 *Dáil debates*, vol. 21, col. 676, 2 November 1927 (Eamon Cooney).

46 UCDA, P176/352, Pamphlet, 14 November 1928.

47 NAI, DT, S8336, Confidential report from superintendent's office in Kinsale, 17 May 1928.

48 NAI, DT, S8336, Confidential report submitted to superintendent's office in Letterkenny, from Inspector James Dowd, 12 February 1929.

49 NAI, DT, S8336, Patrick Hogan to E. Herlihy, 25 June 1929.

50 NAI, DT, S8336, James Fitzgerald-Kenney to Patrick Hogan, 25 June 1929.

51 NAI, DT, S8336, Patrick Hogan to Diarmuid O'Hegarty, 25 June 1929, comment dated 8 July 1929 and initialled by O'Hegarty.

52 Richard Dunphy, *The making of Fianna Fáil power in Ireland, 1923–1949* (Oxford, 1995), 97.

53 Patrick McGilligan to L.S. Amery, 25 January 1929, in Ronan Fanning, Michael Kennedy, Dermot Keogh and Eunan O'Halpin (eds), *Documents on Irish foreign policy* (DIFP), *volume iii, 1926–1932* (Dublin, 2002), 244.

54 Thomas J. Kiernan to Joseph Walshe, 30 January 1929 and 31 January 1929, in Fanning *et al.*, DIFP, vol. iii, 245–7.

55 Patrick McGilligan to L. S. Amery, 14 February 1929, in Fanning *et al.*, DIFP, vol. iii, 252.

56 Patrick McGilligan to Lord Passfield, 19 July 1929, in Fanning *et al.*, DIFP, vol. iii, 351.

57 Harkness, *Restless dominion*, 173.

58 Kennedy, *Ireland and the League of Nations*, 119.

59 Kennedy, *Ireland and the League of Nations*, 129–30.

60 Seán Lester to Patrick McGilligan, 16 January 1930, in Fanning *et al.*, DIFP, vol. iii, 493.

61 Kennedy, *Ireland and the League of Nations*, 143.

62 Seán Murphy to Count Gerald O'Kelly de Gallagh, 19 December 1929, in Fanning *et al.*, DIFP, vol. iii, 483.

[63] Kennedy, *Ireland and the League of Nations*, 144.

[64] Kennedy, *Ireland and the League of Nations*, 149.

[65] UCDA, P80/1411, Desmond FitzGerald to Mabel FitzGerald, 10 October 1930.

[66] O'Kennedy-Brindley, *With the president in America: the authorised record of President Cosgrave's tour in the United States and Canada* (Dublin, 1928).

[67] *Irish Times*, 20 January 1928.

[68] *New York Times*, 21 January 1928.

[69] *New York Times*, 22 January 1928.

[70] Quoted in the *New York Times*, 22 January 1928.

[71] NAI, DT, S4529, Speech at the Irish Fellowship Club, Drake Hotel, Chicago, 21 January 1928.

[72] *New York Times*, 26 January 1928.

[73] *New York Times*, 31 January 1928.

[74] Quoted in the *New York Times*, 29 January 1928.

[75] Quoted in Jordan, *W.T. Cosgrave*, 160.

[76] *New York Times*, 20 January 1928.

[77] Lindsay Crawford to Timothy A. Smiddy, 27 July 1923, in Fanning *et al.*, DIFP, vol. ii, 145.

[78] Constitution of the Irish Free State (Saorstát Éireann) Act, 1922, available from www.statutebook.ie (1 June 2010).

[79] Letitia Dunbar-Harrison was appointed to the position of county librarian in Mayo. That she did not speak Irish, and, more significantly, was a Protestant caused consternation. With the local clergy largely opposed to the appointment, both the library committee and the county council refused to approve it. Cosgrave responded by dissolving the council. Although he later reversed his decision and a compromise position was found for Dunbar-Harrison, his actions—which brought him into conflict with the Church—showed his willingness to support the minority community in the Free State if the cause was just. For further discussion of the affair, see Chapter 6, 185–6.

[80] Patrick McGilligan to J.H. Thomas, 12 September 1930, in Fanning *et al.*, DIFP, vol. ii, 643.

[81] Harkness, *Restless dominion*, 173.

[82] Harkness, *Restless dominion*, 202–04.

[83] Harkness, *Restless dominion*, 215.

[84] Nicholas Mansergh, 'Ireland: external relations 1926–1939', in Francis MacManus (ed.), *The years of the great test, 1926–39* (Cork, 1967), 129.

[85] *Hansard*, vol. 259, col. 1192, 20 November 1931 (Winston Churchill).

[86] *Dáil debates*, vol. 39, col. 2307, 16 July 1931 (Patrick McGilligan).

[87] *Hansard*, vol. 259, col. 1194, 20 November 1931 (Winston Churchill).

[88] NAI, 1065/1/1, Kevin O'Higgins to Frank MacDermot, 18 May 1927.

[89] UCDA, P35/174, Patrick McGilligan to J.H. Thomas, 22 November 1931.

[90] NAI, DT, G2/8, Minutes of fifth Executive Council Cabinet meeting, 3 March 1931.

[91] Keogh, *Twentieth century Ireland*, 51.

[92] Diarmaid Ferriter, *Judging Dev* (Dublin, 2007), 123.

[93] Memorandum on the state seals, 1930, in Fanning *et al.*, DIFP, vol. iii, 642.

[94] Harkness, *Restless dominion*, 230–8.

[95] Lowry, 'New Ireland, old empire and the outside world, 1922–49', 180.

[96] Jackson, *Ireland 1798–1998*, 282.

[97] *Dáil debates*, vol. 29, col. 1553, 8 May 1929 (James Fitzgerald-Kenney).

[98] *Dáil debates*, vol. 29, cols 1556–7, 8 May 1929 (James Fitzgerald-Kenney).

[99] In the Jurys' Act of 1927, Kevin O'Higgins had taken the decision to exclude women

from jury service and to dispense with female shorthand writers in the courts. An amendment was accepted, allowing individual women the right to choose if they wished to serve.

[100] NAI, DT, S5864A, Summary of outrages and activities by members of irregular organisations, 1931.

[101] NAI, DT, S5864B, Report by Eoin O'Duffy, 27 July 1931.

[102] *Irish Times*, 22 January 1931.

[103] *An Phoblacht*, 27 June 1931.

[104] *Irish Times*, 25 July 1931.

[105] *Irish Times*, 10 August 1931.

[106] For a more detailed discussion of the Red scare, see Chapter 6, 176–8.

[107] *An Phoblacht*, 4 June 1932.

[108] UCDA, P39/MIN/3, Minutes of the parliamentary party, 25 June 1931.

[109] UCDA, P39/MIN/3, Minutes of the parliamentary party, 9 July 1931.

[110] *Nationalist and Leinster Times*, 15, 22 and 29 October 1927; *Kilkenny People*, 22 and 29 October 1927.

[111] *Irish Times*, 2 November 1927.

[112] *Kilkenny People*, 15 October 1927.

[113] *Dáil debates*, vol. 22, cols 643–4, 1 March 1928 (Éamonn Duggan).

[114] Kevin Rafter, *The Clann: the story of Clann na Poblachta* (Dublin, 1996), 91.

[115] *Evening Herald*, 14 March 1929.

[116] *Leitrim Observer*, 18 May 1929.

[117] Moss, *Political parties in the Irish Free State*, 175.

[118] *Westmeath Independent*, 21 June 1930.

[119] The last time that the Republican vote exceeded Cumann na nGaedheal's was on 18 November 1924 when Seán Lemass won the Dublin South by-election. On the same day John Madden won the Mayo North by-election, though he later remained a Sinn Féin TD. On 11 March 1925 Oscar Traynor and Samuel Holt, both later Fianna Fáil TDs, took a seat in the Dublin North and Leitrim-Sligo by-elections respectively. In both elections, two seats were being contested. In the two elections, however, Cumann na nGaedheal also took a seat and the party's first preference votes surpassed those of the Republican candidates.

[120] *Kildare Observer*, 6 June 1931.

[121] John A. Murphy, *Ireland in the twentieth century* (Dublin, 1975), 72.

CHAPTER 6

[1] *The Times*, 9 February 1932.

[2] 'Fianna Fáil has a plan' advertisement, *Irish Press*, 15 February 1932, 5.

[3] UCDA, P39/MIN/3, Meeting of the parliamentary party, 3 November and 9 July 1931.

[4] UCDA, P176/352, Reports and correspondence of honorary secretaries, 13 November 1928.

[5] *Kildare Observer*, 23 May 1931.

[6] Keogh, *Twentieth century Ireland*, 59.

[7] *Irish Press*, 4 January 1932.

[8] UCDA, P24/336, Memorandum on the financial position, 9 September 1931.

[9] UCDA, P39/MIN/3, Meeting of the parliamentary party, 5 November 1931.

[10] Donal McCartney, *The dawning of democracy: Ireland 1800–1870* (Dublin, 1987), 153.

[11] Andrew Thorpe, *A history of the British Labour Party* (London, 1997), 55.

[12] *Wicklow People*, 26 December 1931.

[13] Cumann na nGaedheal, *Fighting points 1932*, 70.

[14] Patricia Clavin, *The Great Depression in Europe, 1929–1939* (London, 2000), 105.

[15] CCCA, U404/3, Notes, 24 September 1930.

[16] Mary E. Daly, *Social and economic history of Ireland since 1800* (Dublin, 1981), 144.

[17] Patricia Clavin, *The failure of economic diplomacy: Britain, Germany, France and the United States, 1931–36* (London, 1996), 1.

[18] *People*, 2 January 1932.

[19] Maurice Manning, *The Blueshirts*, (Dublin, 2006), 106.

[20] See Chapter 2, 65.

[21] See for example, *Galway Observer* and *Kerryman*, 30 January 1932, *Anglo-Celt* and *Limerick Leader*, 23 January 1932.

[22] Cumann na nGaedheal, *Fighting points 1932*, 61

[23] *Dáil debates*, vol. 21, col. 379, 26 October 1927 (Daniel Morrissey).

[24] Labour's election statement in Moss, *Political parties*, 209–16.

[25] Labour election statement in Moss, *Political parties*, 216

[26] *Dáil debates*, vol. 40, col. 3026, 17 December 1931 (Eamon de Valera).

[27] Cousins, *The birth of social welfare*, 35–6.

[28] Cousins, *The birth of social welfare*, 49.

[29] See Lemass's criticisms in *Irish Times*, 1 June 1931.

[30] Thorpe, *A history of the British Labour Party*, 69.

[31] Cumann na nGaedheal, *Fighting points 1932*, 61.

[32] *Irish Press*, 4 January 1932.

[33] CCCA, U404/7, Barry Egan to Thomas Buckley, 25 October 1932.

[34] Cumann na nGaedheal, *Fighting points 1932*, 62.

[35] William Norton quoted in *Irish Press*, 4 January 1932.

[36] *Irish Press*, 15 February 1932.

[37] J.H. Whyte, 'Ireland: politics without social bases', in Richard Rose (ed.), *Electoral behaviour: a comparative handbook* (New York, 1974), 622. Speaking in the Dáil in 2004, John Bruton asserted that governments 'should not be judged by things it cannot direct, such as the world economy'. The very fact that he made the statement implied that they often are. *Dáil debates*, vol. 578, col. 124, 21 January 2004.

[38] *Dáil debates*, vol. 337, col. 3112, 16 July 1982 (Charles Haughey).

[39] Mark Mazower, *Dark continent: Europe's twentieth century* (London, 1998), 114.

[40] Clavin, *The Great Depression*, 98.

[41] Robert Blake, *The Conservative Party from Peel to Major* (London, 1997), 245.

[42] *Dáil debates*, vol. 21, col. 378, 26 October 1927 (Daniel Morrissey).

[43] 'I desire to move the motion standing in my name that the Dáil is of opinion that steps should be taken forthwith by the Executive Council to provide work or maintenance to meet the immediate needs of the unemployed', *Dáil debates*, vol. 41, col. 280, 20 April 1932 (Daniel Morrissey).

[44] Cormac Ó Gráda, 'The rise in living standards', in Kieran A. Kennedy (ed.), *From famine to feast: economic and social change in Ireland, 1847–1997* (Dublin, 1998), 14 and 20.

[45] See Chapter 3, 100–01.

[46] Quoted in Fanning, *Independent Ireland*, 109.

[47] Ryan, *Unique dictator*, 240.

[48] Moss, *Political parties*, 33, 125.

[49] Cited in Margaret O'Carroll, 'Cumann na nGaedheal's 1932 election posters: repre-

senting Irish national identity?', unpublished BA dissertation, Waterford Institute of Technology, 2010, 16.

50 O'Carroll, 'Cumann na nGaedheal's 1932 election posters', 17.

51 Paul Richards, *How to win an election: the art of political campaigning* (London, 2001), 46.

52 Quoted in *Irish Times*, 4 February 1932.

53 *Dáil debates*, vol. T, col. 36, 19 December 1921 (Michael Collins).

54 *Dáil debates*, vol. T, col. 224, 4 January 1922 (Eoin O'Duffy).

55 M.A. Busteed, *Voting behaviour in the Republic of Ireland: a geographical perspective* (Oxford, 1990), 10.

56 L.S. Amery, *A plan of action embodying a series of reports issued by the research committee of the empire economic union and other papers* (London, 1932), 1.

57 *Kildare Observer*, 5 December 1931.

58 Cumann na nGaedheal, *Fighting points 1932*, 45.

59 David M. Farrell, 'Ireland: centralization, professionalization and competitive pressures', in Richard S. Katz and Peter Mair (eds), *How parties organise: change and adaptation in party organisations in western democracies* (London, 1994), 221.

60 Gallagher, *Electoral support for Irish political parties*, 19.

61 Ian Budge and Dennis J. Farlie, *Explaining and predicting elections: issue effects and party strategies in twenty-three democracies* (London, 1983), 132.

62 Bowman, *De Valera and the Ulster question*, 112.

63 UCDA, P176/830, General election statement, 1932.

64 Election advertisement, *Irish Independent*, 10 February 1932.

65 Election advertisement, *Irish Independent*, 7 February 1932.

66 See Chapter 5, 159–60.

67 *Irish Times*, 30 January 1932.

68 Dermot Keogh, 'De Valera, the Catholic Church and the "Red scare" 1931–1932', in J.P. O'Carroll and John A. Murphy (eds), *De Valera and his times* (Cork, 1983), 144.

69 *Irish Times*, 1 February 1932.

70 Myrtle Hill, *Women in Ireland: a century of change* (Belfast, 2003), 112.

71 *Irish Independent*, 28 September 1931.

72 CCCA, U404/6, Unsigned letter, [1932?].

73 UCDA, P176/830, Election statement, 1932.

74 Quoted in John Horgan, 'Fianna Fáil & arms decommissioning', *History Ireland* 5 (4) (winter 1997), 53.

75 Keogh, 'De Valera, the Catholic Church and the "Red scare"', 140.

76 Kavanagh, *Election campaigning*, 155.

77 The Daisy advertisement was part of Lyndon Johnson's 1964 presidential campaign. It showed a little girl picking petals from a daisy and miscounting, while a military-style voice, counting down from ten, was played over hers. When it reached zero there was an explosion. The intention was to juxtapose the style of the two candidates, as interpreted by the Democrats. Johnson's leadership of the country was to bring peace, while his Republican opponent, Barry Goldwater, was shown to be trigger-happy. The advertisement, which was later voluntarily withdrawn by the Democrats, was the most controversial of its time. Kavanagh, *Election campaigning*, 155.

78 Kavanagh, *Election campaigning*, 155.

79 James Hogan, *Could Ireland become communist? The facts of the case* (Dublin, 1935), x.

80 Cumann na nGaedheal, *Fighting points 1932*, 122.

[81] Cumann na nGaedheal election advertisement, *Irish Times*, 16 February 1932.

[82] *North Dublin Election News*, 10 February 1932.

[83] Cumann na nGaedheal, *Fighting points 1932*, 123.

[84] Moss, *Political parties*, 129.

[85] Richard Rose, *Influencing voters: a study of campaign rationality* (London, 1967), 180.

[86] *Leitrim Observer*, 20 February 1932.

[87] Moss, *Political parties*, 178.

[88] *Irish Times*, 16 February 1932.

[89] *Irish Press*, 15 February 1932.

[90] Stephen Ansolabehere, Shanto Iyengar, Simon Adam, and Nicholas Valentino, 'Does attack advertising demobilise the electorate?', *American Political Science Review* 88 (4) (December 1994), 834.

[91] Ronan Fanning, *The four-leaved shamrock: electoral politics and the national imagination in independent Ireland* (Dublin, 1984), 10.

[92] Similarly in the 1933 election, the party would emphasize Cosgrave's role in the Easter Rising.

[93] Fanning, *The four-leaved shamrock*, 9.

[94] *Waterford News*, 20 November 1932.

[95] *Roscommon Messenger*, 28 November and 5 December 1931.

[96] Jackson, *Ireland 1798–1998*, 282.

[97] The Roscommon convention in June 1927 was marred by controversy after accusations that the convention had been packed and that the party leadership had tried to influence the outcome. Having failed to secure a place on the ticket, Michael Brennan, along with Michael Killian—despite the undertaking that all candidates would abide by the results—opted to go forward as independents. Both stood as declared supporters of the government, critical only of the convention, and could even be found on government platforms introducing the official candidates. By openly associating themselves with the government party, Brennan and Killian appealed to its supporters on the same grounds as the endorsed aspirants, thus potentially attracting votes that might otherwise have been cast for Cumann na nGaedheal. The party's organisation should have taken decisive action but Cumann na nGaedheal's failure to do so reflected its relaxed attitude towards organisation. Brennan, but not Killian, won a seat, which he retained at the second election of 1927.

[98] Moss, *political parties*, 181.

[99] Sinnott, 'The electoral system', 68.

[100] Cain, Ferejohn and Fiorina, *The personal vote*, 27.

[101] *Dundalk Democrat*, 21 May 1927.

[102] Tom Garvin, 'Nationalist elites, Irish voters, and Irish political development: a comparative perspective', *Economic and Social Review* 8 (1977), 178.

[103] *Dáil debates*, vol. 20, col. 1681, 16 August 1927 (W.T. Cosgrave).

[104] UCDA, P24/336, Memorandum, 9 September 1931.

[105] UCDA, P24/336, Memorandum, 9 September 1931.

[106] *Dáil debates*, vol. 40, col. 1533, 13 November 1931 (Ernest Blythe).

[107] Fanning, *Department of Finance*, 214.

[108] Quoted in *Meath Chronicle*, 23 January 1932.

[109] *Irish Press*, 12 January 1932.

[110] Quoted in *Irish Press*, 14 January 1932.

[111] UCDA, P24/341, Memorandum, January 1932.

[112] *Irish Times*, 19 January 1932.

[113] *Irish Press*, 16 January 1932.

[114] *Irish Press*, 9 January 1932.

[115] *Irish Press*, 11 January 1932.

[116] *Irish Press*, 11 January 1932.

[117] T. J. O'Connell, *A history of the Irish National Teachers' Organisation, 1868–1968* (Dublin, 1969), 281.

[118] Hill, *Women in Ireland*, 100.

[119] Moss, *Political parties*, 177.

[120] *Irish Press*, 2 June 1931.

[121] Lee, *Ireland 1912–1985*, 164–5.

[122] Lee, *Ireland 1912–1985*, 166.

[123] Jordan, *W.T. Cosgrave*, 148.

[124] *Irish Times*, 17 February 1932.

[125] *Irish Times*, 17 February 1932.

[126] *Dáil debates*, vol. 40, col. 1245, 11 November 1931 (Seámus Moore).

[127] *Waterford News*, 20 November 1931.

[128] *Irish Press*, 22 December 1931.

[129] UCDA, P176/352, Circular to all Fianna Fáil deputies, 6 November 1928.

[130] *Irish Press*, 27 January 1932.

[131] *Irish Press*, 26 January 1932.

[132] *Irish Independent*, 18 February 1932.

[133] *Irish Press*, 26 January 1932.

[134] Naturally the *Leitrim Observer* dedicated much space to coverage of the lengthy inquest, which met on five separate occasions and was fraught with difficulties, but the *Irish Times*, *Irish Independent* and *Sunday Independent* also touched on the matter and naturally the coverage was far greater in Fianna Fáil's *Irish Press*. James Vaugh is not listed in Padraic O'Farrell, *Who's who in the Irish War of Independence and Civil War, 1916–1923* (Dublin, 1997). However, according to Seán Farrell—a former Republican deputy for Leitrim-Sligo, who delivered the oration at the first anniversary Mass—Vaugh participated in both the independence struggle and the Civil War. He also assisted in 'maintaining and re-organising the broken remnants of that once, great, powerful and invincible army [the IRA]'. The turnout at the anniversary Mass was estimated to have exceeded (a probably embellished) several thousand people from all parts of Leitrim and Roscommon. See the *Sligo Champion*, 7 January 1933; the anniversary also received brief coverage in the *Irish Independent*, 2 January 1933.

[135] *Roscommon Herald*, 2 January 1932.

[136] Two doctors had treated the deceased. Dr J.H. Flynn initially treated Vaugh for influenza, which he believed subsequently developed into meningitis. The second doctor, J.F. Roden, attributed the cause of death to measles. While Flynn claimed that Vaugh informed him of the alleged maltreatment, Roden asserted that no such complaints were ever made to him. Given the diverging evidence, the jury at the inquest decided that a post-mortem should be undertaken.

[137] *Leitrim Observer*, 20 February 1932.

[138] *Leitrim Observer*, 9 January 1932.

[139] Jackson, *Ireland 1798–1998*, 284.

[140] Sean Edmonds, *The gun, the law and the Irish people* (Kerry, 1971), 146.

[141] Richards, *How to win an election*, xvi.

[142] *Kildare Observer*, 2 January 1932.

[143] Gallagher, *Irish elections 1922–44*, 147.

[144] Munger, *The legitimacy of opposition*, 21.

[145] Carlow-Kilkenny, Cavan, Clare, Cork Borough, Cork West, Donegal, Dublin North, Dublin South, Dublin County, Galway, Leitrim-Sligo, Limerick, Louth, Mayo North, Mayo South, Monaghan, Roscommon, Tipperary, Wicklow and the National University.

[146] For the corresponding analysis for September 1927 see Appendix 1.

[147] Richard Rose and Thomas T. Mackie, *Incumbency in government: asset or liability* (Glasgow, 1980), 2.

[148] Thorpe, *A history of the British Labour Party*, 77.

[149] Harrop, 'Political marketing', 278.

[150] Interview with the *Sunday Dispatch* quoted in the *Irish Press*, 22 February 1932.

[151] *Irish Press*, 15 February 1932.

CHAPTER 7

[1] Mike Cronin, 'The formation of Fine Gael in 1933', unpublished conference paper, The 75th anniversary of the founding of the Fine Gael party 1933–2008 conference, Green Isle Hotel, Dublin, 1 November 2008.

[2] De Vere White, *Kevin O'Higgins*, 228.

[3] Moss, *Political parties*, 194.

[4] CCCA, U404/3, Barry Egan to Liam Burke, 25 May 1932.

[5] CCCA, U404/3, Barry Egan to Liam Burke, 14 May 1932.

[6] *Dáil debates*, vol. 41, col. 738, 28 April 1932 (William Norton).

[7] UCDA, P39/MIN/3, Meeting of the parliamentary party, 28 March 1930.

[8] UCDA, P39/MIN/3, Meeting of the parliamentary party, 27 October 1932.

[9] UCDA, P39/MIN/3, Meeting of the parliamentary party, 5 April 1933.

[10] UCDA, P39/MIN/3, Meeting of the parliamentary party, 22 February, 16 May and 14 June 1934.

[11] Alan J. Ward, *The Irish constitutional tradition: responsible government and modern Ireland, 1782–1992* (Dublin, 1994), 5.

[12] Blake, *The Conservative Party*, 224.

[13] Maye, *Fine Gael*, 29.

[14] Dennis Kavanagh, 'The politics of manifestos', *Parliamentary Affairs* 34 (1981), 13.

[15] *Dáil debates*, vol. 44, cols 1743–8, 15 and 16 November 1932 (W.T. Cosgrave).

[16] *Dáil debates*, vol. 44, col. 1505, 11 November 1932 (P.S. Doyle).

[17] *Dáil debates*, vol. 45, cols 628–9, 1 December 1932 (Eugene O'Brien).

[18] *Dáil debates*, vol. 41, cols 334–5, 21 April 1932 (P.S. Doyle).

[19] Michael Gallagher, 'Parliament', in John Coakley and Michael Gallagher (eds), *Politics in the Republic of Ireland* (New York, 2005), 226.

[20] *Dáil debates*, vol. 21, col. 377, 26 October 1927 (Eamon de Valera).

[21] *Dáil debates*, vol. 22, cols 206–14, 22 February 1928 (Seán Lemass).

[22] *Dáil debates*, vol. 32, cols 533–41, 30 October 1929 (James Ryan).

[23] *Dáil debates*, vol. 30, col. 174, 23 May 1929 (Eamon de Valera).

[24] *Dáil debates*, vol. 39, col. 335, 12 June 1931 (Frank Fahy and Martin Corry).

[25] Patrick Dunleavy, G.W. Jones, Jane Burnham, Robert Elgie and Peter Fysh, 'Leaders, politics and institutional change: the decline of prime ministerial accountability to the House of Commons, 1868–1990', *British Journal of Political Science* 23 (3) (July 1993), 269.

[26] Patrick Dunleavy, G.W. Jones and Brendan O'Leary, 'Prime ministers and the Commons: patterns of behaviour, 1868 to 1987', *Public Administration* 68 (1) (1990), 123–40; Dunleavy *et al.*, 'Leaders, politics and institutional change', 267–98; Robert Elgie and John Stapleton, 'Testing the decline of parliament thesis: Ireland, 1923–2002', *Political Studies* 54 (3) (2006), 465–85.

[27] Spacing scores are calculated by dividing the total number of days that the Dáil was in session during a term of office by the total number of days on which the head of government (or, in this case, the leader of the opposition) was active during that period.

[28] Elgie and Stapleton, 'Testing the decline of parliament thesis', Table 2, 476

[29] Elgie and Stapleton, 'Testing the decline of parliament thesis', 475.

[30] Dunleavy *et al*, 'Leaders, politics and institutional change', 284.

[31] See Figures 1.1 and 1.2 in the Appendix.

[32] Elgie and Stapleton, 'Testing the decline of parliament thesis', 477.

[33] Elgie and Stapleton, 'Testing the decline of parliament thesis', 476.

[34] *Dáil debates*, vol. 41, col. 798, 28 April 1932 (Margaret Collins-O'Driscoll).

[35] *Dáil debates*, vol. 41, col. 727, 28 April 1932 (John Marcus O'Sullivan).

[36] See for example, *Dáil debates*, vol. 41, cols 581, 585, 588, 598–9, 603, 605–10, 616, 621, 27 April 1932 (W.T. Cosgrave and Desmond FitzGerald).

[37] *Dáil debates*, vol. 44, cols 1595–6, 15 November 1932 (W.T. Cosgrave).

[38] Part four of the 'Mr John A. Costello remembers' series, *Irish Times*, 7 September 1967.

[39] *Sligo Champion*, 14 January 1933.

[40] Roger Eatwell and Anthony Wright, 'Labour and the lessons of 1931', *History* 63 (1978), 38–53.

[41] 'Labour manifesto, 1931', in F.W.S. Craig (ed.), *British general election manifestos, 1918–1966* (Chichester, 1970), 69.

[42] Thorpe, *A history of the British Labour Party*, 79.

[43] 'Labour manifesto, 1931', 71.

[44] See for example, *Northern Standard*, 13 January 1933 and *Donegal Vindicator*, 14 January 1933.

[45] Quoted in Lee, *Ireland 1912–1985*, 127.

[46] Paul Smith, 'Political style on film: Neville Chamberlain', in M.J. Clark (ed.), *Politics and the media: film and television for the political scientist and historian* (Oxford, 1979), 88.

[47] See Chapter 2, 45.

[48] David McCullagh, *A makeshift majority: the first inter-party government, 1948–51* (Dublin, 1998), 20.

[49] T.J. Hollins, 'The Conservative Party and film propaganda between the wars', *English Historical Review* 96 (1981), 362

[50] William G. Chrystal, 'Nazi Party election films, 1927–1938', *Cinema Journal* 15 (1) (autumn 1975), 29.

[51] Anthony Seldon and Stuart Ball, 'Introduction', in Anthony Seldon and Stuart Bell (eds), *Conservative century: the Conservative Party since 1900* (Oxford, 1994), 12.

[52] Hollins, 'The Conservative Party and film propaganda between the wars', 360.

[53] *Cork Weekly Examiner*, 14 January 1933.

[54] *Irish Independent*, 14 January 1933.

[55] *Irish Times*, 14 January 1933.

[56] *Irish Times*, 12 January 1933.

[57] *Irish Times*, 13 January 1933.

[58] S.J. Connolly, 'Cinema', in S.J. Connolly (ed.), *The Oxford companion to Irish history* (Oxford, 1998), 93.

[59] Brown, *Ireland: a social and cultural history*, 141.

[60] Hollins, 'The Conservative Party and film propaganda between the wars', 362.

[61] *Irish Independent*, 12 January 1933.

[62] *Irish Times*, 12 January 1933.

[63] Rose, *Influencing voters*, 181.

[64] CCCA, U404/4, Timothy Donovan, Michael O'Sullivan, John P. Meehan, John Florish, Jeremiah Daly, John Corbett, Daniel J. Lynch, Denis P. O'Hara, Joseph Harold, Michael Sheehan and Patrick Twomey to Liam Burke, 4 June 1932.

[65] CCCA, U404/4, Barry Egan to Liam Burke, 9 June 1932.

[66] CCCA, Papers of Séamus Fitzgerald, PR6/455, Statement on position in Cork County, 2 April 1933.

[67] Quoted in *Northern Standard*, 13 January 1933.

[68] UCDA, P39/MIN/6, Meeting of the standing committee of the National Farmers' and Ratepayers' League, 22 September 1932.

[69] John Coakley, 'Minor parties in Irish political life, 1922–1989', *Economic and Social Review* 21 (1990), 280.

[70] Election statement, *Longford Leader*, 7 January 1933.

[71] Centre Party advertisement, *Roscommon Herald*, 21 January 1933.

[72] Maurice Manning, *James Dillon: a biography* (Dublin, 1999), 67.

[73] *Roscommon Herald*, 21 January 1933.

[74] *Sligo Champion*, 14 January 1933.

[75] Until William Redmond joined the party, Cumann na nGaedheal had never managed to win more than one seat in the constituency. Kiersey was unseated by Nicholas Wall who had been elected for the Farmers' Party in 1923 but who had lost his seat in June 1927. Noting the presence of the Centre Party candidate, the *Waterford News* observed that Kiersey had been 'largely supported by the farming classes at the last election, and this support will probably suffer a large diminishment on his occasion'. *Waterford News*, 13 January 1933.

[76] *Waterford News*, 3 February 1933.

[77] *Donegal Vindicator*, 7 January 1933.

[78] The seats were lost in Carlow-Kilkenny, Donegal, Leitrim-Sligo, Longford-Westmeath, Monaghan, Tipperary and Waterford. The loss in Tipperary was more technical than the other, straightforward defeats. Technically the Centre Party candidate won a seat held by the Independent Labour deputy, Daniel Morrissey. In 1933 Morrissey stood on the Cumann na nGaedheal ticket and as there were no independent candidates in that particular constituency, the result must be registered as a Cumann na nGaedheal defeat. Thus his affiliation was of no benefit to his new party.

[79] Manning, *James Dillon*, 66.

[80] *Longford Leader* and *Westmeath Examiner*, 14 January 1933.

[81] *Westmeath Examiner*, 28 January 1933.

[82] *Westmeath Examiner*, 7 January 1933.

[83] *Cork Weekly Examiner*, 14 January 1933.

[84] *Mayo News*, 7 January 1933.

[85] For example, the Mayor of Sligo John Lynch stated 'they had two parties to choose between, one standing for Ireland and the other for England', *Sligo Champion*, 14 January 1933. Similarly, the editor of the *Leitrim Observer* claimed 'in this great contest the fight will not be between one Irish party and another, but between England and Ireland', *Leitrim Observer*, 14 January 1933.

[86] *Waterford News*, 6 January 1933.

[87] *Dáil debates*, vol. T, col. 45, 19 December 1921 (Kevin O'Higgins).

[88] *Waterford News*, 13 January 1933.

[89] *Donegal Vindicator*, 14 January 1933.

[90] For example, J.P. McKinley, who presided over the Cumann na nGaedheal convention in Donegal, in referring to Mulcahy, McEoin, Lynch and Cosgrave, stated 'all ... had been tried, and were not found wanting from the day of the Easter Rising to the present day', *Donegal Vindicator*, 14 January 1933.

[91] Ward, *The Irish constitutional tradition*, 192.

[92] Manning, *James Dillon*, 55.

[93] *Irish Independent*, 13 January 1933.

[94] *Mayo News*, 21 January 1933.

[95] See for example, *Northern Standard*, 20 January 1933, *Donegal Vindicator* and *Longford Leader* 21 January 1933.

[96] See for example, *Waterford News*, 20 January 1933 and *Meath Chronicle*, 21 January 1933.

[97] *Roscommon Herald*, 14 January 1933.

[98] Quoted in *Roscommon Herald*, 14 January 1933.

[99] *Donegal Vindicator*, 14 January 1933.

[100] *Irish Independent*, 7 January 1933.

[101] See for example, *Waterford News*, 13 January 1933, *Sligo Champion*, 14 January 1933, *Tipperary Man*, 21 January 1933.

[102] See for example, *Northern Standard*, 13 January 1933, *Clare Champion*, *Free Press* and *Kilkenny People*, 13 January 1933.

[103] *Northern Standard*, 20 January 1933.

[104] See Chapter 5, 146–7.

[105] Ó Gráda, *Ireland: a new economic history*, 393.

[106] *Mayo News*, 7 January 1933.

[107] See for example, *Donegal Vindicator* and *Sligo Champion*, 7 January 1933.

[108] *Leitrim Observer*, 21 January 1933.

[109] Lee, *Ireland 1912–1985*, 215.

[110] *Mayo News*, 28 January 1933.

[111] *Northern Standard*, 3 February 1933.

[112] *Dáil debates*, vol. 21, col. 24, 11 October 1927 (Seán T. O'Kelly).

[113] Sean Edmonds, *The gun, the law and the Irish people* (Kerry, 1971), 147.

[114] UCDA, LA30/340, Letter from Arthur Vincent [to be delivered as a speech at Killarney], 28 [unknown month] 1932.

[115] *Irish Independent*, 6 January 1933.

[116] Quoted in *Cork Weekly Examiner*, 14 January 1933.

[117] *Longford Leader*, 7 January 1933.

[118] *Northern Standard*, 6 January 1933.

[119] *Westmeath Examiner*, 14 January 1933.

[120] *Irish Independent*, 9 September 1933.

[121] Manning, *James Dillon*, 65.

[122] UCDA, LA30/340, Letter from Arthur Vincent [to be delivered as a speech at Killarney], 28 [unknown month] 1932.

[123] Mike Cronin, *The Blueshirts and Irish politics* (Dublin, 1997), 73.

[124] *Dáil debates*, vol. 50, col. 2547, 2 March 1934 (W.T. Cosgrave).

[125] Maye, *Fine Gael*, 30.

[126] CCCA, U404/6, Unsigned letter [1932?].

[127] *Irish Times*, 29 July 1933.

[128] *Irish Times*, 23 August 1933.

[129] *Irish Times*, 31 July 1933.

[130] Manning, *The Blueshirts*, 77–9.

[131] *Irish Times*, 23 August 1933.

[132] Quoted in *Irish Independent*, 9 September 1933.

[133] Manning, *The Blueshirts*, 88.

[134] John Coakley, 'The significance of names: the evolution of party labels', *Études Irlandaises* 5 (1980), 178.

[135] *Anglo-Celt*, 19 August 1933.

[136] *Anglo-Celt*, 26 August 1933.

[137] Quoted in *Irish Independent*, 9 September 1933.

[138] *Irish Independent*, 8 September 1933.

[139] Manning, *The Blueshirts*, 90.

[140] *Irish Independent*, 9 September 1933.

[141] *Anglo-Celt*, 19 August 1933.

[142] NAI, 1065/4/4, Michael Tierney to Frank MacDermot, 27 November 1934.

[143] Quoted in *Irish Independent*, 9 September 1933.

[144] The delay in his reappointment reflects the degree of demoralisation that had developed in Fine Gael; the party had become reluctant to take any hasty steps.

[145] *Irish Times*, 11 September 1933.

[146] *Irish Press*, 2 September 1933.

[147] *Anglo-Celt*, 9 November 1933.

[148] NAI, 1065/4/4, Michael Tierney to Frank MacDermot, 27 November 1934.

[149] *Dáil debates*, vol. 55, col. 1366, 21 March 1935 (Seán Lemass).

[150] Thorpe argues that the 1931 defeat should have, but did not serve as a learning opportunity for Labour. Consequently, the only thing inevitable about British politics in the 1930s was Labour's presence on the opposition benches. Thorpe, *A history of the British Labour Party*, 78.

[151] For a more in-depth discussion see Meehan, 'Fine Gael's uncomfortable history', 253–66

[152] *Dáil debates*, vol. 272, col. 471 and vol. 363, col. 2497, 30 April 1974 and 12 February 1986 (Jimmy Leonard and Michael Woods).

[153] *Dáil debates*, vol. 582, col. 1478 and vol. 595, col. 577, 30 March and 15 December 2004 (Enda Kenny).

[154] *Dáil debates*, vol. 66, col. 228 and vol. 70, col. 961, 1 April 1937 and 24 March 1938 (Patrick Kehoe and Daniel O'Rourke).

[155] *Dáil debates*, vol. 298, cols 54–5, 22 March 1977 (James Gibbons).

[156] Several references were made; for examples see, *Dáil debates*, vol. 214, col. 5 and vol. 236, cols 2454–5, 10 February 1965 and 7 November 1968 (Brian Lenihan and Neil Blaney). See also *Seanad debates*, vol. 81, col. 351, 3 June 1975 (Jack Garrett).

[157] *Dáil debates*, vol. 60, col. 1778 and vol. 233, col. 1209, 5 March 1936 and 27 March 1968 (Thomas Kelly and Seán MacEntee).

[158] *Dáil debates*, vol. 103, col. 769, 13 November 1946 (Martin Corry).

Bibliography

Primary sources

A. Archives

Cork City and County Archives (CCCA)

Papers of:
Séamus Breathnach—unsorted
Liam de Róiste—U271
Barry Egan—U404
Séamus Fitzgerald—PR6
J. J. Walsh—U355

National Archives of Ireland (NAI)

Papers of:
Department of the Taoiseach—DT
Frank MacDermott—1065

National Library of Ireland (NLI)

Papers of:
Thomas Johnson
William O'Brien

THE NATIONAL ARCHIVES: PUBLIC RECORDS OFFICE (TNA, PRO)

Cabinet minutes—CAB

UNIVERSITY COLLEGE DUBLIN ARCHIVES, SCHOOL OF HISTORY
AND ARCHIVES (UCDA)

Papers of:
Ernest Blythe—P24
Desmond and Mable FitzGerald—P80
Michael Hayes—P53
Patrick McGilligan—P35
Eoin MacNeill—LA1
Richard Mulcahy—P7
Kevin O'Higgins—P197
Michael Tierney—LA30

Miscellaneous:
Cumann na nGaedheal and Fine Gael Party minute books—P39
Records of the Fianna Fáil Party—P176

B. Newspapers, periodicals and magazines

An Phoblacht
Anglo-Celt
Clare Champion
Clonmel Chronicle
Connacht Tribune
Cork County Eagle
Cork Examiner
Cork Weekly Examiner
Crystal, The
Derry People
Donegal Democrat
Donegal Vindicator
Drogheda Independent
Dublin Evening Mail
Dundalk Democrat
Echo

Electric Mail
Enniscorthy Guardian
Evening Herald
Freeman's Journal
Free Press
Galway Observer
Irish Independent
Irishman
Irish Press
Irish Statesman
Irish Times
Kerryman
Kerry People
Kildare Observer
Kilkenny Journal
Kilkenny People
Leader
Leitrim Leader
Leitrim Observer
Limerick Chronicle
Limerick Leader
Longford Leader
Mayo News
Meath Chronicle
Midland Tribune
Nation
Nationalist and Leinster Times
New Ross Standard
New Statesman
New York Times
North Dublin Election News
Northern Standard
Oakland Tribune
Offaly Chronicle
People
Phoenix, The
Realt A'deiscirt
Roscommon Herald

Roscommon Messenger
Sinn Féin
Sligo Champion
Sligo-Leitrim Liberator
Southern Star
Star
Sunday Independent
The Times
Tipperary Man
Voice of Labour
Waterford News
Waterford Standard
Western People
Westmeath Examiner
Westmeath Independent
Wicklow People

C. Official publications

Dáil debates
Hansard
Senate debates
Seanad Éireann debates

D. Other printed primary sources

Cosgrave, William T. 1927 *Policy of the Cumann na nGaedheal party.* Dublin. Cahill and Co.

Craig, F.W.S. (ed.) 1970 *British general election manifestos, 1918–1966.* Chichester. Political Reference Publications.

Cumann na nGaedheal 1932 *Fighting points for Cumann na nGaedheal: speakers and workers, general election 1932.* Dublin. Cumann na nGaedheal.

Fanning, Ronan, Kennedy, Michael, Keogh, Dermot and O'Halpin, Eunan (eds) 2000 *Documents on Irish foreign policy: volume ii, 1923–1926.* Dublin. Royal Irish Academy.

Fanning, Ronan, Kennedy, Michael, Keogh, Dermot and O'Halpin, Eunan (eds) 2002 *Documents on Irish foreign policy: volume iii, 1926–1932.* Dublin. Royal Irish Academy.

Gallagher, Michael 1993 *Irish elections 1922–44: results and analysis.* Limerick. PSAI Press.

Irish Labour and Trade Union Congress 1927 *Thirty-third Annual report of the Irish Labour Party and Trade Union Congress.* Dublin. Irish Labour and Trade Union Congress.

Irish Labour and Trade Union Congress 1928 *Thirty-fourth Annual report of the Irish Labour Party and Trade Union Congress.* Dublin. Irish Labour and Trade Union Congress.

McLoughlin, Michael 1996 *Great Irish speeches of the twentieth century.* Dublin. Poolbeg Press.

Van der Poel, Jean (ed.) 1966–73 *Selections from the Smuts papers* (7 vols). Cambridge. Cambridge University Press.

2. SECONDARY SOURCES

A. BOOKS

Amery, L.S. 1932 *A plan of action embodying a series of reports issued by the research committee of the empire economic union and other papers.* London. Faber & Faber.

Andrews, C.S. 1982 *Man of no property.* Dublin. Mercier Press.

Bew, Paul, Patterson, Henry and Hazelkorn, Ellen 1989 *The dynamics of Irish politics.* London. Lawrence and Wishart.

Bielenberg, Andy (ed.) 2002 *The Shannon Scheme and the electrification of the Irish Free State: an inspirational milestone.* Dublin. Lilliput Press.

Blake, Robert 1997 *The Conservative Party from Peel to Major.* London. Heinemann.

Bowman, John 1982 *De Valera and the Ulster question, 1917–1973.* Oxford. Clarendon Press.

Boyce, D. George 1996 *The Irish question and British politics* (2nd edn). London. Palgrave Macmillan.

Brown, Terence 2004 *Ireland: a social and cultural history 1922–2002.* London. Harper Perennial.

Budge, Ian and Farlie, Dennis J. 1983 *Explaining and predicting elections: issue effects and party strategies in twenty-three democracies.* London. Allen Unwin.

Busteed, M.A. 1990 *Voting behaviour in the Republic of Ireland: a geographical perspective*. Oxford. Clarendon Press.

Cain, Bruce, Ferejohn, John and Fiorina, Morris 1987 *The personal vote: constituency service and electoral independence*. Cambridge. Harvard University Press.

Clark, M.J. (ed.) 1979 *Politics and the media: film and television for the political scientist and historian*. Oxford. Pergamon Press.

Clavin, Patricia 1996 *The failure of economic diplomacy: Britain, Germany, France and the United States, 1931–36*. London. Palgrave Macmillan.

Clavin, Patricia 2000 *The Great Depression in Europe, 1929–1939*. London. Macmillan.

Coleman, Shane 2006 *Foot in mouth: famous Irish political gaffes*. Dublin. Mentor Books.

Collins, Stephen 1996 *The Cosgrave legacy*. Dublin. Blackwater Press.

Connolly, S.J. (ed.) 1998 *The Oxford companion to Irish history*. Oxford. Oxford University Press.

Corish, Patrick (ed.) 1985 *Radicals, rebels, and establishments*. Belfast. Appletree Books.

Cousins, Mel 2003 *The birth of social welfare in Ireland, 1922–52*. Dublin. Four Courts Press.

Cronin, Mike 1997 *The Blueshirts and Irish politics*. Dublin. Four Courts Press.

Cronin, Mike 2008 The formation of Fine Gael in 1933. Unpublished conference paper, 'The 75th anniversary of the founding of the Fine Gael party 1933–2008' conference, Fine Gael.

Cronin, Mike and Regan, John M. (eds) 2000 *Ireland: the politics of independence, 1922–49*. Basingstoke. Palgrave Macmillan.

Daly, Mary E. 1981 *Social and economic history of Ireland since 1800*. Dublin. Educational Company of Ireland.

Davis, Richard 1974 *Arthur Griffith and non-violent Sinn Féin*. Dublin. Anvil Books.

De Vere White, Terence 1968 *Kevin O'Higgins*. London. Anvil Books.

Dolan, Anne 2003 *Commemorating the Irish Civil War: history and memory, 1923–2000*. Cambridge. Cambridge University Press.

Dunphy, Richard 1995 *The making of Fianna Fáil power in Ireland, 1923–1949*. Oxford. Oxford University Press.

Edmonds, Sean 1971 *The gun, the law and the Irish people*. Tralee. Anvil Books.

ESB 2002 *75 years of ESB advertising*. Dublin. ESB.

Eyler, Audrey S. and Garrat, Robert F.(eds) 1988 *The uses of the past: essays on Irish culture*. Newark, DE. University of Delaware Press.

Fanning, Ronan 1978 *The Irish Department of Finance 1922–1958*. Dublin. IPA.

Fanning, Ronan 1983 *Independent Ireland*. Dublin. Helicon.

Fanning, Ronan 1983 *The four-leaved shamrock: electoral politics and the national imagination in Independent Ireland*. Dublin. National University of Ireland.

Farrell, Brian 1971 *Chairman or chief: the role of the Taoiseach in Irish government*. Dublin. Gill & Macmillan.

Ferriter, Diarmaid 2001 *'Lovers of liberty'? Local government in 20ᵗʰ century Ireland*. Dublin. National Archives of Ireland.

Ferriter, Diarmaid 2005 *The transformation of Ireland, 1900–2000*. Dublin. Profile Books.

Ferriter, Diarmaid 2007 *Judging Dev: a reassessment of the life and legacy of Eamon de Valera*. Dublin. Royal Irish Academy.

Ferriter, Diarmaid 2009 *Occasions of sin: sex and society in modern Ireland*. London. Profile Books.

Fisk, Robert 1983 *In time of war: Ireland, Ulster, and the price of neutrality, 1939–45*. London. Andre Deutsch.

Gallagher, Michael 1976 *Electoral support for Irish political parties, 1927–1973*. London. Sage Publications Ltd.

Gallagher, Michael 1985 *Political parties in the Republic of Ireland*. Manchester. Manchester University Press.

Gallagher, Michael and Marsh, Michael 2002 *Days of blue loyalty: the politics of membership of the Fine Gael Party*. Dublin. PSAI Press.

Gallagher, Michael, Marsh, Michael and Mitchell, Paul (eds) 2002 *How Ireland voted 2002*. Basingstoke. Palgrave Macmillan.

Garvin, Tom 1996 *1922: the birth of Irish democracy*. Dublin. Gill & Macmillan.

Garvin, Tom 2009 *Judging Lemass: the measure of the man*. Dublin. Royal Irish Academy.

Garvin, Tom, Maurice Manning and Richard Sinnott (eds) 2004 *Dissecting Irish politics: essays in honour of Brian Farrell*. Dublin. University College Dublin Press.

Girvin, Brian 1989 *Between two worlds: politics and economy in independent Ireland*. Dublin. Gill & Macmillan.

Gorham, Maurice 1967 *Forty years of Irish broadcasting*. Dublin. Talbot Press.

Griffith, Arthur 1918 *The resurrection of Hungary: a parallel for Ireland.* Dublin. Whelan and Son.

Gwynn, Denis 1928 *The Irish Free State, 1922–27.* London. Macmillan.

Gwynn, Denis 1950 *The history of Partition, 1912–25.* Dublin. Browne and Nolan.

Harkness, D.W. 1970 *The restless dominion: the Irish Free State and the British Commonwealth of Nations, 1921–31.* New York. Macmillan.

Hill, Myrtle 2003 *Women in Ireland: a century of change.* Belfast. Blackstaff Press.

Hogan, James 1935 *Could Ireland become communist? The facts of the case.* Dublin.

Horgan, John 2001 *Irish media: a critical history since 1922.* London. Routledge.

Jackson, Alvin 1999 *Ireland 1798—1998: politics and war.* Oxford. Blackwell.

Jordan, Anthony J. 2006 *W.T. Cosgrave, 1880–1965: founder of modern Ireland.* Dublin. Westport Books.

Katz, Richard S. and Mair, Peter (eds) 1994 *How parties organise: change and adaptation in party organisations in western democracies.* London. Sage Publications Ltd.

Kavanagh, Dennis 1995 *Election campaigning: the new marketing of politics.* Oxford. Wiley-Blackwell.

Kennedy, Kieran A. (ed.) 1998 *From famine to feast: economic and social change in Ireland, 1847–1997.* Dublin. IPA.

Kennedy, Michael 1996 *Ireland and the League of Nations, 1919–1946: international relations, diplomacy and politics.* Dublin. Irish Academic Press.

Kennedy, Michael and Morrison Skelly, Joseph (eds) 2004 *Irish foreign policy, 1919–66: from independence to internationalism.* Dublin. Four Courts Press.

Keogh, Dermot 1986 *The Vatican, the bishops and Irish politics, 1919–1939.* Cambridge. Cambridge University Press.

Keogh, Dermot 1988 *Ireland and Europe, 1919–1948.* Dublin. Gill & Macmillan.

Keogh, Dermot 1994 *Twentieth century Ireland: nation and state.* Dublin. Gill & Macmillan.

Kissane, Bill 2002 *Explaining Irish democracy.* Dublin. University College Dublin Press.

Kotsonouris, Mary 2004 *The winding-up of the Dáil courts, 1922–1925: an obvious duty.* Dublin. Four Courts Press.

Laffan, Michael 1983 *The Partition of Ireland, 1911–25.* Dundalk. Dundalgan Press.

Laffan, Michael 1999 *The resurrection of Ireland: the Sinn Féin Party, 1916–1923.* Cambridge. Cambridge University Press.

Laffan, Michael 2006 Illustrious corpses: nationalist funerals in independent Ireland. Unpublished conference paper, 'The politics of dead bodies' conference, University College Dublin.

Lee, J.J. 1989 *Ireland 1912–1985: politics and society.* Cambridge. Cambridge University Press.

MacDonagh, Oliver 1983 *States of mind: a study of Anglo–Irish conflict, 1780–1980.* London. Allen & Unwin.

MacManus, Francis (ed.) 1967 *The years of the great test.* Dublin. Mercier Press.

Mair, Peter 1987 *The changing Irish party system.* London. F. Pinter.

Manning, Maurice 1972 *Irish political parties: an introduction.* Dublin. Gill & Macmillan.

Manning, Maurice and McDowell, Moore 1984 *Electricity supply in Ireland: the history of the ESB.* Dublin. Gill & Macmillan.

Manning, Maurice 1999 *James Dillon: a biography.* Dublin. Wolfhound Press.

Manning, Maurice 2006 *The Blueshirts.* Dublin. Gill & Macmillan.

Mansergh, Nicholas 1991 *The unresolved question.* Yale. Yale University Press.

Martin, F.X. and Byrne, F.J. (eds) 1973 *The scholar revolutionary: Eoin MacNeill, 1867-1945, and the making of the new Ireland.* Cork. Irish University Press.

Matthews, Kevin 2004 *Fatal influence: the impact of Ireland on British politics, 1920–1925.* Dublin. University College Dublin Press.

Maume, Patrick 1995 *D.P. Moran.* Dundalk. Dundalgan Press.

Maye, Brian 1993 *Fine Gael, 1923–1987: a general history with biographical sketches of leading members.* Dublin. Blackwater Press.

Mazower, Mark 1998 *Dark continent: Europe's twentieth century.* London. Penguin.

McCarthy, John P. 2006 *Kevin O'Higgins: builder of the Irish Free State.* Dublin. Irish Academic Press.

McCarthy, Michael 2004 *High tension: life on the Shannon Scheme.* Dublin. Lilliput Press.

McCartney, Donal 1987 *The dawning of democracy: Ireland 1800–1870*. Dublin. Helicon.

McCullagh, David 1998 *A makeshift majority: the first inter-party government, 1948–51*. Dublin. IPA.

McGarry, Fearghal (ed.) 2005 *Eoin O'Duffy: a self-made hero*. Oxford. Oxford University Press.

McNamara, Maedhbh and Mooney, Paschal 2000 *Women in parliament: Ireland, 1918–2000*. Dublin. Wolfhound Press.

Mitchell, Arthur 1974 *Labour in Irish politics, 1890–1930: the Irish Labour movement in an age of revolution*. Dublin. Irish University Press.

Morrissey, Thomas J. 1991 *A man called Hughes: the life and times of Séamus Hughes, 1881–1943*. Dublin. Veritas.

Moss, Warner 1933 *Political parties in the Irish Free State*. New York. Columbia University Press.

Mulcahy, Risteárd 2009 *My father, the general: Richard Mulcahy and the military history of the revolution*. Dublin. Liberties Press.

Munger, Frank 1975 *The legitimacy of opposition: the change of government in Ireland in 1932*. Beverley Hills, CA. Sage Publications Ltd.

Murphy, John A. 1975 *Ireland in the twentieth century*. Dublin. Gill & Macmillan.

Murray, Patrick 2000 *Oracles of God: the Roman Catholic Church and Irish politics, 1922–37*. Dublin. University College Dublin Press.

Nowlan, Kevin B. and Williams, T. Desmond (eds) 1969 *Ireland in the war years and after, 1939–51*. Dublin. Gill & Macmillan.

O'Carroll, J.P. and Murphy, John A. (eds) 1983 *De Valera and his times: political development in the Republic of Ireland*. Cork. Cork University Press.

O'Connell, T.J. 1969 *A history of the Irish National Teachers' Organisation, 1868–1968*. Dublin. Irish National Teachers' Organisation.

O'Farrell, Padraic 1997 *Who's who in the Irish War of Independence and Civil War, 1916–1923*. Dublin. Lilliput Press.

Ó Gráda, Cormac 1995 *Ireland: a new economic history, 1780–1939*. Oxford. Clarendon Press.

O'Hagan, J.W. (ed.) 1981 *The economy of Ireland: policy and performance* (3rd edn). Dublin. Irish Management Institute.

O'Hagan, J.W. 1995 *The economy of Ireland: policy and performance of a small European country*. Dublin. Gill & Macmillan.

O'Kennedy, Brian 1927 *Making history: the story of a remarkable campaign*. Dublin. O'Kennedy-Brindley.

O'Kennedy-Brindley 1928 *With the president in America: the authorised record of President Cosgrave's tour in the United States and Canada.* Dublin. O'Kennedy-Brindley.

O'Leary, Cornelius 1961 *The Irish Republic and its experiment with proportional representation.* Notre Dame. University of Notre Dame Press.

O'Leary, Cornelius 1979 *Irish elections 1918–1977: parties, voters and proportional representation.* Dublin. Gill & Macmillan.

O'Leary, Olivia 2004 *Politicians and other animals.* Dublin. The O'Brien Press.

O'Sullivan, Donal 1940 *The Irish Free State and its senate: a study in contemporary politics.* London. Faber & Faber.

Pine, Richard 2002 *2RN and the origins of Irish radio.* Dublin. Four Courts Press.

Prager, Jeffrey 1986 *Building democracy in Ireland: political order and cultural integration in a newly independent nation.* Cambridge. Cambridge University Press.

Puirséil, Niamh 2007 *The Irish Labour Party 1922–73.* Dublin. University College Dublin Press.

Rafter, Kevin 1996 *The Clann: the story of Clann na Poblachta.* Dublin. Mercier Press.

Regan, John M. 1999 *The Irish counter-revolution 1921–1936: Treatyite politics and settlement in independent Ireland.* Dublin. Gill & Macmillan.

Reynolds, Brian A. 1976 The formation and development of Fianna Fáil, 1926–1933. Unpublished PhD thesis, Trinity College Dublin.

Reynolds, Brian A. 1998 *William T. Cosgrave and the foundation of the Irish Free State, 1922-25: an analysis of the rise to power of William T. Cosgrave and his leadership in creating a structure of government in the Irish Free State.* Kilkenny.

Richards, Paul 2001 *How to win an election: the art of political campaigning.* London. Politico's.

Rose, Richard 1967 *Influencing voters: a study of campaign rationality.* London. St Martin's Press.

Rose, Richard (ed.) 1974 *Electoral behaviour: a comparative handbook.* New York. The Free Press.

Rose, Richard and Mackie, Thomas 1980 *Incumbency in government: asset or liability?* Glasgow. Centre for the Study of Public Policy.

Ryan, Desmond 1936 *Unique dictator: a study of Eamon de Valera.* London. Arthur Barker.

Seldon, Anthony and Bell, Stuart (eds) 1994 *Conservative century: the Conservative Party since 1900*. Oxford. Oxford University Press.

Severn, Bill 1971 *Irish statesman and rebel: the two lives of Eamon de Valera*. Whitstable. Bailey Bros. and Swinfea Ltd.

Sheedy, Kieran 1993 *The Clare elections*. Dun Laoghaire. Bauroe.

Shiel, Michael 2003 *The quiet revolution: the electrification of rural Ireland*. Dublin. The O'Brien Press.

Sinnott, Richard 1994 *Irish voters decide: voting behaviour in elections and referendums since 1918*. Manchester. Manchester University Press.

Sommerville-Large, Peter 1999 *Irish voices: fifty years of Irish life, 1916–1966*. London. Chatto & Windus.

Thorpe, Andrew 1997 *A history of the British Labour Party*. London. Palgrave Macmillan.

Travers, Pauric 1994 *Eamon de Valera*. Dundalk. Dundalgan Press.

Valiulis, Maryann Gialanella 1985 *Almost a rebellion: the Irish Army mutiny of 1924*. Cork. Irish Academic Press.

Walsh, J.J. 1944 *Recollections of a rebel*. Tralee. The Kerryman Ltd.

Ward, Alan J. 1994 *The Irish constitutional tradition: responsible government and modern Ireland, 1782–1992*. Dublin. Irish Academic Press.

B. Articles and papers

Ansolabehere, Stephen, Iyengar, Shanto, Adam, Simon, and Valentino, Nicholas 1994 Does attack advertising demobilise the electorate? *American Political Science Review* **88**(4), 829–38.

Bielenberg, Andy 2002 Seán Keating, the Shannon Scheme and the art of state-building. In Andy Bielenberg (ed.), *The Shannon Scheme and the electrification of the Irish Free State*, 114–37. Dublin. Lilliput Press.

Bowler, Shaun and Farrell, David M. 1991 Party loyalties in complex settings: STV and party identification. *Political Studies* **39**(2), 350–62.

Chrystal, William G. 1975 Nazi Party election films, 1927–1938. *Cinema Journal* **15**(1), 29–47.

Coakley, John 1980 The significance of names: the evolution of Irish party labels. *Études Irlandaises* 5, 171–81.

Coakley, John 1990 Minor parties in Irish political life, 1922–1989. *Economic and Social Review* **21**, 269–97.

Coakley, John 2002 The election and the party system. In Michael

Gallagher, Michael Marsh and Paul Mitchell (eds), *How Ireland voted 2002*, 230–46. Basingstoke. Palgrave Macmillan.

Cockett, Richard 1994 The party, publicity, and the media. In Anthony Seldon and Stuart Bell (eds), *Conservative century: the Conservative Party since 1900*, 547–77. Oxford. Oxford University Press.

Cronin, Mike 2000 Golden dreams, harsh realities: economics and informal empire in the Irish Free State. In Mike Cronin and John M. Regan (eds), *Ireland: the politics of independence, 1922–49*, 144–63. Basingstoke. Palgrave Macmillan.

Cronin, Mike 2003 Projecting the nation through sport and culture: Ireland, Aonach Tailteann and the Irish Free State, 1924–32. *Journal of Contemporary History* **38**(3), 395–411.

Curran, Joseph M. 1966 Ireland since 1916. *Éire-Ireland* **1**(3), 14–28.

Delany, Brendan 2002 McLaughlin, the genesis of the Shannon Scheme and the ESB. In Andy Bielenberg (ed.), *The Shannon Scheme and the electrification of the Irish Free State: an inspirational milestone*, 11–27. Dublin. Lilliput Press.

Dunleavy, Patrick, Jones, G.W., Burnham, Jane, Elgie, Robert and Fysh, Peter 1993 Leaders, politics and institutional change: the decline of prime ministerial accountability to the House of Commons, 1868–1990. *British Journal of Political Science* **23**(3), 267–98.

Dunleavy, Patrick, Jones, G.W. and O'Leary, Brendan 1990 Prime ministers and the Commons: patterns of behaviour, 1868 to 1987. *Public Administration* **68**(1), 123–40.

Eatwell, Roger and Wright, Anthony 1978 Labour and the lessons of 1931. *History* **63**, 34–53.

Elgie, Robert and Stapleton, John 2006 Testing the decline of parliament thesis: Ireland, 1923–2002. *Political Studies* **54**(3), 465–85.

Farrell, David M. 1994 Ireland: centralization: professionalisation and competitive pressures. In Richard S. Katz and Peter Mair (eds), *How parties organise: change and adaptation in party organisations in western democracies*, 216–41. London. Sage Publications Ltd.

Farrell, David M. 2004 Before campaigns were 'modern': Irish electioneering in times past. In Tom Garvin, Maurice Manning and Richard Sinnott (eds), *Dissecting Irish politics: essays in honour of Brian Farrell*, 178–97. Dublin. University College Dublin Press.

The Cosgrave Party

Finnane, Mark 2001 The Carrigan Committee, 1930–31. *Irish Historical Studies* **32** (128), 519–36.

Gallagher, Michael 2005 Parliament. In John Coakley and Michael Gallagher (eds), *Politics in the Republic of Ireland* (4th edn), 211–41. New York. Routledge.

Garvin, Tom 1977 Nationalist elites, Irish voters, and Irish political development: a comparative perspective. *Economic and Social Review* **8**, 161–86.

Hand, Geoffrey J. 1973 MacNeill and the Boundary Commission. In F.X. Martin and F.J. Byrne (eds), *The scholar revolutionary: Eoin MacNeill, 1867–1945, and the making of the new Ireland*, 199–275. Cork. Irish University Press.

Harrop, Martin 1990 Political marketing. *Parliamentary Affairs* **43**(2), 277–91.

Haughton, Jonathan 1995 The historical background. In J.W. O'Hagan (ed.), *The economy of Ireland: policy and performance of a small European country*, 1–48. Dublin. Gill & Macmillan.

Hollins, T.J. 1981 The Conservative Party and film propaganda between the wars. *English Historical Review* **96**, 359–69.

Horgan, John 1997 Fianna Fáil & arms decommissioning. *History Ireland* **5**(4), 49–53.

Kavanagh, Dennis 1981 The politics of manifestos. *Parliamentary Affairs* **34**, 7–27.

Kavanagh, Dennis 1989 The timing of elections: the British case. In Ian Crewe and Martin Harrop (eds), *Political communications: the general election campaign of 1987*, 314. Cambridge. Cambridge University Press.

Keogh, Dermot 1983 De Valera, the Catholic Church and the 'Red scare' 1931-1932. In J.P. O'Carroll and John A. Murphy (eds), *De Valera and his times*, 134–59. Cork. Cork University Press.

Keown, Gerard 2000 Taking the world stage: creating an Irish foreign policy in the 1920s. In Michael Kennedy and Joseph Morrison Skelly (eds), *Irish foreign policy 1919–1966: from independence to internationalism*, 25–43. Dublin. Four Courts Press.

Kennedy, Finola 2000 The suppression of the Carrigan Report: a historical perspective on child abuse. *Studies* **89**(356), 354–62.

Laffan, Michael 1985 'Labour must wait': Ireland's conservative revolution. In Patrick Corish (ed.), *Radicals, rebels, and establishments*, 203–22. Belfast. Appletree Press.

Laffan, Michael 2009 Arthur Griffith. In James McGuire and James Quinn (eds), *Dictionary of Irish biography*, 278. Cambridge. Cambridge University Press.

Laver, Michael 1986 Ireland: politics with some social bases. *Economic and Social Review* **17**(3), 107–31.

Lowry, Donal 2000 New Ireland, old empire and the outside world, 1922–1949: the strange evolution of a dictionary republic. In Mike Cronin and John M. Regan (eds), *Ireland: the politics of independence, 1922–49*, 164–216. Basingstoke. Palgrave Macmillan.

McCarthy, Michael 2002 How the Shannon Scheme workers lived. In Andy Bielenberg (ed.), *The Shannon Scheme and the electrification of the Irish Free State*, 48–72. Dublin. Lilliput Press.

McInerney, Michael 1974 and 1975 Ernest Blythe: a political profile. *Irish Times* (30, 31 December and 1–4 January).

MacNeill, Eoin 1932 Ten years of the Irish Free State. *Foreign Affairs* **10**, 235–49.

Manning, Maurice 1984 The *New York Times* and Irish politics in the 1920s. *Études Irlandaises* **9**, 217–27.

Mansergh, Nicholas 1967 Ireland: external relations, 1926–1939. In Francis MacManus (ed.), *The years of the great test, 1926–1939*, 127–137. Cork. Mercier Press.

Maume, Patrick 1998 Nationalism and Partition: the political thought of Arthur Clery. *Irish Historical Studies* **13**, 222–40.

Maume, Patrick 2009 James Joseph Walsh. In James McGuire and James Quinn (eds), *Dictionary of Irish biography*, 738. Cambridge. Cambridge University Press.

Meehan, Ciara 2009 Fine Gael's uncomfortable history: the legacy of Cumann na nGaedheal. *Éire-Ireland* **43**(3&4), 253–66.

Meenan, James 1967 From free trade to self sufficiency. In Francis McManus (ed.), *The years of the great test, 1926–39*, 69–79. Dublin. Mercier Press.

Mezo, Josu 1994 Nationalist political elites and language in Ireland, 1922–1937. In Justo G. Beramendi, Ramón Máiz and Xosé M. Núñez (eds), *Nationalism in Europe: past and present* (2 vols), 209–22. Santiago de Compostela. Universidade de Santiago de Compostela.

Murphy, John A. 1969 The Irish party system. In Kevin B. Nowlan and T. Desmond Williams (eds), *Ireland in the war years and after, 1939–51*, 147–66. Dublin. Gill & Macmillan.

Ó Brolcháin, A. 1932 The economic problem of the Gaeltacht. In Bulmer Hobson (ed.), *Saorstát Éireann: Irish Free State official handbook*. Dublin. Talbot Press.

O'Callaghan, Margaret 1984 Language, nationality and cultural identity in the Irish Free State, 1922–7: the *Irish Statesman* and the *Catholic Bulletin* reappraised. *Irish Historical Studies* **14** (94), 226–45.

O'Callaghan, Margaret 1999/2000 Old parchment and water: the Boundary Commission on 1925 and the copper fastening of the Irish border. *Búllan: An Irish Studies Journal* **4**(2), 27–55.

Ó Gráda, Cormac 1998 The rise in living standards. In Kieran A. Kennedy (ed.), *From famine to feast: economic and social change in Ireland, 1847–1997*, 12–22. Dublin. IPA.

Ó Gráda, Cormac 2000 The political economy of the old age pension: Ireland *c*. 1908–1940. *Centre for Economic Research: Working Paper Series*, 1–49.

O'Halpin, Eunan 2004 'Weird prophecies': British intelligence and Anglo-Irish relations, 1932–3. In Michael Kennedy and Joseph Morrison Skelly (eds), *Irish foreign policy, 1919–66: from independence to internationalism*, 61–73. Dublin. Four Courts Press.

O'Halpin, Eunan 2009 William Thomas Cosgrave. In James McGuire and James Quinn (eds), *Dictionary of Irish biography*, 881. Cambridge. Cambridge University Press.

Pollock, James K. 1928 The Irish Free State elections of September 1927. *The American Political Science Review* **22**(1), 154–6.

Ruane, F.P. 1981 Review of industrial policies. In J.W. O'Hagan (ed.), *The economy of Ireland: policy and performance* (3rd edn), 291–300. Dublin. Irish Management Institute.

Scott, Peter Hardiman 1979 The development of an approach to the presentation of political and current affairs on television: the experience of the BBC. In M.J. Clark (ed.), *Politics and the media: film and television for the political scientist and historian*, 3–8. Oxford. Pergamon Press.

Sinnott, Richard 1993 The electoral system. In John Coakley and Michael Gallagher (eds), *Politics in the Republic of Ireland* (2nd edn), 67–85. Dublin. PSAI Press.

Smith, Paul 1979 Political style on film: Neville Chamberlain. In M.J. Clark (ed.), *Politics and the media: film and television for the political scientist and historian*, 87–93. Oxford. Pergamon Press.

Staunton, Enda 1996 The Boundary Commission debacles of 1925: aftermath and implications. *History Ireland* **4**(2), 42–5.

Valiulis, Maryann Gialanella 1988 After the revolution: the formative years of Cumann na nGaedheal. In Audrey S. Eyler and Robert F. Garrat (eds), *The uses of the past: essays on Irish culture*, 131–43. Newark, DE. University of Delaware Press.

Whyte, J.H 1974 Ireland: politics without social bases. In Richard Rose (ed.), *Electoral behaviour: a comparative handbook*, 619–52. New York. Free P.

C. Internet resources

Hayes, Brian 2003 Ireland, republicanism and Fine Gael (address to the Ireland Institute). See: www.finegael.ie/news/index.cfm/type/details/nkey/22835 (1 June 2010).

Hyde, Douglas 1926 Address to mark the opening of 2RN (in Irish). See: www.rte.ie/laweb/brc/brc_1920s.html (1 June 2010).

Irish Statute Book is available online to view various legislation at: www.irishstatutebook.com (1 June 2010).

Selected reading

Primary sources

A. Archives

National Library of Ireland (NLI)
Thomas O'Donnell

University College Dublin Archives, School of History and Archives (UCDA)
Papers of:
Frank Aiken—P104
John A. Costello—P190
Eamon de Valera—P150
Seán Lemass—P161
Seán Lester—P203
Seán MacEntee—P67

B. Newspapers, periodicals and magazines

Advertiser
Ballina Herald
Catholic Pictorial
Clonmel Nationalist
Connaught Telegraph
Derry Journal
Dungarvan Observer
East Galway Democrat

Enniscorthy Echo
Free State / An Saorstát
Freeman
Gaelic American
Informer, The
Irish Catholic Herald
Irish Truth
Kerry News
Kerry Reporter
Kilkenny Post
Kingdom
King's County Chronicle
Leinster Express
Leinster Leader
Limerick Echo
Magill
Manchester Guardian
Munster News
Nenagh Guardian
Offaly Independent
Round Table
Roscommon Journal
Saturday Record
South Dublin Chronicle
Strokestown Democrat
Sunday Business Post
Tipperary Star
Waterford Evening News
Waterford Evening Star
Weekly Observer
Westmeath Nationalist
Wexford People
Workers' Republic

C. Other printed primary sources

Cronin, Seán (ed.) 1972 *The McGarrity papers: revelations of the Irish revolutionary movement in Ireland and America 1900–1940*. Tralee. Anvil Books.

Fanning, Ronan, Kennedy, Michael, Keogh, Dermot and O'Halpin, Eunan (eds) 1998 *Documents on Irish foreign policy: volume i, 1919–1922.* Dublin. Royal Irish Academy.

Moynihan, Maurice (ed.) 1980 *Speeches and statements by Eamon de Valera, 1917–73.* Dublin. Palgrave Macmillan.

2. SECONDARY SOURCES

A. BOOKS

Akenson, Donald Harman 1975 *A mirror to Kathleen's face: education in independent Ireland, 1922–1960.* London. McGill-Queens University Press.

Allen, Kieran 1997 *Fianna Fáil and Irish Labour: 1926 to the present.* London. Pluto Press.

Anderson, James and Bort, Eberhard (eds) 1999 *The Irish border: history, politics, culture.* Liverpool. Liverpool University Press.

Andrews, C.S. 1979 *Dublin made me.* Dublin. Mercier Press.

Bax, Mart 1976 *Harp strings and confessions: an anthropological study of politics in rural Ireland.* Amsterdam. Van Corcum.

Bell, J.B. 1987 *The gun in politics: an analysis of Irish political conflict, 1916–1986.* New Brunswick. Transaction Books.

Bew, Paul and Patterson, Henry 1982 *Seán Lemass and the making of modern Ireland, 1945–66.* Dublin. Gill & Macmillan.

Bowler, Shaun and Farrell, David M. (eds) 1992 *Electoral strategies and political marketing.* Basingstoke. Palgrave Macmillan.

Boyce, D. George 1982 *Nationalism in Ireland.* London. Croom Helm.

Boyce, D. George 1990 *Nineteenth century Ireland: the search for stability.* Dublin. Gill & Macmillan.

Brennan, Robert 1958 *Allegiance.* Dublin. Brown and Nolan.

Briscoe, Robert and Hatch, Alden 1959 *For the life of me.* London. Longmans.

Budge, Ian and Farlie, Dennis J. 1983 *Voting and party competition: a theoretical critique and synthesis applied to surveys from ten democracies.* London. Wiley.

Bromage, Mary 1964 *Churchill and Ireland.* South Bend. University of Notre Dame Press.

Cain, P.J. and Hopkins, A.G. 1993 *British imperialism: crisis and decon-struction 1914–1990*. London. Longman.

Canning, Paul 1985 *British policy towards Ireland, 1921–1941*. Oxford. Oxford University Press.

Carty, R.K. 1981 *Party and parish pump: electoral politics in Ireland*. Waterloo, Ont. Wilfrid Laurier University Press.

Chubb, Basil (ed.) 1964 *A source book of Irish government*. Dublin. IPA.

Chubb, Basil (ed.) 1971 *The government and politics of Ireland*. London. Longman.

Chubb, Basil (ed.) 1974 *Cabinet government in Ireland*. Dublin. IPA.

Cronin, Seán (ed.) 1980 *Irish nationalism: a history of its roots and ide-ology*. Dublin. Academy Press.

Cruise O'Brien, Conor (ed.) 1960 *The shaping of modern Ireland*. London. Routledge & Paul.

Curran, Joseph M. 1980 *The birth of the Irish Free State 1921–1923*. Alabama. University of Alabama Press.

Daly, Mary E. 1992 *Industrial development and Irish national identity, 1922–1939*. Dublin. Gill & Macmillan.

De Vere, Joan 1990 *In ruin reconciled: a memoir of Anglo–Ireland, 1913–1959*. Dublin. Lilliput Press.

Dwyer, T. Ryle 2001 *Tans, terror and troubles: Kerry's real fighting story, 1913–1923* Cork. Mercier Press.

English, Richard 1994 *Radicals and the republic: socialist republicanism in the Irish Free State, 1925–1937*. Oxford. Clarendon Press.

Farrell, Brian 1971 *The founding of Dáil Éireann: parliament and nation building*. Dublin. Gill & Macmillan.

Farrell, Brian (ed.) 1973 *The Irish parliamentary tradition*. Dublin. Gill & Macmillan.

Farrell, Brian 1983 *Seán Lemass*. Dublin. Gill & Macmillan.

FitzGerald, Garret 1991 *All in a life: an autobiography*. Dublin. Gill & Macmillan.

FitzGerald, Garret 2003 *Reflections on the Irish state*. Dublin. Irish Academic Press.

Fitzpatrick, David 1998 *The two Irelands, 1912–1939*. Oxford. Oxford University Press.

Flynn, William J. (ed.) 1932 *Free State parliamentary companion for 1932*. Dublin. Talbot Press.

Garvin, Tom 1981 *The evolution of Irish nationalist politics*. Dublin. Gill & Macmillan.

{292}

Gaughan, J. Anthony 1981 *Thomas Johnson 1872–1963: first leader of the Labour Party in Dáil Eireann*. Dublin. Kingdom Books.

Hill, Ronald J. and Marsh, Michael (eds) 1993 *Modern Irish democracy: essays in honour of Basil Chubb*. Dublin. Irish Academic Press.

Hoppen, K. Theodore 1989 *Ireland since 1800: conflict and conformity*. London. Longman.

Horgan, John 1986 *Labour: the price of power*. Dublin. Gill & Macmillan.

Horgan, John 1997 *Seán Lemass: the enigmatic patriot*. Dublin. Gill & Macmillan.

Jackson, Alvin 2003 *Home rule: an Irish history, 1800–2000*. London. Weidenfeld.

Jamieson, K.H. 1992 *Dirty politics: deception, distraction and democracy*. New York. Oxford University Press.

Johnson, David 1985 *The inter-war economy in Ireland*. Dublin. Economic & Social History Society of Ireland.

Kavanagh, Ray 1988 *Labour from the beginning: a short history of the Labour Party, 1912–1987*. Dublin. Elo Press.

Lawlor, Catriona (ed.) 2005 *Seán MacBride: that day's struggle, a memoir 1904–1951*. Dublin. Currach Press.

Lee, J.J. and Ó Tuathaigh, Gearóid 1982 *The age of de Valera*. Dublin. Ward River Press.

Long, Brendan 1999 *Tipperary SR County Council, 1899–1999: a century of local democracy*. Clonmel. Tipperary SR County Council.

Lyons, F.S.L. 1971 *Ireland since the Famine*. London. Weidenfeld and Nicolson.

Lyons, F.S.L. 1979 *Culture and anarchy in Ireland, 1890–1939*. Oxford. Clarendon Press.

McCracken, John L. 1958 *Representative government in Ireland: a study of Dáil Éireann, 1919–48*. London. Oxford University Press.

MacDonagh, Oliver 1977 *Ireland: the union and its aftermath*. London. Allen & Unwin.

McGarry, Fearghal (ed.) 2003 *Republicanism in modern Ireland*. Dublin. University College Dublin Press.

McInerney, Michael 1974 *Peadar O'Donnell: Irish social rebel*. Dublin. The O'Brien Press.

Mair, Peter 1997 *Party system change: approaches and interpretations*. Oxford. Oxford University Press.

Mansergh, Nicholas 1934 *The Irish Free State: its government and politics*. London. George Allen & Unwin.

Mansergh, Nicholas 1941 *Britain and Ireland*. London. Longman.

Martin, Micheál 2009 *Freedom to choose: Cork and party politics in Ireland, 1918–1932* Cork. Collins Press.

Maume, Patrick 1993 *'Life that is exile': Daniel Corkery and the search for Irish Ireland*. Belfast. Institute of Irish Studies, Queen's University Belfast.

Maume, Patrick 1999 *The long gestation: Irish nationalist life, 1891–1918*. Dublin. Gill & Macmillan.

Mauser, Gary A. 1983 *Political marketing: an approach to campaign strategy*. New York. Praeger.

Meenan, James 1970 *The Irish economy since 1922*. Liverpool. Liverpool University Press.

Mulcahy, Risteárd 1999 *Richard Mulcahy (1886–1971): a family memoir*. Dublin. Aurelian Press.

Ní Dhomhnaill, Nuala 2001 *RTÉ 100 years: Ireland in the 20th century*. Dublin. Town House.

O'Brien, Mark 2001 *De Valera, Fianna Fáil and the 'Irish Press'*. Dublin. Irish Academic Press.

Ó Corráin, Donnchadh (ed.) 2000 *James Hogan: revolutionary, historian and political scientist*. Dublin. Four Courts Press.

O'Donnell, Peadar 1963 *There will be another day*. Dublin. Dolmen Press.

O'Mahony, Patrick J. and Delanty, Gerard 1998 *Rethinking Irish history: nationalism, identity and ideology*. Basingstoke. Palgrave Macmillan.

Ó Muircheartaigh, Fionán (ed.) 1997 *Ireland in the coming times: essays to celebrate T.K.Whitaker's 80 years*. Dublin. IPA.

O'Neill, Máire 1991 *From Parnell to de Valera: a biography of Jennie Wyse Power, 1858–1941*. Dublin. Blackwater Press.

O'Sullivan, Harold 2000 *History of local government in the county of Louth: from earliest times to the present time*. Dublin. IPA.

Pakenham, Frank 1935 (1992 edn) *Peace by ordeal: the negotiations of the Anglo-Irish Treaty, 1921*. London. Pimlico.

[Pakenham, Frank] Longford, Lord and O'Neill, Thomas P. 1970 *Eamon de Valera*. London. Gill & Macmillan.

Philipin, C.H.E. (ed.) 1987 *Nationalism and popular protest in Ireland*. Cambridge. Cambridge University Press.

Pronay, Nicholas and Spring, D.W. 1982 *Politics, propaganda and film, 1918–1945*. Basingstoke. Macmillan.

Reid, Austin 1994 *Ireland since 1923: politics or violence?* London. Longman.

Ross, J.F.S. 1959 *The Irish election system.* London. Pall Mall Press.

Rumpf, Erhard and Hepburn A.C. 1977 *Nationalism and socialism in twentieth-century Ireland.* Liverpool. Liverpool University Press.

Sacks, Paul M. 1976 *The Donegal mafia: an Irish political machine.* London. Yale University Press.

Savage, Robert 1999 *Seán Lemass.* Dundalk. Dundalgan Press.

Schmitt, David 1973 *The irony of Irish democracy: the impact of political culture on administration and democratic development in Ireland.* Lexington, MA. D.C. Heath.

Tanner, Duncan, Thane, Pat and Tiratsoo, Nick (eds) 2000 *Labour's first century.* Cambridge. Cambridge University Press.

Townshend, Charles 1999 *Ireland: the twentieth century.* London. Arnold.

Valiulis, Maryann Gialanella 1992 *Portrait of a revolutionary: General Richard Mulcahy and the foundation of the Irish State.* Dublin. Irish Academic Press.

Walker, Brian (ed.) 1974 *Dáil Éireann election results, 1922–1944.* Dublin. Royal Irish Academy.

Walker, Brian (ed.) 1992 *Parliamentary election results in Ireland 1918–92.* Dublin. Royal Irish Academy.

Walsh, Pat 1994 *Irish republicanism and socialism: the politics of the republican movement 1905–1994.* Belfast. Athol Books.

Ware, Alan 1987 *Political parties: electoral change and structural response.* Oxford. Blackwell.

Younger, Calton 1968 *Ireland's Civil War.* London. Muller.

B. Articles and papers

Augusteijn, Joost 2003 Political violence and democracy: an analysis of the tensions within Irish republican strategy, 1914–2002. *Irish Political Studies* **18**(1), 1–26.

Baranczak, Stanislaw 1992 Memory: lost, retrieved, abused, defended. *Ideas* **1**(1), 3–14.

Barrington, T.J. 1967 Public administration, 1927–36. In Francis MacManus (ed.), *The years of the great test 1926–1939,* 80–91. Dublin. Mercier Press.

Busteed, John 1930 Agriculture and employment in the Free State 1926–30. *Studies* **19**, 185–98.

Carty, R.K. 1980 Politicians and electoral laws: an anthropology of party competition in Ireland. *Political Studies* **28**(4), 550–66.

Chubb, Basil 1957 The independent member in Ireland. *Political Studies* **5**, 131–9.

Chubb, Basil 1963 Going about persecuting civil servants: the role of the Irish parliamentary representative. *Political Studies* **11**(3), 272–86.

Coakley, John 1984 Selecting a prime minister: the Irish experience. *Parliamentary Affairs* **37**(4), 403–17.

Coakley, John and Farrell, Brian 1989 The selection of Cabinet ministers in Ireland, 1922–1982. In Mattei Dogan (ed.), *Pathways to power: selecting rulers in pluralist democracies*, 199–218. London. Westview.

Coakley, John 1995 Competing conceptions of legitimacy and the creation of the new state. *Études Irlandaises* **20**(1), 55–65.

Coughlan, Anthony 1966 Public affairs, 1916–66: the social scene. *Administration* **14**(3), 204–14.

Cronin, Mike 1994 The socio-economic background and membership of the Blueshirt movement, 1932–35. *Irish Historical Studies* **29**(144), 234–49.

Cronin, Mike 1995 The Blueshirt movement, 1932–5: Ireland's fascists? *Journal of Contemporary History* **30**(2), 311–32.

Daniel, T.K. 1976 Griffith on his noble head: the determinants of Cumann na nGaedheal economic policy, 1922–32. *Irish Economic and Social History* **3**, 55–65.

Delaney, Enda 1998 State politics and demography: the case of Irish emigration, 1921–71. *Irish Political Studies* **13**, 25–49.

Dunphy, Richard 2000 The enigma of Fianna Fáil: party strategy, social classes and the politics of hegemony. In Mike Cronin and John M. Regan (eds), *Ireland: the politics of independence, 1922–49*, 67–83. Basingstoke. Palgrave Macmillian.

Fanning, Ronan 1986 Britain's legacy: government and administration. In P.J. Drudy (ed.), *Ireland and Britain since 1922: Irish studies 5*, 45–64. Cambridge. Cambridge University Press.

Fanning, Ronan 1998 Small states, large neighbours: Ireland and the United Kingdom. *Irish Studies in International Affairs* **9**, 21–30.

Farrell, Brian 1968 The new state and Irish political culture. *Administration* **16**, 238–46.

Farrell, Brian 1972 The paradox of Irish politics. In Brian Farrell (ed.), *The Irish parliamentary tradition*, 13–25. Dublin. Gill & Macmillan.

Farrell, Brian 1985 Ireland: from friends and neighbours to clients and partisans. Some dimensions of parliamentary representation under PR-STV. In Vernon Bogdanor (ed.), *Representatives of the people? Parliamentarians and constituents in western democracies*, 237–66. London. Gower Publishing.

Farrell, Brian 1988 From first Dáil through Free State. In Brian Farrell (ed.), *De Valera's Constitution and ours*, 18–32. Dublin. Gill & Macmillan.

Gallagher, Michael 1978 Party solidarity, exclusivity, and inter-party relationships in Ireland, 1922–1977. *Economic and Social Review* **10**(1), 1–22.

Gallagher, Michael 1986 The political consequences of the electoral system in the Republic of Ireland. *Electoral Studies* **5**(3), 253–76.

Gallagher, Michael 1999 Politics in Laois-Offaly, 1922–92. In Pádraig G. Lane and William Nolan (eds), *Laois: history and society, interdisciplinary essays on the history of an Irish country*, 657–87.

Gallagher, Tom 1985 Fianna Fáil and Partition, 1926–1984. *Éire-Ireland* **20**(1), 28–57.

Garside, W.R. 1998 Party politics, political economy and British protectionism, 1919-1932. *History* **83** (269), 47–65.

Garvin, Tom 1971 The formation of the Irish political elite. In Brian Farrell (ed.), *The founding of Dáil Éireann: parliament and nation building*, 47–60. Dublin. Gill & Macmillan.

Garvin, Tom 1972 Continuity and change in Irish electoral politics. *Economic and Social Review* **3**, 359–72.

Garvin, Tom 1978 The destiny of the soldiers: tradition and modernity in the politics of de Valera's Ireland. *Political Studies* **26**(3), 328–47.

Greary, R.C. 1951 Irish economic development since the Treaty. *Studies* **11**, 399–418.

Harkness, David 1979–80 Patrick McGilligan: man of Commonwealth. *Journal of Imperial and Commonwealth History* **8**, 117–35.

Harrison, Michael J. and Marsh, Michael 1994 What can he do for us? Leader effects on party fortunes in Ireland. *Electoral Studies* **13**(4), 289–312.

Harrison, William M. 1995 European postcoloniality: *the Saorstát Éireann / Irish Free State official handbook, 1932*. *Éire-Ireland* **30**, 35–42.

Helferty, Seamus 1978 The records of the Fine Gael party. *Irish Archives Bulletin: Journal of the Irish Society for Archives* **8**, 24–31.

Hogan, E.M. 2000 James Hogan: a biographical sketch. In Donnchadh Ó Corráin (ed.), *James Hogan: revolutionary, historian and political scientist*, 1–34. Dublin. Four Courts Press.

Katz, Richard S. 1981 But how many candidates should we have in Donegal? Numbers of nominees and electoral efficiency in Ireland. *British Journal of Political Science* **11** (1981), 117–22.

Kissane, Bill 1981 Majority rule and the stabilisation of democracy in the Irish Free State. *Irish Political Studies* **13**, 1–24.

Kissane, Bill 1995 The not-so-amazing case of Irish democracy. *Irish Political Studies* **10**, 43–68.

Knirck, Jason 2003 Afterimage of the revolution: Kevin O'Higgins and the Irish revolution. *Éire-Ireland* **38**(3/4), 212–43.

Laver, Michael 1986 Ireland: politics with some social bases. *Economic and Social Review* **17**(3), 107–31.

McKay, Enda 1986 Changing with the tide: the Irish Labour Party, 1927–1933. *Saothar* **11**, 27–39.

MacQueen, Norman 1982 Eamon de Valera, the Irish Free State, and the League of Nations, 1919–46. *Éire-Ireland* **17**(4), 110–27.

Mair, Peter 1977 Labour and the Irish party system re-visited: party competition in the 1920s. *Economic and Social Review* **9**(1), 59–70.

Malone, Andrew E. 1929 The development of party government in the Irish Free State. *Political Science Quarterly* **11**(4), 363–78.

Manning, Maurice 1979 Patrick McGilligan: nation builder. *Irish Times* (12 April).

Manning, Maurice 1980 William T. Cosgrave: a forgotten man of lasting attainments. *Irish Times* (5 June).

Martin, Ged 1975 The Irish Free State and the evolution of the British Commonwealth, 1921-49. In Ronald Hyam and Ged Martin (eds), *Reappraisals in British imperial history*, 201–23. London. Macmillan.

Maume, Patrick 1995 The ancient constitution: Arthur Griffith and the intellectual legacy to Sinn Féin. *Irish Political Studies* **10**, 123–37.

Mayer, William G. 1996 In defense of negative campaigning. *Political Science Quarterly* **111**(3), 437–55.

Morris, Ewan 1998 'God save the king' versus the 'Soldier's song': the 1929 Trinity College national anthem dispute and the politics of the Irish Free State. *Irish Historical Studies* **21**(121), 72–90.

Murphy, John A. 1976 Identity change in the Republic of Ireland. *Études Irlandaises* **1**, 143–58.

Nowlan, Kevin B. 1967 President Cosgrave's last administration. In Francis MacManus (ed.), *The years of the great test 1926–1939*, 7–18. Dublin. Mercier.

O'Brien, George 1936 Patrick Hogan. *Studies* **25**, 353–68.

O'Carroll, J.P. 1999 Cork: the political context. In Barry Brunt and Kevin Hourihan (eds), *Perspectives on Cork*, 149–68. Cork. Geographical Society of Ireland.

Ó Cinnéide, Séamus 1998 Democracy and the Constitution. *Administration* **64**(4), 41–58.

O'Connell, D. 1983 Proportional representation and intra-party competition in Tasmania and the Republic of Ireland. *Journal of Commonwealth and Comparative Politics* **11**(1), 45–70.

O'Connor, Emmet 1996 A historiography of Irish Labour. *Labour History Review* **60**(1), 21–34.

O'Connor, Emmet 1999 Jim Larkin and the communist internationals, 1923–9. *Irish Historical Studies* **31** (123), 357–72.

O'Halpin, Eunan 1993 Army politics and society in independent Ireland, 1923-1945. In T.G. Fraser and Keith Jeffery (eds), *Men, women and war: historical studies*, xvii, 158–74. Dublin. Lilliput Press.

O'Halpin, Eunan 1997 Parliamentary party discipline and tactics: the Fianna Fail archives of 1926-32. *Irish Historical Studies* **30**(120), 581–90.

O'Neill, T.P. 1976 In search of a political path: Irish republicanism, 1922–27. In G.A. Hayes-McCoy (ed.), *Historical studies 10: papers read before the eleventh Irish conference of historians*, 147–71. Galway. Clo Chois Fharraige.

Paseta, Senia 2000 Ireland's last Home Rule generation: the decline of constitutional nationalism in Ireland, 1916–1930. In Mike Cronin and John M. Regan (eds), *Ireland: the politics of independence, 1922–49*, 13–31. Basingstoke. Palgrave Macmillan.

Patterson, Henry 1988 Fianna Fáil and the working class: the origins of the enigmatic relationship. *Saothar* **13**, 81–8.

Pyne, Peter 1969 The third Sinn Féin Party, 1923–1926: part I. *Economic and Social Review* **1**(2), 229–57.

Pyne, Peter 1976 The new Irish state and the decline of the Republican Sinn Féin party, 1923-1926. *Éire-Ireland* **11**, 43–7.

Regan, John M. 1997 The politics of reaction: the dynamics of Treatyite government and policy 1922–33. *Irish Historical Studies*, **30**(120), 543–63.

Regan, John M. 2000 The politics of Utopia: party organisation, executive autonomy and the new administration. In Mike Cronin and John M. Regan (eds), *Ireland: the politics of independence, 1922–49*, 32–66. Basingstoke. Palgrave Macmillan.

Tiratsoo, Nick 2000 Labour and the electorate. In Duncan Tanner, Pat Thane and Nick Tiratsoo (eds), *Labour's first century*, 281–308. Cambridge. Cambridge University Press.

Valiulis, Maryann Gialanella 1992 Defining their role in the new state: Irishwomen's protest against the Juries Act of 1927. *Canadian Journal of Irish studies* **18**(1), 43–60.

The Cosgrave Party

Index

Page numbers in italic refer to documents, illustrations and photographs.